REFERENCE ONLY

AMERICAN COUNTERCULTURES

An Encyclopedia of Nonconformists, Alternative Lifestyles, and Radical Ideas in U.S. History

Volume Three

Edited by
Gina Misiroglu

SHARPE REFERENCE
an imprint of M.E. Sharpe, Inc.

SHARPE REFERENCE

Sharpe Reference is an imprint of M.E. Sharpe, Inc.

M.E. Sharpe, Inc.
80 Business Park Drive
Armonk, NY 10504

Library of Congress Cataloging-in-Publication Data

American countercultures: an encyclopedia of nonconformists, alternative lifestyles, and radical
ideas in U.S. history/Gina Misiroglu, editor.
    p. cm.
Includes bibliographical references and index.
ISBN 978-0-7656-8060-0 (hardcover: alk. paper)
1. Counterculture—United States—History. 2. United States—Social life and customs. 3. Popular
culture—United States—History. I. Misiroglu, Gina Renie.

HM647.A44 2009
306'.1—dc22   2008026227

Cover images (clockwise, starting in upper left corner) provided by the following: Bob Gomel/Stringer/
Time & Life Pictures/Getty Images; Silver Screen Collection/Hulton Archive/Getty Images; John Olson/
Stringer/Time & Life Pictures/Getty Images; Library of Congress; Stringer/Getty Images; Library of
Congress.

Printed and bound in the United States of America

The paper used in this publication meets the minimum requirements of
American National Standard for Information Sciences
Permanence of Paper for Printed Library Materials,
ANSI Z 39.48.1984.

(c) 10 9 8 7 6 5 4 3 2 1

Publisher: Myron E. Sharpe
Vice President and Director of New Product Development: Donna Sanzone
Vice President and Production Director: Carmen Chetti
Executive Editor and Manager of Reference: Todd Hallman
Executive Development Editor: Jeff Hacker
Project Manager: Laura Brengelman
Program Coordinator: Cathleen Prisco
Text Design: Carmen Chetti and Jesse Sanchez
Cover Design: Jesse Sanchez

Contents

Documents

Topic Finder

Arts and Artists, Visual

Abstract Expressionism
Advertising
Armory Show
Ashcan School
Black Arts Movement
Body Arts
Chick, Jack
Comics, Underground
Conceptual Art
Crumb, Robert
Doonesbury
Fashion
Federal Art Project
Graffiti
Guerrilla Girls
Harlem Renaissance
Lost Generation
Luhan, Mabel Dodge
Mapplethorpe, Robert
Max, Peter
O'Keeffe, Georgia
Outsider Art
Patchen, Kenneth
Pop Art
Poster Art
Ray, Man
Rivers, Larry
Sloan, John
Surrealists
Warhol, Andy

Biographies

Abbey, Edward
Alcott, Amos Bronson
Ali, Muhammad
Alison, Francis
Anderson, Laurie
Anderson, Margaret
Andrews, Stephen Pearl
Backus, Isaac

Baez, Joan
Baker, Chet
Baker, Josephine
Baldwin, James
Baldwin, Roger
Baraka, Amiri
Barnes, Djuna
Barnum, P.T.
Beach, Sylvia
Bellamy, Edward
Berkman, Alexander
Berrigan, Daniel, and Philip Berrigan
Bierce, Ambrose
Blavatsky, Helena
Bowie, David
Brando, Marlon
Brautigan, Richard
Brisbane, Albert
Brown, H. Rap
Brownson, Orestes
Bruce, Lenny
Bukowski, Charles
Buntline, Ned
Burns, Otway
Burroughs, William S.
Carlin, George
Carmichael, Stokely
Carroll, Jim
Carson, Rachel
Cash, Johnny
Castaneda, Carlos
Chávez, César
Cheech and Chong
Chick, Jack
Chomsky, Noam
Claflin, Tennessee
Clapp, Henry
Clare, Ada
Collins, Judy
Conroy, Jack
Coyote, Peter

Crumb, Robert

Cummings, E.E.

Cushman, Charlotte

Davis, Andrew Jackson

Davis, Angela

Davis, Miles

Dean, James

Debs, Eugene V.

Deganawidah

Delany, Martin R.

Dick, Philip K.

Douglass, Frederick

Du Bois, W.E.B.

Dyer, Mary

Dylan, Bob

Eastman, Max, and Crystal Eastman

Ellison, Harlan

Emerson, Ralph Waldo

Father Divine

Ferlinghetti, Lawrence

Fitzgerald, F. Scott

Fitzgerald, Zelda

Foster, Charles H.

Fox, Kate, Leah Fox, and Margaret Fox

Friedan, Betty

Fuller, Margaret

Fuller, R. Buckminster

Garrison, William Lloyd

Garvey, Marcus

Gaye, Marvin

Ginsberg, Allen

Goldman, Emma

Gonzales, Rodolfo "Corky"

Gorton, Samuel

Graham, Sylvester

Greeley, Horace

Gregory, Dick

Guthrie, Woody

Harris, Thomas Lake

Hatch, Cora Scott

Hawthorne, Nathaniel

Haywood, William "Big Bill"

Hecker, Isaac

Hefner, Hugh

Hemingway, Ernest

Hendrix, Jimi

Hester, Carolyn

Hoffman, Abbie

Holiday, Billie

hooks, bell

Hopper, Dennis

Houdini, Harry

Hughes, Langston

Hurston, Zora Neale

Hutchinson, Anne

Huxley, Aldous

Ingersoll, Robert

James, C.L.R.

Jemison, Mary

Joplin, Janis

Kerouac, Jack

Kesey, Ken

King, Martin Luther, Jr.

Kunstler, William

Le Sueur, Meridel

Leary, Timothy

Lee, Ann

Lennon, John

Lippmann, Walter

London, Jack

Lovecraft, H.P.

Ludlow, Fitz Hugh

Luhan, Mabel Dodge

Lumpkin, Grace

Macfadden, Bernarr

Malcolm X

Manson Family

Mapplethorpe, Robert

Marcuse, Herbert

Max, Peter

McCarthy, Eugene

McKenna, Terence

McLuhan, Marshall

McPherson, Aimee Semple

Menken, Adah Isaacs

Millay, Edna St. Vincent

Miller, Henry

Miller, William

Mills, C. Wright

Moore, Michael

Morrison, Jim

Morrison, Toni

Morton, Thomas

Nader, Ralph

Neolin

Newton, Huey

Noyes, John Humphrey

O'Brien, Fitz-James

Ochs, Phil

O'Keeffe, Georgia

O'Neill, Eugene

Owen, Robert Dale

Palahniuk, Chuck
Palmer, Phoebe
Patchen, Kenneth
Piñero, Miguel
Pirsig, Robert M.
Poe, Edgar Allan
Pop, Iggy
Pound, Ezra
Presley, Elvis
Priestley, Joseph
Pryor, Richard
Purple, Adam
Pynchon, Thomas
Rand, Ayn
Randolph, A. Philip
Rankin, Jeannette
Ray, Man
Reed, John
Reed, Lou
Reich, Wilhelm
Rexroth, Kenneth
Rice, Thomas Dartmouth
Ripley, George
Rivers, Larry
Robbins, Tom
Robeson, Paul
Rubin, Jerry
Salinger, J.D.
Sanger, Margaret
Saxton, Alexander P.
Seeger, Pete
Shakur, Tupac
Sinclair, Upton
Sloan, John
Smith, Joseph
Smith, Patti
Smothers Brothers
Snoop Dogg
Snyder, Gary
Spock, Benjamin
Stein, Gertrude
Thoreau, Henry David
Turner, Nat
Twain, Mark
Unabomber
Vonnegut, Kurt, Jr.
Vorse, Mary Heaton
Ward, Nancy
Warhol, Andy
Waters, John
Watson, Thomas E.

Watts, Alan
Wavy Gravy
Whitman, Walt
Wilkinson, Jemima
Williams, Roger
Woodhull, Victoria
Woolman, John
Wright, Frances
Wright, Richard
Young, Brigham
Zappa, Frank

Civil Rights and Social Protest Movements
Abolitionism
African Americans
Ali, Muhammad
American Indian Movement
Baldwin, Roger
Berkman, Alexander
Berrigan, Daniel, and Philip Berrigan
Black Panthers
Black Power Movement
Brown Berets
Brown, H. Rap
Carmichael, Stokely
Catholic Worker Movement
Chávez, César
Chicago Seven
Chicano Moratorium
Chicano Movement
Civil Rights Movement
Daughters of Bilitis
Davis, Angela
Delany, Martin R.
Douglass, Frederick
Du Bois, W.E.B.
Eastman, Max, and Crystal Eastman
Feminism, First-Wave
Feminism, Second-Wave
Feminism, Third-Wave
Feminism, Social Justice
Free Speech Movement
Friedan, Betty
Garrison, William Lloyd
Garvey, Marcus
Gay Liberation Movement
Goldman, Emma
Gonzales, Rodolfo "Corky"
Gray Panthers
Haywood, William "Big Bill"
Hippies

Hoffman, Abbie
Industrial Workers of the World
John Reed Clubs
King, Martin Luther, Jr.
Kunstler, William
Mattachine Society
Movimiento Estudiantíl Chicano de Aztlán
Nader, Ralph
New Left
Newton, Huey
People for the Ethical Treatment of Animals
Queer Nation
Randolph, A. Philip
Rankin, Jeannette
Riot Grrrl
Robeson, Paul
Rubin, Jerry
Sanger, Margaret
Social Gospel
Socialism
Spock, Benjamin
Students for a Democratic Society
Turner, Nat
Underground Railroad
Universal Negro Improvement Association
Up Against the Wall Motherfucker
Vietnam War Protests
Weatherman
Yippies

Communities, Settlements, Neighborhoods

Amana Society
Amish
Andrews, Stephen Pearl
Aurora Commune
Austin, Texas
Berkeley, California
Berlin Heights Commune
Bethel Commune
Brisbane, Albert
Brook Farm
Cambridge, Massachusetts
Communes
Communitarianism
East Village, New York City
Ephrata Cloister
Eugene, Oregon
Farm, The
Fruitlands
Gorton, Samuel
Greenwich Village, New York City

Haight-Ashbury, San Francisco
Harmony Society
Harris, Thomas Lake
Icarians
Los Angeles
Madison, Wisconsin
Modern Times
Mole People
Noyes, John Humphrey
Oneida Community
Owen, Robert Dale
Ripley, George
San Francisco
Seattle
Settlement Houses
Taos, New Mexico
Venice, California
Wavy Gravy
Williams, Roger
Wright, Frances

Consumer Goods and Products

Absinthe
Advertising
Apple Computer
Ben & Jerry's
Bicycles
Birth Control Pill
Bookstores, Alternative
Comics, Underground
Cooperatives, Consumer
Fashion
Health Foods
Magazines, Little
Smoking, Tobacco
Volkswagen Beetle
Zines

Cultural/Historical Periods and Events

Altamont Free Concert
Armory Show
Baby Boomers
Beat Generation
Be-Ins
Burning Man Festival
Chautauqua Movement
Chicano Moratorium
Generation Gap
Generation X
Generation Y
Ghost Dance

Goth Culture
Graffiti
Grateful Dead
Gray Panthers
Groupies
Hackers
Harlem Renaissance
Hasidim and Hasidism
Hells Angels
Hippies
Industrial Workers of the World
Jehovah's Witnesses
Knights of the Golden Circle
Ku Klux Klan
Latino and Latina Culture
Lesbian Culture
Lost Generation
Lowriders
Mafia
Magic and Magicians
Manson Family
Mattachine Society
Me Decade
Medieval Reenactment
Men's Movements
Merry Pranksters
Mod
Mole People
Native Americans
New Age
Nudism and Nudist Colonies
Organic Farming
Physical Culture Movement
Queer Nation
Rastafari Movement
Rave Culture
Regulators
Riot Grrrl
Role-Playing Games
Sex Trade and Prostitution
Skateboarders
Slang
Slave Culture
Slow Movement
Smoking, Tobacco
Squatters and Squatting
Straight Edge Culture
Students for a Democratic Society
Suffragists
Surfing and Surfer Culture
Surrealists

Survivalists
Tramps and Hoboes
Transsexuals
Transvestites
Trekkies
Up Against the Wall Motherfucker
Weatherman
White Supremacists
Yippies
Yoga
Zoot-Suiters

Ideologies and Theories

Abolitionism
Abstract Expressionism
Afrocentrism
Anarchism
Antinomianism
Astrology
Atheism
Bohemianism
Communism
Communitarianism
Consciousness Raising
Conspiracy Theories
Deep Ecology
Environmentalism
Existentialism
Exorcism
Extrasensory Perception and Parapsychology
Feminism, First-Wave
Feminism, Second-Wave
Feminism, Third-Wave
Feminism, Social Justice
Free Love
Freemasonry
Fundamentalism, Christian
Gonzo Journalism
Harmonialism
McCarthyism
Medicine, Alternative
Mesmerism
New Age
New Left
New Thought
Omphalism
Pacifism
Pentecostalism
Populism
Pseudoscience
Social Gospel

Socialism
Spiritualism
Swedenborgianism
Transcendentalism
UFOs
Unitarianism
Utopianism
Vegetarianism

Literature and Literary Figures
Algonquin Round Table
Baldwin, James
Baraka, Amiri
Barnes, Djuna
Beach, Sylvia
Beat Generation
Bellamy, Edward
Bierce, Ambrose
Black Arts Movement
Brautigan, Richard
Bukowski, Charles
Buntline, Ned
Burroughs, William S.
Carroll, Jim
Castaneda, Carlos
Catcher in the Rye, The
City Lights Books
Clare, Ada
Conroy, Jack
Cummings, E.E.
Cyberpunk
Delany, Martin R.
Dick, Philip K.
Douglass, Frederick
Du Bois, W.E.B.
Ellison, Harlan
Emerson, Ralph Waldo
Federal Writers' Project
Ferlinghetti, Lawrence
Fitzgerald, F. Scott
Fitzgerald, Zelda
Fuller, Margaret
Ginsberg, Allen
Harlem Renaissance
Harris, Thomas Lake
Hawthorne, Nathaniel
Hemingway, Ernest
hooks, bell
Hughes, Langston
Hurston, Zora Neale
Huxley, Aldous

Kerouac, Jack
Kesey, Ken
Le Sueur, Meridel
London, Jack
Lost Generation
Lovecraft, H.P.
Ludlow, Fitz Hugh
Luhan, Mabel Dodge
Lumpkin, Grace
Magazines, Little
McLuhan, Marshall
Menken, Adah Isaacs
Millay, Edna St. Vincent
Miller, Henry
Morrison, Toni
O'Brien, Fitz-James
Palahniuk, Chuck
Patchen, Kenneth
Piñero, Miguel
Pirsig, Robert M.
Poe, Edgar Allan
Pound, Ezra
Presses, Small Book
Pulp Fiction
Pynchon, Thomas
Rand, Ayn
Rexroth, Kenneth
Robbins, Tom
Salinger, J.D.
Saxton, Alexander P.
Science Fiction
Sinclair, Upton
Snyder, Gary
Stein, Gertrude
Thoreau, Henry David
Twain, Mark
Vonnegut, Kurt, Jr.
Vorse, Mary Heaton
Whitman, Walt
Wright, Richard

Media: Film, Television, Radio, Alternative
Advertising
Alice's Restaurant
Bloggers
Brando, Marlon
Cheech and Chong
Coyote, Peter
Cushman, Charlotte
Dean, James
Easy Rider

AMERICAN COUNTERCULTURES

Volume Three

Radio

From its early use as a Morse code transmission device to its modern mass-media role as a source of news, music, and information, radio has both shaped and been shaped by America's countercultural movements and trends. The tensions between the scientific exploration, artistic expression, business interests, and altruism that combine in radio have made it not only a revolutionary medium of communication but a manifestation of counterculture itself.

When radio entered mainstream America in the early twentieth century, commercial interests generally viewed it as a novelty, likely to be useful only for minimal communication between businesses and Wall Street. Amateur ham radio operators, however, viewed the new technology as an intellectual challenge. Clubs sprang up across the nation with members as young as ten years old building and operating their own transmitters.

The camaraderie and sense of community that developed among ham operators became the hallmark of countercultural influences in radio. Despite government restrictions and fierce opposition from emerging commercial networks, amateur interest in radio provided the impetus for radio's expansion and maturation.

The Golden Age and Beyond

Technological advances made during World War I allowed commercial stations to broadcast a greater variety of programming during the 1920s and 1930s, primarily on the AM (amplitude modulation) band. The widespread availability of affordable receivers ushered in the golden age of radio with hours of dramas, slapstick comedies, newscasts, and musical performances. An increasing number of performers on the radio were African American. Although the rigid segregation of the Jim Crow era applied to the host venues, there was no way to differentiate between white and black music on the ra-

dio. Whites grew to appreciate the talent and originality of black performers, especially jazz artists. The assimilation of black music into white America's youth culture helped soften racial barriers.

As commercial radio expanded after World War II, the gradual integration of black and white culture continued. The social and economic mobility of the emerging black middle class offered too ripe a prize for commercial operators. Despite seemingly inflexible racial limitations, station WDIA in Memphis, Tennessee, beginning in the late 1940s, operated with an exclusively African American broadcast staff and catered to an enormous African American audience, at times as high as 10 percent of the total black population of the United States. It also reached a significant segment of the white population of the rural South. The anonymous accessibility to black culture provided by stations such as WDIA paved the way for "crossover" music and the rock and roll revolution that inundated white America in the 1950s, forever altering the political, social, and musical landscape of America.

Although white disc jockeys (DJs) such as Alan Freed and Wolfman Jack were credited with creating the rock and roll phenomenon, undoubtedly black music was the true object of white teenagers' fascination. DJs attempted to use "race ventriloquism" to sound blacker and therefore more authentic to their white audiences.

As rock became the lingua franca of teenagers, DJs held more sway over teenagers' decisions than did their parents, let alone societal norms and customs. As white youth embraced black culture and civil rights, the establishment attempted to rein in the forces of cultural change. Many influential DJs fell to the infamous payola scandals involving pay-for-play transactions with record labels, a common practice since the early days of commercial radio. Strict Top 40 playlists and homogenized copy neutralized the DJs' cult of personality, reinstituting the monotony of pre-rock mainstream radio.

FM Revolutions

One of the DJs ousted in the payola fiasco, Tom Donahue, resurfaced in San Francisco, where by 1967 the mix of drugs, innovative music, and barren airwaves prompted him to embrace an alternate form of transmission, FM (frequency modulation). With his wife, Rachael, Donahue pioneered a free-form style of broadcasting.

Giving DJs complete freedom of choice and action, the new FM stations not only introduced such legendary artists such as the Doors and Jimi Hendrix, but they also provided a voice and source of information for the hippie counterculture and other movements of the time. From broadcasting public-service announcements concerning tainted drugs to spearheading protests against the Vietnam War, FM radio served as the conduit of communication among, as well as the harbinger of trends within, the various factions of the movement. Ultimately, however, free-form FM's success became its undoing, as corporate control soon stifled DJ creativity and silenced alternate voices much as it had in the 1950s.

As commercial rock became the mainstay of the FM band, its former home, the AM band, saw the development of a novel concept, which, ironically, had its roots in the freewheeling ramblings of the free-form FM DJs. Talk radio stations gained increasingly larger shares of bandwidth and listeners throughout the 1980s and 1990s.

By the mid-1990s, AM talk radio was a bastion of conservative counterculture. Bombastic hosts such as Rush Limbaugh used the airwaves to counter what they perceived as an erosion of morality in American politics and culture through the domination of all forms of media by liberal elites. Ironically, while conservatives vilified National Public Radio (NPR) as liberal and countercultural, most liberals and noncommercial broadcasters viewed the network as not only a tool of the government, but as a collaborator with commercial radio.

In 2004, liberal activists launched an alternative to both NPR and AM talk radio, Air America Radio. Using the deep pockets and name recognition of celebrities such as Al Franken and Robert Kennedy, Jr., Air America created instant buzz and attracted franchise investors across the country.

As talk radio staked its flag on the AM dial, the institution of formats and increasing consolidation of corporate holdings saw FM radio lose its influence among not only the counterculture, but among main-

stream listeners as well. Although college radio stations attempted to sustain a modified free-form style, disgust with the state of radio led to the emergence of pirate radio stations.

Although the practice of "squatting" on frequencies dates back to the early days of the ham operators, pirate stations specialize in thumbing their noses at the Federal Communications Commission's (FCC's) regulations as well as at society in general. From call letters to playlists to publicity tactics, pirate stations stand for the fringes, the off-the-beaten-track listeners. Stations such as KPBJ San Francisco and KBLT Los Angeles play cat-and-mouse games with the FCC, while enjoying rabidly loyal followings.

Playing within the law are micro FM stations, low-wattage stations that cater to small geographic areas and often provide the only access to local news and events. Others serve as the voice of political outsiders, such as Radio Conciencia, connecting the embattled Immokalee tomato workers of Florida while transmitting vital weather and news bulletins in Central American dialects. Higher power but geographically limited stations operating as nonprofits, collectively called community radio, also provide alternative voices. Nevertheless, micro FM stations and community radio both lack the range and money to compete with commercial stations.

New technology has continued to revolutionize commercial broadcasting. Some dissatisfied with the state of mainstream radio create Internet-only stations, avoiding the cost and hassle of acquiring a broadcasting license. Disputes with record labels over royalty payments often silence the stations before fan bases can be built, however.

An older broadcasting method, satellite radio, has emerged as an important commercial player. A subscriber-based format outside the jurisdiction of the FCC, satellite provides cover for nationally syndicated shock jocks such as Howard Stern, who had faced increasing pressure from the FCC to clean up his show's language and content on the FM band. Major satellite networks Sirius and XM Radio have become standard issue in American cars as well as being aired on cable and satellite television, virtually guaranteeing an increasing share of the listening market.

The emergence of satellite and Internet as alternative media outlets has not diminished the impact or allure of traditional radio. Hundreds of thousands of citizens have bombarded the FCC with complaints about consolidation and lobbied for expansion of micro FM licensure. Community stations around the country enjoy robust membership and provide vital community services while crafting innovative programming. If anything, the availability of affordable satellite service and the advent of Internet streaming have only enhanced the reach and mission of alternative radio, ensuring the continuation of the romance between the airwaves and the counterculture.

Ann Youngblood Mulhearn

See also: Pirate Radio.

Further Reading

Carpenter, Sue. *40 Watts from Nowhere: A Journey into Pirate Radio.* New York: Scribner's, 2004.

Douglas, Susan J. *Listening In: Radio and the American Imagination: From Amos 'n' Andy and Edward R. Murrow to Wolfman Jack and Howard Stern.* New York: Times Books, 1999.

Ladd, Jim. *Radio Waves: Life and Revolution on the FM Dial.* New York: St. Martin's, 1991.

Savage, Barbara Dianne. *Broadcasting Freedom: Radio, War, and the Politics of Race, 1938–1948.* Chapel Hill: University of North Carolina Press, 1999.

Walker, Jesse. *Rebels on the Air: An Alternative History of Radio in America.* New York: New York University Press, 2001.

Ramones, The

Formed in 1974 in Forest Hills (Queens), New York, the Ramones were an iconic punk rock band. Regarded by many as the first punk band, they remained at the heart of the American counterculture for almost twenty years. Famously hardworking, the band produced furiously fast cartoon punk-pop music influenced by early punk artists such as the Stooges, Iggy Pop, and the New York Dolls, as well more mainstream rock bands such as the Who, the Rolling Stones, and the Beatles.

The band included singer Joey Ramone (Jeffrey Hyman); lead guitarist Johnny Ramone (John Cummings); bassist Dee Dee Ramone (Douglas Colvin), who left the group in 1989; and, variously, drummers Tommy Ramone (Thomas Erdelyi), Marky Ramone (Marc Bell), Elvis Ramone (Clem Burke), and C.J. Ramone (Christopher Joseph Ward). In addition to the Ramone surname, inspired by a pseudonym of Beatles singer-songwriter Paul McCartney, band members shared uniform long hair and leather jackets.

The Ramones began playing in the New York City punk club CBGB alongside early versions of the bands the Talking Heads and Blondie. By 1975, the Ramones had earned full-page coverage in *Rolling Stone* magazine. Their eponymous first album was released in 1976 on Sire records, with which they remained signed until 1992, when they moved to the Radioactive label. The Ramones recorded more than twenty-five albums, fourteen of which were original studio recordings.

They rarely reached the singles charts in the United States. However, they gained cult status in South America, Japan, and Europe. They were particularly influential on the British punk scene, where they inspired bands such as the Clash, the Damned, and the Sex Pistols. The pared-down style of songs such as "Sheena Is a Punk Rocker" stood out at a time of musical flamboyance. Meanwhile, the excesses of the members' rock and roll lifestyle became legendary, particularly their relationship with music producer Phil Spector, who produced four of their singles, including "Baby I Love You."

Ever ready to deal with marginal or taboo subject matter, the Ramones often were denied airplay on commercial radio stations. Concurrently, their cult status grew, encouraged by celebrity fans such as horror writer Stephen King, who mentioned the band in a number of his books. In turn, the band wrote and recorded a song for the soundtrack of the film *Pet Sematary* (1989), based on King's novel of the same title. In addition, the Ramones had appeared in the 1979 film *Rock 'n' Roll High School.*

In later years, the band toured alongside U2, Pearl Jam, White Zombie, and Soundgarden. In 1985, Joey Ramone joined Steven van Zandt (guitarist for Bruce Springsteen's E-Street Band and an actor on the hit television show *The Sopranos*) and other musicians in recording for Artists Against Apartheid, a group founded by van Zandt to denounce apartheid in South Africa. And Dee Dee, while still writing songs for the Ramones, recorded a rap album as Dee Dee King in 1989.

The longevity of the group's touring career, compounded by health problems and increasing personal animosity, finally led the Ramones to disband after a farewell tour in 1996. They reunited for two final appearances in 1997 and 1999. Three of the band's original members died in the ensuing years: Joey of Hodgkin's lymphoma in 2001, Dee Dee of a heroin overdose in 2002, and Johnny of prostate cancer in 2004. The Ramones were inducted into the Rock and Roll Hall of Fame in 2002, and their legacy continues through the music and style of bands on both sides of the Atlantic.

Lucy Robinson

See also: CBGB; Punk Rock.

Further Reading

Bessman, Jim. *Ramones: An American Band.* New York: St. Martin's, 1993.

Osgerby, Bill. "'Chewing Out a Rhythm on My Bubble-Gum': The Teenage Aesthetic and Genealogies of American Punk." In *Punk Rock: So What?* ed. Roger Sabin. New York: Routledge, 1999.

Ramone, Dee Dee. *Poison Heart: Surviving the Ramones.* Wembly, UK: Firefly, 1997.

Rand, Ayn (1905–1982)

Novelist and philosopher Ayn Rand, founder of the philosophic system known as Objectivism, was a quintessential counterculture thinker. She often said that she was challenging 2,500 years of traditionalist, Judeo-Christian culture by proclaiming a secular standard of morality for human life and declaring rational self-interest as the means to its achievement. According to Objectivism, reality is what it is, independent of what human beings think or feel, and reason is the only means to knowledge. In novels such as *We the Living* (1936), *The Fountainhead* (1943), and *Atlas Shrugged* (1957), Rand dramatized her views that individual rights are essential to survival in a social context, and that laissez-faire capitalism is the only social system consonant with such rights. In these and other works, she celebrated the fully integrated individual, who recognizes no conflict between mind and body, reason and emotion, thought and action, or morality and prudence.

Rand was born Alisa Zinov'yevna Rosenbaum on February 2, 1905, in St. Petersburg, Russia. Her father's pharmacy was confiscated by the Soviets after the Bolshevik Revolution of 1917, and the family moved to Crimea. She returned to St. Petersburg to study philosophy and history at the University of Petrograd (later St. Petersburg State University), earning her degree in 1924.

In February 1926, having been granted a visa to visit relatives in the United States, she traveled to New York and Chicago—and resolved not to return home. Moving to Hollywood in hopes of becoming a screenwriter, she changed her name to Ayn Rand and found odd jobs as a script reader. She married the actor Frank O'Connor in 1929 (the couple would remain together until his death in 1979) and became a U.S. citizen two years later.

Given her background, Rand's advocacy of capitalism was no mere apologia for the American status quo. She was a radical critic of what she characterized as the mystical, altruist, and collectivist roots of contemporary culture and the "New Fascist" statist politics that it made possible. In nonfiction anthologies such as *The Virtue of Selfishness* (1964) and *Capitalism: The Unknown Ideal* (1966), Rand maintained that government intervention had been the cause of socioeconomic injustice and instability, including militarism, monopolies, business cycles, and ever-increasing social fragmentation along material, racial, ethnic, sexual, generational, and other lines. Conflict among groups was inevitable in the current system, argued Rand, requiring the sacrifice of some groups for the benefit of others and leading to the triumph of groupthink in social life.

Rand's advocacy of free-market capitalism suggested little common ground with the radical left counterculture of the 1960s and 1970s. And while she repudiated the New Left for its "Hegelian" and "Marxist" ideology, and the hippie student rebels of the 1960s for their "emotionalism," "subjectivism," and "nihilism," her work had a certain kinship with the counterculture revolt against authoritarianism and social conformity. Rand shared with the student rebels an opposition to the Vietnam War and the military draft, and she joined in their rejection of social hypocrisy. At the same time, Rand contended that counterculture activists of the time merely reflected the bankruptcy of the establishment by blaming science, technology, and capitalism for the woes of society and by proposing an "anti-Industrial Revolution" as the antidote.

Despite the disdain that Rand heaped on the counterculture, students of the 1960s ranked her as among those who had most influenced, or were most admired by, that generation. Among writers, Rand was tied for sixth place with feminist Germaine Greer, behind satiric novelist Kurt Vonnegut, Lebanese American poet Kahlil Gibran, journalist Tom Wolfe, French philosophers Jean-Paul Sartre and Albert Camus (tied for fourth place), and Beat poet Allen Ginsberg.

Many in the counterculture responded favorably to Rand's attacks on intellectual, political, and educational elites. Her influence would extend to popular artists of the era, including rock musicians such as Neil Peart, drummer and lyricist for the band Rush, which paid tribute to "the genius of Ayn Rand," and comic-book artists and writers Steve Ditko and Frank Miller, whose stories expressed a Randian politics of rebellion.

Although Rand rejected many of the collectivist social and political claims of 1960s sexual liberationists, she also influenced a generation of individualist feminist writers (such as Joan Kennedy Taylor, Wendy McElroy, and Sharon Presley) and gay libertarian writers (including those affiliated with the Independent Gay Forum) who were inspired by her heroic vision of individual authenticity. Ayn Rand died in New York City on March 6, 1982.

Chris Matthew Sciabarra

See also: Feminism, Second-Wave; Gay Liberation Movement; New Left.

Further Reading

Gladstein, Mimi Reisel, and Chris Matthew Sciabarra. *Feminist Interpretations of Ayn Rand.* University Park: Pennsylvania State University Press, 1999.

Riggenbach, Jeff. *In Praise of Decadence.* Amherst, NY: Prometheus, 1998.

Sciabarra, Chris Matthew. *Ayn Rand, Homosexuality, and Human Liberation.* Cape Town, South Africa: Leap, 2003.

———. *Ayn Rand: The Russian Radical.* University Park: Pennsylvania State University Press, 1995.

Randolph, A. Philip (1889–1979)

One of the twentieth century's foremost labor organizers and civil rights activists, Asa Philip Randolph was the founder of the first black labor union in the United States, the Brotherhood of Sleeping Car Porters (BSCP), in 1925, and he played a central role in bringing African Americans into the labor movement.

A native of Florida born in Crescent City on April 15, 1889, and raised in nearby Jacksonville, Randolph joined the Great Migration and relocated to New York City in 1911, searching for greater economic and educational opportunities. In his early twenties, Randolph worked a variety of odd jobs to support himself while studying Shakespeare, socialism, public speaking, and other subjects of interest at the free City College.

Along with Chandler Owen, a fellow traveler in New York City's vibrant political and cultural scene during the early twentieth century, Randolph launched a monthly magazine called *The Messenger.* Through the magazine's pages, he denounced U.S. participation in World War I, encouraged African Americans to resist enlistment in a segregated military, and provided an opportunity for scores of writers to articulate a socialist-influenced program for black liberation.

Randolph put his principles into action by dedicating his talents to the BSCP, a predominantly African American labor union representing Pullman porters. As the union's president, Randolph situated himself in the vanguard of a decade-long struggle by black workers to represent themselves in collective bargaining. In addition to confronting a corporation with a strong reputation for hostility to independent unions, Randolph and the BSCP regularly came to loggerheads with the American Federation of Labor (AFL) about racial discrimination in local affiliates, a problem that Randolph would confront throughout his career, well into the 1950s.

In addition to being his generation's premier African American labor leader, Randolph made other significant contributions to the struggle for black equality. Most important among these was the 1941 founding of the March on Washington Movement (MOWM). Supported by African American leaders of the mid-twentieth century, including Walter White, Lester Granger, and Mary McLeod Bethune, the movement threatened widespread public protest during World War II and forced President Franklin D. Roosevelt to issue an executive order prohibiting racial discrimination in defense industries.

Although there was no actual march on the capital, Randolph's harnessing of pressure to force the federal government to address racial inequality was pioneering. Additionally, the MOWM was a training ground for African American activists of the 1940s to discuss and implement Gandhian nonviolent civil disobedience, a protest tactic that would later be widely employed in the civil rights movement.

Randolph's lifetime dedication to struggle included newspaper publishing, labor organizing, spearheading the MOWM and an effective postwar campaign to desegregate the armed forces, and joining Martin Luther King, Jr., in the Prayer Pilgrimage of May 1957 (the largest civil rights demonstration in America to that date). Randolph's final major battle against racial inequality was the 1963 March on Washington for Jobs and Freedom. Organized by Randolph with activist Bayard Rustin, this mass demonstration would prove to be emblematic for many observers of the civil rights movement. Although the day is best remembered for King's historic and moving "I Have a Dream" speech, it was Randolph who, in the demonstration's keynote address, declared, "The civil rights revolution is not confined to Negroes; nor is it confined to civil rights." It is fitting that a protest embodying the goals of the civil rights movement marked the culmination of Randolph's career as an activist.

In more than half a century of struggle, Randolph was guided by progressive socialist principles, but he remained virulently anticommunist, and his faith in American democracy never wavered. As a labor leader, trailblazer in the use of nonviolent mass-protest tactics, and shaper of African American thought, he sought not to destroy capitalism but to incorporate African Americans into the nation's capitalist democracy on equal footing with whites. Randolph died on May 16, 1979, in New York City.

David Lucander

See also: African Americans; Civil Rights Movement; King, Martin Luther, Jr.

Further Reading

Kersten, Andrew E. *A. Philip Randolph: A Life in the Vanguard.* Lanham, MD: Rowman & Littlefield, 2006.

Pfeffer, Paula F. *A. Philip Randolph: A Pioneer of the Civil Rights Movement.* Baton Rouge: Louisiana State University Press, 1990.

Taylor, Cynthia. *A. Philip Randolph: The Religious Journey of an African-American Labor Leader.* New York: New York University Press, 2006.

Rankin, Jeannette (1880–1973)

Jeannette Rankin was the first woman to be elected to the U.S. Congress and the only member to vote against U.S. entry into both World War I and World War II. A suffragist, pacifist, and worker for social reform, she assumed roles that were counter to both the prevailing culture and traditional views of femininity.

Rankin was born on June 11, 1880, near Missoula, Montana, where she attended local public schools and graduated from the University of Montana in 1902. She taught school for several years before entering the New York School of Philanthropy in 1908, and she later served as a social worker in Montana and Washington.

Discontented with social work, Rankin enrolled at the University of Washington and while a student there became involved in the woman suffrage movement. Eventually, she became legislative secretary of the National American Woman Suffrage Association, an organization that, through a series of well-orchestrated state campaigns, was active in securing ratification of the Nineteenth Amendment in 1920, guaranteeing women the right to vote.

A member of the Republican Party, Rankin ran for Congress in Montana in 1916, campaigning for universal suffrage, prohibition, child welfare reform, an end to child labor, and keeping the United States out of World War I. One of her first actions was to introduce a bill that would have allowed women citizenship independent of their husbands.

On the evening Congress convened in April 1917, President Wilson called for a resolution for the United States to enter the Great War. Although Rankin had not been previously identified as a pacifist, she decided to vote against U.S. participation in the conflict. Carrie Chapman Catt of the National American Woman Suffrage Association tried to change Rankin's mind, because she thought that a vote against war would brand suffragists as unpatriotic. By contrast, Alice Paul of the Woman's Party thought that women in politics should speak for peace. In the end, Rankin voted with forty-eight other members of Congress against war with Germany.

Her controversial views on World War I, trade union rights, equal pay for men and women, and birth control cost her the Republican nomination for the U.S. Senate in 1918. She ran as an independent, but was easily defeated without the support of the party.

After leaving Congress in 1919, Rankin campaigned for the Sheppard-Towner Maternity and Infancy Protection Act of 1921, which provided federal funding for the health and welfare of women and children; the Child Labor Amendment, which proposed to limit and regulate child labor; and a variety of pacifist causes and organizations, such as the Women's International League for Peace and Freedom, the oldest women's peace organization in the world. In addition, she served as a field representative for the National Council for the Prevention of War, established in 1921 by representatives of seventeen national pacifist organizations to serve as a clearinghouse for the peace movement.

In 1940, Rankin won reelection to the House of Representatives, again as a Republican from Montana, but this time on an explicitly antiwar platform. After the Japanese attack on Pearl Harbor the following December, she was the only member of Congress to vote against the United States entering World War II. She was convinced that President Franklin D. Roosevelt had deliberately provoked the attack. After casting her vote on FDR's war measure, Rankin hid from angry crowds in a nearby phone booth until police could escort her home. Her vote made her extremely unpopular, and she did not seek reelection in 1942.

In the years after World War II, Rankin traveled to India to study the pacifism of spiritual leader Mohandas Gandhi. In the 1960s, she established a self-sufficient women's cooperative in Georgia and actively campaigned against the Vietnam War. In January 1968, at age eighty-seven, she led 5,000 peace protestors—calling themselves the "Jeannette Rankin Brigade"—in a demonstration against the Vietnam War in Washington, D.C. She died in Carmel, California, on May 18, 1973.

Kathy Warnes

See also: Pacifism; Suffragists.

Further Reading

Davidson, Sue. *A Heart in Politics: Jeannette Rankin and Patsy T. Mink: Women Who Dared.* Seattle, WA: Seal, 1994.

Giles, Kevin. *Flight of the Dove: The Story of Jeannette Rankin.* Beaverton, OR: Touchstone, 1980.

Lopach, James J., and Jean A. Luckowski. *Jeannette Rankin: A Political Woman.* Boulder: University Press of Colorado, 2005.

Rapp, George

See Utopianism

Rap Music

Rap music is a genre defined by the presence of "rapping" (also known as "MCing" or "rhyming"). The term describes a popular form of syncopated, rhythmic street poetry that first gained popularity in the United States through young urban poets in the late 1960s and early 1970s. The art form gained momentum in New York City during the remainder of the 1970s. The term *rap* is commonly understood as an abbreviation of *rapid,* in reference to the comparatively quick, poetic delivery of the genre. In the 1970s and 1980s, rap artists typically infused lyrics with an easy-to-follow rhyme scheme, blunt self-referential humor, and brutal honesty about the harsh circumstances of inner-city life, including gang violence and drug abuse. Rap music, along with emerging affiliated trends such as break dancing, graffiti art, and "turntablism," formed the elements of a new and accessible hip-hop counterculture movement that was embraced in many urban circles across the nation, primarily in the 1980s.

Young listeners in urban centers, including New York City, Chicago, Los Angeles, and Detroit, often were attracted to early rap music, as many failed to relate to the hollow concepts of love and picturesque good times portrayed in mainstream music. In the wake of the civil rights movement of the 1960s, many African American artists and audiences embraced the genre as a revelatory and definitive new voice in American media. Since the late 1960s, many rap artists have used the genre to explore and comment upon inner-city poverty, violence, race relations, gender issues and roles, urban drug use, and rampant materialism. They have intertwined lyrics with autobiographical touches, particularly in relation to poverty, violence, and romance, and often with humor. Rap artists have addressed these topics from many different perspectives with widely varying aims, including sheer entertainment, political motivation, and shock value.

Iconic figures in rap music throughout the genre's history include pioneers Kool DJ Herc (Clive Campbell), Afrika Bambaataa (Kevin Donovan), Ice-T (Tracy Marrow), and Dr. Dre (Andre Young), along with groups like the Sugar Hill Gang, Run DMC, N.W.A. (Niggaz With Attitude), Public Enemy, and A Tribe Called Quest.

Roots

Rap music in America began with the formation and success of the African American, New York City–based group the Last Poets in the late 1960s and early 1970s. Formed in 1968 on Black Muslim leader Malcolm X's birthday in response to the urban turmoil of the civil rights movement, the group relied heavily on primitive, noninvasive rhythms to showcase rapid-fire poetic delivery. In songs such as "When the Revolution Comes" (1970) and "This Is Madness" (1971), the group's furious lyrics and delivery were used to explore the circumstances of African Americans living in urban centers. The success of the Last Poets was a watershed event in the history of rap music, as the group's reliance on harsh tribal rhythms, racially charged lyrics, and frenetic delivery earned it a tremendous following. The Last Poets embraced and endorsed traits that would be further popularized by successful groups such as Public Enemy and the Jungle Brothers in the following decade.

As the 1970s progressed, artists such as New York–based Jamaican refugee Herc solidified the success of the genre through the promotion of rap-based block and club parties in urban centers of the Northeast. Herc, inspired by the uplifting work of black activist and poet Gil Scott-Heron, occupies a dual place in the history of the genre as the first hip-hop disc jockey and one of the first popular American rap artists. Artists who followed closely in Herc's footsteps, including Coke La Rock and Melle Mel (Melvin Glover), focused primarily on MC duties while allowing DJs to provide beats and samples.

By the close of the 1970s, artists such as Herc, La Rock, and Mel solidified a New York City following at parties and in clubs. A thriving rap-devoted club following developed in the city as the disco movement thrived simultaneously.

In 1979, rap experienced a thunderous embrace from new demographic groups with the release of the Sugar Hill Gang's first single, "Rapper's Delight," on Sugar Hill Records. The nine-member Sugar Hill Gang was formed primarily of workers at a New York City pizzeria. Upon the single's release, the group gained an immense following from performances at New York City block parties. Often considered the first commercially successful rap single, the group's sixteen-minute tour de

Slain hip-hop star Tupac Shakur, symbol of the West Coast rap style and subculture, is memorialized in urban graffiti art. West Coast rap emphasized heavy bass music and edgy lyrics about ghetto life. *(Al Pereira/Michael Ochs Archives/Getty Images)*

force continues to hold the record as the best-selling single in rap history. Through its easy-to-follow rhyme structure, autobiographical subject matter, and aurally-familiar sampling of Chic's disco hit "Good Times" (1979), "Rapper's Delight" offered solid proof of the genre's appeal among young audiences, across economic and gender boundaries. Many Sugar Hill artists progressed to success in the early 1980s.

Golden Era

The years 1980 to 1997 are often called the Golden Era of rap music, primarily due to the barrage of genre-defining material that was released then. Many of the rap artists who surfaced in the 1980s reached a degree of critical and commercial acclaim that remains unrivaled by contemporary musicians within the genre.

In 1982, *The Message,* an album by Grandmaster Flash and the Furious Five, married the DJ-produced sound of late Sugar Hill records with the social consciousness and ferocity of the early-1970s work by the Last Poets. This trend continued throughout the decade,

as material by artists such as EPMD, Erik B. and Rakim, Run DMC, Biz Markie (Marcel Hall), Slick Rick (Richard Walters), and LL Cool J (James Smith) formed the standard by which critics and audiences judge the majority of contemporary rap music. All of these artists employed the successful formula of "Rapper's Delight" to some degree, combining creative DJ-driven implementation of samples from popular music with straightforward and accessible rhyme delivery.

Golden Era artists, primarily groups, also had an influence on 1980s urban fashion and humor as well as the lifestyles of many teenagers and young adults across the nation. Audiences in New York donned matching leather jackets and gold chains in mimicry of Run DMC. (New York–based artists already had influenced fashion earlier in the decade, when groups of friends across the city purchased matching jumpsuits in emulation of groups such as the Sugar Hill Gang.)

Many Golden Era groups relied on fashion gimmicks, along with humorous lyrics, to win the hearts and minds of increasingly large audiences. This trend was most evident in the work of the George Clinton–inspired, California-based 1980s rap group the Digital

Underground, in songs like "The Humpty Dance" and "The Way We Swing" from the album *Sex Packets* (1989). Like Clinton's 1970s-era bands Parliament and Funkadelic, the Digital Underground embraced stage theatrics; during performances, group leader Shock-G (Gregory Jacobs) would often change into contextually specific costumes for different material. Many artists in the Golden Era were also scathingly autobiographical, often with humor and particularly in reference to subjects such as heartbreak. Both of these trends are evident in Biz Markie's "Just a Friend" (1989), in which the rapper leaves behind the genre's traditional romantic boasting to offer consecutive personal tales of unrequited love.

In the late 1980s and early 1990s, as news of the HIV/AIDS epidemic spread, many Golden Era artists, including the California artists Dr. Dre, Snoop Dogg (Calvin Broadus), and Ice Cube (O'Shea Jackson), consistently alluded to safe sex practices. As was the case in the 1970s for limited audiences, Golden Era rap music offered a compelling alternative for listeners tired of the trite themes of more radio-friendly fare. Many young African American teenagers across the country mimicked the style (in humor, fashion, and behavior) of Golden Era MCs, particularly in the case of Run DMC. Rap-exclusive labels such as Tommy Boy Records and Def Jam Records emerged during the 1980s as a result of the genre's overwhelming popularity among young audiences.

In the late 1980s and early 1990s, an interesting dichotomy emerged in American rap music. On the one hand, the emergence of East Coast gangsta rappers, whose violent lyrics were inspired by pioneers like Ice-T, Schoolly D (Jesse Weaver), and KRS-One (Lawrence Parker), gained mainstream appeal in the work of such groups as California's N.W.A. The gangsta subgenre became popular in the 1990s primarily through the efforts of labels such as Death Row Records and Bad Boy Records. The violent, often misogynistic material by California artists such as Eazy E (Eric Wright), Ice Cube, and Dr. Dre was embraced by many West Coast gangs, while Bad Boy Records artists like Biggie Smalls (Christopher Wallace) were embraced by similar audiences on the East Coast. In both regions, gangsta rap labels relied on use of popular hooks and samples in an attempt to increase mainstream appeal and record sales.

On the other end of the rap spectrum, the success of politically and emotionally charged rap artists such as Public Enemy, the Pharcyde, and A Tribe Called Quest in the late 1980s and early 1990s gave way to an emerging independent rap movement in the 1990s.

Defining record labels emerged for the independent movement, including Quannum Projects and Definitive Jux Records. Gangsta rap flourished until 1997, a year punctuated by the murder of two of the subgenre's biggest names, West Coast rap artist and actor Tupac Shakur in September 1996 and East Coast gangsta Biggie Smalls (or Notorious B.I.G.) in March 1997.

Mainstream Leanings

While independent rap production continues to capture the attention of primarily college-aged audiences, mainstream interest in gangsta rap has given way to an era of label-controlled, homogenized, radio-friendly fare. Overall, critics and audiences often see independent rap music as a continuation or elaboration of traditions and techniques established during the Golden Era. Artists such as Blackalicious, Dead Prez, Jedi Mind Tricks, Sage Francis, and the People Under the Stairs have attained cult followings in recent years. Many of today's mainstream artists continue to maintain popularity despite a hollow lyrical focus on materialism. Traditional rap events in the style of Kool DJ Herc's parties also surface in large-city competitions between lyricists, primarily in California and along the East Coast, where audiences often judge artists on lyrics and rhyme delivery.

On the other hand, many of the artists and producers who embraced the gangsta rap trend either have softened their abrasive lyrics or have catered to mainstream demands to increase popular appeal. In the 2000s, widely diverse styles of rap emerged from mainstream and independent rap artists. Despite the pervasive commercial success of the genre, the countercultural aspects of rap music, including direct inspiration from Golden Era artists, independent record distribution, and rap competitions in large cities, no doubt will continue to flourish.

Wesley French

See also: Gangsta Rap; Hip-Hop; Malcolm X; N.W.A.; Shakur, Tupac; Snoop Dogg.

Further Reading

Keyes, Cheryl L. *Rap Music and Street Consciousness.* Music in American Life. Urbana: University of Illinois Press, 2004.

McQuillar, Tayannah Lee. *When Rap Music Had a Conscience: The Artists, Organizations and Historic Events That Inspired and Influenced the "Golden Age" of Hip-Hop from 1987 to 1996.* New York: Thunder's Mouth, 2007.

Watkins, S. Craig. *Hip Hop Matters: Politics, Pop Culture and the Struggle for the Soul of a Movement.* Boston: Beacon, 2006.

Rastafari Movement

Rastafarianism is a millenarian religious and cultural movement that arose in the 1930s among black Jamaicans and continues to the present day. According to Rastafarian belief, former Ethiopian Emperor Haile Selassie (originally known as Ras Tafari and accepted as the "Lion of Judah" as referred to in the Hebrew Bible) was God incarnate. Crucial to the emergence and spirit of Rastafarianism were the black separatist teachings of Jamaican liberationist Marcus Garvey, who advocated the formation of separate black businesses and social institutions, and came to be regarded as a Rastafarian prophet. Other lifestyle practices associated with Rastafarians include growing the hair into long braids known as dreadlocks, not eating certain foods thought to be unclean, such as pork, and the ritual use of ganja (marijuana). The Rastafari movement has spread throughout the world, largely on the strength of its popular musical style, reggae.

Origins

The crowning of Haile Selassie I as emperor of Ethiopia in 1930—making him the monarch of Africa's only independent nation—was regarded by many working-class and peasant Jamaicans as fulfillment of the biblical prophecy that a black king would be crowned in Africa. Although evidence is scant, it appears that several individuals had simultaneously begun to promote Haile Selassie I as a black liberator and messianic figure. The most famous of these was Leonard Howell, who regarded Selassie as the incarnation of God and claimed to be his divine messenger. From 1933 to 1940, Howell preached the tenets of Rastafarianism. His message asserted the superiority of blacks to whites and advocated resistance to white oppression. His advocacy of violent revolution attracted the attention of Jamaican authorities, and in 1933 he was sentenced to a two-year prison term for sedition. In 1940, he established a Rastafarian community known as Pinnacle on an abandoned colonial estate. By the mid-1950s, there were a dozen or more small (20 to 200 members) Rastafarian groups in the Kingston area. By the 1970s, the number had grown to fifty or more.

Rastafarians believe that they are the descendants of the Israelites, whom they see as God's chosen people, and that they will someday be returned to Zion (Ethiopia). Many organized religions throughout history have instructed their downtrodden followers to suffer silently while awaiting their heavenly reward. Rastafarianism, by contrast, teaches that heaven is on Earth and that political struggle can be used to improve social conditions. This philosophy proved appealing to thousands of poor Jamaicans, who could relate to the Rastafarian emphasis on the present human condition as opposed to a mythical afterlife.

The basic tenets of Rastafarianism, according to George Simpson's classic 1955 article "Political Cultism in West Kingston," are as follows: (1) black people were exiled to the West Indies because of their transgressions; (2) whites are inferior to blacks; (3) the Jamaican situation is hopeless—that is, there is no way Jamaican blacks can ever be truly liberated as long as they remain in Jamaica; (4) Ethiopia is heaven; (5) Haile Selassie is the living God; (6) the emperor of Abyssinia (now Ethiopia) will arrange for expatriated persons of African descent to return to the homeland; and (7) blacks will soon get their revenge by compelling whites to serve them.

Despite influences such as Garvey's, modern-day Rastafarianism is a diffuse movement with a wide range of beliefs. Many Rastafarians believe in some but not all of the tenets. For example, some believe in the divinity of Haile Selassie while others do not; some Rastas eat meat while others are vegetarians (although most follow Ital, or "vital," rules for the procurement and preparation of food); and some Rastas smoke ganja while many others choose not to. The variations in belief reflect the loose, decentralized nature of the movement itself. There is no universal structure or central authority and no single leader. Followers, both in the United States and in Jamaica, tend to gather in small, informal groups, and often refuse to take part in elections. This has changed in recent decades, as more Rastafarians have become politically active. Socialist Prime Minister Michael Manley attempted to win Rastafarian votes during the elections of the 1970s by addressing their concerns and adopting reggae songs, most notably Delroy Wilson's "Better Must Come" (1971), as campaign anthems.

Growth and Influences

The mid- to late 1950s was a period of rapid growth for Rastafarianism in Jamaica, as more traditional Afro-Caribbean religions, such as revivalism, went into decline. The growth continued into the 1970s and 1980s. While older Rastafarians believed strongly in the repatriation of Jamaican blacks to their ancestral African homelands, the return-to-Africa movement was de-emphasized in later years as younger Rastafarians insisted that improvements in the living conditions of the Jamaican poor must stem from changes in Jamaican society. Rastafarians believe that "Babylon," usually identified with the United States, Great Britain, the Jamaican government, and organized religion, is the root cause of the poverty of Jamaican blacks.

Rastafarianism has had a profound influence on reggae, Jamaica's indigenous popular music. Rastafarian themes are common in both ska and reggae, and the movement even has its own form of music, known as *nyabinghi*, which makes heavy use of African percussion and polyrhythms. Awareness of African identity and culture is a predominant theme in several forms of Rastafarian cultural expression. Rastafarian culture has spread throughout the Caribbean, the United States, and the world, in large part through reggae music but also through art, literature, and philosophy. Reggae music in general and singer Bob Marley's work in particular have gained wide popularity all over the world, especially in Africa. Elements of Rastafarian culture also have become popular among non-Rasta American youth, including the dreadlocks hairstyle, ganja smoking, and Rasta-influenced clothing styles.

Rastafarianism in the United States

Although there have been no comprehensive studies of Rastafarianism in the United States, it is believed that the movement was a largely Jamaican phenomenon until the mid-1960s. Many Caribbean people migrated to the United States in the 1960s and 1970s, increasing the visibility of Rastafarians in U.S. cities with substantial Jamaican populations, such as Boston, New Haven, New York, Philadelphia, Washington, D.C., Miami, Chicago, Houston, Los Angeles, and the San Francisco Bay Area. New York City has historically been the most important U.S. urban center for Rastafarianism, in large part because of Marcus Garvey's early work in that city. Early black leaders such as Leonard Howell also spent significant periods of time in New York.

After a period of growth in the 1970s and 1980s, Rastafarianism in the United States today remains a limited phenomenon. National surveys conducted in 1990 and 2001 indicate that between 10,000 and 15,000 self-identified Rastafarians live in the United States.

These numbers are comparable to those for such other folk religions such as Wicca and Eckankar, though many researchers believe that estimates severely underrepresent actual numbers of followers. In the earliest days of Rastafarianism in the United States, the movement's adherents were often portrayed in the mainstream media as violent, drug-addicted criminals.

Most U.S. Rastas are Caribbean immigrants, though others are African, African American, Native American, and even white American. Due partially to their emphasis on self-reliance, many Rastafarians in the United States have started their own businesses, including reggae record stores, health food stores, Rasta accessory stores, and Ital restaurants.

As in Jamaica, the Rastafarian community in the United States is a decentralized and leaderless movement, unaffiliated with any organized church or congregation. Nevertheless, there are several important Rastafarian and Afrocentric churches and other organizations in the United States, among them the Ethiopian World Federation (established in New York City in 1937), the Twelve Tribes of Israel, the Ethiopian Orthodox Church, and the Church of Haile Selassie I.

Paul Kauppila

See also: Garvey, Marcus; Universal Negro Improvement Association.

Further Reading

Barrett, Leonard E. *The Rastafarians.* 20th anniv. ed. Boston: Beacon, 1997.

Clarke, Peter B. *Black Paradise: The Rastafarian Movement.* San Bernardino, CA: Borgo, 1988.

Edmonds, Ennis Barrington. *Rastafari: From Outcasts to Culture Bearers.* New York: Oxford University Press, 2003.

Simpson, George E. "Political Cultism in West Kingston." *Social and Economic Studies* 4 (June 1955): 133–49.

Rave Culture

Rave culture is the underground music and dance scene associated with raves, all-night parties typically held in warehouses, clubs, or outdoor venues and featuring laser light shows, electronic music, and, in many cases, ecstasy and other drugs. With antecedents in the 1960s, rave emerged as a distinctive culture and style in the 1980s. Rave parties reflect a collective sense of well-being and enthusiasm that, despite the opposition of politicians and law enforcement in the early years, transcends ethnicity, social-economic class, and sexual orientation. It is an inclusive culture in which up to thousands of partiers dance until the sun comes up, at which time they part ways and return to their jobs, schools, neighborhoods, and separate lives.

In the spirit of 1960s psychedelic rock culture, English club-goers in the 1980s combined acid house and techno music with the drug ecstasy in a series of large, outdoor dance events. These raves, as they came to be called, attracted thousands of people to venues in London and Manchester during the summer of 1988. By the early 1990s, New York DJ Frankie Bones shared his English club-scene experiences with America through his STORMraves, huge raves that also attracted thousands of partygoers. British DJ Steve Levy brought raves to Los Angeles, while Dianna Jacobs, Preston Lytton, and Mark Heley (an English expatriate) brought Toon Town parties (cartoon-themed raves) to San Francisco.

Most early raves were held illegally on private property in places such as brickyards, warehouses, parking garages, and even churches, or outdoors on beaches or in deserts, wooded areas, or cow pastures. The illicit and unconventional nature of the events, not to mention the drug use, added elements of danger and excitement that only increased the allure to rebellious partygoers. However, chronic shutdowns by law enforcement proved to be a disappointment for both partygoers and promoters. As a result, promoters such as Les Borsai and his archrival, Daven "the Mad Hatter" Michaels, turned to promoting large, extravagant, themed raves in legally reserved venues.

DJs, or so-called digital shamans, such as Doc Martin, Jenö, Richie Hawtin, and Sven Vath, utilize a combination of synthesizers, turntables, and computer programs to set the mood and control the crowd as it writhes, bounces, and surges to the techno, house, and electronica beats under laser light and artificial fog. A DJ may incorporate punk, pop, funk, rock, movie themes, and even nursery rhymes into the music, laying down a seamless soundtrack for the night's experience. The DJ's role is so crucial to the ambience that good ones are sought after, catered to, and widely celebrated in the rave world.

As the music pulses, ravers—who may be waving glowsticks, wearing "kandi" necklaces and bracelets made of plastic beads, clad in "phat pants," and sporting nostalgic backpacks and clothing with childhood favorites such as Winnie the Pooh and Teletubbies on them—dance alone, with friends, or with strangers. Drugs such as ecstasy induce a sense of euphoria and unity, while heightening the senses (causing sounds to become sharper and colors more vibrant); some ravers

wear dust masks smeared with Vicks VapoRub to enhance the effects of ecstasy. The marathon dancing and drug use carry the risk of dehydration, so many ravers take breaks to lounge together in "chill out" areas with bottles of water. The experience, for some spiritual and for others tribal, culminates in a sense of PLUR (an acronym for peace, love, unity, and respect) that promotes acceptance, connection, and oneness with fellow beings.

The increasing commercialization of raves since the 1980s has led many old-school ravers to lament that "rave is dead." By its very nature, they argue, rave rejects popular culture and entrenched social mores. Nevertheless, as raves have gained in popularity, event promoters and corporate sponsors have mainstreamed the experience. Organized raves are regarded by purists as formulaic in presentation, expensive (with promoters charging upwards of $50 a ticket), and commercialized. Another factor in the changing nature of rave culture is the increased use of harder drugs, such as crystal meth, ketamine ("Special K"), and LSD, as well as alcoholic beverages, such as Vex and Gruv, and highly caffeinated nonalcoholic drinks such as Red Bull. The edgier scene created by harsher drugs, alcohol, and direct marketing is said to detract from the utopia-like environment and has alienated many original ravers.

Jennifer Aerts Terry

See also: Ecstasy.

Further Reading

Green, Jared F., ed. *DJ, Dance, and Rave Culture.* Detroit, MI: Greenhaven, 2005.
McCall, Tara. *This Is Not a Rave: In the Shadow of a Subculture.* New York: Thunder's Mouth, 2001.
Reynolds, Simon. *Generation Ecstasy: Into the World of Techno and Rave Culture.* New York: Routledge, 1999.
Sylvan, Robin. *Trance Formation: The Spiritual and Religious Dimensions of Global Rave Culture.* New York: Routledge, 2005.

Ray, Man (1890–1976)

One of the most influential American artists of the early twentieth century (though he lived for much of his life in Paris, France), Man Ray is known primarily for his avant-garde photography, but he also worked as an assemblage artist, draughtsman, painter, and filmmaker. He is credited with founding the American arm of the Dada "anti-art" movement, which began in Europe as a rejection of the aesthetics of modern visual art, and was a central figure as well in the surrealist and abstract art movements.

Born Emmanuel Rudnitsky in Philadelphia on August 27, 1890, to Russian immigrants, he moved with his family to Brooklyn, New York, at an early age. It was there that he developed interest and inclinations in art. Moving to Manhattan after high school to pursue his career as an artist, he eventually befriended the French Dadaists Marcel Duchamp and Francis Picabia, photographer and Gallery 291 owner Alfred Stieglitz, and other members of the early-twentieth-century American avant-garde.

In 1921, after publishing one issue of a magazine called *New York Dada* and helping found a modernist organization called Société Anonyme, Man Ray famously declared that "Dada cannot live in New York" and moved to the Montparnasse section of Paris. While making his mark as an avant-garde photographer, he became deeply involved with both the French Dada and the surrealist art movements. Especially during the interwar years in Paris, Man Ray experimented extensively with photographic technique. This led him to the highly innovative use of solarization—the partial reversal of tones in a photographic image—grain enlargement and prints made without a camera, which he called Rayographs. These, he produced by placing objects directly on photographic paper and exposing them to light to capture their silhouettes.

With a growing reputation for portraiture as well, he documented some of the most famous literary figures of the period, including James Joyce, T.S. Eliot, Ernest Hemingway, and Gertrude Stein. In addition to the surrealists and other members of the Paris vanguard, such as Pablo Picasso and Constantin Brancusi, Man Ray's artistic circle included the photographer Lee Miller and the Parisian singer Kiki de Montparnasse, both of whom were his lovers.

Man Ray once said, "I paint what cannot be photographed. I photograph what I do not wish to paint." Many of his works have become icons in the history of modern Western art. Among these are "Tears" (1932), the close-up image of an eye "crying" glass tears; "Ingres' Violin" (1924), picturing Kiki's back with sound holes like those of a stringed instrument; "Gift" (1921), a menacing surrealist object consisting of a flatiron with nails attached to its surface; "Object to Be Destroyed" (1923), an assemblage consisting of a metronome with the photograph of an eye attached to it; and "At the Observatory Hour—The Lovers" (1934), a Magritte-like painting of a pair of disembodied lips floating in the sky.

Man Ray also produced an arresting and impressive body of fashion photographs for *Vanity Fair, Harper's Bazaar,* and *Vogue* magazines. His film credits include several surrealist productions of the 1920s, including *Le Retour à la Raison* (*The Return of Reason,* 1923), *Emak Bakia* (1926); *L'Etoile de Mer* (*The Starfish,* 1928), and *Les mystères du Chateau du Dé* (*The Mysteries of the Chateau of Dice,* 1929).

To escape the Nazi occupation of Paris, Man Ray returned to America to live in 1940. He went back to Paris in 1951, and remained a resident until his death on November 18, 1976.

Julia Pine

Further Reading

Ray, Man. *Self Portrait.* London: André Deutsch, 1963.
Schaffer, Ingrid. *The Essential Man Ray.* New York: Harry N. Abrams, 2003.
Ware, Kate. *Man Ray: 1890–1976.* Cologne, Germany: Taschen, 2000.

Realist, The

Edited and published by social critic and stand-up comic Paul Krassner, *The Realist* was one of the most influential and durable underground publications in America during the latter half of the twentieth century. Beginning with its first issue in 1958, the magazine quickly established itself as a consistently readable source of satire, news, commentary, conspiracy theory, and hoax. Published out of the same building as the satirical *MAD* magazine, *The Realist* was viewed in many ways as the adult counterpart to the teen magazine.

In its most bracing moments, the magazine blurred the line between fiction and reality, often leaving readers questioning what they were willing to accept as true. In perhaps the paper's most outrageous and infamous article, Krassner used a real vignette from the 1960 Democratic Party leadership race between John F. Kennedy and Lyndon B. Johnson to introduce a report claiming that Kennedy's widow, Jacqueline, had caught Johnson having sex with the dead president's neck wound while on the flight from Dallas to Washington following Kennedy's assassination in 1963. The May 1967 article, titled "The Parts That Were Left Out of the Kennedy Book," was presented as unpublished excerpts from historian William Manchester's controversial book about the killing, *The Death of a President.*

Another piece that brought a great deal of attention to *The Realist,* ranging from the wildly positive to the harshly critical, was the Disneyland Memorial Orgy poster in 1967. Illustrated by *MAD* artist Wally Wood and published shortly following the death of Walt Disney, the poster depicted beloved Disney characters in varying states of undress and engaged in a variety of sexual activities. Designed as a statement against the repressive social codes and conservatism of the later 1950s and early 1960s, as represented by Disney, the poster would become probably the most popular, and most enduring, work to appear in the magazine. It has proven such a lasting image that digitally colored versions of the poster still sell in the twenty-first century.

The Realist provided a home for the critical voices of writers and activists who were denied publishing opportunities in the mainstream press. Among those who were given space within its pages were sex-worker organizer Margo St. James and conspiracy theorist Mae Brussell, who detailed the operation of the Watergate break-in well before the mainstream media took notice of it. The magazine also published social commentary by playwright Norman Mailer, novelist Ken Kesey, philosopher Robert Anton Wilson, and satirical novelist Joseph Heller.

In no ways a journal of detached satire, *The Realist* maintained a connection with real-world social developments and movements. Editorship of issue 81 in August 1968 was turned over to the anarchist-communalist Diggers collective, providing them with an opportunity to present their radical egalitarian philosophies to a broader public.

Through *The Realist*, Krassner developed an influential form of what he called "participatory journalism." When, following the publication in 1962 of an interview with humane abortionist Dr. Robert Spence, women called Krassner in search of safe abortions, he provided an underground abortion referral service. While covering the anti–Vietnam War movement in the United States, Krassner ended up cofounding the Youth International Party with Abbie Hoffman and Jerry Rubin in 1967. With money raised by selling "Fuck Communism" posters through *The Realist*, Krassner sent to Southeast Asia a reporter critical of the U.S. war effort.

After publishing regularly throughout the 1960s and into the early 1970s, *The Realist* was forced to suspend publication due to financial constraints in 1974. Krassner revived *The Realist* as an irregular newsletter in 1985 and continued publishing until the final issue, number 146, in 2001.

Jeff Shantz

See also: MAD; Yippies.

Further Reading

Krassner, Paul. *How a Satirical Editor Became a Yippie Conspirator in Ten Easy Years.* New York: Putnam, 1971.
———. *Murder at the Conspiracy Convention and Other American Absurdities.* Fort Lee, NJ: Barricade, 2000.
———. *One Hand Jerking: Reports From an Investigative Satirist.* New York: Seven Stories, 2005.
———. *Paul Krassner's Impolite Interviews.* New York: Seven Stories, 1999.

Recycling

Recycling is the practice and industry of separating, collecting, and breaking down domestic and industrial waste for the purpose of manufacturing new items from the same raw material. In theory, the practice allows ecologically savvy citizens and businesses to cut back on the amount of waste produced by society at large. The motivation for recycling, ultimately, is to reduce energy consumption and conserve the earth's natural resources. Glass, paper, aluminum, and plastic have been the most commonly recycled materials since the practice was widely adopted in the United States in the latter decades of the twentieth century.

Recycling was implemented in a number of countries during both World War I and World War II, as citizens on the home front were encouraged or required to limit their consumption of vital commodities and to collect others for reuse. Although recycling continued to be encouraged after the wars in areas with depleted resources (such as Japan), Americans became entrenched in a massive cycle of environmental abuse.

Rather than expand or even continue its recycling campaigns, or seeking other solutions for its growing waste problem, the United States continued to open large waste dumps in the late 1940s. The Fresh Kills Landfill in New York, for example, built in 1948, reached such heights that it became the only man-made object visible from outer space besides the Great Wall of China. Other environmentally unsound American innovations of the 1940s included aerosol sprays, Styrofoam, and aluminum beverage cans.

As the suburbs expanded and mass consumption continued to increase in the 1950s and early 1960s, many people began to recognize that rampant waste and environmental destruction had become a fact of everyday life in America. Environmentalists such as Rachel Carson published books that called attention to the damage being caused to the natural world and the threats to human health. Carson's *Silent Spring* (1962), which focused on the indiscriminate use of chemical pesticides and fertilizers, was one of the first books to warn of the danger of ecological carelessness and to suggest recycling as a means of preserving nature. The warnings of Carson and others gave birth to the modern environmental movement.

The first wave of modern recycling programs were drop-off arrangements: participants brought aluminum, paper, and plastic materials to a collection site located in a shopping area or other easily accessible place. There, workers crushed or otherwise prepared the different materials for transport. Generally, brokers bought the recyclable materials and sold them to manufacturers, who in turn used them to create new products.

Federal officials tried several options in the mid-1960s to curb the unparalleled accumulation of waste, starting with the Solid Waste Disposal Act of 1965, which restricted the use of landfills. In 1969, a Modesto, California, group called Ecology Action organized a "Survival Walk" across the state, during which participants, led by environmentally conscious citizens Cliff and Mary Humphrey, created recycling collection sites along the way.

At the turn of the decade, Senator Gaylord Nelson (D-WI) called for the establishment of an annual teach-in called Earth Day. The first Earth Day was held in spring 1970. Modeled after the large-scale antiwar protests of the 1960s, the event attracted 20 million people to activities that promoted environmental education and encouraged Americans to embrace recycling. Within six months, approximately 2,000 collection programs were started nationwide.

As energy prices rose to unprecedented heights during the 1970s, glass bottle return centers and other recycling facilities began to surface in large cities, particularly in the states of California, Oklahoma, and Rhode Island, which offered cash for raw materials. In 1976, the Resource Conservation and Recovery Act mandated the sanitization of existing landfills by establishing Environmental Protection Agency regulations to protect citizens from potentially toxic overflows.

Recycling gradually increased in popularity among average citizens, and curbside collection made it easier to recycle from home. By 1986, San Francisco met its goal of recycling 25 percent of the city's waste. That same year, Rhode Island instituted the first statewide legislation to require citizens to use recycling centers for metal, glass, newspapers, and plastic. In 1987, Philadelphia became the nation's first large city to mandate citywide recycling; other municipalities have followed suit.

Since the late twentieth century, many major corporations, including McDonald's, Coca-Cola, and Pepsi, have switched to recycled packaging material in an attempt to improve their public images and environmental "footprints." Recycling retains a positive social connotation in the early twenty-first century, thanks in part to television commercials and films designed to increase environmental awareness. Community services, such as public recycling bins, scheduled pickup of various recycled materials, and the operation of recycling centers in most areas, have made it increasingly easy for citizens to participate in recycling programs.

Wesley French

See also: Carson, Rachel; Environmentalism.

Further Reading

Bisio, Attilio, Adam Weinberg, David Pellow, and Allen Schnaiberg. *Urban Recycling and the Search for Sustainable Community Development*. Princeton, NJ: Princeton University Press, 2000.

Carless, Jennifer. *Taking Out the Trash: A No-Nonsense Guide to Recycling*. New York: Island, 1992.

Rome, Adam. "Give Earth a Chance: The Environmental Movement and the Sixties." *Journal of American History* 90:2 (September 2003): 525–54.

Stein, Kathi. *Beyond Recycling: A Re-User's Guide*. Santa Fe, NM: Clear Light, 1997.

Reed, John (1887–1920)

The journalist and Communist sympathizer John Reed was a war correspondent, friend of the Russian revolutionist Vladimir Lenin, and founder of the U.S. Communist Labor Party in 1919, one of the predecessors of the Communist Party USA. He is perhaps best known as the author of *Ten Days That Shook the World* (1917), a sympathetic account of the Bolshevik Revolution of 1917, which he experienced firsthand.

Reed was born on October 22, 1887, in Portland, Oregon, in the mansion of his maternal grandparents. Both of his parents were of prominent families; his father sold agricultural implements and insurance. As a boy, Reed attended public schools in Portland and suffered frequent bouts with a kidney ailment.

After graduating from Harvard in 1910, Reed moved to New York, where he worked on the *American Magazine* and published his poetry. During this period, he became acquainted with the work of muckraking journalists Ida Tarbell and Lincoln Steffens, but he felt that they were not doing enough to help oppressed workers. Drawn into socialist circles, Reed joined the staff of Max Eastman's radical journal *The Masses,* in 1913, contributing more than fifty articles and reviews. He also experienced his first arrest that year, as a result of supporting striking garment workers in Paterson, New Jersey.

In 1914, Reed went to Mexico to report on that country's revolution. He was sympathetic to Pancho Villa's revolt there. Villa took a liking to the earnest young American and made him a staff officer with the rank of brigadier general. With the outbreak of World War I in Europe, Reed traveled overseas as a reporter for *Metropolitan Magazine,* serving as a war correspondent on several fronts.

In 1917, his reporting took him and his wife, fellow journalist and feminist Louise Bryant, to Petrograd (later Leningrad and St. Petersburg), Russia, to witness the October Revolution. His coverage of the activities of revolutionary leaders and the rise to power of the Bolsheviks led to his close friendship with Lenin, who wrote a preface to the original edition of *Ten Days.*

Reed returned to New York as the Russian consul in 1918, but the U.S. government refused any dealings with him. Expelled from the Socialist Party the following year, he joined with a number of other radicals in forming the American Communist Labor Party, the first communist party in the United States. His activities, speeches, and several articles in the *Voice of Labor* led to his indictment for sedition in 1919.

Reed fled the United States for the newly formed Soviet Union in hopes that Lenin would grant him asylum and perhaps even a position in the government. However, Reed's opposition to the increasingly dictatorial nature of the Soviet regime strained relations between him and the Bolsheviks. He attempted to return to the United States several times, hoping to resume his communist agitation at home. During one such attempt, he was arrested in Finland and held for thirteen weeks before being returned to the Soviet Union.

In 1920, Reed contracted typhus. He died on October 20 while still in the Soviet Union. He was given a state funeral and became the only American to be buried at the Kremlin Wall in Moscow.

Leigh Kimmel

See also: Communism; *Masses, The.*

Further Reading

Duke, David C. *John Reed.* Boston: Twayne, 1987.
Homberger, Eric. *John Reed.* Manchester, UK: Manchester University Press, 1990.
———, ed. *John Reed and the Russian Revolution: Uncollected Articles, Letters, and Speeches on Russia.* New York: St. Martin's, 1992.

Reed, Lou (1942–)

Lou Reed is an iconoclastic rock musician who was an inspiration to a generation of New Wave and punk musicians during the 1970s and 1980s, both as a founding member of the band the Velvet Underground and as a solo performer.

He was born Lewis Alan Reed on March 2, 1942, in Brooklyn, New York, the first of two children. In 1953, his conservative Jewish family moved to the middle-class suburb of Freeport, Long Island, where the rebelliously eccentric and moody Reed channeled his energies into music. Concerns about his emotional health, however, led his parents to have him undergo electroshock treatment from 1959 to 1960.

Reed entered Syracuse University in 1960. The beatnik milieu, drug culture, and writings of Beat poets and writers Allen Ginsberg, Jack Kerouac, and William S. Burroughs, as well as figures from popular culture (such as actors Marlon Brando and James Dean, comic Lenny Bruce, and folk singer-songwriter Bob Dylan) reinforced his existing penchant to challenge the conventions of contemporary college life. At Syracuse, Reed formed rock and roll bands, composed, and presented a morose persona. He also met the self-destructive poet and professor Delmore Schwartz, who became a lifelong mentor. Reed graduated from Syracuse in 1964.

A year later, Reed met the musical prodigy, bassist, and keyboardist John Cale, with whom he formed what many consider to be one of the most influential bands in rock history, the Velvet Underground. Reed received managerial direction from pop artist Andy Warhol, who ensconced the band in New York's seedy avant-garde counterculture and played off Reed's bisexuality. Warhol would remain a strong influence on Reed's life and career.

Although the Velvet Underground achieved little commercial success with the four albums it released before Reed left the group in 1970, the band's cult following continued to grow, especially in Europe. Its music, ranging from punk to rock and lyrical to experimental, is characterized by Reed's deadpan vocals and his searching lyrics about drug abuse, deviant sexuality, and bleak emotions; the dark, urban romanticism that marked Reed's identity was central to the band's distinctiveness.

From its inception, the Velvet Underground was closely associated with the avant-garde art and music scene in New York City, which was influenced by surrealism and experimental art, including underground

Rock and roll veteran Lou Reed, who founded the Velvet Underground in 1965, is accompanied by performance artist Laurie Anderson at his 2006 photography exhibit. As of 2008, Reed continues to write and record music, as well as publish poetry. *(Andrew H. Walker/Stringer/Getty Images)*

cinema. The Velvet Underground worked with several filmmakers to create a multimedia experience of music and visual art during its performances. In 1966, the Velvet Underground began working with Warhol on his Exploding Plastic Inevitable multimedia tour. The group provided the music during screenings of Warhol's films and during dance performances. Through a suggestion by Warhol, Christa Paffgen, also known as Nico, sang a number of songs on the group's début album *The Velvet Underground and Nico* (1967). This album became known for Warhol's progressive cover art of a banana with the words "peel slowly and see"; when it was peeled, a pink peeled banana was revealed.

The group's second album, *White Light/White Heat* (1968), embraced a more aggressive sound not found on its first album. Tension developed between Reed and Cale as they struggled to influence the musical direction of the band. By the time the group recorded its third album, *1969: The Velvet Underground Live* (recorded in 1969; released in 1974), Doug Yule had replaced Cale. Before the group released its fourth album, *Loaded* (1970), Reed left the group.

Reed's sullen intensity and unpredictability continued in his solo recordings and performing career in the 1970s. The musical styles in his numerous albums include punk, pop, glam rock, art rock, rock and roll, hints of doo-wop, heavy metal, and, in one eccentric double album, pure electronic noise. Despite growing but uneven commercial recognition (beginning especially in 1973 with the album *Transformer,* produced by music icon David Bowie), Reed's discontent and disaffection remained part of his music: he was anxiously ambivalent about fame and artistic pretension.

Reed's second marriage, to Sylvia Morales in 1980, led to some stability (the couple would later divorce) and his recording and performing continued, but he struggled to control drug-addiction problems. Since the early 1980s, a seriousness has been apparent in Reed's music and lifestyle, which includes benefits for various causes as well as recording soundtracks. In early 2008, Reed married his longtime companion, performance artist Laurie Anderson, and he continued to tour, perform, and record.

G. Kim Blank and Michael LaMagna

See also: Anderson, Laurie; Beat Generation; Bowie, David; Rock and Roll.

Further Reading

Bockris, Victor. *Transformer: The Lou Reed Story.* New York: Simon and Schuster, 1994.

Bockris, Victor, and Gerard Malanga. *Up-Tight: The Story of the Velvet Underground.* London: Omnibus, 1997.

Clapton, Diana. *Lou Reed and the Velvet Underground.* New York: Proteus, 1983.

Doggett, Peter. *Lou Reed: Growing Up in Public.* New York: Omnibus, 1992.

Heylin, Clinton. *All Yesterdays' Parties: The Velvet Underground in Print: 1966–1971.* Cambridge, MA: Da Capo, 2005.

Reed, Jeremy. *Waiting for the Man: A Biography of Lou Reed.* London: Picador, 1994.

Regulators

In the mid-eighteenth century, disgruntled farmers in the Piedmont backcountry of the Carolinas who called themselves "Regulators" challenged what they regarded as inequitable treatment at the hands of colonial elites. Active in the western territories of current-day North Carolina and South Carolina, the Regulators mobilized by the hundreds, then by the thousands, to intimidate local sheriffs and other royal officials. Their anger at the perceived tyranny of urban elites, both British and American, was testimony to the egalitarian radicalism in the colonies during the 1760s and 1770s.

Backcountry German, Scottish-Irish, and Welsh settlers fought to preserve their traditional ways of life.

Rural families in the region put a premium on economic cooperation, self-sufficiency, and isolation from city affairs. The absence of hard currency in their barter system, however, placed them at the mercy of tax collectors, who demanded payments to the British Crown in silver and gold.

As taxes rose to pay for government salaries, the sheriff's wagon filled with items from a recently foreclosed farm was an increasingly frequent and distressing sight. The settlers' pleas for issuance of paper money with which to pay taxes fell on deaf ears among nonelected local officials, who could increase their own salaries either by collecting more taxes than required or by selling off rural property to speculators.

Piedmont farmers felt compelled to restore accountability for corrupt authority. Drawing upon longstanding European traditions of popular resistance, they proposed to "regulate" the Crown's tyrannical hold over them. Leaders and organizers, foremost among them the outspoken Quaker Herman Husband, emerged in the early 1760s to channel rural grievances against the courts. Regulator ideology spread rapidly by means of songs and ballads. In an age when common people were expected to defer to the wisdom and virtue of political elites, thousands embraced radical democratic principles in the name of preserving their accustomed livelihoods.

New taxes to pay for an expensive statehouse and governor's residence proved the catalyst for widespread Regulator revolt in 1768. Their petitions ignored, the farmers took up arms against perceived abuses of power. Seven hundred Regulators from Orange County marched on the town of Hillsborough in April after Husband and another Regulator were arrested for "inciting to rebellion." Later that month, 100 men shut down the court in Anson County and refused to pay taxes.

Temporary measures by the royal governor to satisfy Regulator demands eventually broke down, and on May 16, 1771, 2,000 poorly armed and organized farmers confronted 1,000 North Carolina militiamen at the Battle of Alamance. The Regulators were quickly routed, with each side losing about nine persons. Seven leaders of the movement were executed by the state, and the spirit of Regulation quickly receded.

The Regulators vividly demonstrate the complex popular origins of the American Revolution. The same sentiments that drove farmers to resist local and state corruption would fuel the colonial break from England. In 1776, the backcountry would arise again to defend its liberties.

The Regulator drama, rehearsed in North Carolina, was reenacted after the Revolutionary War in Daniel Shays's 1786 rebellion against the Massachusetts tax system. The last Regulator-style revolt occurred in 1791 in western Pennsylvania, where President George Washington and 15,000 cavalrymen eventually arrested and then pardoned a still-fiery Herman Husband. The Regulators are the subject of former president Jimmy Carter's historical novel, *The Hornet's Nest* (2003).

Mark Edwards

Further Reading

Kars, Marjoleine. *Breaking Loose Together: The Regulator Rebellion in Pre-Revolutionary North Carolina.* Chapel Hill: University of North Carolina Press, 2002.

Nash, Gary B. *The Unknown American Revolution: The Unruly Birth of Democracy and the Struggle to Create America.* New York: Viking, 2005.

Reich, Wilhelm (1897–1957)

Wilhelm Reich was a psychoanalyst, political theorist, and experimental scientist whose theories of human sexuality and its relationship to broader social problems made him one of the boldest and most controversial figures in the history of modern psychiatry. He came to be regarded by the mainstream psychoanalytic community as a renegade, chiefly for his concept of "orgastic potency"—the surrender of the human organism to the emotion of love and sexual excitement—as the basis of mental health.

Reich was born on March 24, 1897, in Dobrzcynica, Austria. He attended medical school at the University of Vienna, where he became interested in the work of Sigmund Freud. He became a regular member of the Vienna Psychoanalytic Association in 1920 and received his M.D. degree two years later.

Reich's most important psychoanalytic work concerned character theory, in particular the observation that neurotic patients tend to develop routinized patterns of behaviors and reactions—what he termed "character armor"—as a way of deflecting the pain of traumatic events from the past. In Reich's view, character armor is a major barrier to the healthy integration of the ego.

Despite the positive reception accorded to this theory, Reich's psychoanalytic colleagues did not treat his other main interest nearly as warmly. That interest was the link between human sexuality and neurosis. Reich argued that many neurotic symptoms are not so much the result of repressed childhood trauma, as Freud had posited, but the product of an unhealthy sex life in the present. According to Reich, social mores that stigmatize sex and force people to express their sexuality only in the confines of the family lead to a deficiency of "orgastic potency." This, in turn, contributes to the process of character armoring and helps produce neuroses.

Reich's increasing involvement in politics did not help his cause within the psychoanalytic community. In 1928, he joined the Austrian Communist Party, while in his theoretical work he increasingly made the link between sexual repression and social oppression. Indeed, he called for a sexual revolution as a necessary complement to social and political revolution. In 1930, Reich published one of his best-known books, *The Sexual Revolution,* in which he praised the sexual liberalism of the early Soviet Union.

Reich set up a number of sexological clinics designed to offer sex education and contraceptive devices specifically to working-class youth. In 1933, he published his greatest political work, *The Mass Psychology of Fascism,* in which he argued that Adolf Hitler's rise to power in Germany was made possible by his manipulation of the sexual frustration and character armor of the masses.

Reich's work was cause for embarrassment on the part of the Austrian Communist Party as well as the International Psychoanalytic Association, both of which began to view his ideas as dangerous and heretical. He was expelled from the former in 1933 and from the latter in 1934. Professional setbacks and the increasing Nazi repression of Jews and political dissidents (Reich was both) prompted him to flee Germany in 1933. He bounced between several European countries before finally landing in the United States in 1939.

By the time Reich arrived in America, the focus of his work had become more biological in orientation. Spurred by his interest in the orgasm, he embarked upon a quest to identify the biological energy source that "flowed" during orgasms. After a series of experiments, he claimed to have identified what he called "orgone energy," or the primordial energy underpinning all organic forms of life. Reich considered his discovery of paramount scientific importance, claiming that many of humankind's problems could be alleviated by using orgone energy to cure all types of diseases.

Although his ideas were not given much credence by the scientific community, Reich was able to gather around himself a dedicated group of young researchers who took his work seriously and who sought to advance this new field of "orgonomy." In succeeding years, Reich and his collaborators produced what he called an "orgone accumulator": a large wooden compartment lined with metal, with an opening through which orgone energy was said to enter; it would then accumulate. The idea was for patients to sit inside and reap the therapeutic benefits of the concentrated orgone energy.

During the 1940s and 1950s, Reich's work took on an increasingly mystical tone, as he began to regard orgone energy as a cosmic force. Humanity as a whole was suffering from an "emotional plague," he contended, and only the successful harnessing of orgone energy could cure it. Reich's marketing of the orgone accumulator as a medical device drew the attention of the U.S. Food and Drug Administration, and in 1954 he was served with a court injunction to stop selling the device. In 1956, Reich was arrested for violating the injunction and sentenced to federal prison. He died of a heart attack there on November 3, 1957.

Despite the academic discrediting of orgonomy and the prosecution for his device, many of Reich's young collaborators continued his work, training new generations of Reichian therapists and orgonomists. In the 1960s, the republication of many of Reich's political writings influenced the protest movements that challenged traditional institutions and social relationships, especially the conventional family. He was also widely cited by intellectuals exploring the relationship between Marxism and psychoanalysis.

Michael F. Gretz

See also: Communism; Medicine, Alternative; New Age.

Further Reading

Osborn, Reuben. *Marxism and Psychoanalysis.* New York: Delta, 1965.

Robinson, Paul A. *The Freudian Left: Wilhelm Reich, Geza Roheim, Herbert Marcuse.* New York: Harper & Row, 1969.

Rycroft, Charles. *Wilhelm Reich.* New York: Viking, 1971.

Sharaf, Myron. *Fury on Earth: A Biography of Wilhelm Reich.* New York: Da Capo, 1994.

Wolfenstein, Eugene Victor. *Psychoanalytic-Marxism: Groundwork.* New York: Guilford, 1993.

R.E.M.

R.E.M. is a pioneering alternative rock band. It was formed in Athens, Georgia, in 1980, and features Michael Stipe on vocals, Peter Buck on guitar, Mike Mills on bass, and Bill Berry on drums. The group became a staple of college radio and built a large fan base during the early and mid-1980s, before emerging as a superstar in the late 1980s.

The group built upon folk roots to create a rhythmic, guitar-enriched sound that was a far cry from the synthesizer-heavy Top 40 music of the time. Many R.E.M. songs contain lyrics that are hard to understand, especially those on the early albums (including the appropriately titled *Murmur,* 1983); lyrics were not provided with the albums. The band evolved as it became famous, yet it refused to become subject to the whims of pop music, instead charting its own course.

The band's style changed with each album. Its folk rock songs are infused with lush harmonies and twanging guitars, while its harder rock songs feature a relentless, electric garage-band sound (especially on the multiplatinum seller *Monster,* 1994). After Berry left the band for health reasons in 1997, it recorded the somber and dense album *Up* in 1998 without a replacement drummer.

R.E.M. addressed a number of sensitive issues in its music, in statements to the press, and through participation in the activities of left-wing-leaning nonprofit organizations. Among the topics on which R.E.M. has expressed its views are American imperialism, freedom of speech, and the destruction of ecological systems. The band felt that each of its albums should serve as a snapshot of the time during which it was recorded. During the administrations of presidents Ronald Reagan and George H.W. Bush in particular, R.E.M. found strong inspiration for social commentary. Lead singer Stipe became known for his counterculture views on a number of subjects, including the environment and the activities of the federal government.

The album *Fables of the Reconstruction* (1985) includes the song "Green Grow the Rushes," about the plight of Latino migrant workers in the United States. *Document* (1987) is packed with overtly political songs, including "Exhuming McCarthy" (a reference to the rabidly anticommunist Republican Senator Joseph McCarthy of the 1950s), "Welcome to the Occupation" (about the U.S. role in Nicaragua during the 1980s), and "Disturbance at the Heron House" (about revolution). Also on that album is the song "It's the End of the World as We Know It (and I Feel Fine)," an uptempo laundry list of the ills of the modern world.

With the release of the album *Green* on election day in 1988, R.E.M.'s message continued to carry political and social themes. The song "Orange Crush" alludes to the use of the herbicide-defoliant Agent Orange by the U.S. military during the Vietnam War. In 1991, R.E.M. released the album *Out of Time,* which contains the hit single "Losing My Religion."

The Best of R.E.M., a greatest-hits album released in 2003, features the song "Bad Day," begun in the 1980s and finished during the presidency of George W. Bush, about the games played by both the media and the political establishment. R.E.M. toured on behalf of Democratic presidential candidate John Kerry in 2004; an album released just before the 2004 election, *Around the Sun,* contained a number of songs inspired by the U.S. war in Iraq.

R.E.M. also favors the offbeat. Prolific outsider artist Reverend Howard Finster designed the cover art for the album *Reckoning* in 1984. The band's 1992 album *Automatic for the People* includes the song "Man on the Moon," about the eccentric comedian Andy Kaufman. When the movie *Man on the Moon* was released in 1999, the band contributed another song about Kaufman, "The Great Beyond." The *Monster* album contains the song "What's the Frequency, Kenneth?" based on the bizarre incident in October 1986 in which newscaster Dan Rather was beaten by an unknown attacker who kept asking that question. In addition, Stipe has produced several offbeat feature films, including *Being John Malkovich* (1999), *American Psycho* (2000), and *Saved!* (2004).

Richard Panchyk

See also: Environmentalism; McCarthyism.

Further Reading

Bowler, Dave, and Bryan Dray. *R.E.M.: From "Chronic Town" to "Monster."* New York: Carol, 1995.

Sullivan, Denise. *R.E.M.: Talk About the Passion: An Oral History.* New York: Da Capo, 1998.

Rexroth, Kenneth (1905–1982)

The American poet Kenneth Rexroth, recognized as a catalyst of the post–World War II San Francisco Renaissance in poetry and art, had a major creative and intellectual influence on the Bay Area's literary and radical subcultures during the mid-twentieth century and beyond. The model he provided for younger writers and artists in both politics and aesthetics contributed to a flowering of cultural activity, establishing a link between twentieth-century modernists such as Ezra Pound and William Carlos Williams, and the West Coast wing of the iconoclastic Beat Generation.

Born on December 22, 1905, in South Bend, Indiana, Rexroth was orphaned at the age of twelve and sent to live with an aunt in Chicago. As he matured, Rexroth became increasingly involved in Chicago's radical bohemian and artistic circles; he soon decided that he would devote his life to art and poetry. When he moved to San Francisco in 1927, he carried with him the memory of Chicago's intense cultural ferment, which he ultimately tried to replicate.

San Francisco's radical political legacy, however, heightened Rexroth's interest in developing an overall social and political vision. After flirting with communism in the 1930s, he slowly pieced together an anarchist philosophy that provided a strong critique of American capitalism and militarism. He then spent much of the rest of his life trying to inculcate this vision in a new and youthful "alternative society" in the San Francisco Bay Area.

This began during World War II, when Rexroth provided a haven for conscientious objectors (COs) in the Pacific Northwest who came to the city on weekend leaves from their CO camps. Many of these were writers and artists whom he befriended. They would later play a role in the postwar cultural renaissance in San Francisco.

In the late 1940s, Rexroth held a weekly salon at his apartment, where he educated a varied group of writers and artists in the tenets of anarchism, communal living, and aesthetics. This public function continued in the 1950s through idiosyncratic book reviews he broadcast on KPFA radio. A recurring theme in these reviews was that all cultures are possessed of a transcendental social vision, carried forth in the writings of its most cultivated individuals. Rexroth also was a regular contributor to the two leading anarchist periodicals of the time, George Leite's *Circle* and the more militant *Ark* magazine.

Because of his stature in the community, Rexroth was the natural choice to be emcee of the famous Six Gallery reading of October 1955, at which Allen Ginsberg kicked off the San Francisco Renaissance by reading his poem *Howl* for the first time. Rexroth's elder statesman role in relation to the Beat poets, however, portended his decline as an active member of the San Francisco scene.

In 1968, he moved south to Santa Barbara, where he collected his poetry, essays, and social criticism in books that would continue to have a strong influence on West Coast counterculture movements. After a lifetime of activism and art, Rexroth died in Montecito, California, on June 6, 1982.

Michael Van Dyke

See also: Anarchism; Beat Generation; Conscientious Objectors, Draft Dodgers, and Deserters; San Francisco.

Further Reading

Gibson, Morgan. *Revolutionary Rexroth: Poet of East-West Wisdom.* North Haven, CT: Shoe String, 1986.

Hamalian, Linda. *A Life of Kenneth Rexroth.* New York: W.W. Norton, 1991.

Rexroth, Kenneth. *World Outside the Window: The Selected Essays of Kenneth Rexroth.* Ed. Bradford Morrow. New York: New Directions, 1987.

Rice, Thomas Dartmouth (1808–1860)

The actor Thomas Darmouth ("Daddy") Rice made a fortune "blacking up" as the rebellious, raunchy figure of Jim Crow, who mobilized his racial otherness to lambaste the white culture set on disenfranchising black subjects. In fact, Rice became the most popular actor in the United States and Britain from the 1830s to the 1850s by playing a figure whose comic unruliness thrilled audiences even while exposing to ridicule the malignant racism that led up to the American Civil War. Thus Rice came to be known as the "father of American minstrelsy."

Rice was born on May 20, 1808, in New York City. He got his start in acting in the 1820s in Noah M. Ludlow's company in Louisville, Kentucky, playing characters such as the subservient black Sambo in English farces. But Rice's legacy would be the theatrical reversal of traditional black subservience, using blackface, biting satire, and elements of African American folk culture.

He returned to New York in 1830 and performed a popular song-and-dance routine as the old black slave "jumping Jim Crow" in *The Kentucky Rifle* at the Bowery Theatre. Audiences flocked to see a black character who punctured Sambo's air of gracious servility and whose power depended on understanding black subjects as obedient figures content to exist on the periphery. In Rice's play *Oh Hush! or, The Virginny Cupids!* (1833), his Jim Crow character smashes his minstrel's violin over the head of the Sambo character, garnering applause through physical humor even as he smashes the way blacks were perceived. Rice's performances were not invested in performing black authenticity, but rather in using race to critique a society of slavery. "The words Jim Crow," one reviewer perfectly summarized, "are a nom de guerre."

Throughout plays such as *The Virginia Mummy* (1835) and *Bone Squash* (1839), Rice engaged in theatrical warfare by exploding white Americans' convictions about black sexuality, slavery, miscegenation, and white authority. Through the Jim Crow character, he condemned chattel slavery and championed abolitionism, all while confronting his audience with the fact that America's dominant culture was becoming risible. In plays such as *Bone Squash,* for instance, Jim Crow evades a white devil figure through lowbrow comedy, fantasy, and stage magic, casting himself all the while as a real—and rebellious—runaway slave. Jim Crow not only dodged white authority, but he also staged for an eager audience the methods by which one might perform one's resistance to the power of the white devil.

Perhaps Rice's most rebellious role, however, was his burlesque version of the title role in William Shakespeare's *Othello* (1604–1605), which he performed in the early 1850s. Not only did Rice mock white culture's deep investment in Shakespeare as a cultural authority, but he also used the play's focus on the relationship between black and white identity to ask pointed questions about the racial politics of antebellum America.

Rice achieved these goals by recasting *Othello* in significant ways. For instance, while Desdemona is famously murdered by Othello, who is himself killed at the end of the original, both characters live in Rice's reworked version. Thus, by presenting not racial annihilation but racial union, he underscored a theme of racial integration rather than division. Moreover, in a subversive coup de théâtre, Rice presented for his American audience Desdemona and Othello's child, a literal embodiment of interracial productivity and thus a provocative challenge to the nation's burgeoning miscegenation statutes and regulations.

Rice died on September 19, 1860. By the end of his career, he had developed a stage tradition that had taken the United States by storm and whose legacies still can be seen today in everything from television programs such as *Chappelle's Show* (2003–2006), to films such as Spike Lee's *Bamboozled* (2000), and to plays such as Suzan-Lori Parks's Pulitzer Prize–winning *Topdog/Underdog* (2001). Rice's Jim Crow provided a crucial figure in the early to mid-nineteenth century for interrogating racial stereotyping and repression, and thereby offered a productive challenge to cultural institutions that worked—and continued to work—to control and contain black culture.

Matthew Rebhorn

See also: African Americans.

Further Reading

Lhamon, W.T., Jr. *Jump Jim Crow: Lost Plays, Lyrics, and Street Prose of the First Atlantic Popular Culture.* Cambridge, MA: Harvard University Press, 2003.

Lott, Eric. *Love and Theft: Blackface Minstrelsy and the American Working Class.* New York: Oxford University Press, 1993.

Rogin, Michael. *Blackface, White Noise: Jewish Immigrants in the Hollywood Melting Pot.* Berkeley: University of California Press, 1998.

Riot Grrrl

Riot Grrrl is a punk feminist movement developed primarily by white, middle-class female youth on the East Coast of the United States during the early 1990s. A subculture within the larger punk music scene, Riot Grrrl is a more complex countercultural community that involves other activities and forms of expression—group meetings, support groups, self-defense courses (such as Home Alive), and a thriving underground zine culture—as well as political activism that often involves benefit concerts. As evidenced by their allegiance to the do-it-yourself ethic, Riot Grrrls embrace a variety of radical ideologies, particularly those associated with feminism and socialism, while also reconfiguring them in an effort to galvanize, celebrate, and support female youth, a demographic group whose members are doubly disenfranchised because of their sex and age.

Riot Grrrl formed unofficially during the spring of 1991 in Washington, D.C., where members of two Northwest punk bands, Bikini Kill and Bratmobile, were living temporarily. When a race riot erupted in the neighborhood, a local friend and early Bratmobile member, Jen Smith, suggested that the male-dominated punk scene could use a "girl riot," or more active participation by females.

Emboldened by that concept and wanting to communicate with other female youth marginalized in the punk community, as well as in the rest of society, Allison Wolfe and Molly Neuman of Bratmobile started a zine, or underground magazine, *Riot Grrrl.* Meanwhile, Kathleen Hanna and other members of the bands solicited girls in the D.C. punk scene for weekly get-togethers. Much like feminist consciousness-raising groups of the 1960s and 1970s, these meetings allowed girls to share their experiences of the patriarchy, misogyny, and homophobia prevalent in both mainstream society and their punk communities.

As a result of the *Riot Grrrl* zine and these girls-only meetings, more friends were made, more support groups were developed, and more zines, music, and work in other media were produced, as more girls realized the political power and necessity of their self-expression and solidarity. The name eventually attached to this counterculture and its members was Riot Grrrl.

Another significant moment in early Riot Grrrl history was the August 1991 indie music festival, the International Pop Underground (IPU) convention held in Olympia, Washington. During what has come to be known as "Grrrl Night," female members of the bands Bikini Kill, Bratmobile, Heavens to Betsy, 7 Year Bitch, Mecca Normal, Suture, and others performed as part of an all-female billing called "Love Rock Revolution Girl Style Now," and encouraged female youth in the crowd to become politically and culturally active. At this event, many youth who had conversed by mail or phone finally met in person. As a result, more music, zines (including *Satan Wears a Bra, Princess Charming, Diabolical Clits, Pussycat Rag,* and *The Bad Girl Club*), and videos were created within this community, and production and distribution companies run by feminist youth, such as Horse Kitty Records, Riot Grrrl Press, and Big Miss Moviola, were founded.

In 1992, Riot Grrrls began organizing annual conventions so that larger groups of girls could meet each other, discuss issues of common concern, organize for political action, and experience an alternative culture created by and for feminist youth. One of the first Riot Grrrl conventions was held in Washington, D.C., in July and August 1992.

The mainstream press lost interest in Riot Grrrl in 1992 when its members initiated a media blackout in an effort to stop their misrepresentation and commodification. Although the Riot Grrrl movement had splintered by the mid-1990s, the counterculture continued to thrive in a number of countries in the 2000s, offering female youth a safe and supportive network through which to explore radical identities, ideologies, and cultural practices. Riot Grrrls have increasingly turned to the Internet, especially fan sites and message boards, to converse, organize, and distribute products.

Mary Celeste Kearney

See also: Feminism, Third-Wave; Punk Rock; Zines.

Further Reading

Gottlieb, Joanne, and Gayle Wald. "Smells Like Teen Spirit: Riot Grrrls, Revolution, and Women in Independent Rock." In *Microphone Fiends: Youth Music and Youth Culture,* edited by Andrew Ross and Tricia Rose. New York: Routledge, 1994.

Rosenberg, Jessica, and Gitana Garo. "Riot Grrrl: Revolutions from Within." *Signs: Journal of Women in Culture and Society* 23:3 (1998): 809–41.

Whitely, Sheila, ed. *Sexing the Groove: Gender and Popular Music.* New York: Routledge, 1997.

Ripley, George (1802–1880)

A Unitarian minister, transcendentalist thinker, journalist, and social reformer, George Ripley is best known as the founder in 1841 of the utopian cooperative community Brook Farm in West Roxbury, Massachusetts, near Boston. Modeled on the ideas of the French socialist Charles Fourier, Brook Farm became a self-sufficient community whose economic strength lay in farming and light industry. Although Ripley's experiment in secular cooperative living flourished for less than a decade, Brook Farm is considered one of the antecedents of the antiestablishment communes prevalent in the United States during the latter part of the twentieth century.

Ripley was born in Greenfield, Massachusetts, on October 3, 1802. As the son of an affluent New England businessman, he was educated at Harvard College, graduating with highest honors. He pursued graduate studies at the Harvard Divinity School, while teaching mathematics courses for his alma mater. In 1826, he became an ordained minister and began serving at the newly formed Purchase Street Unitarian Church in Boston. The following year, Ripley married Sophia Willard Dana, who capably assisted him in the establishment of the utopian community of Brook Farm.

Ripley's breadth of knowledge and writing talents provided him entrée into the elite social and literary circles of Boston. There, he met such contemporaries as Henry David Thoreau, Ralph Waldo Emerson, Nathaniel Hawthorne, and Karl Marx; many of these notable acquaintances would lecture at the Brook Farm school. During this time, Ripley was one of the editors of the fourteen-volume work *Specimens of Foreign Standard Literature* (the first two volumes of which were published in 1838), which contained the English translations of many important works by European writers. He also assisted in editing the transcendentalist magazine *The Dial*.

According to an anonymous pamphlet, *An Essay on Transcendentalism,* often credited to Charles Mayo Ellis, "Transcendentalism . . . maintains that man has ideas, that come not through the five senses, or the powers of reasoning, but are either the result of direct revelation from God, his immediate inspiration, or his immanent presence in the spiritual world" and "it asserts that man has something besides the body of flesh, a spiritual body, with senses to perceive what is true, and right and beautiful, and a natural love for these, as the body for its food." As the transcendentalists became disenchanted with the Unitarian Church, their literary pursuits and common activities increased steadily. Ripley—whose own home since 1836 had been the meeting place of the Transcendentalist Club, the core of the movement—resigned from the ministry in 1841 and founded Brook Farm.

A fire that swept through Brook Farm in 1846 caused devastating damage from which the community never recovered; it disbanded the following year. George and Sophia Ripley moved to New York City, where he continued to publish and edit *The Harbinger,* a journal first issued at Brook Farm in 1845, and wrote for Horace Greeley's *New York Tribune* and the *Christian Register.* Later, Ripley helped establish and edited *Harper's New Monthly Magazine* and the *New American Cyclopaedia.*

Four years following his wife's death in 1861, Ripley married Louisa Schlossberger, and together they remained active in New York social and literary circles. During the last year of his life, he was beleaguered by ill health. On July 4, 1880, Ripley died while writing an editorial for *Harper's.*

Denise A. Seachrist

See also: Brook Farm; Communes; *Dial, The;* Transcendentalism.

Further Reading

Crowe, Charles. *George Ripley: Transcendentalist and Utopian Socialist.* Athens: University of Georgia Press, 1967.

Golemba, Henry L. *George Ripley.* Boston: Twayne, 1977.

Rivers, Larry (1923–2002)

Larry Rivers was a painter and sculptor whose works have been described by critics as a combination of abstract and pop art. His subjects were far reaching, including portraits of friends and family members; historical figures and themes, including the Russian Revolution and the Holocaust; everyday items; and sex and eroticism. Rivers's work marked a crucial transition in mid-century painting, from the abstract expressionism of the 1950s to the pop art of the 1960s. Rivers was also known in New York's mid-century bohemian counterculture as a jazz musician, filmmaker, actor, and provocateur, pushing the boundaries of taste as well as aesthetics.

Rivers was born Yitzroch Loiza Grossberg in the Bronx, New York, on August 17, 1923. His most important early passion was jazz. After serving in the U.S. Army Air Corps during World War II, he studied at the prestigious Juilliard School of Music in New York, where he met many of the finest musicians of his generation. Among these was Miles Davis, who gave Rivers an entrée into the city's flourishing jazz counterculture. Rivers subsequently began touring with various groups as a jazz saxophonist.

In 1945, an encounter with a book on modern painting redirected Rivers's interest from music to art. He took up painting, studying at the Hans Hofmann School as well as at New York University, from which he graduated in 1951. Rivers quickly became part of the New York School of painters and poets, meeting such rising stars as painter Jackson Pollock and poet and art critic Frank O'Hara, with whom he became close friends.

Rivers's best-known early works are semi-abstract paintings that reimagine traditional, historical subjects. For example, his *Washington Crossing the Delaware* (1953), a painting that measures 10 feet (3 meters) long, features washed-out colors and an urgent, half-drawn, half-painted appearance that would become a trademark style. His fifty-three-piece mixed media work *The History of the Russian Revolution: From Marx to Mayakovsky* (1965) features portraits of Russian rulers, maps, and vignettes of Russian history. Rivers's work subsequently began to incorporate images from popular culture—such as dinner menus, cigarette packs, and banknotes—prefiguring the trend of pop art to come in the 1960s.

Sex and eroticism were other frequent subjects of Rivers's works. In 1965, he was commissioned by *Playboy* magazine to interpret the playmate (the magazine's nude models) in a work of art. The result was the semi-naked *Plexi Playmate,* made of Plexiglas and vinyl. He followed that work with a graphic lamp-sculpture called *Lampman Loves It* for an erotic exhibition. Using the shock factor of sexuality to draw attention, Rivers often painted male and female nudes; the physical beauty or age of his subjects was unimportant. In 1964, he painted *The Greatest Homosexual,* a mixed-media work depicting Napoleon that was inspired by Jacques-Louis David's classic *Napoleon in His Study* (1812).

In both his art and lifestyle, Rivers earned a reputation as a contrarian. He also was well known for his uninhibited enjoyment of marijuana and sex, and for his extensive associations with other artists and writers of mid-century bohemian countercultures. Among his acting credits is a starring role in *Pull My Daisy* (1959), a short film about a raucous bohemian party written by Beat writer Jack Kerouac and costarring poet Allen Ginsberg, among others. Rivers lived at New York's

Hotel Chelsea during the 1960s, a spot famous for housing eccentric artists and writers.

Rivers continued to work on his own and collaborative projects into his seventies. He designed art for the windows of the Lord & Taylor department store in New York and attended the opening in 2001, saxophone in hand to perform for fans. The techniques of his work had changed over time, but what remained consistent was his energy in critiquing entrenched artistic styles and forms. He was and continues to be the object of harsh criticism by some, who consider his renown to be more a function of his eccentric lifestyle and famous friends than of his own artistic innovation and talent. Rivers died on August 14, 2002.

Susanne E. Hall and Richard Panchyk

See also: Jazz; Pop Art.

Further Reading

Duyck, John. *Larry Rivers: Paintings and Drawings, 1951–2001.* New York: Marlborough Gallery, 2006.

Livingstone, Marco. *Pop Art: A Continuing History.* New York: Harry N. Abrams, 1990.

Rivers, Larry, and Arnold Weinstein. *What Did I Do: The Unauthorized Biography of Larry Rivers.* New York: Thunder's Mouth, 2001.

Robbins, Tom (1936–)

The American novelist Tom Robbins, known for a uniquely inventive, humorous, highly charged style, became an icon of post–World War II counterculture literature for works of offbeat social and political satire beginning in the 1970s, the best known of which is *Even Cowgirls Get the Blues* (1976; film version, 1993).

Born on July 22, 1936, in Blowing Rock, North Carolina, Thomas Eugene Robbins was the oldest child of a utility company executive, George T. Robbins, and an author of children's stories, Katherine (Robinson) Robbins. He was raised in North Carolina and Virginia but, like many characters in his novels, Robbins was an adventurer. After withdrawing from Washington and Lee University, he hitchhiked across the United States and then settled in New York's Greenwich Village, where he hoped to become a poet. Unable to support himself and facing the prospect of being drafted, he joined the U.S. Air Force and served for three years in South Korea in the late 1950s.

Upon completion of military service, he returned to school at the Richmond Professional Institute (now Virginia Commonwealth University) and received his degree in 1960. After a brief stint as a journalist in Richmond, he moved to Seattle, Washington, to pursue a master's degree in Far Eastern Studies and write for the *Seattle Times* and *Seattle Post-Intelligencer.* Even as he continued mainstream journalistic pursuits, Robbins took his adventures in new directions, including experimenting with LSD—an event that shaped his personal philosophy and writing style, and led to his friendship with Timothy Leary.

Robbins's first novel, *Another Roadside Attraction* (1971), is the wild, eccentric story of the mummified body of Jesus Christ, which ends up in a hot dog stand/wildlife preserve in the Pacific Northwest. His second novel, *Even Cowgirls Get the Blues,* solidified his reputation as an innovative storyteller and caught the attention of younger readers and others rooted in the counterculture sensibility of the 1960s and 1970s. The novel recounts the adventures of a large-thumbed hitchhiker named Sissy Hankshaw, from the fashion scene of New York to a health spa in North Dakota, where she joins a rebellious band of feminists.

Still Life with Woodpecker (1980), subtitled "Sort of a Love Story," is the tale of a modern-day princess and her unlikely match with a terrorist named Woodpecker. *Jitterbug Perfume* (1984) is the story of the search for the perfect scent, combining heavy doses of absurdity and mysticism with a touch of political commentary. Similar elements are also central to *Skinny Legs and All* (1990), in which a spoon, a sock, and a can of beans play roles as critical as those of their human counterparts in assessing and solving the situation in the Middle East. In *Half Asleep in Frog Pajamas* (1994), Robbins enlists another oddball cast of characters who comment collectively on the state of society, again only slightly removed from absurdity.

International intrigue, central to many of Robbins's novels, figures prominently in *Fierce Invalids from Hot Climates* (2000) and *Villa Incognito* (2003), both of which capture the eccentricities of the Tom Robbins style. Robbins's major works convey many of the central themes of the counterculture—drugs, sexual promiscuity, and communal living—and track political and social trends over the course of more than three decades with consistently poignant sarcasm.

James J. Kopp

See also: Leary, Timothy.

Further Reading

Hoyser, Catherine E., and Lorena Laura Stookey. *Tom Robbins: A Critical Companion.* Westport, CT: Greenwood, 1997.

Whitmer, Peter O. *Aquarius Revisited: Seven Who Created the Sixties Counterculture That Changed America—William Burroughs, Allen Ginsberg, Ken Kesey, Timothy Leary, Norman Mailer, Tom Robbins, Hunter S. Thompson.* With Bruce VanWyngarden. New York: Macmillan, 1987.

Robeson, Paul
(1898–1976)

Through both his personal achievements and his radical politics, Paul Robeson defied cultures of white supremacy in America and abroad. He earned international fame as an actor and bass-baritone singer, but in the years leading up to World War II, he dedicated his efforts to the liberation of African peoples worldwide. Although Robeson is still celebrated by the American left in the twenty-first century, his outspoken criticism of President Harry S. Truman's postwar foreign policy made him one of the nation's most unpopular and tragic figures of the cold war era.

Paul Robeson was born on April 9, 1898, in Princeton, New Jersey, to William Drew Robeson, a pastor who was a former slave, and Maria Louisa Bustill. After the young Robeson's mother died in a household fire, he and his family settled in Somerville, New Jersey, in 1909. A distinguished student, performer, and athlete while in high school, Robeson entered Rutgers University in 1915 on a four-year scholarship, becoming the third African American ever to attend that school, and the only one on campus at the time. Facing sometimes violent racism, he nevertheless excelled in football, basketball, baseball, and track, and graduated as valedictorian of his class in 1919.

Robeson moved on to Columbia Law School, where he earned his degree in 1923, and took up the practice of law in New York City. His legal career proved short-lived. When white colleagues and office staff refused to work with him, he left the profession to pursue a full-time career in entertainment.

Performances in the title role of *The Emperor Jones* (1924) and other works by playwright Eugene O'Neill in the 1920s established Robeson as an actor of note. His rendition of the song "Old Man River" in the Jerome Kern musical *Show Boat* (1927) became legendary, and his performance in the lead role of *Othello* (1943–1945) made it the longest-running Shakespeare production in Broadway history.

From 1925 to 1942, Robeson also appeared in thirteen motion-picture films, though only four of them were made in the United States. Dismayed by the treatment of African Americans in all walks of life and

Scholar, athlete, actor, and renowned bass-baritone Paul Robeson championed the cause of oppressed peoples and became a friend of the Soviet Union. In 1949, he stirred controversy with remarks at the Communist-supported Paris World Peace Congress. *(Nat Farbman/Stringer/Time & Life Pictures/Getty Images)*

increasingly attracted to radical politics, he spent much of the 1930s in England and the Soviet Union.

While abroad, Robeson befriended politically radical Africans and gained a lifelong appreciation for perceived Soviet egalitarianism and antiracism. He joined African American educator W.E.B. Du Bois and other black activists in forming the pan-African Council on African Affairs (CAA) in 1937. Its goal was to unite people of African descent in support of African liberation from Western European colonialism. As chairman of the CAA, Robeson spoke to audiences worldwide and raised funds for the cause. The United States officially supported decolonization during World War II, and few Americans seemed to object to Robeson's new political views. In fact, his performance of the patriotic "Ballad for Americans" on the CBS network in 1939 received the longest applause in radio history.

The resurgence of anticommunism in cold war America would prove to be Robeson's undoing. He openly criticized racial segregation after World War II and argued that American aid to Europe through the Marshall Plan would extend colonialism in Africa. Such remarks brought him under the close scrutiny of the Federal Bureau of Investigation (FBI) and the House Committee on Un-American Activities (HUAC).

With the exception of the progressive press, the white media censored Robeson's activities, and he was blacklisted from performing in the nation's concert halls. After several newspapers reported that he had made pro-Soviet remarks while attending the Paris World Peace Congress in 1949, the U.S. State Department promptly revoked his passport.

Robeson's reputation was further damaged when, at the apparent instigation of U.S. State Department officials, some of the African American press disparaged him as a Communist sympathizer. That impression seemed confirmed in 1952, when the Soviet government awarded him the Stalin Peace Prize.

When Robeson's U.S. passport finally was renewed in 1958, he left the country for Great Britain, performing and traveling extensively. He did not return to the United States until 1963, plagued by ill health and chronic depression. He made few public appearances during the remaining years of his life, not even attending a seventy-fifth birthday celebration held for him at New York's Carnegie Hall in 1973. He died of a stroke two years later, on January 23, 1976, in Philadelphia.

Mark Edwards

See also: African Americans; Communism; Du Bois, W.E.B.

Further Reading

Duberman, Martin. *Paul Robeson: A Biography.* New York: W.W. Norton, 2005.

Von Eschen, Penny M. *Race Against Empire: Black Americans and Anticolonialism, 1937–1957.* Ithaca, NY: Cornell University Press, 1997.

Rock and Roll

The term *rock and roll,* previously used as a sexual allusion in popular song lyrics, was first applied by Cleveland disc jockey Alan Freed in 1951 to an emerging wave of music that mixed both "black" and "white" American traditions. The merging of blues, hillbilly, gospel, Tin Pan Alley, and other styles is perhaps best seen in the early music of Elvis Presley, Chuck Berry, Jerry Lee Lewis, and Little Richard. In addition to mixing previously segregated musical styles, the early rock and roll performers challenged mainstream culture with their flamboyant, sexually charged, rebellious style and public personae. The focus of their lyrics on leisure-time activities from dancing to cars to sex and a casual, free lifestyle flew in the face of middle-class cultural values in postwar America.

By the beginning of the 1960s, however, a new type of rock and roll musician had emerged: the social com-

mentator. First in folk music and later in psychedelic rock, the construct of popular music itself was challenged by singers and songwriters who had a message as well as a song in their hearts. Whether unplugged (armed just with an acoustic guitar, a voice, and maybe a harmonica) or plugged in (playing in a band with an electric guitar, bass, drums, and vocals, all projected through a microphone and amplifier), the emerging artist-critic attacked the institutions of contemporary society.

Thus, in differing ways, rock and roll was at the center of the American counterculture throughout the 1950s, 1960s, and 1970s. In its early days, the music was countercultural in that it challenged the conventional norms of mainstream society and placed young people in opposition to both adults and institutions by focusing on leisure, consumption, and sexuality. The rock and roll music of the 1960s was countercultural in that it had strong political overtones, which openly opposed the foreign and domestic policies of the U.S. government and gave the youth of America—during a rebellious movement in the nation's history—a voice, a channel through which to communicate and be heard, and a place to find a common identity. As the anti–Vietnam War movement peaked in the late 1960s and early 1970s—during the administrations of presidents Lyndon B. Johnson and Richard M. Nixon, a Democrat and a Republican, respectively—rock and roll music was an instrument of change and source of generational identity as much as a form of entertainment.

One of the main reasons rock and roll survived and continued to grow was the purchasing power of American teenagers. Songs such as Chuck Berry's "Sweet Little Sixteen" and Little Richard's "Lucille" (both 1957) played an important role in the creation of a distinct youth identity and consumption ethic. As the recording industry aggressively marketed its product, the new youth market became a mainstay of the American economy. The rise in annual gross revenues of the U.S. recording industry—from $109 million in 1945 to $213 million in 1954 to $603 million by 1959—mirrored the explosion in overall consumer spending in the period after World War II. In the words of *American Bandstand* host Dick Clark, "Teenagers have nine billion dollars a year to spend."

Influences on the Counterculture

Up-and-coming folk and rock musicians in the 1950s and 1960s both heralded the political and social changes of the emerging counterculture and were products of it.

Musicians who helped inspire the new way of thinking included leading voices of the folk revival such as Pete Seeger, Joan Baez, and Bob Dylan (who alienated more traditional fans by going electric in the mid-1960s), followed by British Invasion bands such as the Beatles and the Rolling Stones, and homegrown psychedelic-rock groups such as the Grateful Dead, Jefferson Airplane, and the Doors, among others.

Dylan, for one, appeared to view himself more as a poet than a singer, and the lyrics of his songs were rife with political commentary. His was the voice and music of youthful energy, political and social awareness, and challenge to the status quo. "The times they are a-changin'," he sang, and few could disagree. For Dylan and his legions of successors and counterculture comrades-in-arms, the Vietnam War became a rallying point, and opposition to it became the basis of shared moral conviction and generational identity.

The seriousness of the times—including other heady issues such as Black Power, the plight of inner cities, political corruption, and the perceived enervation of the "establishment"—also helped transform the innocent pop entertainer of earlier times into the musical artist and earnest troubadour. By 1966, the term *artist* had begun to be applied to rock musicians, denoting a growing separation from the cultural and commercial mainstream, or bohemianism.

The evolution from "mere" entertainment to social commentary and musical artistry coincided with the replacement of the single by the LP (long-playing album) as the dominant medium, thereby giving the artist forty minutes of canvas instead of the traditional three-minute record. With the LP came eleven-minute songs and concept records, and the notion that music could be made for art's sake, instead of primarily for commercial purposes. The Beatles and their landmark album *Sgt. Pepper's Lonely Hearts Club Band* (1967) were seen as the catalysts of this transition.

An example of the transition from entertainers to artists can be seen the changes in the Beatles' cover art and music, from *Meet the Beatles* (1964) to *Sgt. Pepper's*. As the band took a hiatus from touring to focus on studio recordings, their themes shifted from love to social criticism; the graphics, production values, and musical energy of their LP efforts reflected greater interest in artistic music than commercial sales, as well as increased drug use and spiritual searching. At this time the Beatles also began producing their own music and designing their own cover art, rather than allowing their label to do the work. The entire transition, not coincidentally, paralleled the transition of American

youth from consumer-oriented teenage frivolity to political engagement, social criticism, and increased drug use at university campuses and musical events across the country.

What followed the Beatles' explosion into mainstream rock was the movement of acid rock and psychedelic rock. Built on the social critiques of Dylan and the artistry of the Beatles, this music is perhaps best known for its association with the mind-altering drug LSD. It was a new sound that mixed jazz, Latin, and blues music with electric guitars and distortion. The vanguard of this movement—including Jimi Hendrix and his ripping guitar solos, which were full of distortion and unlike anything ever heard before in popular music—challenged the conventional notions of musical form in much the same way the Beats and the bebop jazzers had a decade earlier. Hendrix played the guitar with his teeth or behind his head. At the end of his performances, he smashed his guitar against the stage or set it on fire.

Perhaps the pinnacle of the counterculture movement in rock and roll came at the Woodstock music festival, held in Bethel, New York, in August 1969, an event that was supposed to draw only a small number of fans but instead drew hundreds of thousands and lasted three days. The festival showcased many of the icons of the counterculture, including San Francisco bands such as the Grateful Dead and Jefferson Airplane, singers such as Janis Joplin and Joan Baez, and guitarists such as Hendrix and Carlos Santana. Other musicians who performed included the Who, Joe Cocker, Sly and the Family Stone, Ravi Shankar, Richie Havens, Blood, Sweat and Tears, and Creedence Clearwater Revival.

The 1970s brought further change in rock and roll music and its connection with American youth and counterculture. Disillusionment over the perceived lack of success of the 1960s protest movements coupled with the aging of the baby boom generation—now reentering mainstream society by finding jobs and having families—moved rock and roll in two different directions.

On the one hand, some rock music got "harder," with a stronger emphasis on escapism—as reflected in the music of artists from Led Zeppelin to Black Sabbath. On the other hand, rock musicians took an even greater interest in technical artistry, focusing on innovative sound productions and special effects, as in the case of supergroups Pink Floyd and Genesis. In both cases, while rock and roll still appealed primarily to younger audiences, it had lost some of the rebellious and counterculture energy that was central to its identity and success in the 1960s.

Stephen Gennaro

See also: Beatles, The; Dylan, Bob; Grateful Dead; Hendrix, Jimi; LSD; Woodstock Music and Art Fair.

Further Reading

Bromell, Nicholas Knowles. *Tomorrow Never Knows: Rock and Psychedelics in the 1960s.* Chicago: University of Chicago Press, 2000.

Clymer, Kenton J., ed. *The Vietnam War: Its History, Literature and Music.* El Paso: Texas Western Press, 1998.

Hersch, Charles. *Democratic Artworks: Politics and the Arts from Trilling to Dylan.* Albany: State University of New York Press, 1998.

Szatmary, David P. *Rockin' in Time: A Social History of Rock-and-Roll.* 4th ed. Englewood Cliffs, NJ: Prentice Hall, 2000.

White, Ralph. *Nobody Wanted War: Misconceptions in Vietnam and Other Wars.* New York: Doubleday, 1970.

Rocky Horror Picture Show, The

The Rocky Horror Picture Show, directed by Jim Sharman and released by 20th Century Fox in 1975, is considered the quintessential cult movie. Based on a stage musical by Richard O'Brien, *Rocky Horror* was first performed at the London Royal Court Theatre Upstairs in 1973. Initial enthusiasm for the play brought it to the United States, where it was adapted for the screen with many members of the original cast. At first a box-office flop, the movie developed a cult following that rescued it from obscurity. Special screenings after regular features, typically at midnight, created a highly ritualized viewing experience that has continued for more than three decades.

The plot of *Rocky Horror* involves a fresh-faced couple—Janet (played by Susan Sarandon) and Brad (Barry Bostwick)—who stumble upon a "castle" in the woods (really a spaceship) inhabited by aliens posing as an eccentric household. There, Janet and Brad encounter a parade of larger-than-life characters: Dr. Frank-N-Furter (Tim Curry), the megalomaniacal cross-dressing scientist; Rocky (Peter Hinwood), his Aryan sex toy; Magenta (Patricia Quinn) and Riff Raff (O'Brien himself), the incestuous brother-sister servant team; Columbia (Little Nell), the fuchsia-haired groupie; and Eddie (the overstuffed Meat Loaf), who is the object of Columbia's rock and roll desire.

During the course of the film, Brad and Janet, both seduced by Frank-N-Furter, become increasingly uninhibited sexually. In the film's climax, most of the cast performs the cancan in fishnets and boas, Magenta and Riff Raff take over the castle, Frank-N-Furter os-

tensibly repents, Rocky dies, and the castle returns to Transsexual Transylvania, leaving Brad, Janet, and their friend Dr. Scott (Jonathan Adams) dazed and confused in its wake.

A send-up of B-level science-fiction and horror movies, drag shows, coming-of-age stories, rock operas, and popular culture in general, *Rocky Horror* struck a chord with mid-1970s youth sensibility, creating a carnivalesque space where social pressures were lifted and sexuality was unleashed. Fans began to appear at screenings dressed as characters in the film, sang along with the music, ritually injected dialogue at key moments, and tossed around any number of props—from confetti to toast to teddy bears—transforming film attendance into one great costume party.

Rocky Horror is an intriguing study in cult phenomena: the film itself, and much of the audience participation, has remained consistent, while the fan base is forever changing. Many Americans admit to having gone through a *"Rocky Horror* phase" at some point in their young adulthood but—other than the diehards who claim to have seen the film hundreds of times—few make it a prolonged pastime.

Still a popular stage play in the twenty-first century, productions of *Rocky Horror* continue to be staged throughout North America and Europe. Its influence is seen in productions such as the *Sing-Along Sound of Music* (2000), the audience-participation version of the 1965 Academy Award–winning film *The Sound of Music,* which encouraged costume wearing as well as singing, and the film *Moulin Rouge* (2001), a postmodern pastiche of camp, costumes, and cultural references in a fantasy atmosphere.

Julia Pine

See also: Film, Cult.

Further Reading

Evans, David, and Scott Michaels. *Rocky Horror: From Concept to Cult.* London: Sanctuary, 2002.

Piro, Sal, Merylene Schneider, and Richard O'Brien. *Creatures of the Night: The Rocky Horror Experience.* Livonia, MI: Stabur, 1990.

Role-Playing Games

Role-playing games (RPGs) are board games that focus on storytelling, characterization, and cooperation among players, rather than on winning and competition, as in more traditional board games. In most RPGs, the game is controlled by a central storyteller, or "gamemaster," who monitors the ebb and flow of the game. The other players control the central characters, working as a team to solve puzzles and challenges put forth by the gamemaster.

Popular role-playing games began with the first incarnation of *Dungeons and Dragons* in 1974, a high-fantasy game created by Gary Gygax and Dave Arneson, and distributed by Tactical Studies Rule (TSR). *Dungeons and Dragons* quickly gained in popularity, spawning a number of spin-offs and new editions over the next three decades. Many companies had joined the RPG market by the 1980s, when film tie-ins became especially marketable; game titles based on film franchises, such as *Star Wars, Star Trek,* James Bond, and *The Lord of the Rings,* all debuted in this era. Marketing tie-ins soon included popular novels, cartoons, and television series.

In the early 1980s, computer-game companies began using the RPG model of storytelling and characterization as a new paradigm for computer games, also known as RPGs. Strategic Simulations, Inc. (SSI), with its licensed *Dungeons and Dragons* games, and Sierra with its King's Quest series, were early leaders in the computer RPG market. Since then, the number of games and their sales have exploded. By the early 2000s, hundreds of computer RPGs were available. The Internet also has spawned Massively Multiplayer Online Games (MMOG), in which hundreds of players can log on and interact in the game format.

RPGs began to take on a darker cast in the 1990s, in both subject matter and graphic design. In 1991, Mark Rein-Hagen and the publishing company White Wolf introduced the revolutionary gothic-horror RPG, *Vampire: The Masquerade.* Based on its horror RPG line, White Wolf also debuted the first mass-market Live-Action Role Playing (LARP) game, in which players act out their characters' roles in a setting best described as guided improvisational theater.

Another innovation took the gaming industry by storm during the early 1990s: *Magic: The Gathering* achieved instant success as the first collectible card game (CCG). Combining elements of role playing with marketing hype for the collectibles, *Magic* cards sold in vast quantities and made Wizards of the Coast the richest game manufacturer in the United States. Many imitators followed, and, by the 2000s, tie-in CCGs were standard elements in major film and television marketing campaigns.

By the end of the 1990s, however, a slew of bankruptcies and corporate buyouts signaled a slump in the gaming industry. Industry giant TSR declared bankruptcy in 1997; it was followed by other major companies such as West End Games. New management

teams were brought in, bringing a greater emphasis on commercial appeal and profit margins, and many flagging RPG manufacturers were revitalized. As of the early 2000s, the RPG industry was showing strong signs of recovery, with revivals of classic RPGs and innovative new ones leading the way.

Jeffrey Sartain

Further Reading

Fine, Gary Alan. *Shared Fantasy: Role Playing Games as Social Worlds.* Chicago: University of Chicago Press, 1983.

Mackay, Daniel. *The Fantasy Role-Playing Game: A New Performing Art.* Jefferson, NC: McFarland, 2001.

Rolling Stone

Rolling Stone magazine rose from obscurity in the late 1960s to become the primary source for information on rock and popular music in America. The magazine was started in San Francisco by Jann Wenner—still the editor and publisher today—and the noted music critic Ralph Gleason. Its first managing editor was *Newsweek* journalist Michael Lydon, and its first photographic editor was Baron Wolman. The first issue was published on November 9, 1967, and featured the Beatles' John Lennon on the cover. Of 40,000 copies shipped to newsstands, 34,000 were returned unsold.

Despite its inauspicious beginnings, the magazine continued and eventually thrived, largely due to the tenacity of publisher Wenner, the dearth of credible youth music magazines, and advertising revenue from the major record labels. By early 1968, *Rolling Stone* could number almost every major record company among its advertising accounts, including Atlantic, Capitol, Columbia, Reprise, Elektra, A&M, Warner, and RCA.

In February 1969, the magazine's issue on the groupie subculture, often referred to as "The Groupie Issue," was published. Using the company's last $7,000, Wenner bought a full-page ad in *The New York Times* and, with ballyhoo worthy of nineteenth-century showman P.T. Barnum, situated his magazine as the ultimate source on the subject. By November 1969, the monthly publication had turned a corner and reported a paid circulation of nearly 60,000.

Rolling Stone may have had considerable cultural capital, but its financial fortunes in the 1970s were not assured. Indeed, the magazine almost went into bankruptcy in 1977. This was also the year that *Rolling Stone* moved its offices from San Francisco to New York City; issue number 248 was the first to be produced from its new offices at 745 Fifth Avenue in Manhattan. By the close of the 1980s, Robert Draper, author of *Rolling Stone Magazine: The Uncensored History* (1990), described the magazine as "respected but no longer relied upon, a force among other forces—an institution, surely, and like many such institutions, disregarded." Despite this lukewarm analysis, *Rolling Stone* continues as a successful publication in the late 2000s.

To cognoscenti of the counterculture of the 1960s and early 1970s, the words *Rolling Stone* conjure up some unforgettable achievements, including the gonzo journalism of Hunter S. Thompson or the prose of Greil Marcus, both of which graced the magazine's pages. Others may wax poetic about the music reviews of Ed Ward and Lester Bangs, or the interviews of Ben Fong-Torres. Still others remember the hard-hitting investigative journalism of Joe Eszterhas and the sublime photography of chief photographer Annie Leibovitz, whose rock celebrity portraits helped define the look of the magazine. Although the focal points of their memories may vary, to people who were under thirty during this era and involved in music and the counterculture, *Rolling Stone* was a relied-upon source of news and counterculture commentary.

Lisa Rhodes

See also: Rock and Roll.

Further Reading

Anson, Robert Sam. *Gone Crazy and Back Again: The Rise and Fall of the* Rolling Stone *Generation.* New York: Doubleday, 1981.

Burks, John, Jerry Hopkins, and Paul Nelson. "The Groupies and Other Girls." *Rolling Stone,* February 15, 1969, 11–26.

Draper, Robert. Rolling Stone *Magazine: The Uncensored History.* New York: Doubleday, 1990.

Rhodes, Lisa. *Electric Ladyland: Women and Rock Culture.* Philadelphia: University of Pennsylvania Press, 2005.

Rolling Stones, The

The British rock group the Rolling Stones, originally formed in 1962, has remained one of rock and roll's most enduring and popular bands on the strength of their driving, blues-influenced style, the creative songwriting of lead singer Mick Jagger and guitarist Keith Richards, high-energy concert performances, and an edgy, defiant image. First achieving notoriety alongside the Beatles and other bands from England as part of the so-called British Invasion, the Stones have consistently maintained their place in the public eye with the release of new music, frequent worldwide concert tours, and the enduring popularity of their older songs.

Lead singer Mick Jagger (left) and guitarist Keith Richards are original members of the Rolling Stones. The duo is also responsible for writing many of the band's hit recordings. In their fifth decade, the Stones have released over forty original albums. *(George Rose/Getty Images)*

Although they have achieved commercial success equaled by few other musical acts of any kind—with fifty-five albums released and hundreds of millions of copies sold as of 2007—the Rolling Stones have persistently flouted social convention and produced some of the most innovative, radical music of their time.

Early Days

While the Beatles began their career with cheery pop tunes, the Rolling Stones got their musical start singing about the darker side of love. Playing blues standards by the likes of Howlin' Wolf and Muddy Waters (from one of whose songs the band takes its name), the Stones quickly became one of England's best-known blues bands.

The composition of the band changed several times during its first year of existence, but by 1963 the lineup had been set. The quintet included singer and front man Michael Phillip (Mick) Jagger, guitarist Keith Richards, multiple-instrument-playing Lewis Brian Hopkin (Brian) Jones, bassist William George Perks (Bill Wyman), and drummer Charles Robert (Charlie) Watts.

It was in this form that the Rolling Stones began their first club residency, at the Crawdaddy in London, England. During their tenure at the Crawdaddy, the band attracted the attention of businessman and Beatles publicist Andrew Loog Oldham, who became their manager soon thereafter. Oldham's efforts ultimately resulted in the group's first recording contract, with Decca Records, as well as in the somewhat manufactured and highly promoted image of the Rolling Stones as the bad boys of Britain. This image stood in stark contrast to the more clean-cut appearance of the Beatles.

The group's self-titled first album, *The Rolling Stones* (1964), contained a number of blues and rock and roll covers and only one original song. The album did well, however, and, by the end of the year, the band had released two more albums, resulting in a number of hit singles and increasing airplay in England and the United States.

By the summer of 1965, the Rolling Stones began to break away from recording covers in favor of more original work. The songwriting team of Jagger and Richards gained their first big hit with "(I Can't Get No) Satisfaction" (1965), melding their blues roots with a rock and roll sound, and the group quickly rose to superstardom.

Rock and Roll as Counterculture

Like rock and roll music itself, the Rolling Stones were fond of thumbing their noses at societal norms, such as puritanical attitudes regarding sex and the consumerist mind-set that seemed commonplace in 1950s and 1960s America. Although their music was less overtly political than that of the Beatles and certain other groups, it was no less radical, because they sang about taboo subjects, especially sex, drugs, and disrespect for authority figures, and discussed them openly in interviews.

The Stones refused to censor themselves, and their music was aggressively frank in its portrayal of these subjects. Beyond that, band members flouted social norms in their overt sexuality and drug use, including Jagger's periodic sporting of women's clothing and makeup and Richards's flagrant drug use and multiple arrests. In short, not only did the band seem to seek out controversy in their music and public life, but they seemed to revel in the publicity and understand that they did not have to please the public in order to be highly successful.

With the growing attention being paid to Eastern thought and music in the mid-1960s, Jones began experimenting with more exotic musical sounds and instruments, especially the sitar. Following the Beatles' success with the psychedelic *Sgt. Pepper's Lonely Hearts Club Band*, the Stones released *Their Satanic Majesties' Request* in 1967. Also an experiment into psychedelia, the album was recorded soon after a visit to India by Jagger to meditate with the Maharishi Mahesh Yogi

and after multiple drug arrests of Jagger, Richards, and Jones.

The foray into psychedelic music was to prove brief, however, as the music of the Rolling Stones continued to evolve. Refining what has become a signature of their sound, Richards began using open guitar tunings. This evolution led to some of the band's most recognizable sounds, such as those heard in "Honky Tonk Women," which appeared on their album *Get Yer Ya-Ya's Out!* (1970).

While most of the band was pleased with the emerging sound, Jones was growing disenchanted with the new directions the band was taking. He left the group in June 1969 and was found dead in his pool a month later. Mick Taylor took Jones's place in the group, and in 1975 Ron Wood replaced Taylor, creating what would become the longest-running incarnation of the Rolling Stones.

Tragedy and Resurgence

The death of Jones was not the band's only tragedy in 1969. The Woodstock music festival held in Bethel, New York, that August, and billed as "three days of peace and music," had been such a success that the Rolling Stones hoped to create a similar concert experience on the West Coast.

Held at the Altamont Speedway in Northern California, the concert was planned as a free, all-day event featuring several acts and culminating with the Rolling Stones. At the suggestion of members of the Grateful Dead, the Stones hired the Hells Angels biker gang to provide security for the concert, in exchange for alcohol. By the time the Stones took the stage, there had already been altercations between the drunk and violent Hells Angels, several musicians, and the crowd. During the Rolling Stones' set, a young man was fatally beaten and stabbed before Jagger's eyes by several of the Hells Angels.

The disaster at Altamont might have been a death knell for many bands, but for the Rolling Stones it became merely a footnote. Continuing to record and perform in the aftermath of the killing, the band produced much of its most enduring music in the years immediately following, including the albums *Sticky Fingers* (1971) and *Exile on Main Street* (1972).

No longer perceived as a threat to the dominant culture, the Stones have continued to create provocative new music, as evidenced on such albums as *Some Girls* (1978) and *Tattoo You* (1981), which included such hits as "Beast of Burden," "Shattered," and "Start Me Up." In the twenty-first century, they have released *Forty Licks*

(2002), a greatest-hits album with four new tracks, and *A Bigger Bang* (2005), which lyrically took on neoconservative politics in America. Recording and touring to the present day, the Rolling Stones have been one of the most enduring yet innovative rock groups of all time.

Kathryn L. Meiman

See also: Beatles, The; Rock and Roll.

Further Reading

Booth, Stanley. *The True Adventures of the Rolling Stones.* Chicago: Chicago Review, 2000.

Davis, Stephen. *Old Gods Almost Dead: The 40-Year Odyssey of the Rolling Stones.* New York: Broadway, 2001.

Decurtis, Anthony, et. al. *The Rolling Stone Illustrated History of Rock & Roll.* New York: Random House, 1992.

Jagger, Mick, Keith Richards, Charlie Watts, and Ronnie Wood. *According to the Rolling Stones.* San Francisco: Chronicle, 2003.

Rowan & Martin's Laugh-In

Rowan & Martin's Laugh-In was a comedy television series that ran on the NBC network from January 1968 to May 1973. Hosted by comedians Dan Rowan and Dick Martin, *Laugh-In* consisted primarily of short, rapid-fire, often unconnected comedy sketches filled with jokes and innuendo-laden wordplay. The program frequently ventured into political satire, lampooning current events and poking fun at politicians and other establishment figures. The title *Laugh-In* alluded to the teach-ins, be-ins, and love-ins of the 1960s hippie counterculture, as well as the sit-ins of civil rights and anti–Vietnam War protestors, invoking the irreverent and antiauthoritarian attitude of these public demonstrations.

The weekly program followed a predictable format, recycling similar scenarios and characters. Rowan and Martin highlighted their two-man stand-up comedy act, with Rowan as the straight man and Martin as his clownish comic foil. Other regular actors established recurring characters, including Goldie Hawn as a stereotypically ditzy, giggling blonde, Lily Tomlin as an irritating telephone switchboard operator, and Flip Wilson as the cross-dressing Geraldine. During breaks between sketches, the show often featured clips of bikini-clad female cast members dancing to go-go music and displaying jokes, flowers, and other decorations painted on their bodies.

Another regular feature was "*Laugh-In* Looks at the News," a parody of network news broadcasts that commented on current events, poked fun at historical events,

and predicted future events and news stories. (*Laugh-In's* news parodies owed much to the early-1960s British satire *That Was the Week That Was* and later inspired the "Weekend Update" segments on *Saturday Night Live.*) *Laugh-In* also was known for creating a number of popular catchphrases that passed into everyday parlance:

> "Look *that* up in your Funk 'n' Wagnalls!" (referring to the *Funk and Wagnalls* encyclopedia, as well as hinting at the perceived obscenity of the word *funk*)

> "You bet your sweet bippie!" (another hint at obscenity, with *bippie* replacing a crude anatomical reference)

> "Sock it to me!" (a generally meaningless phrase used mostly for emphasis, though it also could carry a vaguely sexual meaning depending on the context)

Laugh-In's status as a counterculture media phenomenon rests on its comedic, satirical, and often flippant attitudes toward authority figures and current events, a perspective that helped to make it especially popular with younger television audiences. Federal Bureau of Investigation (FBI) files on the show were later turned up, specifically in connection with jokes made on the show about the bureau and its longtime director, J. Edgar Hoover.

Laugh-In went off the air in May 1973 after 140 episodes, but the format of the comedy-sketch variety show would appear again about two years later with the first airing of *Saturday Night Live,* which was created by Lorne Michaels, a veteran *Laugh-In* writer.

Shannon Granville

See also: Television.

Further Reading

Erickson, Hal. *From Beautiful Downtown Burbank: A Critical History of* Rowan and Martin's Laugh-In, *1968–1973.* Jefferson, NC: McFarland, 2000.

"Laugh Trackers." Readings. *Harper's Magazine* (March 2006).

World Publishing. Rowan and Martin's Laugh-In: *The Burbank Edition.* New York: World, 1969.

Rubin, Jerry (1938–1994)

A founder of the radical theatrical political group Youth International Party, whose adherents were known as yippies, Jerry Rubin mobilized American youth of the 1960s with his outrageous rhetoric, including "Don't trust anyone over thirty." His infamous use of street theater and his antics as a defendant in the Chicago Seven trial following antiwar demonstrations at the Democratic National Convention in Chicago in August 1968 put him at the forefront of the counterculture revolution.

Rubin was born on July 14, 1938, in Cincinnati, Ohio. His father was a bread delivery truck driver and a member of the International Brotherhood of Teamsters. Rubin studied at Oberlin College and the University of Cincinnati before moving with his younger, teenaged brother, Gil, to Israel upon the deaths of their parents. Rubin enrolled as a graduate student in sociology at Hebrew University.

The year 1964 marked the beginning of counterculture radicalism for Rubin. He moved back to the United States in January and began graduate studies at the University of California, Berkeley. Six weeks later, he withdrew from his graduate program to walk a picket line against a grocery store that was not hiring African Americans. Within the next few months, he volunteered to travel illegally to Cuba, where he had the opportunity to hear President Fidel Castro speak and to interview the Argentine-born Marxist revolutionary Che Guevara. Upon Rubin's return, the U.S. government confiscated his passport.

Having been involved in the student-led Free Speech Movement at Berkeley in 1964 and 1965, Rubin sought to harness the same energy in the movement against the U.S. war in Vietnam. In 1966, subpoenaed to testify before the House Committee on Un-American Activities (HUAC), Rubin showed up for the hearings dressed as a soldier from the American Revolution and distributed copies of the Declaration of Independence to emphasize the patriotism of the antiwar movement.

Rubin's theatrics made headlines with increasing frequency over the course of the next several years. He was sent to prison for thirty days for spilling blood on the limousine of a U.S. Army general. Upon his release in early 1967, after moving to New York City, Rubin and fellow activist Abbie Hoffman created havoc on the floor of the New York Stock Exchange, when they scattered dollar bills from a balcony above. The crush of stockbrokers scrambling for the money brought the exchange to a halt and—in the eyes of the perpetrators, at least—perfectly illustrated the rampant greed on Wall Street.

In collaboration with Hoffman's wife, Anita, Paul Krassner, and Nancy Kurshan, Rubin and Hoffman conceived the Youth International Party to lend a more formal, organized image to the antiwar counterculture movement. In August 1968, the group's presence in Chicago for the Democratic National Convention diverted media attention from the political proceedings and drew the spotlight to antiwar demonstrations. The yippies' "Festival of Life" rally resulted in physical violence between protestors and police.

Among those arrested were eight protest organizers, who went on trial for conspiracy and inciting a riot. Bobby Seale, cofounder of the Black Panther Party, was gagged under order of the judge for his inflammatory courtroom remarks and tried separately; the remaining defendants, including Rubin and Hoffman, became known as the Chicago Seven. Represented by radical attorney William Kunstler, the Chicago Seven rose to national celebrity for their courtroom antics. Five of the defendants were found guilty of related offenses, but their convictions were later overturned on appeal.

Rubin summarized his antiestablishment philosophy and advocacy of revolution in a 1970 handbook, *Do It!: Scenarios of the Revolution*. The volume became a best seller, helping perpetuate the youth counterculture in a new decade. In the Yippieland of the future, Rubin wrote, "police stations will blow up. Revolutionaries will break into jail and free all the prisoners. Clerical workers will ax their computers and put chewing gum into the machines. . . . Kids will lock their parents out of their suburban homes and turn them into guerrilla bases, storing arms."

Rubin was accused of selling out to the mainstream establishment in the 1980s. In a startling change of stripes, he became an unabashed businessman, entrepreneur, and investor, taking a job on Wall Street and starting innovative business ventures to encourage corporate networking.

On November 14, 1994, while jaywalking on a six-lane boulevard in Los Angeles, he was hit by an automobile and seriously injured. He did fourteen days later.

Nathan Zook

See also: Chicago Seven; Free Speech Movement; Yippies.

Further Reading

Alonso, Karen. *Chicago Seven Political Protest Trial: A Headline Court Case.* Berkeley Heights, NJ: Enslow, 2002.

Rubin, Jerry. *Do It! Scenarios of the Revolution.* New York: Simon and Schuster, 1970.

———. *Growing (Up) at Thirty-Seven.* Toronto: M. Evans, 1976.

Sacco and Vanzetti Case

Nicola Sacco and Bartolomeo Vanzetti, two Italian-born U.S. anarchists, were arrested on May 5, 1920, on suspicion of robbery and murder. The victims, shoe-factory employees Alessandro Berardelli and Frederick Parmenter, were shot dead in South Braintree, Massachusetts, on April 15 of that year while delivering the factory's payroll. Despite evidence of Sacco and Vanzetti's apparent innocence, another man's confession, and the fact that the money could be traced to neither of the accused, the two were found guilty at trial and executed on August 23, 1927. The case was one of the most controversial in American history, causing outrage among those who believed the defendants had been convicted because of their political beliefs and immigrant status.

Sacco and Vanzetti originally were taken into custody based only upon their loose association with a fellow anarchist who was suspected of having participated in a similar crime. Although both men provided heavily corroborated alibis for the South Braintree robbery and murders, and despite inconclusive ballistics evidence that may have been tampered with by the prosecution, Sacco and Vanzetti were found guilty after only five hours of jury deliberation.

Presiding Judge Webster Thayer, who admitted apparently faulty evidence and allowed for nearly abusive cross-examination by prosecutor Frederick Katzmann, was widely suspected of bias against the two men due to their radical political affiliations. Thayer's presumed bias may have been exacerbated by the flamboyant personality and indecorous courtroom manner of the defendants' lawyer, radical labor advocate Fred Moore. While Moore was able to turn Sacco and Vanzetti's case into a cause célèbre among the left, he was unable to save his clients.

At the time of Sacco and Vanzetti's arrest and conviction, America was in the grip of its first Red Scare, characterized by rampant fear of Communists and Communist activity, especially the infiltration of Communists into the U.S. government. After the Russian Revolution of 1917, many Americans feared that immigrants would foment a similar revolution in the United States. Europeans associated in any way with leftist politics or the labor movement were especially suspect. Terms such as *Bolshevik, Communist, anarchist,* and *radical* were used interchangeably in reference to anyone who appeared to pose an ideological or physical threat to the establishment.

Both Sacco and Vanzetti were active radicals who subscribed to the ideology of Italian anarchist Carlo Tresca, and counted among their compatriots a number of radicals who had been scooped up in recent raids by the federal government. One such compatriot, Andrea Salsedo, had died under suspicious circumstances while in police custody. When arrested, Sacco and Vanzetti were not informed of the crimes with which they were being charged; they merely were asked if they were anarchists—which they denied. Although the denials were made in fear for their lives, the defendants later testified, their credibility was cast in doubt with jurors. The tactics of the prosecution and bias of the judge, moreover, made it all but impossible for the defendants to overcome the stigma of their political leanings.

Sacco and Vanzetti's defense team submitted multiple motions for a new trial but was rebuffed each time, even when one Celestino Madeiros freely confessed to the crimes. Nor did a scathing exposé of the trial's shortcomings by *Atlantic Monthly* reporter and future U.S. Supreme Court Justice Felix Frankfurter sway the Massachusetts court system.

Leftists and civil libertarians throughout the United States made Sacco and Vanzetti a focus of public discourse from shortly after their arrest through their execution in 1927. Meanwhile, in response to extraordinary worldwide support, Massachusetts governor Alvan T. Fuller assembled an independent commission to review the case. Once again, the appeal to justice was denied. Sacco and Vanzetti finally were sentenced to death on April 9, 1927. On August 23, they were electrocuted amid a torrent of worldwide indignation and sympathy.

It was not until half a century later, in 1977, that Massachusetts governor Michael Dukakis signed a proclamation clearing the names of Sacco and Vanzetti, admitting the abuses of Judge Thayer and the prosecution, and naming August 23 Sacco and Vanzetti Day.

Nicole Zillmer

See also: Anarchism; Communism.

Further Reading

Feuerlicht, Roberta Strauss. *Justice Crucified: The Story of Sacco and Vanzetti.* New York: McGraw-Hill, 1997.
Russell, Francis. *Tragedy in Dedham: The Story of the Sacco-Vanzetti Case.* New York: McGraw-Hill, 1971.

Salem Witch Trials

See Witchcraft and Wicca

Salinger, J.D. (1919–)

J.D. (Jerome David) Salinger is a reclusive American writer best known for his only published novel, *The Catcher in the Rye* (1951), the story of sixteen-year-old Holden Caulfield and his experiences in New York City in the days following his expulsion from preparatory school. The cynical and complex Caulfield, who abhors everything he sees as "phony" in the adult world, has become an enduring symbol of the alienation felt by many adolescents.

Salinger was born in New York City on January 1, 1919. As a child, he lived with his father, Sol, mother, Marie, and older sister, Doris, and attended public schools in Manhattan. He entered the McBurney prep school there in 1931 but failed to advance past the tenth grade. Happy to get away from his family, he attended Valley Forge Military Academy in Wayne, Pennsylvania, and received his diploma in 1936.

Following graduation, Salinger enrolled at New York University but dropped out after completing only one semester. Briefly pursuing the same trade as his father, he worked as a meat importer in Vienna, Austria, before returning to the United States in 1938

(months before the Nazis assumed power). After attending Ursinus College in Collegeville, Pennsylvania, for a semester, he took a writing class at New York's Columbia University with Whit Burnett, the editor of the magazine *Story.* In 1940, *Story* published Salinger's story "The Young Folks." Drafted into the U.S. Army in 1942, shortly after the United States entered World War II, Salinger participated in the D-day invasion of Normandy in 1944 and the Battle of the Bulge. During the course of the war, he continued publishing stories in magazines, among them *The Saturday Evening Post, Collier's, Harper's, Good Housekeeping, Cosmopolitan,* and *The New Yorker,* where his stories were published almost exclusively by the late 1940s. One story he wrote during the war, not published in *The New Yorker* until 1946, was titled "Slight Rebellion Off Madison." This story's main character was Caulfield, later the protagonist of *The Catcher in the Rye.*

Near the end of the war, after helping liberate Jews from a concentration camp, Salinger suffered a nervous breakdown. Following his recovery, he married a woman he had met while serving overseas. Their marriage lasted only a few months, however, and, in 1946, he returned to New York City. In 1952, after studying the writings of religious philosopher Sri Ramakrishna and his disciple, Swami Vivekananda, Salinger converted to Advaita Vedanta Hinduism. His second marriage, to Claire Douglas in 1955, produced two children, Margaret Ann and Matthew. The couple divorced in 1967. In the following decades, Salinger was romantically linked to the actress Elaine Joyce and the writer Joyce Maynard. Then, in the late 1980s, he met his third wife, Colleen O'Neill, a nurse. These sparse details are among the few pieces of personal information known about Salinger.

The Catcher in the Rye chronicles Holden Caulfield's activities after he is expelled from an elite private school as he heads off seeking to understand the adult world and his role in it. He checks into a New York City hotel, gets drunk in a nightclub, has an encounter with a prostitute, and attempts to rekindle several old relationships. Each event leads to disaster and takes an increasing emotional toll on the ever-sympathetic young hero.

The book was an almost immediate commercial success despite markedly mixed reviews from critics. While many praised its effective use of satire and other forms of humor and its telling portrayal of adolescence, others criticized the work for its glorification of alcohol abuse, premarital sex, prostitution, and foul language. Despite the controversy surrounding the book, it has sold hundreds of thousands of copies, and is widely regarded as a modern American literary classic.

Following the publication of *The Catcher in the Rye*, Salinger became a virtual recluse and published only sparingly. Subsequent works include three collections of short stories—*Nine Stories* (1953), *Franny and Zooey* (1961), and *Raise High the Roof Beam, Carpenters and Seymour: An Introduction* (1963)—and a novella, *Hapworth 16, 1924* (*The New Yorker*, June 19, 1965). A number of his thirty-five published short stories feature a group of characters called the Glass family. As of 2007, Salinger was said to be residing in Cornish, New Hampshire.

Lindsay Schmitz

See also: Catcher in the Rye, The.

Further Reading

Alexander, Paul. *Salinger: A Biography.* Los Angeles: Renaissance, 1999.

Alsen, Eberhard. *A Reader's Guide to J.D. Salinger.* Westport, CT: Greenwood, 2002.

San Francisco

Since the middle of the nineteenth century, when the forty-niners of the California Gold Rush descended upon the region to prospect for riches, San Francisco has been a haven for society's dreamers and outcasts. It thus has been the site of a variety of alternative cultural movements and activities, some of which have been labeled radical or extreme. As a port city, however, San Francisco also has been one of the foremost centers of commerce on the West Coast, and the necessity of establishing structures and institutions for the management of capitalist activities has existed in perpetual tension with the constant influx of new groups, ideas, and vitalities.

In the half century before the earthquake of 1906, San Francisco developed a reputation for boisterous living amid reckless entrepreneurship. It was the place where Samuel Clemens became Mark Twain (literally), after encountering an atmosphere that set him loose to be a thorn in the side of bourgeois society.

By the turn of the twentieth century, several bohemian and radical subcultures had grown up around Montgomery Block, a large office building in the city. Authors such as Ambrose Bierce, George Sterling, Jack London, and Edwin Markham traded ideas about socialism and utopianism while having a drink at Coppa's restaurant (later the site of the Transamerica Pyramid). The city also attracted practitioners of various occultisms, from astrology and palm reading to the nature mysticism of outdoorsmen such as John Muir.

The 1906 earthquake reshuffled the cultural deck in San Francisco. Rebuilding the city gave the upper hand to commercial interests, and most bohemian or radical activities were dispersed. A budding organized-labor movement was stopped in its tracks and did not reassert itself until the maritime and general strike of 1934.

It was not until the 1930s that countercultural activities within the city began to grow again, too. The Black Cat Café on Montgomery Street became a popular bohemian hangout, presaging the café culture of the 1950s Beat and 1960s hippie movements.

In the North Beach section of the city, Italian anarchists, still bitter about the murder convictions of Nicola Sacco and Bartolomeo Vanzetti in 1927, began to nurture a wider affinity for anarchist thought among younger writers and artists. During and after World War II, the poet Kenneth Rexroth was instrumental in forming several anarchist clubs that kept this legacy alive.

The San Francisco poetry renaissance and the Beat movement of the 1950s—which established the works of poets and novelists Allen Ginsberg, Philip Whalen, Jack Kerouac, and William S. Burroughs—were built, philosophically, on the foundation of anarchist social criticism that Rexroth and radical periodicals such as *Circle* and *Ark* helped to establish. But the demographics of San Francisco also were changing dramatically. A deep Asian influence was showing itself in the arts and in the religious perspectives of the city's counterculture, and Mexican and African American migrants chipped away at the predominately white, Anglo-Saxon character of the city's population. The deportation of Japanese Americans during World War II, along with a large contingent of conscientious objectors, solidified radical sentiments in the region.

Thus, the generation that grew up after World War II found in the Bay Area a mixture of radical dissent and mystical religion. This environment was attractive to East Coast poets and writers such as Ginsberg and Kerouac, who were were transformed by their San Francisco experiences, ultimately providing a bridge between the emerging Beat, or beatnik, movements on both coasts. Though the Beats were criticized in the media for their seeming "know-nothing bohemianism," they were actually attempting to create a synthesis of Asian religious traditions (especially Zen

Buddhism) with European literary traditions, an effort which was in keeping with the way San Francisco seemed to present a combination of the two cultures. Many of the Beats' activities were not recorded in books, however, since much occurred in poetry readings at bars such as the Cellar and the Black Hawk, where the verse often was declaimed to the accompaniment of a jazz band.

In the 1960s, with the advent of the Vietnam War era, the Beat movement gradually gave way to the hippie phenomenon in San Francisco. The word *hippie* initially was a derogatory term applied to "little hipsters" by the older, more literary Beats, but it was quickly embraced by the younger runaways and artists who congregated near the area of the city where Haight and Ashbury streets intersected.

Though the hippies were often associated negatively with drugs and psychedelic experiences, the more articulate in the Haight-Ashbury scene saw themselves as primarily concerned with mind expansion and expression of their most personal selves. This impulse can be most clearly seen in the drug experiments and road trips of writer Ken Kesey and his group of Merry Pranksters, as well as in the music of the Grateful Dead and their lead guitarist, Jerry Garcia, a native San Franciscan.

A high point of the San Francisco hippie era was an antiwar rally called the Gathering of the Tribes at Golden Gate Park in January 1967, a "Human Be-In" that brought together members of the 1960s counterculture and encouraged them to "question authority" in regard to civil, women's, and consumer rights. During the subsequent Summer of Love, young people from all over the United States came to San Francisco to camp out, make and listen to music, take drugs, and have sex.

During the transitional period between the heydays of the Beats and the hippies, the anarchist impulse in the Bay Area also was kept alive by a group that called itself the "Diggers," taking their name from a seventeenth-century English group of agrarian communists. The San Francisco Diggers operated stores that gave out free food and communicated their ideas through an aggressive form of street theater. The radical political stance of the Diggers, soon was engulfed in more widespread Bay Area activism against the Vietnam War. For a while, Berkeley, on the other side of the San Francisco Bay, became the center of American countercultural activity.

In the 1970s, gay pride activists in the Castro district and other neighborhoods south of Market Street in San Francisco turned the city once again into a symbol of dissent and a haven for alternative lifestyles. Yet it is possible to see their political activities as part of a larger cultural trend, centered in San Francisco, to celebrate diversity, multiculturalism, and a militant ecological ethos—a trend that continued throughout the 1980s, 1990s, and into the 2000s, despite a fervent conservative backlash.

Michael Van Dyke

See also: Anarchism; Beat Generation; Be-Ins; City Lights Books; Ginsberg, Allen; Grateful Dead; Haight-Ashbury, San Francisco; Hippies; Kerouac, Jack; Kesey, Ken; Merry Pranksters; Rexroth, Kenneth.

Further Reading

Brook, James, et al. *Reclaiming San Francisco: History, Politics, Culture: A City Lights Anthology.* San Francisco: City Lights, 1998.

Ferlinghetti, Lawrence, and Nancy J. Peters. *Literary San Francisco.* San Francisco: Harper & Row, 1980.

McGloin, John Bernard. *San Francisco: The Story of a City.* San Rafael, CA: Presidio, 1978.

Starr, Kevin. *The Dream Endures: California Enters the 1940s.* New York: Oxford University Press, 2002.

Sanger, Margaret (1879–1966)

Social activist, author, and nurse Margaret Sanger is known for her pioneering work to help women in America gain access to birth control, a term she coined. She was the founder of the National Birth Control League (1914), the American Birth Control League (1921), and the Birth Control Clinical Research Bureau (1923), the first legal birth control clinic run by doctors in the United States. The American Birth Control League and the Birth Control Clinical Research Bureau merged in 1942 to become Planned Parenthood Federation of America, based in New York City, which, by the early 2000s, had more than 800 health centers nationwide. Sanger later (1953) served as the founding member of the International Planned Parenthood Federation. She was the author of *What Every Girl Should Know* (1916), *What Every Mother Should Know* (1916), *Family Limitation* (1916), *Woman and the New Race* (1920), *The Pivot of Civilization* (1922), *Happiness in Marriage* (1926), *My Fight for Birth Control* (1931), and *Margaret Sanger: An Autobiography* (1938). She also founded the newspapers *The Woman Rebel, Birth Control Review,* and *Birth Control News.*

Born Margaret Louise Higgins on September 14, 1879, in Corning, New York, she was the sixth of

Margaret Sanger coined the term *birth control* and pioneered the movement. She faced criminal charges for distributing literature on the subject through the U.S. mail and for opening the nation's first family-planning clinic in 1916. *(Library of Congress)*

believed was due to eighteen pregnancies and eleven live births), and her work with social causes among New York City's working class. According to biographer Esther Katz, she came to believe that "family limitation [was] as a tool by which working-class women would liberate themselves from the economic burden of unwanted pregnancy."

Legally prosecuted for her public speaking, for mailing and distributing contraceptives and birth control information (illegal under the federal Comstock Law of 1873, which classified all contraceptive pamphlets as pornographic and forbade their distribution through the mail), and for opening the nation's first birth control clinic (in Brooklyn, New York, in 1916), Sanger was jailed several times and on other occasions fled the country. Her efforts, and the public support of her work, eventually led to changes in the legal system regarding the ways birth control information and contraceptive devices could be distributed, and allowing physicians the right to prescribe birth control for medical reasons.

Throughout her adult life, Sanger fought for cheaper, easier-to-use, more accessible means of contraception, at times smuggling devices from Europe. Her efforts ultimately led to funding for the development of the birth control pill in the mid-1950s and approval by the U.S. Food and Drug Administration in 1960. Sanger died in Tucson, Arizona, on September 6, 1966.

Emily C. Martin-Hondros

See also: Birth Control Pill; Bohemianism; *Document: The Woman Rebel* (1914), Margaret Sanger.

Further Reading

Kennedy, David M. *Birth Control in America: The Career of Margaret Sanger.* New Haven, CT: Yale University Press, 1970.

Sanger, Margaret. *The Selected Papers of Margaret Sanger.* Ed. Esther Katz. Urbana: University of Illinois Press, 2003.

eleven children. Margaret attended Claverack College, the Hudson Institute, and the nursing program at White Plains Hospital. In 1902, she married architect William Sanger. Together, they had three children and, upon moving to New York City, became part of the prewar radical bohemian culture, identifying with socialist and early labor movements, including labor strikes led by the Industrial Workers of the World; the couple separated in 1914.

Margaret Sanger came to her activism for birth control due to her observations working as a nurse, her mother's early death from tuberculosis (which Sanger

Santería

Santería, also known as Lukumi, is a syncretistic or "creolized" folk religion that developed among African slaves in Cuba. Santería is derived from the traditional Yoruba culture of West Africa, from which a large proportion of Cuban slaves had been captured. Lukumi, which can be translated from the Yoruba language as "friends," is still practiced in West Africa; the term is also used to identify adherents of Yoruba beliefs who have been dispersed around the world due to slave trading and later migrations. In recent times, some practitioners of Santería have attempted to reunite the faith with seminal Lukumi beliefs of Africa, in an attempt to decrease the effects of slavery and colonialism.

During the slavery era, Cuban authorities outlawed the practice of Lukumi and compelled the slaves to convert to Christianity. Adherents of Lukumi responded by claiming that their revered spiritual leaders, the Orishas, were in fact Catholic saints—a subterfuge that allowed them to secretly worship the Orishas while carrying out the required Christian rituals. The term *Santería* was used derisively by the Spanish to describe this practice and to criticize Lukumi's over-devotion to "saints" rather than to a single deity.

The original practitioners of Lukumi in Cuba, like slave owners, were scattered throughout the island. This led to an ongoing fragmentation and dilution of beliefs until the early eighteenth century, when Cuban authorities allowed slaves to intermingle in societies called *cabildos.* The slaves had the opportunity to reconstitute their belief systems, which came back together as Santería, essentially an evolved version of Lukumi with New World influences.

After the abolition of slavery, Santería spread beyond Cuba to other areas of the Americas with large Afro-Latin populations. Adherents were found in the United States, Canada, Mexico, several nations in South America, and many Caribbean islands. A similar religion, called Cadomble, is widely practiced in Brazil, and a number of similarities also can be found with Haitian Vodun (Voodoo), the historical development of which was comparable to that of Santería.

The core beliefs of Santería are directly descended from the Lukumi faith. A supreme deity known as Olorun or Olodumare is believed to be the creator of the universe and the immediate authority figure over the Orishas. Religious rituals include animal sacrifice and sung invocations. An initiated priest may enter a trance state brought on by music and dance, during which the priest channels an Orisha, communicates with spirits, and performs healing.

Santería does not stipulate judgments of good and evil or right and wrong; instead, it professes that all things, people, and events are mixtures of both and must be judged in context. Most of the rituals are dedicated to respecting and communicating with one's ancestors. The belief system places great responsibility on the individual practitioner for developing good character. Santería is practiced in secret and the rituals are kept off limits to nonadherents.

There are several large American churches, particularly in the South, in which Santería is practiced in the present day. Of particular note is the Church of the Lukumi Babalu Aye in Hialeah, Florida, whose animal sacrifices were outlawed by the city in the late 1980s. The church won back the right to follow such practices in a landmark 1993 ruling by the U.S. Supreme Court (*Church of Lukumi Babalu Aye v. City of Hialeah*), in which the justices unanimously recognized Santería as a legitimate, organized, legally protected religion. While not legalizing animal sacrifice per se, it declared the Hialeah ordinance unconstitutional for targeting the practices of a particular religious group.

Other important Santería churches in the American South include South Carolina's African Theological Archministry and Florida's Church of Seven African Powers. There is also a noteworthy Santería community in New York City, where shrines and totems are highly visible in the homes and businesses of practitioners. All told, an estimated 5 million or more people in America observe Santería/Lukumi.

Benjamin W. Cramer

See also: Voodoo, Hoodoo, and Conjure.

Further Reading

Bascom, William R. "The Focus of Cuban Santería." *Southwestern Journal of Anthropology* 6:1, 1950.

Brown, David H. *Santería Enthroned: Art, Ritual, and Innovation in an Afro-Cuban Religion.* Chicago: University of Chicago Press, 2003.

Gonzalez-Wippler, Migene. *Santería: The Religion, Faith, Rites, Magic.* St. Paul, MN: Llewellyn, 1994.

Lefever, Harry G. "When the Saints Go Riding In: Santería in Cuba and the United States." *Journal for the Scientific Study of Religion* 35:3, 1998.

Murphy, Joseph M. *Santería: African Spirits in America.* Boston: Beacon, 1993.

Saxton, Alexander P. (1919–)

A professor emeritus of history at the University of California, Los Angeles, Alexander P. Saxton spent his early years as a radical novelist and member of the American Communist Party. His novels, though constituting only one aspect of his life's work and personal history, nonetheless occupy an important place in the genre of radical literature.

Alexander Plaisted Saxton was born on July 16, 1919, into a middle-class family in Great Barrington,

Massachusetts. As a college student at the University of Chicago, he joined the Communist Party in about 1940. Intensely interested in issues of socioeconomic class and labor, Saxton's firsthand observances during the Great Depression added to his desire to join the party. Saxton served in the U.S. Merchant Marine during World War II and, upon his return, settled in California.

His first book, *Grand Crossing* (1943), was favorably received, and he immediately began work on a second, *The Great Midland,* which was published in 1948. *The Great Midland* is the story of American Communist Party activists and their attempts to unionize and promote better working conditions on the Great Midland Railroad. Saxton himself admitted that the novel was an attempt to portray the party and its participants in a favorable light. Many of the characters are based on comrades who Saxton encountered in the course of his own activities, lending a vital authenticity to the novel. Published after the conclusion of World War II, at a time when anti-Communist sentiments were running high in the United States, *The Great Midland* was shunned by reviewers, booksellers, and even the publisher. When the novel did not do well financially, Saxton began working as a carpenter to support himself, continuing to write novels and stories on the side.

Because of his membership in the Communist Party, Saxton was called before the House Committee on Un-American Activities (HUAC), the special congressional committee formed in 1938 to investigate communist and other extremist political organizations in the United States, in 1951. When questioned about his politics and comrades, Saxton revealed nothing and claimed protection under the Fifth Amendment right to avoid self-incrimination. While the committee did not charge Saxton with any crime, the fallout from his refusal to testify was severe. His third novel, *Bright Web in Darkness,* was not published until 1958.

It was around this time that Saxton resigned his membership in the Communist Party, primarily because it no longer seemed effective in meeting its goals. Earning his master's and Ph.D. degrees in history from the University of California, Berkeley, in 1962 and 1967, respectively, Saxton began his career as a history professor. In 1976, he joined the faculty of the University of California, Los Angeles, where he remained more than forty years later.

Although he discontinued writing the radical novels for which he first became known, Saxton's legacy in that genre has endured. *The Great Midland* remains a compelling examination of race, class, and gender exploitation in America during the first half of the twen-

tieth century. His involvement in the Communist Party informed his work with a firsthand understanding of the state of radical politics in America, and his insights into racial consciousness and the immigrant working experience were reflected in fictional characters who worked side by side to promote radical politics, better working conditions, and racial and ethnic equality at a time when these values were widely sought but feared by mainstream American society.

Lisa A. Kirby

See also: Communism.

Further Reading

Saxton, Alexander. *Bright Web in the Darkness.* New York: St. Martin's, 1958.
———. *The Great Midland.* 1948. Urbana: University of Illinois Press, 1997.

Schools, Alternative and Experimental

Alternative education typically refers to any and all options outside the mainstream educational system. Alternative schooling can be designed around a particular educational or life philosophy or a unique approach to curriculum, or to meet the needs of a specific population, or some combination of these. Historically, the alternatives have been offered in private school settings or outside of school entirely, as in homeschooling.

Many alternatives to mainstream schooling were introduced or revived during the 1960s and 1970s, often organized around principles of self-determination and lack of central authority. These were principles that appealed to the counterculture community of the time, which criticized conventional education for contributing to the problems of American society. In the 1970s and 1980s, critics also began to examine the reverse process—that is, how the problems of mainstream society were affecting the school system. Today, some of these alternatives are offered via the educational establishment in the form of charter schools.

Many of the alternative schooling experiments in the United States have been inspired by the work of Progressive Era educators and philosophers such as John Dewey. Dewey's writings from the early twentieth century, including *The Child and the Curriculum* (1902) and *Democracy and Education* (1916), promoted the ideal of the school as a vital component in maintaining a vibrant democracy. As such, Dewey argued, school ought to encourage self-motivation and problem-solving skills. Rather than having the teacher or administration be the locus of control, Dewey believed the focus ought to be on the learner. He also believed that school should provide an environment in which children could mature into socially responsible citizens.

While Dewey was promoting progressive education in the United States, A.S. Neill was exploring similar ideals in Europe. In 1921, he founded an alternative, coeducational boarding school in England called Summerhill, where students were not required to attend classes and everyone, staff and students alike, had one vote at weekly administrative meetings. Because the students were allowed to choose what they would do or not do, whether to study or not study, Neill called the experiment a "free" school. Summerhill did not receive much public support and had only about twenty-five students by the late 1950s. Then, in 1960, Neill published a book about the school, *Summerhill*, which was an instant sensation in the United States. Not only did the Summerhill school survive, but it inspired many other such schools around the world.

Among the philosophical descendants of Summerhill is Sudbury Valley School in Framingham, Massachusetts, founded in 1968 along the philosophical lines promoted by Dewey and Neill. Sudbury is a day school, where students can choose what they want to learn and how they want to learn it. The school also has a weekly meeting at which each student and each staff member has one vote.

Another form of alternative education, emphasizing early learning, is based on the theories of the Italian physician and educator Maria Montessori. In 1907, Montessori opened a day-care center in a poor area of Rome, where she adapted the objects and materials she had used with disabled children for use with preschoolers. With the classroom arranged as a collection of activity centers designed to engage the interest and challenge the abilities of the children, young pupils were then free to move about the room at will and choose their own activities. The interior and exterior environments of the school were designed on a child-sized scale.

Montessori's methods enjoyed widespread popularity in the United States in the early 1900s, lost popularity in the 1930s and 1940s, and enjoyed a revival in the late 1950s. Today, there are approximately 4,000 Montessori schools in the United States, some of which are charter schools.

Another notable innovator in modern education was Rudolf Steiner, founder of the Waldorf School in Stuttgart, Germany, in 1919. The school was based on Steiner's spiritual-scientific theory of the developmental stages of childhood in roughly seven-year increments, with the curriculum designed accordingly. One unique feature of the Waldorf method was the teaching of eurythmy, a kind of language through movement. Introduced to the United States in 1928, Waldorf education did not catch on quickly. By 1965, the United States still had only eight Waldorf schools. Most of the more than 150 Waldorf schools in the United States today have been formed since 1980. Some of these are charter schools.

An increasing number of American parents choose to educate their children at home. They may have philosophical or religious differences with the way schools are run, they may not live near or be able to afford alternative schools that share their views, or they may be opposed to public schooling altogether. Homeschooling was the norm in America through the nineteenth century, until compulsory education laws and the expansion of formal public schooling in the early part of the twentieth century made it all but obsolete.

In the 1960s, however, many critics of the public school system began reconsidering the homeschool option. Some were influenced by the writings of educator John Holt, including *How Children Fail* (1964) and *How Children Learn* (1967). Although these works were critical of public education, Holt did not specifically advocate homeschooling in them. Other thinkers of the time did, including Ivan Illich in his book *Deschooling Society* (1971) and Hal Zina Bennett in *No More Public School* (1972). By 1976, Holt had joined the cry for alternatives to compulsory education, and in 1977 he began publishing a magazine for homeschooling families called *Growing Without Schooling.*

In the early 1980s, more and more parents decided to school their children at home. Between 1982 and 1993, thirty-four states passed laws allowing parents to legally teach their children at home. By 1998, all fifty states had passed such laws.

Diana Stirling

Further Reading

Dewey, John. *Democracy and Education: An Introduction to the Philosophy of Education.* New York: Macmillan, 1916.

Holt, John. *Instead of Education: Ways to Help People Do Things Better.* New York: Dutton, 1976.

Montessori, Maria. *The Montessori Method.* Cambridge, MA: R. Bentley, 1965.

Neill, A.S. *Summerhill: A Radical Approach to Child Rearing.* New York: Hart, 1960.

Science Fiction

Science fiction (or *sci-fi*) is a broad term applied to a cluster of related yet heterogeneous subgenres of contemporary popular literature spanning virtually every medium, including novels, short fiction, film, television, comics, and games. Although precise genre definitions remain subject to vociferous debate by both writers and readers, science fiction generally speculates about scientific, technological, and ethical issues, including those related to space travel, extraterrestrial contact, robotics and artificial intelligence, telepathy and other psionic (paranormal psychic) abilities, cloning, time travel, nanotechnology, alternate history, and the general and specific effects of technological change (negative or positive) on individuals and on the human condition. Robert A. Heinlein, widely considered the dean of modern science fiction, described the genre as "realistic speculation about possible future events, based solidly on adequate knowledge of the real world, past and present, and on a thorough understanding of the nature and significance of the scientific method."

Golden Age and Beyond

Early science fiction was characterized by turgid and inelegant prose stylings, and lurid illustrations depicting bug-eyed alien monsters menacing scantily-clad Earth women. Although it took many decades before any serious cultural respectability would accrue to the field, it nevertheless gathered much of its enduring power as an American pop-culture touchstone and countercultural force during the first half of the twentieth century.

This is largely attributable to that era's relentless, headlong march of science, technology, and industry, all of which drove the sales of innumerable pulp sci-fi periodicals from the 1920s through the post–World War II years, with *Amazing Stories* (established in 1926 and published intermittently until 2005) and *Astounding Science Fiction* (1930–), and later *The Magazine of Fantasy & Science Fiction* (1949–) and *Galaxy Science Fiction* (1950–1980), at the forefront. The genre spread throughout American culture, owing largely to a profusion of sci-fi comics, radio shows, feature films, and movie serials.

Prose science fiction's first great period of creative fecundity, broadly described as the Golden Age, arrived in 1937 with John W. Campbell's assumption of the editorship of *Astounding* and arguably lasted through the 1950s. Campbell nurtured some of the genre's most influential writers, including Heinlein, many of whose works comprise one of the field's first and greatest "future history" timelines (much of it available today in a volume titled *The Past Through Tomorrow*, published in 1967).

As the launch of the first space satellite, the Soviet Union's Sputnik, in 1957, catalyzed an acceleration of technological progress that would take the United States to no less a science-fictional destination than the Moon by 1969, interest in sci-fi among America's youth hit its high-water mark. This was the era of Heinlein's "juveniles," short, youth-oriented adventure novels marked as much by their inculcation of math and science (*Rocket Ship Galileo*, 1947; *Red Planet*, 1949; and *Have Space Suit, Will Travel*, 1958) as by their libertarian notions of self-reliance and individual rights (*Starship Troopers*, 1959).

In addition to Heinlein, Campbell mentored a cadre of younger up-and-coming sci-fi stylists known collectively as the "Futurians," a group that included genre luminaries such as Poul Anderson, Isaac Asimov, James Blish, Damon Knight, Judith Merril, Frederik Pohl, and Donald A. Wollheim. Campbell pushed his writers to achieve a significantly higher level of characterization and literary quality than the customary pulp-era norm, and he emphasized the use of plausible science, believable aliens, and the primacy of humanity in most human-alien conflicts. Although his influence unquestionably challenged sci-fi to transcend its adolescent roots, Campbell's belief in Earth's "cosmic manifest destiny" might have betrayed the editor's parochial racial attitudes, whether conscious or unconscious, or this belief simply may have revealed him to be a product of his time.

Other seminal authors in sci-fi's putative Golden Age included Arthur C. Clarke, most famous for writing the novel and coauthoring the screenplay for the Stanley Kubrick film *2001: A Space Odyssey* (1968), as well as for conceptualizing the modern telecommunications satellite; A.E. Van Vogt, whose feared-and-hated superhuman mutants portrayed in *Slan* (1940) provided the template for generations of fictional alienated superhumans; Jack Williamson, perhaps best remembered for his Humanoids, Legion of Space, and Legion of Time series; and L. Ron Hubbard, renowned not only for his best-selling *Battlefield: Earth* series of alien-invasion novels (which debuted in 1982), but also for founding the controversial organization known as the Church of Scientology.

Williamson scorned Scientology as "a lunatic revision of Freudian psychology," and Campbell's preoccupation with Hubbard's new belief system prompted author Alfred Bester to stop writing for *Astounding* in favor of the other pulps of the period. Whatever its merits (or lack of same), Scientology, as laid out in Hubbard's best-selling *Dianetics* (1950), proved greatly influential over Campbell, whose *Astounding* published one of Hubbard's earliest articles explicating the subject. More than two decades after his death, Hubbard maintains the distinction of being the only sci-fi writer to have created something that, arguably, amounts to a world religion.

Film and Television

The increased sophistication of the genre began creeping slowly into film and even invaded the new medium of television. Sci-fi used the visual media as an allegorical mirror for society's concerns rather than to serve up thoroughgoing escapism. Robert Wise's *The Day the Earth Stood Still* (1951) made trenchant observations about the tragic human predilection for aggression and self-destruction. George Pal's *When Worlds Collide* (1951) allowed a cosmic, Earth-destroying disaster to stand in for America's growing anxieties about nuclear annihilation. Pal's 1953 adaptation of the seminal 1898 H.G. Wells novel, *The War of the Worlds*, provided cathartic escape from the era's seemingly omnipresent Red Menace (via a metaphorical Martian invasion), as did Don Siegel's much-imitated *Invasion of the Body Snatchers* (1956), in which pernicious humanlike alien doppel-gängers represented either lurking Communists or authoritarian red-baiters of the Joseph McCarthy era.

Films such as Bruno VeSota's *The Brain Eaters* (a 1958 adaptation of Heinlein's 1951 novel of humans covertly enslaved by aliens, *The Puppet Masters*), the amusingly dreadful *Plan 9 From Outer Space* (1956) from Edward D. Wood, Jr., and *I Married a Monster from Outer Space* (1958) from Gene Fowler, Jr., all demonstrated the prevalence in the 1950s of a fear of American society being quietly subverted from within. Other general anxieties of the Atomic Age were worked out in the national pop-cultural psyche in films such as Gordon Douglas's *Them!* (1954), which depicted desert nuclear weapons tests that spawned terrifyingly destructive giant ants.

Despite its often dismal track record with sci-fi in terms of both seriousness and quality, television allowed the science-fictional literary zeitgeist to penetrate even further into the American consciousness with the advent of such generally well-crafted, anthology-format series as Rod Serling's *The Twilight Zone* (1959–1964) and *The Outer Limits* (1963–1965), both of which frequently employed significant genre

writers such as Jerome Bixby, Harlan Ellison, Damon Knight, Richard Matheson, and Norman Spinrad.

September 8, 1966, marked the premiere of *Star Trek,* the brainchild of writer-producer Gene Roddenberry. Likewise retaining the services of a number of influential genre writers, including Bixby, Ellison, Theodore Sturgeon, and Robert Bloch, the series served up an optimistic and ecumenical future despite the manifold social upheavals of the day. Although low ratings killed the original *Star Trek* after three seasons, persistent fan interest resurrected the show, both as a Saturday morning animated series (1973–1974) and as a film franchise (1979–2008), ultimately leading to four more live-action television series.

Maturation and Modernity

Unsurprisingly, prose sci-fi advanced far ahead of both film and television sci-fi as the 1960s ushered in the genre's New Wave movement, named after the work of such innovative French filmmakers as Jean-Luc Godard and François Truffaut. During this period of intense creative ferment, the 1950s Beat writers and mainstream modernist and surrealist fiction such as that of William S. Burroughs also were extraordinarily influential on American writer Philip K. Dick, probably best remembered for the existentially tortured androids ("replicants") and android hunters of his 1968 novel *Do Androids Dream of Electric Sheep?* (the basis for Ridley Scott's stylish, dystopian 1982 film *Blade Runner*). Dick created a body of fiction infused with paranoia over the unreliability of memory, personal identity, and even reality itself, as in *Flow My Tears, the Policeman Said* (1974), *A Scanner Darkly* (1977), and "We Can Remember It for You Wholesale" (1966).

African American sci-fi writer Samuel R. Delany explored themes relating to social mobility, employed the "soft sciences" of linguistics and sociology, and weaved both mythology and alternative sexuality into works such as *Nova* (1968), *Dhalgren* (1975), and *Stars in My Pocket Like Grains of Sand* (1984). Groundbreaking feminist authors such as Ursula K. Le Guin, Joanna Russ, and James Tiptree, Jr. (also known as Alice B. Sheldon), gained unprecedented prominence by further opening up the genre to themes impelled by the social sciences, straying from sci-fi's more traditional stomping ground of physics, astronomy, and chemistry. Le Guin's *The Left Hand of Darkness* (1969) and *The Dispossessed* (1974) explore, respectively, the issues of gender identity and communal living versus individual rights. Russ's *The Female Man* (1975) offers a satirical feminist perspective on gender issues. And Tiptree routinely fuses sophisticated New Wave prose stylings, feminist, and "soft" (or sociological) science-fiction themes with the rivets-and-rockets tech more commonly associated with earlier epochs of "hard" science fiction (as in "Houston, Houston, Do You Read?" 1976).

New Wave sensibilities unleashed a veritable torrent of sci-fi creativity, with authors such as Spinrad, J.G. Ballard, John Brunner, Philip José Farmer, Kurt Vonnegut, Jr., and Roger Zelazny examining religion, mythology, politics, and sex to an unprecedented degree. Even the conservative Heinlein loosened up with *Stranger in a Strange Land* (1961), the saga of a man raised from childhood by Martians who becomes a religious icon upon his return to Earth. Reading and "grokking" (Martian for "understanding") *Stranger in a Strange Land* became an almost mandatory rite of passage in the 1960s hippie counterculture.

Meanwhile, space opera collided with both ecological concerns and messianic religion with the publication of Frank Herbert's *Dune* (1965). This novel spawned an enduring series set on the harsh but resource-rich desert planet Arrakis.

Traditional hard science fiction received a new breath of life from the cutting-edge science literacy and storytelling skills of Anderson and Larry Niven. The former may be remembered best for his Time Patrol series and numerous stories and essays advocating human space exploration as a survival necessity. The latter is renowned for committing wild but scientifically plausible speculations in such novels as *Ringworld* (1970), a tale set on an artificially constructed, solar-system-sized torus built around a star, and *The Integral Trees* (1984), in which humans live weightlessly in forests suspended in a planetless bubble of atmosphere in orbit around a star. Niven also has distinguished himself by applying the rationality of hard sci-fi to the fantasy milieu, effectively transforming sorcery into an alternate form of science in *The Magic Goes Away* (1978) and its sequels.

In film, Kubrick's *2001: A Space Odyssey* (1968) set new standards for style, production values, and scientific rigor (for the first time in cinematic history, spaceships made no sound in the vacuum of space). Like the best of the era's print science fiction, Kubrick's other sci-fi-tinged works covered important sociological ground; *Dr. Strangelove or: How I Learned to Stop Worrying and Love the Bomb* (1964) commented on the absurdity of the cold war nuclear doctrine of Mutually Assured Destruction, while 1971's *A Clockwork Orange* (based on a 1962 novel by Anthony Burgess) presented a convincingly wrought future British dystopia in which street gangs and an authoritarian government vie for supremacy.

Whatever later blockbuster movies such as George Lucas's *Star Wars* (1977) and its sequels and prequels may have lacked in sophistication compared to the earlier groundbreaking sci-fi films mentioned above, they compensated for with a sense of adventurous fun that evoked the movie serials of the 1930s. The *Star Wars* franchise garnered enormous audiences, whetting the appetites of millions for more similar sci-fi film fare while spreading sci-fi tropes farther into the mainstream culture, sometimes arguably to the detriment of "real" science fiction.

The Modern Era

By the 1980s, the term *science fiction* had come to encompass such a broad array of styles, subgenres, and subject matter as to nearly defy definition entirely. The fin-de-siècle anarchism of the cyberpunk subgenre, inaugurated by William Gibson's 1984 novel *Neuromancer* and continued in the works of Rudy Rucker and others, influenced the explosive real-world growth of modern Internet culture while building upon the alienation themes of earlier authors such as Bester and Dick. A related variant subgenre known as "steampunk," practiced by Gibson, Bruce Sterling, Neal Stephenson, and others, transposes cyberpunk's "rebel hacker" sensibilities onto other times and technologies, most notably the Victorian Era, thereby making Wells and Jules Verne in vogue.

Science fiction, its tropes, and its current real-world offspring (rockets, robots, computers, cell phones, etc.) now so suffuses mainstream culture that divisions within the genre are more artifacts of publishers' marketing departments than the natural creations of authors. The fact that much of the output of contemporary mainstream novelists such as Jonathan Lethem or Thomas Pynchon is considered by many to be sci-fi of the modern or postmodern stripe (Letham's *Gun, with Occasional Music*, 1994, and Pynchon's *Gravity's Rainbow*, 1973, stand out as conspicuous examples) seems to have freed such works from their customary confinement to the sci-fi ghetto—or at least from booksellers' science-fiction sections.

What Dreams May Come

Whatever meaning the increasing trend toward cross-genre promiscuity might hold for science fiction's future, or for its artistic purity, remains open to debate. But despite the trumpetings of impending doom so often heard among both writers and fans, whether because of allegedly declining American literacy levels or the perceived threat to "serious" science fiction posed by the proliferation of media tie-in novels (e.g., *Star Trek* and *Star Wars* "franchise fiction"), a diverse and lively core of hard science fiction—defined loosely as literature in which the absence of a story's scientific content would cause the entire narrative to collapse—persists in reaching a robust American audience.

Science fiction partisans can draw hope from the fact that the number of sci-fi and fantasy titles published annually continues to rise, even if sci-fi unit sales do not. And while the audience for sci-fi magazines, once the genre's very lifeblood, continues its decades-long decline, occasional smash successes such as J.K. Rowling's Harry Potter novels suggest that the steadily graying readership of fantastic literature may replenish itself as youthful, new readers seek more challenging fare. Hope may yet remain of rejuvenating science fiction's aging fandom, and of keeping both entropy and dystopia at bay for yet another generation.

Michael A. Martin

See also: Burroughs, William S.; Cyberpunk; Pulp Fiction; Pynchon, Thomas; Trekkies; UFOs; Vonnegut, Kurt, Jr.

Further Reading

Aldiss, Brian W. *Billion Year Spree: The True History of Science Fiction.* Garden City, NY: Doubleday, 1973.

Amis, Kingsley. *New Maps of Hell.* New York: Harcourt, Brace, 1960.

Asimov, Isaac. *Asimov on Science Fiction.* Garden City, NY: Doubleday, 1981.

Clute, John, and Peter Nicholls, eds. *The Encyclopedia of Science Fiction.* New York: St. Martin's, 1995.

Disch, Thomas M. *The Dreams Our Stuff Is Made Of: How Science Fiction Conquered the World.* New York: Touchstone, 1998.

Gunn, James. *Alternate Worlds: The Illustrated History of Science Fiction.* Englewood Cliffs, NJ: Prentice Hall, 1975.

Lundwall, Sam J. *Science Fiction: What It's All About.* New York: Ace, 1971.

Pringle, David. *The Ultimate Guide to Science Fiction.* New York: Pharos, 1990.

Scientology

Conceived by American science fiction author L. Ron Hubbard in the early 1950s as an extension of his self-help system, Dianetics, Scientology is a nonmainstream religion whose adherents claim to help people achieve full awareness of their spiritual existence and, in the process, become more effective in the contemporary world. A controversial presence in American popular and religious culture, Scientology finds its institutional identity in the beliefs and practices of the Church of Scientology (founded in 1953), essentially a network of affiliated organizations that claim sole authority to disseminate beliefs and principles and to monitor religious practice. Characterized by Hubbard as an "applied religious philosophy," Scientology is, according to the church, "the study and handling of the spirit in relationship to itself, others and all of life." Based on the principle that "Man is an immortal, spiritual being" whose "experience extends well beyond a single lifetime" and whose "capabilities are unlimited," the goal of Scientology is to achieve certain knowledge of one's spiritual existence and thereby attain "higher states of awareness and ability."

Church teachings, referred to as "Tech" or "Technology," thus suggest that adherents can be relieved of

Scientology, an "applied religious philosophy," was founded in the early 1950s by former pulp and science fiction writer L. Ron Hubbard. He is seen here in 1968 using his Hubbard Electrometer (or E-meter) to determine if tomatoes feel pain. *(Evening Standard/Stringer/Hulton Archive/Getty Images)*

their everyday miseries and become more successful in business and other areas of life. This can be accomplished by disposing of the "bank" of traumatic memories known as "engrams" said to inhibit one's success. Through the process of "auditing," one can reach the state of "Clear" and, following that, the even higher level of "Operating Thetan." (Thetan is the immortal spirit, the source of life, and individual identity, akin to what other religions refer to as soul.) Each successive state represents the recovery of native spiritual abilities and confers dramatic mental and physical benefits as well.

Led by a trained Scientology counselor, each step in the process of auditing is a personal instruction session. The eventual goal is to return the human soul to its native condition of spiritual freedom, gaining direct control over matter, energy, time, and space. Many members claim that the practices of Scientology have left them with an improved intelligence quotient, a greater ability to articulate their needs, and enhanced memory. Others credit the religion with alleviating dyslexia and attention deficit problems, as well as a host of other problems. Many other members have abandoned the religion entirely.

Among Scientology's most controversial positions is its opposition to conventional psychiatry and psychotherapy, both of which are regarded as abusive. At the same time, Scientology owes a debt to the psychological theories of Sigmund Freud and Carl Jung, while also drawing upon Buddhism, Hinduism, and the heretical form of Christianity known as Gnosticism.

This mix of doctrines and attendant practices has led many former members and outside observers to charge the Church of Scientology with being little more than a commercial enterprise that has perverted religion, exploited its own members, and harassed defectors. Now practiced around the world, Scientology is regarded by some governments as a legitimate religious movement fully entitled to legal protections, and by others as a pseudoreligion, a dangerous cult, or, at best, a fraudulent and exploitative corporation.

Contemporary critics and some former members believe that Scientology is not a church at all, but an enormous and well-organized cult that fleeces the gullible and the vulnerable by enslaving them in an army of followers who live under a form of mind control. One means by which the group recruits new members, they maintain, is to showcase the lives and beliefs of members who happen to be Hollywood celebrities. Actors Tom Cruise, Kirstie Alley, John Travolta, and others have become fixtures in Scientology campaigns to solicit new members. Celebrity Scientologists not only help identify and locate potential new members, but they also publicly endorse the teachings of Hubbard and provide Scientology greater legitimacy in mainstream America.

The Church of Scientology claims anywhere from 7 to 15 million members worldwide—estimates that some observers regard as greatly exaggerated. Scientology organizations and missions have been established in dozens of countries, with the "worldwide spiritual headquarters" located in Clearwater, Florida, and the highest concentration of U.S. adherents and church activities in Los Angeles.

Although there is no single, formal scripture associated with the religion, its principles and practices are laid out in a number of books by, or based on the writings of, L. Ron Hubbard, beginning with *Dianetics* (1950) and including *Science of Survival* (1951), *Dianetics 55!* (1954), *Scientology: The Fundamentals of Thought* (1956), *Have You Lived Before This Life?* (1960), *Scientology: A New Slant on Life* (1965), *Dianetics Today* (1975), *The Way to Happiness* (1981), *The Future of Scientology and Western Civilization* (1985), and *The Scientology Handbook* (1994), among others.

Bart Dredge

Further Reading

Church of Scientology. http://www.scientology.org.

Corydon, Bent, and L. Ron Hubbard, Jr. *L. Ron Hubbard: Messiah or Madman?* Secaucus, NJ: Lyle Stuart, 1987.

Hubbard, L. Ron. *Scientology: The Fundamentals of Thought.* 1956. Los Angeles: Bridge, 1997.

Melton, J. Gordon. *The Church of Scientology.* Studies in Contemporary Religions. Salt Lake City: Signature Books in cooperation with CESNUR, 2000.

Seattle

As the major population center of the Pacific Northwest region of the United States, the city of Seattle, Washington, has long provided a home for a diversity of thriving countercultures. At the same time, its general isolation from other American urban centers and its status as a so-called secondary city has meant that countercultural activity in Seattle developed along its own unique lines and beyond the media focus received by the counterculture in larger cities, such as New York and Los Angeles.

Given the city's status as a Pacific port and hub for resource industries, the earliest countercultures in Seattle had a strong working-class character. In the early decades of the twentieth century, Seattle was an important organizing base for the Industrial Workers of the World (IWW), a revolutionary union that made innovative use of music, poetry, and public performance to develop a working-class counterculture in opposition to the exploitative economic culture of capitalism.

The Seattle General Strike of 1919 stands as the first citywide labor shutdown in American history. The strike began with demands by shipyard workers for increased wages and spread, through sympathy strikes, to calls for social revolution. It ended with raids on IWW social centers, union halls that served as schools, meeting spaces, and hubs of working-class culture.

During the 1960s and 1970s, Seattle was home to numerous local countercultures, echoing the development of countercultures nationally during that period. The epicenter for countercultural activity was the so-called Hippie Hill area, a piece of land on the edge of the University of Washington campus. Hippie Hill quickly became a popular counterculture destination, rivaled on the West Coast only by San Francisco's Haight-Ashbury district. Other important counterculture spaces during this period included El Centro de La Raza, a formerly abandoned school that was occupied and turned into a community center and base for Chicano organizing.

Seattle countercultures came to national prominence during the late 1980s and early 1990s with the emergence of grunge rock, also called the "Seattle sound." Locally based bands such as Nirvana, Mother Love Bone, Screaming Trees, Soundgarden, Green River, and Tad provided a creative mix of heavy metal, punk, and psychedelic rock in an era of synthesizer pop and light rock. Influenced by the earlier hippie and punk movements, grunge bands also espoused counterculture values of collaboration, independence from the mainstream music industry, and do-it-yourself recording, production, and promotion.

Seattle gained a central place in the history of early-twenty-first-century global countercultures with the tumultuous protests against the Ministerial Conference of the World Trade Organization (WTO) in November 1999. Plans by the WTO to launch a new round of trade negotiations were halted for the first time ever when demonstrators, numbering at least 50,000, blockaded streets outside the Seattle convention center and delegates' hotels and took direct action against symbols of corporate globalization. The Battle of Seattle, as it came to be known, marked the emergence into broad public consciousness of new counter-

cultures, ones with global connections and organizing capacities, especially through the Internet and a willingness to engage in militant activities against police, corporations, and government officials.

The Battle of Seattle also stirred an old and seemingly vanquished countercultural specter, that of anarchism. Striking media coverage of angry, black-clad, balaclava-wearing youth demonstrating outside the global meetings of government and corporate power holders stirred memories of the moral panic over anarchism that marked the beginning of the twentieth century.

The so-called uncivil disobedience, especially where it concerned damage to corporate property, was attributed to "black bloc" anarchists at the 1999 WTO meetings. It returned anarchists to the headlines and landed them on the covers of *Time* and *Newsweek* in addition to a feature story on television's *Sixty Minutes II*. As well, police assaults on anarchists in Seattle, using pepper spray, tear gas, rubber bullets, and mass arrests, suggested to the general public that anarchists were something to be feared.

Jeff Shantz

See also: Grunge Rock; Industrial Workers of the World.

Further Reading

Azerrad, Michael. *Come As You Are: The Story of Nirvana.* New York: Doubleday, 1994.

Notes from Nowhere, eds. *We Are Everywhere: The Irresistible Rise of Global Anti-capitalism.* London: Verso, 2003.

Thomas, Janet. *The Battle in Seattle: The Story Behind and Beyond the WTO Demonstrations.* Golden, CO: Fulcrum, 2003.

Tyler, Robert L. *Rebels of the Woods: The IWW in the Pacific Northwest.* Eugene: University of Oregon Press, 1967.

Seeger, Pete (1919–)

Singer, songwriter, banjo player, and music collector Pete Seeger served as a role model for many folk musicians who became prominent in the late 1950s and early 1960s, and he is a vital force in the revival of the folk music tradition in America. In the course of his long musical career, Seeger also has become known as a labor activist, outspoken advocate of peace, and ardent environmentalist.

Born on May 3, 1919, in New York City to Juilliard School of Music professors Charles and Constance Seeger, Seeger was surrounded by music from the beginning. When he was sixteen, he and his father attended a square dance festival in Asheville, North

Carolina, where Pete first heard the five-string banjo. He fell in love with its sound and the folk-oriented music he heard at the festival. The five-string banjo became his instrument of choice, and folk music became his devotion.

Seeger enrolled at Harvard University in 1936 to study journalism and sociology, but left in the middle of his sophomore year to pursue his growing interest in folk music. He traveled extensively, selling original watercolors to help support himself, playing wherever he could and learning all he could about the genre.

During parts of 1939 and 1940, he worked at the Archive of American Folk Song in the Library of Congress as an assistant to folklorist John Lomax and served as a field assistant to Lomax and his son Alan, traveling around the country to record traditional folk music. On March 3, 1940, Alan Lomax introduced Seeger to legendary folk artist Woody Guthrie at a migrant-worker benefit concert in New York City. The two became fast friends and later that year formed the Almanac Singers, a folk group that also included Sonny Terry, Brownie McGhee, Lee Hays, and Sis Cunningham.

In 1941 and 1942, Seeger and Guthrie toured the United States playing for labor unions and other politically oriented groups. They both joined the American Communist Party in 1942, because they opposed the system of private profit and thought their efforts would help people find jobs. Seeger left the party in 1950, but his career would suffer for his membership and for his political and social views. In the meantime, he was drafted into the U.S. Army Special Services in 1942 and served for the rest of World War II entertaining soldiers in the South Pacific and at home.

Seeger first came to national prominence in 1948 as a member of the Weavers, a folk-singing group he formed with Hays, Ronnie Gilbert, and Fred Hellerman. The Weavers's second recording, "Goodnight Irene," went to number one on the charts in 1950 and sold more than 2 million copies. Other Weavers's hits included "On Top of Old Smokey," "So Long, It's Been Good to Know You," "Wimoweh (The Lion Sleeps Tonight)," "Rock Island Line," and "Kisses Sweeter Than Wine," all of which were recorded by numerous other artists.

With all of their success, however, the Weavers were blacklisted in 1952 because of Seeger's previous membership in the Communist Party and the left-wing political views of Seeger and other members. The group disbanded, and Seeger continued performing as a solo artist, mostly on the college circuit and to left-oriented political groups. He rejoined the resurrected Weavers in 1955 but left again in 1958 after opposing their participation in a cigarette commercial.

The House Committee on Un-American Activities (HUAC), a congressional body appointed to investigate communist and other radical groups in America, subpoenaed Seeger to testify in 1955. Many witnesses who appeared before the committee invoked their Fifth Amendment rights against self-incrimination, but Seeger refused to testify on First Amendment grounds, arguing that to be forced to discuss his political views and answer questions about his friends would violate his rights of free speech and free association. The next year, he was indicted on ten counts of contempt of Congress.

It was more than five years before the case came to trial; in 1961, Seeger was convicted and sentenced to a year in jail. He appealed the verdict, and in May 1962 the charges were dismissed. Seeger continued to be blacklisted, however, and he was barred from appearing on radio and television for more than fifteen years.

Meanwhile, Seeger worked tirelessly to promote the American folk music tradition. In 1946, he founded People's Songs, a kind of labor union for folk singers. In 1950, the organization began producing *Sing Out! The Folk Magazine*, which remains in publication in the 2000s. Seeger also helped found the music magazine *Broadside* in 1961, which helped bring attention to such folk artists as Bob Dylan, Phil Ochs, Tom Paxton, and Eric Anderson. He was also instrumental in founding the Newport Folk Festival in 1959.

Several of Seeger's songs covered by folk artists in the early 1960s became countercultural, then popular, standards. Among these were Peter, Paul and Mary's recording of "If I Had a Hammer" and the Byrds's recordings of "The Bells of Rhymney" and "Turn, Turn, Turn." Seeger himself received extensive radio play in 1964 with "Little Boxes," a song against cultural conformity written by Malvina Reynolds.

Pete Seeger also is known for his lifelong struggle for social justice. Supporting the civil rights movement in the 1960s, he spent significant time in the South as a volunteer and activist. His rendition of the old spiritual "We Shall Overcome" became the anthem of the entire movement. An early and vocal opponent of the Vietnam War, Seeger also generated overnight national controversy when he sang the protest song "Waist Deep in the Big Muddy" on the *Smothers Brothers Comedy Hour,* a popular television show, in 1967. His appearance on that program marked the end of his blacklisting by the American media, and he began appearing regularly thereafter, primarily on public television.

After reading Rachel Carson's book *Silent Spring* (1962), which called attention to environmental degradation, Seeger became more interested in environmental activism. He formed the Clearwater Organization in 1969, dedicated to cleaning up New York's highly polluted Hudson River, and helped raise money to build the *Clearwater,* a replica of the river sloops that navigated the Hudson in earlier centuries.

In addition to recording more than eighty albums, many of them for children, Seeger has compiled a number of folk songbooks. His many awards and honors include the National Medal of Arts, Kennedy Center Award, and Harvard Arts Medal (all 1994); induction into the Rock and Roll Hall of Fame (1996); and a Grammy Award for Best Traditional Folk Album, for *Pete* in 1997. The words written on his famous five-string banjo exemplify Seeger's commitment to social justice through his music: "This machine surrounds hate and forces it to surrender."

Jerry Shuttle

See also: Broadside; Communism; Dylan, Bob; Folk Music; Guthrie, Woody; Peter, Paul and Mary.

Further Reading

Dunaway, David King. *How Can I Keep from Singing: Pete Seeger.* New York: McGraw-Hill, 1981.
Seeger, Peter. *Where Have All the Flowers Gone: A Musical Autobiography.* Ed. Peter Blood. Bethlehem, PA: Sing Out, 1997.

Settlement Houses

Settlement houses were community-based organizations that served the urban poor during the late nineteenth and early twentieth centuries. They emphasized independent, urban living and offered a range of cultural services and educational programs, including courses in English language, art, music, nutrition, and family planning. Settlement houses were considered a radical experimental approach to solving the problems of urban poverty. They directly challenged the established assumption that poverty is the result of personal shortcomings and moral failings, such as laziness, drunkenness, or gambling, and embraced the philosophy that the working poor, including recent immigrants, could learn effective methods of helping themselves. In settlement house workers' efforts to find more effective solutions to social issues relating to poverty, they pioneered the social work profession.

Social settlement houses were nondenominational community centers for the urban poor, offering such services as day care, child recreation, and language instruction. The movement represented a radical, new approach to urban poverty. *(Library of Congress)*

Rather than following the reigning model of established charity organizations, in which the more economically stable volunteers would visit those in poor neighborhoods to provide moral uplift, workers in the settlement house movement took up residency (thus, the settlement house designation) in these neighborhoods. The settlement house movement especially attracted young women who were educated in fields such as nursing, social work, and education. Through the use of such methods as group work, residence empowerment, social action, community organization, and lobbying for urban policy and legislation, young settlement house participants sought to use their skills and education to directly effect change in the poor neighborhoods of major cities.

The first settlement house was Toynbee Hall, founded in East London in 1883 by two Oxford University students, Frederick Denison Maurice and Charles Kingsley, both socialists. Toynbee Hall inspired several Americans, most notably Stanton Coit, to establish the Neighborhood Guild (later the University Settlement) on the Lower East Side of New York City in 1886. By 1897, there were seventy-four settlements in the United States, and by 1910 there were 400.

The most prominent of the early settlement houses were Hull-House, founded in 1889 by Jane Addams and Ellen Gates Starr in an impoverished neighborhood of Chicago, and the Henry Street Settlement, established in New York in 1893 by Lillian Wald. Besides social services and community action efforts, activities at Hull-House included a kindergarten for children and activities for adults that focused on building social relationships. Administrators encouraged socializing by providing an environment in which people from different ethnic groups could engage in conversation, friendship, and a sense of community. Hull-House became a model for other settlement house experiments; its influence extended far into the twentieth century through the work of Dorothy Day and the Catholic Worker Movement, a social-services organization.

Settlement houses demonstrated that neighborhood organization could have a positive effect on the problems of urban poverty, and thus presented a clear challenge to conservative assumptions about the sources and nature of poverty. Beyond this, their importance to the American counterculture lies in the fact that, during the period from 1880 to 1930, America was producing a generation of talented, idealistic, and educated young women within a socioeconomic system that had no real place for them. Many of these young women found their way into the settlement house movement.

As settlement house workers, these young women had their first experiences of social independence, program management, alternative living conditions, and political organization and action. They also were exposed to the reality that there are many other ways to live than according to the norms and mores of middle- and upper-class American society. It was, in short, an entry point into public life for a number of young women, many of whom went directly into other social movements and ushered in the first wave of feminism.

Rebecca Tolley-Stokes and Daniel Liechty

See also: Catholic Worker Movement; Socialism.

Further Reading

Axinn, June, and Mark J. Stern. *Social Welfare: A History of the American Response to Need.* 6th ed. Boston: Pearson/Allyn and Bacon, 2005.

Cash, Floris Barnett. "Radicals or Realists: African American Women and the Settlement House Spirit in New York City." *Afro-Americans in New York Life and History* 15:1 (1991): 7–17.

Davis, Allen F. *Spearhead for Reform: The Social Settlements and the Progressive Movement 1890–1914.* New York: Oxford University Press, 1967.

Seven Arts, The

The Seven Arts was a literary journal founded by poet and author James Oppenheim in 1916 as a tool to transform American society through literature and criticism. Criticized by more mainstream publications for its radical bias, *The Seven Arts* ceased publication in 1917 after antiwar essays and a pacifist editorial position frightened financial backers and brought threats of criminal action for treason.

The Seven Arts owed its existence to what historians refer to as the Little Renaissance between about 1910 and 1919. New styles and movements became popular in the arts, and a greater appreciation developed among many Americans for creative expression of all kinds.

Influenced by Sigmund Freud's new psychoanalytic movement, many young American artists believed that truth and value could be found in expressing their inner selves. Inspiration came from experience, many held, and art should be as realistic as possible. Additionally, writers, painters, and other artists of the Little Renaissance believed that American subjects and traditions had unique, intrinsic value and that art should adopt a "cultural nationalism" as opposed to imitating European norms.

Oppenheim was a poet and writer who subscribed to this view, and he sought to create a magazine that would help reshape American society and make it more humane. Oppenheim's dream was shared by novelist and critic Waldo Frank and musician Paul Rosenfeld, and the trio managed to convince Annette Rankine, a wealthy patron of the arts, to provide financial backing.

Rankine sold part of her art collection for start-up money and accepted a clerical position on the magazine. Oppenheim became the editor, assisted by Frank. A distinguished seven-person advisory board was named that included the literary critic Van Wyck Brooks, anthropologist and poet Louis Untermeyer, and poet Robert Frost. Oppenheim named the new magazine *The Seven Arts* in reference to medieval terminology referring to the division of knowledge into arts and sciences.

In the first issue, published in November 1916, Oppenheim laid out the purpose and principles of the magazine in a manifesto: "We have no tradition to continue; we have no school of style to build up. What we ask of the writer is simply self-expression without regard to current magazine standards. We should prefer that portion of his work which is done through a joyous necessity of the writer himself." Poetry, short stories, and plays were featured in its pages. Criticism and essays also appeared and soon became the most prominent material in the journal. Oppenheim and his contributors believed that cultural and social criticism could be used to initiate dialogue among readers and thereby promote the goals the editors espoused.

The Seven Arts attracted a number of young, unknown writers who would eventually become famous and influential, among them Amy Lowell, Robert Frost, Sherwood Anderson, Stephen Vincent Benét, and Walter Lippmann. Others whose work appeared in its pages included Eugene O'Neill, John Reed, John Dos Passos, and H.L. Mencken. Most contributors shared the anticapitalism and anti-industrial philosophy of the editors.

One of the most outspoken authors in *Seven Arts* was Randolph Bourne, who published a series of essays in its pages that opposed American involvement in World War I and eventually led to the magazine's collapse. In his most critical essay, "The War and the Intellectuals," published in the June 1917 issue, Bourne attacked liberal intellectuals, such as his own mentor, philosopher John Dewey, for changing their attitudes to support the war. He criticized the restrictions on speech and open discussion imposed by the federal government and argued that democratic freedoms were being jeopardized. Oppenheim, also a militant pacifist, did not hesitate to print Bourne's essays as well as other antiwar writings.

The journal's open antiwar position ran counter to general sentiment in the United States as well as to official government policy. The Espionage Act, passed on June 15, 1917, made it a crime to engage in disloyal acts, and Rankine, fearing prosecution for the antiwar articles, withdrew her financial support for *The Seven Arts*. The journal was never financially self-sufficient, and Oppenheim was forced to cease publication with the September 1917 issue.

Tim J. Watts

Further Reading

Oppenheim, James. "The Story of the *Seven Arts*." *American Mercury* 20 (1930): 156–64.

Sex Trade and Prostitution

The sex trade refers to any commercial enterprise in which there is an exchange of sexual services or other sexually oriented activity for money, including prostitution, stripping, sexual massage, pornography, live and Internet sex shows, and phone sex operations. In America as elsewhere, historically the sex trade has been predominantly operated by, and for the financial benefit of, males, while prostitution and other types of sex work have been predominately feminized occupations. While rarer, men who provide sexual services to women are known as gigolos.

Today, a person who supervises mostly female prostitutes—in legal or illegal settings—is known as a pimp. Pimps take a portion of the prostitute's income as their own, perhaps providing protection and support in exchange. Supervised prostitution in brothels or so-called houses of ill repute is often under the direction of other women, referred to as madams. Male patrons of prostitutes are known as johns.

In many periods of American history, children, teenagers, and young adults in their twenties were especially desired as sex workers. Young workers were regarded as more likely to be virginal or pure, and a female's virginity was a valuable commodity—one that might be advertised and sold several times over. Youths also were regarded as less likely to carry a sexually transmitted disease, a significant concern before the advent of medical treatments such as antibiotics.

Prostitution has been a part of life in America since the early days of the republic. Historical documents of New York City and Boston indicate the existence of prostitution dating to the late eighteenth century, likely the result of soldiers being stationed there during wartime. Prostitution and sex work in various other forms became increasingly available with urbanization in the mid- to late nineteenth century, most often geared to male consumers. Prostitution was so prevalent that political and religious officials were known to frequent brothels; regarded as normative male behavior, this was hardly even noted in gossip circles.

The most prominent locale for prostitution and brothels in New York City from 1770 into the early 1800s was the Holy Ground, located uptown near King's College (later Columbia University). Other cities known for their brothels during the 1800s were St. Louis, Philadelphia, New Orleans, and Chicago. While prostitution was generally tolerated during this period, it was practiced predominantly by young women and concentrated in specific neighborhoods.

During the course of the nineteenth century, the sex trade expanded significantly, particularly with the advent of industrialization. Restricting and regulating prostitution have been attempted sporadically during the course of American history, and this was especially true during the Victorian Era of the late 1800s.

Prostitution also proliferated in Western territories during the period of settlement in the nineteenth century. The early decades, in particular, brought large numbers of men and relatively few women, a demographic skew that produced enormous economic opportunity in prostitution. The gold rushes of midcentury likewise were a boon to prostitution. And later, with the arrival of railroads and construction of port facilities, cities on the West Coast attracted growing populations and an increasing sex trade, especially for railroad workers and sailors.

The occupation of prostitution always has been characterized by several levels of prestige, today ranging from high-class call girls or escorts, who may be self-managed or work for an escort service, to streetwalkers, who may or may not be managed by a pimp. In many towns of the early West, women who worked in brothels were considered of higher prestige, while streetwalkers were regarded as having the lowest status. With the advent of the Internet, the culture and practice of prostitution and other sex work, such as pornography, has become increasingly visible and accessible.

In most of the United States today, prostitution is illegal. Notable exceptions are some counties of Nevada, where legalized "Bunny Ranches," or brothels, provide prostitution service to men. However, legal prosecution of prostitutes has historically focused on streetwalkers, who are more visible, and less on brothel workers or escorts.

Pornography and other aspects of the sex trade, meanwhile, have become increasingly legitimized and prevalent. With the advents of still photography and then the motion picture industry, nude modeling and film pornography became areas of especially significant growth, which continued throughout the twentieth century and into the twenty-first century.

While estimates are unreliable, it is believed that more than 1 million persons in the United States are employed in prostitution today, and many millions more are involved in the rest of the sex trade. More than 100,000 arrests occur annually for illegal prostitution alone. Most likely to be arrested are the prostitutes themselves, while patrons and pimps are at much lower risk.

Daniel Farr

Further Reading

Bullough, Vern, and Bonnie Bullough. *Women and Prostitution: A Social History.* New York: Prometheus, 1987.

Gilfoyle, Timothy J. *City of Eros: New York City, Prostitution, and the Commercialization of Sex.* New York: W.W. Norton, 1992.

Murphy, Alexandra K., and Sudhir Alladi Venkatesh. "Vice Careers: The Changing Contours of Sex Work in New York City." *Qualitative Sociology* 29 (2006): 129–54.

Weitzer, Ronald. *Sex for Sale: Prostitution, Pornography, and the Sex Industry.* New York: Routledge, 1999.

Sexual Revolution

The sexual revolution of the 1960s and 1970s was a movement that entailed sweeping changes in American sexual mores, encompassing a newfound acceptance of sex outside of marriage, the replacement of procreation with pleasure as the perceived function of sex, and the integration of sexual themes into the media and public discourse.

This shift was not an abrupt transition but the culmination of a lengthy process. Accelerated urbanization near the start of the twentieth century allowed for greater sexual freedom for young people. Working girls explored romance and relationships in new environments—from the workplace to amusement parks to speakeasies—with a freedom previously unknown to them, while city life also facilitated the formation of an urban gay subculture. Outside the cities, automobiles brought new opportunities for mobility, privacy, and sexual exploration to small-town and rural teens in the 1920s.

While terms such as *necking* and *petting* became familiar, however, sex itself remained highly regulated in mainstream American culture. Religious values continued to exert great influence, as did the cultural tenet that "good" girls preserved their virginity until marriage. As a practical matter, birth control methods either were unreliable (such as the rhythm method or withdrawal) or were seen as awkward (diaphragms and condoms).

Kinsey Reports and the Pill

This cultural regulation of sex maintained its hold on Americans for another two decades, but the years following World War II brought upheaval. Two groundbreaking empirical studies—*Sexual Behavior in the Human Male* (1948) and *Sexual Behavior in the Human Female* (1953), by Indiana sociologist Alfred Kinsey—revealed the true extent and variety of American sexual activity on the basis of massive research, revealing widespread premarital, extramarital, homosexual, and autoerotic activity on the parts of both men and women. These revelations shocked the nation, but the publicity the reports received ensured general public awareness of their content.

In the 1950s, American media followed Kinsey's lead in addressing sex more frankly. Magazine publisher Hugh Hefner introduced *Playboy* in 1953, combining pictures of naked women with quality writing. Best-selling novels such as Grace Metalious's *Peyton Place* (1956) dealt with sex overtly. Films also grew bolder. In 1953, Otto Preminger's film *The Moon Is Blue* challenged convention by using the word *virgin*; by 1959, Russ Meyer's *The Immoral Mr. Teas* featured bountiful shots of naked women.

These developments clearly challenged convention, but it was the 1960 approval of the birth control pill (known as "the Pill") by the Food and Drug Administration that heralded what came to be known in the media as the sexual revolution. Suddenly, women could control their own reproduction easily and effectively. The impact of the Pill was massive; by 1965, some 5 million women—both married and single—were using it.

The technological severing of sex from procreation was mirrored by cultural indications of a new focus on pleasure. Examples include Helen Gurley Brown's book *Sex and the Single Girl* (1962), which climbed the best-seller lists and was produced as a major motion picture two years later.

Students, Hippies, and Swingers

In universities, students challenged the in loco parentis tradition by which schools served as proxy parents, implementing curfews and prohibiting opposite-sex visits to dormitory rooms. Coed dorms grew increasingly common during the 1960s—even the staunchly conservative University of Kansas had two by 1964. Unmarried female students at Brown University in Providence, Rhode Island, received prescriptions for oral contraceptives from the director of the school's health services in 1965. And in 1968, undergraduate Linda LeClair defied the rules at Barnard College in New York City by living off campus with her boyfriend; the resulting flap led Barnard to change its rules to allow off-campus living. The following year, protests by students at the University of Tennessee in Knoxville resulted in the end of dormitory curfews for female students.

While universities gradually accommodated shifting sexual mores by allowing more student freedom, other groups displayed new sexual attitudes as well. Hippies celebrated nudity and free love, while "swinging" and "wife swapping" became the marks of liberated couples in the middle-class suburbs. Sandstone, a 15-acre (6-hectare) retreat in Southern California, opened in 1969 as a swinger utopia and hosted hundreds of couples every weekend.

These new attitudes carried over into other spheres as well. In *Griswold v. Connecticut* (1965), the U.S. Su-

preme Court struck down a state anticontraceptive law, indicating official recognition of sex as an activity for more than procreation. Human-sexuality researchers William Masters and Virginia Johnson carried on the Kinsey tradition, overturning conventional wisdom in their groundbreaking text *Human Sexual Response* (1966), which explained that female orgasms stem from the clitoris, not the vagina. And when New York police raided the Stonewall Inn, a gay bar in Greenwich Village, in June 1969, the patrons revolted, starting a two-day riot that lead to the formation of the Gay Liberation Front, the umbrella name for a number of gay liberation groups.

Much of the political radicalism of the 1960s failed to carry into the 1970s, but the sexual revolution continued unabated. By 1970, a reported two-thirds of all Catholic women were using birth control methods disavowed by the church. Alex Comfort's *Joy of Sex,* an explicit, how-to book about sex published in 1972, quickly reached best-seller status and went on to sell 12 million copies in two-dozen languages. The pornographic film *Deep Throat* (1972) earned a record-breaking box office and spawned a spate of X-rated feature films referred to as the "porno chic" movement. The following year, the U.S. Supreme Court ruling in *Roe v. Wade* institutionalized women's control over their bodies by legalizing abortion. Clubs such as Plato's Retreat, which opened in New York City in 1977, institutionalized heterosexual swinging, while a plethora of gay bathhouses offered anonymous public sex to patrons. Disco clubs, too, such as the famous Studio 54 in New York City, created sexual space for both straight and gay attendees.

Backlash

Not everyone embraced the sexual revolution. Many women felt anger at the widespread male chauvinism of 1960s, seen in such draft-protest slogans as "Girls Say Yes to Guys Who Say No." Robin Morgan's 1970 manifesto, "Goodbye to All That," dismissed the sexual revolution as a sham, used by men to obtain sexual favors from women, who could be chastised as prudish, frigid, or "unhip" if they rejected male overtures. Dissatisfaction with the sexual revolution helped the women's liberation movement coalesce and grow. Many lesbians, too, took exception to the gay male insistence on public sex as integral to gay identity, leading to tensions within the gay liberation movement.

Perhaps the most powerful voice of opposition to the sexual revolution was the New Right, a coalition of the Republican Party and the Christian conservative movement that acquired unprecedented power in the late 1970s. Antigay measures, such as singer Anita Bryant's 1977 battle to repeal a gay rights amendment in Dade County, Florida, and the failed 1978 Briggs initiative in California to allow the firing of gay teachers, became staples of the New Right. Opposition to abortion and support of abstinence-only sex education also marked the New Right, which sought to restore the connection between sex and procreation. The election of conservative Ronald Reagan as president in 1980 constituted a major victory for the New Right and highlighted the traditional values of Republican America.

Most destructive to the sexual revolution, however, were the new medical threats of the 1980s. Herpes emerged as a noncurable venereal disease in 1979, and it was quickly represented by the mainstream media as a sign of the risks of promiscuity. *Time* magazine in 1982 called it "the new scarlet letter." Far more threatening, however, was the HIV/AIDS crisis, which first appeared in the early 1980s among urban gay populations but quickly spread to other groups, especially intravenous-drug users and hemophiliacs, who contracted the disease through contaminated needles or blood samples.

While conservative politicians exploited the HIV/AIDS epidemic to advance their religiously based agendas, mainstream culture also restored some of the moral and behavioral norms of a previous generation as an imperative of public health. The sexual revolution would not be reversed or undone, as sexual activity had been divorced, perhaps forever, from its purely procreative function, but the spirit and direction of change seemed over.

Whitney Strub

See also: Birth Control Pill; Free Love; Hefner, Hugh; Hippies.

Further Reading

Allyn, David. *Make Love, Not War: The Sexual Revolution, an Unfettered History.* Boston: Little, Brown, 2000.

Bailey, Beth. *Sex in the Heartland.* Cambridge, MA: Harvard University Press, 1999.

Heidenry, John. *What Wild Ecstasy: The Rise and Fall of the Sexual Revolution.* New York: Simon and Schuster, 1997.

Watkins, Elizabeth Siegel. *On the Pill: A Social History of Oral Contraceptives, 1950–1970.* Baltimore: Johns Hopkins University Press, 1998.

Shakers

A hardworking, communal religious sect in the eastern United States that peaked in popularity during the mid-1800s, the Shakers came into existence in England as an offshoot of the Quakers during the mid-1700s. They were first called the "Shaking Quakers," after the shaking movement they made during the "testimonial" portion of their communal prayers. Their first and most important leader was a charismatic woman known as "Mother" Ann Lee, who immigrated to America in 1774 just before the Revolutionary War, along with other Believers, as they also called themselves.

Although she was illiterate and married (her husband left her and the movement not long after arriving in America), Lee was believed to embody the feminine principle of the divine. With her guidance, the Shakers, originally known as the United Society of Believers in Christ's Second Appearing, established a foothold in upstate New York. Their first village was built at Niskayuna (later Watervliet), near Albany, in 1776. The early days of the Shakers were marred by strife. Mother Ann was imprisoned on charges of spying for the British. As the Shakers tried to spread the word of their beliefs, they were, at times, verbally abused and physically injured by suspicious crowds. William Lee, Ann's brother, died of a skull fracture he received in such a conflict. Despite some continued opposition, the Shakers won converts in the years following the Revolution.

Over time, the Shaker lifestyle was no longer seen as a threat to society, and the religious sect attracted hundreds of people. The first organized Shaker community, New Lebanon, was established in 1787, and became the guiding authority of all later settlements. The governing principles developed there were adopted in other Shaker villages. Each community included respected elders, men and women with seniority to whom others could go for spiritual guidance and conflict resolution. Villages were divided into two to eight distinct living groups called "families."

During the eighteenth and early nineteenth centuries, the Shakers formed communities in New York, Connecticut, Massachusetts, Maine, New Hampshire, Kentucky, Ohio, and Indiana—more than any other religious group of the time. The last new community was formed in the mid-1820s. At its peak, in the mid-nineteenth century, the Shaker population in America numbered between 4,000 and 6,000 members.

Even after Ann Lee's death in 1784, Shaker leaders continued to hold Mother Ann's teachings in the highest esteem. The Shaker faith and lifestyle were based on principles of hard work and continual prayer, following the mandate of Mother Ann, who had said, "Hands to work and hearts to God." Work was seen as a path to salvation and the most useful way to expend one's energy. The Shakers raised their own crops, and their villages were largely self-sufficient. It was common for the Shakers to make their own nails and bricks to build meetinghouses.

The Shakers expressed prayer daily through the spoken word and numerous hymns and spirituals. They also craved simplicity. Their best-known hymn is "Simple Gifts," which begins with the words "'Tis the gift to be simple, 'tis the gift to be free." As had been dictated by Lee, order and neatness were an integral part of the Shaker lifestyle. Dirt and dust were considered mortal enemies.

Although they lived in their own communities, the Shakers did not shun contact with the outside world. Indeed, they allowed outsiders to visit and to watch their religious ceremonies. Committed pacifists, they requested and received exemption from service in the American Civil War from President Abraham Lincoln.

The Shakers cultivated a thriving trade with the outside world. They kept their hands busy in every spare moment by making craft items and furniture that could either be used within the community or labeled as "worldly goods" and sold to outsiders. Shaker design emphasized basic, straight lines and fine craftsmanship. Their furniture and crafts have been imitated for more than a century, including the ubiquitous ladder-back chair and the oval, fingered wooden box.

Although they valued handiwork, Shakers did not shun technology. By the mid- to late nineteenth century, they had adopted several modern technologies to assist them in their daily lives. In fact, they were at the forefront of the technology of the time. Their industrious nature and communal problem-solving abilities led to the invention of numerous machines and improvements in tools, including the circular-saw blade, a mechanical washing machine, and the flat broom.

Perhaps most important in distinguishing Shakers from the rest of society was one of the primary rules of their religion: Shakers were not to marry or have children. In taking the vow of celibacy and in leaving one's family behind to join the community, a new Shaker was in effect trading in his or her biological family for a new family of strangers who were fellow Believers. Thus,

The Shakers were a celibate millenarian sect that established communal settlements in upstate New York during the American Revolution. They got their name from the shaking and dancing that characterized their worship services. *(Library of Congress)*

Shaker communities grew only by the taking in of orphaned children or by outside adults choosing to join. Personal effects and wealth also were banned; converts donated all of their worldly goods to the community.

By the 1870s, largely because of the practice of celibacy, the Shaker population in America had declined to about 2,500 members; by 1900, it had fallen to about 2,000 members. Ten Shaker settlements, once thriving, were abandoned between 1900 and 1930. By 1945, there were only a few hundred Shakers left in the United States.

Tourist interest and an appreciation for Shaker culture and arts revived in the latter decades of the twentieth century, and some villages have been preserved as museums. The last surviving Shaker community is at Sabbathday Lake Shaker Village in New Gloucester, Maine, where a few Believers still carry on the centuries-old traditions in earnest.

Richard Panchyk

See also: Communes; Lee, Ann.

Further Reading

Foster, Lawrence. *Religion and Sexuality: The Shakers, the Mormons, and the Oneida Community.* Urbana: University of Illinois Press, 1981.

Panchyk, Richard. *American Folk Art for Kids.* Chicago: Chicago Review Press, 2004.

Shea, John G. *The American Shakers and Their Furniture.* New York: Van Nostrand Reinhold, 1971.

Sprigg, June. *Shaker Design.* New York: Whitney Museum of American Art, 1986.

Wertkin, Gerard C. *The Four Seasons of Shaker Life.* New York: Simon and Schuster, 1986.

Shakur, Tupac (1971–1996)

Tupac Amaru Shakur was a hip-hop artist and actor known for his outlaw identity, hard-edged songs about racism and ghetto violence, and death by shooting in September 1996. Recognized as a best-selling rap recording artist, and by many fans and critics as the most accomplished of all rappers, Shakur was central to the development of West Coast rap style, which emerged in the 1990s to challenge the popularity of East Coast rap music, emphasizing bass-heavy music and "reality" lyrics that chronicle the struggles of ghetto life. Shakur remains a revered figure in hip-hop culture.

He was born Lesane Parish Crooks in East Harlem, New York City, on June 16, 1971. His mother, Afeni Shakur, was a member of the Black Panther Party who had just been acquitted of multiple charges of conspiracy against the U.S. government; his stepfather, Mutulu Shakur, later became known for planning the $1.6 million robbery of a Brink's Company armored truck in New York in 1981. Tupac Shakur was renamed in honor of the Incan ruler and revolutionary leader Tupac Amarú II (ca. 1742–1781), who was executed after leading an indigenous rebellion against the Spanish colonization of Peru.

After living in New York and Baltimore, Shakur and his family moved in 1988 to Marin City, California, where he served as a lyricist for the local hip-hop group Strictly Dope, before joining the Oakland-based group Digital Underground. He gained national recognition as a rap artist for his contribution to Digital Underground's "Same Song" (1991). Shortly thereafter, Shakur launched his solo career with the album *2Pacalypse Now* (1991). He released a total of five more studio albums during his brief career: *Strictly 4 My N.I.G.G.A.Z.* (1993), *Thug Life* (1994), *Me Against the World* (1995), *All Eyez on Me* (1996), and *The Don Killuminati: The 7 Day Theory* (1996). As his music career took off, Shakur also ventured into acting, starring in such feature films as *Juice* (1992), *Poetic Justice* (1993) with costar Janet Jackson, and *Above the Rim* (1994).

Shakur was the preeminent figure in the development of what was called the "East Coast versus West Coast rivalry" in rap music. Shakur signed with Death Row Records in 1995, a Los Angeles recording label headed by Suge Knight, a controversial CEO with Mob Piru Bloods gang connections and a dislike for the East Coast hip-hop label Bad Boy Records (headed by Sean Combs).

While driving with Knight in Las Vegas, Nevada, Shakur was shot. He died from the wounds six days later, on September 13, 1996, at the age of twenty-five. The murder was never solved, but many suspected the involvement of New York–based rapper Notorious B.I.G. (of Bad Boy Records), whom Shakur had earlier accused of arranging a 1994 New York recording studio robbery during which Shakur had been shot several times. The suspicions over Shakur's murder stirred growing animosity, until Notorious B.I.G. himself was killed in Los Angeles six months later, on March 9, 1997. In the aftermath of that incident, many hip-hop artists and social activists began a concerted and successful effort to quell the East-West rivalries.

Venerated as a hip-hop cultural icon, Shakur is regarded by fans and critics of the genre as a "ghetto saint." His songs intimately and eloquently express the joys and the pains of African American life in the inner city. On the one hand, songs such as "Brenda's Got a Baby" (1991) and "Dear Mama" (1995) celebrate and pay homage to women, especially mothers, while "Keep Ya Head Up" (1993) and "Life Goes On" (1996) offer a broad message of hope and spiritual uplift for everyone facing hard times. On the other hand, songs such as "I Get Around" (1993) glamorize Shakur's sexual exploits, while "Hit 'Em Up" (1996) champions the violence and intimidation needed to live a successful "thug life." The complexities and contradictions in his music and his personal life secured Shakur a loyal following among those who respected his lyrical honesty and welcomed his representation of their own lives.

More than a decade after his death, Shakur's vocals continued to garner significant album sales. Since 1997, several successful albums have been released using previously recorded songs or lyrics. In addition, Shakur's poetry was published in *The Rose That Grew from Concrete* (1997) and *Inside a Thug's Heart* (2004); the documentary film *Tupac: Resurrection*, about his life and death, was released in 2003. A majority of his albums, produced both before and after his death, have achieved platinum and multiplatinum certification.

Natchee Blu Barnd

See also: Gangsta Rap; Hip-Hop; Rap Music.

Further Reading

Dyson, Michael Eric. *Holler If You Hear Me: Searching for Tupac Shakur.* New York: Basic Civitas, 2001.
Joseph, Jamal. *Tupac Shakur Legacy.* New York: Simon and Schuster, 2006.

Simpsons, The

Starting its television life as a series of short, animated sketches on *The Tracey Ullman Show* in 1987, *The Simpsons* graduated to network-show status on the then-burgeoning Fox Network in 1989. An animated nuclear-family sitcom, the show has served as a richly developed mouthpiece of social, political, cultural, consumer, and media satire and parody. Challenging the very notion of counterculture, *The Simpsons* arguably has become one of the counterculture's most mainstream texts, attaining widespread fame and notoriety both in America and abroad, and becoming one of television's longest-running and most easily recognizable programs.

Creator and animator Matt Groening poses with a cutout of everyman Homer Simpson, the father character in his animated hit television series *The Simpsons*. The sitcom has broken new ground in satirizing politics, society, media culture, and family life. *(Alan Levenson/Time & Life Pictures/ Getty Images)*

The Simpsons follows the lives of parents Homer and Marge and children Bart, Lisa, and Maggie in the never-precisely-located suburban landscape of Springfield, U.S.A. Originally written by Matt Groening, previously known for the subversive cartoon "Life in Hell," *The Simpsons* continued its predecessor's interest in contesting authority figures. Springfield's mayor, Joe Quimby, Principal Seymour Skinner, and local nuclear power plant owner Montgomery Burns form a triumvirate of corrupt, self-serving leadership, surpassed only by the most dysfunctional authority figure of all, Homer Simpson as father.

Hearkening back to the Springfield of television's 1950s family series *Father Knows Best* and to the barrage of whitewashed, perennially happy sitcoms that preceded it, *The Simpsons* centers its family on the ignorant, overeating, ill-fated antifather, and offers up the "underachieving, yet proud of it" son, Bart, as its initial moral engine. Bart's rebellious platitudes and unruly attitude drew quick focus from parent groups and schools nationwide, and even inspired comment from family values–oriented presidential candidate George H.W. Bush, who in 1992 called for "a nation closer to the Waltons than to the Simpsons." Over time, the show challenged patriarchal authority more convincingly by shifting greater emphasis to the precocious and environmentally, ecologically, and socially aware Lisa. Indeed, one episode studies a family gene that renders all its men stupid but the women geniuses.

Ultimately, however, the program's greatest offering to the counterculture, and that which has won it a cult following among college students and liberal academics nationwide, is its predilection to comedically attack capitalist consumerist values. Frequently mocking the form and content of advertising in particular, *The Simpsons* depicts consumerism as gluttony.

Using its four-fingered yellow characters to comment on reality, the program also often lampoons other genres of television, such as the news show and the documentary, as well as celebrity. While *The Simpsons* has hosted major celebrities, including pop star Michael Jackson, *Harry Potter* author J.K. Rowling, *Star Wars* star Mark Hamill, and rock band U2, it often mocks them in the process.

Meanwhile, *The Simpsons* habitually mocks itself and its own position in the cultural and economic mainstream, even occasionally taking satiric swipes at Fox owner Rupert Murdoch. The show has spawned a wealth of commercial merchandise ranging from T-shirts to bottle openers, but similarly ridicules its own act of selling out, most notably by offering the figure of debased children's television icon and product-pusher Krusty the Clown as its on-screen stand-in.

Reflecting a certain postmodern cynical chic, *The Simpsons* is iconic of its age. It has given birth to numerous followers, most notably the animated television shows *King of the Hill* (1997–), *South Park* (1997–), and *Family Guy* (1999–).

Jonathan Gray

See also: South Park.

Further Reading

Alberti, John, ed. *The Simpsons and the Possibility of Oppositional Culture.* Detroit, MI: Wayne State University Press, 2003.

Gray, Jonathan. *Watching with the Simpsons: Television, Parody, and Intertextuality.* New York: Routledge, 2006.

Turner, Chris. *Planet Simpson: How a Cartoon Masterpiece Defined a Generation.* Cambridge, MA: Da Capo, 2005.

Sinclair, Upton (1878–1968)

Upton Sinclair was one of America's great crusading writers and a vocal supporter of socialism in the twentieth century. A prolific author, he wrote ninety novels, thirty plays, and countless articles, stories, and pamphlets. Well known for his polemical concern for progressive reform, he was a firm believer in the power of literature to improve the human condition. As one of the prominent social critics—popularly known as "muckrakers"—of his time, he displayed an intense interest in social and industrial reform by exposing injustice and corruption with his pen.

Upton Beall Sinclair was born on September 20, 1878, in Baltimore, Maryland. He graduated from City College of New York in 1897 and attended graduate school at Columbia University while supporting himself by writing for newspapers and magazines.

In 1904, he was sent by the socialist newspaper *Appeal to Reason* to report on the unsanitary conditions in the meatpacking industry in Chicago. His report in fictional form was serialized in the paper during the summer of 1905. It was published in early 1906 as *The Jungle,* a brutally graphic novel of the Chicago stockyards in which Sinclair describes the wretched sanitary and working conditions of the industry.

The book is based on Sinclair's eyewitness accounts and interviews with workers, who revealed the tuberculosis and cholera that developed as a result of exposure to and repurposing of spoiled meat, a result of what Sinclair saw as the "monstrous disease" of industrial capitalism. After living a life of poverty, death, and destruction, the book's main character, factory worker and Lithuanian immigrant Jurgis Rudkus, turns to socialism.

The Jungle soon became a national sensation. Although Sinclair had hoped that his writing would arouse sympathy for the worker, it created tremendous public indignation at the deplorable quality of food industry standards. Sinclair was quoted as saying, "I aimed at the public's heart and by accident I hit it in the stomach." The book's popularity is believed to have been instrumental in passage of the Pure Food and Drug Act of 1906 by the U.S. Congress.

Publication of the novel placed Sinclair in the ranks of such leading muckraking writers as Ida Tarbell, Lincoln Steffens, and others. Proceeds from the book provided Sinclair with the finances to open the

Upton Sinclair's 1906 novel *The Jungle,* an especially graphic example of "muckraking" fiction, exposed the unsanitary conditions and corruption in the Chicago meatpacking industry. The public outcry led to passage of the Pure Food and Drug Act of 1906. *(Library of Congress)*

cooperative-living community Helicon Hall (Helicon Home Colony) in Englewood, New Jersey, a utopian-socialist project that lasted until 1907, when a fire destroyed the hall and the venture was abandoned.

Sinclair continued writing muckraking novels that attacked social evils. Representative works, in addition to *The Jungle,* include *King Coal* (1917), which reveals the conditions of Western coal miners of the time; *Oil!* (1927), loosely based on the Teapot Dome oil scandal of the Warren G. Harding administration; *Boston* (1928), about the Sacco and Vanzetti murder case; and *Little Steel* (1938), which explores union resistance in the oil industry.

He also wrote eleven historical novels, known as the Lanny Budd series, beginning with *World's End* (1940), which examines the life of an antifascist hero. One of the Lanny Budd novels, *Dragon's Teeth* (1942),

about Adolf Hitler's rise to power in Nazi Germany, won Sinclair the 1943 Pulitzer Prize. His final novel in the series, *The Return of Lanny Budd* (1953), explores the United States's hostile sentiment toward post–World War II Soviet Russia.

During the Great Depression of the 1930s, Sinclair played a part in organizing a socialist reform movement in California called EPIC (End Poverty in California), which proposed that the state repurpose idle factories and farmland into cooperatives that would hire the unemployed. In 1934, he entered politics by running as a Democrat for governor of California; he lost the election to Republican candidate Frank Merriam.

Upton Sinclair died on November 25, 1968, in Bound Brook, New Jersey.

Yuwu Song

See also: Socialism.

Further Reading

Bloodworth, William A. *Upton Sinclair.* Boston: Twayne, 1977.
Harris, Leon. *Upton Sinclair: American Rebel.* New York: Crowell, 1975.
Yoder, Jon A. *Upton Sinclair.* New York: Ungar, 1975.

Ska

Ska is an upbeat, horn-driven style of music that emerged in Jamaica during the 1950s, drawing upon aspects of mento (the indigenous folk music), calypso, jazz, and American rhythm and blues. Ska and the subcultures associated with it are often divided into three waves. Jamaican ska thrived until the mid-1960s, when it was replaced in popularity by rock steady and reggae music. The second-wave ska revival, in the form of the Two-Tone movement, occurred in the 1970s and 1980s in the United Kingdom. A third revival took place in the 1990s, this time largely based in the United States. Ska music and style were popular in the Jamaican Rude Boy subculture, as well as among some members of the punk, mod, and skinhead movements.

Jamaican ska arose in the context of the Jamaican independence movement, which inspired a nationalistic yearning for music based on island traditions. During the same period, portable sound systems (mobile discotheques) proliferated in Jamaica, playing dance music for crowds of people. As sound system operators became more competitive, they began producing their own records that emphasized a "Jamaican feel" and aesthetic; ska music flourished. Of the numerous groups of the time, the Skatalites dominated the scene as true pioneers of ska and epitomized the sound.

Others influential in the movement included Laurel Aitken, Clement "Coxsone" Dodd, Don Drummond, Desmond Dekker and the Aces, Prince Buster, Roland Alphonso, Toots and the Maytals, Bob Marley's band the Wailers, the Duke Reid Group, the Ethiopians, and Peter Tosh, among others. While early ska music often entailed the instrumental reworking of popular American and British songs, much of it drew upon local culture and folk traditions, and sometimes took the form of social commentary, addressing the hardships faced by the poor and marginalized in Jamaican society.

In the 1960s, ska music was embraced by the Rude Boy (or "Rudie") subculture that emerged in the ghettos of Kingston. In response to poverty, unemployment, and oppression, Rude Boys became gangsters and petty thieves with a reputation as stylish street hooligans who lived by their wits and tried to beat the system. Some Rude Boys were armed with knives or handguns and, when organized in gangs, would roam through West Kingston on foot or stripped-down chrome motorbikes.

Ska music both celebrated and criticized the Rude Boys' subterranean lifestyle, alluding to street fights, the ghetto, crime, sexual encounters, gambling, guns, prison life, and dying young. The Rude Boys' unique street style involved a streamlined, hard-edged, trimmed-down look, with sharply cut suits, cropped slim trousers, porkpie hats, tightly cropped haircuts, wraparound hipster sunglasses, white socks, polished black shoes, and leather jackets. Rude Boys also favored mohair, and "tonic" suits that shimmered with the two-tone effect of contrasting colors, such as black-red or electric blue.

Ska music and Rude Boy style were brought by Jamaican immigrants to the United Kingdom and North America in the late 1960s and 1970s. In the United Kingdom especially, the sound and style of ska were appealing to white youth (such as hard mods and nonracist skinheads) who disliked the styles and values of the hippies and other youth movements of the time; it also influenced a number of musicians, such as the Clash, the Police, and Elvis Costello.

In the late 1970s, the ska revival movement known as Two-Tone (after the influential 2 Tone record label) drew upon punk ethos and style, and emphasized racial harmony, societal problems, and social justice. Black and white youth, often in black and white suits, "skanked" (danced) together at dance halls to the music of racially integrated groups such as the Specials and, later, the Selecter, Madness, and the Beat (also known as the English Beat). These bands and the associated subculture did not just revitalize the style of ska; they directly confronted racial prejudices. More politically oriented than most movements of the time, they faced violent confrontations with racist skinheads, conservative nationalists, and others at dance halls and elsewhere.

The Two-Tone ska movement resulted in the formation of ska bands in the United States, such as the highly influential Toasters (in existence since the early 1980s and led by Robert Hingley, who later created Moon Ska Records). This led to the third wave of ska music, in the 1990s, further popularized by bands such as the Untouchables, Fishbone, Bim Skala Bim, Operation Ivy, the Scofflaws, the Mighty Mighty Bosstones, the Slackers, Hepcat, the Pietasters, the Voodoo Glow Skulls, Reel Big Fish, Skankin' Pickle, Let's Go Bowling, Save Ferris, Less Than Jake, and the Aquabats. Some of these bands achieved commercial success, with musical styles that reflect a range of influences including punk, hard core, heavy metal, funk, soul, surf, and others. Ska-influenced bands such as Rancid, No Doubt, and Sublime also popularized and commodified the ska sound.

After the mainstreaming of pop-ska sounds on MTV and commercial radio, popular interest peaked and then declined in the late 1990s, as other styles were promoted to capture mainstream attention. Out of the limelight, the ska scene continued to develop at a more grassroots level, with some enthusiasts taking an inclusive, hodgepodge approach in innovating on the style. Others, more traditionalist in attitude, embraced the Jamaican 1960s-style ska, while some bands and fans were deeply committed to the Two-Tone movement and Rude Boy style, sometimes with mod culture influences.

Although the American third-wave ska is often depicted as being solely party music—skanking to catchy rhythms and having fun—some of it offers relevant social commentary. The appearance of a fourth wave of ska came to be debated in fanzines and on Web pages, as subcultural events and tours of ska bands promoted the eclectic range of contemporary ska. Though separated from ska's original context and related social conditions, the various forms of ska style continued to signify a subcultural identity for some youth, offering a sense of community, creativity, and aesthetic pleasure.

Daniel Wojcik

See also: Folk Music; Jazz; Punk Rock.

Further Reading

Barrow, Steve, and Peter Dalton. *The Rough Guide to Reggae.* 2nd ed. London: Rough Guides, 2001.

Hebdige, Dick. *Cut 'n' Mix: Culture, Identity, and Caribbean Music.* London: Methuen, 1987.

Potash, Chris, ed. *Reggae, Rasta, Revolution: Jamaican Music from Ska to Dub.* New York: Schirmer, 1997.

Skateboarders

Skateboarders are mostly, although not exclusively, young males who practice the sport of skateboarding and who belong to a broader youth subculture defined by the "skater" identity. While the specific content of this identity has shifted since it first emerged in the 1950s—moving from a heavily surf- and punk-inspired image of destructive rebelliousness to a more urban, hip-hop–influenced image of personal creative expression—the skater identity has consistently challenged dominant social and cultural norms and values.

While a profitable skateboard industry has existed for decades and produces some wealthy professional skateboarders, most skaters are urban and suburban youth who reject "adult" values of career advancement and who struggle to escape the discipline of alienated labor in the job market. For most skaters, life is about advancing their sport, enjoying life through the associational experience of belonging to an underground movement, and reclaiming public space through the creative use of the skateboard itself.

History

As a recreational activity, skateboarding got its start in Southern California during the late 1950s when surfers attached roller-skate wheels to wooden planks in an effort to simulate surfing on land. Dubbed "sidewalk surfing," skateboarding was originally part of Southern California's larger surf and beach culture.

During the 1960s and 1970s, skateboarding emerged as an independent form of recreation when several companies began to market skateboards and skating equipment to suburban youth. As part of their marketing campaigns, companies promoted skateboard competitions, which, in turn, gave rise to a number of amateur and professional skateboard athletes. During this period, the dominant technical practice of skateboarding featured mostly handstands and spins or downhill racing.

In Southern California, however, surfers continued to practice a form of skateboarding very different from that of the official contest circuit. Based largely in the ethnically diverse working-class beach communities of Venice and Santa Monica, these surfer-skaters sought to emulate the smooth-flowing style of surfing on land, developing long carving and sliding maneuvers to re-create the motion and sensation of riding the waves. These youth skated the banked and sloped terrains of the city, where they practiced a form of boarding that was aggressive and smooth at the same time. They also began a process of creatively reappropriating urban space, which has been a hallmark of skater culture ever since.

The first significant confrontation between the two poles in skateboarding culture occurred in 1975, when the Zephyr team from Santa Monica entered a slalom and freestyle contest in Del Mar, California. The Zephyr team, or "Z-Boys," brought the aggressive style of skating they practiced on the streets into the public eye. Their maneuvers evidenced an aggressive slashing, grinding, and sliding style that was largely foreign to the figure-skating–like practice of skateboarding at the time.

During the same period, skateboarding also expanded to suburban backyards, where skaters took their craft to the smoothly sloped and vertical terrains of swimming pools drained during the drought of 1976. Often, skaters did not have the permission of the property owners, bringing them into direct conflict with police and the idea of private property itself, and indicating the subversive character skateboarding culture was taking on.

As the more aggressive style of skating became popular, corporate interests were quick to see it as an opportunity to expand their market. Many of the original members of the Z-Boys team were signed to lucrative contracts with manufacturing companies that exploited their image to increase market share. At around the same time, entrepreneurs and municipalities across the country began to open skate parks that emulated the concrete terrains of the city and the backyard pool. By the close of the 1970s, skateboarding had penetrated popular culture and become a multimillion-dollar business.

Nevertheless, in the late 1970s and early 1980s, a rash of liability and insurance problems forced many of the skate parks to close. As public interest in the sport waned and its profitability declined, skateboarding was once again driven underground. With the decline of the concrete skate parks, die-hard skaters began to build "half-pipes" from plywood and two-by-fours in backyards and in abandoned or fallow spaces. Often built to heights of 12 feet (3.7 meters) or more, these half-pipes allowed skaters to take vertical aerial maneuvers to new levels of skill and complexity.

Following the nationwide recession of the mid-1980s, a new consumer-driven mentality took root in America, and young people across the country began to rediscover skateboarding. However, the boarding scene that emerged was quite different from the preceding one. For one thing, a widening of the skateboard allowed companies to print more elaborate graphics on the bottom of the deck, and they chose provocative, even demonic, graphics that were shocking to many suburban parents.

Skating Subculture

During the mid-1980s, skateboarding solidified as more than a merely recreational activity. Spurred by manufacturers' exploitation of the emerging suburban youth market, boarding became a powerful adolescent subculture that often determined everything about skaters' personal identities—from the clothes they wore to the music they listened to and the attitudes they professed about the meaning and purpose of life.

During this time, skateboard culture existed in a kind of liminal space, somewhere between the rampant suburban consumerism of the Me Generation of the 1980s and an underground subversiveness that rejected the traditional family mores of academic success and career preparation. For many skaters, life was about living for the day and avoiding the alienation of school and work as long as possible. More politically conscious skaters even drew an explicit connection between skateboarding and the anarchist tradition of refusing labor.

As the 1980s progressed, street skaters—many from urban environments on the East Coast—continued to redefine the sport, using the "ollie" maneuver to jump over planters, slide down handrails, and even ride walls. In doing so, the street skaters of the mid- to late 1980s took skateboarding back to its origins and resumed the decolonization of urban space that their predecessors had begun a decade earlier.

A definite divide between "street skaters" and "vert skaters" became evident during the late 1980s and early 1990s. The latter were much more likely to retain links to the surf and punk cultures, while the former emerged as part of a newly insurgent urban culture that some considered part of the wider hip-hop movement. Many street skaters were young African

Americans or Hispanics, and the budding rap music scene of the time became popular among street skaters of all ethnic and social backgrounds.

The rise in popularity of street skating was fueled in large measure by the release of several team videos by new, independent skateboard companies. The videos showed previously unknown amateur skaters performing skillful street maneuvers that many older, vert-skating pros could not even contemplate. With their gritty, underground feel, the videos fueled the new urban street-skating orientation of many young skaters.

Despite the economic recession of the early 1990s and the often bitter competition between newer, independent skateboard manufactures and older, vert-based firms, skateboarding has survived until the present day, even as the gap between the two distinct axes that have marked it since its inception has been exacerbated. The inclusion of skateboarding in the rising genre known as Xtreme sports during the 1990s—including in regular

Tony Hawk (bottom) and other champion competitors contributed to the Generation X counterculture image of skateboarding and helped transform the sport into a mass-culture commercial phenomenon. *(Matt Stroshane/Getty Images)*

coverage of the annual X Games on the all-sports television network ESPN—has provided a broad media outlet and ensured that the sport itself has commercial viability and corporate sponsorship.

At the same time, a vibrant underground culture of street skaters has persisted in most major cities. Many of these skaters subscribe to the dropout philosophy of their predecessors, even as it is expressed in an increasingly urban and hip-hop–oriented idiom.

Michael F. Gretz

See also: Me Decade; Venice, California.

Further Reading

Borden, Iain. *Skateboarding, Space and the City: Architecture and the Body.* New York: Berg, 2001.

Brooke, Michael. *The Concrete Wave: The History of Skateboarding.* Toronto, Canada: Warwick, 1999.

Davis, James. *Skateboarding Is Not a Crime: Fifty Years of Street Culture.* Richmond Hill, Canada: Firefly, 2004.

Skinheads

See White Supremacists

Slang

One of the main ways in which a subculture distinguishes itself from the rest of society is by devising its own vocabulary, or slang. Slang is primarily made up of words and phrases that are not part of standard, formal language but are derived from a foreign language, dialect, or other special language for informal, colloquial use. Slang terms often refer to objects or activities considered inappropriate for polite conversation, and the terms themselves sometimes are considered vulgar, obscene, or otherwise offensive by mainstream society. Over time, however, many slang words become accepted as standard language, finding their way into dictionaries and formal usage.

Even generally accepted words can be used as slang if they are given meanings other than their formal ones. For example, the original, formal definition of the word *cool* refers to temperature, but the word also developed a slang usage in which it means "excellent." *Bad* means "the opposite of good" in formal English, or even "evil"; in contemporary street slang, however, *bad* means "excellent," making it a synonym for *cool.*

The members of any group may invent their own slang to communicate among themselves. Hence, slang serves as a kind of secret language that cannot be readily understood by the rest of society. Members of the group can identify themselves to one another merely by their use and understanding of slang words and phrases. Slang, therefore, is particularly important to American countercultures, whose members regard themselves as outsiders, alienated from society at large.

For example, one of the earliest known forms of slang is English "criminal cant," which originated in the sixteenth century and was used as a secret language by criminals and beggars. In the present day, members of organized crime continue to have their own semiprivate vocabulary, using the term *whacked,* for example, as a synonym for *killed.*

Slang is especially common among racial and ethnic minority groups, who use it to distinguish themselves from mainstream culture and reinforce cultural identity. African Americans have contributed countless slang words to the English language throughout their history, and today the hip-hop culture has its own extensive slang vocabulary. For example, the term *dead presidents* refers to paper currency, which features images of deceased presidents George Washington, Abraham Lincoln, and others.

The 1960s Counterculture

Traditionally, teens and young adults have developed and used slang to have a vocabulary that adults do not understand. Slang was an important element of the American counterculture created by the generation that came of age following World War II. The Beat culture of the 1950s and early 1960s generated slang words such as *cats* and *Daddy-o* (for "cool" people) and *square* (for people who were not cool). Adjectives were turned into place names, such as *dullsville* and *weirdsville.*

The youth movement of the 1960s proved to be a rich source of slang. New phrases were devised to express the counterculture philosophy of the decade, such as *do your own thing* and *turn on,* and there were new terms for the people who practiced it, including *hippies* and *yippies.*

Likewise, the underground drug culture spawned an endless series of slang words to disguise their meaning from outsiders. Marijuana has been called "pot," "weed," and "Mary Jane," among a myriad of other terms. The California surfer culture of the early 1960s contributed such words as *bummer* (for depressing) and *gnarly* (for good). Young people sent to fight in Vietnam also contributed: American soldiers were "grunts," and the Vietcong were referred to as "Charlie."

Going Mainstream

It is not just members of countercultures who create slang. Even groups considered part of the cultural mainstream devise their own vocabularies. Regional slang is used by people across the United States. An example is the infamous Valley Girl–speak of Southern California.

Members of virtually every profession invent their own slang as well. Doctors and nurses have an extensive slang vocabulary, including *stat* (meaning immediately). In show business, the trade publication *Variety* is famous for inventing slogans and slang terms, such as *sitcom* for situation-comedy series.

The rise of the Internet has brought a new, widely used form of slang, including such now-familiar terms as *surfing the Web* or *lurker* (someone who reads posts on a Web site without contributing). Internet slang terms are distinctive in that many of them are abbreviations, such as *LOL* (laughing out loud).

When slang words become accepted parts of the language, they cease being slang. Hence, the continual development of new slang words ultimately serves to enrich and revitalize the language. In 1888, the great poet and inventor of American vernacular Walt Whitman hailed the creation of slang as "the wholesome fermentation or eructation of those processes eternally active in language, by which froth and specks are thrown up, mostly to pass away; though occasionally to settle and permanently crystallize."

A good example of the process Whitman described is the history of *cool*. Slang use of the word to mean "excellent" originated among African Americans and was first recorded in the early 1930s. In the 1940s, the general public became aware of how African American jazz musicians used the word. White hipsters thereupon adopted this version in the 1950s, and hippies readily embraced it in the 1960s. By the 2000s, if not before, the usage had become common throughout the English-speaking world. Indeed, while this use of *cool* is still informal, it is arguably no longer slang.

Cool is also a notable exception to the rule that the majority of terms introduced as slang are ephemeral and eventually fall from fashion. If a slang term is adopted by mainstream society, it usually loses its outsider cachet.

Moreover, as each new generation invents its own slang words to distinguish its members from their elders, slang becomes dated. However hip the slang of the 1950s sounded to the youth of that time, today,

much of it seems quaint, if not ridiculous. Ultimately, slang—characterized by Whitman as "the start of fancy, imagination and humor, breathing into its nostrils the breath of life"—either is assimilated into the mainstream language over time or vanishes into obscurity.

Peter Sanderson

See also: Beat Generation; Drug Culture; Hippies; Jazz.

Further Reading

Dickson, Paul. *Slang: The Popular Dictionary of Americanisms.* New York: Walker, 2006.

Lighter, Jonathan E., ed. *Historical Dictionary of American Slang.* 2 vols. New York: Random House, 1994, 1997.

Partridge, Eric. *A Dictionary of Slang and Unconventional English.* 8th ed. Ed. Paul Beale. New York: Macmillan, 1984.

Spears, Richard A. *American Slang Dictionary.* 4th ed. New York: McGraw-Hill, 2006.

Slave Culture

Slave culture was a complex amalgamation of Central and West African traditions and practices tempered by the social, political, and economic exigencies of the British North American plantation system. Language, religion, family, and community were critical components of a largely oppositional culture that enabled slaves to endure extreme hardship, separation, and loss.

Slave culture was not monolithic, but important changes during the early national period helped forge an increasingly distinct African American slave experience. During the eighteenth century, slavery was a profitable but still relatively small institution in North America, and slave culture varied considerably by region. By the early nineteenth century, however, slavery became a distinctively Southern institution, with most slaves filling the labor needs on Southern plantations. Although three-quarters of Southerners did not own slaves, and most slaveholders owned fewer than five, three-quarters of slaves lived in groups of ten or more, and half of all slaves lived in groups of twenty or more.

Even after the constitutional ban on the African slave trade went into effect in 1808 and slavery became illegal in the North, the slave population continued to grow. Illegal imports combined with births resulted in a population of nearly 4 million slaves by 1860. Increased cotton production and the expansion of slavery into places such as Mississippi and Louisiana resulted in the growth of an internal slave trade that wreaked havoc in the lives of slaves in the Upper South, jeopardized the newly acquired freedom of many Northern blacks, and ultimately created a slave culture rooted in deep South plantation agriculture.

Language

Language played a critical role in the creation and maintenance of slave culture. The many languages of peoples from West and Central Africa often were so different that communication between Africans initially was difficult. Over time, numerous African languages and English mingled on the plantations of British North America, combining to form a language that made communication between Africans and whites possible. Slaves living in coastal South Carolina and Georgia, for example, spoke Gullah, a creole language that consisted primarily of English words but retained the pronunciation and grammar rules of various West African languages. The more time slaves lived among each other and their white masters, the more familiar they became with the English language and with the society of their captors.

African-born and American-born slaves who were able to communicate with one another, and with whites, benefited from increased knowledge of European ways and more sophisticated understanding of the slave system, which better equipped them to oppose white domination. Slaves who could communicate could form strong kinship and community networks; they could educate themselves; and, perhaps most importantly, they could sustain a distinct, oppositional slave culture rooted in their African past and traditions and their experience as slaves.

Language, like all elements of slave culture, became a complex means of resistance. Although the most readily identifiable forms of slave resistance usually involved direct confrontations or overt refusals to submit to the authority of owners or overseers, resistance also could be much more subtle. Language, as well as other forms of lyrical and nonverbal means of communication, enabled slaves to defy masters who sought to strip them of their culture and their identities.

Resistance often meant using language, song, and other gestures and postures to forge strong bonds with family, friends, and other fellow slaves, and ultimately pass on that knowledge and sense of loyalty and community to succeeding generations. Trickster tales, stories conveyed around a campfire or in the darkness of the slave quarters that pitted characters such as John the Slave or Brer (brother) Rabbit against Old Master or Brer Fox, often were used by slaves as a means of metaphorically defying or outwitting their masters and as a way of transferring important life lessons to younger slaves.

Religion

Religion, like language, contributed to the foundation of slave culture. Often, special talents or abilities, such as storytelling or healing, helped some slaves gain respect and authority among their fellow slaves; slave conjurers and preachers who ministered to the spiritual needs of the community held a special place of privilege.

Most owners insisted that their slaves convert to Christianity, and most slaves did indeed profess a faith in Christianity by the mid-nineteenth century, but slaves did not simply adopt European religious beliefs. Those who did generally adapted their religious beliefs and practices to their own African cultural and spiritual traditions and used them for their own practical and spiritual purposes.

Slaves lived in a sacred world in which their lives and their natural environment were intimately connected to their ancestors and to powerful religious or spiritual figures that often had very human qualities. Although planters encouraged the acceptance of a form of Christianity that emphasized obedience, sin, and gentleness, slaves were drawn to stories in the Hebrew Bible such as those from Exodus that featured themes of escape from bondage and freedom from oppression. Owners hoped to use religion as a means of reinforcing their power over slaves by arguing that God commanded slaves to obey their masters and to be loyal, and used religion to justify holding slaves in bondage for life. Instead, slaves used Christianity, as well as older African traditions and beliefs, to form a powerful oppositional culture.

African Americans not only adapted Christian beliefs to their previous belief systems and present condition, but they also incorporated African styles of worship that included singing, dancing, storytelling, and the call-and-response style of communication into their Christian services. For instance, the ring shout, a ritual originally performed in Africa that remained an important part of New World slave culture, symbolized oneness with nature and with ancestors, and the solidarity of the community. Far less stolid and solemn than Europeans in their worship, Africans celebrated their religion.

Family and Community

Along with language and religion, the family proved essential to the maintenance of slave culture and community. Family life for slaves was always problematic, since they had no legal rights to protect their family or keep it intact. In slave marriages, husbands and wives survived on an equal footing: Neither had any property rights or legal standing. Slave masters had absolute authority to punish with impunity, to separate the family, and to reward a family member, theoretically making parental authority and marriage rights meaningless. Nevertheless, slaves devised their own rituals, customs, and social boundaries regarding marriage and family, and they worked hard to maintain kin networks.

Slaves performed their own marriage ceremonies, often consisting of older African traditions such as "jumping the broomstick," in slave quarters, away from the master's gaze. Slaves used African naming customs to honor relatives and denote familial lineage. They also followed certain prohibitions, such as not marrying one's "blood kin," or first cousin.

By the 1840s, three-quarters of slaves in Louisiana lived in what one historian has referred to as simple family households, consisting of a couple with or without children or a single parent, usually a mother, with children. The Louisiana slaves were not alone; most slaves lived in families. The fact that slave families existed and endured well after the tremendous upheaval caused by the Civil War and emancipation is testimony to the power of the oppositional culture formed by slaves, despite white society's efforts to dehumanize them.

At the center of the oppositional slave culture lay the slave community. Two separate but intricately connected slave communities developed on plantations during the nineteenth century. One centered around the "big house," where the master and his family exercised the greatest control over slaves and where slaves were most likely to appear to acquiesce to the master's authority. This was where most white people gained their impressions of slavery and of Southern black people, as well as of the Southern slave owner as genteel and patriarchal.

There was a very different plantation community in the slave quarters, however, where white people held far less direct power and authority over their slaves. It was within the slave quarters that slaves could maintain a greater degree of dignity and control over their lives. Freed from the master's gaze, slaves developed and maintained a complex oppositional culture rooted in rituals, practices, traditions, songs, storytelling, and beliefs born in Africa and reconstituted in the New World.

Whether they were attending a clandestine religious service, participating in a wedding ceremony, or surreptitiously making plans to escape or engage in some other unlawful act, slaves acted within a complex cultural milieu that was formed in opposition to the larger white culture. Slave communities were not without conflict and confrontation, but the common bond of servitude often proved to be a powerful uniting force among slaves.

Michael A. Rembis

See also: African Americans.

Further Reading

Fett, Sharla M. *Working Cures: Healing, Health, and Power on Southern Slave Plantations.* Chapel Hill: University of North Carolina Press, 2002.

Genovese, Eugene D. *Roll, Jordan, Roll: The World the Slaves Made.* New York: Pantheon, 1974.

Hall, Gwendolyn Midlo. *Africans in Colonial Louisiana: The Development of Afro-Creole Culture in the Eighteenth Century.* Baton Rouge: Louisiana State University Press, 1995.

Levine, Lawrence W. *Black Culture and Black Consciousness: Afro-American Folk Thought from Slavery to Freedom.* New York: Oxford University Press, 1977.

White, Deborah Gray. *Ar'n't I a Woman?: Female Slaves in the Plantation South.* New York: W.W. Norton, 1999.

Wood, Peter H. *Black Majority: Negroes in Colonial South Carolina from 1670 through the Stono Rebellion.* New York: Alfred A. Knopf, 1974.

Sloan, John (1871–1951)

John Sloan was a distinguished American artist whose sympathy for the common people put him on the side of those artists hoping for progressive change in turn-of-the-twentieth-century America. His subject matter, drawn from everyday life, on many occasions challenged mainstream artistic norms and made his art a potential tool for social justice. His naturalistic style gave new aesthetic insights into the modern urban landscape.

John French Sloan was born in Lock Haven, Pennsylvania, on August 2, 1871. His family moved to Philadelphia when he was still a boy, and it was there that he was raised and educated. While at the city's Central High School, he became friends with another aspiring artist, William Glackens.

Primarily self-taught, Sloan obtained work as an illustrator with the *Philadelphia Inquirer* in 1891; he moved to the *Philadelphia Press* in 1895 and remained there until 1903. Increasingly, newspaper illustrations were being replaced by photography, a reality that helped persuade Sloan to become a full-time artist.

Sloan's formal art education had begun in the early 1890s at the Pennsylvania Academy of the Fine Arts, where he studied oil painting with the influential artist and teacher Robert Henri, and with Thomas Anshutz, an equally significant masculine realist. It was also during these studies that he became friends with some of the other young artists who would later become known as The Eight—the group of painters who participated in an exhibition at the Macbeth Gallery in New York City in February 1908 in response to the National Academy's rejection of their work for its 1907 spring exhibition.

In 1904, joining other artists such as Glackens, George Luks, and Everett Shinn, Sloan settled in New York City, where the bustle of daily life provided a new creative inspiration. Sloan's newspaper work had introduced him to everyday life from the bottom up, giving him an appreciation for both narrative and naturalism in art.

Sloan began to exhibit in 1906 and joined the other members of The Eight in the Macbeth Gallery exhibit. The show helped seal the group's identity as the Ashcan School, a name associated with their realistic and challenging take on urban life. The Ashcan School stuck its collective finger in the eye of academic convention, which meant defying the art critics of the day. As a group, they embraced the urban backdrop of American life and saw that unfashionable reality could be the legitimate subject of art. Through the use of thick and rapidly applied brushstrokes, they created a dark vision, in which common people were central and everyday events and lifestyles were legitimate materials for artistic expression.

Along with his artistic style, Sloan's politics made him something of a rebel. He moved in early socialist circles, although his independent streak would cause him to break with formal politics and pursue his own artistic style free from the dictated rigidities of socialist realism. In 1912, he joined the radical magazine *The Masses* as art director; the following year, his artwork was included in the critically important New York Armory Show. In addition, he began teaching at the Art Students League, where he taught a large number of America's next generation of artists.

During World War II, Sloan took up outdoor painting and, with his wife, Dolly, took part in the artists' colonies of Gloucester, Massachusetts, and Santa Fe, New Mexico. Sloan was elected to the National Academy in 1929, and he gained further accolades in 1931, when he became president of the Art Students League. During the Great Depression, he supported campaigns to improve artists' economic prospects but avoided association with the Communist Party USA, then exercising influence over certain artists.

After Dolly's death, in 1943, Sloan married a former student, Helen Farr, who had assisted him in assembling his thoughts and theories for his 1939 book, *The Gist of Art*. In recognition of his lifetime's contribution to American culture and his promotion of artistic independence, Sloan was awarded the Gold Medal by the American Academy of Arts and Letters in 1950.

At the time of his death on September 7, 1951, in Hanover, New Hampshire, a retrospective of Sloan's work was being planned at New York's Whitney Museum. His varied body of work remains popular and is still largely identified with urban realism. He is well represented in major national museums and collections, and the continued sale of his art has long been associated with the Kraushaar Gallery in New York.

Theodore W. Eversole

See also: Ashcan School; Communism.

Further Reading

Loughery, John. *John Sloan: Painter and Rebel.* New York: Henry Holt, 1995.

Perlman, Bennard B. *Painters of the Ashcan School: The Immortal Eight.* Mineola, NY: Dover, 1988.

Sloan, John. *The Gist of Art: Principles and Practise Expounded in the Classroom and Studio.* Mineola, NY: Dover, 1977.

Slow Movement

The Slow movement consists of a number of separate and diverse efforts in the 1990s and 2000s by individuals and groups who share the central goal of resisting what they perceive as the accelerating pace of modern life and the destructive effects of commercialization and globalization. In addition to a general slowing down of the pace of life, the movement's goals include preserving distinctive local customs, de-emphasizing conspicuous consumption, strengthening familial and social structures, and preserving the local physical environment.

Proponents of the Slow movement often state their goals in opposition to what they regard as the tendencies of a technology-driven modern lifestyle with an over-emphasis on efficiency and uniformity, and a concomitant tendency to discard what is unique or local in favor of that which can be mass-produced and mass-distributed. Some individuals and groups within the Slow movement see themselves as part of the worldwide anti-globalization movement and have organized around causes such as opposition to the opening of fast-food restaurants in European cities. Others have chosen to focus entirely on personal concerns, such as limiting the intrusion of workplace concerns into the home, or promoting leisure activities such as yoga or gardening, rather than watching television.

The beginnings of the Slow movement have been traced to the efforts of Carlo Petrini, an Italian who in 1986 organized a demonstration against building a McDonald's restaurant near the Piazza di Spagna in Rome. Protestors brandished bowls of penne, a traditional Italian pasta dish, as a symbol of their opposition to the standardized foods to be offered by the American, corporate, fast-food restaurant. Petrini became a spokesperson for the importance of meals as a social ritual and the preservation of local foods and customs.

Another well-known spokesperson is the French farmer José (Joseph) Bové, who became famous for his role in dismantling a McDonald's restaurant in Millau, France, in 1999. Bové is an anti-globalization activist and politician who was a candidate for the French presidency in 2007 and had previously been an anti-military and antinuclear activist. Groups such as Slow Food USA and Local Harvest, who support the principles of Petrini and Bové, came to be known as the Slow Food movement.

From its birth in the Slow Food movement, the Slow movement in the United States has grown rapidly to embrace many facets of modern life. Slow Travel advocates vacations that avoid well-known tourist destinations and long-distance, short-duration travel in favor of leisurely travel within smaller, less heavily traveled areas. The Slow Schools movement believes that American schools have become overly competitive and standardized and should instead adopt a cooperative and child-centered approach to education.

Advocates of the Slow Living movement attempt to adapt the principles of the Slow Food movement to many aspects of daily life, emphasizing the quality and individuality of each person's life rather than the amount of work accomplished or prestige garnered. They advocate a greater emphasis on family, social, and recreational activities; reserving time each day during which one is unavailable through electronic technologies such as e-mail and pagers; and taking up leisurely hobbies such as gardening or knitting.

Part of the movement's growth has been due to the recognition of common concerns among preexisting elements within U.S. counterculture. The Voluntary Simplicity movement, begun in the 1980s, advocates decreased consumption of material goods, increased simplification of daily life, and increased focus on personal growth and awareness. It is represented by organizations such as the Simple Living Network.

The Slow movement's concern with preserving the local environment has its roots in the ecology movement of the 1960s and 1970s. The New Urbanism movement, begun in the 1980s as an alternative to the automobile-based suburban model of community development prevalent in the United States, shares with the Slow movement concerns with the human scale of design and the local quality of life. These include building or preserving traditional neighborhoods that encourage social interaction and provide a safe environment for walking and bicycling.

Sarah Boslaugh

See also: Anti-Globalization Movement.

Further Reading

Honoré, Carl. *In Praise of Slow: How a Worldwide Movement Is Challenging the Cult of Speed.* New York: HarperSanFrancisco, 2004.
Petrini, Carlo. *Slow Food Revolution: A New Culture for Eating and Living.* With Gigi Padovani. Trans. Francesca Santovetti. New York: Rizzoli, 2006.

Smith, Joseph
(1805–1844)

Joseph Smith was the founder of the Church of Jesus Christ of Latter-day Saints (commonly known as the Mormon Church) and the publisher of its defining text, the *Book of Mormon,* in 1830, which he claimed to have translated from golden plates he found buried near Palmyra, New York. As a "seer, a Translator, a Prophet, and Apostle of Jesus Christ and Elder of the Church," Smith later moved with the growing Mormon Church to Ohio, Missouri, and, finally, Illinois, facing persecution by non-Mormons in each locale. At the time of his death in 1844, there were more than 30,000 Mormons worldwide. By the early 2000s, there were more than 10 million, making it one of the most successful new religions of the past several centuries.

Smith was born on December 23, 1805, in Sharon, Vermont. His parents, struggling farmers, moved Joseph and his nine siblings all over the Northeast, landing near Palmyra, New York, by the time Joseph was a teenager. The sectarian infighting inspired by the religious revivals sweeping across upstate New York at the time confronted Joseph and his family with the question of which Christian sect to join. In his personal history, later canonized as part of the Mormon scriptural book the *Pearl of Great Price* (1851), Smith described how, at the age of fourteen, he had a vision in which God and Jesus told him that all of the sects were wrong.

Smith's divinely appointed rejection of Protestant sectarian culture characterized Mormonism's relationship to mainstream American Christianity through the rest of Smith's life. He presented Mormonism as the true Christianity in opposition to the babble of competing sects, a view many disgruntled sectarians found appealing. With divine assistance, Smith retranslated the King James Version of the Hebrew Bible and the New Testament because, he asserted, the version Protestants were reading was corrupt. In addition, Smith offered converts the *Book of Mormon,* a more-than-500-page narrative of the 1,000-year history of a family of Israelites who fled from Jerusalem to America in 600 B.C.E.

Smith asserted that the *Book of Mormon* was an ancient compendium of historical documents written by the kings and prophets of a lost people, the only descendants of whom were Native Americans. The volume's deft combination of Hebrew Bible and New Testament milieus attributed Christian knowledge to pre-Christian characters and enabled Mormon converts to read the newly restored, entire Bible (composed of the Hebrew Bible, the *Book of Mormon,* and the New Testament) as a single, continuous Christian narrative.

Detractors pointed to the similarities between the *Book of Mormon* and nineteenth-century Christian conceptions as evidence of Smith's own authorship, but the early Mormons cited the *Book*'s agreement with mainstream Christianity as proof of its authenticity. Many interpreters, Mormon and non-Mormon alike, also have asserted that the book departs from nineteenth-century Christian understandings. Smith presented his miraculous reception and translation of the *Book* as proof of the Mormon tenet that God continues to communicate divine truth to man. In this way, the very physical presence of the *Book* was said to validate Smith's later revelations.

Smith's revelations during the fourteen years he led the Mormon Church were published in the scrip-tural book *Doctrine and Covenants* (1835), which developed Mormonism into a complex religion that agreed with some aspects of nineteenth-century Protestantism but sharply distinguished itself from the mainstream. The practice of plural marriage, which Smith justified as a divine revelation and surrounded with secrecy, fomented controversy and posed a moral challenge to the communities in which the Mormons first settled. But it was the political dimension of Smith's leadership that would contribute most to anti-Mormon sentiment and the Mormons' expulsions from Ohio (1838), Missouri (1839), and Illinois (1846).

Instead of isolating the Morman Church from local politics, as had other nineteenth-century American separatist religious sects, Smith aggressively pursued political control. He encouraged Mormons to run for local office and instructed them on how to vote so that, as a bloc, they could influence state politics. In Missouri, the perception that the Mormons were too numerous and politically powerful led to persecution and violent conflict, as did hostility to the practice of men having multiple wives, which Mormons claimed was divinely ordained. A full-scale war would have followed if the Mormons had not retreated to Illinois.

In 1838, the Mormons settled the river town of Nauvoo, Illinois, and instituted a town charter that gave Smith unusual control. The Nauvoo Legion, which Smith commanded, was the largest local militia in the state of Illinois. While Smith often attributed divine sanction to U.S. laws and to the Constitution itself, the combination of his near-absolute political control and the doctrine of continuous revelation left the door open to the rejection of government authority. The perception that Nauvoo was a state-sanctioned theocracy with its own army troubled the Mormons' neighbors in Illinois. Smith's earnest run for president of the United States in 1844 further exacerbated negative sentiment toward the Mormons.

Not long after the Mormons arrived in Illinois, former Missouri Governor Lilburn Boggs was assassinated, and Smith was named as a suspected conspirator in the murder. Smith avoided extradition to Missouri, but when anti-Mormon pressure climaxed in 1844, he turned himself in to Illinois authorities. An angry mob stormed the jail where Smith and his brother Hyrum were being held and, with the compliance of the guards, killed the two men on June 27, 1844.

Joshua Goren

See also: Mormonism.

Further Reading

Bushman, Richard. *Joseph Smith and the Beginnings of Mormonism.* Urbana: University of Illinois Press, 1984.

Hill, Marvin S. *Quest for Refuge: The Mormon Flight from American Pluralism.* Salt Lake City: Signature, 1989.

Lesueur, Stephen C. *The 1838 Mormon War in Missouri.* Columbia: University of Missouri Press, 1987.

Smith, Patti (1946–)

Patti Smith is an American poet, rock singer, songwriter, and performance artist widely regarded as a forerunner of the New York punk movement. Variously referred to as the "high priestess of punk" and "punk's poet laureate," she is perhaps best known for a series of 1970s recordings that blurred the line between rock and roll and performance poetry, including *Horses* (1975). Long a leading figure in New York City's downtown art and music scene, Smith first gained prominence for her poetry readings and performances in such East Village venues as the Poetry Project at St. Mark's Church and the club CBGB. Her work, which also includes visual art, theater, rock criticism, and several books of poetry, has had significant international influence, particularly in such genres as alternative rock, spoken word, and performance art. Smith is also known for her activism in support of various environmental, social justice, and human rights causes; some consider her a feminist icon.

Patricia Lee Smith was born in Chicago, Illinois, on December 30, 1946, the oldest of four children. Her father, Grant Smith, was a factory worker, and her mother, Beverly, was a waitress. Raised in Woodbury, New Jersey, near Philadelphia, in high school Smith was drawn to the work of Arthur Rimbaud, Bob Dylan, James Brown, and the Rolling Stones.

Dropping out of Glassboro State College (now Rowan University), she moved to New York City in 1967, where she worked as a clerk at the Strand bookstore, frequented the Hotel Chelsea and Max's Kansas City nightclub, wrote rock criticism for publications such as *Creem,* and lived with the photographer Robert Mapplethorpe, who would go on to design the cover of her first album. During this period, she also lived with the playwright Sam Shepard, with whom she collaborated on the play *Cowboy Mouth* (1971). Shortly thereafter, she published her first volumes of poetry, *Seventh Heaven* (1972) and *Witt* (1973).

In 1971, backed by guitarist and rock critic Lenny Kaye, Smith opened for poet Gerald Malanga at the Poetry Project. The collaboration was a success, and

Smith and Kaye continued playing throughout the city, eventually recruiting piano player Richard Sohl. The trio soon developed a potent mix of rock, jazz, and poetry, epitomized by their early track "Piss Factory" (1974) and fleshed out the following year in her debut album, *Horses,* produced by John Cale, former cellist for the Velvet Underground. Critics praised the album's bold merger of garage rock abandon with Beat and symbolist sensibility, and it has since become a rock classic. Around the same time, Smith and her group began playing with the band Television at CBGB, ushering in the era of New York punk and New Wave.

Smith followed up the success of *Horses* with three more albums—*Radio Ethiopia* (1976), *Easter* (1978), and *Wave* (1979)—and the Patti Smith Group, as it was now called, toured extensively in the United States and Europe. In 1978, the song "Because the Night," a collaboration with singer Bruce Springsteen, became Smith's only Top 20 hit—a rare instance of a punk-identified artist crossing over into the pop charts.

Soon thereafter, Smith married Fred Smith, the former guitarist of the influential 1960s rock band MC5, and she withdrew from the spotlight. She released only one album in the 1980s, focusing instead on raising her two children.

In the mid-1990s, following the deaths of her husband and brother, Smith resumed recording and touring. By 2007, she had released four more albums and several compilations and had toured and collaborated with such artists as Bob Dylan, R.E.M., and Television. In 2005, France named Smith a Commandeur dans l'Ordre des Arts et des Lettres, and in 2007 she was inducted into the Rock and Roll Hall of Fame.

Urayoán Noel

See also: Punk Rock.

Further Reading

McNeil, Legs, and Gillian McCain, eds. *Please Kill Me: The Uncensored Oral History of Punk.* New York: Penguin, 1997.

Rock and Roll Hall of Fame and Museum. "Patti Smith." http://www.rockhall.com/inductee/patti-smith.

Smith, Greg. " 'And All the Sinners, Saints': Patti Smith, Pioneer Musician and Poet." *Midwest Quarterly: A Journal of Contemporary Thought* 41:2 (Winter 2000): 173–90.

Smoking, Tobacco

The use of tobacco has been tainted by controversy ever since the Native Americans who were encountered by Christopher Columbus gifted him and his fellow

European adventurers with the plant. When tobacco use is in general favor, opponents tend to be overlooked as a sometimes vocal minority. Historically, however, tobacco has been unpopular with the majority of American society, and proponents of its use have had to fight to have their views heard or respected. Public opinion on the subject of tobacco use has often been hostage to clashes between big government and big businesses, and their struggles over profits, taxes, and the general health and welfare of the American population.

History and Countercultural Roots

The true nature of smoking was misunderstood by the European explorers who ventured to the Americas and were introduced to tobacco by Native Americans. Smoking tobacco had traditionally been part of a ceremonial ritual, but Europeans regarded it as a vice.

From colonial times, many European Americans considered smoking a filthy habit. Its value as an export to the Old World outweighed its vileness, however, and tobacco plantations flourished in America. Indeed, it became an economic mainstay, escalating the slave trade from Africa even before the infamous cotton plantations that proliferated across the South during the early years of nationhood.

Photographs of former slaves often show both men and women smoking, their pipes hand carved from corncobs. It is not inconceivable that many slaves smoked clandestinely, gaining a small consolation from partaking of the master's fortune and reducing, however infinitesimally, the profit of the plantation—and perhaps, thereby, creating an early counterculture of smoking.

In the early twentieth century, most smokers were men; smoking tobacco continued to be viewed as immoral and a sign of especially bad character among women. The 1920s, however, was a time of sweeping change for American women, who had just won the right to vote (under the Nineteenth Amendment, ratified in 1920) and were determined to show their independence in other ways as well. Tobacco companies encouraged them to smoke, and "flappers," the modern women of the Roaring Twenties, wore skimpy clothes, drank (prohibited) alcohol, and openly smoked cigarettes and cigars.

The encouragement to smoke was perhaps the impetus to engage in other independent behaviors as well. Women drank, wore what they wanted to, owned property, and were no longer content to stand on the pedestal of virtuous wife and mother. This, it is important to note, applied exclusively to well-to-do white women; poorer white women and women of color remained beneath the notice of the elite and powerful (white men). Nevertheless, disenfranchised women enjoyed a freedom in their powerlessness that rich white women tried to emulate. Photographs of poor rural women in the early twentieth century often showed them with corncob pipes between their lips.

Cigarette smoking emerged more visibly among the economically distressed people of the Great Depression as a way to escape their dire circumstances. Another popular escape was going to the movies, in which heroes and heroines indulged heavily in smoking. Theatergoers in those days would light up in sympathy with smoking protagonists. Vicariously through smoking, desperately poor men and women prevailed against evil, lived, loved, and even died with their celluloid counterparts, forgetting the hardships of the day and gaining a feeling of command over events beyond their control.

In films and in the theater of the era, the trappings and mannerisms of smoking—filling, tamping, and lighting a pipe, tamping down a cigarette and lighting it, or clipping the end of a cigar—were emphasized. These activities enabled the smoker to take control of situations, to punctuate words and silences with subtle meaning, and to underscore points and create emphasis where needed.

Mid-Twentieth Century to the Present

During World War II, soldiers fighting in the trenches, in ships, and in the air were issued free cigarettes from the maker of Lucky Strikes. Women working in factories during the war also were encouraged to smoke. Indeed, cigarette ads helped to popularize "Rosie the Riveter," a cultural icon extolling the ability of women to keep the economy going at home while the men were away fighting for freedom. Smoking in this instance was seen as a symbol of competence.

When the men came back from fighting overseas, advertisements encouraged women to return to the home, while continuing to smoke. Smoking was promoted as a social activity, and advertisements reinforced this. The characters portrayed by tough-guy film star Humphrey Bogart, in *Casablanca* (1941) and other popular releases of that decade, lent a particular cachet and nightclub glamour to smoking cigarettes.

After World War II, free thinkers such as the Beat writers offered an alternative to the prevailing conservative lifestyle of the 1950s, and were often seen with cigarettes dangling from their mouths. The nonconformist, rebellious young man was further exemplified by the brief career and tragic death of movie actor James Dean, best known for his role in *Rebel Without a Cause* (1955) and often pictured with cigarette in hand. Tobacco advertising was quick to target smoking as de rigueur for young men who wanted to show off their own nonconformist, rebellious ways. The onslaught of ads focused on teenagers as consumers who would smoke to emulate popular antiheroes.

Smokers in the 1960s rebelled vicariously, emulating fictional superspy James Bond and other larger-than-life characters of the big screen. To smoke was to become a hero. Cigarette ads reflected this, and the branding of the Marlboro Man tapped into the American ideals of rugged individualism and the romance of life on the open range. Camel, a rival company, used the phrase "I'd Walk a Mile for a Camel" to signify determination in the face of obstacles, again appealing to men. With the rise of the feminist movement in the 1960s, Virginia Slims targeted liberated women with slogans such as "You've Come a Long Way, Baby!" All in all, smoking became a more accepted social activity, a means of bonding, through the shared enjoyment of smoking, and projecting a desired image in atmospheres as diverse as the workplace, the restaurant, and the bar.

Meanwhile, hippies preferred smoking marijuana to smoking tobacco, certain that marijuana, not being physically addictive, was less damaging physically than tobacco and its nicotine. Nor was tobacco deemed to fit their search for a natural, simple lifestyle. Many dreamed of a day when tobacco would be illegal and marijuana would be the smoke of respectability.

By the 1970s, the pendulum of smoking in America began to swing back to the status of unacceptable, for both men and women. Congress passed the Federal Cigarette Labeling and Advertising Act in 1965, followed by the requirement to print a warning from the Surgeon General on all cigarette packs, advising purchasers of the health risks associated with smoking.

Tobacco companies persisted in downplaying the health risks of smoking and the addictiveness of nicotine for the next several decades, but by the end of the century, class-action suits won large reparations from the industry. In 1998, forty-six states signed an agreement with America's five largest tobacco corporations, whereby the states would receive $206 billion over twenty-five years to use at their discretion to educate the public about the risks of smoking and to discourage tobacco use.

As of 2008, New York, Boston, and Chicago were among the major U.S. cities that had banned smoking in indoor public places. At issue is the right of the individual to breathe clean air versus an individual's right to smoke in the pursuit of happiness. Belmont, a city near San Francisco, proposed an even stricter ban, effectively forbidding smoking any place other than on the property of a single-family, detached home.

Smokers have banded together in the face of widespread ostracism, as tobacco use has once again become the underdog rather than an accepted social activity. Groups such as FORCES (Fight Ordinances and Restrictions to Control and Eliminate Smoking), Cigar World, the United Smokers Association, American Smokers Alliance, and the National Smokers Alliance view antismoking measures as infringements on individual rights as guaranteed by the Constitution. Moreover, say such groups, the antismoking movement is commercially motivated, benefiting large corporations such as pharmaceutical companies that manufacture nicotine-replacement therapy products, such as patches and gum.

Other groups, including the MATCH (Mobilize Against Tobacco for Children's Health) Coalition, the Foundation for a Smokefree America, Action on Smoking and Health (ASH), Children Opposed to Smoking Tobacco (COST), and numerous others, claim that breathing clean air and living in a smoke-free environment, as well as other benefits from banning smoking, are the rights of every American. As such, they have pushed to make the general public aware of other issues related to smoking, such as secondhand smoke, to which children and young adults are especially susceptible.

Janis Lyman

See also: Beat Generation; Dean, James; Feminism, Second-Wave; Flappers and Flapper Culture; Great Depression.

Further Reading

Gately, Iain. *Tobacco: A Cultural History of How an Exotic Plant Seduced Civilization.* New York: Grove, 2003.

Kluger, Richard. *Ashes to Ashes: America's Hundred-Year Cigarette War, the Public Health, and the Unabashed Triumph of Philip Morris.* New York: Alfred A. Knopf, 1996.

Rabin, Robert L., and Stephen D. Sugarman. *Regulating Tobacco.* New York: Oxford University Press, 2005.

———. *Smoking Law Policy: Law, Politics, and Culture.* New York: Oxford University Press, 1993.

Rafferty, Sean, and Rob Mann, eds. *Smoking and Culture: The Archeology of Tobacco Pipes in Eastern North America.* Knoxville: University of Tennessee Press, 2004.

Smothers Brothers

The folk singing comedy duo of Tom and Dick Smothers, known as the Smothers Brothers, stood up against network television censorship in the 1960s and were important in promoting the disaffected youth culture of the time. The Smothers Brothers first performed professionally as a music-and-comedy team at San Francisco's Purple Onion club in 1958, and made their national television debut on *The Jack Paar Show* in 1961. Tom, the older of the two (born on February 2, 1937), played guitar and portrayed himself as mentally slow; his catchphrase was "Mom always loved you best." Dick (born on November 20, 1938) played stand-up bass and was the straight man in their routines. They usually began with a song duet, which was interrupted by Tom or Dick and led to a comedy dialogue, and then a return to the song.

The brothers had made several successful albums and numerous television appearances before their own show, *The Smothers Brothers Comedy Hour,* debuted on the CBS television network on February 5, 1967. Some politically and culturally sensitive material was aired the first season, but it was mostly diffused by comedic counterpoints. The show proved to be a ratings success, especially with the youth demographic of sixteen-to twenty-four-year-olds, and was renewed for a second season.

Then, the tenor of the show changed dramatically. The second show of the new season, aired on September 1, 1967, featured folk singer and political activist Pete Seeger, who had been blacklisted from television for more than fifteen years for his political beliefs. Seeger was to sing "Waist Deep in the Big Muddy," a thinly disguised criticism of the war in Vietnam. CBS censored the song, but strong opposition from the public and the press prompted the network to backtrack and let Seeger perform the song on the February 16, 1968, show.

Throughout the season the Smothers Brothers continued to include material designed to denounce the war and mock mainstream American culture. The recurring routine "Share a Little Tea with Goldie" featured Leigh French portraying a pothead named Goldie O'Keefe. Ironically, most of these segments got past the censors, because they did not understand the code language being used, such as "tea" for marijuana.

The third season, premiering on September 19, 1968, marked a sharp escalation of the show's political radicalism and the network's attempts to silence its dissenting voice. The spring of that year had seen the assassinations of civil rights leader Martin Luther King, Jr., and Democratic presidential candidate Robert F. Kennedy, and the Chicago police had publicly beaten demonstrators at the Democratic National Convention in August. As a sign that their own attitudes had also changed, Tom and Dick returned to the air with longer hair, moustaches, and unconventional clothing. On the season's opening show, Harry Belafonte's song "Don't Stop the Carnival" was censored, because he had changed the lyrics to refer to events in Chicago. CBS, meanwhile, also had refused to air any convention footage that showed police violence.

Throughout the season, the brothers pushed material that seemed to dare CBS to censor them. Their musical guests also were geared to the views of counterculture youth, with appearances by the Beatles, Jefferson Airplane, the Doors, Donovan, and Peter, Paul and Mary.

On March 9, 1969, CBS refused to show an entire episode in which singer Joan Baez spoke about her husband's imprisonment on draft-evasion charges. Finally, on April 3, 1969, the network canceled the show entirely. The Smothers Brothers sued for breach of contract and eventually won, but the radical programming so loved by the counterculture was gone.

The Smothers Brothers had short-lived series in later years on ABC and NBC, and they even returned to CBS for a twenty-year reunion show. But none of the revivals was particularly successful in terms of viewer ratings, nor important in terms of political or cultural commentary. They continue to perform live in the 2000s.

Jerry Shuttle

See also: Baez, Joan; Chicago Seven; Seeger, Pete; Television.

Further Reading

Bodroghkozy, Aniko. *Groove Tube: Sixties Television and the Youth Rebellion.* Durham, NC: Duke University Press, 2001.

Snoop Dogg (1971–)

Snoop Dogg, formerly known as Snoop Doggy Dogg, is a leading figure in West Coast rap culture as an artist, record producer, and actor. He personifies 1990s gangsta rap, a subgenre of hip-hop associated with urban gangs and characterized by violent and misogynistic lyrics. Terse, laid-back, hip-hop rhyming is a defining feature of this controversial artist, whose

California hip-hop artist and producer Snoop Dogg (Calvin Broadus) is a leading figure in the rise of gangsta rap, the controversial subgenre known for violent, misogynistic, sexually explicit lyrics. *(Greetsia Tent/WireImage/Getty Images)*

lyrics about violence and pimping seem to both reflect and foreshadow events that have marked his everyday life off stage. Many of his song lyrics have played out in his own life, and his appearances in feature films and video games placed him squarely in the mold of the underground, streetwise hustler and smooth-talking player.

Snoop Dogg was born Calvin Broadus in Long Beach, California, on October 20, 1971. He was given the name "Snoopy" by his mother after the dog in the comic strip *Peanuts.* He became a member of the Long Beach Rollin' 20s Crips, one of several street gangs that sprang from the original Crips.

In his post–high school years, he was jailed for several offenses, including drug trafficking. Meanwhile, he was recording his own rap tapes and eventually worked with Dr. Dre, a hip-hop artist formerly of the band N.W.A. (Niggaz With Attitude), performing on Dre's popular album *The Chronic* (1992).

Doggystyle (1993) was Snoop Dogg's first solo album, released on the heels of his arrest in the shooting death of a member of a rival gang. It entered the charts at number one and set a trend in terms of graphic lan-

guage, allusions to violence, and gangsta motifs. A video with fellow artist Tupac Shakur, *2 of Amerikaz Most Wanted* (1996), captured the anguish and bravado of the era, featuring the two artists posturing and enveloped in a chaotic world of hustling and gunplay. A concept video, *Murder Was the Case* (1994), dramatized Snoop Dogg's death. That year, during a tour in England, tabloid newspapers and some members of Parliament requested that the government expel the rapper for his growing notoriety.

Snoop Dogg was a participant in the gangsta rap feud between the East Coast's Bad Boy Records and the West Coast's Death Row Records, which turned violent in the mid-1990s. Snoop's stage persona and alter ego offstage were at the heart of the all-out contest for power, money, and notoriety. The rivalry culminated in the murder of West Coast rap icon Shakur in November 1996 and East Coast counterpart Notorious B.I.G. six months later. Snoop Dogg's second album, *The Doggfather* (1996), did not sell as well as his first, partly because the industry and fan base seemed tired of the East Coast–West Coast feud.

In the aftermath, Snoop Dogg began altering his image, appearing to move away from purely gangsta motifs, broadening his audience and influence. The effort included participation in the 1997 tour of Lollapalooza, the traveling music festival. But Snoop did not give up his radical posture and lifestyle. In fact, he only seemed to further embed his career in controversy. In 2000, he directed the near-pornographic film *Snoop Dogg's Doggystyle,* and, two years later, released the film *Snoop Dogg's Hustlaz: Diary of a Pimp.*

In 2003, he was embroiled in a highly publicized civil rape case, and in 2006, he and members of his entourage were arrested at London's Heathrow airport for unruly behavior and vandalizing a shop. Thereafter, he was variously charged with and arrested for possession of firearms and drugs and with disruptive behavior. In April 2007, he was found guilty of gun and drug charges, and sentenced to five years on probation.

In 2004, meanwhile, Snoop Dogg had left Death Row Records and signed with Geffen Records, releasing *R&G: Rhythm & Gangsta* with Geffen that year. Critics hailed the album—which featured the enormously popular song "Drop It Like Its Hot"—as hardcore and commercially appealing, featuring jazz guitars and mainstream collaborations.

Snoop Dogg hosted a kind of peace summit for the hip-hop community in 2005, calling on West Coast rappers to "end all their beefs" and "protect the West." The event also attracted some rival artists and led Snoop

Dogg to end his rivalries with Death Row founder Suge Knight and rappers Jayo Felony and Kurupt.

Between 1991 and early 2007, Snoop Dogg's albums sold 18.5 million copies in the United States alone. Throughout his career, his public persona has exuded both the cool and the perverse, a paradox he brought to the rap stage and to hip-hop culture in general. In spite of his overtures to other genres and subgenres within hip-hop, his work is still widely known for espousing violence and misogyny.

Curwen Best

See also: Gangsta Rap; Hip-Hop; Rap Music.

Further Reading

Carlson-Berne, Emma. *Snoop Dogg.* Broomall, PA: Mason Crest, 2006.

Light, Alan. *The Vibe History of Hip Hop.* New York: Three Rivers, 1999.

Snoop Dogg. *Tha Doggfather: The Times, Trials, and Hardcore Truths of Snoop Dogg.* With Davin Seay. New York: William Morrow, 1999.

Snyder, Gary (1930–)

Poet Gary Snyder is one of the most prominent figures to emerge from the San Francisco Renaissance of the 1950s. In 1975, he became the first poet of the American West to be awarded the Pulitzer Prize, for his collection *Turtle Island.* By merging his practice of Buddhism with an ecological perspective rooted in Native American understandings and an intimate knowledge of western U.S. topography, Snyder became a modern-day Henry David Thoreau whose writings and personal example helped shape American countercultural thought from the 1950s onward.

Gary Sherman Snyder was born on May 8, 1930, in San Francisco and raised in Lake City, Washington, and Portland, Oregon. As a youth, he became deeply interested in the wilderness of the surrounding mountain ranges and in Native American lifestyles and approaches to the land. He graduated from Reed College in 1951 with a double major in anthropology and literature, and spent the next few years taking graduate classes, writing poetry, and working as a lookout at various national forests.

Soon after taking part in the famous October 1955 Six Gallery reading in San Francisco at which Allen Ginsberg first recited his poem *Howl,* Snyder boarded a freighter for Kyoto, Japan. He lived in Japan for most of the next twelve years, deepening his understanding of Buddhist practice under the tutelage of Zen master Oda Sesso Roshi and continuing to write the poems that would be published in *Riprap* (1959), *Myths and Texts* (1960), *Mountains and Rivers Without End* (1965), *A Range of Poems* (1966), and *The Back Country* (1967; first U.S. edition, 1968).

During these years, Snyder was was able to maintain his relationships with the Beat writers he had helped launch in the mid-1950s. He often gave readings with Ginsberg, and he participated in such antiwar demonstrations as the Gathering of the Tribes in San Francisco's Golden Gate Park in 1967. During the 1970s, 1980s, and 1990s, Snyder became increasingly outspoken about ecological concerns and collected his essays on Buddhism, poetry, and land use in such influential volumes as *Earth House Hold* (1969), *The Real Work* (1980), and *The Practice of the Wild* (1990). He also continued to collect his poetry in several more volumes.

In a 1977 interview published in *East-West Journal,* Snyder commented:

> What it comes down to simply is this: If what the Hindus, the Buddhists, the Shoshone, the Hopi, [and] the Christians are suggesting is true, then all of industrial/technological civilization is really on the wrong track, because its drive and energy are purely mechanical and self-serving—*real* values are someplace else. The real values are within nature, family, mind, and into liberation.

Snyder's life, politics, and poetry consistently have been devoted to elucidating the "real" values that he discerns within the core of every truly holistic religion. The meditative calm, zest for life, and wise humor he brought to this task has made him one of the most admired and iconic figures of the late-twentieth-century American counterculture.

Michael Van Dyke

See also: Beat Generation; Be-Ins; Buddhism; Ginsberg, Allen; San Francisco; Thoreau, Henry David.

Further Reading

Halper, Jon. *Gary Snyder: Dimensions of a Life.* New York: Random House, 1991.

Snyder, Gary. *The Gary Snyder Reader: Prose, Poetry, and Translations, 1952–1998.* Washington, DC: Counterpoint, 1999.

———. Interview. By Peter Barry Chowka. *East–West Journal* (Summer 1977).

Social Gospel

The Social Gospel, arising in the second half of the nineteenth century, refers to the ideology of social service promoted by a broad, transatlantic movement of Protestants. (Roman Catholics maintained their own social Christian tradition at that time.) Advocates of the Social Gospel would proceed to challenge America to apply the ethical imperatives of Judeo-Christianity creatively to their economic, political, and international activities during the Progressive Era (1890–1919) and after. Pastors, theologians, and lay activists united in demanding a "beloved community" characterized by respect for workers, civil rights for minorities, and an end to war.

The Social Gospel crusade emerged after the American Civil War in response to problems arising from unregulated industrialization and urbanization. Episcopalians, Congregationalists, Methodists, and Baptists in the Northeast and Midwest, witnessing firsthand the hardships of new working and immigrant classes, were its earliest proponents. Through sermons and numerous books, Ohio pastor Washington Gladden championed "Applied Christianity" in opposition to unjust employers and corrupt urban politicians. Frances Willard, leader of the Woman's Christian Temperance Union (WCTU), argued that the Christian middle classes should "do everything" to combat class inequalities. For them, the "fatherhood" of God and resulting "brotherhood" of humankind negated all exploitative relationships.

Gladden and Willard were soon joined by pioneering social scientists such as University of Wisconsin professor Richard T. Ely, who founded the American Economic Association (AEA) in 1885 on a Christian socialist foundation. Ely and other Social Gospel pioneers received significant inspiration from British and German social Christians, including journalist William T. Stead. Reprints of Stead's 1893 address, "If Christ Came to Chicago," described and condemned the horrible conditions under which millions in European and U.S. cities were living.

The Social Gospel also was spread at this time by popular fiction. Elizabeth Stuart Phelps Ward, a feminist author and the daughter of a prominent Massachusetts theologian, won instant celebrity for her 1868 novel, *The Gates Ajar.* She called upon middle-class churchgoers to become involved in labor movements, temperance, and other social reforms through novels such as *The Silent Partner* (1871) and *A Singular Life*

(1894). The latter highlighted the New Testament command to follow Christ's example of sacrificial service and suffering. In that regard, Ward's work was superseded by that of Kansas pastor Charles Sheldon, whose collection of sermon-stories, *In His Steps* (1896), asked readers, "What would Jesus do?" Sheldon's work eventually sold 30 million copies and remains the ninth best-selling book of all time.

The Social Gospel was institutionalized between 1900 and 1920, as leading Protestant denominations followed the Catholic Church in formulating public statements on Christian involvement in social justice efforts. The Federal Council of Churches (FCC), representing thirty-three denominations and roughly 20 million Protestants, issued its first "Social Creed of the Churches" in 1908. The Social Creed, borrowed from Northern Methodists, endorsed many of the aims of Progressive reformers, especially recognition of the rights of labor, minimum wage legislation, and federal social insurance programs.

FCC members could be found working to effect social justice in each of the major political parties (including many through the Progressive and Socialist parties), as well as through their own religious organizations, such as the WCTU. "Labor" and "socialist" churches also were established in several major cities to represent the concerns of working-class families before local and state officials. Pacifism became an integral component of the Social Gospel in light of the devastation of World War I, as the FCC campaigned hard for the success of the new League of Nations.

The countercultural aspects of the Social Gospel at this time were most clearly articulated in the writings of New York pastor and seminary professor Walter Rauschenbusch. In his landmark *Christianity and the Social Crisis* (1907), Rauschenbusch demonstrated how passion for social justice had been central to the Old Testament prophets and the Gospels. To Protestant churches long preoccupied with personal salvation from hell, he counseled greater concern for "Christianizing" economic and political life in the here and now. The Kingdom of God was not merely an object of prophecy but something to be made a lived reality in the world.

For Rauschenbusch and other adherents, the Social Gospel demanded the rewriting of old theologies, reconstruction of church practices, and the overcoming of class, racial, and ethnic barriers in religious fellowships. Social Christians, furthermore, prayed for America to replace its competitive and acquisitive society with one founded upon cooperation and social service.

Whether through membership in the Socialist Party (Rauschenbusch), the preaching of socially relevant sermons (Gladden), or following the lead of Jesus (Sheldon), they hoped religion might make significant contributions to a better future throughout the world.

Post–World War I

The Social Gospel continued to grow in the tumultuous decades after World War I. The pacifists of the Fellowship of Reconciliation (FOR) coordinated and defended social Christian thought nationwide during the 1920s. College-student Christian groups, led by the Young Men's Christian Association (YMCA), lent their support to various experiments in interracial cooperation and radical economic reform.

Given the worldwide collapse of capitalism during the 1930s, Protestant and Catholic leaders alike celebrated President Franklin D. Roosevelt's New Deal program as either the embodiment of Judeo-Christian concern for the oppressed, or as a trend toward that concern. German American pastor and New York seminary professor Reinhold Niebuhr, in his controversial *Moral Man and Immoral Society* (1932), criticized utopian social Christian expectations even as he reiterated Rauschenbusch's main point that the Social Gospel was the only gospel there ever was. Niebuhr later led several church leaders in a break from pure pacifism when the need to resist Nazi aggression militarily presented itself. Nevertheless, millions of Americans supported the FCC's position of a "just and durable peace," developed during the war years, which set out postwar goals eventually fulfilled by the creation of the United Nations in 1945.

The Social Gospel movement split into competing camps under cold war pressures. Veteran social Christians opposed Soviet Communism yet refused to bless unprecedented militarization and national security measures. Rather, through the newly formed World Council of Churches (WCC) in 1948, they advocated a "Responsible Society" characterized by decentralized economic power, extensive welfare programs, and superpower coexistence. That Social Gospel tradition was challenged during the 1960s by South American liberation theologians, Black Power theologians, and younger Protestants involved in civil rights and anti–Vietnam War protests. The voices of young and old social Christians alike were quickly drowned out, however, by the flood of religiously and politically conservative Christians during the ascendancy of President Ronald Reagan in the 1980s.

Today, the Social Gospel movement has become so diverse and contradictory that one term can hardly be applied to it. All the same, the host of resilient social Christians bears witness to a desire voiced by their brothers and sisters more than a century ago that their faith has relevance beyond one's belief about the afterlife.

Mark Edwards

See also: Socialism.

Further Reading

Curtis, Susan. *A Consuming Faith: The Social Gospel and Modern American Culture.* Columbia: University of Missouri Press, 2001.

Dorrien, Gary. *Soul in Society: The Making and Renewal of Social Christianity.* Minneapolis, MN: Fortress, 1995.

McCarraher, Eugene. *Christian Critics: Religion and the Impasse in Modern American Social Thought.* Ithaca, NY: Cornell University Press, 2000.

Warren, Heather A. *Theologians of a New World Order: Reinhold Niebuhr and the Christian Realists, 1920–1948.* New York: Oxford University Press, 1997.

Socialism

Advocates of socialism—a political philosophy with a long history in many countries—believe that society should not be divided into social classes and that social wealth should be shared equally by all. Many socialists today trace their roots to the philosophy of the German economist and revolutionary Karl Marx, but they distinguish themselves from communists, who also trace their heritage to Marx, in their belief that social transformation can be achieved through democratic politics.

In many countries, the Socialist Party is a major national political organization that regularly competes for and often wins national political office. This is not the case in the United States. Indeed, why there is no socialist party of national importance in the United States has been a source of fascination and discussion among comparative historians and sociologists for some time. Few academics disagree, however, that, with the exception of a brief period of relative national importance in the early twentieth century, socialism as a political ideology and way of life has been relegated to the sidelines of American history and culture.

Early History

As a counterculture on the margins of American politics and society, socialism—or at least its core principles—has a long history in the United States. It dates back to the colonial era, when those at the bottom of society rose up on several occasions to challenge the class-based societies that were taking shape in both the North and the South. As early as the late seventeenth century, frontier rebels in Virginia led by Nathaniel Bacon rose up against the colonial authorities to protest against high taxes, high prices for imported goods, and the monopolization of farmland by the coastal elites.

Although the immediate causes of Bacon's Rebellion were complex, many historians argue that it is a powerful symbol of the alternative lifestyle that developed among frontier people during the colonial era. This lifestyle emphasized freedom from state oppression and economic cooperation in a way that challenged the highly regulated class societies of the Atlantic Coast.

Although Bacon's Rebellion was ultimately defeated, similar episodes of organized protest from frontier people continued throughout the next three centuries of American history. These protests reflected the stark disconnect between the highly structured class relationships of the coasts and the more level communities of the frontiers. Often influenced by Native American ways of life, many frontier communities lived by a social ethic that reflected the cooperation and principles of equitable distribution championed by socialists.

Still, it was not until the early nineteenth century that socialism as a distinct social and political doctrine arrived in the United States from Europe. In the 1820s, the British social reformer Robert Owen—who was influenced by a brand of socialism that would later be called "utopian socialism"—arrived in the United States to set up a community that would live by a new set of moral standards radically different from the greed and competition that marked the newly emerging industrial capitalism of the day.

Having already set up a model communitarian factory town in Scotland, Owen purchased land in Indiana with the goal of establishing an ideal society there. He envisioned the settlement, called New Harmony, as a respite from the world where residents would work cooperatively and abide by a code of social ethics that excluded money and most commodities. Owen's experiment did not last long, but his example stood out for other utopian- and religious-inspired socialists, many of whom established ideal communities of their own on a smaller scale in subsequent decades.

In many ways, the utopian socialists of the nineteenth century were an extension of the frontier communities for the industrial age. They also prefigured the dropout culture that would develop in the twentieth century, whose proponents chose to isolate themselves from the outside world in what they viewed as their citadels of moral virtue.

Turn-of-the-Century Socialism

In the later half of the nineteenth century, with industrial capitalism spreading across the country at a rapid pace, socialism entered the American lexicon for the first time in a specifically political and programmatic fashion. The development of an industrial working class gave the Marxist version of socialism, first articulated in Europe, a social base in America.

Initially, the new form of socialism would be marked by many specifically American features, in particular the heavily immigrant composition of the new working class. For much of the nineteenth century, socialism mostly was expressed in the form of small clubs of immigrant workers, many from Germany, who had become radicalized during the frequent revolutionary outbreaks in Europe during this period.

The new type of socialism, which emphasized class struggle from below in order to change the state and economy over self-imposed isolation, gained an increasingly loud echo among American workers as the nineteenth century progressed and the industrial working class congealed. In 1876, the first specifically socialist political party in the United States was founded in Newark, New Jersey. Originally called the Workingmen's Party of America (WPA), it was renamed the Socialist Labor Party (SLP) the following year. The SLP reflected the heavily immigrant character of American socialism at the time, as it was largely a federation of small groups of radical German workers.

In 1890, the SLP came under the leadership of Daniel De Leon, a lawyer who left the profession to devote himself full-time to socialist politics. De Leon's name still is heard frequently in socialist circles as the founder of "De Leonism." This is an interpretation of Marxism that rejects war and accommodation with capitalist political parties, but argues that the path to a socialist society lies in winning a majority in Congress and amending the U.S. Constitution to recognize the importance of industrial unions in organizing society.

The SLP remained a relatively small party in the last decades of the nineteenth century, but it did run candidates for various political offices, including president (with little success). In addition, its members worked inside trade unions in the effort to spread socialist ideas among the working class.

A new American socialist party founded toward the end of the nineteenth century, the Social Democratic Party (SDP), was modeled on the many European socialist parties that were rapidly growing and becoming more active in the political life of their nations. The SDP, however, was a small party compared to its European cousins. In 1901, elements from the SLP and the SPD united to form the Socialist Party of America (SPA).

Socialist Party of America

With industrial capitalism spreading rapidly and the American working class growing increasingly radicalized, the SPA quickly developed a significant level of importance in national political life during the first two decades of the twentieth century. One of the original members of the SDP, Eugene V. Debs, emerged as the party's main spokesman and strategist. Coming from a labor union background, Debs was a skillful orator who knew how to stoke a crowd. The SPA ran Debs as its candidate for president a total of four times during this period (1904–1912, 1920). Although he never came close to winning office, he received hundreds of thousands of votes on every occasion.

During this period, the SPA, and Debs in particular, presided over a growing countercultural movement that challenged the prevailing social norms of the time. Industrial capitalism, with its emphasis on material acquisition and personal gain, was at its height. Socialists preached a new social creed that emphasized the collective solidarity of humanity led by the working class.

Socialists, firmly rooted in the traditions of the labor movement, published numerous periodicals and pamphlets dedicated to the new gospel, including the *Appeal to Reason*, which reached a circulation of up to 600,000 copies. Debs and other leaders traveled the country, giving impassioned speeches to motivate support for the party's political candidates, but also to inspire a sense of optimism among the exploited workers that the world could be a better place.

In areas where there was a high concentration of workers, Socialists often set up schools and meeting halls to serve as the infrastructure of the new culture. They also led retreats in order to give life to the idea of social solidarity. On occasion, it was difficult to determine the SPA's exact role in this, as much of the activity emanated from the local, grassroots level, with only guidance and support from the national political organization.

SPA candidates did win a number of local offices, including the mayoralty of such cities as Bridgeport, Connecticut, and Milwaukee, Wisconsin. Several SPA members even won election to Congress. All in all, however, the SPA did not play a central role in the national political culture, its influence generally limited to ethnic enclaves in working-class areas.

During this period, American Socialists developed a somewhat tense relationship with the labor movement. Most shunned the established American Federation of Labor (AFL), and both De Leon and Debs participated in the founding of the competing Industrial Workers of the World (IWW) in 1905. The IWW was set up as a different type of union, one that would regroup workers regardless of race, origin, sector, or nation. However, the emergence of the IWW sparked an intense debate and even a theoretical crisis in the workers' movement, about the relative importance of politics and political parties versus industrial action and the unions. Eventually, most socialist leaders would break with the IWW's philosophy of direct industrial action and argue for the continued importance of electoral politics for the attainment of socialism.

The outbreak of World War I was a watershed moment in the history of socialism. While most European socialist parties abandoned the principle of working-class internationalism and supported their own nation's war effort, most American Socialist leaders opposed the nation's involvement in the war. Debs was one of the most outspoken critics of the war and the capitalist system that had produced it.

In 1919, Debs was convicted of violating the 1917 Espionage Act for his speeches against the war, and he was sentenced to ten years in federal prison. This did not stop him from running for president from prison, and he received nearly 1 million votes in the 1920 election. Since the World War I era, antimilitarism has been a key component of American socialism; many socialists took a central role in the movement against the Vietnam War some fifty years later.

Nevertheless, the crisis that gripped the world socialist movement as a result of World War I also would affect the SPA. Radicals, inspired by the Russian Revolution of 1917, the new Communist regime, and the ideology of its new leader, Vladimir Lenin, split off from the Socialist Party and founded several American communist parties in the early 1920s. From that point on, communists and socialists would exist in a tenuous relationship on the extreme left of American politics.

The events of the war years, the leftist split, and Debs's death in 1926 took their toll on the American socialist movement. While the SPA and the SLP continued to exist, they would never duplicate the electoral influence achieved in previous decades. As the century progressed, American socialism slipped further and further into the counterculture, even as the ideology became more and more mainstream in Europe.

Socialists would play a part in both the 1948 presidential bid of Henry Wallace on the Progressive Party ticket and in the antiwar movement of the 1960s. For the most part, however, the torch of the left was passed to the communists, whose strict theories on party discipline helped ensure some level of organizational continuity in the face of the factional disputes and splits that would rock the left during the twentieth century.

Mid-Twentieth-Century Activism

In terms of social activism, the 1960s saw socialists play a key part in the opposition to the Vietnam War, as they had to World War I. However, socialist ideas tended to become subsumed to more strictly pacifist ones and there was no specifically socialist opposition to the war. This did not prevent individual socialists from playing key roles in various organizations such as the War Resisters League (WRL), but there was no socialist party of any size or influence opposing the war.

The 1960s and 1970s did see a burgeoning of socialist intellectual life in the United States, primarily in the universities, with many leftist intellectuals attempting to merge socialist theory with other theories in vogue at the time. These ideas would come to play key roles in the emerging dropout counterculture of the late 1960s and early 1970s.

Such theories as "socialist feminism" (which argues that women's oppression cannot be solved by mere legal and political reform, and that true women's liberation requires the creation of a society based not on capitalist competition but on socialist solidarity) and "socialist humanism" (which argues that capitalist society is responsible for dehumanizing civilization and that only a socialist society would allow people to assume their full creative human potential) were popular among many on the left at the time.

Even today, adherents of these attempts to merge socialist ideas with other radical philosophies can be found on many university campuses. In the 2000s, one of the most popular of these hybrid philosophies merges socialist ideas with radical environmental theory in so-called eco-socialism. This version blames capitalism for the degradation of the biosphere and argues that only a socialist society, by controlling greed and profit, can protect and rehabilitate the environment.

Despite the theoretical advances of the 1960s and 1970s, the widening of the counterculture represented another watershed for socialism in the United States. While many innovative ideas were incorporated in the new dropout culture, members of the old line socialist parties tended to regard the young hippies with suspicion and kept their distance. For the most part, socialist culture in the United States split into three groups: members of the old line socialist parties, with tenuous links to the labor movement; socialist academics and intellectuals, largely confined to university campuses; and the dropout counterculture, which was not specifically socialist in all of its aspects, but instead hearkened back in some ways more to anarchist ideas of personal fulfillment than socialist ones of collective solidarity.

By the 1980s, the SPA changed its name to the Social Democrats USA and began to function more as a discussion circle than a political party. The SLP continues to function in the twenty-first century, with De Leonism still a point of reference for those who seek a less authoritarian alternative to Marxism.

Legacy

In twenty-first-century America, there is not much of a socialist counterculture. The SLP continues to exist and some communist groups call themselves socialist in order to avoid identification with the discredited Soviet Union. However, most socialist theorizing has been subsumed under the more recent academic trend of "radical democracy," which claims to continue socialism's emphasis on the equitable distribution of power and resources without reference to the industrial working class.

While there are still individuals who practice a form of dropout culture influenced by socialist ideas, there is no singular socialist counterculture outside of the SLP and other small groups. Moreover, the absence of any real organizational discipline in these groups problematizes the identification of those individuals who adhere to socialist culture and others who "visit" temporarily as they sample different radical ideas.

Perhaps the most important remainder of socialist counterculture in the United States is the annual Socialist Scholars Conference (SSC) held at the Cooper Union school in New York City. Renamed in 2005 the Global Left Forum (GLF) following a split in the organizing committee, the GLF gathers a very eclectic group of academics, activists, and organizations, only some of whose commitments can properly be called socialist in the legacy of Robert Owens, Daniel De Leon, or Eugene V. Debs.

Michael F. Gretz

See also: Communism; Debs, Eugene V.; Industrial Workers of the World; Owen, Robert Dale; Social Gospel; Temperance Movement; Utopianism.

Further Reading

Bell, Daniel. *Marxian Socialism in the United States.* Ithaca, NY: Cornell University Press, 1996.

Buhle, Paul. *Marxism in the United States: Remapping the History of the American Left.* New York: Verso, 1991.

Le Blanc, Paul. *A Short History of the U.S. Working Class: From Colonial Times to the Twenty-First Century.* Amherst, NY: Humanity, 1999.

Salvatore, Nick. *Eugene V. Debs: Citizen and Socialist.* Urbana: University of Illinois Press, 1982.

Seretan, Glenn L. *Daniel De Leon: The Odyssey of an American Marxist.* Cambridge, MA: Harvard University Press, 1979.

South Park

Trey Parker and Matt Stone's animated cable television show, *South Park,* began as a video Christmas card for Fox Television executive Brian Graden in 1995, and two years later premiered as a half-hour animated sitcom on the cable television channel Comedy Central. The premier tells the story of the alien abduction of third grader Eric Cartman and the subsequent implantation of a massive satellite beacon into his anus. It illustrated why all of network television passed on the show and why *South Park* would soon become one of cable television's most controversial and objectionable shows. Focused on young Eric and fellow third graders Kyle, Stan, and Kenny, living in the seemingly wholesome rural nowheresville of South Park, Colorado, the program became best known for its utter vulgarity and defiant disinterest in respecting social taboos.

South Park uses its crudely drawn animation to transgress social boundaries that its live-action brethren are forced to observe. Over its multiple-year run, it has broached all manner of scatological and risqué topics, including preteen breast implants, bestiality, child abuse in a scouting group, exploitation of the physically and mentally handicapped, child drug use, and anti-Semitism. More than just a collection of bathroom humor and shock value, though, most episodes mount a wry and intelligent satiric attack on multiple aspects of American life, particularly small-town conservative values and cultural delusions.

The show's deep-seated suspicion of authority and of American-Dream optimism shows itself most visibly in the town's parents, all of whom are too ineffective, ignorant, self-righteous, or morally bankrupt to serve as adequate role models. Eric's mother is a prostitute and porn actress, and the teacher, the mayor, the principal, the school counselor, and even Jesus Christ (starring in a local public-access-channel talk show) prove similarly ineffective. The only adult figure respected by the children is Chef, his "wisdom" taking the form of graphically explicit songs about his sexual escapades and fantasies.

Media savvy to the core, the show reserves much of its satire for contemporary media culture. Taking aim at televisual rules of political correctness, for instance, the lone black child in town is named simply Token, while the sitcom's impervious disregard for chronology is mocked by the weekly murder and uncommented-upon resurrections of Kenny. Other episodes examine moral panics surrounding violence in the media, irrational parental fears of the media, and media-inspired cultlike activity. Meanwhile, the show has savagely attacked numerous celebrities, turning Sally Struthers into a grotesquely overweight glutton, for example, and Mel Gibson into a psychotically disturbed narcissist, obsessed with torture.

Despite widespread condemnation by church groups, parents, and cultural conservatives, and even occasional censorship from Comedy Central, the show's fame grew over time, spawning a feature film that grossed $53 million domestically, and multiple T-shirts, toys, CDs, and other tie-in merchandise. Moreover, although primarily for adults, the program attracts a large following among children.

Arguably one of the first television shows truly to exploit the leeway allowed by cable television, *South Park* remains one of that medium's bolder experiments, as well as a loud and well-respected, if simultaneously filthy and crude, voice of dissension against accepted cultural and televisual norms of propriety, conduct, and thought.

Jonathan Gray

See also: Television.

Further Reading

Arp, Robert, ed. *South Park and Philosophy: You Know, I Learned Something Today.* Malden, MA: Blackwell, 2006.

Johnson-Woods, Toni. *Blame Canada!: South Park and Contemporary Culture.* New York: Routledge, 2006.

Spiritualism

Spiritualism, the belief that it is possible to communicate with the spirits of the dead, has long been an element of folk religious practice. In the 1850s, however, spiritualism became a national obsession and part of the mainstream popular culture of the United States. Mediums, those who purport to communicate with the dead, toured the country performing for large and small audiences. Many others were exposed to spiritualism through articles and editorials in newspapers such as *The New York Times* and popular magazines such as *Harper's* and *The Atlantic Monthly.* Spiritualist themes also found their way into the work of such notable authors as Nathaniel Hawthorne, Ralph Waldo Emerson, and Henry James. During the 1850s, thousands of Americans were active believers in spiritualism; as many as 1 million explored the movement in some way. The belief in a contactable spirit realm and the perfectibility of humanity became part of a reformist countercultural movement during the nineteenth century.

Although ghost stories had long been a part of American culture, the emergence of the modern spiritualist movement is commonly dated to events at Hydesville, New York, on March 28, 1848. Young sisters Kate and Margaret Fox reported hearing loud raps on the walls and floorboards of their bedroom in the family farmhouse near town. Assuming that the noises were being made by spirits attempting to communicate, the girls asked questions out loud. The spirits, according to their account, rapped their answers in a code. Reports of these "manifestations" spread quickly, and the Fox sisters became famous. It was not long before they were appearing before large audiences in New York City and staying at the posh Barnum Hotel.

The Fox girls were only the first of a number of well-known mediums during that time. Other men and women soon claimed to be able to contact the world beyond the grave. Some performed elaborate physical manifestations in front of large audiences, including automatic writing, the production of mysterious noises, the movement of furniture by unseen forces, the evocation of ghostly figures, and claims of clairvoyance or clairaudience (the ability to see and hear things happening at great distances).

Other spiritualists moved beyond demonstrations of spiritual contact, exploring the philosophical and social ramifications of spiritual manifestations. Among the most notable of these was Andrew Jackson Davis, who became famous in New York as the "Poughkeep-

The modern spiritualist movement is traced to events at the Fox farmhouse in Hydesville, New York, in March 1848. Two young girls, Kate and Margaret Fox, reputedly made contact with the spirit of a dead man who communicated by rapping on walls. *(Library of Congress)*

sie Seer." Even before the events in Hydesville, Davis had used mesmerism, an early form of hypnosis, to explore to world of the spirits. In 1847, he published *The Principles of Nature, Her Divine Revelation, and a Voice to Mankind,* a collection of communications he delivered while in a mesmerized state.

Seizing on the popularity generated by the performances of mediums such as the Foxes, Davis began to lay out his spiritual system, which he called Harmonialism. This philosophy, and the view of the spirit world he described, borrowed heavily from religious thinkers such as Emanuel Swedenborg, the Swedish visionary who had also described his encounters with spiritual beings. Davis saw his contacts with the spiritual realm as a way to better society, using the wisdom of the higher spirit realms to perfect and harmonize religion, medicine, and all of American society. Like many other spiritualists, Davis believed that the spirits condemned traditional systems of medicine, economics, and religion as barbaric and endorsed alternative medical systems such as homeopathy and social reforms such as the abolition of slavery.

The popularity of spiritualism derived partly from its flexibility. It was a religious movement with no dogma that adherents were forced to accept, no priests or authority figures, and no formal places of worship. Séances, intimate gatherings where people met to contact the spirit world, could take place at anyone's home, and people could either visit mediums or try to contact the spirit world on their own. Some Americans regarded the entire affair as a parlor game; others viewed it as a scientific form of religion and saw the séance room as a laboratory in which the existence of an afterlife could be proven. Still others made spiritual communication part of existing Christian practice, and a few organized communal spiritualist societies, for example in Mountain Cove, Virginia. Because of the considerable authority that spiritualism gave female mediums, thought to be better spirit channelers than men because of their more "passive" nature, spiritualism also became associated with the movement for women's rights.

For all its popularity, the spiritualist movement also caused a backlash. As adherents claimed spiritual authority for controversial social reforms, and as the physical demonstrations became more and more dramatic, skeptics and critics began to expose mediums as frauds. The claim that séances provided indisputable evidence of spirit communication invited scrutiny by skeptics. Several magazine and newspaper exposés during the 1850s showed how many of the most popular manifestations were performed. In later decades, even the Fox sisters would admit that they had faked the rappings that had started the movement—though Margaret Fox would later retract the confession.

The popularity of spiritualism declined after the American Civil War. Although it never again reached the pinnacle of popularity it had reached in the 1850s, the movement's notoriety rose and fell throughout the rest of the nineteenth century. Even when interest waned, small groups of spiritualists continued to meet.

The investigation of the spirit world continued in other forms, including the scientific exploration of paranormal phenomena by Harvard professor William James (brother of novelist Henry James) and the founding of the American Society for Psychical Research in 1885. Spiritualism remained an issue of debate and speculation, bringing together ardent devotees such as author Arthur Conan Doyle and equally dedicated debunkers such as the illusionist Harry Houdini.

In 1893, spiritualists, who had long debated the value of organizing themselves into a more coherent church, founded the National Spiritualist Association of Churches (NSAC). A number of churches still exist in this loose framework, and the NASC continues to offer minister education, provide organizational assistance, and publish a national magazine for children, *The Lyceum Spotlight.* Beyond formal spiritualist churches, mediums continue to contact the spirits in communities dedicated to spiritualism such as Lily Dale, New York, and Cassadaga, Florida.

Stephen D. Andrews

See also: Davis, Andrew Jackson; Emerson, Ralph Waldo; Fox, Kate, Leah Fox, and Margaret Fox; Hawthorne, Nathaniel.

Further Reading

Braude, Ann. *Radical Spirits: Spiritualism and Women's Rights in Nineteenth-Century America.* Boston: Beacon, 1989.

Caroll, Bret E. *Spiritualism in Antebellum America.* Bloomington: Indiana University Press, 1997.

Cox, Robert S. *Body and Soul: A Sympathetic History of American Spiritualism.* Charlottesville: University of Virginia Press, 2003.

Moore, R. Laurence. *In Search of White Crows: Spiritualism, Parapsychology, and American Culture.* New York: Oxford University Press, 1977.

Spock, Benjamin (1903–1998)

Benjamin McLane Spock was an American pediatrician and the author of the best-selling book *The Common Sense Book of Baby and Child Care* (1946), a groundbreaking text said to mold the character of the entire baby boom generation in America. The first American practitioner to have completed training in both pediatrics and psychiatry, Spock applied theories of psychology to understanding the needs of children within the family and the dynamics between parents and children. The wildly popular book—which was retitled *Dr. Spock's Baby and Child Care* and which has sold more than 50 million copies throughout the world—calls for greater leniency and permissiveness on the part of parents and advocates a commonsense, pragmatic approach to child-rearing, in which parents are encouraged to trust themselves and treat their children as equals.

Spock was born on May 2, 1903, in New Haven, Connecticut, and studied medicine as an undergraduate at Yale University. In 1924, he and seven fellow Yale rowers competed at the Olympic Games in Paris and won the gold medal for the United States. Spock went on to attend medical school at New York's Columbia University, graduating at the top of his class in 1929. He had residency training in both pediatrics and psychiatry, and served as a psychiatrist for the U.S. Navy during World War II.

Although many young parents of the 1950s and 1960s regarded him as the ultimate authority on proper parenting, Spock's philosophy came under fire when his political views and public activities began running counter to the prevailing mood of the day. Spock was one of the founders of the Committee for a Sane Nuclear Policy, created in 1957 to protest the

Dwight D. Eisenhower administration's nuclear weapons policy and to campaign for nuclear disarmament. He was also an active anti–Vietnam War protestor, writing letters to the White House and frequently attending antiwar demonstrations. In 1967, he was arrested in New York City for crossing a police line in an act of civil disobedience and protest against a military recruitment center.

Spock's conspicuous role in the antiwar movement eventually brought him into conflict with the federal government. In 1968, he and four other men were prosecuted by Attorney General Ramsey Clark for conspiracy to promote resistance to the draft and to aid young men who wished to avoid conscription. Spock had been one of the signers of "A Call to Resist Illegitimate Authority," an antiwar petition carrying the names of more than 20,000 individuals and printed in newspapers across the country the previous year. Signing the declaration was prosecuted as a criminal misdemeanor and used against him at trial. Despite the lack of hard evidence to support the charge of conspiracy, Spock and three of the others were convicted. He was sentenced to two years in prison, but he appealed, and a federal court overturned the conviction in 1969.

Spock remained active in the antiwar movement, even as top military, political, and social leaders blamed the outpouring of social and political discontent among American youth on the lenient, permissive style of parenting that Spock had advocated in *Baby and Child Care.* Conservative commentators such as Vice President Spiro T. Agnew and Christian author Norman Vincent Peale blamed Spock for the disobedient and rebellious attitudes of "Spock-marked" American teenagers and young adults in the late 1960s—and, by extension, for the excesses of counterculture. Spock claimed to have had only a mild influence on the changes in American attitudes toward child-rearing, but his opponents declared that the generation of children who had been brought up under his theories had learned that it was acceptable to defy authority and ignore traditional social values.

In 1972, Spock ran in the U.S. presidential election on the People's Party ticket, capturing barely 78,000 votes. In the years that followed, he continued to speak out against nuclear weapons and criticize American foreign policy, and he called for greater women's rights and the legalization of homosexuality, abortion, and marijuana. Spock died at his home in La Jolla, California, on March 15, 1998.

Shannon Granville

See also: Baby Boomers; Pacifism; Vietnam War Protests.

Further Reading

Maier, Thomas. *Dr. Spock: An American Life.* New York: Basic Books, 2003.

Spock, Benjamin. *The Common Sense Book of Baby and Child Care.* 1946. New York: Pocket Books, 1957.

Spock, Benjamin, and Mary Morgan. *Spock on Spock: A Memoir of Growing Up with the Century.* New York: Pantheon, 1989.

Sports

If sports are a microcosm of society, as is often observed, they will include reflections of the counterculture as well as the mainstream. Indeed, while spectator sports in America have come to represent big business as well as being a source of popular entertainment, issues of politics and social justice have made their way onto the ball field and gym floor for decades.

In the realm of professional sports, individual athletes frequently spark national debates when they use their celebrity to confront social conventions regarding issues such as race, gender, sexuality, or even public health. Examples of twentieth-century American sports figures who, intentionally or unintentionally, served as spokespersons or symbols of political and social causes are legion—from the black boxing champions Jack Johnson and Muhammad Ali to baseball's Jackie Robinson, who broke the game's so-called color line in 1947, to women's tennis player Billie Jean King and basketball stars Dennis Rodman and Magic Johnson.

Race and Politics

Among the most outspoken sports figures to openly address the issues of race, war, and religion in America is the gregarious boxer Cassius Clay, now Muhammad Ali. He was inspired by the daring Jack Johnson, the first African American heavyweight champion (1908), who brushed aside personal fears of white supremacist threats, brazenly flaunted his wealth and celebrity status, and openly dated white women (which landed him in a federal penitentiary in 1920).

In the 1960s and 1970s, Clay gained notoriety for joining the Nation of Islam (Black Muslims) and changing his name to Muhammad Ali, then refusing to serve in the U.S. Army after being drafted for the Vietnam War. Banned from professional boxing as a result, he continued to speak out against the war, the draft, and racial discrimination in America. He would refuse to fight in the war, he declared in 1966, because "no Vietcong ever called me nigger." And, he added, "I am not going 10,000 miles to help murder, kill, and burn other people to simply help continue the domination of white slavemasters over dark people the world over."

Following Ali's example, two U.S. track-and-field stars at the 1968 Olympic Games in Mexico City, Tommie Smith and John Carlos, used the medal-awarding ceremony (they had won the gold and bronze medals, respectively, for the 200-meter dash) to spotlight the cause of Black Power. As the U.S. national anthem began playing, the two athletes bowed their heads and raised their black-gloved fists defiantly into the air.

Whereas Ali, Smith, and Carlos had boldly declared their political views and racial pride, earlier athletes inclined to challenge the forces of racism in America relied on their mere participation on the field of play to make their point. The Penobscot Indian Louis Sockalexis and Colombian native Louis Castro defied daily harassment and abuse from players, fans, and the media to succeed as the first Native American (in 1897) and Latino (in 1902) players in professional baseball. Likewise, when Jackie Robinson joined the Brooklyn Dodgers in 1947, he ushered in the official era of desegregation in professional baseball. "America's pastime" had actively barred African Americans to that time.

Gender, Homosexuality, and HIV/AIDS

Athletes and activists also have used sports as a vehicle for exposing and challenging gender inequities. In 1973, tennis professional Billie Jean King championed the burgeoning women's movement and scored a public victory in the so-called Battle of the Sexes, in which she took on and defeated former men's champion Bobby Riggs before a national television audience. In 1972, federal legislation known as Title IX (authored by Japanese American Congresswoman Patsy Mink of Hawaii) mandated a balance between the educational resources spent on men and women (including for athletics) and set off a national debate about the roles of men and women in society, the scope of gender inequities, and the impact of sexism. One major result has been an exponential increase in the number and variety of women's sports in American public schools and universities, as well as the growth of professional wom-

en's sports, as with the Women's National Basketball Association (formed in 1996).

Male-dominated sports traditionally have demanded hyper-masculinity from participants, but some male athletes have openly challenged the boundaries of "acceptable manhood." In the 1960s, for example, quarterback Joe Namath of football's New York Jets was a prototypically brash, hard-partying playboy who drew heavy criticism from some quarters—and ridicule behind locker-room doors—for his willingness to appear in a television commercial wearing a pair of women's pantyhose.

Still, if Namath's leg display bothered many viewers, countless more were repulsed in the 1980s and 1990s by the public rebellion against mainstream values of masculinity on the part of all-star basketball player Dennis Rodman. As a player for the San Antonio Spurs and the Chicago Bulls of the National Basketball Association, Rodman sported bold, elaborately-dyed hair, elaborate tattoos, and prominent body piercings. In 1997, when he promoted his first autobiography, *As Bad as I Wanna Be*, Rodman signed books while in full makeup, wearing a white wedding dress and bride's veil.

Billie Jean King, after her triumph in the Battle of the Sexes, struck a second blow to mainstream values in 1981, when she publicly confirmed that she was a lesbian, bringing attention to antigay sentiment in the sports world and society at large. Like King, tennis star Martina Navratilova, who came out as bisexual in 1981, expressed the view that athletes "have a responsibility" to be activists and vocal spokespersons for important social and cultural issues. Houston Comets basketball all-star and former Olympic gold medalist Sheryl Swoopes came out as a lesbian in 2005, her status as a celebrity athlete making her a model of defying homophobia.

By contrast, no major American male sports figure has announced his homosexuality during his playing days (a number came out of the closet after retiring). Like athletes of earlier generations who faced overt racial and gender discrimination, gay male athletes remain reluctant to directly confront the aggressive homophobia in male sports.

Postretirement announcements of homosexuality by male athletes began in the early 1970s, when former professional football player David Kopay threw aside a potential coaching career by becoming one of the first male athletes to come out. Since then, public admissions have been made by former football players Roy Simmons (1992), who talked about feeling "tortured" during his playing years, and Esera Tuaolo (in 2006), who was hired by the National Football League to promote sensitivity training in the sport. However, as recently as 2007, former basketball player John Amaechi's autobiography about his experiences as a gay player met with harsh criticism by other players, including one who stated publicly that he would not want a gay teammate and that he "hate[s] gays."

Basketball legend Magic Johnson announced in 1991 that he had contracted HIV (human immunodeficiency virus), and became one of the most prominent athletes to address the health issues of the virus. Johnson used his immense celebrity to help dispel lingering beliefs that HIV was a "gay disease" that only affected homosexuals and to bring much-needed attention to the increasing rates of contraction among African Americans. Continuing a productive life as an athlete, coach, businessman, and public speaker, Johnson also has fostered greater awareness of the viability of living with HIV.

Natchee Blu Barnd

See also: Ali, Muhammad.

Further Reading

Kopay, David, and Perry Dean Young. *The David Kopay Story: The Coming-out Story that Made Football History.* Los Angeles: Advocate, 2001.

Powers-Beck, Jeffrey. *The American Indian Integration of Baseball.* Lincoln: University of Nebraska Press, 2004.

Robinson, Jackie, and Alfred Duckett. *I Never Had It Made: An Autobiography of Jackie Robinson.* New York: HarperPerennial, 2003.

Ward, Geoffrey. *Unforgivable Blackness: The Rise and Fall of Jack Johnson.* New York: Vintage Books, 2006.

Zirin, Dave. *What's My Name, Fool? Sports and Resistance in the United States.* New York: Haymarket, 2005.

Squatters and Squatting

Squatting is the act of occupying property, either public or private, without authorization or payment. A squatter, therefore, is a person who occupies an uninhabited area, abandoned building, or other vacant space that he or she does not own, rent, or otherwise have permission to inhabit. Squatting is typically an urban phenomenon, closely linked to poverty, the lack of adequate, affordable housing, and other social and economic ills.

Squatters may occupy property individually or in communities; squatter settlements are often referred to as shantytowns or tent cities. Such properties typically are located at the margins of mainstream communities and, due to their unsanctioned and often illegal nature, are lacking in sanitation and utilities such as electricity, heat, and running water. Other critical social services are typically unavailable, such as schools and health care. Squatters generally fall into lower socioeconomic groups. Those who have jobs at all are typically employed in wage labor or informal employment, typically the social sectors deemed most at risk for homelessness.

Although squatting in America dates to the nineteenth-century practice of settling land on the Western frontier—which, under the Preemption Act of 1841, squatters became entitled to buy—the modern urban practice is a relatively recent phenomenon. As an ideological construct and counterculture, squatting in North America dates to the mid-1960s and the writings of Charles Abrams on housing reform and civil rights. The term generally carries the implication and stigma of violating social and cultural norms; that is, operating outside expected and acceptable behavior. As such, squatting also can be a political statement, in response to the cultural, social, political, and economic causes of homelessness and marginalization in urban areas. Abrams, for example, who referred to squatting as the necessary "conquest" of urban properties for shelter, advocated support and legal protection rather than hostility and resistance.

The new perspective was evident in the case of Tompkins Square Park in New York City during the late 1980s, when residents of the East Village neighborhood, displaced by gentrification, actively relocated to the park in a refusal to relinquish their neighborhood. Hundreds of squatters, with support from other groups and community members, resisted local officials' attempts to remove them. This gave rise to the Tompkins Square Park riots in August 1988, which ended with dozens of injuries and the forcible displacement of hundreds of squatters.

This practice of "open squatting" is far less common than its covert counterpart. The most common practice is the "back window (or back door) squat," in which the squatters attempt to conceal their residence. The "front door squat," in which squatters are open about their occupation of a property, as in Tompkins Square Park and other settlements, is increasingly less common, as cities enact increasingly rigid laws against vagrancy. In a front door squat, squatters often consult with neighbors prior to taking up residence, creating an alternative approach to constructing a community.

The modern squatters' rights movement in America—in which unauthorized occupants of land or buildings, generally in cities, claim rightful possession—entails a political and social statement against gentrification, treatment of the homeless, and economic injustice. *(Carolyn Schaefer/Getty Images)*

A number of advocacy and awareness-raising initiatives have emerged from the increasing prevalence of squatting in urban areas. One example is Homes Not Jails, an activist group with chapters in Boston, San Francisco, and Washington, D.C., that has actively occupied abandoned properties with the intent of transforming them into housing for the homeless. At least two independent documentaries, *The Homeless Home Movie* (1996) and *Dark Days* (2000), have provided awareness-raising narratives about the lives of homeless individuals squatting in tunnels, parking lots, partially occupied buildings, and abandoned properties.

Cynthia J. Miller

See also: Mole People.

Further Reading

Abrams, Charles. *Man's Struggle for Shelter in an Urbanizing World.* Cambridge, MA: MIT Press, 1964.

Mele, Christopher. *Selling the Lower East Side.* Minneapolis: Minnesota University Press, 2000.

Stein, Gertrude (1874–1946)

Although she fashioned herself a literary genius and published a number of books and plays in her own right, Gertrude Stein generally is remembered as a patron of the arts and literature whose legendary home in Paris was a center for expatriate artists and writers between the two world wars. A celebrated personality, Stein befriended, encouraged, helped, and influenced—through her patronage and her works—many literary and artistic figures.

Stein was born on February 3, 1874, in Allegheny, Pennsylvania (now part of Pittsburgh), the last of five children of a German Jewish family. Hers was a somewhat unsettled childhood. She was raised in Vienna and Paris. Her parents died in 1888 and 1891, and Stein was left with a modest income.

At the age of nineteen, she entered Radcliffe College in Cambridge, Massachusetts, and majored in psychology, studying under William James. After graduating in 1897, she went to Johns Hopkins Medical School in Baltimore, Maryland. Relinquishing her studies, she moved to London in 1902 and to Paris the following year.

In Paris, Stein became a permanent expatriate, establishing a literary salon in the city's bohemian Left Bank. Except for time spent in the French village of Culoz during World War II, Paris was her home for the rest of her life.

With America providing the subject matter and France the freedom to write, she eventually made herself into one of the most original figures of twentieth-century literature. Early on, Stein also became interested in the fledgling modern art movement. She and her brother, art critic Leo Stein, were among the first to appreciate and collect the works of such modernist painters as Pablo Picasso, Paul Cézanne, and Henri Matisse.

In addition to her involvement in the arts, Stein entertained writers such as Ernest Hemingway and F. Scott Fitzgerald, and authored experimental works that fit Mark Twain's definition of a classic, "a work that everyone admires and nobody reads." Her early works include the novel *The Making of Americans,* written between 1903 and 1911 and published in 1925. Her first published book, *Three Lives* (1909), describes the lives of three working-class women.

Her best-known work is *The Autobiography of Alice B. Toklas* (1933). Although the name in the title refers to Stein's secretary and lover, the book is by and about Stein herself. Alice B. Toklas's own autobiography, *What Is Remembered* (1963), was published seventeen years after Stein's death. Stein also wrote the librettos for two operas by Virgil Thomson, *Four Saints in Three Acts* (1934) and *The Mother of Us All* (1947). *Brewsie and Willie* (1946), her last book, is based on her memory of visits by American servicemen during the war.

Inspired by the stream-of-consciousness psychology of William James and the geometry of Cézanne and the cubist painters in Paris, Stein developed a "continuous present" style characterized by constant repetition and variation of simple phrases. Her work had great influence on other expatriate American writers such as Hemingway, Fitzgerald, and Sherwood Anderson. Stein died on July 27, 1946, in Paris from stomach cancer.

Yuwu Song

See also: Fitzgerald, F. Scott; Hemingway, Ernest; Lost Generation.

Further Reading

Greenfeld, Howard. *Gertrude Stein: A Biography.* New York: Crown, 1973.

Hobhouse, Janet. *Everybody Who Was Anybody: A Biography of Gertrude Stein.* New York: Putnam, 1975.

Simon, Linda. *Gertrude Stein Remembered.* Lincoln: University of Nebraska Press, 1994.

Steinem, Gloria

See Ms.

Straight Edge Culture

The straight edge movement, popularly known by the acronym sXe, emerged during the 1980s out of the East Coast hard-core punk scene. Straight edge rejected the hedonistic substance abuse associated with punk rock, proclaiming self-improvement and discipline as its central tenets. Most straight edgers share a rejection of alcohol, tobacco, drugs, and sexual promiscuity. While committed to individual self-discipline, members of the straight edge culture rely heavily on communities of mutual support to maintain their alternative lifestyle, utilizing peer pressure and positive cultural reinforcement within the straight edge hard-core scene. Over the years, straight edge has evolved in distinct ways, while retaining a common self-help morality based on sobriety and responsibility. Although it started as a secular movement, straight edge has incorporated elements of Eastern philosophy and has influenced Christian youth culture.

Straight edge culture originated in the Washington, D.C., hard-core music scene around 1980 in reaction to a policy of local club owners to mark the hands of minors with Xs to prevent them from purchasing alcohol. The X mark was co-opted as a rallying symbol for punks, both minors and legal adults, who rejected the substance abuse associated with punk. Ian MacKaye, lead singer of the band Minor Threat, popularized straight edge themes and symbols in his poignant lyrics and album art. The straight edge movement expanded north to Boston through bands such as DYS and to the West Coast through Uniform Choice and 7 Seconds.

In 1985, a new breeding ground for straight edge coalesced around the band Youth of Today and the New York hard-core scene. The membership of Youth of Today was in constant flux, but the band maintained consistent positive messages of straight edge and vegetarianism through the lyrics of Ray Cappo. Revelation Records, Cappo's label, became the main promoter of straight edge hard-core music, supporting influential bands such as Gorilla Biscuits, Bold, Chain of Strength, Shelter, Side by Side, and Judge.

During the 1990s, straight edge and hard-core music went through a profound transition. Diverging from its punk origins, hard-core music began borrowing stylistic elements from heavy metal, adding a more aggressive edge to its sound. Victory Records and the band Earth Crisis began promoting a militant style of hard core, blending together traditional straight edge values with activist themes of veganism, antiracism, and environmentalism. Some critics claimed that Earth Crisis had abandoned the "positive hard-core" vision of straight edge, inadvertently encouraging a subculture based on militancy and intolerance, which was called "hardline."

The most notorious hardline scene emerged in Salt Lake City during the 1990s, as Utah law enforcement officials claimed that straight edge "gangs" were physically assaulting smokers and drinkers in public. Another militant trend emerged out of Dayton, Ohio, with the formation of the Courage Crew, a group that was intended by its founders to be a defensive organization but instead became known for the violent behavior of some of its members. Most straight edgers express hostility or outright condemnation of these intolerant and aggressively masculine minorities in the movement.

Despite its controversial elements, straight edge continues to thrive as a distinct youth culture with adherents throughout the world in the 2000s. The movement's unique blend of youth rebellion, Eastern spiritualism, secular humanism, social consciousness, and positive lifestyles is likely to continue making it an attractive counterculture.

Joel A. Lewis

See also: Punk Rock.

Further Reading

Haenfler, Ross. *Straight Edge: Clean-Living Youth, Hardcore Punk, and Social Change.* New Brunswick, NJ: Rutgers University Press, 2006.

Wood, Robert. *Straightedge Youth: Complexity and Contradictions of a Subculture.* Syracuse, NY: Syracuse University Press, 2006.

Streaking

Streaking is the act of running nude—alone or en masse—from one point to another in public view. The term gained its modern cultural connotation in the early 1970s, as the streaking fad became a popular symbol of the sexual revolution. Unlike nudists (who typically shy away from public attention) or flashers (who often gain sexual gratification from randomly shocking members of the public), streakers of the 1970s often practiced the act in support of the era's loosening of repressed standards of sexuality.

The trend gained popularity in the early 1970s on many newly coed college campuses. In celebration of coed life, students of both genders often gathered to streak through campus libraries and dormitories, across school grounds, and through active class sessions. Beyond mere celebration, many early-1970s college students saw streaking as a fun and inventive way to meet members of the opposite sex.

The trend started on campuses in and around Los Angeles, including the University of California, Los Angeles (UCLA), and quickly spread to other regions of the country. Students at schools such as Florida State University and the University of Missouri engaged in mass streaks, with participants numbering in the hundreds or thousands. In 1974, University of Notre Dame students went so far as to establish a "streaking Olympic games" race.

The streaking fad gained a wealth of media coverage in the 1970s, appearing, for example, in a late-1973 issue of *Time* magazine. The trend became so popular that Maine enacted a law against streaking. In other areas, streakers often were arrested and simply charged with indecent exposure.

Popular novelty-music artist Ray Stevens recorded a song about the fad, "The Streak," which reached number one on American pop music charts in 1974. Around the same time, Robert Opel streaked across the stage of the 1974 Academy Awards ceremony flashing a peace sign to the audience. Opel's act occurred so quickly that broadcasters were unable to censor the national telecast. Streaking also became a hallmark of early 1970s sporting events, and devoted sports fans still occasionally streak at contemporary games.

Although it is practiced far less frequently in the 2000s, the tradition of streaking remains an occasional student activity at schools such as Princeton University, Lewis and Clark College, Dartmouth College, and others. At the University of Michigan, for example, students gather every April to streak across campus in the "Naked Mile." Contemporary groups of streaker students from rival universities often organize into teams and compete to see who can stage the largest and most public instances of streaking.

Although some schools (beginning with Lewis and Clark in 1999) have started to dissuade students from participating by ordering campus police to arrest streakers, many students simply view this as encouragement to run faster. At Lewis and Clark, students have taken to "streaking" in underwear to avoid the threat of campus police.

In the 2000s, the streaking fad has been memorialized as a quirky, lighthearted moment in the annals of 1970s popular culture, as in such television series as *That '70s Show* (1998–2006) and such films as *Old School* (2003). Despite its occasional, sudden reappearance, the trend is fondly recalled as one of the benign expressions of the American sexual revolution.

Wesley French

See also: Sexual Revolution.

Further Reading

Garner, Gerald C. *The Streaking Book.* New York: Bantam, 1974.
Pleasant, George. *The Joy of Streaking: A Guide to America's Favorite Pastime.* New York: Ballantine, 1974.

Students for a Democratic Society

Students for a Democratic Society (SDS) was one of the largest and most influential American New Left organizations of the 1960s. The group took a prominent activist role, especially on college and university campuses, in protesting the U.S. role in the Vietnam War and the Selective Service draft of young men to fight in it. With more than 100,000 members, the SDS grew from an organization that sought to reform American society into a radical one that called for political and social revolution. From its first national convention in 1962, to its factional split in 1969, the SDS set the context and political agenda for the radical counterculture of that decade.

The origins of the organization date to 1960 and the annual congress of the National Student Association, at which University of Michigan student Alan Haber began mobilizing student activists. Haber had been a member of the youth auxiliary of the liberal, prolabor organization League for Industrial Democracy (LID). From its inception, the SDS took an important step distancing itself from older, anticommunist leftist groups, particularly the LID, which was damaged by 1950s government investigations. Within a

year or two, Haber had recruited a core membership from various colleges and universities.

At the first national SDS convention, its members, both undergraduates and graduate students, produced the Port Huron Statement, a manifesto named after the Michigan town in which the convention was held. A core document of the American New Left, it began: "We are the people of this generation, bred in at least modest comfort, housed now in universities, looking uncomfortably to the world we inherit." The text went on to call for "participatory democracy," that is, the full voice of all members of society in decisions that affect them.

The SDS advocated nonviolent civil disobedience and was heavily critical of both U.S. foreign policy and the government's failure to address civil rights reform and poverty. In addition to Haber, early leaders included Tom Hayden (the drafter of the Port Huron Statement and SDS president, 1962–1963), Todd Gitlin, Rennie Davis, Bob Ross, Sharon Jeffrey, and Paul Potter.

In the early 1960s, the SDS drew inspiration from the civil rights movement and began to focus on urban community projects. Among these was the Economic Research and Action Project (ERAP), which sought to provide disenfranchised blacks and whites with jobs, education, and housing. By 1965, as President Lyndon B. Johnson escalated the war in Vietnam, SDS chapters across the country led localized demonstrations in protest, culminating in the first March on Washington that April, in which 25,000 people participated. Later that year, SDS members helped organize more than 100,000 protestors in the International Days of Protest (October 15–16) and a second March on Washington (November 27). By this time, many of the founding members were no longer students and a new generation of campus leadership had taken over, including Carl Oglesby, an Akron, Ohio, student.

The year 1966 marked a turning point, with a new influx of members from the Midwest and large state institutions, bringing with them new priorities for the organization. The new members also were more connected to the emerging counterculture of rock music and drugs, with a particular emphasis on personal freedom and challenging societal norms.

The SDS began to develop a broader social critique, linking multiple struggles. In this radical new perspective, all of American society and culture was regarded as flawed, corrupt, and immoral. In the face of the ever-escalating war in Southeast Asia, the membership in 1968 and 1969 began to see itself as part of a worldwide revolutionary struggle.

Mark Rudd, strike organizer and head of the local chapter of Students for a Democratic Society, addresses campus radicals during the spring 1968 uprising at Columbia University. *(Hulton Archive/Getty Images)*

SDS rhetoric became more politically radical and explicitly Marxist. Its activities became more militant, moving from protest rallies to the occupation or burning of buildings. The occupation of administrative offices at Columbia University in the spring of 1968 epitomized the shift. SDS students led by Mark Rudd seized the buildings in response to the university's sponsorship of war-related research and a perceived disrespect for the nearby impoverished black area of Harlem.

At the SDS national conference in 1969, the group split into two factions over the direction of the counterculture and the tactics of the movement. The Progressive Labor (PL) faction stressed traditional organizing of the working class and the building of a mass party. The other faction eventually emerged as the revolutionary guerrilla group Weatherman, later renamed the Weather Underground; its most famous members included Rudd, Bill Ayers, and Bernardine Dohrn. PL was antagonistic to the counterculture. The Weathermen wanted to create a sense of a common cause between themselves and working-class youth. During the 1960s, they engaged in a campaign of radical, violent protest, including rioting and the bombings of government buildings.

While the factional split effectively ended the SDS as a national organization, individual chapters continued working for several years. Even in its splintered state, the SDS formed the context against which the counterculture of the 1960s framed itself. Drawing on old members for guidance and a blessing, high school and college students in 2006 who opposed the U.S. military occupation of Iraq began efforts to reconstitute the SDS, declaring their intentions in a public statement on Martin Luther King, Jr., Day.

Andrew Hannon

See also: Chicago Seven; New Left; Vietnam War Protests; Weatherman; *Document:* Port Huron Statement (1962).

Further Reading

Hayden, Tom. *Reunion: A Memoir.* New York: Random House, 1988.

McMillian, John, and Paul Buhle, eds. *The New Left Revisited.* Philadelphia: Temple University Press, 2003.

Miller, Jim. *Democracy Is in the Streets: From Port Huron to the Siege of Chicago.* Cambridge, MA: Harvard University Press, 1994.

Sale, Kirkpatrick. *SDS.* New York: Vintage Books, 1974.

Varon, Jeremy. *Bringing the War Home: The Weather Underground, the Red Army Faction, and Revolutionary Violence in the Sixties and Seventies.* Berkeley: University of California Press, 2004.

Studio 54

The epicenter of New York City nightlife during the late 1970s and early 1980s, Studio 54 was the most famous disco in the United States, with a worldwide reputation as a notorious den of decadence and celebrity excess. The nightclub was housed at 254 West 54th Street in a building that was originally built as the Gallo Opera House in 1927. The structure served as a theater under various names until the 1950s, when the Columbia Broadcasting System (CBS) purchased it and turned it into a radio and television studio. The company used the location for about twenty years before Steve Rubell and Ian Schrager purchased the building and made plans to open a nightclub. Rubell and Schrager were entrepreneurs who owned a chain of steak houses and nightspots in Boston and New York.

After an expensive renovation of the building, Studio 54 opened on April 26, 1977. It was an immediate success from the standpoint of being perceived as the place to be seen in New York City. The nightclub drew celebrities and New Yorkers who were screened by doormen, and sometimes by Rubell himself, outside the entrance.

Every night, crowds gathered in front of the club with many people literally begging to be allowed in the door. Inside, there was loud disco music, flashing lights, an expansive dance floor, semi-clad bartenders, and an ample supply of alcohol and drugs. A large, decorative "man in the moon" (complete with a cocaine spoon) hung over the dance floor, and men and women routinely had sex in the balcony. The outgoing Rubell, in particular, was in his element as he personally played host to pop-culture icons Liza Minnelli, Cher, Andy Warhol, Bianca Jagger, and other celebrities who frequented the club.

Mismanagement and Rubell's uninhibited personality finally brought down Studio 54 as the 1970s drew to a close. After he suggested in an interview that the business had not paid its share of taxes to the Internal Revenue Service, dozens of federal agents raided the nightclub in December 1979. Among other things, they found garbage bags full of unreported currency stashed in the ceiling and elsewhere. The Studio, as it had become known, shut down in February 1980, and Rubell and Schrager eventually served time in prison for tax evasion.

The club reopened in September 1981 under new ownership, but it failed to generate the unbridled excitement—or hedonism—that had made it famous originally. The disco craze itself began to fade, and Studio 54 closed its doors permanently in 1986. Since then, the building has hosted a variety of tenants. As for the owners, Rubell died in 1989 of complications from AIDS, and Schrager later found success in the hotel business. In 1998, Mike Myers starred as Rubell the motion picture *54,* depicting Studio 54 at its peak of popularity.

Ben Wynne

See also: Disco.

Further Reading

Haden-Guest, Anthony. *The Last Party: Studio 54, Disco, and the Culture of the Night.* New York: William Morrow, 1997.
Miller, Bobby. *Fabulous!: A Photographic Diary of Studio 54.* New York: St. Martin's, 1998.

Suffragists

The term *suffragist* generally refers to those, mostly women, who agitated on behalf of women's voting rights in the nineteenth and early twentieth centuries. Sometimes referred to as "suffragettes" (especially for more radical activists in England), the suffragists constituted the first wave of American feminists.

Suffrage itself was initially part of a larger complex of issues aimed at reversing women's social, political, and economic liabilities. By the late nineteenth century, suffrage overshadowed other women's issues, in part because women had been granted some legal rights at midcentury and their educational opportunities had expanded, and in part because proponents held that suffrage would make the other pro-woman reforms possible.

Roots

Historians generally cite the 1848 Seneca Falls Convention in upstate New York, under the guidance of reformers Elizabeth Cady Stanton and Lucretia Mott, as the beginning of the campaign for woman suffrage. At the time, however, it was the most controversial issue on the woman's rights agenda.

In fact, woman suffrage was the only issue cited in the Seneca Falls Convention's Declaration of Sentiments that did not receive the unanimous approval of the assembly. Modeled after the Declaration of Independence, the new document declared "that all men and women were created equal." Nevertheless, in the days following the convention, many attendees revoked their pledge for suffrage; the thought of women voting was simply too radical for the time.

A series of national conventions were held during the decade after Seneca Falls, with one occurring each year except from 1857 until 1860, near the start of the

American Civil War. Many of the most prominent woman's rights advocates devoted themselves to the Union cause, in the belief that they would be awarded their full citizenship rights after the war. When the fighting was over, however, the radical Republicans who had been promoting the rights of former slaves claimed it was "the Negro's Hour" and that women would have to wait for the franchise.

This mindset split the emerging movement for woman suffrage: The American Woman Suffrage Association (AWSA), led by suffragists Lucy Stone, her husband, Henry Blackwell, and Julia Ward Howe, was formed in 1869 to champion the rights of former slaves and women. Feeling betrayed by the politicians, Stanton and reformer Susan B. Anthony created the National Woman Suffrage Association (NWSA), also in 1869, to promote woman's rights exclusively and to work for a woman suffrage amendment to the Constitution. The two organizations maintained separate memberships until 1890, when they merged as the National American Woman Suffrage Association (NAWSA).

The two organizations also differed on other cultural and political matters. For example, the AWSA allowed men to assume leadership roles in the organization and focused on achieving suffrage on a state-by-state basis. In the NWSA, by contrast, males were not permitted to hold top offices in the organization, and its focus was on a federal approach to woman suffrage. Both organizations published a journal, peti-

tioned the government, and held meetings; some women, such as Anthony, attempted to vote and were promptly arrested. Their appeals to lawmakers fell on deaf ears.

Beginning in the 1890s, suffrage began the long, slow process of state passage in the West, where the harsh conditions were felt equally by women and men. In the more culturally settled, urban East, the doctrine of separate spheres segregated the sexes and relegated women to the home. Sporadic victories and defeats at the state level continued for the next thirty years.

Twentieth-Century Victories

The new century claimed the lives of many of the founding mothers, who did not live long enough to realize their dreams of woman suffrage. With renewed energy and leadership, however, the movement was revived.

In the 1910s, Anna Howard Shaw and Carrie Chapman Catt expanded the membership base of NAWSA and began organizing at the state level. Alice Paul and Lucy Burns, two young, well-educated activists who had participated in the suffrage movement in England, in 1913 assumed control of the NAWSA's Congressional Union (CU), a committee created to press the U.S. Congress to pass a woman suffrage amendment.

The CU stole president-elect Woodrow Wilson's thunder by staging a parade in Washington, D.C., on the eve of his March 1913 inauguration. But the parade turned ugly: Men in the streets harassed and harangued the marchers, while the police stood idly by.

The methods of the CU, influenced by the often violent actions of the English movement, were too radical for the growing NAWSA. As the latter organization expanded, it brought in more conservative women, including many from the South and the larger Woman's Christian Temperance Union (WCTU). This change in composition came at the cost of including black women, who were forced into segregated clubs and organizations.

Before long, the CU broke with the mother organization over differences of opinion regarding membership and tactics. NAWSA President Catt urged respectability and continued organizing. CU suffragists eschewed mere public speaking for the publicity of the spectacle, including parades, pageants, and picketing. Aiming for a national amendment, the CU believed that only militant tactics could awaken the complacency of the NAWSA and uncommitted American women. A true counterculture was born.

Suffragists in New Jersey lobby for the women's vote in 1915. The measure was defeated there, though the movement had achieved victories in other states. Final success came with ratification of the Nineteenth Amendment in 1920, granting the right nationwide. *(FPG/Hulton Archive/ Getty Images)*

When the United States entered World War I in 1917, many NAWSA women engaged in war work. Paul's CU crowd refused to abandon its commitment to suffrage, however, holding bonfires and pickets at the White House and silently displaying placards that described their plight: "Resistance to Tyranny Is Obedience to God"; "Mr. Wilson, How Long Must Women Wait for Liberty?"; and even an inflammatory reference to "Kaiser Wilson." The public was enraged. The protestors were harassed by passersby and their patriotism impugned. Eventually, the women were jailed for their activism, only to be replaced by fresh CU legions.

Local law enforcement officials enhanced the punishment for the protestors' public campaigning by ordering them to fulfill their sentences at the Occoquan Workhouse in Virginia. There, the women endured harsh conditions. Claiming they were political prisoners, Paul demanded like treatment and refused to eat her rancid daily rations, resulting in violent force-feedings. When news of the women's treatment became public, President Wilson intervened and the suffragists were released, having served hard time on the trumped-up charge of obstructing traffic. The brutality both radicalized the protestors and roused the public's sympathy.

After many years and many failed attempts, the Nineteenth Amendment to the U.S. Constitution—according to which the right to vote "shall not be denied by the United States or by any State on account of sex"—passed both the Senate and the House in 1919, and was sent to the states for ratification. Catt's organizing paid off, as advocates were in place to petition the statehouses. In 1920, with two-thirds of state legislatures voting for approval, the Nineteenth Amendment was officially ratified, and women joined the American electorate with the same rights and responsibilities as men.

The 1920 elections showed little difference in voting patterns between men and women, but the cultural contributions of the suffragist movement are undeniable. Women's activism inspired both Indian spiritual leader Mohandas Gandhi and civil rights leader Martin Luther King, Jr., and served as a living testament to the power of nonviolent civil disobedience. In addition, the suffrage movement exploded the myth that women were shrinking violets in need of protection, and it empowered many women to take charge of their own lives.

Once suffrage was achieved, many women were assimilated into mainstream political organizations. Others began to agitate for the Equal Rights Amendment, a hallmark of the second wave of American feminism. By the 1980s, a distinct gender gap in voting patterns began to emerge, promising the political potential of women as a voting bloc.

Janet Novak

See also: Feminism, First-Wave.

Further Reading

Campbell, Karlyn Kohrs, ed. *Man Cannot Speak For Her.* New York: Praeger, 1989.

Flexner, Eleanor. *Century of Struggle: The Woman's Rights Movement in the United States.* 1959. Enlarged ed. with Ellen Fitzgerald. Cambridge, MA: Belknap Press, 1996.

Ford, Linda G. *Iron-Jawed Angels.* Lanham, MD: University Press of America, 1991.

Lumsden, Linda J. *Rampant Women.* Knoxville: University of Tennessee Press, 1997.

Surfing and Surfer Culture

Surfing, the sport of standing on a flat board while gliding along the crest of a breaking wave, made its way from Polynesia to the Hawaiian Islands by approximately 400 C.E. At first a religious ritual of native nobles, surfing would thrive in Hawai'i, unseen by Western eyes, until the English explorer Captain James Cook arrived nearly 1,400 years later.

Early explorers and visitors to the islands were impressed by the skill and daring of the surfers, but native customs were repressed with the arrival of Christian missionaries and European and American settlers. Surfing was all but eliminated by the early nineteenth century, kept alive only by a few locals as a means of passive resistance to the moral values espoused by the Westerners. The sport languished until the turn of the century, when American businessmen began to replace missionaries as the controlling force on the Hawaiian Islands. Entrepreneurs called on the few Hawaiians who still possessed the ability to surf to revitalize the sport as a means of catalyzing the islands' tourism appeal.

One of these locals was young Duke Kahanamoku, the grandson of a native chief and an Olympic swimming champion. While hardly the only Hawaiian to take part in the revival of the pastime, Kahanamoku was surfing's most visible figure and effective popularizer. A superb surfer from childhood, he went on to establish the first surfing club in Waikiki and gave exhibitions around the world. His demonstrations in Southern California laid the foundations of the sport in the mainland United States.

Surfing took firm root in America in the late 1950s and early 1960s, as teenagers took to the waves at beach towns such as Santa Monica, Huntington Beach, and Malibu, California, and developed leisure-centered lifestyles that embraced surfing as both sport and catharsis. Shaggy-haired, suntanned surfers in Hawaiian shirts descended on the beach in Volkswagen vans. They developed their own jargon as well, including such terms of the art as *peak* and *offshores* and *mellow.*

Films such as *Gidget* (1959) and *Beach Party* (1963) glorified the carefreeness of surfer life, the camaraderie between surfers and beach girls, and the nights of bonfires and beach parties. Even documentaries on surfing became box-office successes. For example, Bruce Brown's masterpiece, *The Endless Summer* (1966), about two surfers going around the globe in search of the "perfect wave," was embraced by audiences across the United States.

Musical artists such as Dick Dale, the Chantays, the Ventures, and the Surfaris pioneered "surf rock," a genre noted for its rapidly oscillating guitar instrumentals and loud, fast beat. The surfing influence on pop music reached its zenith in the 1960s with the Beach Boys, who performed such family-friendly songs as "Surfin' U.S.A.," "Surfin' Safari," and "Surfer Girl."

The popular success of surfing, however, did not sit well among the core members of the subculture. With the establishment of a competitive professional circuit in 1976 came money, sponsorships, and throngs of aspiring surfers threatening to compromise the sport's ideals of a serene and private experience. "Soul surfers" began to distinguish themselves by shunning technological advances in the sport—primarily by refusing to wear a wet suit to stay warm or a leash to keep the board nearby after a wipeout.

Likewise, dramatic increases in the sheer numbers of surfers led to the social phenomenon of "localism." Outsiders to an area's usual crowd generally were unwelcome by the core fraternity and sometimes were driven off by violence in the water, or returning to broken car windows and slashed tires.

Into the 2000s, surfing remains a popular source of entertainment for much of America. Yet the sport's underlying cliquishness remains strong among hard core participants.

Chris Rutherford

See also: Slang.

Further Reading

Finney, Ben, and James D. Houston. *Surfing: A History of the Ancient Hawaiian Sport.* Rohnert Park, CA: Pomegranate Artbooks, 1996

Warshaw, Matt. *Surfriders: In Search of the Perfect Wave.* Del Mar, CA: Tehabi, 1997.

Surrealists

A term coined by French writer Guillaume Apollinaire in 1917, *surrealism* refers to an avant-garde cultural movement in the early twentieth century most prominently manifested in the realms of literary and visual arts. The movement's arrival in the United States, through exhibitions such as the Newer Super Realism show (1931) in Hartford, Connecticut, coincided with the personal presence of European surrealists such as André Masson and Marcel Duchamp, who in their opposition to Fascism and Nazism sought exile in the United States and joined forces with the American art community. Highly publicized and celebrated artists such as Salvador Dali, as well as art and museum patrons such as Peggy Guggenheim (who was married to émigré German surrealist Max Ernst), helped to popularize surrealism, which became a vital force in American art during the Great Depression and the cold war.

From its arrival on U.S. shores, many critical voices attacked surrealism as a foreign and even mad decadence in danger of corrupting American ideals and national art. With Freudian psychoanalysis becoming increasingly fashionable, however, others, in search of creative freedom and techniques for gaining access to the unconscious mind, enthusiastically turned to surrealism's openness to formal experimentation and personal interpretation.

While typically associated with the arts, surrealism has never been restricted to them. Indeed, from the start, proponents have aimed at transcending the arts. Like the earlier Dada movement, from which it partly derived, surrealism took part in a modernist avant-garde aesthetics of forcefully disrupting traditional rationalist ways of thinking, seeing, and feeling. But whereas the Dadaists, shell-shocked by the disillusionment and mass destruction of World War I, produced anti-art defying reason, the surrealists believed strongly in the positive, mind-changing force of artistic expression and assaulted public sensibility.

Drawing heavily on Freudian theory, as well as Marxist thinking and the Marquis de Sade's and Arthur Rimbaud's radically sexualized poetics, French poet André Breton, the major spokesperson of the surrealist movement and later a New York refugee himself, declared in "The Surrealist Manifesto" (1924) that surrealism is "psychic automatism in its pure state, by which one proposes to express—verbally, by means of the written word, or in any other manner—the actual functioning of thought. Dictated by the thought, in the absence of any control exercised by reason, exempt from any aesthetic or moral concern."

For Breton and the group of artists surrounding him (among them Louis Aragon, Philippe Soupault, Paul Éluard, Robert Desnos, Pierre Naville, Roger Vitrac, Gala Éluard, Man Ray, Hans Arp, Antonin Artaud, Raymond Queneau, Joan Miró, Jacques Prevert, and Yves Tanguy), the term *surreality* aimed at a revolutionary unification of conscious and unconscious realms of experience into one new and marvelous "absolute reality." A more precise translation of French *surréalisme*, therefore, would thus correspond more closely with the English *supernatural* or *super real*. As much as surrealism stems from artistic roots, Breton made it clear that surrealist activity can be performed in any circumstance of life—making practitioners thoroughgoing nonconformists.

From the movement's center in Paris, surrealism by the end of the 1920s began to spread around the globe, with North and South America getting their fair share of major surrealist artists. While surrealism as a historical avant-garde movement formally came to an end with Breton's death in 1966, its influence lasted long after.

One proof of this was the founding in the same year of the Chicago Surrealist Group by Franklin and Penelope Rosemont as an official offshoot of the Paris group. Initially coming from left-wing or anarchist backgrounds, the Chicago Group, which includes photographer Clarence John Laughlin, artist Gerome Kamrowski, and poet Philip Lamantia, became an agitating force in the arts sector and beyond. The Chicago Group has continually identified itself with the cause of black liberation, including its early participation in the civil rights movement of the 1960s, the struggle against white supremacists in Chicago's Marquette Park neighborhood and elsewhere in the 1970s, and efforts to free African American political prisoner Mumia Abu-Jamal in the early 2000s.

It also has been associated with the Chicago-based labor organization Industrial Workers of the World (IWW), especially with the publication of the periodical *Rebel Worker* in the 1960s; it was allied with the antiwar activist group Students for a Democratic Society (SDS) in the 1960s, with an entire issue of the group's leading journal, *Radical America*, devoted to the Chicago surrealists; and it was directly linked to the women's movement, specifically with Penelope Rosemont's groundbreaking anthology *Surrealist Women* (1998), the first and largest collection ever to represent the many women who participated in surrealism from its origins.

Social Surrealism

Besides the California post-surrealists Lorser Feitelson, Helen Lundeberg, Philip Guston, Reuben Kadish, Harold Lehman, and Knud Merrild—who in the 1930s used such surrealist devices as scale contrasts and odd juxtapositions of objects, but rejected European surrealism's irrationality—the first distinct manifestation of a genuine American surrealist movement adopted a political agenda: American social surrealism.

In the 1930s, during the Great Depression, artists such as O. Louis Guglielmi, Walter Quirt, James Guy, Peter Blume, Francis Criss, and David Smith drew on the experience of everyday life as nightmare, employing the radical aesthetics of surrealism to intensify the power of their social-political critique. Lacking the sexual overtones of European surrealism, the American social surrealists concentrated on presenting familiar aspects of American life in new, frightening, and hallucinatory perspectives. Attacking national problems such as poverty, workers' rights, and, later, the threat of fascism, the social surrealists created easy-to-read art with clear messages.

The group thus followed an overall trend of aligning leftist politics with communism. It supported Leon Trotsky and his International Left Opposition (including communist artists like Mexican Frida Kahlo, whose paintings of physical pain and suffering combined personal experience with the depictions of indigenous culture from a decidedly feminine and surrealist perspective). It also supported the negritude movement and anticolonial, revolutionary writers such as Aimé Césaire of Martinique, taking up surrealism as a method of cultural critique.

American social surrealism followed the veristic branch of surrealism by stressing representation and clarity over automatism and abstraction. At times merging with magic realism (notably Jared French, Henry Koerner, George Tooker, Charles Rain) in its reliance on mystery and the marvelous, and translating everyday experience into strangeness as well as celebrating a revival of Renaissance techniques like tempera painting, veristic surrealism has resurfaced since the 1960s. Key artists, such as Irving Norman, Paul Pratchenko, Lynn Randolph, Phyllis Davidson, and Vaclav Vaca, claim a century-long tradition of art as symbolic narration, disparate juxtapositions of representational imagery, concern for audience, personal content, and classical technique.

Post-Surrealists

During the 1940s, the other main strand of surrealism in its American variation developed the idea of psychic automatism into the New York School of abstract expressionism. Arshile Gorky, Jackson Pollock, Robert Motherwell, Adolph Gottlieb, Mark Rothko, Roberto Matta, and Barnett Newman, among others, celebrated the instantaneous human act (free play and improvisation) as the wellspring of creativity. Later developments of this strand, taking up the humorous aspects of surrealism, developed into 1950s pop art (as seen in the work of Andy Warhol). Robert Rauschenberg was a key transitional figure, making use of surrealism in his Combine Paintings (collages of found objects bridging the gap of life and art by including everyday objects).

Already Breton's assumption that surrealism "acts on the mind very much as drugs do . . . and can push man to frightful revolts," as well as his observation that a surrealist act is like "dashing down into the street, pistol in hand, and firing blindly, as fast as you can pull the trigger, into the crowd," account for the movement's appeal to post–World War II counterculture and antibourgeois generations. All aimed to revolutionize multiple aspects (personal, cultural, social, political, sexual, religious) of human experience. False rationality and restrictive customs were sworn enemies of the surrealists' successors.

Latter-day surrealists can be found in diverse artistic fields, as in the works of the Beat Generation writers (Ted Joans, Bob Kaufman, Gregory Corso, Allen Ginsberg, and William S. Burroughs); free jazz (Don Cherry, Sun Ra, and Cecil Taylor); popular and experimental music (Bob Dylan and Laurie Anderson); film and television (David Lynch's *Twin Peaks* television series, 1990–1991, and Gregg Araki's New Queer Cinema films, such as *The Doom Generation,* 1995); and the stage, ranging from Richard Foreman's Ontological-Hysteric Theater and the camp and transvestite aesthetics of the Ridiculous Theater (Kenneth Bernard, Ronald Tavel, Charles Ludlam) in the 1970s to dance theater (Merce Cunningham, Meredith Monk) and Robert Wilson's Theater of Images. French surrealist Louis Aragon praised Wilson as being "what we, from whom Surrealism was born, dreamed would come after us and go beyond us."

Surrealism from the start has been criticized as artistically avant-garde yet ultimately chauvinistic, misogynist, and male centered. Thus, whenever women have adopted surrealism as their chosen method, they have done so mostly with ironic and parodic intent. Feminist subversion of patriarchal hierarchies has been a driving force in surrealist works as different in time, form, and content as Gertrude Stein's landscape plays of the 1920s and 1930s (with their radical aesthetics all but veiling their inherent homosexual politics), Cindy Sherman's *Untitled Film Stills* series (1977–1980), and Kathy Acker's post-punk porn novels.

In turning stereotypical sexist attitudes toward women into ironic commentaries on society's misgivings, these post-surrealists take part in the overall surrealist notion of a countercultural movement—one that links radical aesthetics with revolutionary politics by emphasizing the links between freeing imagination and mind and liberation from repressive and archaic social structures.

Ralph J. Poole

See also: Abstract Expressionism; Beat Generation; Great Depression; Industrial Workers of the World.

Further Reading

Breton, André. *Manifestoes of Surrealism.* Trans. Richard Seaver and Helen R. Lane. Ann Arbor: University of Michigan Press, 1972.

Caws, Mary Ann, ed. *Surrealist Painters and Poets: An Anthology.* Cambridge, MA: MIT Press, 2001.

Nadeau, Maurice. *The History of Surrealism.* Trans. Richard Howard. New York: Macmillan, 1965.

Sakolsky, Ron, ed. *Surrealist Subversions: Rants, Writings and Images by the Surrealist Movement in the United States.* Brooklyn, NY: Autonomedia, 2003.

Suleiman, Susan R. *Subversive Intent: Gender, Politics, and the Avant-Garde.* Cambridge, MA: Harvard University Press, 1990.

Survivalists

Survivalists are individuals or groups who aim to outlast an anticipated widespread catastrophe by stockpiling goods, learning self-sufficiency skills, and/or arranging to defend themselves from the government or those who did not prepare. Elements of survivalism are found among more radical groups on both the left (including Earth First! and homesteaders) and the right (including Aryan Nations, Michigan Militia) of the political spectrum, although white supremacist groups have received the vast majority of media and academic attention. Expected calamity can take a number of permutations, ranging from religious millennial events to nuclear holocaust, environmental destruction (such as that brought by Hurricane Katrina in 2005 to areas of the Gulf Coast), or societal collapse. The defining aspects of the movement, however, are the intended responses to the perceived threats. Survivalism most commonly entails such actions as the storage of extra water and food in case of an emergency, but it can escalate to engaging with other survivalists to prepare for catastrophic scenarios. At the most extreme end, this entails living "off the grid" of the normal power supply in a communal situation, such as a militia or cult. The survivalist movement is dominated by white males.

Modern examples of the survivalist movement began during the cold war over fears of an impending nuclear holocaust. Government agencies urged preparedness and the construction of fallout shelters in case of an attack within the United States. In the 1960s and 1970s, with the rise and peak of the counterculture movement, survivalists became increasingly focused on other forms of collapse such as environmental and economic ones.

In the 1980s, attention shifted back to nuclear weapons amid their proliferation in the final years of the cold war. During this time, survivalist conventions (often sponsored by, and advertised in, gun magazines) also proliferated. The 1990s saw an increasing dependence on information technology, giving rise to a growing sense of impending "technocalypse." Survivalists started to focus more on surviving without the complexities of a technology-driven society around them. Earth First!, which had held regional training camps since the 1970s, began to shift attention toward sustainable lifestyles and wilderness skills.

The most recent popular manifestation of the survivalist movement came after the terrorist attacks of September 11, 2001, with a focus on preparing for widespread devastation at the hands of Islamic fundamentalists. In the early 2000s, "freegans" (people whose aim is to survive a prospective crisis of capitalism by scavenging food from dumpsters and other free sources) received increased media attention.

In the United States, the federal government often has been involved in the popular survivalist movement, providing guides on surviving multiple forms of catastrophes. The advice of government agencies is almost always geared toward short-term survival, a period of several days at most, which is why more serious survivalists often disregard these suggestions. Emergency response workers, who work with the government to prepare for disasters and emphasize working with others to restore order, often disparage survivalists who foresee a longer-term collapse of civilization.

Although mainstream survivalists often focus on ways to respond to disasters at their homes, more extreme survivalists tend to focus on ways to escape urban areas and head for rural retreats where they can survive long-term societal collapse. To this end, many survivalists form semi-clandestine clubs with whom they plan to meet up during a catastrophe and escape to a less densely populated area. At the most extreme end of this spectrum are militias such as the Montana Freemen, millennial cults such as the Branch Davidians, and back-to-earthers who attempt to live outside U.S. society in preparation for the coming apocalypse.

Literature of the movement proliferates on both sides of the spectrum, with the radical right producing the likes of Andrew MacDonald's novel *The Turner Diaries* (1978) and *Soldier of Fortune* magazine, and the left producing books and zines on urban salvaging, wilderness survival, and cultural resistance.

The survivalist community is heavily represented on the World Wide Web, which disseminates information on products (often with a focus on firearms), strategies, and works of literature, and provides space for the interaction of different points of view among survivalists. Survivalist themes are occasionally presented in the American mass media, as in the case of Edward Abbey's novel *Good News* (1980), the hit movie *Red Dawn* (1984), and the television series *Lost* (2004–).

Matthew Branch

See also: Branch Davidians; Environmentalism; Transcendentalism; White Supremacists.

Further Reading

Barkun, Michael. *Disaster and the Millennium.* Syracuse, NY: Syracuse University Press, 1986.

Lamy, Philip. *Millennium Rage: Survivalists, White Supremacists, and the Doomsday Prophecy.* New York: Plenum, 1996.

Mitchell, Richard G., Jr. *Dancing at Armageddon: Survivalism and Chaos in Modern Times.* Chicago: University of Chicago Press, 2004.

Swedenborgianism

The writings and teachings of the eighteenth-century visionary Emanuel Swedenborg became the basis of a religious system called Swedenborgianism. Swedenborg's religious writings describe an accessible spiritual world populated by entities that interact with humans and offer guidance and wisdom. His encounters with this world inspired various countercultural thinkers and artists and influenced later movements that claimed contact with spiritual teachers and guides.

Swedenborg's Life

Swedenborg was born in Stockholm, Sweden, on January 29, 1688, to a wealthy and prominent Lutheran family. Since his father was a Lutheran bishop, he received an excellent education and grew up intensely aware of the conflicts between Catholics and Protestants and the many divisions among Protestant denominations that roiled the religious world of the late seventeenth century. Swedenborg showed promise as a student and graduated at an early age from the University of Uppsala. Following graduation, he traveled in Europe while studying astronomy, physics, mathematics, and physiology. Taking careful notes during his travels, he returned to Sweden and published books on chemistry, mathematics, and mineralogy.

In 1744, Swedenborg began a period of spiritual transformation that started with a series of increasingly powerful dreams. These nighttime visions expanded into his waking hours, where he encountered a divine being who explained that he was to receive the true meaning of the Bible. After these experiences, Swedenborg claimed, he was able to look into the spirit or heavenly realm and converse with the wide variety of beings he found there.

Over the next decade, Swedenborg wrote and published his eight-volume work *Arcana Coelestia* (1749–1756), which began to lay out his spiritual system. He wrote of his encounters and documented them as meticulously as his physical journeys and produced several works of mystical theology, producing nearly twenty works after his spiritual awakening. Among the most important was *Heaven and Its Wonders and Hell* (1758), which presented his vision of a spiritual realm divided into an organized hierarchy of seven spheres of ascending purity and divinity, with the mundane physical world at the center.

While producing this large body of written material, Swedenborg also worked in various scientific fields, edited a scientific magazine, served in the Swedish legislature, and held a government position as assessor to the Royal College of Mines. He later resigned the latter post to pursue his writing and lived an ascetic life on half-pension.

Although he published his spiritual works anonymously, the 1768 revelation of his identity as the author of the books and pamphlets that had become something of a sensation in Europe led Swedish Lutheran ministers to accuse him of heresy. Swedenborg, known and respected by many prominent political, religious, and scientific figures in Sweden, used his connections to escape punishment.

He continued to travel, write, and publish until 1771, when he suffered a stroke while visiting London. He died there the following year.

Swedenborgianism in the United States

Following Swedenborg's death, many of his followers organized a branch of Christianity modeled on his works that they called the Church of the New Jerusalem. Although it had some popularity in France and Central Europe, Swedenborgianism as an organized religious movement had its greatest successes in England and the United States. The Church of the New Jerusalem remained a small but viable denomination throughout the nineteenth and twentieth centuries, but Swedenborgianism's greatest impact on countercultural groups occurred outside the boundaries of any organized church.

Swedenborg's writings became popular in the United States during the nineteenth century, and he became a notable influence on many who would become involved in such countercultural movements as transcendentalism and spiritualism. His vivid descriptions of a world both internal and spiritual led to his popularity among a wide variety of Americans who were pursuing an interest in mesmerism, communal settlements, and medical practices such as homeopathy.

Some of those who were active in disseminating Swedenborg's ideas in the United States during the 1840s, such as New York University professor of theology George Bush, became attracted to the emerging spiritualist movement, which centered on communications with the dead. Over the next decade, many spiritualists praised Swedenborg as a seer and medium, arguing that the angelic communications he described in his writings actually were the same types of contacts with the spirit world that they experienced. Andrew Jackson Davis, one of the most prominent of the antebellum spiritualists, claimed that the spirit of Swedenborg appeared to him in the 1840s as a kind of spiritual guide.

Swedenborg's reputation as a serious scholar, his erudite theological works, and his systematic treatment of the spirit world made him a revered figure among many spiritualists. Some, like the Reverend Thomas Lake Harris, made Swedenborgianism a major part of their own spiritual systems. However, this popularity eventually created tensions. While spiritualists were happy to consider Swedenborg's experiences a harbinger of the manifestations of the mid-nineteenth century, more doctrinaire Swedenborgians objected to having him treated as simply another medium.

Swedenborg's influence also extended to transcendentalist thinkers such as Ralph Waldo Emerson, who was so impressed by the Swedish seer that he included an essay titled "Swedenborg, the Mystic" (alongside essays on Plato, Napoleon, and Shakespeare) in his 1859 book *Representative Men*. Long before the appearance of that essay, however, several well-known figures associated with transcendentalism, such as the writer Margaret Fuller and the New England teacher Amos Bronson Alcott, read and discussed Swedenborg's works and theological system. Another prominent New England intellectual, philosopher Henry James, Sr. (the father of Harvard professor of psychology William James and novelist Henry James), became one of the most well-known and ardent devotees of Swedenborg.

Beyond his obvious influence on familiar countercultural movements such as spiritualism and transcendentalism, Swedenborg's writings have inspired poets and artists in the United States and overseas for more than two centuries, including William Blake, William Butler Yeats, and Honoré de Balzac. Outside the arts, Swedenborg influenced the development of New Thought, the late-nineteenth-century religious movement that taught that spirit was the only reality and that individual thoughts exercised power over the physical world, and other alternative philosophical systems.

While the most important influence of Swedenborgianism, both on mainstream culture and on countercultural movements, was exercised by Swedenborg's writings, churches organized around his beliefs remain active to the present day. Since their founding, these churches have faced a number of schisms over whether Swedenborg's writings should be seen as a lens through which to understand the Christian Scriptures or should be considered infallible, divinely inspired documents.

By the twenty-first century, such divisions fractured the Church of the New Jerusalem into a number of smaller groups. Two of the largest are the General Church of the New Jerusalem, headquartered near Philadelphia, which claims about 5,000 members, and the Swedenborgian Church of North America, based near Boston, which has about 1,500 members. Swedenborgian-influenced denominations in Europe, Asia, and Africa brought the total number of members to about 30,000 as of 2008.

Stephen D. Andrews

See also: Alcott, Amos Bronson; Davis, Andrew Jackson; Emerson, Ralph Waldo; Fuller, Margaret; Harris, Thomas Lake; Spiritualism; Theosophy; Transcendentalism.

Further Reading

Brock, Erland J., ed. *Swedenborg and His Influence*. Bryn Athyn, PA: Academy of the New Church, 1988.

Silver, Richard. "The Spiritual Kingdom in America: The Influence of Swedenborg on American Society and Culture, 1815–1860." Ph.D. diss., Stanford University, 1983.

Toksvig, Signe. *Emanuel Swedenborg, Scientist and Mystic*. New York: Swedenborg Foundation, 1983.

Trobridge, George. *Swedenborg: Life and Teaching*. New York: Swedenborg Foundation, 1968.

T

Talking Heads

The Talking Heads were seminal figures in the history of the New York punk music scene, pioneering the more commercially friendly New Wave genre. More than any other band in this musical milieu, the Talking Heads had an exceptionally enduring connection to the avant-garde of New York. Musically, the band members became early innovators in incorporating dance rhythms, both funk and African polyrhythms, into their sound.

Singer David Byrne, bassist Tina Weymouth, and drummer Chris Franz (who later married Weymouth), attended the Rhode Island School of Design in Providence, Rhode Island, where they formed the band in 1974. In 1976, they achieved early success, based on riveting live performances at Hilly Kristal's club on Bowery Street in New York City, CBGB, the epicenter of New York's burgeoning punk movement. Seymour Stein of Sire Records was so impressed that he immediately signed the group. The following year, guitarist Jerry Harrison, who had studied architecture at Harvard University, joined them, and that same year, the band released its first album, *Talking Heads '77.*

The Talking Heads' early minimalist, terse sound was based on Byrne's yelping vocals and Weymouth's deliberate bass lines. Harrison had played with Jonathan Richman and the Modern Lovers, and the Talking Heads were influenced by the Modern Lovers' preppy visual style and simple, pared-down music, which was often accompanied by surreal and naive lyrics. The Talking Heads, in contrast to most early New York City punk bands, did not embrace the rebellious, romantic rock aesthetic or pose as anti-intellectual, working-class toughs or dissipated junkies.

The Talking Heads' edgy pop music and surreal lyrics of alienation evolved from the tradition of New York City art rock that originated in the late 1960s with the Velvet Underground, and later the New York Dolls and Patti Smith—all of whom had strong connections with the art and literary worlds. Byrne was inspired by the creative strategies of the Dadaists and surrealists, and he used games and chance elements to create lyrics. From the band's inception, every album design was conceived and created by some or all of the band members. Later, pop artist Robert Rauschenberg was enlisted to design a limited-edition LP package for *Speaking in Tongues* (1983). *True Stories* (1986) was a full-length film conceived by, directed by, and starring Byrne.

In 1983, the band found mass popularity with the hit "Burning Down the House." The cable television network MTV (Music Television) had been launched just two years earlier, and the Talking Heads' popularity was enhanced by their visually arresting music videos.

Alternative-music producer Brian Eno had introduced the band to African music, which is reflected on the albums *Fear of Music* (1979) and *Remain in Light* (1980). Byrne and Eno further explored the use of sub-Saharan and northern African sounds in *My Life in the Bush of Ghosts* (1981) and a collaboration with dancer-choreographer Twyla Tharp titled *The Catherine Wheel* (1981). The three other members of the band all released side projects, and Weymouth and Franz were unexpectedly successful with their white rap project, the Tom Tom Club.

As the Talking Heads found commercial success, however, the members grew increasingly at odds with each other. Soon after producing a final album in 1988, *Naked,* the band broke up. Its legacy of musical boundary breaking has influenced the work of such later performers as Beck, Radiohead, Phish, and others.

Monica Berger

See also: CBGB; Punk Rock.

Further Reading

Bowman, David. *This Must Be the Place: The Adventures of the Talking Heads in the Twentieth Century.* New York: HarperCollins, 2001.
Rockwell, John. "Art-Rock, Black vs. White and Vanguard Cross-Pollination." In *All American Music: Composition in the Twentieth*

Century, edited by John Rockwell. New York: Alfred A. Knopf, 1983.

Taos, New Mexico

First in the 1920s and again in the 1960s, the remote mountain village of Taos, New Mexico, acquired an international reputation for artistic experimentation, while hosting such well-known counterculture residents as American patron of the arts Mabel Dodge Luhan and actor Dennis Hopper.

Pueblo Indians have inhabited Taos Pueblo, the multifamily, adobe structure on the edge of town, since the pueblo's construction in about 1400 C.E. Spanish settlers, priests, and soldiers arrived in the 1500s. The Taos Revolt in 1680 led to their expulsion, but the Spanish returned in 1690. Taos then became a fortified trade city, bustling with the activity of Spanish merchants from Chihuahua, French and American fur trappers, and Indian traders from tribes across the region. Kit Carson, the American scout who settled in town in the 1840s, was typical of many in Taos in having an interethnic marriage.

The flags displayed in town changed with Mexican independence in 1821, and again upon U.S. annexation in 1846, but little else changed until railroad construction connected Taos with other parts of the country in the 1880s. It was during this time that popular fascination with Western and Native American themes drove Taos's rebirth as an art colony. Artists Ernest Blumenschein and Bert Phillips settled there in 1889, and in 1915 they joined with recently arrived artists Joseph Henry Sharp, Bert Harwood, Nicholai Fechin, and Joseph A. Fleck in founding the Taos Society of Artists cooperative. The Atchinson, Topeka and Santa Fe railroad purchased much of their work to promote regional tourism.

The 1916 arrival of Mabel Dodge, a wealthy New York socialite, transformed Taos. Soon thereafter, Dodge married local Pueblo Indian Tony Lujan (Luhan), and over the next decade built a rambling complex in which she housed painters, writers, and photographers. Her financial independence allowed her to offer guests (who sometimes stayed years) a respite from the commercial art market, resulting in a vibrant center of avant-garde experimentation. During the 1920s and 1930s, Dodge hosted a cross-section of the most innovative minds of the era, among them Ansel Adams, Willa Cather, John Collier, Carl Jung, D.H. Lawrence, John Marin, Georgia O'Keeffe, Elsie Clews Parsons, Gertrude Stein, Alfred Stieglitz, and Paul Strand. She remained in Taos until her death in 1962.

In the 1960s, Taos again became a center of cultural experimentation. The population doubled as more than two dozen communes appeared on the outskirts of town, including Morningstar, Lama, and the Reality Construction Company. The communes varied widely in terms of philosophy and lifestyle, but all were perceived as being more accepting of experimentation with drugs and sex than was the broader Taos community. Iris Keltz's *Scrapbook of a Taos Hippie* (2000) is one of several memoirs on the Taos commune scene, where, the author recalls, young people hoped to change the direction of American culture by rejecting materialism and violence.

The New Buffalo Commune became the most famous of the Taos communities when it provided the backdrop for the 1969 film *Easy Rider,* which brought actors Dennis Hopper and Jack Nicholson to town. Hopper bought the Dodge-Luhan ranch and used the "Mud Palace" as a studio for experimental filmmaking, while hosting Bob Dylan, Janis Joplin, Timothy Leary, Andy Warhol, and other icons of the era.

Despite the national attention, this was a tense time. Some of what communalists viewed as natural human behavior—including nudity, free love, and religious syncretism—the Pueblo Indians considered offensive to their indigenous traditions, and the town blamed newcomers for rising rates of drug use and delinquency. Federal Bureau of Investigation (FBI) investigations of the communes, tribal political groups, and Chicano activists, who sought to organize Hispanic residents of the town to resist discrimination, contributed to the tension.

By the 1970s, the commune era was in decline, but Taos retained its reputation as a center of creativity. Writer John Nichols (author of *The Milagro Beanfield War,* 1974) and Navajo artist R.C. Gorman acquired national reputations with their New Mexico-centered art. By the 1990s, many of the town's communes had evolved into centers for sustainable agriculture, New Age spiritualism, and global education.

In the twenty-first century, these communities have continued to attract visitors interested in alternative lifestyles, while the many workshops run by these groups help spread the Taos ethic of cultural experimentation. The local art community remains active, and the town remains home to the Taos Pueblo Indians, as it has for centuries.

Janice Lee Jayes

See also: Communes; Hopper, Dennis; Luhan, Mabel Dodge; O'Keeffe, Georgia; Stein, Gertrude.

Further Reading

Keltz, Iris. *Scrapbook of a Taos Hippie: Tribal Tales from the Heart of a Cultural Revolution.* El Paso, TX: Cinco Puntos, 2000.

Luhan, Mabel Dodge. *Edge of Taos Desert: An Escape to Reality.* Albuquerque: University of New Mexico Press, 1987.

Rudnick, Lois Palken. *Utopian Vistas: The Mabel Dodge Luhan House and the American Counterculture.* Albuquerque: University of New Mexico Press, 1996.

Taggett, Sherry Clayton, and Ted Schwarz. *Paintbrushes and Pistols: How the Taos Artists Sold the West.* Santa Fe, NM: John Muir, 1990.

Television

Although television technology had been successfully demonstrated as early as 1927 and the first regular programming began in 1939, the medium did not become a popular source of entertainment and news in the United States until after World War II. In the years that followed, however, television's popularity increased dramatically. As of 1948, an estimated 1 million U.S. households had television sets; by 1969, some 95 percent of homes contained a television, and Americans watched an average of six hours of television daily.

As a function of its universality and audiovisual format, television has been regarded as an extremely effective medium for the dissemination of information and maintaining mainstream values and ideologies. Nevertheless, in the history of the medium, countercultures have wrought significant changes in the structure and content of television programming.

The 1960s, when television was still relatively young and counterculture groups were growing in popularity, was a particularly important period for such changes. News coverage of counterculture movements and entertainment content drawing on countercultural stereotypes represented commercial efforts to profit from the public interest. Ultimately, however, the countercultures of the period succeeded in changing television, especially by making it a medium more attuned to youth culture. As the civil rights, anti–Vietnam War, and hippie movements succeeded in bringing their goals and values into American living rooms via the small screen, television itself had a direct and dramatic impact on the strategies of the political counterculture and the course of events.

Television is alluring to anyone with a message to spread, because its extensive and intimate penetration into the daily lives of Americans makes it an effective way to share ideas on a large scale. At the same time, many of the practices that have come to be associated with television—including situation comedies that reinforce the nuclear family and heterosexuality, entertainment programming with racist depictions of minorities, the perceived bias of mainstream news, and the use of commercials to support the costs of most programming—represent values that countercultures have opposed.

Moreover, with large corporations owning the three major networks in the United States during the 1960s, counterculture groups had little direct access to the means of production or channels of distribution. Direct, objective representations of alternative political, social, and cultural points of view thus depended largely, and tenuously, on the objectivity of news organizations.

Counterculture Depictions

The youth-based movements of the period prompted the quest for programming that relied on rock music and other cultural artifacts to capture the interest of younger viewers. NBC launched *The Monkees* (1966–1968) in an attempt to capture some of the hysteria over the Beatles. The Monkees were purely a TV creation with recording spin-offs; the show consisted of band members portraying themselves in comical fashion. The series was devoid of any politically, socially, or morally objectionable content, but it strove to retain the style of the hip culture associated with rock music.

This tendency to repackage the culture of recreational drug use and brazen sexuality into a harmless, stylish entertainment product was dominant. Other popular programs that presented a sanitized version of the rock world included the Beatles' Saturday morning cartoon show (1965–1968), Dick Clark's *American Bandstand* (1952–1989), and *The Partridge Family* (1970–1974).

The Mod Squad (1968–1973) made clear that youth counterculture was changing traditional television. The show took a conventional format, the buddy cop show, and altered it by including a woman character and an African American character in addition to a white male. Though juvenile delinquents recruited to do police work to save themselves from jail, the three were hip and fashionable, and they mingled easily with the Southern California youth subculture to fight crime. The show's logline, or capsule summary, advertised its multicultural emphasis: "One black, one white, one blonde." *Mod Squad* was an instant hit, perhaps because it could not only draw interest from countercultural viewers, but also seem to give a mainstream viewer entrée into the youth subculture while maintaining the strong sense of morality that drove cop shows in its era.

Some television personalities earnestly sought to infuse their programs with countercultural messages, though generally with minimal success. The Smothers Brothers used the platform of their comedy variety show *The Smothers Brothers Comedy Hour* (1967–1969) to protest against the Vietnam War. As a result, the Columbia Broadcasting System (CBS) network president decided to censor the show, and the withdrawal of advertisers finally forced cancellation. Gene Roddenberry, creator of NBC's science fiction series *Star Trek* (1966–1969), was likewise prevented from writing shows that implied opposition to the Vietnam War.

Television programs also lampooned the counterculture for entertainment value. *The Many Loves of Dobie Gillis* (1959–1963) featured a recurring beatnik character named Maynard G. Krebs, a harmless free spirit who loved jazz and playing the bongos and had an aversion to work of any kind. *Rowan & Martin's Laugh-In* (1968–1973) was a sketch comedy show that drew on hip imagery of the swinging 1960s for laughs. And many other series included single episodes in which the main characters encountered versions of beatniks, hippies, feminists, or Black Power activists, who would inevitably display markers of countercultural stereotypes without giving voice to the substance.

The televised media also effected change in mainstream political perceptions and was a factor in precipitating strategies adopted by the New Left. As the nightly television news brought the Vietnam War into the living rooms of the American people, the antiwar movement found ways to use media coverage to their own ends.

Organizers, especially, came to appreciate the value of visual spectacle in protest events, recognizing that outrageous or unusual stunts could lead to increased coverage by the televised media. Notable among the counterculture groups who recognized the power of televised spectacle were the yippies. In October 1967, the March on Washington to protest the Vietnam War attracted an estimated 100,000 activists. Still, the claim by yippie leader Abbie Hoffman that he would "levitate" the Pentagon, accompanied by poet Allen Ginsberg's Tibetan chants and a musical "exorcism" by the band the Fugs, drew as much media attention as the march itself.

Another event—among many—that reflected the counterculture's recognition of the power of television was the protest of track-and-field athletes Tommie Smith and John Carlos at the 1968 Olympic Games. By lowering their heads and raising their fists on the medal stand during the playing of the national anthem, Smith and Carlos created a visual image of Black Power that was broadcast globally and became instant history.

Since the 1960s, television has continued to be a medium that caters to interests of youth culture and tends to represent threatening social movements in a politically neutered manner for its own financial profit. Advances such as color television and the advent of cable and satellite service have only made television a more profitable and ubiquitous source of information. Countercultures have most recently seen representation on cable networks, whose proliferation has meant an increasingly diverse representation of U.S. cultures on television. Notably, Home Box Office (HBO) brought viewers seemingly realistic depictions of mob life in *The Sopranos* (1999–2007) and polygamous countercultures in *Big Love* (2006). Showtime's *Queer as Folk* (2000–2005) opened up a frank look at gay culture, and its *The L Word* (2004–) did the same for lesbian culture. Reality television also sometimes attempts to offer insight into the lives of marginalized groups previously unrepresented on television.

Despite the presence of independent public television stations, the ongoing trend has been toward consolidation of television network ownership by multinational corporations. And this trend is likely to continue making television an even narrower platform for direct resistance to mainstream culture.

Susanne E. Hall

See also: Beatles, The; *Mod Squad, The*; New Left; *Rowan & Martin's Laugh-In*; Science Fiction; Smothers Brothers; Trekkies.

Further Reading

Gitlin, Todd. *The Whole World Is Watching: Mass Media in the Making and Unmaking of the New Left.* Berkeley: University of California Press, 1980.

Himmelstein, Hal. *Television Myth and the American Mind.* New York: Praeger, 1984.

Watson, Mary Ann. *Defining Visions: Television and the American Experience Since 1945.* Fort Worth, TX: Harcourt Brace College, 1998.

Temperance Movement

Emerging in the early decades of the nineteenth century, the U.S. temperance movement sought to limit consumption of alcohol, moving between an emphasis on voluntary individual behavior and coercive legislation. The movement focused on alcohol's negative impact on both society and individuals, especially the moral, economic, and medical effects of overindulgence. Gaining momentum in the latter part of the nineteenth century, the struggle culminated in ratification of the Eighteenth Amendment to the U.S. Constitution, which became law on January 16, 1920. National Prohibition lasted until the amendment was repealed, with ratification of the Twenty-First Amendment in 1933, but the ban on alcohol remained a local option and remained in effect in some locations.

Origins

After independence, American annual per capita consumption of absolute alcohol rose from 3 gallons (11.34 liters) in 1790 to 4 gallons (15.12 liters) in 1830. Although there had been efforts to restrict alcohol sales during the colonial period, the publication of Dr. Benjamin Rush's *An Inquiry Into the Effects of Ardent Spirits* (1784), which advocated total abstinence from distilled liquors, provided the intellectual basis for the temperance movement.

The Massachusetts Society for the Suppression of Intemperance, founded in 1813, advocated moderation, but the American Society for the Promotion of Temperance, founded in 1826, followed Rush in calling for complete abstinence from distilled spirits. Appealing to the masses through tracts, newspapers, and circulars, the latter organization gained 1.5 million members by 1835. It soon became clear that no legitimate distinction could be made between distilled and fermented beverages; by 1836, the American Temperance Union, as the national society renamed itself, was promoting teetotalism. The movement proved effective, with the nation's annual per capita consumption of alcohol dropping to 2 gallons (7.56 liters) by 1840.

The 1840s saw both the growth of temperance efforts and the broadening of their appeal. The Washingtonian Total Abstinence Society, or Washingtonians, an organization of reformed alcoholics, originated in Baltimore in 1840; by the following year, it was sending speakers to cities throughout the Northeast. Recounting their personal struggles with drink, the Washingtonians developed a support network for common people who sought help in overcoming alcohol dependence.

In Maine, industrialist Neal Dow worked through the Washingtonian movement to achieve both local and statewide restrictions on the sale of alcohol by 1846. In 1851, he obtained stronger state legislation that outlawed the manufacture of alcohol and limited its use to medicine and industry. Over the next four

years, twelve additional states and territories adopted similar prohibition laws. This legislation prompted organized opposition, however, which succeeded in eliminating or weakening prohibitions in five of these states and territories prior to the American Civil War.

Between 1850 and 1900, American drinking habits stabilized, as annual per capita consumption of absolute alcohol dropped to about 1.5 gallons (5.67 liters). While the decline was accounted for in part by the increasing popularity of beer over whiskey with the influx of German immigration, this change also reflected the influence of the temperance movement.

Tactics

With the stalling of early prohibition efforts, temperance forces moved in several directions. In the 1850s, Dr. Joseph E. Turner began describing habitual drunkenness as a disease and called for the establishment of specialized treatment facilities, the first of which was the New York State Inebriate Asylum, established in 1864. In the 1870s, lectures by Dr. Dio Lewis helped inspire the Women's Temperance Crusade, which organized mass marches that focused on closing down saloons and other liquor retailers. Appearing in thirty-one states and the District of Columbia, the crusade involved at least 56,000 women.

Meanwhile, prohibition advocates continued their efforts, organizing the Prohibition Party in 1869 and achieving prohibition in six states toward the end of the century. With the emergence of the Populist Party in the early 1890s and the failure of the Prohibition Party to form a coalition with it, the Prohibition Party was relegated to permanent minor-party status.

More significant was the Woman's Christian Temperance Union (WCTU), established in 1874. Under the leadership of educator and reformer Frances Willard, the WCTU approached alcohol as a social problem. The organization ran jail visitation programs, established departments to work with miners and timber laborers, encouraged children to take temperance pledges, and promoted "scientific temperance instruction" in the public schools. In addition, the WCTU circulated petitions for statewide prohibition as well as local option laws that allowed counties to prohibit the sale of alcohol. Its efforts helped push Kansas in 1880 and Iowa in 1881 to adopt prohibition. Although the WCTU was a largely white, upper middle-class organization, lower-class women were active on the state and local levels, and the organization's Departments of Colored Work took part in both national efforts and in several state unions. The temperance activities of the WCTU also brought it into contact with a variety of social problems that widened its concerns, leading the organization to seek such additional objectives as woman suffrage and an increase in the legal age for sexual consent.

Responding to lax enforcement of prohibition in Kansas, temperance agitator Carry Nation helped organize a local chapter of the WCTU in Medicine Lodge in 1900. Claiming to be inspired by visions, she launched a campaign of direct action in which she entered local saloons wielding an ax, destroying liquor bottles, kegs, and furnishings. She soon expanded her actions to other cities in Kansas and eventually to such places as San Francisco and New York City. Although she gained national notoriety, Nation was a controversial figure within the temperance movement itself, and she had little lasting influence.

In contrast to the WCTU, the Anti-Saloon League of America (1905) focused on the single issue of prohibition. It argued that the way to achieve this goal was through national policy rather than attempting to change personal behavior. Although it ultimately sought an end to all trafficking in liquor, it chose its goals pragmatically, seeking local option in some places and statewide prohibition in others. The league worked through local churches, both to solicit financial pledges and to identify church members willing to vote for "dry" political candidates. It organized voters at the precinct level, sought to influence the caucuses and conventions of both the Democratic and Republican parties, distributed circulars to industrial employees, and published a variety of papers in several languages. By 1915, it had helped pass prohibition legislation in several Southern and Western states. Meanwhile, in 1913, the league gained passage of a federal law that prohibited the interstate shipment of alcohol into dry counties.

This success led the Anti-Saloon League to begin lobbying for a constitutional amendment to establish national Prohibition—a goal achieved in December 1917, when Congress voted to submit the Eighteenth Amendment to the states. The ratification process was completed in January 1919, and the amendment went into effect one year later. Annual alcohol consumption in America fell from 1.7 gallons (6.43 liters) per capita in 1916 and 1917 to about .75 gallons (2.83 liters) in 1921 and 1922, rising again to 1.1 gallons (4.16 liters) in the years 1927 through 1930.

Resistance to Prohibition arose quickly. Opponents, known as "wets," argued that the restriction was ineffective and impossible to enforce, as well as an unnecessary restriction on personal freedom. Bootlegging,

Members of the Woman's Christian Temperance Union join in song as part of its dry California activities of 1914. From its founding in 1874, the WCTU played a leading role in the campaign for prohibition. *(Peter Stackpole/Time & Life Pictures/Getty Images)*

rum-running, and speakeasies (illegal underground drinking establishments) all flourished, giving rise to unprecedented levels of organized crime.

By 1932, nine states had repealed their prohibition laws. The following year, thirty-seven states held referenda on an amendment that would repeal national Prohibition, and thirty-five states voted for repeal (the exceptions being North Carolina and South Carolina). The national experiment was over upon ratification of the Twenty-First Amendment, but the annual per capita consumption of alcohol changed little until after World War II, when it again leveled off at about 1.5 gallons (5.67 liters).

Although its efforts to establish permanent Prohibition were ultimately unsuccessful, the temperance movement had a major effect on American drinking behavior. By the mid-twentieth century, U.S. consumption of alcohol had dropped to approximately half of what it had been in the early days of the republic.

Gary Land

See also: Prohibition; Social Gospel; *Document:* Woman's Christian Temperance Union "Do Everything" Policy (1893).

Further Reading

Blocker, Jack S. *American Temperance Movements: Cycles of Reform.* Boston: Twayne, 1989.

Bordin, Ruth. *Woman and Temperance: The Quest for Power and Liberty, 1873–1900.* Philadelphia: Temple University Press, 1981.

Szymanski, Ann-Marie. *Pathways to Prohibition: Radicals, Moderates, and Social Movement Outcomes.* Durham, NC: Duke University Press, 2003.

Tyrell, Ian R. *Sobering Up: From Temperance to Prohibition in Antebellum America, 1800–1860.* Westport, CT: Greenwood, 1979.

Theater, Alternative

Alternative theater—variously referred to as experimental, avant-garde, or fringe theater—has provided a counterpoint to the commercialism, conventionality, and high ticket prices of mainstream American theater, including Broadway and off-Broadway, since at least the early twentieth century. Among the hallmarks of American alternative theater in its many forms and expressions are the use of the stage to dramatize a particular ideology or point of view, whether political, social, or artistic; innovative approaches to staging and production; and affordability for ordinary people. Early institutions of this type were founded in New York City, including the experimental Provincetown Playhouse (1917) and Cherry Lane Theatre (1924). From these, the alternative theater movement of the 1950s and 1960s would evolve and achieve more enduring success.

Committed to a democratic model, postwar alternative theater has tended to adhere to a policy of low-price or even free entry fees. At the same time, producers and others working in the business have explored new methods, materials, and dramatic devices, using a variety of physical spaces for performances, erasing boundaries between production crew and actors by making each participant perform a variety of roles, and otherwise resisting the commercialism of middle-class theater.

As a vital element of the postwar American counterculture, the alternative theater also has been a venue for addressing such political and social issues as race relations, U.S. involvement in the Vietnam War, women's rights, and economic justice. Prominent examples include political street theater, epitomized in the 1960s in rural California by El Teatro Campesino, a bilingual farmworkers' theater that criticized the exploitation of farmworkers by grape growers; and the Diggers in San Francisco, an improvisational guerrilla theater group that opposed private property and provided free food, medical supplies, and transportation for the urban poor.

Early Twentieth Century

With antecedents in European traveling shows and other improvisational groups, experimental theater in America took root in New York's Greenwich Village in 1917 with the arrival of the Provincetown Players. The group had been organized two years earlier under the leadership of playwrights Susan Glaspell and George Cram Cook in Cape Cod, Massachusetts, with the shared goal of breaking away from contemporary commercial melodrama and supporting new voices and new directions in American drama. The Provincetown Players produced the early works of Eugene O'Neill, among others, and became closely associated with the little theater movement of the times, with its themes of left-wing politics, feminism, and the bohemian lifestyle. After closing for three years in the early 1920s, the Provincetown Players disbanded in 1929.

Meanwhile, in Greenwich Village, the bohemian poet and playwright Edna St. Vincent Millay, with other members of the Provincetown Players, opened another venue of experimental theater, the Cherry Lane Theatre, in a converted warehouse in March 1924. Now the oldest extant off-Broadway theater in New York, the Cherry Lane has showcased the works of countless aspiring playwrights who became leading innovators of American drama.

Nor was the movement confined to New York. Among the notable innovative theater groups to spring up around the country, some of which still operate, were the Little Theatre of Chicago (1912), the Vagabond Players in Baltimore (1916), the Arts and Crafts Theatre of Detroit (1916), the Des Moines (Iowa) Playhouse (1919), and many others.

Postwar Era

The period following World War II brought a kind of revival in alternative American theater, which continued to gain momentum in the 1950s, 1960s, and onward. Innovative new productions were being mounted by the Living Theatre, founded in 1947 by actress Judith Malina and her husband, painter Julian Beck. The Living Theatre was among the first American companies to stage modernist European works by the likes of Bertolt Brecht and Antonin Artaud, and it remains the oldest experimental theater group still operating in the United States. Also noteworthy in the immediate postwar years was Theatre '47 in Dallas, Texas, founded in 1947 by the innovative stage director and regional-theater pioneer Margo Jones.

It was in the early 1960s, however, that American alternative theater began to recognize itself as an independent group and cohesive movement. Much of the alternative theater forged during the 1960s and 1970s remains very much alive in the twenty-first century, if in different forms.

The work of Judith Malina and colleagues at the Living Theatre was especially noteworthy for questioning the terms of conventional theatrical performance and subverting the psychological realism that had dominated mainstream stage drama in America. Plays such as Paul Goodman's *Faustina* (1952) and Jack Gelber's *The Connection* (1959) experimented with forms of "direct address," in which actors speak directly to the audience and make it part of the play, in some cases suggesting that the actors were not acting at all. Highly experimental in form, the Living Theatre often patterned its performances on readings and interpretations of modernist poetry and art, including the work of such writers as Gertrude Stein.

The New York City–based Open Theater, founded in 1963 by playwright Joseph Chaikin, director Peter Feldman, and a group of actors, pursued many of the same directions as the Living Theatre. A primary emphasis from the outset was on improvisational live performance, focusing on the actors rather than the characters; the cooperative method brought together the impulses and creative directions of individual actors in a kind of living collage. The Open Theater also was groundbreaking in its exploration of contemporary political, social, and cultural issues, exemplified by such productions as *Viet Rock* (1966) and *The Serpent* (1967).

The San Francisco Mime Troupe, founded in 1959 by R.G. Davis, extended the idea that theater can advance a political agenda through such works as the anti–Vietnam War drama *L'Amant militaire* and a critique of American racism in *The Minstrel Show, or Civil Rights in a Cracker Barrel,* both in 1965. Emphasizing physical action on stage, the troupe invokes the imagery and style of the circus, carnival, parades, and medieval European *commedia dell'arte* (which featured the use of masks and exaggerated movements). Emerging from Davis's original mime troupe, the guerrilla theater movement of the 1960s took a consistent and radical political position with the student-led New Left, opposing the Vietnam War, mocking the cultural establishment, and promoting Marxism. In addition to the Diggers, local guerrilla theater groups included the aptly named Haight-Ashbury Vietnam Committee and the San Francisco Red Theater.

Luis Valdez's El Teatro Campesino, or Farmworkers' Theater, developed out of his involvement in the San Francisco Mime Troupe. In 1965, his ideas to explore the subject of workers' rights led him first to join Davis's company and then to begin envisioning his own theater group, with a separate social agenda. As a play-

wright, Valdez began drafting *actos,* or brief scenarios in Spanish and English that were meant to support striking Latino farmworkers on the picket line. That year labor activist César Chávez organized a strike against grape growers in Delano, California, the same place where Valdez organized and created his theater in conjunction with union members. El Teatro Campesino later incorporated Aztec and Mayan traditions in dramatizing themes and events in Latino culture.

The Free Southern Theatre was established in 1963 as a cultural extension of the civil rights movement, advancing the causes of desegregation and freedom by staging works, starting that year, such as Martin Duberman's *In White America* and Beckett's *Waiting for Godot.* Founded by Gilbert Moses and John O'Neal, the company was established at Toogaloo University in Jackson, Mississippi, with the intention of bringing live theater to people who had never experienced it before. The company toured in predominantly rural, black areas of the South before moving to New Orleans in 1965.

Many African Americans took a more radical political position, promoting an African American theater movement completely organized and run by their own community. Seeing the potential to effect real political and social change through the theater, poet and playwright Amiri Baraka (LeRoi Jones) founded the Black Arts Repertory Theater (1965) in Harlem and Spirit House (1967) in Newark, New Jersey. Baraka's best-known plays include *Dutchman* (1964), in which a middle-class African American man is murdered by a white woman, and *Slave Ship* (1967), about the suppression of a slave revolt on the Middle Passage.

Theater groups whose primary objective has been to promote change in the perception of gender and sexuality include such feminist companies as It's Alright to Be a Woman Theatre, the Spiderwoman Theatre Workshop, Lilith: A Woman's Theatre, Women's Experimental Theatre, and Split Britches; gay and lesbian companies such as the Gay Theatre Collective, the Cockettes, and the San Francisco Angels of Light; and transvestite and transsexual groups such as the Play-House of the Ridiculous and the Ridiculous Theatrical Company. The Women's Experimental Theatre is best known for a trilogy of plays, *The Daughters Cycle* (1977–1981)—*Daughters, Sister/Sister,* and *Electra Speaks*—which recast classical tragedy from a woman's perspective. Both the Play-House of the Ridiculous's *Indira Gandhi's Daring Device* (1966), about overpopulation and the malnourishment of India's Untouchables (lower caste), and the San Francisco Angels of Light's *Razzmatazz* (1974), an example of gay theater that includes the intentional misremembering of lines, push the boundaries of sexuality in live performance, with a strong dose of absurdity and humor.

Pacifist theater groups are tied together by the innovative use of physical space for staging performances, integrating their plays into such settings as peace marches, college campuses, and even laundromats. Another innovation is "invisible theater," in which the production is seamlessly integrated into its setting so that viewers do not know they are watching a performance. The group most associated with the Pacifist movement is the Bread & Puppet Theater, established in New York City (later relocated to Glover, Vermont) by artist Peter Schumann in 1962. While the majority of Pacifist theater groups developed out of the anti–Vietnam War protest movement, the Bread & Puppet Theater pursued a unique aesthetic vision and emphasized more basic human needs—reflected by its practice of distributing free fresh bread at its performances. New York's Pageant Players, on the other hand, levied more direct political criticisms in productions such as *The Paper Tiger Pageant* (1965), meant to be performed at peace rallies, and an anti-corporation play, *King Con* (1966).

The late 1970s brought a surge of formalist theater—that is, theater that is self-conscious about how it is represented and perceived—with a series of plays about human thought and perception. Robert Wilson, a painter, architect, and director whose work encouraged varying levels of attention and participation from the audience; Richard Foreman, who wrote plays about his thought process; Michael Kirby, a sculptor and theorist of structuralist drama; and the Wooster Group, established in Soho, New York City, in 1980, all played a role in re-conceptualizing the theater as formalist. Productions such as *Deafman Glance* (1970), which used no sound and whose central character was a deaf-mute, and *Photoanalysis* (1976), which employed multiple projectors and the repetition of lines by each character, forced audiences to consider and question their own perceptions of what was taking place on stage.

The formalist trend reflected a transition in American alternative theater from an emphasis on political and social themes in the 1960s and early 1970s to a greater focus on the individual in the late 1970s and 1980s. Actors and playwrights such as Spalding Gray of the Wooster Group made themselves the central focus of the performance; each of Gray's plays is based on an experience in his own life, so much so that he ultimately resisted ever playing a character other than himself.

By the 1990s, however, nonmainstream American theater returned to the more political-social impulse of the 1960s and 1970s. Thus, reflecting the trend toward globalization—and the counterculture movement against it—the San Francisco Mime Troupe's *Off Shore* (1993) addressed issues of foreign policy and free trade. Other alternative theatrical groups continue to explore themes and trends in public life, innovations in stage production and the theater (or non-theater) experience, and original, new themes and voices in the dramatic arts.

Christine M. Connell

See also: Cherry Lane Theatre; Greenwich Village, New York City; Guerrilla Theater; Haight-Ashbury, San Francisco; Provincetown Players; United Farm Workers.

Further Reading

Canning, Charlotte. *Feminist Theaters in the U.S.A.: Staging Women's Experience.* New York: Routledge, 1996.

Doyle, Michael William. "Staging the Revolution: Guerrilla Theater as a Countercultural Practice, 1965–1968." In *Imagine Nation: The American Counterculture of the 1960s and '70s,* edited by Peter Braunstein and Michael William Doyle. New York: Routledge, 2002.

McNamara, Brooks, and Jill Dolan, eds. *The Drama Review: Thirty Years of Commentary on the Avant-Garde.* Ann Arbor, MI: UMI Research Press, 1986.

Shank, Theodore. *Beyond the Boundaries: American Alternative Theater.* Ann Arbor: University of Michigan Press, 2002.

Yordon, Judy E. *Experimental Theatre: Creating and Staging Texts.* Long Grove, IL: Waveland, 1997.

Theosophy

Theosophy—from the Greek *theos* ("God") and *sophos* ("wise"), and thus literally translated as "knowledge of the divine"—is a term used in reference to any number of religious or philosophical systems professing mystical knowledge of the nature of God and the universe. Religious mystics and philosophers Jacob Boehme and Emanuel Swedenborg, for example, are commonly referred to as Theosophists. Although true believers trace the origin of Theosophy to the writings of the ancient Greek philosopher Plato and the Roman Neoplatonic philosopher Plotinus, Theosophy gained its greatest notoriety in the nineteenth century with the founding of the Theosophical Society by Helena Petrovna Blavatsky in New York City in 1875.

Blavatsky's books *Isis Unveiled* (1877), based on her extensive travels in Asia, Europe, and the Middle East, and *The Secret Doctrine* (1888), based on esoteric Buddhism and Hinduism, became the fundamental texts of the nontheistic theosophical movement. Madame Blavatsky, who claimed numerous psychic powers, eventually settled in India, where she established the headquarters of the Theosophical Society. Directly or in spirit, the late-twentieth-century New Age movement, with its emphasis on meditation, reincarnation, the mystical properties of crystals, and psychic phenomena, is based significantly on the teachings of Madame Blavatsky.

A central principle of Theosophy is the belief that a boundless, unchanging reality and immutable truth—akin to what people have called God—is inherent in all life and transcends human understanding. Another central, and related, tenet is that nothing happens by chance; all events—past, present, and future—occur as a result of the universal laws of nature. Thirdly, Theosophists believe in the principle of reincarnation; that is, human development is guided by the law of karma and the attainment of spiritual growth through innumerable reincarnations of spirit. Good and evil are understood as the result of separation of the spirit and the body throughout the life cycle. The soul, or spirit, is a universal, unifying aspect of nature, joining all humanity in brotherhood.

With Blavatsky's death in 1891, several theosophical societies emerged, following a cycle of numerous schisms. English social reformer Annie Besant became leader of the society based in Adyar, India, while Irish-born mystic William Quan Judge directed the American Section of the Theosophical Society in New York, which later relocated to Pasadena, California, under a succession of leaders. At its peak in the 1920s, the parent Theosophical Society (or Theosophical Society Adyar) had approximately 7,000 members in the United States. The largest branch of the Theosophical Society, the Indian section, at one time had more than 20,000 members; as of the early 2000s, the figure stood at just under 10,000. In India, Theosophy was closely associated with the Indian independence movement from the early days of both; indeed, the Indian National Congress was founded during a theosophical conference in 1885.

Membership in the Theosophical Society is open to all who support its Three Objects: a universal brotherhood regardless of race, creed, sex, caste, or color; the comparative study of religion, philosophy, and science; and investigation into the unexplained laws of nature. Members, who are not required to renounce the teachings and beliefs of their own faiths, either belong to a local lodge or study center or are members-at-large. Lodges are formally organized groups that consist of a minimum of seven members and meet regularly to study Theosophy and arrange theosophical programs for the public. Study centers are informal groups of at least three members who meet regularly and who may offer occasional public programs.

The study of Theosophy directly influenced the works of several well-known composers, artists, and authors, including Ruth Crawford-Seeger, Alexander Scriabin, Wassily Kandinsky, Piet Mondrian, Franz Kafka, and T.S. Eliot. References to Theosophy, often in satire or parody, have appeared in a number of literary, dramatic, and cinematic works, including E.M. Forster's novel *Howard's End* (1910), James Joyce's novel *Ulysses* (1922), Sean O'Casey's play *Juno and the Paycock* (1924), H.P. Lovecraft's short story "The Call of Cthulhu" (1928), Mohandas Gandhi's autobiography, *The Story of My Experiments with Truth* (1927–1929), John Crowley's novel *Little, Big* (1981), Mark Frost's novel *The List of 7* (1993), and the film *FairyTale: A True Story* (1997), directed by Charles Sturridge.

Denise A. Seachrist

See also: Blavatsky, Helena; New Age; New Thought.

Further Reading

Blavatsky, Helena Petrovna. *Isis Unveiled.* 2 vols. 1877. Wheaton, IL: Theosophical University Press, 1999.
———. *The Key to Theosophy.* 1889. Wheaton, IL: Theosophical University Press, 1998.
———. *The Secret Doctrine: The Synthesis of Science, Religion, and Philosophy.* 2 vols. 1888. Wheaton, IL: Theosophical University Press, 1999.
Theosophical Society in America. http://www.theosophical.org.
Washington, Peter. *Madame Blavatsky's Baboon: A History of the Mystics, Mediums, and Misfits Who Brought Spiritualism to America.* New York: Schocken, 1995.

Thompson, Hunter S.

See Gonzo Journalism

Thoreau, Henry David (1817–1862)

Transcendentalist essayist and theorist Henry David Thoreau was a radical abolitionist and anti-imperialist who pioneered the practice of civil disobedience in America. He was perhaps best known for his 1854 book *Walden, or Life in the Woods,* an account of his two-year experiment in "simple living" in a cabin in the woods. A philosopher and practitioner of American individualism in a pure sense, an advocate of ethics over conformity and of nature over materialism, and a critic of the "busyness" of American life, he was a counterculture of one for his brief adult life.

Born on July 12, 1817, in Concord, Massachusetts, Thoreau inhabited his home there perhaps more intensively than anyone before or since has ever inhabited a locale. He claimed he had "traveled a good deal in Concord" and applied his searching, critical mind to everything he encountered. He addressed his fellow townspeople throughout his life, asking them about their "condition or circumstances in this world, in this town, what it is, whether it is necessary that it be as bad as it is, whether it cannot be improved. . . ."

Concord was the site of one of the first battles of the American Revolution in April 1775. During Thoreau's life, the egalitarian ideals that had inspired the Revolution not only had been deeply undermined by the spread of slavery, but also faced a new challenge. Industrialization had produced new kinds of class inequality and poverty for workers in the rapidly growing cities of the Northeast. When Thoreau graduated from Harvard University in 1837, the United States had just entered an economic depression that left many out of work. Americans began to wonder whether the new capitalist social order could deliver on its promises of prosperity.

Thoreau addressed this question in his Harvard commencement essay, titled "The Commercial Spirit of Modern Times," declaring "this world is a place of business. What an infinite bustle! I am awaked almost every night by the panting of the locomotive. It interrupts my dreams. . . . I think that there is nothing, not even crime, more opposed to poetry, to philosophy, ay, to life itself, than this incessant business." Thoreau believed that in such a materialistic world, writers and artists had an especially important role to play: to keep in view transcendental truths that had been forgotten in a competitive scramble for profit and prestige.

For the first decade of his life as a writer, Thoreau thought of himself mainly as a poet working in the tradition of the English Romantic William Wordsworth. At first, Thoreau's themes and style were closely modeled after the transcendental idealism of American essayist and Concord neighbor Ralph Waldo Emerson, but he soon began to develop his own voice and vision. At its best, his verse is firmly anchored in the physical specifics of New England, and its angular rhythms combine with striking vernacular to produce musical language that was innovative and powerful for its time.

Thoreau's most widely read book, *Walden,* is a kind of long poem in prose. It records his two years, two months, and two days living in a one-room cabin on the shores of a small pond outside of Concord. Thoreau explains, "I went to the woods because I wished to live deliberately, to front only the essential facts of life, and see if I could not learn what it had to teach, and not, when I came to die, discover that I had not lived."

During his sojourn at the pond, Thoreau experimented with cultivating beans for personal consumption and for sale. If this smacked too much of competition and consumerism, he scaled back his farming during the second year, replacing it with walks in the woods to harvest wild huckleberries. He advocated vegetarianism, abstinence from sex, and stimulant beverages such as coffee, tea, and alcohol. Above all, his work at the pond was to write, and he completed many poems, several essays, the manuscript of *A Week on the Concord and Merrimac Rivers* (1849), and the first draft of *Walden.*

Henry David Thoreau's *Walden, or Life in the Woods* (1854), an account of his two years living alone at Walden Pond, Massachusetts, is a criticism of the "busyness" of American life and a reflection on the simple joys and transcendental laws of nature. *(Library of Congress)*

As a response to the bleak reality of life during the depression, *Walden* makes a sustained exploration of the religious philosophy of pantheism. According to this way of thinking, the physical world incarnates the transcendental laws of nature ordained by God. The poet or writer who walks or lives in the woods can become sensitively attuned to these higher laws. He (this was imagined as a gendered role) can then use them to understand and reform a society that has slid into avarice, greed, and hypocrisy.

One way that American society demonstrated its loss of contact with the divinity in nature, in Thoreau's eyes, was by its treatment of the land. *Walden* features meditations on the railroad's invasion of the woods and on the destructive profit seeking of ice packers. It is from Thoreau's essay "Walking" that the influential environmental organization, the Sierra Club, takes its motto, "In wildness is the preservation of the world."

In Thoreau's view, chattel slavery was the most outrageous example of the depths to which a materialistic society could slide. Following his belief that individual conscience overrides social law, he frequently acted as a conductor on the Underground Railroad, concealing escaped slaves in his home and accompanying them to the next safe haven northward. He also turned his talents to supporting the abolitionist cause, publishing fiery antislavery essays that began as lectures.

"Slavery in Massachusetts" (1854), for instance, delivers an unrelentingly harsh attack on Northern complicity with the slavocracy, especially criticizing those who obeyed Fugitive Slave Laws that required Northerners to return escaped slaves. Thoreau concluded the essay by describing a white water lily as an "emblem of purity" growing from "the slime and muck of earth"—a symbol of the redemption he felt was possible should his audience break unjust laws and take direct action to abolish slavery.

During the last decade of his life, Thoreau dedicated himself to learning as intimately as possible the natural cycles of the woods around Concord. He took long daily walks and gathered voluminous notes for a "Kalendar," or guidebook to the seasons, that he hoped would help his neighbors regain their communal intimacy with nature. He was unable to complete this ambitious project, nor did he live to see the end of the Civil War and the emancipation of the slaves.

On his deathbed in Concord in spring 1862, he was asked if he could see the other side. He replied, "One world at a time." Henry David Thoreau died on May 6, 1862.

Lance Newman

See also: Abolitionism; Transcendentalism; *Document:* "Where I Lived, and What I Lived For," *Walden* (1854), Henry David Thoreau.

Further Reading

Buell, Lawrence. *The Environmental Imagination: Thoreau, Nature Writing, and the Formation of American Culture.* Cambridge, MA: Harvard University Press, 1995.

Richardson, Robert D., Jr. *Henry Thoreau: A Life of the Mind.* Berkeley: University of California Press, 1986.

Schneider, Richard J. *Henry David Thoreau.* Boston: Twayne, 1987.

Thoreau, Henry David. *The Portable Thoreau.* Ed. Carl Bode. New York: Penguin, 1977.

Tramps and Hoboes

The terms *tramp* and *hobo* refer to members of the American subculture of wanderers, in particular those whose movement from place to place is tied to the railroad system. The tramp and hobo also exist as cultural tropes, familiar figures in the mythology of the American West—on one hand valued for symbolizing freedom and the pioneer spirit; on the other vilified for resisting the conventions of the American work ethic and meritocracy.

The beginnings of tramp and hobo culture generally are traced to post–Civil War America, with their roots in the expansion of the railroad system, the Depression of 1873, the arrival of the Industrial Revolution, and the movement West to explore the frontier, seek adventure, and find jobs. The construction of a national rail network, along with general westward expansion, meant an abundance of work for men willing to travel significant distances from job to job, creating a culture of mobility and flexibility in wage earning. With the financial panic of 1873, that new culture of mobility was adapted by unemployed workers, who used the rail system to "hop rides" to whatever location promised the next month's wages.

By 1890, train-hopping became an art and a culture unto itself, existing outside the boundaries of mainstream American culture, with its own norms, values, and codes. The hobo culture, with its distinctive "rules of the road" and techniques for survival, was passed from veteran to fledgling wanderer via stories, songs, and slang in "jungle camps"—squatter campsites on the outskirts of towns, near the railway tracks, where hoboes could eat, sleep, and create a community in relative safety. All were welcome, so long as the rules of the "jungle" were obeyed.

A particularly significant aspect of hobo and tramp culture was the complex system of signs, which resembled hieroglyphs, used for communication. For the most part, hoboes and tramps did not use mainstream means of communication, such as mail, telegraph, and telephone; these signs were used to pass along insider information to other members of the subculture. Hobo signs communicated positive messages about safe and welcoming resting places and where food might be easily obtained, as well as warnings about thieves, vicious dogs, or police.

The terms *hobo* and *tramp* originally held little of the social stigma or exoticism they took on in the latter part of the twentieth century. They merely signified individuals, usually men, who "tramped" from town to town in search of work.

Within the subculture itself, however, distinctions were sometimes made. Hoboes were typically unskilled migrant laborers or seasonal workers who traveled by rail from one job to the next. Tramps wandered but, unlike the hobo, did not work. Tramps typically relied more on their wiles, as well as handouts and petty crime. The actual social boundaries between the two groups, however, were more fluid, depending upon the availability of work.

Small numbers of self-ascribed hoboes and tramps continue to maintain the subculture today, although they are socially and statistically subsumed in the wider homeless population.

Cynthia J. Miller

See also: Drifters; Great Depression; Guthrie, Woody.

Further Reading

Bruns, Roger A. *Knights of the Road: A Hobo History.* London: Methuen, 1980.

Spence, Clark C. "Knights of the Tie and Rail—Tramps and Hoboes in the West." *Western Historical Quarterly* 2:1 (January 1971): 4–19.

Williams, Clifford. *One More Train to Ride: The Underground World of Modern American Hoboes.* Bloomington: Indiana University Press, 2003.

Transcendental Meditation

Transcendental meditation (TM) is a relaxation technique that was introduced to the United States in 1958 by Maharishi Mahesh Yogi, an Indian Hindu monk, and popularized by the Beatles and other celebrities who visited the Maharishi's ashram in the 1960s and 1970s. Transcendental meditation, a proprietary term in the United States, is said to promote relaxation through chanting a mantra, or secret Sanskrit word, assigned to the individual by a TM instructor. Meditators

Indian ascetic Maharishi Mahesh Yogi (center) introduced the relaxation and consciousness-raising technique of transcendental meditation. Popularized by Beatles stars George Harrison (left) and John Lennon (right), TM became a counterculture craze. *(Keystone/Hulton Archive/Getty Images)*

chant for twenty minutes twice a day in a relaxed, comfortable position of their choosing, with eyes closed.

According to its founder, TM is based on ancient Vedic traditions from India; daily practice leads to a higher level of consciousness and a state of "true bliss." The Maharishi claims that TM allows practitioners to transcend their own consciousness, rising to a state of "restful alertness." He describes seven states of consciousness, which range from the commonly understood to those reached through the long-time practice of TM, after which one arrives at a state of true enlightenment.

Maharishi consistently has rejected any notion that TM is a form of religious mysticism, denying any connection to a particular belief or creed and insisting that TM requires no change in lifestyle. However, TM can only be learned from a qualified program teacher, who is the only authorized source for an individualized mantra. The costs of the initial program in the United States begin at $2,500 (as of July 2007); optional lifetime follow-up programs are available to meditators at an additional charge.

Adherents of TM claim substantial positive results from the practice, including improved physical and mental health due to lowered blood pressure, increased heart function, and reduced stress. Additional claims include reduced cigarette and alcohol use, decreased insomnia and anxiety, and an increased sense of well-being and calmness. Much research has been done on the benefits of TM, including a 1999 study on its effects on heart disease funded by the National Institutes of Health. Although TM has been found to lower blood pressure, reduce stress, and promote good health, similar meditation techniques have been found to be equally effective.

Surrounded by controversy from its introduction in the United States, TM has been accused of such practices as overstating its benefits, including a type of levitation supposedly achieved by advanced practitioners called Yodic Flying. It also has been condemned outright as a cult, although research has shown that TM adherents do not demonstrate behaviors traditionally associated with cults.

In 1973, the Maharishi founded the Maharishi University of Management, located in Fairfield, Iowa, a "consciousness-based" educational institution relying heavily on the practice of TM. Through its adherence to and daily practice of TM, the university and adjacent secondary school, the Maharishi's School of the Age of Enlightenment, claim to have won academic and athletic recognition and awards. In the twenty-first century, the Maharishi has expanded the practice of Vedic tradition to include the incorporation of Maharishi Vedic City, Iowa, where transcendental meditation is used to promote peace and harmony.

Pat Tyrer

See also: Beatles, The; Hippies; Yoga.

Further Reading

Cunningham, C., S. Brown, and J.C. Kaski. "Effects of Transcendental Meditation on Symptoms and Electrocardiographic Changes in Patients with Cardiac Syndrome X." *American Journal of Cardiology* 85:5 (March 2000): 653–5.
Mahesh Yogi, Maharishi. *Science of Being and Art of Living: Transcendental Meditation.* New York: Plume, 2001.
Transcendental Meditation Program. http://www.tm.org.

Transcendentalism

A prominent intellectual, literary, and cultural movement in New England during the 1830s and 1840s, American transcendentalism was an idealist reaction against British empiricism, or the idea that all knowledge comes from the senses, reason, and reflection on experience, as well as a turning against the dominant Protestant doctrine and secular intellectualism of the time. As America's first cultural revolution, transcendentalism emphasized the innate, intuitive power of the human mind, a spiritual state that transcends the material plane, the immanence of the divine, and the moral insight and creative energy of the individual.

Challenging contemporary religious beliefs, literary norms, and even social practices, New England transcendentalists such as Amos Bronson Alcott, Ralph Waldo Emerson, Margaret Fuller, and Henry David Thoreau, changed the way Americans thought about culture and society, including religion, community, education, literature, and politics, and the individual. These men and women elevated the borrowing and melding of religions, philosophies, and literatures into a literary, intellectual, and educational renaissance. The impact of transcendental idealism on the national culture was widespread and enduring, producing a new voice and direction in American letters.

While the movement never had a written set of rules or became popular with the masses, transcendentalism was a powerful idea that confounds many people to the present day. The only certainty is the depth and variety of thought among proponents and the sharing of a few broad principles regarding the question "How do we see the world?" The root word, *transcendent,* is sometimes mistaken as suggesting its traditional religious association with a divine being above or apart from life on earth. For the transcendentalists, by contrast, the immanence of the divine, in living creatures and in objects considered inanimate, is a shared spiritual conviction, realized not by material sense perception but by a higher, innate intuition.

Among the underlying principles and influences were those of Eastern religions; the *Bhagavadgita,* the ancient Hindu spiritual text, was revered and referenced by several of the transcendentalists. Unitarianism was another powerful influence, with its belief in revealed religion based on history and the development of an active individual mind—a culture of the self, independent thinking, and creative expression that, in the mind of Emerson at least, called for a radical break from European tradition, the Bible, and any other handed-down constraints.

In addition to religion, morality was also a central concern, with transcendentalists espousing the individual's responsibility for his or her own morality, the necessity of being true to one's own divine nature, and distinguishing between doing good and being good (in other words, doing good deeds because religion or law demands it does not make an individual good).

Transcendentalists believed that nature was the ultimate source of knowledge and moral clarity, the only true place to discover God's will, because God and nature are one. To immerse oneself in the natural world was good for the soul. As a result, utopian social experiments such as Walden and Brook Farm embodied this ideal oneness with nature and the divine.

Walden Woods and Brook Farm

Walden Woods outside Concord, Massachusetts, was the location of Thoreau's experiment in transcendental living from 1845 to 1847. *Walden, or Life in the Woods* (1854) is his record of those two years, during which he lived in a one-room cabin on the shores of a small pond. In that account, Thoreau made his intention clear: to prove "the mass of men lead lives of quiet desperation" in the overcrowded cities. He set out to "live deliberately" in the woods by the strength of his back and will alone.

Indeed, as Americans were flooding to cities in search of work and wealth, Thoreau embodied the transcendental ideal by becoming one with nature and his own mind, referring to "wildness" as a "tonic." He sought to experience only the necessities of life—food, shelter, clothing, and fuel—in a state of "voluntary poverty." Emerson owned property around Walden Pond and also valued the area, walking there often. With the publication of *Walden,* reading Americans were exposed to Thoreau's rebellious lifestyle and inward-directed mindset, causing some to question the value of urbanization and the health of their own minds and spirits.

Another attempt at social reform was Brook Farm, which operated from 1841 to 1847 in West Roxbury, Massachusetts. Unlike Thoreau's solitary pursuit of moral self-improvement, Brook Farm sought to change society by combining the thinker and the worker, the intellectual and the laborer, into one person via communal effort. Author Nathaniel Hawthorne was an original member and shareholder, staying six months before losing interest in the visionary, but ultimately impractical, community. (His 1852 novel, *The Blithedale Romance,* is based heavily on his experiences there.)

The early years at Brook Farm were characterized by the transcendentalist goal of self-culture and spiritual renewal. The farm, while providing a high quality of life and enjoyment for members, eventually shifted from transcendentalist ideals to the more rigid structure of Charles Fourier's socialist utopian doctrines, which blended with financial troubles to end farm operations by 1847. Later counterculture movements in the United States referred to the Brook Farm experiment for communal living ideas.

Antislavery

While transcendental idealism in physical form, such as Walden and Brook Farm, may have faltered under the weight of unrealistic expectations, the new way of thinking had an enormous and beneficial impact on the abolition movement, adding momentum and moral fortitude to the fight in the antebellum period.

Many Bostonians of the early 1800s had considered abolitionists to be extremists. The efforts on the part of the transcendentalists, however, contributed significantly to the spread of the movement and its mainstreaming in the Boston area. Their efforts took largely written and verbal form, the most explosive example being Thoreau's "Resistance to Civil Government" (1849). In this aggressive essay, Thoreau railed against unjust laws, government hypocrisy, and the right of men "to refuse allegiance to and to resist the government, when its tyranny or its inefficiency are great and unendurable."

Other influential antislavery writings by transcendental thinkers include William Ellery Channing's "Slavery" (1835), Thoreau's "A Plea for Captain John Brown" (1859), and Theodore Parker's "Letter to a Southern Slaveholder" (1848). In addition to their essays, speeches, and letters, the Emersons, Alcotts, Thoreaus, and other families in and around Concord covertly offered safe haven and passage for runaway slaves as part of the Underground Railroad.

Education Reform

In a time when rote repetition of facts and figures dominated American education, Alcott used the Socratic method of questioning to draw out his students' knowledge, rather than treating them as empty containers to be filled with dates and formulas. Alcott's Temple School, which he opened in Boston in 1834, went decidedly against the grain of 1800s American education.

Elizabeth Palmer Peabody recorded Alcott's organic teaching methods on such subjects as sexuality, religion, geography, writing, math, and languages in her book, *Record of a School: Exemplifying the General Principles of Spiritual Culture* (1836). Particularly disturbing to Alcott's traditional contemporaries were his discussions with students about the human body and his two-volume *Conversations with Children on the Gospels* (1836–1837).

Despite shock at Alcott's methods, the public clamored for educational reform beginning in the 1820s.

Now, teacher training, curriculum, discipline, teacher salaries, and working conditions all seemed ripe for reform. In 1837, the Massachusetts Board of Education was created to address the demands for improvement. Alcott, Peabody, and other transcendental reformers believed in students' inherent moral goodness, but they felt that industrialization had weakened the ability of church and family to influence young people. Encouraging individual moral development as part of the school curriculum thus became a transcendentalist benchmark in education reform.

Literature

In addition to effecting fundamental changes in educational philosophy, the transcendentalists breathed new vitality into American literature, placing greater emphasis on private thoughts, the intuitive sense of spiritual immanence, and, perhaps above all, an original, organic, native, *American* voice that eventually evolved into literary realism. A greater premium was placed on life and nature as they are experienced and observed firsthand, without the inhibitions and moral strictures of Old World religious, cultural, and literary traditions.

The new intellectual freedom was declared by Emerson in his groundbreaking address at Harvard University in 1837, "The American Scholar," which Oliver Wendell Holmes called "America's intellectual Declaration of Independence." The spiritual underpinnings of transcendentalism were articulated in Emerson's essay of the previous year, "Nature," which literary and intellectual historians widely regard as the closest thing to a fundamental text of the movement. Thoreau's writings explored another broad theme, the distinctions between wild nature and the humanized landscape.

Also notable was a journal called *The Dial* (1840–1844), a quarterly publication edited first by Fuller and Emerson. Notable transcendental thinkers whose writings appeared in its pages included James Freeman Clarke, Orestes Augustus Brownson, George Ripley, Jones Very, Frederic Henry Hedge, Peabody, Channing, Theodore Parker, as well as Fuller, Emerson, Thoreau, and Alcott.

In addition to writing for publication, the transcendentalists also valued conversation, a frequent theme throughout their works. Much of the published work was originally written for the pulpit and lyceum circuit, or public oratory and educational venues. The transcendentalists, to a person, sought to communicate in real, spoken language, valuing the democratic give-and-take quality of personal conversation.

In November 1839, Peabody and Fuller began hosting meetings for women at which participants could discuss a wide array of philosophical issues, such as "What are we born to do?" and "How shall we do it?" Alcott held meetings throughout his life for male participants to discuss topics such as planets, talents, temptations, and culture and tendencies.

Women's Rights

One institutionalized conversation that involved transcendental ideals with a positive and long-term result had to do with the women's rights movement. Arguably, the most influential transcendentalist woman was Fuller, a journalist, critic, and educator who had taught at Alcott's Temple School and edited *The Dial* for its first two years.

The primary intent of Fuller's parlor sessions with Peabody and others was nothing more or less than to promote women's right to think. Through conversation, she sought to influence the way men and women thought about women in America by focusing on the female identity; namely, that women had an identity beyond sex and gender definitions, based on an independent, individually discovered relationship with God. In consonance with the broader spiritual principles of the movement, women were recognized as intelligent, rational, independent beings with value outside of men's regard, worthy of an equal voice in politics, art, religion, and community.

Radical Ideology

Ultimately, American transcendentalism promoted a hard-line individualism, protesting traditional social, religious, and intellectual systems of the early nineteenth century. From social and education reform to literature and politics, transcendentalism introduced Americans to a new way of thinking. Relying on one's individual intuition, trusting oneself to discover truth and make the right decisions without the external influence of church and state, and recognizing God's immanent presence in nature remain radical ideas in many intellectual, religious, and social circles to the present day.

Amanda L. Morris

See also: Alcott, Amos Bronson; Beat Generation; Brook Farm; *Dial, The*; Emerson, Ralph Waldo; Fuller, Margaret; Hawthorne, Nathaniel; Hippies; Survivalists; Swedenborgianism; Thoreau, Henry David; *Document:* "Where I Lived, and What I Lived For," *Walden* (1854), Henry David Thoreau.

Further Reading

Baker, Carlos, and James R. Mellow. *Emerson among the Eccentrics: A Group Portrait.* New York: Penguin, 1997.

Capper, Charles, and Conrad Edick Wright, eds. *Transient and Permanent: The Transcendentalist Movement and Its Contexts.* Boston: Massachusetts Historical Society, 1999.

Mott, Wesley T. *Encyclopedia of Transcendentalism.* Westport, CT: Greenwood, 1996.

Myerson, Joel, ed. *Transcendentalism: A Reader.* New York: Oxford University Press, 2000.

Richardson, Robert D., Jr. *Emerson: The Mind on Fire.* Berkeley: University of California Press, 1996.

Schreiner, Samuel A., Jr. *The Concord Quartet: Alcott, Emerson, Hawthorne, Thoreau, and the Friendship That Freed the American Mind.* New York: John Wiley and Sons, 2006.

Transsexuals

Transsexuals are individuals who identify with a gender other than the physical one with which they were born and who alter their bodies to achieve the physical norms associated with the chosen gender. The emphasis on bodily transformation is essential to the definition. Generally, *transsexual* refers specifically to those people who, with the aid of surgery and hormone therapy, transform their bodies in order to more comfortably inhabit another gender. The term *transsexual* should not be conflated with *transgender,* which also refers to an identification with non-birth gender but does not imply surgical or hormonal transformation. *Transgender* thus has broader applicability than *transsexual,* with some people using it as an umbrella term for a wide array of gender variance, including people who identify as transsexual. According to a 1998 article in *The New York Times,* more than 50,000 Americans at that time were living in a gender other than their birth gender; approximately 28,000 Americans had undergone sex-change surgery.

Dr. David O. Cauldwell is credited with introducing the term *transsexual* in a 1949 journal article titled "Psychopathia Transexualis." Dr. Harry Benjamin popularized the term in the early 1950s and developed standards of medical care still in use in the twenty-first century. The medical community initially considered these standards radical because Benjamin's treatments accommodated his patients' desires to transition into another gender, rather than use electroshock therapy and medication to subdue the desires.

In the early 1970s, the American Psychological Association introduced into its *Diagnostic and Statistical Manual* (*DSM*) the condition "gender dysphoria," later changed to "gender identity disorder," as the standard diagnosis for a range of cross-gender identifications that might produce a desire to change physical sex. Like Benjamin's treatments, the introduction of this condition into the *DSM* was perceived as a departure from previous psychological perspectives, which insisted on the immutability of assigned biological gender (often defined according to reproductive capacity).

Since the 1980s, many self-identified transsexuals have protested the persistence of diagnoses such as gender identity disorder, as well as the strict medical processes through which one must proceed in order to have surgery. Many transsexuals argue against the classification of transsexuality as a disorder subject to medical intervention. They suggest instead that transsexuality should be understood as one of many commonplace variations of gender and sex that can be addressed with a range of therapeutic options. In the 1990s and 2000s, organizations such as Transsexual Menace and the Gender Public Advocacy Coalition (GenderPAC), have provided education, support, and legal action to improve the quality of life, standards of care, and civil rights of transsexuals.

Transsexual Menace was founded in 1994 by Riki Wilchins in response to the failure to name the transgendered community as part of Stonewall 25, a festival celebrating the 1969 Stonewall riots in New York, which many consider the birth of the contemporary queer movement. Since its founding, Transsexual Menace has organized protests against trans exclusion, held vigils to remember transgendered people who have been victims of physical violence, including murder, and raised awareness by encouraging members to "out" (reveal) themselves as transgendered in their daily lives.

Wilchins founded GenderPAC, a public advocacy group based in Washington, D.C., that lobbies for the rights of transsexuals and the greater transgender community, in 1995. GenderPAC also maintains a youth education program to reach out to transgender youth, who may be isolated and lack support in their homes. Mainstream media coverage of transsexual people and the discrimination they face has increased in recent years, for example in popular depictions such as the film *Boys Don't Cry* (1999), which documents the life and murder of Brandon Teena.

Transsexual and transgendered groups frequently organize with gay and lesbian or queer groups, and transsexuals were centrally involved in the seminal gay and lesbian protests of the 1960s and 1970s. However, these communities remain distinct in many ways and, at times, even may be hostile. For example, the Michigan

Womyn's Festival, a well-known lesbian music festival, continues to refuse entry to transsexual women, who protest the policy annually by setting up Camp Trans across the street from the festival.

Margaux Cowden

See also: Fetish Culture; Gay Liberation Movement; Lesbian Culture; Transvestites.

Further Reading

Devor, Holly. *FTM: Female-to-Male Transsexuals in Society.* Bloomington: Indiana University Press, 1999.

Gender Public Advocacy Coalition. http://www.gpac.org.

Meyerowitz, Joanne. *How Sex Changed: A History of Transsexuality in the United States.* Cambridge, MA: Harvard University Press, 2002.

Stryker, Susan, and Stephen Whittle, eds. *The Transgender Studies Reader.* New York: Routledge, 2006.

Transvestites

The term *transvestite,* coined in 1910 by German sex researcher Magnus Hirschfeld, refers to a person who regularly wears clothing associated in his or her society with the opposite sex. It is equivalent to the English term *cross-dresser,* although *transvestite* is more often used in psychiatric, medical, legal, and academic contexts, while *cross-dresser* is more often the term of choice for those who engage in the practice. The slang term *tranny* is used to refer to all transvestites, transsexuals, and transgendered people. Although cross-dressing is often equated with homosexuality, many experts believe that more heterosexuals than homosexuals engage in cross-dressing.

Cross-dressing is known in many societies and has been practiced throughout history. Thus, any attempt to assign a meaning to this behavior must consider carefully the historical and cultural context. Today, people engage in cross-dressing for many reasons: as a source of sexual satisfaction, a generalized protest against social norms, a refusal to accept the dichotomous division of gender or gender identity, an expression of identification with the opposite sex, or preparation for gender-reassignment surgery, among others.

Some people customarily dress in accordance with their biological gender and only occasionally engage in cross-dressing, while for others cross-dressing is the norm. Although both men and women engage in cross-dressing, it is more associated with men, in part because in modern Western countries it is socially ac-

ceptable for women to wear men's clothing while the reverse is less often the case.

Virginia Charles Prince is generally regarded as the founder of the transvestite movement in the United States. Born in Los Angeles to an upper-middle-class family in 1913, Prince, a biological male, began secretly cross-dressing at home in his late teens. In 1961, he founded Hose and Heels (also known as the Society for Personal Expression), the first support group for male cross-dressers. Heterosexuals, including Prince, formed the majority of members of Hose and Heels. In subsequent years, hundreds of social and support groups that cater to heterosexually identified male cross-dressers have emerged in the United States. Additionally, scores of conventions provide the opportunity for transvestites from all over the country to meet one another and cross-dress for extended periods of time.

The gay community has long had an equivocal relationship with cross-dressers, who were sometimes despised for their nonconformity and the unwanted attention they drew to the community. This has led to the ironic consequence that some gay cross-dressers keep the transvestite aspect of their identity concealed within the gay community, or only reveal it among selected peers known to be sympathetic. One might say that they are "out of the closet" as gay men but still "in the closet" as transvestites.

Heterosexual cross-dressers face even greater social disapproval. The overall lack of social acceptance encouraged transvestites to form their own networks, support groups, and communities, which in the 2000s include Web sites such as Trannyweb.com and organizations such as Tri-Ess, the Society for the Second Self and the Renaissance Transgender Association. Such organizations perform many functions, including counseling and support to cross-dressers, providing a social context and community, educating others about transvestite issues, and advocating for social and legal acceptance of cross-dressing.

At the start of the twenty-first century, one of the best-known transvestite organizations was the International Foundation for Gender Education (IFGE) in Waltham, Massachusetts. Transgender activist Merissa Sherrill Lynn founded IFGE in 1987 as a nonprofit advocacy organization to combat ignorance that encourages intolerance of transvestitism and transsexualism. IFGE has subsequently expanded to educate all people about restrictive gender viewpoints. IFGE publishes a quarterly journal, *Transgender Tapestry.*

Sarah Boslaugh and Caryn E. Neumann

See also: Drag; Fetish Culture; Gay Liberation Movement; Lesbian Culture; Transsexuals.

Further Reading

Fausto-Sterling, Anne. *Sexing the Body: Gender Politics and the Construction of Sexuality.* New York, NY: Basic Books, 2000.

Garber, Marjorie. *Vested Interests: Cross-dressing and Cultural Anxiety.* New York: Routledge, 1992.

Meyerowitz, Joanne. *How Sex Changed: A History of Transsexuality in the United States.* Cambridge, MA: Harvard University Press, 2002.

Suthrell, Charlotte. *Unzipping Gender: Sex, Cross-Dressing and Culture.* Oxford, UK: Berg, 2004.

Trekkies

Trekkies is the familiar term for the large, enthusiastic (some might say obsessed or cultlike) fan base of the *Star Trek* science-fiction television shows and movie series. While the original show failed to find long-lasting network success, it attracted devoted fans who worked to keep the show and its progressive, multicultural view of the future on the air. The Trekkies' devotion to and participation in the *Star Trek* franchise demonstrates the deep cultural connection that can develop between a television show and its audience.

The *Star Trek* television series debuted on the NBC network in 1966, at a time when the concept of space exploration and science in general were permeating American popular culture. Audiences, reeling from the effects of the ongoing Vietnam conflict and civil unrest at home, connected with the vision of *Star Trek* in which humanity had overcome its social woes and embraced a philosophy of tolerance toward those—including aliens—outside the mainstream.

Science fiction itself also was in the process of evolving from a genre that extolled the virtue of technological utopias to one that focused on the cultural relevance of the societies portrayed in its stories. Americans who had been turned off by tech-heavy sci-fi literature were attracted to the social and cultural messages of *Star Trek.* At the surface, the show—pitched as a "wagon train to the stars," according to creator Gene Roddenberry—was an action series geared toward the young; however, the provoking philosophical debates between thoughtful characters, dressed in edgy costumes and presented in campy and alien settings, prompted viewers of all ages to consider the shortcomings of modern-day culture.

Cancellation rumors plagued the show from its beginning, as studio executives failed to see its appeal.

Fans, led by Los Angeles science-fiction aficionado Bjo (Betty Jo) Trimble, mounted a spirited write-in campaign to keep the show on the air. Estimates of the number of fan letters that arrived at the studio range from 114,000 to 500,000. The response from viewers countered the common industry belief that Nielsen ratings were the best measure of television audiences and demonstrated the connection between the show's audience and its creators. Before the show even aired, Roddenberry had courted the fanzine community, in which fans wrote their own stories, thereby building a devoted audience infrastructure. Upon cancellation of the show by NBC in June 1969—after three seasons and seventy-nine episodes—devotees of the series, led by the fanzine community, united in an effort to meet at conventions. The first was held in New York City in 1972, with organizers expecting about 300 attendees. Several thousand showed up, and the zeal of fans became evident to the creators and the press. The term *Trekkies* is believed to have been coined by a science-fiction editor, Art Saha, after he saw attendees at a science convention wearing pointy ears (in honor of the pointy-eared character Spock, half-human, half-Vulcan, played by Leonard Nimoy).

Trekkies saw in the series a call to change their lives for the better, to seek infinite possibilities, question them, and build a better future. Many credited the show with inspiring them to become activists for civil rights, peace, women's rights, or gay and lesbian rights; others were inspired to seek careers in the sciences.

Thanks to their efforts, the original *Star Trek* series grew into a popular media franchise that included four additional live-action television series, an animated series, ten feature films, books, comics, and conventions across the country where Trekkies (many of whom prefer to be called Trekkers) could meet the stars and purchase the latest *Star Trek* merchandise.

Laura Finger

See also: Science Fiction; Television.

Further Reading

Bacon-Smith, Camille. *Science Fiction Culture.* Philadelphia: University of Pennsylvania Press, 2000.

Lichtenberg, Jacqueline, Sondra Marshak, and Joan Winston. Star Trek *Lives! Personal Notes and Anecdotes.* New York: Bantam, 1975.

Tulloch, John. *Science Fiction Audiences: Watching* Doctor Who *and* Star Trek. New York: Routledge, 1995.

Whitfield, Stephen, and Gene Roddenberry. *The Making of* Star Trek. New York: Ballantine, 1968.

Turner, Nat (1800–1831)

Nat Turner was a leader in the slave community of eastern Virginia who issued a call for rebellion after witnessing a solar eclipse in 1831. His rebellion led to the deaths of nearly sixty white people and almost 300 black people, most of whom were unconnected to the uprising. Captured and sentenced to death, Turner comported himself with dignity and left a moving final statement, the publication of which made him a martyr and inspiration to antislavery forces.

Turner was born on the plantation of Benjamin Turner in Southampton County, Virginia, on October 2, 1800. A skilled carpenter and exhorter, or lay preacher, he displayed a keen intellect and sense of conviction that made him a leader to fellow slaves, who referred to him as "The Prophet" or "General Nat." In February 1831, Turner interpreted a solar eclipse as a sign from God that he was an instrument through whom his people could achieve violent retribution against slave owners and gain their freedom.

Launching the rebellion on August 22, 1831, Turner and six fellow slaves murdered the family that owned his plantation and moved through the area from farm to farm, gathering a force of about seventy slaves. Over the course of four days, the rebels killed approximately sixty white people—making theirs the deadliest slave uprising in U.S. history—before being routed by white militia.

Poorly armed and untrained, Turner's men were unable to withstand the militia guarding the county seat of Jerusalem. Turner, who fled and was captured in mid-October, was executed on November 11. In the general hysteria that followed the revolt, hundreds of slaves were killed by white mobs or their own owners.

During his imprisonment, Turner made a lengthy statement that was published as *The Confessions of Nat Turner* (1832). Spelling out the brutality and inhumanity of growing up and living as a slave, *Confessions* describes the night of the rebellion and Turner's life before it in stark terms. It is, perhaps above all, the portrait of a man secure in his convictions and confident in the rightness of his actions. This work, and his reputation as the leader of America's most significant slave rebellion, made Turner a hero to slaves throughout the United States and to many who were working to end slavery.

There were more than 200 similar attempts to raise slave rebellions throughout the United States before the abolition of slavery in 1865. Other than Turner's, only a handful achieved even relative success. In 1739, an uprising in South Carolina led by a slave named Cato gathered about eighty followers at the Stono River (the incident came to be called the Stono Rebellion), resulting in the deaths of twenty whites and forty-four slaves. In 1800, Gabriel Prosser, a slave, planned to seize Richmond, Virginia, but he was captured before he was able to execute his strategy. A plan to capture Charleston, South Carolina, was devised in 1822 by freed slave Denmark Vesey, who was hanged with more than thirty followers when their plan was betrayed. In 1859, the white abolitionist John Brown led an assault on the federal arsenal at Harpers Ferry, Virginia (now West Virginia), hoping to arm a slave militia that would negotiate or shoot its way to freedom; finally surrounded and forced to surrender, Brown was sentenced to death and executed—gaining instant status as a martyr to the abolitionist cause.

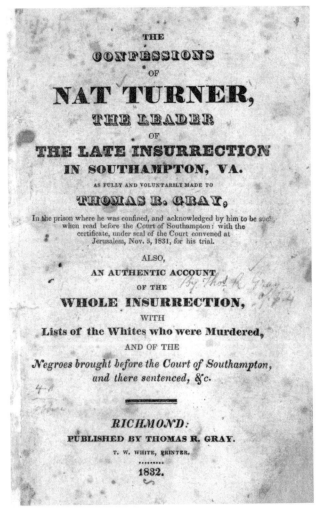

The Confessions of Nat Turner (1832) is an account of the deadliest slave uprising in U.S. history. The book recounts Turner's life as a slave and the revolt of August 1831, as described to his lawyer during imprisonment. *(Library of Congress)*

Outright rebellion was the most visible form of slave resistance; murder, arson, and theft were everyday worries for slave owners throughout the United States, who understood that Turner's example was all too easy to replicate. Turner's rebellion and the reprisals that followed galvanized both slave owners and the abolition movement. Many slave owners believed that white abolitionists had incited the rebellion or aided Turner, and the U.S. Senate called for the arrest of abolitionist leader William Lloyd Garrison. State governments throughout the South passed harsh laws controlling the behavior of slaves and free blacks. Liberal leaders, who believed that Turner's rebellion was part of a larger movement toward liberty, used Turner as an example of the violence that would continue if the United States failed to end slavery. In this larger context, Turner's rebellion helped to solidify the divide between the North and South that led to the American Civil War.

James L. Erwin

See also: African Americans; Slave Culture; *Document: The Confessions of Nat Turner (1832).*

Further Reading

Carroll, Joseph Cephas. *Slave Insurrections in the United States, 1800–1865.* Mineola, NY: Dover, 2004.

Franklin, John Hope, and Loren Schweninger. *Runaway Slaves: Rebels on the Plantation.* New York: Oxford University Press, 1999.

Greenberg, Kenneth S., ed. *Nat Turner: A Slave Rebellion in History and Memory.* New York: Oxford University Press, 2003.

Twain, Mark (1835–1910)

Mark Twain was the pen name of Samuel Langhorne Clemens, a self-taught humorist, novelist, and social observer who rose from lowly printer's apprentice in his native Missouri to internationally celebrated author of several works that continue to grace canon lists. In these writings, Twain spared no theme or subject, bringing an often jaundiced eye and stingingly satiric perspective to mainstream social mores and controversial issues of the time. His fearlessness in exploring sometimes sensitive subjects and ideas in a winningly blunt, down-to-earth way was anathema to some contemporaries but helped make his works timeless and essential reading. Nevertheless, some of Twain's works have found their way onto lists of banned reading in some U.S. schools and libraries.

Twain was born on November 30, 1835, in Florida, Missouri. His family moved four years later to nearby Hannibal, a town on the banks of the Mississippi River

that would appear prominently as a setting in his books. When his father died, in 1847, he quit school and joined his brother's printing business. He set type for local and national newspapers as well as literary and humor volumes.

The humor pieces published in these works sparked the boy's interest and figured prominently in his later writings. A commission to write comic travel letters for an Iowa weekly under the pen name Thomas Jefferson Snodgrass allowed him to develop his satirical style, in which he creatively used misspellings, grammar, and syntax. Twain also served as a local and traveling reporter for many weekly publications as he crossed the United States following his interests.

As Twain's writings turned from journalism to autobiographical sketches and fiction, the many sides of his personality began to shine through. Sensitive, humane, and conscientious, his writings also were known to shock readers with their irreverence toward traditional religious and cultural beliefs. Two of his most famous novels, *The Adventures of Tom Sawyer* (1876) and *The Adventures of Huckleberry Finn* (1884), for instance, promote youth mischief, deception, and manipulation of authority figures, openly satirize religious affiliation, and accentuate the racist leanings of many late-nineteenth-century Americans.

In 1873, Twain's playful social critiques turned toward social criticism. *The Gilded Age* (1873), written by Twain in collaboration with Charles Dudley Warner, attacked political corruption and the vices of wealth, even as its author was building a lavish home in Hartford, Connecticut. While some of his literary works—such as *Tom Sawyer, Huckleberry Finn,* and *Life on the Mississippi* (1883)—brought to life fond memories and imaginings of his Missouri childhood, Twain's criticism of American society became acute. *Huck Finn,* perhaps his most famous and most controversial novel, is also a powerful satire of Southern slavery and racism, the failures of Reconstruction, and evangelical spiritualists, among other elements of post–Civil War life.

Following the deaths of two of his four children, Twain's writings took a dark turn. Human failings and inhumanity became the focus in place of the lighthearted sarcasm for which he had been known, as evident in works such as *What Is Man?* (1906). Antigovernment writings and speeches included his introduction of Winston Churchill at a reception committee meeting on December 13, 1900, during which he declared the United States a meddling sinner in global affairs. Such inflammatory remarks led some to call Twain a traitor. Others merely dismissed him, and several of his works were denied publication during his lifetime.

Twain's global travels opened his eyes to the exploitation of weaker nations by the Western world, a perspective highlighted in subsequent writings. In 1900, he declared himself an anti-imperialist. In 1901, he became vice president of the American Anti-Imperialist League (established in 1898 to fight the U.S. annexation of the Philippines and other territories); he held that position until his death on April 21, 1910, near Redding, Connecticut.

Beyond the characters he created, the times and places he evoked, and the cultural sensibilities he portrayed, Twain's greatest legacy, perhaps, lay precisely in bucking tradition, speaking down-home truth in the American vernacular, and giving birth to a unique, unfettered national literature. There is perhaps no better example of a countercultural writer whose works became mainstream.

Sueann M. Wells

Further Reading

Ayres, Alex, ed. *The Wit and Wisdom of Mark Twain.* New York: HarperPerennial, 2005.

Neider, Charles, ed. *The Complete Short Stories of Mark Twain.* New York: Bantam, 1984.

Powers, Ron. *Mark Twain: A Life.* New York: Free Press, 2005.

UFOs

UFOs are mysterious airborne objects whose nature and origin remain unknown even after close investigation. Their name is a military acronym that stands for "unidentified flying object." While the vast majority of UFOs are explainable as misidentified aircraft or natural meteorological or astronomical phenomena (becoming "identified flying objects," or IFOs), the more difficult-to-categorize UFOs are thought by believers and advocates—known as UFOlogists—to be extraterrestrial spacecraft.

Stories of UFO sightings date back to ancient times. UFOlogists have posited that an 8,000-year-old painting from the Sahara Desert depicts an extraterrestrial visitor. Tales of inexplicable objects have been widely documented throughout history, ranging from China in the twentieth century B.C.E. to Rome in the third century C.E., Japan in the twelfth, thirteenth, and eighteenth centuries, and North America in the late nineteenth and early twentieth centuries.

UFOs of the familiar "flying saucer" variety seem to be a phenomenon of the nuclear age. They achieved widespread publicity after pilot Kenneth Arnold spotted what he described as nine circular airborne objects on June 24, 1947, while flying near Washington State's Mount Rainier. Arnold likened the motions of these mysterious flyers to those of saucers being skipped across water, and his account gave rise to the term *flying saucer.* Since Arnold's encounter, thousands of sightings of saucer-shaped UFOs have been reported all over the world, as well as observations of flying objects resembling cigars, squares, triangles, and more irregular shapes.

On July 8, 1947, newspapers reported the recent crash of a flying saucer near New Mexico's Roswell Army Air Field. Although the fallen craft was most likely part of a U.S. military surveillance program intended to spy on the Soviet Union, the shroud of cold war secrecy with which the government surrounded the crash gave rise to an all-but-inexhaustible wellspring of UFO legend and mythology. UFOlogists believe that the crashed object was an alien spacecraft and that the debris and bodies of the dead alien crew had been whisked away to a high-security government installation for study. No amount of scientific debunking (such as that of the fraudulent alien autopsy videos of the mid-1990s) has been sufficient to dissuade those who subscribe to this theory.

Over the years since the Roswell incident, countless science fiction films, pulp magazine stories, novels, television shows, and comic books have bolstered the popular image of UFOs and their alien occupants. Believers frequently posit that the aliens responsible for

An officer at Roswell Army Air Field in New Mexico examines debris from a nearby crash in July 1947. The military identified the material as the remains of a radar surveillance system. To this day, UFOlogists insist it was the wreckage of an alien spacecraft. *(AFP/GettyImages)*

the UFOs in our skies are concerned about humankind's propensity toward violence, as is Klaatu in Robert Wise's 1951 film *The Day the Earth Stood Still*. Other alien visitors are reputed to have less altruistic motives for visiting us, such as the exploitation of Earth's resources or even the plundering of the human genome.

Some aliens are portrayed as being preoccupied with briefly abducting humans, conducting invasive but impermanent medical procedures on them, then releasing their victims with convenient memory gaps that are later filled in via hypnosis. The case of Betty and Barney Hill, a New Hampshire couple who claimed to have been kidnapped for several hours in 1961 by aliens from the Zeta Reticuli star system, are perhaps the most famous of these so-called alien abductees. Although the physical descriptions of the aliens allegedly encountered vary, the tall, slender, hairless humanoids seen by millions in films such as Steven Spielberg's *Close Encounters of the Third Kind* (1977) and television's *The X-Files* (1993–2002) appear frequently enough in the abduction literature to suggest a strong pattern of pop-cultural influence over the UFO phenomenon.

Like many other episodes of mass hysteria, UFO reports tend to occur in waves, such as the flying saucer heyday of the few years following the Roswell crash, or the "ancient astronaut" UFO renaissance of the early 1970s, which was fueled greatly by the success of the U.S. edition of Erich von Däniken's *Chariots of the Gods?* (1970), a best-selling book of speculations about alien visitations of Earth during ancient times.

Despite the complete absence of definitive proof of extraterrestrial visitation thus far, the sheer volume of UFO reports has received attention from many legitimate scholars and investigators over the years, including agencies of the federal government. In 1948, the U.S. Air Force launched Project Sign, a task force formed to evaluate UFO sightings. The government evidently placed enough credence in the UFO phenomenon to follow up its initial investigations with Project Grudge (1948) and Project Blue Book (1952–1970). After years of gathering and sifting through eyewitness reports, however, these investigative bodies found no conclusive answers to the UFO question. Other countries also have studied the phenomenon, though none have actually endorsed the idea of "aliens among us" as yet.

Several "contactee cults" have arisen since Roswell, beginning in the 1950s. These UFO-oriented spiritual sects usually have formed around a leader who claimed to have made either direct or telepathic contact with alien visitors. George Adamski, who in 1965 established a UFO-inspired foundation that still exists, built a cult

around his alleged relationship with Orthon, a Venusian committed to preventing Earth's nuclear destruction. The Unarius Foundation and the Aetherius Society were formed in 1954 and 1956, respectively, around a similar message of altruistic aliens determined to save us from the dangers of nuclear proliferation. During recent years, UFO cults such as Heaven's Gate and the Raëlians have garnered sensational headlines, the former by committing mass suicide in 1997 with the expectation of deliverance by an alien mothership, and the latter by making yet-unproven claims in 2001 about creating human clones.

The existence of such cults suggests that the UFO phenomenon may be rooted in the human religious impulse rather than in the vastness of the cosmos. The aliens that UFO adherents report encountering simply may be the angels, devils, and gods of antiquity dressed up in the modern pseudoscientific raiment of popular culture. To those who believe in alien visitations, they may be as real and as emotionally affecting as any deeply religious experience inspired by belief in a Supreme Being.

Michael A. Martin

See also: Heaven's Gate; Science Fiction; *X-Files, The.*

Further Reading

Curran, Douglas. *In Advance of the Landing: Folk Concepts of Outer Space.* Rev. ed. New York: Abbeville, 2001.
Picknett, Lynn. *The Mammoth Book of UFOs.* New York: Carroll & Graf, 2001.
Sagan, Carl, and Thornton Page, eds. *UFOs: A Scientific Debate.* Ithaca, NY: Cornell University Press, 1972.
Thompson, Keith. *Angels and Aliens: UFOs and the Mythic Imagination.* Reading, MA: Addison-Wesley, 1991.

Unabomber

Theodore John Kaczynski, the notorious and elusive Unabomber of the 1990s, was responsible for developing and sending sixteen mail bombs that claimed the lives of three people and injured another twenty-three. The motivation for this self-proclaimed anarchist and former mathematics professor, as articulated in letters and a lengthy manifesto sent to government authorities and the press, was to attract attention to the dangers of high-tech industrial society. His targets therefore tended to be associated with universities, airlines, and computers. The Unabomber moniker was derived from the FBI code name UNABOMB (university and airline bomber) during the early years of the case.

He was born to Richard and Wanda Kaczynski in Chicago on May 22, 1942. When he was ten years old, the family moved from Chicago to suburban Evergreen Park. His childhood was generally uneventful, although he later attested to being maltreated by his family and having suffered permanent emotional harm.

Kaczynski was described as a bright child—he scored 167 on an intelligence quotient (IQ) test before entering high school—but not very sociable. Ironically, it was his superior aptitude that propelled him away from his peers at a young age, possibly exacerbating his antisocial predisposition. Kaczynski skipped the sixth and eleventh grades and was admitted to Harvard University when he was only sixteen.

College life was without significant incident, although there are records of his participation in a longitudinal (years-long) study on stress that may have affected him negatively. Otherwise, during his four years at Harvard, Kaczynski studied intensely, joined the swimming and wrestling teams, and played the trombone, while apparently avoiding social bonds. Later, most of his peers could not recall Kaczynski with any specificity. After graduating from Harvard in 1962, he attended graduate school at the University of Michigan, where he completed his Ph.D. in mathematics by the age of twenty-five.

In the fall of 1967, he accepted an assistant professorship at the University of California, Berkeley, where he taught math until 1969. He resigned as a result of apathy toward a profession he believed lacked "relevancy."

In 1971, Kaczynski moved to Lincoln, Montana, after purchasing a piece of land with his brother, David. Kaczynski later said he was inspired by Henry David Thoreau, the nineteenth-century naturalist and writer whose two years alone in a cabin are recounted in *Walden, or Life in the Woods* (1854), to build a 10-by-12-foot (about 3.05-by-3.66-meter) cabin on the plot. The Lincoln community came to refer to him as "the hermit" because of his reclusive lifestyle.

Meanwhile, in his self-imposed isolation, Kaczynski was committing terrorist acts against individuals he believed were perpetuating the destruction of society. He rationalized the sometimes-fatal bombings as the only remedy to societal problems impelled by technology and those who sought to advance it. Kaczynski was a nihilist who objected to all forms of technological development that, in his view, had become an end rather than a means to greater social good. Society valued individuals only in accordance with the "social machine" of modern capitalism, he argued, and the prevailing institutions exacerbated the ills of the human condition while pretending to do the opposite. Consequently, he did not regard his victims as innocent, seeing them as leaders in the technology industry that was most responsible for the incremental destruction of mankind and nature.

The first bombing incident took place in May 1978 when Kaczynski mailed a bomb to Professor Buckley Crist of Northwestern University. Upon receiving the package, Crist was immediately suspicious of the contents and contacted campus police. Officer Terry Marker responded and suffered minor injuries when he opened the package and a bomb exploded. Over the next seventeen years, Kaczynski sent sixteen more bombs. The last one sent before his capture resulted in the death of Gilbert P. Murray, a timber-industry lobbyist from Sacramento, California, on April 25, 1995.

The Unabomb case entailed the longest and costliest search for a serial killer in U.S. history, including 3,600 volumes of information, 20,000 telephone tips, 200 suspects, 175 computer databases, 82 million records, 12,000 event documents, and 9,000 evidence photographs. Kaczynski was meticulous in engineering the explosives and employed several measures to elude detection. He removed identification numbers from all batteries used in bombing devices, used only wires that were no longer in production, and never licked stamps so that he could not be identified by DNA testing.

In the summer of 1995, Kaczynski threatened to bomb a plane during the Fourth of July weekend unless his essay *Industrial Society and Its Future* was published in *The New York Times* and the *Washington Post*. The U.S. Justice Department urged publication to avoid risking public safety, but the appearance of the 35,000-word manifesto was criticized in other circles for setting a precedent of appeasement for future terrorists.

As it turned out, publishing the essay proved to be the critical step in solving the case, because the Unabomber's brother David Kaczynski recognized the ideology and rhetoric. They resembled the ideas and language in writings by Theodore that had been discovered in their mother's attic. David's attorney contacted the FBI and provided them with information leading to his brother's arrest on April 3, 1996.

The FBI confiscated more than seven hundred pieces of incriminating evidence from the cabin, including a half-constructed and a fully assembled bomb, as well as the typewriter used to draft the manifesto. In return, David Kaczynski received the $1 million reward, which he apportioned to the families of victims and his brother's defense counsel.

A court-appointed psychiatrist diagnosed Theodore Kaczynski as a paranoid schizophrenic prone to delusions and violence, but found him mentally competent to stand trial. A full trial was precluded, however, when Kaczynski pleaded guilty to thirteen federal bombing offenses. After insisting that his faculties were rational, he conceded to pleading insanity to circumvent the death penalty.

In May 1998, the Unabomber was sentenced to four consecutive life terms and remanded to a maximum-security facility in Florence, Colorado. He continued appealing the case to the United States Court of Appeals for the Ninth Circuit on various grounds, including the grounds that his Sixth Amendment rights—including the right to a speedy and public trial by an impartial jury—were violated.

Giuseppe M. Fazari

Further Reading

Chase, Alston. *Harvard and the Unabomber: The Making of an American Terrorist.* New York: W.W. Norton, 2003.

Morrow, Lance, Nancy Gibbs, Richard Lacayo, and Jill Smolowe. *Mad Genius: The Odyssey, Pursuit and Capture of the Unabomber Suspect.* New York: Warner, 1996.

Underground Railroad

The Underground Railroad was a vast, secret network of individuals and safe houses and other facilities that helped slaves escape from their owners in the American South to freedom in the North and Canada before and during the Civil War. A scattered system had begun to take shape in the late eighteenth century, but it was not referred to as the Underground Railroad until the early 1830s. In the decades that followed, the network helped tens of thousands of slaves reach freedom.

The early system consisted primarily of free blacks, escaped or freed slaves, and a few white abolitionists. With the spread of the abolitionist movement, more whites joined in the clandestine effort. The network was most active in Ohio, Pennsylvania, and Indiana, with efforts and facilities throughout the Northern states.

The Underground Railroad was neither underground nor a railroad, but adopted the nomenclature of the newly emerging rail system. Individuals who helped slaves begin their journey to freedom were termed "agents." Those moving fugitives between stations were called "conductors," and the places providing food and shelter were known as "stations." The "stationmasters" who ran them were themselves undertaking great risk

by their involvement. Once escaping slaves made connection with the railroad or "obtained a ticket," they were referred to as "passengers" or "cargo." Others, not directly associated with the railroad itself, provided financial support and were referred to as "stockholders."

Although the connections to the North were well organized, utilizing regular routes, individuals were seldom aware of stations beyond their own immediate locations, which provided security for those working the railroad and for those escaping to freedom. Demand from the South for effective legislation to reduce escapes resulted in the Fugitive Slave Law of 1850 requiring runaways to be returned to their owners, thus increasing the danger for those trying to escape to the North as well as for those assisting them.

Fugitives generally would travel from 10 to 20 miles (16 to 32 kilometers) a day, mostly at night and by foot or wagon. Occasionally, transportation was arranged and paid for by Northern supporters, who would provide appropriate clothing for the fugitives to be transported by ship or rail. Routes often were indirect to avoid discovery, with information passed only by word of mouth; however, fugitives frequently followed routes parallel to common landmarks, such as the Appalachian Mountains or the Mississippi River.

The Underground Railroad spanned a number of states, including Kentucky and Virginia, Ohio and Indiana, and traversed north from Maryland, across Pennsylvania to New York and New England. Often, the journey was too arduous for women and children, whose numbers were far below those of men who successfully fled north. According to some estimates, between 80,000 and 100,000 slaves escaped to the North between 1800 and 1850. Once freed, many men worked to earn sufficient funds to purchase their families out of slavery.

Religious supporters of the Underground Railroad belonged to several denominations including Congregationalists, Methodists, Presbyterians, Quakers, and Wesleyans. Additionally, Northern vigilance committees were established in many of the larger cities to raise money to support the railroad. Well-known figures associated with the Underground Railroad include Isaac Hopper, David Ruggles, William Still, Josiah Henson, John Fairfield, Levi Coffin, the legendary Harriet Tubman, and many others.

Hopper, a Quaker, began helping slaves escape north in the late 1890s. He was active in the antislavery movement in New York and Philadelphia and utilized nonviolent methods for hiding and protecting fugitives.

Charles Webber's painting *Fugitives Arriving at Levi Coffin's Indiana Farm* (1850) dramatizes the ordeal of runaway slaves and the Underground Railroad operatives who led them to freedom. The secret network constituted America's first civil rights movement. *(MPI/Stringer/Hulton Archive/Getty Images)*

By the late 1830s, Hopper was joined in the antislavery movement by Ruggles, a New Yorker and America's first black bookseller, publisher of the antislavery magazine *Mirror of Liberty,* and author of several antislavery pamphlets, including *Extinguisher, Extinguished* (1834) and *Abrogation of the Seventh Commandment by the American Churches* (1835). Ruggles is credited with helping escaped slave Frederick Douglass upon his arrival in New York as well as with assisting over 1,000 slaves who traveled on the New York portion of the Underground Railroad.

Still, a slave until his family's escape to New Jersey, taught himself to read and eventually became the secretary of the Pennsylvania Abolition Society; his home became one of the busiest stations on the Underground Railroad. Known as the "father of the Underground Railroad," Still is credited with helping more than 600 slaves to freedom, the account of which he published in the most comprehensive contemporary book on the subject, *The Underground Railroad* (1872).

Henson, like Still, had been born a slave (in Maryland). He escaped to Canada. His life changed when he was introduced to Harriet Beecher Stowe and became the inspiration for Uncle Tom in Stowe's novel *Uncle Tom's Cabin* (1852). Henson traveled extensively throughout the remainder of his life, lecturing and writing about his experiences as Uncle Tom.

Douglass, born a slave and hired out by his master, learned to read under the tutelage of his master's wife. After many years of enslavement, Douglass eventually escaped to New York, where he became one of the nation's most prominent abolitionists and spokesmen against slavery. Also one of the most sought-after runaway slaves, eventually he was forced to flee to England, where his freedom was purchased by other abolitionists. Upon his return to America, as a free man, Douglass began publishing the influential antislavery newspaper *The North Star.* His home in Rochester became a frequent station on the Underground Railroad.

Another Quaker and abolitionist well known for his work on the Underground Railroad was Coffin, often referred to as the "president of the Underground Railroad." His home in Fountain City (then Newport), Indiana, became known as the "Grand Central Station" of the Underground Railroad. With his wife, Catharine, Levi Coffin assisted over 2,000 slaves to safety, most going north to Canada.

The best-known conductor on the railroad was undoubtedly Tubman, a former slave who became known as "Moses" for the nineteen trips she made into the South to escort hundreds of slaves, including her parents and other family members, to freedom. A resolute leader, Tubman carried a revolver, navigated by the North Star, told time by the positions of the sun and moon, and outwitted pursuing slave catchers. With the passage of the Fugitive Slave Law in 1850, Tubman was forced to escort fugitives farther north into Canada. During the Civil War, she worked as a Union spy, commanding a group of black soldiers who worked as spies and scouts. Sometimes referred to as "Old Chariot" because of the spirituals she sang to inform slaves of her presence, Tubman remained active after the war, working for the rights of blacks and women and establishing a home for the aged and indigent in Auburn, New York.

The Underground Railroad was perhaps the largest act of civil disobedience to take place in the United States in support of the rights of black Americans, and it constituted an unparalleled protest against slavery. At the conclusion of the Civil War, in 1865, with the Underground Railroad no longer needed, many of the conductors and other volunteers, like Tubman, turned their attention to working for the economic, social, and political equality of the newly freed Americans.

Pat Tyrer

See also: Abolitionism; African Americans; Douglass, Frederick; Oberlin College; Quakers.

Further Reading

Blight, David W., ed. *Passages to Freedom: The Underground Railroad in History and Memory.* Washington, DC: Smithsonian Institution, 2004.

Bordewich, Fergus M. *Bound for Canaan: The Epic Story of the Underground Railroad, America's First Civil Rights Movement.* New York: Amistad, 2006.

Snodgrass, Mary Ellen. *The Underground Railroad: An Encyclopedia of People, Places, and Operations.* Armonk, NY: M.E. Sharpe, 2007.

Still, William. *The Underground Railroad: Authentic Narratives and First-Hand Accounts.* 1872. Ed. Ian Frederick Finseth. Mineola, NY: Dover, 2007.

Unification Church

See Moonies

Unitarianism

In the broadest and earliest sense, Unitarianism refers to a version of Christian belief that rejects the concept of trinitarianism (the belief that God is a singular being who exists simultaneously as a holy trinity—Father, Son, and Holy Ghost), a dominant doctrine in Western Christianity since it was declared at the Council of Nicea in 325 C.E. More narrowly, however, Unitarianism describes a liberal Christian denomination that over the years has become a creedless religious community that attracts people from across the spectrum of belief. It emerged in the late eighteenth century and has, at various times, been an important part of the counterculture of the United States.

Rejection of Orthodoxy

American Unitarianism emerged primarily from a schism among the Calvinist Congregationalist churches of New England during the eighteenth century. One issue that set the stage for the development of Unitarianism was the emotional revivals of the Great Awakening that swept through the American colonies between about 1720 and 1750. In New England, these religious revivals stressed traditional aspects of Calvinist theology—the need for faith, the salvation offered to a select few though the death of Jesus Christ, and the damnation that awaited those not of the elect.

Many questioned this theology, and some ministers began to reject Calvinist orthodoxy. As these religious liberals gained ground in New England, they came into conflict with more conservative religious leaders. The antagonism erupted into open combat when a religious liberal, Henry Ware, was appointed to the prestigious Hollis Chair of Divinity at Harvard University in 1805. Many conservatives left the university in protest and formed their own institution, the Andover Theological Seminary, in 1808. In the years that followed, Harvard became the center of nineteenth-century American Unitarianism.

The antagonism between conservatives and Unitarians among New England Congregationalists continued for decades. One crucial moment came in 1819, when the prominent minister William Ellery Channing gave his sermon "Unitarian Christianity," setting out the tenets of this brand of liberal faith. Then in 1825, the Unitarians broke away and formed the American Unitarian Association (AUA). By this time, Unitarianism had become very popular in New England, and the vast majority of Congregationalist churches in Massachusetts joined the new organization.

Although Unitarianism started as a liberal Christian denomination, adherents gradually rejected more concepts associated with Christian orthodoxy. In the decades following the organization of the AUA, they abandoned original sin, the virgin birth, the inerrancy of the Bible, the belief in Jesus Christ as a divine savior and belief in his miracles, the tenant of predestination, the anticipation of Judgment Day, and the existence of hell. In place of traditional doctrine, Unitarian ministers presented a rational form of Christianity that celebrated human nature and human reason and made no claims for exclusive possession of religious truth. Unitarians held that both religion and reason were essential to determining truth and believed that science, far from being a challenge to religious belief, offered another way to better understand God and nature.

In the nineteenth century, Unitarianism's abandonment of many traditional Christian doctrines made it an attractive denomination for those with radical religious beliefs or reformist goals. Many of the most well-known countercultural movements of the period had extensive connections with Unitarianism. In the 1830s, many notable transcendentalists, including minister Theodore Parker and poet Ralph Waldo Emerson, were Harvard-trained Unitarian clergymen. Both movements were centered in New England, and Unitarianism's views of God and nature drew strongly from transcendentalist writers and thinkers. During the antebellum years, the Unitarian rejection of tradition also made it a natural home for many like Adin Ballou, who worked for the abolition of slavery, and Susan B. Anthony, who campaigned for women's rights and suffrage.

Modern Developments

Since the nineteenth century, Unitarians have held as one of their primary tenets that the church should not impede each individual's freedom of conscience in spiritual matters. Because of this belief, the Unitarians abandoned expectations that members have any particular beliefs, including in the existence of God. Unitarianism, therefore, attracts many who believe in the importance of communal cooperation to reach individual spiritual or social goals but reject the imposition of religious dogma.

In 1961, the American Unitarian Association united with the Universalist Church of America to form the Unitarian Universalist Association (UUA), bringing together two liberal denominations with a shared opposition to the imposition of doctrine. Since that time, Unitarian Universalists have described themselves in a variety of ways, most often claiming identities as humanist, agnostic, atheist, Buddhist, Pagan, and Christian. Given their varied identifications, Unitarians have been champions of religious pluralism and have sought to build bridges among various denominations and religious groups.

The wide variance of individual beliefs, however, has not prevented Unitarians from working together for social causes. In the twentieth century, the UUA was an active part of movements for peace, environmental protection, human rights, and social justice. During the 1960s, many Unitarian Universalist churches were outspoken in their opposition to the Vietnam War and joined the effort to freeze nuclear-weapons production. In 1967, the General Assembly of the UUA passed a resolution to urge the federal government to "broaden the concept of conscientious objection" and formally extended "support to those persons who in the exercise of their moral choice . . . refuse to register for Selective Service."

Unitarians were also a vocal part of the campaign for civil and political rights for African Americans. James Reeb, a Unitarian minister serving in Washington, D.C., was beaten to death by segregationists during the march on Selma, Alabama, in 1965. His murder added to the national outrage over the violence that met the civil rights movement in the Deep South.

More recently, Unitarian ministers have played a leading role in performing wedding ceremonies for same-sex couples and in 2004 presided over the first legally sanctioned same-sex marriage, at the Arlington Street Church in Boston, Massachusetts.

Throughout the twentieth century, the membership of the UUA has varied greatly, expanding significantly after the merger in 1961 before declining in the following decade. At the beginning of the twenty-first century, there were more than 1,000 UUA congregations in the United States, with the estimated number of Unitarian Universalists ranging from 250,000 to 500,000.

Stephen D. Andrews

See also: Emerson, Ralph Waldo; Transcendentalism; Vietnam War Protests.

Further Reading

Conkin, Paul. *American Originals: Homemade Varieties of Christianity.* Chapel Hill: University of North Carolina Press, 1997.

Howe, Daniel Walker. *The Unitarian Conscience: Harvard Moral Philosophy, 1805–1861.* Cambridge, MA: Harvard University Press, 1970.

Olds, Mason. "Unitarian-Universalism: An Interpretation Through Its History." In *America's Alternative Religions,* ed. Timothy Miller. Albany: State University of New York Press, 1995.

United Farm Workers

The United Farm Workers Organizing Committee (UFWOC) emerged during the formational years of the Chicano Movement, the unprecedented mobilization of Chicanos across the United States on behalf of their civil rights in the 1960s and 1970s. Formed in August 1966, the UFWOC became the leading force for farmworkers' rights in the United States, especially the Southwest. Although some attempts at organizing farmworkers in California predated the UFWOC (which later changed its name to the United Farmworkers of America, or UFW), it was not until 1966 that these attempts merged under the union affiliation of the American Federation of Labor–Congress of Industrial Organizations (AFL-CIO).

Origins

The struggles for worker rights in the California agricultural system during the 1960s were about more than labor. The larger target was the ideology of a dominant American culture that treated migrant workers as less than human, robbing them of fair wages, education, and basic living conditions.

In the early 1960s, two groups worked diligently to redress institutional discrimination against field workers, the majority of whom were Mexicans, Mexican Americans, and Filipinos, with small minorities of blacks and whites. One of the two groups, the Agricultural Workers Organizing Committee (AWOC), largely a Filipino organization, was having trouble standing up to California growers, especially grape growers in the Delano area. The other group, co-founded by César Chávez and Dolores Huerta in 1962, was called the National Farm Workers Association (NFWA). In 1965, the NFWA, a heavily Mexican American organization, voted to join the Filipinos in their strike against grape growers.

Together, the AWOC and the NFWA fought discrimination and stereotypes, while also pressing for the right to unionize. Chávez led the striking workers in nonviolent demonstrations as they tried to enlist the support of more workers. This was an uphill battle, as the growers had access to strikebreakers and injunctions against the picketing. However, the Chicano Movement as a larger cultural phenomenon was emerging at about the same time, with Chicanos from all walks of life becoming committed to the cause of economic and social freedom. One of the most significant alliances formed during this period was between the NFWA/AWOC and El Teatro Campesino (The Farmworkers' Theater), an activist theater group under the leadership of Luis Valdez, himself a native of Delano and son of migrant laborers.

El Teatro Campesino had members who traveled with the NFWA/AWOC into the fields and on marches, and it was central to the effort, recruiting workers as actors in its plays and then into the movement. The early productions were of short, one-act plays (called *actos*) designed to allow workers to express themselves and describe their conditions by taking on a variety of roles and improvising based on their experiences.

Other artistic alliances also were formed, as artists created posters and banners to be carried in the fields and displayed in the cities in support of the cause. Many plays and art pieces recalled Mexican and Aztec heritage, celebrating the Chicanos' "brown" racial ancestry. Thus, rather than being ashamed of their racial identity, Chicanos reminded themselves through art that they could be and would be proud of that heritage.

Also central to the UFW's formation was a march led by Chávez from Delano to Sacramento, California,

César Chávez, the founder and leader of the United Farm Workers, leads a union rally in California during the late 1970s. Chávez and the UFW won gains for migrant workers through strikes, boycotts, protests, and lobbying. *(FPG/Hulton Archive/Getty Images)*

in early 1966. The march took demonstrators across a stretch of the San Joaquin Valley, which was notoriously hostile to the workers' cause, and constituted a direct challenge to the segregation historically practiced and enforced there.

Moreover, the identity of the workers as Mexican Americans was evident in many aspects of this march and throughout the campaign. A banner of the Virgin of Guadalupe, the patroness of Mexicans and a figure central to their native heritage, was held high at the front of the procession. At the same time, however, the workers expressed their dual heritage as both Mexicans and Americans—while not fitting completely in either culture or social milieu.

From this contradiction emerged the Chicano voice and sensibility. Signs and flags representing Chicano identity, from the Aztec eagle to the Mexican and U.S. flags, along with such slogans as *"Peregrina, Penitencia, Revolución"* ("Pilgrimage, Penitence, Revolution"), called attention to the history and determination of the Mexican American people.

Here and elsewhere, Chávez and his followers also professed their Roman Catholic faith by attending mass regularly, sometimes daily. This often angered the growers, whose families attended the same churches as workers and who resented the strikers' use of religious imagery to suggest that God was on their side.

Growth and Merger

After the NFWA and AWOC officially merged under the UFW in mid-1966, its leaders and members had much work ahead with respect to the grape strikes. Their efforts for fair working conditions and an end to racism and oppression in labor ultimately brought national attention to the organization and much of national sentiment to their side. Young Chicano activists, including the influential Eliseo Medina, traveled east and eventually rallied a number of mayors and other civic leaders to the farmworkers' cause. The boycott of California non-union-label grapes even extended overseas. Finally, in 1970, the grape growers, who had held out for years, sat down to sign new contracts.

While the issue of racism against Mexican American workers was not fully resolved by the farmworkers' victory, it was significant that the UFW had managed to convince wholesalers and retailers, not just shoppers, to boycott nonunion grapes. This was a sign that mainstream American society was listening to a greater degree than ever before to what Chicanos were saying about the work they did and the treatment they re-

ceived in the fields. The strikes and demonstrations became the foundation of the fledgling Chicano civil rights movement and labor organization across the United States.

Significantly, strides on behalf of civil rights continued to be made under Chávez's model of nonviolent organizing. Beyond the successes on behalf of Chicano workers in the 1960s and 1970s and its continued advocacy on behalf of all field workers, the legacy of the UFW is far-reaching. Where it continues to operate, the UFW lobbies for fair living and working conditions for field workers and their communities, along with serving outreaches such as La Campesina Radio Network (Farmworker radio). As one of the moving forces in the social, economic, and cultural history of the American Southwest, the UFW continues to pursue the vision of Chávez and Huerta, and to serve their legacy of hope for marginalized peoples.

Jean Anne Lauer

See also: Chávez, César; Chicano Movement.

Further Reading

Broyles-González, Yolanda. *El Teatro Campesino: Theater in the Chicano Movement.* Austin: University of Texas Press, 1994.

Gutiérrez, David G. *Walls and Mirrors: Mexican Americans, Mexican Immigrants, and the Politics of Ethnicity.* Berkeley: University of California Press, 1995.

Maciel, David R., and Isidro D. Ortiz, eds. *Chicanas/Chicanos at the Crossroads: Social, Economic, and Political Change.* Tucson: University of Arizona Press, 1996.

Universal Negro Improvement Association

The Universal Negro Improvement Association (UNIA) was a black nationalist organization of the early twentieth century that advocated building commercial ties between African Americans and Africa, as well as the emigration of African Americans to Africa. The association was founded in Jamaica by the charismatic black separatist Marcus Garvey in 1914, and it moved its headquarters to New York City in 1916, eventually expanding internationally.

Beginnings

Garvey, a native of Jamaica, had just returned from four years of travel in Central America and Europe when he organized the association, originally intended as a benevolent organization devoted to social and economic reform. Garvey had witnessed the racism that pervaded the "new imperialism" of Europeans in Africa and the massive pressures that expanding capitalism and governments placed on rural blacks, whether from America, the West Indies, or Africa. For workers who felt disenfranchised from society at large, the UNIA, like other nationalist and Pan-African organizations, provided a sense of belonging.

When Garvey relocated to New York in 1916, the UNIA was still a fledgling organization, not having yet amassed a substantial membership. This changed when Garvey settled in Harlem and brought the UNIA headquarters to New York. Starting with fewer than twenty members, its strong advocacy for black economic and political independence attracted many new members within the first year. New branches began to emerge across the country and would later take hold worldwide. To circulate the ideas of the organization, the UNIA began publishing *The Negro World,* a weekly newspaper, in 1918; circulation would eventually exceed 500,000. By 1920, membership had so expanded that there were nearly 1,000 branches in over forty countries throughout the Americas and Africa.

In 1920, the UNIA held its first international convention, at Madison Square Garden in New York City. At the convention, members promulgated the *Declaration of Rights of the Negro Peoples of the World,* seeking to uplift the black race by encouraging self-reliance and nationhood. The declaration listed a number of grievances and demanded their resolution. Demands were made for ending racially motivated practices such as lynching, standardizing the capitalization of the N in the word Negro, and teaching children black history in public schools. Among the declarations was the adoption of a red, black, and green flag as the official banner of the UNIA and a symbol of the entire African race.

Culture

In an attempt to unify the black community, the UNIA sought inclusive participation by creating a place for men, women, and children in the organization. Male members were able to join the Universal African Legion and the Black Eagle Flying Corps, both uniformed paramilitary groups.

Women, although subordinate to male members, were given a place of their own within the movement: membership in the Black Cross Nurses and the Universal African Motor Corps. The Black Cross Nurses, modeled on the Red Cross, were organized at the local

level. The group performed benevolent work, providing public health-care services in black communities. The Universal African Motor Corps was a female auxiliary that was affiliated with the all-male African Legion. Members of the Motor Corps were trained in military discipline and automobile driving and repair.

Youth divisions were organized according to age and, after the age of seven, by gender. The youngest children, ages one through seven, were taught the Bible, the doctrine of the UNIA, and the history of Africa. Between the ages of eight and thirteen, all children received further education in black history and etiquette. After the age of thirteen, education for girls included lessons on hygiene and domestic service in preparation for participation in the Black Cross Nurses. Boys of this age received military training, preparing them for admission to the African League.

Garvey instituted several auxiliary business ventures within the UNIA. The Negro Factories Corporation, incorporated in 1919 with capitalization of $1 million, generated income and provided jobs in its varied commercial enterprises—grocery stores, restaurants, laundries, tailor and dress-making shops, and a publishing house. The Black Star Steamship Line, a Delaware corporation financed by selling shares to UNIA members and public investors, was also incorporated in 1919. The Black Star Line did not have unanimous support, however, and opponents questioned Garvey's veracity, calling for an accounting of UNIA funds.

The Back to Africa Program, endorsed by the UNIA, had a multifaceted purpose. On one hand, the goal was to uplift and redeem Africa with American blacks taking the lead. From another perspective, the goal was to repatriate African Americans. Beginning in 1921, efforts were made to establish a site in Liberia for UNIA members who were interested in living in Africa. In 1921, an official delegation traveled to Liberia to survey a potential location for those desiring to immigrate.

Initial interaction between the UNIA and Liberian officials was positive. Later, however, Liberian president Charles D.B. King ordered all of the nation's ports closed to members of the UNIA. Some have suggested that King's reversal of attitude was the result of an agreement between Liberia and the Firestone Rubber Company granting Firestone the use of land originally intended for the UNIA. In any event, the lockout by the Liberian government dealt a harsh blow to the UNIA and virtually ended the African repatriation program.

While the UNIA was likely the largest unified black organization of its time, it was not without its problems. Garvey governed the association absolutely, intolerant of even the smallest challenges to his authority, a fact that caused dissension among some of its members. The U.S. government, meanwhile, suspected the UNIA of being subversive and allowed J. Edgar Hoover and the Bureau of Investigation (the forerunner of the Federal Bureau of Investigation, or FBI) to investigate the activities of the association, coordinating their efforts with other federal agencies. European governments distrusted Garvey and his organization because they threatened European colonization. The National Association for the Advancement of Colored People (NAACP) and other organizations advocating integration spoke out against the UNIA because it favored black separatism rather than integration.

Perhaps the greatest blows to the association were Garvey's incarceration (1925–1927) for federal mail fraud in connection with the Black Star Line and his subsequent deportation. Upon his return to Jamaica, Garvey continued his involvement with the UNIA until his death in 1940.

As subsequent leaders directed the UNIA, Garvey's ideas continued to hold sway with the black masses in America. Roi Ottley, a Harlem journalist, explained this influence, noting that Garvey was responsible for instigating the race and color consciousness that continues to inspire black reform efforts.

Joann M. Ross

See also: African Americans; Garvey, Marcus.

Further Reading

Clarke, John Henrik, ed. *Marcus Garvey and the Vision of Africa.* New York: Random House, 1974.

Cronon, Edmund David. *Black Moses: The Story of Marcus Garvey and the Universal Negro Improvement Association.* Madison: University of Wisconsin Press, 1968.

Gates, Henry Louis, Jr., and Cornel West. *The African-American Century: How Black Americans Have Shaped Our Country.* New York: Free Press, 2000.

Lewis, Rupert, and Patrick Bryan, eds. *Garvey: His Work and Impact.* Trenton, NJ: Africa World Press, 1991.

Martin, Tony. *Race First: The Ideological and Organizational Struggles of Marcus Garvey and the Universal Negro Improvement Association.* Westport, CT: Greenwood, 1976.

Stein, Judith. *The World of Marcus Garvey: Race and Class in Modern Society.* Baton Rouge: Louisiana State University Press, 1986.

Up Against the Wall Motherfucker

Up Against the Wall Motherfucker (UAW/MF) was an artistically oriented, anarchist street gang that formed in New York City's Lower East Side in 1967. Colloquially referred to as the Motherfuckers, the group championed an aggressive "politics of confrontation" and was well known in the neighborhood until its demise in mid-1969.

Although the UAW/MF had no formal hierarchy, many regard Ben Morea as the group's de facto leader. Morea, who grew up on the streets of New York City, became friends in the early 1960s with Julian Beck and Judith Malina, cofounders of the Living Theatre, an experimental, politically radical stage group.

In 1966, Morea launched *Black Mask,* a short-lived, crudely mimeographed arts magazine. He also was peripherally involved with Angry Arts Week, a January 1967 festival that brought together hundreds of New York City artists in condemnation of the Vietnam War. The UAW/MF emerged out of *Black Mask,* Angry Arts Week, and the influence of the militant Black Power movement of the late 1960s, which inspired an outpouring of Afrocentric expression in the realms of art, literature, fashion, verbal expression, and other cultural arenas.

The Motherfuckers, which took its name from a poem by LeRoi Jones (later Amiri Baraka) titled "Black People," never had more than a few dozen full-time members. Their ranks included an Ivy League dropout, autodidacts, and barely literate street people, who together carved out a unique niche in the counterculture. While generally sympathetic to the hippies, they often chided the flower children for weakness. The Motherfuckers had a tenuous connection with the Students for a Democratic Society (SDS), the New Left's main political organization, but they recoiled from the group's sectarian political debates and regarded even the most militant students as cloistered and unreliable. Probably the countercultural group the UAW/MF most resembled was the Diggers, an artistically inclined, utopian-minded collective that championed an ethos of maximum personal freedom and set up various counterinstitutions around the Haight-Ashbury neighborhood of San Francisco.

For all their connections to other countercultural movements, the UAW/MF set itself apart with a dark and angry temperament. Some members owned guns and knives, and their broadsheets—frequently published in a militant underground newspaper, *The Rat*—trumpeted the most extreme formulations of the counterculture cosmology. Some of their actions included dumping garbage near the fountain at Lincoln Center for the Performing Arts in midtown Manhattan; cutting the fences and raiding the concession stands at the August 1969 Woodstock music festival in Bethel, New York; strong-arming promoter Bill Graham into letting East Village denizens have free use of his rock club, the Fillmore East; and building support for Valerie Solanas, the tormented feminist who tried to assassinate pop artist Andy Warhol in 1968. The group also set up crash pads for teenage runaways, and it briefly ran a "free store" and a radical coffee shop, the Common Ground.

In 1968, Morea was involved in a melee on Boston Common in which two men were stabbed; in January 1969, he was acquitted of assault and battery with a dangerous weapon. By early 1969, many Motherfuckers sensed that increasing crackdowns by New York City's Ninth Precinct's Tactical Police Force (TPF) and the influx of heroin and amphetamines into the Lower East Side meant that the neighborhood was no longer ideal as a base of operations. As a result, the group slowly disbanded.

A few former members affiliated with the Hog Farm, a famous commune in Northern California. Others spent time in Canjilón, New Mexico, among followers of the militant Indio-Hispanic activist Reies Tijerina (also known as "King Tiger"). Morea and his wife moved to the Sangre de Cristo Mountains in the American Southwest, where they lived, illegally and traveling mostly on horseback, for several years.

John McMillian

See also: Anarchism; Black Power Movement; Living Theatre; Students for a Democratic Society.

Further Reading

Hahne, Ron. *Black Mask and Up Against the Wall Motherfucker: The Incomplete Works of Ron Hahne, Ben Morea, and the Black Mask Group.* London: Unpopular Books and Sabotage Editions, 1993.

McCarthy, Timothy Patrick, and John McMillian, eds. *The Radical Reader: A Documentary History of the American Radical Tradition.* New York: New Press, 2003.

Patterson, Clayton, ed. *Resistance: A Radical Social and Political History of the Lower East Side.* New York: Seven Stories, 2007.

Utopianism

Utopianism is the pursuit of an ideal society or community in which the inhabitants live under seemingly perfect conditions. Hence *utopia* and *utopian* are words used to denote an ideal that is likely to be unrealistic and ultimately unattainable.

The word *utopia* first appeared as the title of Sir Thomas More's book-length essay, published in Latin in 1516, about an ideal island community called Utopia. More fashioned the name for his mythical island from an amalgamation of the Greek words *ou* (no) and *topos* (place), and thus "utopia" was "nowhere." However, the concept of utopia is considerably older than its name; Plato's *Republic,* written during the fourth century B.C.E., was perhaps the first comprehensive description of an ideal society. Plato's version of utopia served as the model for countless others, including Tomaso Campanella's *The City of the Sun* (1623), Sir Francis Bacon's *The New Atlantis* (1627), Samuel Butler's *Erewhon* (1872), Edward Bellamy's *Looking Backward: 2000–1887* (1888), William Morris's *News from Nowhere* (1891), and H.G. Wells's *A Modern Utopia* (1905).

Utopianism in the United States, whether based on religious tenets, secular idealism, or economic necessity, has been manifested most often in planned residential communities founded and run by individuals who desired to withdraw from society and to live together harmoniously in their quest for perfection. For nonconformists forced to flee Europe for reasons of religious and political persecution, pre-colonial America—with its vast and relatively inexpensive land and an ideology of tolerance espoused by William Penn in Pennsylvania, Lord Baltimore in Maryland, and Roger Williams in Rhode Island, among others—was an extremely attractive refuge.

The first documented utopian community in the United States was founded in 1663 on the Delaware shore, near the present-day town of Lewes. Dutch Mennonite Pieter Cornelisz Plockhoy van Zierikzee established the settlement, known as the Valley of the Swans or Horekill. At that site, Plockhoy attempted to realize his utopian vision, as outlined in his treatise of 1659, *The Way to the Peace and Settlement of These Nations.* The text included two petitions for peaceful utopian existence to England's lord protector, Oliver Cromwell. Although the community failed after one year, the Valley of the Swans is recognized as the first colony in North America to ban slavery.

Religious Utopias

Many religious utopian societies established in North America were millennial groups preparing for the Second Coming of Christ. Johann Conrad Beissel established the community of Ephrata in Lancaster County, Pennsylvania, in 1732. The celibate brothers and sisters of Ephrata subscribed to an ideal of moral perfectionism that could be attained only through self-denial and strenuous labor. Noted for its printing facilities and accomplishments in calligraphy and choral music, the community declined after the American Revolution and was legally disbanded in 1814. However, smaller settlements in the Ephrata tradition flourished well into the nineteenth century.

The most successful of the nineteenth-century American utopian communities was established by the Shakers, officially known by several names, including the United Society of Believers in Christ's Second Appearing and the Shaking Quakers. Led by Ann Lee, they were a radical offshoot of English Quakers who had adopted the French Camisards' ritual practices of shaking, shouting, dancing, whirling, and singing in tongues when the Spirit came upon them. Shakers attempted to create a utopian existence in which feminism, pacifism, and abolitionism were the ideals. The first Shaker community was established in 1776 at Niskayuna (later Watervliet), New York. At its zenith in the 1840s, between 4,000 and 6,000 members resided in twenty Shaker villages from Maine to Indiana and Kentucky. Known for the simple beauty and craftsmanship of their furniture, the Shakers flourished economically. Two communities, in Maine and New Hampshire, existed into the late 1970s. The practice of celibacy, along with the inability to attract new members, led to increasingly fewer numbers of Shaker followers.

Several other religious utopian communities prospered in the United States during the nineteenth century. The attempt to create "heaven on earth" while striving to attain spiritual and physical perfection were ideals common to such societies as Harmony, Zoar, Amana, and Oneida.

Johann Georg Rapp's Harmony Society, similar to the Shakers in core beliefs, was one of the most successful. It flourished in Harmony, Pennsylvania (1805–1814), New Harmony, Indiana (1815–1825), and Economy, Pennsylvania (1825–1906). In Economy (present-day Ambridge), Rapp and his followers, known as Rappites, purchased 3,000 acres (1,214 hectares) of land and established themselves as industrious leaders on an ideal trade route on the Ohio River near Pittsburgh. In 1906, a century after its founding, the Harmony Society was officially dissolved.

Joseph Bimeler's Society of Separatists of Zoar, established in 1817, was another economic success. The Zoarites purchased a 5,500-acre (2,200-hectare) tract of land along the Tuscarawas River in east central Ohio.

Its magnificent community garden, which occupied an entire village square, symbolized their desire to create an Eden-like utopia. By 1852, the society's assets were valued at more than $1 million. In 1898, the remaining members decided to dissolve the society.

The Community of True Inspiration, later known as the Amana Society, established at Ebenezer, New York in 1844, and reestablished in Iowa in 1854, differed from the other religious communal societies in at least one key respect. The group did not have one strong individual as leader; rather, its Grand Council made the operational decisions. For the Inspirationists, the economic activity was subordinate to their religious ideal of living a devout and pious life. Money, property, and goods were shared by all members, as in other utopian organizations. In 1932, however, the members voted to disband the communal society and adopted a capitalistic economy.

John Humphrey Noyes's Oneida Perfectionists, relocated from Putney, Vermont, to Oneida, New York, in 1848, also differed from the other religious utopian societies. Noyes believed that only by living in a perfect environment could one live a life without sin. The inhabitants at Oneida lived together with all things, including marriage partners, in common. Noyes' belief in so-called complex marriage was viewed by outsiders as adulterous and sexually immoral. In 1881, Oneida became a joint-stock company involved primarily in the production of flatware, which has continued to the present.

Secular Utopias

Generally more short-lived than their religious counterparts, secular utopias typically were connected with a political or economic revolution. Significant secular communities included New Harmony, established in 1825 in Posey County, Indiana, by Robert Owen, a Welsh industrialist, who purchased the 30,000-acre (12,150-hectare) community, buildings and all, from the Harmony Society for the sum of $150,000 in an attempt to create a social utopia there; and Brook Farm, founded in 1841 at West Roxbury, Massachusetts, by George Ripley, a Unitarian minister and journalist who based his ideas on those of the French socialist Charles Fourier in an attempt to create a transcendentalist utopia.

Even though both New Harmony and Brook Farm became well established as self-sufficient communities with economic strength in agriculture and industry, these communities lasted less than a decade. However, these secular utopias were the ancestors of the antiestablishment communes prevalent in the United States during the twentieth century. These communes, most popular during the late 1960s, were largely created by antiestablishment protesters opposed to the Vietnam War, capitalism, and mainstream culture. Most of these communes, whose inhabitants were called hippies, dissolved within a few years. Several still flourish today.

Denise A. Seachrist

See also: Amana Society; Brook Farm; Communes; Ephrata Cloister; Harmony Society; Lee, Ann; Noyes, John Hunphrey; Oneida Community; Shakers.

Further Reading

Friesen, John W., and Virginia Lyon Friesen. *The Palgrave Companion to North American Utopias.* New York: Palgrave Macmillan, 2004.

Pitzer, Donald E., ed. *America's Communal Utopias.* Chapel Hill: University of North Carolina Press, 1997.

Sutton, Robert P. *Communal Utopias and the American Experience: Religious Communities, 1732–2000.* Westport, CT: Praeger, 2003.

———. *Communal Utopias and the American Experience: Secular Communities, 1824–2000.* Westport, CT: Praeger, 2004.

Vegetarianism

Vegetarianism—the practice of eating only foods from plants and avoiding all red meats, poultry, and even dairy products—dates back thousands of years. It has been variously adopted for religious, spiritual, ethical, and nutritional reasons. In the United States, the practice first gained a major following in the nineteenth century, out of concern for general health, wellness, and psychological well-being. It was not until the counterculture movement of the 1960s and 1970s, however, that vegetarianism became a widespread movement—albeit one still out of the mainstream.

The potential health benefits of vegetarianism began to be noted in eighteenth-century America, with Benjamin Franklin being an early advocate. General practice was limited, however, until various reform movements of the nineteenth century provided the catalysts for broader awareness.

Among the earliest of these was a dietary reform and temperance campaign initiated by a Presbyterian minister, Sylvester Graham, in the 1830s. Later called the "Father of Vegetarianism" in America, Graham preached on the dangers of alcohol and declared a link between the consumption of meat and the craving for alcohol. During the cholera epidemic of 1832, Graham began advocating a meatless diet to combat the general ill effects of meat on the human body. He went on to advocate a diet that banned not only meat but coffee, tea, spices, and white flour, as well as alcohol and tobacco. The coarse, whole wheat flour preferred by the Grahamites was made into a special bread, which eventually led to the development of the graham cracker.

Some advocates of other reform movements during the mid-nineteenth century, such as abolitionism and feminism, also adopted vegetarianism, as did members of various utopian communities in the 1840s. One such settlement was the Fruitlands community in Harvard, Massachusetts, founded in 1843 by the educator and transcendentalist Bronson Alcott. Residents of the community followed a strict vegetarian diet and ate Graham bread with fruit and vegetables grown on site. Although Fruitlands lasted less than two years, many of the ideas put into practice at the community would carry over to other reform activities.

Alcott helped to establish the Physiological and Health Association, essentially a vegetarian society. The Vegetarian Society of the United Kingdom was founded in 1847, followed three years later by the American Vegetarian Society. These organizations highlighted the interest in vegetarianism from several quarters, including the Grahamites, followers of Bronson, and advocates of a growing number of other health reform trends, such as hydropathy, or water cure. Also significant during this period was the rise of such religious groups as the Seventh-Day Adventists, who adopted vegetarianism under the leadership of cofounder Ellen G. White.

Following the American Civil War, vegetarianism continued to be advocated in a wide range of organizations, publications, and communities, such as Joyful News in California. Individuals such as brothers Dr. John Harvey Kellogg and W.K. (Will Keith) Kellogg helped push vegetarianism to new levels of awareness and acceptance, primarily concerning health-related issues. At the Battle Creek Sanitarium, run by John Harvey Kellogg in Michigan, the brothers developed toasted wheat flakes and other health foods that became popular with vegetarians. In 1906, W.K. Kellogg founded the Battle Creek Toasted Corn Flake Company (later the Kellogg Company) to merchandise the products.

Other aspects of vegetarianism became the principal causes of other groups, including animal rights; Professor J. Howard Moore, in particular, was one of the leading activists in the ethical treatment of animals in the early twentieth century. During the Progressive Era, the issue of the treatment of animals became a focal point of muckrakers such as Upton Sinclair, whose novel *The Jungle* (1905) presented a graphic representation of animal slaughter in the meatpacking plants in Chicago. And the early twentieth century also saw a number of other individuals picking up the message of vegetarianism, including the Boston socialite Maude R.L. Sharpe (later Freshel). Sharpe hosted vegetarian dinners and showed films of slaughterhouses at her home, and was known in the community for organizing an annual vegetarian Thanksgiving dinner at Boston's Copley Plaza Hotel.

From the Great Depression to the early 1960s, vegetarianism faded in popularity in the United States. The economic decline of the Depression era certainly played a role, but the influence of the medical profession and promotional efforts by the meat industry also were important factors. Physicians argued for the health benefits of eating meat, and the meat industry used an aggressive advertising campaign to promote its products. Vegetarian societies and publications continued to attract interest in some quarters, and the American Vegetarian Party was founded in 1948, but popular interest in vegetarianism remained minimal overall.

The rise of the youth counterculture in the mid-1960s led to a revival in vegetarianism for several reasons. The nonviolent focus of the movement and the emphasis on pacifism went beyond an antiwar focus to include the treatment of animals and their consumption. Coincidental with this was a rediscovery of Eastern philosophies and belief systems that endorsed meatless diets.

There also was increased concern about the health aspects of eating meat, poultry, and fish, not just because of the nature of the foods but also because the use of chemicals in the raising of these animals and of preservatives in packaging and distribution was increasing. Colorful personalities, such as Gypsy Boots, emerged on the West Coast, advocating a meatless diet and organic foodstuffs. To the ethical, religious, and health factors previously connected to vegetarianism was added that of concern for the environment, another movement rising from the counterculture movement.

James J. Kopp

See also: Fruitlands; Graham, Sylvester; Health Foods.

Further Reading

Iacobbo, Karen, and Michael Iacobbo. *Vegetarian America: A History.* Westport, CT: Praeger, 2004.
Spencer, Colin. *Vegetarianism: A History.* New York: Four Walls Eight Windows, 2002.
Stuart, Tristram. *The Bloodless Revolution: A Cultural History of Vegetarianism from 1600 to Modern Times.* New York: W.W. Norton, 2007.

Velvet Underground

See Reed, Lou

Venice, California

Venice, California, an incorporated part of the city of Los Angeles, is located 14 miles (22 kilometers) west of downtown on the Pacific Ocean, directly south of Santa Monica. A vibrant tourist destination whose Ocean Front Walk has attracted beachgoers, shops and restaurants, and a lively bohemian culture, Venice has been home to several distinctive countercultures, including the Beats of the 1950s and skate culture in the 1970s.

At the turn of the twentieth century, tobacco millionaire Abbot Kinney envisioned a "Venice of America" in the image of Italy's famous city of canals. Kinney had canals dug to drain marshland near the beach on which to build the town, creating an instant tourist attraction. When it opened on the Fourth of July in 1905, Venice of America featured an amusement pier, as well as gondolas and an arcaded street in the Venetian style. While the beach was a significant attraction, the town continued to grow in popularity with the addition of more amusement park attractions in the years that followed.

Local political problems plagued Venice in the early years, and it was annexed by the city of Los Angeles in October 1925. Most of the canals were filled in by the city, and the popular Venice Amusement Pier was closed when its lease expired in 1946. Little money was invested to rebuild the infrastructure of Venice, and the resulting cheap rents began attracting both European immigrants and young artists and writers.

As a result, Venice emerged during the 1950s as Southern California's most vibrant countercultural literary community. It is often linked with San Francisco's North Beach and New York's Greenwich Village as a center of Beat culture and art.

This movement centered on coffeehouse poetry readings, for which two notable venues in the area were the Gas House on Ocean Front Walk and the Venice West Café on Dudley Street. Lawrence Lipton, whose

The Pacific beach community of Venice, California—a haven for bohemians, Beat writers, artists, musicians, surfers, bodybuilders, and skateboarders through the twentieth century—continues to thrive on its countercultural image. *(David McNew/Getty Images)*

book *The Holy Barbarians* (1959) helped popularize the Beats, was a prominent figure in the Venice literary scene and an early proponent of poetry as an oral practice. Other writers associated with the scene included Charles Foster, "Mad Mike" Magdalani, Stuart Perkoff, and Alexander Trocchi.

The Los Angeles municipal government, meanwhile, came to regard the countercultural community as a threat and worked tirelessly to harass the young writers and artists in Venice. In 1961, the city adopted a new building code with the intent of tearing down 1,600 buildings in Venice. By 1965, one-third of the buildings had been razed.

During the 1970s, the area of Venice around the former Pacific Ocean Park, known as Dogtown, became home to a vibrant surf and skateboard community. The local Z-boys, a skateboarder team, are now credited with the creation of the skateboard counterculture, as well as with the practice of aerial skateboarding. Initially evincing the punk rock values of do-it-yourself culture, many of the Z-boys parlayed their passions for skating and surfing into lucrative careers as both sports skyrocketed in popularity during the 1980s and 1990s.

Venice also is well known as the home of Muscle Beach, the center of the postwar bodybuilding and fitness subculture. Originally based in Santa Monica and moving south in the 1950s, Muscle Beach Venice originally featured a small weight pen, which was replaced by a more modern facility in the 1990s. Despite rapid gentrification in recent years, Venice still remains home to many artists, surfers, skaters, and a variety of colorful personalities.

Susanne E. Hall

See also: Beat Generation; Los Angeles; Skateboarders; Surfing and Surfer Culture.

Further Reading

Maynard, John Arthur. *Venice West: The Beat Generation in Southern California.* New Brunswick, NJ: Rutgers University Press, 1993.

Stecyk, C.R., III, and Glen E. Friedman. *DogTown: The Legend of the Z-Boys.* New York: Burning Flags, 2002.

Vietnam War Protests

In response to the U.S. military involvement in the Vietnam War—specifically President Lyndon B. Johnson's decision to escalate fighting, by increasing the number of American troops in Southeast Asia in 1964 and 1965, and the drafting of young men to fight the war—protests involving thousands of antiwar and peace organizations sprang up across the United States. The protestors included citizens of all ethnicities, of all ages, and from all socioeconomic backgrounds. And although the antiwar campaign represented only one element of the broader civil rights and countercultural movements of the era, its actions generated much greater visibility, changed perceptions of the war at home, and caused a significant rent in American political and social life.

In spring 1965, faculty and activists at the University of Michigan organized the first of many "teach-ins," consisting of lectures and seminars aimed at educating the public about the Vietnam War and focusing attention on the issue of U.S. involvement. The practice soon spread to dozens of universities and colleges around the nation, attracting tens of thousands of participants who came to hear and see such well-known figures as radical journalist I.F. Stone, Dr. Benjamin Spock, novelist Norman Mailer, Senator Ernest Gruening (D-AK), well-known pacifist A.J. Muste, folk singers Phil Ochs and Joan Baez, and scores of other intellectuals, academics, and artists.

As the war escalated, it tended to consume the energies of activists involved in other groups and movements. Thus, established organizations such as the Students for a Democratic Society (SDS), the Women's International League for Peace and Freedom (WILPF), the Fellowship of Reconciliation (FOR), the War Resisters League (WRL), the American Friends Service

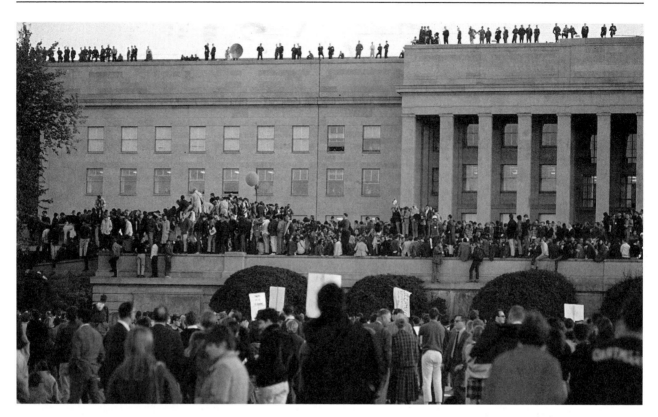

In October 1967, tens of thousands of Vietnam War protestors took part in an action called the March on the Pentagon. The declared intent was to physically levitate the building by exorcising the evil contained inside. Armed federal troops stood guard on the roof. *(Dick Swanson/Time & Life Pictures/Getty Images)*

Committee (AFSC), and others refocused their efforts on bringing about an end to the Vietnam War. These were just a few of the approximately 17,000 organizations that, by 1969, helped focus dissent and organize opposition to U.S. military efforts in Southeast Asia.

The proliferation of organizations reflected a highly decentralized, amorphous antiwar campaign. Decentralization, in fact, was perhaps the one constant and most outstanding feature of the movement. Anyone could belong to the movement, simply through his or her participation in an event. Thus, both large and small protests retained a local quality, while remaining part of large-scale national efforts such as the annual Spring Mobilizations, primarily nonviolent demonstrations involving people in cities across the nation.

Participation took a variety of forms. Protestors expressed their views by signing petitions, refusing to pay taxes, boycotting, marching, burning draft cards, attending teach-ins, refusing induction into the armed services, writing letters to political leaders, engaging in guerrilla street theater, and, on at least eight occasions, burning themselves to death in public. Such was

the nature of the movement. No national-level organization could hope to set a specific agenda or control the activities of countless individuals around the nation, each of whom held an indeterminate level of personal commitment.

The portrayal of the movement by the national media helped to create a caricature of its participants that has persisted into the twenty-first century: Antiwar counterculture types wore bell-bottomed blue jeans, sported facial hair and long manes, smoked marijuana and used other psychedelic drugs to excess, and generally were societal dropouts. In reality, participants in the antiwar movement came from all walks of American life. They were hippies, socialists, liberals, radicals, students, housewives, and working people. The anti–Vietnam War movement was one of the few social movements in American history in which anyone could find a place.

The movement continued to gain momentum and was increasingly a thorn in the side of the federal government, which was spending $1 million per day on the war and downplaying the number of dead being returned home. The movement grew in legitimacy as well, as figures such as Senator Robert Kennedy

(D-NY) and the Reverend Martin Luther King, Jr., publicly broke with the Johnson administration over its Vietnam policies in 1967.

Civil rights groups such as the Congress of Racial Equality (CORE) and the Student Nonviolent Coordinating Committee (SNCC) also denounced the government, condemned the war, and demanded the immediate withdrawal of all U.S. forces. In 1967, returning GIs formed the Vietnam Veterans Against the War (VVAW), adding considerable clout to the movement. The Spring Mobilization of 1967 attracted 250,000 protestors to a demonstration in New York City, while other events around the country attracted tens of thousands of marchers each.

Despite such momentum, the war continued. Antiwar activists grew increasingly frustrated and impatient with a federal government that seemed indifferent to the demands of millions of people.

The peace movement and the government fought an increasingly divisive and bitter battle over the war in Vietnam from the late 1960s to the early 1970s. As part of its Counter Intelligence Program, COINTELPRO, the Federal Bureau of Investigation (FBI) conducted a fierce secret campaign against movement members and participants. Thousands of Americans were spied on, harassed, intimidated, and jailed.

As the movement began to splinter in the late 1960s, activists fought back. Some, such as the radical Weathermen, resorted to violence. Others continued to express their views through public demonstrations and marches. A relative few quit altogether. The movement against the Vietnam War continued to fracture, however, its various factions pursuing different agendas and employing different tactics. By 1971, the movement was in complete disarray.

The antiwar campaign essentially ended as a national political force before the end of the war in 1975, but its influence was certain, if an enduring matter of controversy among participants and historians alike. To many in the military community, proponents of the war, and critics of the counterculture, the Vietnam War protestors had undermined the military effort, cast shame on the soldiers who had served their country, and abetted the interests of the enemy. In the view of participants and sympathizers, however, the protest movement hastened the end of an ill-fated, politically mistaken, immoral war.

James M. Carter

See also: Baez, Joan; Conscientious Objectors, Draft Dodgers, and Deserters; King, Martin Luther, Jr.; Pacifism; Spock, Benjamin; Stu-

dents for a Democratic Society; *Document:* Student Nonviolent Coordinating Committee Position Paper: On Vietnam (1966).

Further Reading

Buzzanco, Robert. *Vietnam and the Transformation of American Life.* Malden, MA: Blackwell, 1999.
DeBenedetti, Charles. *An American Ordeal: The Anti-War Movement of the Vietnam War.* Syracuse, NY: Syracuse University Press, 1990.
Small, Melvyn. *Antiwarriors: The Vietnam War and the Battle for America's Hearts and Minds.* Wilmington, DE: Scholarly Resources, 2002.

Village Voice, The

The Village Voice is a weekly, tabloid-sized, free, alternative newspaper based in New York City. Taking an antiestablishment perspective from the outset, *The Voice* has maintained a gadfly stance toward politics, government, and culture despite evolving into a larger, more commercial publishing enterprise. The paper was acquired in 2005 by the publishing conglomerate New Times Media.

The Voice was founded in New York's Greenwich Village in October 1955 by novelist Norman Mailer, journalist Dan Wolf, and financier Ed Fancher. Although its original focus was the cultural, political, and social scene in the Village, the focus of its investigative reporting, cultural criticism, and social commentary expanded over the years to include New York City and the nation. Originally an independent newspaper, *The Voice* has been owned by several successive corporations, among them Rupert Murdoch's News Corporation from 1977 to 1985, and by businessman Leonard Stern from 1985 to 2005, when it was sold to the Southwest-based alternative newspaper chain New Times Media.

The Voice is sometimes confused with the underground newspapers of the late 1960s, such as *Yarrowstalks* and *The East Village Other.* While clearly and intentionally an alternative newspaper, *The Voice* has always maintained a highly professional approach to its political and arts coverage, winning numerous Pulitzer Prizes and other journalistic awards.

Its news writers and political commentators over the years have included such notables as Murray Kempton, Wayne Barrett, and Nat Hentoff; writers on the arts have included theater critic John Lahr, movie critic Andrew Sarris, dance writer Deborah Jowitt, gossip columnist Michael Musto, and press critic Alexander Cockburn. The paper ran a cartoon strip by Jules Feiffer for many years; cartoonists Lynda Barry and

Robert Crumb have also contributed. Prestigious contributors from the literary world have ranged from Ezra Pound, Henry Miller, and E.E. Cummings to James Baldwin, Allen Ginsberg, and Tom Stoppard.

The Obie Awards, which the paper has bestowed annually since 1956, honor the best of off-Broadway theater. Its Pazz & Jop music awards recognize alternatives to the mainstream music honored by the Grammy Awards.

When the 1960s counterculture began to supplant the Beat movement of the 1950s, *The Voice* was there to chronicle social protest in New York City. Theater critic John Lahr, for example, covered the Living Theatre and other alternatives to traditional Broadway fare; in film, Jonas Mekas covered experimental filmmakers such as Jordan Belson and Stan Brakhage; and, in general, the newspaper chronicled, sometimes with cynicism, the rise of celebrities associated with Andy Warhol's The Factory, such as Viva.

The Voice has always aligned itself with left-wing causes. Editorially, it supported the civil rights movement and opposed the war in Vietnam. Later, it supported the feminist movement and gay liberation, while covering and advocating for the city's diverse ethnic communities. Even its sports coverage was unpredictable, emphasizing the inequities caused by corporate ownership and featuring peculiar sports stars over conventional heroes.

Through its numerous editors, the paper has sometimes strayed toward strict political correctness, especially in the late 1970s. In recent years, it has strayed into conventionality, highlighted by competition from such papers as the *New York Press* and from the Internet.

D.K. Holm

See also: Greenwich Village, New York City; Living Theatre; Theater, Alternative.

Further Reading

Frankfort, Ellen. *The Voice: Life at* The Village Voice. New York: William Morrow, 1976.
MacAuliffe, Kevin M. *The Great American Newspaper: The Rise and Fall of* The Village Voice. New York: Scribner's, 1978.
The Village Voice. http://www.villagevoice.com.

Volkswagen Beetle

The Volkswagen Beetle, affectionately known as the Bug, was a German import that became one of the most popular cars in America during the 1960s. Economic, efficient, and quirkily designed—shaped like a beetle, with a round frame—it appealed to the masses of counterculture youth coming of age in the late 1960s and 1970s.

In the mid-1930s, German dictator Adolf Hitler had requested the creation of an affordable automobile that could be mass-produced for the German population. A prototype of the compact, two-door Volkswagen "People's Car," developed in Germany by Dr. Ferdinand Porsche, was test-driven extensively (a total of 3 million miles, or 4.8 million kilometers). Construction of a factory model began in 1938, but production was halted due to World War II. Production resumed in 1945, but only about 10,000 cars were produced in that first year. Once full-fledged production began in the late 1940s, the Beetle was quickly embraced by the German public.

By 1951, Volkswagens were being exported to twenty-nine countries but had not yet reached the U.S. market. Imports continued to lag through mid-decade, with only about 1,000 of the cars making it to U.S. shores.

In the early 1960s, however, a clever and highly effective advertising campaign began highlighting the benefits of the Beetle and changing its image. Unlike large American cars, for which new models were introduced every year, the Beetle gained cachet for being small (economical) and unchanging (reliable). A print ad in 1963, for example, depicted the "Volkswagen Theory of Evolution" by showing the Beetle unchanged year after year. An ad in 1964 proclaimed, "It makes your house look bigger."

By the early 1960s, the popularity of the VW was soaring, as many Americans rejected the hulking, gas-guzzling cars made in Detroit and embraced the Beetle with its small, air-cooled engine. The Beetle, which reached a top speed of 82 miles (131 kilometers) per hour, became especially popular with the baby boom generation as they came of driving age and attended college, for both its aesthetics and affordability. The 1969 Walt Disney film *The Love Bug,* starring a Beetle named Herbie with a mind of its own, helped cement the Beetle's place in American counterculture.

By 1978, annual American sales of the Beetle had fallen to only 5 percent of what they had been during the peak year of 1968, when 400,000 had been sold in the United States. Japanese imports and the decline of the free-lifestyle hippie culture had taken a toll on sales. The last German model rolled off the assembly line in 1978, but the Beetle continued to be made in Mexico for many years thereafter.

In 1972, a modified model called the Cabriolet was introduced; a convertible, it was instantly popular with college students and beachgoers. Other related Volkswagen models have been the larger fastback and wagonback, and the VW minibus, itself a cultural icon of the 1960s and 1970s. In 1998 a new, more streamlined, and somewhat larger, more powerful Beetle (made in Mexico) was introduced. Consumer reaction to this modernized Beetle, in part based on nostalgia for the old Beetle, has been favorable.

Richard Panchyk

See also: Advertising; Flower Children; Hippies.

Further Reading

Hinckley, Jim, and Jon G. Robinson. *Big Book of Car Culture: The Armchair Guide to Automotive Americana.* St. Paul, MN: Motorbooks, 2005.

McLeod, Kate. *Beetlemania: The Story of the Car that Captured the Hearts of Millions.* New York: Smithmark, 1999.

Seume, Keith. *VW New Beetle Performance Handbook.* St. Paul, MN: MBI, 2001.

Vonnegut, Kurt, Jr. (1922–2007)

Kurt Vonnegut, Jr., was an American novelist and essayist best known for blending science fiction archetypes with social observation and dark satire. Vonnegut is widely credited with helping to move the genre of science fiction away from escapism and adventure and into more political and humanistic themes. His idiosyncratic plots and writing style, as well as his antiwar politics, made him especially popular with counterculture youth.

Born on November 11, 1922, in Indianapolis, Indiana, Vonnegut began his writing career at Shortridge High School, where he worked on the first daily student newspaper in the United States. He later worked as an editor of the student newspaper at Cornell University and served with the U.S. Army during World War II. His wartime experiences, particularly after he was captured by the Nazis, would heavily influence his literary works.

Vonnegut served time as a prisoner of war at a meatpacking facility in Dresden, Germany, that was nicknamed Slaughterhouse Five. He was on hand during the massive Allied bombing of Dresden in 1945 and was one of the few prisoners of war to survive. The Nazis then put Vonnegut to work collecting and disposing of civilian bodies. This horrific experience led him to ruminate on the violence and futility of war, which became the major theme of the semiautobiographical novel *Slaughterhouse-Five* (1969), as well as the focus of several later works.

After returning from the war, Vonnegut attended the University of Chicago and worked as a reporter in that city. He turned to writing science fiction in his spare time, and his first short story was published in 1950. His first novel, *Player Piano* (1952), was a dystopian tale of human workers being replaced by machines. A similar theme was later the centerpiece for Vonnegut's best-selling, breakthrough novel, *Cat's Cradle* (1963), in which he explored ideas of technological hubris and its effects on human society.

Vonnegut further expanded the field of science fiction by adding absurd and surreal elements, one of which is the literary device of including himself as a character that interacts with his own alter ego, an unsuccessful science fiction writer named Kilgore Trout. These elements were introduced in the best-selling *Breakfast of Champions* (1973), with Trout and Vonnegut becoming recurring characters in subsequent works.

Vonnegut's novels and short stories are widely cited both inside and outside the science fiction community for their explorations of humanity and humanism, moral issues, and the influence of the state on the individual. His short story "Harrison Bergeron" (in the 1968 collection *Welcome to the Monkey House*) is a particularly influential look at the repression resulting from even the most egalitarian social structures, while the novel *Jailbird* (1979) is a thinly veiled commentary on the social effects of the Watergate scandal.

Vonnegut announced his retirement from writing upon publication of his 1997 novel *Timequake*. He then began contributing essays periodically to the left-wing political magazine *In These Times*. Many of these essays are sharply critical of the George W. Bush administration and the Iraq War; others address more whimsical matters, including the art of writing and everyday experiences.

Vonnegut's last book was an essay collection titled *A Man Without a Country* (2005). Before his death on April 11, 2007, he served as honorary president of the American Humanist Association.

Benjamin W. Cramer

See also: Science Fiction.

Further Reading

Klinkowitz, Jerome. *The Vonnegut Effect.* Columbia: University of South Carolina Press, 2004.

Marvin, Thomas F. *Kurt Vonnegut: A Critical Companion.* Westport, CT: Greenwood, 2002.

Morse, Donald E. *The Novels of Kurt Vonnegut: Imagining Being an American.* Westport, CT: Praeger, 2003.

Voodoo, Hoodoo, and Conjure

In the United States, the terms *voodoo, hoodoo,* and *conjure* are used more or less synonymously for syncretistic folk religions or magic systems of communities of the African diaspora.

Voodoo, or vodou, is a West African belief system adopted in Haiti and elsewhere. When the term is used in the U.S. South, it refers to a system of magic highly syncretized with Christianity (especially Catholicism, because of its popularity in Louisiana). By any spelling, voodoo is an essentially practical system. That is, it focuses not on self-betterment, enlightenment, or moral guidance, but on changing the course of events in the world.

This is demonstrated by the popular image of the voodoo doll: The principle of sympathetic magic is a simple and evocative one, whereby the target can be controlled or influenced through some connection (such as the hair or blood) and by manipulating a look-alike doll. Other voodoo practices incorporate the Catholic notions of the novena, the intercession of saints, and the lighting of candles to aid in bringing about a desired effect.

This influence is key. Much of what a voodoo practitioner does is called "rootwork," referring to the use of the roots of plants such as mandrake and High John the Conqueror (*Ipomoea jalapa,* taking its familiar name from an African prince who was sold into slavery). Such roots may be used medicinally, making the line between folk magic and folk medicine a thin one. In times when professional doctors called for the letting of blood, the shock of hot and cold baths, and the application of leeches, folk medicine's use of natural remedies was no less "scientific" or effective. But what has kept voodoo popular—especially when it is called "conjure," referring to the conjuration of or communion with spirits and other supernatural entities—is its claim to influence the lives of unwilling individuals.

Love charms always have been popular, but so have curses. Indeed, much of the language and lore of voodoo concerns charms and curses. The mojo bag (containing one or more magical items) of a rootworker or his or her client not only brings good luck, it provides protection from evil and curses. A cursed mojo bag can render a man sick, unlucky, or impotent (a popular curse upon men guilty of sexual transgressions).

New Orleans is famous for its voodoo, a reputation that is justified. For generations, Catholic clergy in the city have been scandalized, at least in the pulpit, by the popularity of voodoo among whites. Therein lies much of the durability of folk magic. It provided a source of power and influence to otherwise disenfranchised African Americans.

Two women named Marie Laveau were the most prominent voodoo practitioners in the city for most of the nineteenth century. The elder Laveau was born to a white man and a free Creole. Her date of birth is placed anywhere from the 1780s to the turn of the nineteenth century. She married Jacques Paris, also a free Creole, in Saint Louis Cathedral in 1819. It is widely speculated that the second Marie Laveau was her daughter, perhaps born out of wedlock. The existence of a daughter is not confirmed, however, although someone continued to use the name after the elder Laveau's death in 1881, and two different New Orleans cemeteries have authentic gravestones bearing the name.

The elder Laveau was instrumental in emphasizing the syncretic Catholic/African/magical nature of voodoo, using rituals to invoke Catholic saints and claiming that benefiting from her work was not at odds with being a Catholic. While many rootworkers in the South catered mostly to the rural poor and working class, those desperate to buy affection or revenge, Laveau worked for the wealthy whites of the city, discovering their secrets by offering free or cheap services to their Creole servants and slaves. For at least two generations, she could be said to be the most well-informed person in the city when it came to the lives of the elite. And this was at a time when those lives were especially rich and secretive, with the traditions of Mardi Gras and krewes forming during the course of the century. Laveau was well respected and, whatever she did to keep her clients happy, it worked well enough to keep her and her successor in business from the beginning of Louisiana's statehood (1812) through the Civil War, Reconstruction, and the early days of the Progressive Era.

In the twentieth century, the visibility of voodoo decreased significantly, even—or especially—in New Orleans, where it became muddled in the city's tourist trade. Certainly one explanation for the decline was the dismantling, intentional and otherwise, of the church's monopoly on moral authority in the first few

A shop window in the French Quarter of New Orleans displays voodoo dolls and other ritual objects. An African folk religion that evolved in the West Indies, voodoo found its strongest U.S. following in and around New Orleans. *(David Seelig/Time & Life Pictures/Getty Images)*

decades of the century. As a countercultural magical practice, voodoo thrives in climates governed by strict authorities that it can subvert or bypass for its clients. But the enfranchisement of blacks also may have something to do with it. The black middle and upper classes have thrived in Louisiana, and there is less need for the sort of unofficial influence wielded by voodoo practitioners.

Those are local explanations. Nationally, the end of the nineteenth century and beginning of the twentieth saw the end of the Third Great Awakening—the cyclical, climactic shift in American religion that brought the renewal of old faiths and the creation of new ones. Though the obvious effects of this were the birth of fundamentalism, Reform Judaism, and other major religious denominations, the Awakening also brought with it a strong interest in mysticism, the occult, and various European magical practices.

This interest was at first associated with secret societies and parlor games, such as the Ouija board, but, by the end of the twentieth century, every major bookstore had a New Age or mysticism section. Such groups and practices answered the same practical concerns that voodoo had, often without requiring an intermediary. Thus, while voodoo continues to be practiced in some quarters, it has become even more decentralized. Hundreds of books are available on the subject, some more dubious than others, for the would-be practitioner; anthropological studies have demystified much of

it; and it must compete with more than just the mainstream church to attract newcomers.

Though associated by some with animal sacrifice, in the United States this is more often the province of Santería, a similar folk religion but one with a distinct history of its own. The animal sacrifices publicized and litigated in the last decades of the twentieth century—such as in *Church of the Lukumi Babalu Aye v. City of Hialeah* (Florida), decided by the U.S. Supreme Court in 1993—have involved Santería or Lukumi ritual, not voodoo.

Bill Kte'pi

See also: Santería.

Further Reading

Hurston, Zora Neale. *Tell My Horse.* New York: HarperPerennial, 1990.

Moro, Pamela, James Myers, and Arthur Lehmann. *Magic, Witchcraft, and Religion: An Anthropological Study of the Supernatural.* New York: McGraw-Hill, 2006.

Stein, Rebecca L., and Philip L. Stein. *Anthropology of Religion, Magic, and Witchcraft.* New York: Allyn and Bacon, 2004.

Ward, Martha. *Voodoo Queen: The Spirited Lives of Marie Laveau.* Jackson: University Press of Mississippi, 2004.

Vorse, Mary Heaton (1874–1966)

As a pioneer of labor journalism and a correspondent on international events from 1912 to the late 1940s, Mary Heaton Vorse appealed to readers' emotions by humanizing strikers, while making the news of labor unrest palatable to the general public. The publicity methods she developed during the Passaic, New Jersey, textile strike of 1926, the first major strike in the United States in which workers accepted Communist leadership, provided a prototype for successful labor protests of the next decade.

Born in New York City on October 9, 1874, to Hiram Heaton and Ellen Cordelia Blackman, she was raised in Amherst, Massachusetts, during the summer and in Europe during the winter. Schooled mostly at home, at age sixteen she studied art in Paris as a means to escape parental control. Moving to New York City, she immersed herself in the Art Students League, which was the heart of the bohemian movement in Greenwich Village. A charter member of the Liberal Club, Vorse was also active in the Heterodoxy Club, a proto-consciousness-raising gathering of New Women.

After marrying Albert White Vorse, a journalist and writer, in 1898, she began writing. Her talent eventually surpassed her spouse's, and she became the sole support of the family. In 1905, she published work in *The Atlantic Monthly* that she later developed into a novel, *The Breaking of a Yachtsman's Wife* (1908).

Vorse and her husband helped establish the A Club, an experiment in communal living that drew liberal reformers and visitors such as novelists Mark Twain and Theodore Dreiser, labor leader Mother Jones, and Russian writer Maxim Gorky. In 1910, when her mother and her husband tragically died within a day of each other, Mary Heaton Vorse entered the ranks of single working mothers.

The magazines *Harper's, Scribner's,* and *The Atlantic Monthly* bought almost every short story Vorse wrote. For several decades, she was one of the most popular writers of women's fiction in America. Impassioned by the Lawrence, Massachusetts, textile strike of 1912, she turned her interest to labor journalism and placed articles on the subject in *The Nation, The New Republic,* and *The Masses.*

What distinguished Vorse from other labor journalists was that she befriended the workers and marched in the strikes, sometimes being arrested and assaulted in the process. Present at all the major strikes of the period, she organized shirtmakers in Pennsylvania in 1919 and served as publicist of the Great Steel Strike the same year. She also lent her writing and publicity skills at major strikes in Gastonia, North Carolina (1929), Harlan, Kentucky (1937), and Flint,

Michigan (1939). Her pen also illuminated the forgotten victims of labor unrest: women and children. In her writings, Vorse emphasized the vital assistance of women in advancing the cause of labor unionism, a perspective not covered by male journalists.

Vorse played a key role in the founding of the Woman's Peace Party in 1915, in the cause of woman suffrage, and in the pacifist movement during World War II. In the arts, her summer home at Provincetown, Massachusetts, became a gathering spot for left-wing and bohemian writers; her wharf was transformed into the initial stage venue of the Provincetown Players, an experimental theater group that introduced the plays of Eugene O'Neill and others.

By the end of her career, Vorse had published sixteen books, two plays, 190 short stories, and numerous articles in national, international, and radical magazines and newspapers. Despite her notable involvement in groundbreaking movements in labor, pacifism, feminism, literature, and theater, she fell into relative obscurity upon her death on June 14, 1966.

Rebecca Tolley-Stokes

See also: Communes; Communism.

Further Reading

Garrison, Dee. *Mary Heaton Vorse: The Life of an American Insurgent.* Philadelphia: Temple University Press, 1989.

Vorse, Mary Heaton. *A Footnote to Folly: Reminiscences of Mary Heaton Vorse.* 1935. Rev. ed., with Mary H. Borse. New York: Arno, 1980.

W

Walden

See Thoreau, Henry David

Ward, Nancy (c. 1738–1822)

As a tribal leader and revered figure of the Cherokee Nation, Nancy Ward—or Nanye'hi Ward—served as a peacemaker between the Cherokee and white settlers in Tennessee during a tumultuous period of cultural shift at the end of the eighteenth century. She challenged Anglo-American assumptions about the roles of women in leadership and in the military.

She was born in Chota, Tennessee, in about 1738 to Tame Doe, a member of the Wolf Clan, and Francis Ward, a white man. Raised by her mother, Ward entered a society troubled by issues of encroaching settlers and forced assimilation into white culture. Her uncle, Little Carpenter, compromised with the whites by accepting missionaries into the village, but only on Cherokee terms. As a biracial child, Ward learned languages of the Cherokee and the English, which later facilitated her position in connecting both worlds.

When she was still a teenager, Ward married a warrior named Kingfisher, a member of the Deer Clan, with whom she had two children. At his side in battle, Ward maintained his firearms, chewing the lead bullets to render them more lethal to the enemy. During the Battle of Taliwa in 1755, in which the Cherokee fought the Creek, Kingfisher received a mortal wound. Grabbing his firearm, Ward assumed his place in combat and rallied the other Cherokee warriors. For her valor, she was bestowed the honorific *Ghihau* ("Beloved Woman") and became a member of the tribal council.

Entering each tribal decision or negotiation with a pacifist viewpoint, which was in part modeled after her uncle's, Ward sided with white settlers when her cousin,

Dragging Canoe, fought with the British against the settlers in 1775. In July of the next year, Ward warned white settlers near the Holston River along Virginia's southwest border of a planned attack by the Cherokee. Ward's village was spared militia retaliation because she rescued a Mrs. Bean, who introduced Ward to the principles of dairy farming, which Ward then shared with the Cherokee. Again in 1780, Ward warned American soldiers of Cherokee plans to attack; she was taken as a prisoner of war and returned to Chota.

Ward's successful peace negotiations between the Cherokee and Americans brought military occupation of their villages to an end, while allowing the army to reallocate soldiers to the front lines of the American Revolution. In the 1785 Treaty of Hopewell, Ward promoted partnership between the Cherokee and settlers by advancing her idea that the Cherokee become farmers, which would make them more like the white settlers and allow them to cement their property rights with legal deeds.

Ward's second husband was her cousin, Bryant Ward, with whom she had two more children. After he deserted them, she opened an inn near Benton, Tennessee.

Ultimately, Ward believed that it was not in the Cherokee's best financial or social interests to sell land to settlers. In 1817, Ward, too ill to travel, sent a letter to the tribal council, urging them to enlarge their farms, never part with tribal land, and stay where they belonged rather than move to the west. She died in 1822.

Rebecca Tolley-Stokes

See also: Native Americans; *Document:* Message by Nancy Ward to the Cherokee Council (1817).

Further Reading

Alderman, Pat. *Nancy Ward, Cherokee Chieftainess, Dragging Canoe, Cherokee-Chickamauga War Chief.* Johnson City, TN: Overmountain, 1978.

Felton, Harold W. *Nancy Ward: Cherokee.* New York: Dodd Mead, 1975.

Warhol, Andy (1928–1987)

A pioneering avant-garde artist, filmmaker, magazine publisher, and celebrity, Andy Warhol revolutionized the American and international art world during the post–World War II era. He was a founder and leading creative force of the pop art movement, which supplanted abstract expressionism as the prevailing trend in the Western visual arts of the mid-twentieth century.

Controversial for his public persona and fascination with celebrity no less than for his creative vision, Warhol became known for his repetitive depictions of everyday commercial objects, colorful portraits of famous people, and prediction that "In the future everyone will be famous for fifteen minutes." Fascinated with fame, Warhol became a celebrity of the 1960s counterculture.

Born Andrew Warhola on August 6, 1928, in Pittsburgh, Pennsylvania, to working-class parents of Eastern European descent, Warhol earned a bachelor of arts degree in pictorial design from the Carnegie Institute of Technology (now Carnegie Mellon University) in 1949. Soon after graduation, he left Pittsburgh for New York, where he lived for the rest of his life. Changing his surname to Warhol, he established himself as a highly successful commercial artist in the early 1950s, designing advertisements, magazine illustrations, book jackets, and covers for record albums. His work appeared in such upscale, high-profile magazines as *Vogue, Glamour,* and *Harper's Bazaar.*

Warhol's early work in the pop art genre mirrored postwar America's emphasis on consumerism, individualism, and celebrity. By the early 1960s, he gained notoriety by producing pieces that depicted commonplace items such as Campbell's soup cans and Coca-Cola bottles in a variety of formats. He also produced colorful images of celebrities such as Marilyn Monroe, Elizabeth Taylor, and Jacqueline Kennedy. The silkscreened, repetitious, nearly identical and often colorful images reflected the American value of mass production and elevated the mundane to high art. By mid-decade, Warhol, now a celebrity in his own right, produced sculptures based on Brillo soap pad and Kellogg's Corn Flakes boxes. He also created a series of death and disaster paintings that revealed the contemporary American preoccupation with violent death.

The Factory, Warhol's downtown studio, whose walls were covered in aluminum foil and silver paint, became the center of the artist's activity and the place

Pop artist, experimental filmmaker, and exemplar of the celebrity culture on which he commented, Andy Warhol was a counterculture of one. His life was as controversial as his art; his techniques were as groundbreaking and unfettered as his creative vision. *(Jill Kennington/Hulton Archive/Getty Images)*

where he often found creative inspiration. It also became famous for attracting celebrities and for its lavish, star-studded parties. Artists, musicians, and celebrities frequented the loft, where Warhol's assistants produced his work in assembly-line fashion. The spirit was captured by *The New Yorker* magazine: "Warhol became a hero to many young people in the sixties because he seemed to be the ultimate anti-parent. Anything you did was O.K. even if you killed yourself doing it." The Factory thus became an icon of the counterculture movement of the 1960s.

Buoyed by his newfound celebrity status in the mid-1960s, Warhol began to concentrate his creative energies on filmmaking. Producing more than sixty films between 1963 and 1974, he addressed a variety of subjects, from the routine to the controversial. His work was influential in the underground cinema, reflecting the values and aesthetic of the avant-garde counterculture.

Sleep (1963), for example, shows one of his male lovers sleeping for six hours; *Empire* (1964) records eight hours in the life of the Empire State Building. Other controversial films include *Blow Job* (1963), *Bike Boy* (1967–1968), and *Lonesome Cowboys* (1968), which highlight homosexuality, an unacceptable topic for film during the 1960s. Sexual themes were also explored in works such as *Blue Movie* (1969), a film that depicts Viva, one of Warhol's superstars and frequent guests at The Factory, engaging in an extended sexual encounter with a male partner. *Andy Warhol's Frankenstein* (1973), a horror-comedy, and *Andy Warhol's Dracula* (1974), a horror film, were directed by Paul Morrissey and enjoyed limited commercial success. Warhol's own most innovative film was *The Chelsea Girls* (1966), a production consisting of two different stories exhibited simultaneously on split screens.

Warhol also ventured into the world of magazine publishing, cofounding *Andy Warhol's Interview* (now *Interview*) in 1969. The large-format publication featured interviews with prominent celebrities and was on the cutting edge of popular culture. In 1966, Warhol became the manager of the Velvet Underground, a rock band that provided the music for his multimedia presentation titled Exploding Plastic Inevitable.

On June 5, 1968, Valerie Solanas, the founder of the radical feminist organization S.C.U.M. (Society for Cutting Up Men) and a Warhol acquaintance, shot the artist in the chest and abdomen while visiting The Factory. "He had too much control over my life" was all she offered by way of explanation. The assassination attempt required Warhol to remain in the hospital for two months, and he never completely recovered from the wounds.

The 1970s marked the low point of Warhol's career. In order to support his endeavors, he focused primarily on portraits commissioned by wealthy clients such as rock stars Mick Jagger and Michael Jackson. He also produced two photographic collections and pieces created by urinating on bronze, a technique that shocked many people. His photography appeared in two collections: *Andy Warhol's Exposures* (1979) and *Andy Warhol: Portraits of the '70s* (1979).

Warhol died on February 22, 1987, in New York of complications following routine gall bladder surgery. By the 1980s, his paintings, sculptures, and other works had been added to the collections of major museums throughout the world, and his philosophy of the mass production of art as a moneymaking enterprise was well established. In *The Philosophy of Andy Warhol* (1975) he wrote, "Making money is art, and working is art and good business is the best art."

An inveterate shopper and collector, Warhol amassed an eclectic assemblage of objects such as artworks, jewelry, and cookie jars over the course of his life. Following his death, an auction of his possessions at Sotheby's netted more than $25 million. The auction benefited the Andy Warhol Foundation for the Visual Arts, an organization dedicated to fostering innovative artistic expression. In 1994, the Andy Warhol Museum opened in Pittsburgh; it is the largest museum in the United States dedicated to a single artist.

Jeffrey S. Cole

See also: Film, Cult; Film, Independent; Pop Art; Reed, Lou.

Further Reading
Bockris, Victor. *Warhol: The Biography.* New York: Da Capo, 2003.
Hackett, Pat, ed. *The Andy Warhol Diaries.* New York: Random House, 1991.
Tomkins, Calvin. "Comment." *The New Yorker,* 27 April 1987, 27–28.
Watson, Steven. *Factory Made: Warhol and the Sixties.* New York: Pantheon, 2003.

Waters, John (1946–)

Generally associated with the transgressive cinema of the 1970s, John Waters is a film producer, director, screenwriter, and actor whose works have carried him to iconic cult status in American cinema. Waters's work is widely recognized, celebrated, and vilified for its exploitation and mockery of social norms, taboos, and traditional middle-class sensibilities. His projects typically champion the marginalized and excluded, particularly those with low social status, who are cast as pioneers of bad taste.

He was born John Samuel Waters on April 22, 1946, in Baltimore, Maryland, to a working-class family. In his youth, Waters began his friendship with Harris Glenn Milstead, who would become his long-time collaborator and later gained infamy as the overweight drag queen Divine. Waters received his first 8mm film camera for his sixteenth birthday.

Waters attended New York University for "about five minutes," soon realizing that he was drawn to the fringe films he attended in the city, rather than the classics discussed in the classroom. He was expelled from the university in 1966 for smoking marijuana on school grounds.

At the time of his departure, Waters had already created his first film, the 8mm *Hag in a Black Leather Jacket* (1964), an ironic tale of an African American man who courts a Caucasian woman by carrying her around in a trash can and later weds her, in a ceremony conducted by a Ku Klux Klansman. This film, along with his other early black-and-white films, *Roman Candles* (1966) and *Eat Your Makeup* (1968), would chart Waters's course into transgressive cinema. Each of these films was set in Baltimore, a location he favored as the ideal low-culture backdrop for his ironic social commentary on classism, social pretension, and unabashed bad taste.

Waters's aesthetic arose from a period of cultural self-reflexiveness in American art. Artifice, exaggeration, and the parody of values and icons were mobilized as significant components of artistic theory and production in the 1960s, celebrating that which mainstream culture had cast off or rejected. Among the key influences on Waters's career are American exploitation directors Herschell Gordon Lewis, William Castle, George and Mike Kuchar, and Russ Meyer, all known for their visually shocking, low-budget productions. Also important are Kenneth Anger and Andy Warhol, icons of the underground art and social scene whose films and photography drew the everyday into sharp focus and dealt with controversial subject matter such as the occult, exclusion, and death, revolutionizing the relationship between art and society.

Widespread distribution of Waters's films began in 1969, with the feature-length *Mondo Trasho,* starring Divine. Waters's successive films with Divine in the 1970s, *Pink Flamingos* (1972) and *Female Trouble* (1974), which feature all manner of grotesque fetishism, sexual and religious perversion, and fringe criminality, soon earned the filmmaker a reputation for transgressing the boundaries of good taste.

The 1980s, however, marked a turn toward the mainstream for Waters. With films such as *Polyester* (1981) and *Hairspray* (1988)—the latter of which inspired the Tony Award–winning Broadway musical and 2007 feature-film remake of the same name—Waters's camp sensibility took aim at suburban America in more circumspect fashion, toning down his leanings toward the shocking and grotesque in favor of more ironic social commentary.

This moviemaking formula continued into the 1990s, with his musical homage to juvenile delinquency, *Cry-Baby* (1990), the dark celebrity-killer satire, *Serial Mom* (1994), and *Pecker* (1998), which exploits the eccentricities of a working-class family in ways that transform them into caricatures of low-life outsiders. In spite of Waters's move into more mainstream filmmaking, his films in the 2000s—such as *Cecil B. DeMented* (2000) and *A Dirty Shame* (2004)—retain his trademark focus on bad taste, sexuality, and his characters' descents into darkness.

Waters's controversial career in cinema has spanned more than three decades and has included seventeen films, numerous television shows, including a 1997 episode of *The Simpsons,* five publications of his writings, CD music collections, a one-man touring show, and commentary on a number of DVD releases. Harkening back to pop-art icon Andy Warhol's influence on his career, Waters turned his attention to visual media besides film in the 1990s, creating photography-based artwork and installations that have been exhibited nationally and internationally, including in a retrospective of his art at New York City's New Museum in 2004.

In 2007, Waters became the host (called "The Groom Reaper") of *'Til Death Do Us Part,* a program on America's Court TV network featuring dramatizations of real-life marriages that ended in murder.

Cynthia J. Miller

See also: Drag; Film, Cult; Film, Independent; Transvestites.

Further Reading

Pela, Robert. *Filthy: The Weird World of John Waters.* Los Angeles: Alyson, 2002.

Waters, John. *Shock Value: A Tasteful Book About Bad Taste.* New York: Thunder's Mouth, 1995.

Watson, Thomas E. (1856–1922)

As a champion of the farm protest movement of the nineteenth century and an outspoken opponent of wealth and privilege, Thomas E. Watson rallied crowds to his side with an inveterate passion and gift for oratory. He attacked the complementary Southern institutions of the Democratic Party and segregation, but the failure of his efforts caused him to turn toward the very things he had attacked. Watson's career demonstrated both the great potential and the inherent difficulties of upsetting the established order during the Populist era of the 1890s.

Thomas Edward Watson was born in Thomson, Georgia, on September 5, 1856, to an upwardly mobile slaveholding family. His parents suffered financially along with many others in the South after the Civil War, but they managed to spare enough money to send him to Mercer University in October 1872. Even as a student, Watson displayed a passion for speaking to an audience.

After studying law and gaining admission to the Georgia bar in 1875, Watson joined the Democratic Party and won election to the state General Assembly in 1882. As a member of the legislature, he fought several losing battles against the exploitation of sharecroppers and convict laborers. Meanwhile, the Farmers' Alliance movement was spreading across the agrarian states, a trend regarded by the Democratic Party as harmless until farmers began forming cooperatives, organizing politically, and working together across racial lines. For years, the Democratic Party had controlled the South by exploiting white fears of "Negro domination" to prevent Southern farmers from uniting against it. Watson never joined the alliance himself, but he was involved in some of its activities, including an 1888 boycott of the jute-bag monopoly.

The spirit of farm protest during this period expressed itself politically as the Populist movement. Watson ran for U.S. Congress in 1890 on a Populist platform, embracing agrarianism, declaring war on the elites who ran the South, and promising an alliance with black farmers. His Congressional career mirrored his time as a state legislator, marked by doomed attempts to end special treatment for elites and to obtain protections for farmers and workers. As a Populist in Congress, Watson was at odds with both the Democratic and Republican parties; as a Southerner, his fight lay with the Democrats who ran the South as a feudal state.

Watson fought against several attempts to merge the Populists with the Democratic Party, realizing that this would mean the death of populism as an independent movement. He was defeated for reelection in 1894 after local Democrats employed mostly illegal campaign tactics. The Populists finally merged with the Democrats by endorsing their candidate, William Jennings Bryan, in the 1896 presidential election. Watson, who ran as the Populist vice-presidential nominee in that contest, was forced to preside over the disintegration of the movement he had fought so long to preserve.

Watson's career reflected the anger of American farmers, who had been pushed to the brink during the late nineteenth century. The lean decades of the 1880s and 1890s caused farmers and those who sympathized with them, such as Watson, to revolt against the Democratic Party, racism, and the elite. Their continued electoral defeats and their inability to overcome the race issue eventually returned many Populists to the Democratic Party. Watson reflected this as well, emerging by 1908 as a bitter racist who championed the Ku Klux Klan and ranted against blacks, Jews, and Catholics. The transformation was complete in 1920, when Watson rejoined the Democratic Party and won reelection to the U.S. Senate.

Less than two years into his term, Watson died, on September 26, 1922. His rise and fall reflected the fortunes of the protest movement that attempted to unite the laboring classes in the South during the Populist era.

Charles E. Delgadillo

See also: Democratic Party; Farmers' Alliance.

Further Reading

Bryan, Ferald Joseph. *Henry Grady or Tom Watson?: The Rhetorical Struggle for the New South, 1880–1890.* Macon, GA: Mercer University Press, 1994.

Woodward, C. Vann. *Tom Watson: Agrarian Rebel.* Savannah, GA: Beehive, 1973.

Watts, Alan (1915–1973)

The American philosopher and theologian Alan Watts was instrumental in bringing awareness of Asian cultures to the West and in explaining and popularizing Eastern religious philosophies, particularly Taoism and Zen Buddhism. Watts's writings and lectures on Eastern religious philosophy found a receptive audience in the American youth culture of the 1950s and 1960s.

Born in Chislehurst, England, on January 6, 1915, Watts became interested in Eastern cultures and Buddhism during his early teenage years. After graduating from public school in 1932, he moved to London, where he immersed himself in the study of religion and psychology and began his lifelong attempt to synthesize Eastern and Western thought as a basis for psychological healing. Largely self-taught, he was active in the Buddhist Lodge and guided by the Buddhist scholars Christmas Humphreys and D.T. Suzuki. He published his first book, *The Spirit of Zen: A Way of Life, Work and Art in the Far East* (1936) at age twenty-one.

In 1938, he married Eleanor Everett, daughter of American Buddhist Ruth Fuller Everett, and moved to the United States the following year. He first lived in New York City and then moved to Illinois, where he attended Seabury-Western Theological Seminary in Evanston. After completion of his studies, he was ordained in the Episcopal Church and from 1944 to 1950 served as a chaplain at Northwestern University. He became disaffected with Christianity and left the church and divorced his wife in 1950. He moved temporarily to Millbrook, New York, with his new wife, Dorothy DeWitt, and then to San Francisco in 1951, where he taught comparative philosophy and psychology at the American Academy of Asian Studies (AAAS).

It was in the San Francisco Bay Area that Watts began to exert a significant influence on the emerging counterculture. He met poet and Zen Buddhist Gary Snyder, who introduced him to people who would form the nucleus of the Beat Generation. In addition to teaching, he lectured regularly throughout the Bay Area and became a popular speaker, noted for his clarity, wit, and entertaining style. In 1953, he began *Way Beyond the West,* a weekly radio show on KPFA in Berkeley that spread his influence even farther. *The Way of Zen,* published in 1957, became a best seller and gave him the financial freedom to leave the AAAS and devote his full attention to writing and lecturing.

In 1958, Watts began experimenting with the mind-altering drug LSD. He thought it useful as a tool for expanding consciousness, though he cautioned against its casual use. In 1959, he hosted *Eastern Wisdom and Modern Life,* a weekly program broadcast nationally on public television for two years. He divorced again in 1963 and married Mary Jane Yates.

Watts was a central figure in the cultural phenomenon known as the San Francisco Renaissance, which he characterized in his autobiography as "a huge tide of spiritual energy in the form of poetry, music, philosophy, painting, religion, communication techniques in radio, television, and cinema, dancing, theater, and general life-style [which] swept out of this city and its environs to affect America and the whole world." His interpretations of Asian philosophies played a prominent role in the development of Beat counterculture philosophy and the hippie subculture of the 1960s, but his influence went far beyond those movements.

His twenty-five books, his radio and television shows, and his extensive public lectures were vital in bringing knowledge of Eastern philosophies to Western consciousness. Watts was at the height of his popularity when he died of heart failure on November 16, 1973, at age fifty-eight.

Jerry Shuttle

See also: Beat Generation; Buddhism; Hippies; LSD.

Further Reading

Furlong, Monica. *Zen Effects: The Life of Alan Watts.* Woodstock, VT: Skylight Paths, 2001.

Watts, Alan. *In My Own Way: An Autobiography, 1915–1965.* New York: Pantheon, 1972.

———. *The Way of Zen.* 1957. New York: Vintage Spiritual Classics, 1999.

Wavy Gravy (1936–)

Wavy Gravy is the founder of the Hog Farm Collective—identified as the longest-running hippie commune in the United States—and a hippie activist strongly identified with the Woodstock music festival of August 1969. His clown-like antics, irreverent attitude toward authority, and eccentric personality have made him a notable figure in the history of American counterculture.

Born Hugh Romney on May 15, 1936, in East Greenbush, New York, he grew up in and around New York City. The German-born physicist Albert Einstein was a family friend and took young Hugh on walks around the neighborhood. Romney was educated at William Hall High School in West Hartford, Connecticut, and by the time he finished his schooling he was already attracted to the Greenwich Village counterculture of Beat and jazz poetry.

In his early adult years, he befriended counterculture entertainment figures such as folk musician Bob Dylan, writer Ken Kesey, activist Paul Krassner, and comedian Lenny Bruce. He moved to San Francisco in 1963 as the hippie movement was just beginning to gain momentum.

In 1965, he founded the Hog Farm Collective on top of a mountain near Tujunga, California. As its name suggests, daily life in the commune included the job of breeding and raising pigs. As more people joined the commune, Wavy Gravy helped form a traveling show called "Hog Farm and Friends in Open Celebration." He and the other members of the collective began to tour the country giving free performances, protesting the Vietnam War, and emphasizing the need to address poverty and social injustice in America.

Members of the collective acted as an unofficial security team at the 1969 Woodstock music festival in Bethel, New York. They were later dubbed the "Please Force," referring to their habit of politely requesting that festivalgoers follow certain rules for safety and security. Wavy Gravy served as an unofficial master of ceremonies for Woodstock (and at the anniversary festivals that took place in subsequent years); his high-profile position at the event firmly established him as a well-known member of the hippie counterculture.

Wavy Gravy is also known as the founder of Camp Winnarainbow, a performing arts summer camp near Laytonville, California. The volunteer-run camp teaches a variety of performing arts, particularly circus arts such as juggling and tightrope walking, to children and adults in separate summer sessions. The camp offers scholarships for financially disadvantaged children, and many of the volunteers who run the camp are former campers themselves.

People who are unaware of Wavy Gravy's status as a counterculture icon may recognize his name in another context: the Ben and Jerry's ice-cream flavor named after him. Wavy Gravy ice cream, first produced in 1991 and dedicated to the "Woodstock Generation's ultimate camp counselor," features a combination of caramel, cashews, almonds, and chocolate hazelnut fudge. Though the ice cream was later taken out of production, Wavy Gravy has remained one of the most popular Ben and Jerry's ice-cream flavors ever sold. It was so well liked that fans successfully petitioned Ben and Jerry's to bring it back and sell it by the scoop in local retail outlets. A portion of the proceeds from the sale of the ice cream goes to Camp Winnarainbow to fund camp programs and activities.

Shannon Granville

See also: Communes; Hippies.

Further Reading

Wavy Gravy. *The Hog Farm and Friends. By Wavy Gravy as told to Hugh Romney and vice versa.* New York: Links, 1974.
———. *Something Good for a Change: Random Notes on Peace Thru Living.* New York: St. Martin's, 1992.

Weatherman

Weatherman—also know as the Weathermen and later as the Weather Underground Organization—was a radical, leftist organization of the late 1960s and early 1970s that was an offshoot of Students for a Democratic Society (SDS). The group took its name from the Bob Dylan song "Subterranean Homesick Blues," which contained the lyrics "You don't need a weather man to know which way the wind blows," reflecting its members' conviction that the necessity for world revolution was obvious.

The collective referred to itself as a "revolutionary organization of communist women and men" and dedicated itself to carrying out a series of militant actions, including bombings and armed robberies, in hopes of overthrowing the U.S. government. The Weathermen represented a broader turn toward violent resistance by late 1960s activists who were frustrated with the lack of progress achieved through peaceful protest.

Formed in 1960, SDS was initially a small group of primarily middle-class college students who adopted protest strategies from the civil rights movement. By the late 1960s, SDS had a membership of more than 100,000 and was one of the most powerful opponents of the Vietnam War. At its annual meeting in 1969, the escalating violence in America's cities, as well as the escalating war in Vietnam, led Weatherman, a group within SDS's Revolutionary Youth Movement, to demand more aggressive forms of antiwar action than the then-prevalent methodology of sit-ins and peaceful demonstrations of civil disobedience. This debate and others led to the fragmentation and effective collapse of SDS at the height of its power, and the members of Weatherman seized the remains of the organization.

The leaders of Weatherman were among the most charismatic figures of the New Left, which was in no small part a factor in their initial success. They were considered alluring because of their perceived combination of youth, physical attractiveness, and radical strength. Leader Bernardine Dohrn was a lawyer known for her aggressive statements to the press. Mark Rudd led demonstrations that closed down Columbia University in 1968. Other prominent members of the group include Kathy Boudin, a former community organizer for the Economic Research and Action Project (ERAP); Cathy Wilkerson, editor of the SDS newspaper *New Left Notes* and a founder of the SDS regional office in Washington, D.C.; Bill Ayers, a University of Michigan graduate; and Naomi Jaffe, Eleanor Raskin, David Gilbert, Bob Tomashevsky, and Laura Whitehorn.

In the summer of 1969, several hundred Weathermen moved into group homes in major U.S. cities in order to implement the group's agenda of executing large-scale violent demonstrations. The Weathermen hoped to organize and revolutionize U.S. working-class youth, but such efforts were largely unsuccessful. The first major event planned by the Weathermen was the October 1969 "Days of Rage" protest in Chicago, at which they claimed tens of thousands of young people would violently rise up and oppose the police. Only

Members of the radical Weatherman group threatened violence against Chicago police during the so-called Days of Rage in October 1969. Organized in response to the Chicago Seven trial, the four-day event resulted in widespread property damage. *(David Fenton/Hulton Archive/Getty Images)*

several hundred protesters showed up, but the small number of participants charged into Chicago's wealthy Gold Coast, breaking windows. The protesters were violently subdued by Chicago police, and six people were shot.

After the December 1969 murder of Black Panther Fred Hampton by a Cook County State Attorney's Office unit and the Chicago Police, the Weathermen adopted the name Weather Underground Organization (WUO) and made efforts at becoming a more covert group. This was in part because the Federal Bureau of Investigation (FBI) now perceived the Weathermen as a credible threat, and began harassing them.

One of the covert actions being planned by a Weatherman unit was the bombing of a noncommissioned officers' dance at Fort Dix in New Jersey. On March 6, 1970, during the preparation of the bomb at a Greenwich Village townhouse, it exploded, killing members Terry Robbins, Ted Gold, and Diana Oughton. Members Wilkerson and Boudin survived the bombing and immediately disappeared underground.

After this event, membership in the Weather Underground declined significantly, and those who remained went fully underground, adopting fake identities and abandoning their families and friends in hopes of evading arrest. A secretive leadership group called the Weather Bureau coordinated information among various Underground groups.

After the townhouse disaster, later bombings were scrupulously planned so as to damage property, but not to hurt or kill people. A bombing was planned to protest the shooting of prisoner George Jackson, a Black Panther, in 1971 at the Ferry Building offices of the state police in San Francisco. The bombing was executed successfully, and without injury.

Other WUO bombings included those of May 1970 at the National Guard Office to protest the student killings at Kent State; June 1970 at New York City Police headquarters to protest police brutality; July 1970 at the Presidio Army Base in San Francisco to mark the eleventh anniversary of the Cuban Revolution; October 1970 at the Harvard Center for International Affairs to protest the Vietnam War; and March 1971 at the U.S. Capitol to protest the invasion of Laos. Communiqués to the press usually accompanied these bombings, and none of them resulted in injury or death.

One of the group's most famous acts was to help LSD guru and counterculture icon Timothy Leary escape from a California prison in 1970, for which the WUO was given $20,000 by the pro-drug group the Brotherhood of Eternal Love. The FBI eventually captured and re-imprisoned Leary.

The remaining members of the group continued to evade police and set off bombs at strategic locations in protest until 1975. With the withdrawal of troops from Vietnam, a key organizing principle of many New Left groups ceased to exist, and activism around identity-based groups began to flourish. The burden of living underground led the remaining members of the Underground to turn themselves in or attempt to reintegrate into society. Few WUO members were ever imprisoned, because the evidence gathered against them by the FBI had been collected using illegal methods.

Susanne E. Hall

See also: Leary, Timothy; New Left; Students for a Democratic Society.

Further Reading

Berger, Dan. *Outlaws of America: The Weather Underground and the Politics of Solidarity.* Oakland, CA: AK, 2006.

Dohrn, Bernardine, Bill Ayers, and Jeff Jones, eds. *Sing a Battle Song: The Revolutionary Poetry, Statements, and Comminiqués of the Weather Underground, 1970–1974.* New York: Seven Stories, 2006.

Grathwohl, Larry. *Bringing Down America: An FBI Informant with the Weathermen.* New Rochelle, NY: Arlington House, 1976.

White Supremacists

Proponents of the white supremacy movement subscribe to the racist ideology that whites are inherently superior to members of other races, and take organized action, including acts of violence, to advance their beliefs. While the movement is fragmented and acts of racial violence have been perpetrated by ad hoc organizations or mobs, the fundamental beliefs of white supremacy have remained constant throughout American history.

Origins

White supremacy as an organized movement in the United States dates to the beginning of Reconstruction and the birth of the Ku Klux Klan (KKK) in Pulaski, Tennessee, in 1865. While the political goal of the organization was to thwart newly enfranchised black Southerners from putting Republicans in power, Klan members routinely indulged in gratuitous and clandestine beatings, rapes, and lynchings of African American citizens.

In the twentieth century, the assumptions and justifications that underlay institutional racism began to crumble as black Americans and then other minorities gained political power and visibility. This provoked a series of violent backlashes, beginning with a resurgence of the Klan in the 1920s. The civil rights movement of the 1950s and 1960s likewise spawned a violent reaction from supremacist groups, such as the next generation of the Ku Klux Klan, the States Rights Party, and the American Nazi Party.

Despite local victories and defiant gestures, however, the white supremacist groups of the 1950s and 1960s failed to stop the collapse of institutionalized racism. The failures of the white supremacist movement and the continued shift in public opinion against its ideals and goals finally drove the Klu Klux Klan and other white supremacist groups underground.

Reemergence

The failure of organized white supremacist groups led to a vacuum on the far right, and it took several decades for the white supremacist movement with which Americans are now familiar to take shape. A strong early influence was the Posse Comitatus, a right-wing militia group founded in 1971. Posse Comitatus adherents believe that the federal government has illegally usurped powers belonging to American citizens, that there is no legitimate government in America above the county level, and that all actions undertaken by the federal government since the Civil War—including the abolition of slavery and the extension of

civil rights to nonwhite Americans—are therefore void. Building on anger in rural areas, where the economic slowdown of the 1970s hit hard, Posse Comitatus spread rapidly.

The mid-1980s brought another major influence: the skinhead movement. The skinheads took their signature shaved-head look—along with a loose, ganglike organization, music, and brutal racism—from working-class British teens. The British skinhead movement had been galvanized by the music and lyrics of Skrewdriver, which mixed heavy metal with the cultural ideals of Nazism.

In the United States, Tom Metzger, a television repairman and former leader of the Knights of the Ku Klux Klan, reinvented himself as the organizer and spokesman of an American skinhead movement he called White Aryan Resistance. The group quickly expanded, with a magazine and a public access television program disseminating white supremacist views and helping to build a small California skinhead gang into a nationwide movement. Metzger and his son, John, were also instrumental in establishing an online presence through bulletin boards and text archives. The anonymity and ease of organization and communication over the Internet was a major spur to the white supremacy movement in general, enabling isolated adherents and groups to coordinate and communicate as never before possible. In the 2000s, the World Wide Web is home to a thriving white supremacist subculture.

The 1980s, meanwhile, also saw the rise of the Aryan Nations, an international neo-Nazi organization founded by Richard Girnt Butler. The Aryan Nations espoused the idea of Christian Identity, a belief that Anglo-Saxons are the lost tribe of Israel and that they, not the Jews, are God's Chosen People. While this belief was first laid out in the nineteenth century, it was not until Butler's Aryan Nations began to disseminate it that the ideology of Christian Identity gained wide acceptance.

The white supremacist movement of the 1980s and 1990s was thus a fusion of three separate cultural trends: the right-wing populist libertarianism of Posse Comitatus, the street muscle of the skinhead movement, and the Christian Identity movement. The combination of racism with a cult of individualism led to the development of armed compounds and entire communities. The archetype was the Aryan Nations compound in Hayden Lake, Idaho. Although there were never more than a handful of these compounds, with a combined population in the hundreds, they seized the public imagination.

The drumbeat of attention played directly into the hands of Metzger, Butler, and other white supremacist leaders. The various white supremacist movements continued to gain supporters and media attention into the 1990s. The militia movement, which adopted the antigovernment views of Posse Comitatus and at its fringes spawned several small secessionist groups such as Montana's Justus Township, often shared views and members with white supremacist movements.

In 1995, militia sympathizers Timothy McVeigh and Terry Nichols were responsible for the massive truck bombing of the Alfred P. Murrah Federal Building in Oklahoma City, killing 168 and wounding more than 800 people. The militia movement virtually collapsed—or went farther underground—in the aftermath of that incident, as the federal government imprisoned some leaders, many members left, and public opinion turned even more strongly against them. The vision of armed resistance lost its appeal for many would-be white supremacists.

Clumsily handled government interventions at places such as northern Idaho's Ruby Ridge in 1992 and the Branch Davidian compound in Waco, Texas, in 1993, which had helped to recruit new members, suddenly became object lessons. The revelation that the two students who killed thirteen people at Columbine High School in Colorado in 1999 were fascinated with white supremacy was another major blow to the movement. In the wake of these events, the federal government stepped up efforts to infiltrate and monitor white supremacist and antigovernment groups.

In 2001, the Aryan Nations lost their property (in a lawsuit by an Idaho woman and her son who had been attacked by Aryan Nations guards) and declared bankruptcy. Also, the terrorist attacks of September 11, 2001, made talk of secession extremely unpopular. The organization splintered, went into decline, and essentially collapsed after Butler's death in 2004. Several of the few remaining militia groups disbanded, and those that survived were subject to intensified federal surveillance.

Despite these and other setbacks, a number of white supremacist groups continue to exist in the twenty-first century, albeit in more decentralized and secretive form. Large-scale demonstrations, terrorist attacks, and other highly visible acts have dropped significantly. A new generation of white supremacist leaders, much warier of government interference and publicity, presides over a movement that is smaller and much more fragmented than that of the previous decades.

James L. Erwin

See also: Ku Klux Klan; White Supremacists.

Further Reading

Chalmers, David M. *Hooded Americanism: The History of the Ku Klux Klan.* New York: New Viewpoints, 1976.

Dray, Philip. *At the Hands of Persons Unknown: The Lynching of Black America.* New York: Modern Library, 2003.

Hamm, Mark S. *American Skinheads: The Criminology and Control of Hate Crime.* Westport, CT: Praeger, 1993.

Levitas, Daniel. *The Terrorist Next Door: The Militia Movement and the Radical Right.* New York: Thomas Dunne, 2002.

Whitman, Walt (1819–1892)

Walt Whitman was the most famous, influential, and controversial American poet of the nineteenth century. Abandoning literary conventions and creating a distinctive American idiom, he captured in verse the pulse of a young nation with subject matter as free as the democratic principles he championed, rhythms and forms as unfettered as the masses of humanity, and a breaking of cultural barriers that was shocking to many contemporaries. His attention to everyday experience—labor, sexuality, and the joys of living—evoked images that some believed threatened American social values but ultimately others embraced, including aspiring writers and artists.

The son of a Quaker carpenter, Whitman was born on May 31, 1819, on Long Island in New York. While growing up in Huntington and Brooklyn, New York, he wrote various works of fiction and was published in the magazines *American Review* and *Democratic Review.* Early in his life, he enjoyed a successful career as a newspaper journalist in and around New York City, editing and writing for a variety of publications, including the *Brooklyn Daily Eagle* (1846–1848).

As a contributor to the *New Orleans Crescent* in 1848, Whitman made an extended trip to the South, where he witnessed slavery firsthand, experienced the music and nightlife of the French Quarter, and was inspired by the majestic Mississippi River. Upon returning to New York in 1859, Whitman began to write and study an increasing amount of poetry. He created his own style of writing, using more free verse than had ever been used before.

His first and most famous collection, *Leaves of Grass,* consisting of twelve poems, was published in 1855. Whitman continued to revise, extend, and republish the collection for the rest of his life; at least six editions were published over the course of the next

Abandoning literary and cultural convention, nineteenth-century poet Walt Whitman is credited with nothing less than the invention of a national idiom. His verse was an affirmation of the freedom and energy of the "American masses." *(Library of Congress)*

three decades. Among the original twelve poems was one that would become his most famous, "Song of Myself" (untitled in the first edition).

Each new edition of *Leaves of Grass,* universally acclaimed as one of the seminal works of American literature, depicted the changing face of the American people, tested the limits of artistic expression in new ways, and forced readers to recognize new aspects of the emerging national counterculture. With each expanded edition, Whitman included more extensive portrayals of and allusions to sexuality, including homoerotic themes. Many credit Whitman with writing some of the first openly gay American literature.

During the American Civil War, Whitman served as a nurse for the Union Army in Washington, D.C. He wrote poems that focused on the war, many of which were included in his book *Drum-Taps* (1865, later incorporated in *Leaves of Grass*). His writings of this period focus mainly on battle experiences, especially the devastating effects on individual soldiers that became apparent after the smoke cleared from the battlefields. His now-classic poem of 1865, "O Captain,

My Captain," pays homage to President Abraham Lincoln after his assassination in April of that year.

When the war was over, Whitman worked as a clerk in the office of the U.S. attorney general in Washington, D.C., where he was said to be involved in a romantic relationship with Peter Doyle, a former Confederate soldier, that would last a number of years. Whitman continued to write literary pieces about the state of the United States, celebrating the American workingman in the poem "Passage to India" and expressing his frustration with Reconstruction in "Democratic Vistas."

Moving to Camden, New Jersey, in 1873 after suffering a stroke, Whitman began to study photography; subsequent editions of *Leaves of Grass* included photographs of himself. By this time, Whitman was famous throughout the world, not least among homosexual activists in Great Britain and elsewhere. Among those who visited Whitman at his Camden home were homosexual activist Edward Carpenter and Irish writer Oscar Wilde.

The 1881–1882 edition of *Leaves of Grass* was arguably the most controversial. The book was banned in Boston because of its many sexual innuendos, but Whitman stood firm in not changing the controversial verses. His final edition—referred to as the "deathbed edition"—appeared in 1892. Whitman died on March 26 of that year in Camden.

Gavin J. Wilk

See also: Pfaff's Cellar.

Further Reading

Blake, David Haven. *Walt Whitman and the Culture of American Identity.* New Haven, CT: Yale University Press, 2006.
Loving, Jerome. *Walt Whitman: The Song of Himself.* Berkeley: University of California Press, 1999.

Whole Earth Catalog

The *Whole Earth Catalog,* described by publisher Stewart Brand as "a survival manual for the citizens of planet earth," appeared twice annually from 1968 to 1972 and intermittently thereafter, becoming a counterculture standard manual of the early environmental movement, and, according to Apple Computer founder Steve Jobs, an antecedent of the Internet search engine. Brand, a biologist by training, was disenchanted with the cold war political establishment and offered his catalog as a sourcebook of tools for "conducting one's own education, finding one's own inspiration, and shaping one's own environment."

Winner of a National Book Award in 1972, the *Whole Earth Catalog* appealed to former radicals who had lost faith in their ability to effect social change and were pursuing radical self-sufficiency. As a University of Chicago student explained in 1969, "the point is that it's the culture that's sick. . . . One way to change that is to live differently . . . just drop out and live in the way you think it ought to be."

Some of these pioneers went "back to the land," and the catalog became their guidebook. It advertised mail-order wood stoves, wind generators, well-digging and welding equipment, farm implements, maps, waterproof boots, Danish Earth shoes, amplifiers, and strobe lights. It featured articles on home construction, building hot water heaters (and guitars), organic gardening, glass blowing, natural childbirth, and meditation. Brand used five criteria for choosing the items he included in the catalog: usefulness as a tool, relevance to independent education, high quality, low cost, and easy accessibility by mail.

From the first issue in 1968, Brand offered such high-tech tools as hand calculators and radio telephones. Unlike many disillusioned hippies, who considered computers dehumanizing instruments of governmental and organizational control, Brand was optimistic that collaborative networking could link like-minded individuals and actually enhance personal liberation. The introduction of the Internet and the World Wide Web in the mid-1990s affirmed that faith. Brand was also confident that alternative technologies could deal with long-standing environmental issues, and indeed the energy crisis of the 1970s revived interest in wind power, solar energy, biofuels, and waste recycling as environmentalism found a place on the national agenda.

The *Whole Earth Catalog* essentially linked the technological legacy of cold war military and industrial engineering with the counterculture's vision of personal liberation. The outcome was not entirely positive, however, since the resulting techno-revolution inspired a generation of young entrepreneurs whose commercial over-reaching led to the dot-com bust of the early 2000s.

In his 2005 commencement address at Stanford University, Steve Jobs cited the *Whole Earth Catalog* as one of the bibles of his generation. It was "like Google in paperback," he said, "overflowing with neat tools and great notions" whose message was "'Stay hungry. Stay foolish.'"

Mary Stanton

See also: Apple Computer; Hippies; Organic Farming.

Further Reading

Kirk, Andrew. *Counterculture Green: The* Whole Earth Catalog *and American Environmentalism.* Lawrence: University Press of Kansas, 2007.

Rheingold, Howard, ed. *The Millennium Whole Earth Catalog: Access to Tools and Ideas for the Twenty-first Century.* San Francisco: Harper San Francisco, 1994.

Turner, Fred. *From Counterculture to Cyberculture: Stewart Brand, the Whole Earth Network, and the Rise of Digital Utopianism.* Chicago: University of Chicago Press, 2006.

Wilkinson, Jemima (1752–1819)

Jemima Wilkinson was a charismatic eighteenth-century female evangelist who began the first communal society founded by a native-born American, in western New York State. Born into a Quaker family, Wilkinson had a visionary experience in her early twenties that led her to adopt the name "Publick Universal Friend" and to begin an itinerant preaching mission focused primarily in New England and eastern Pennsylvania. As the number of her followers grew, Wilkinson, aided by a few wealthy converts, bought land in western New York and established the community where she would spend the rest of her life. Although most of her religious messages were not particularly innovative or heretical—a mix of Quaker ideals, millennialism, and a belief in personal divine revelation—her appearance and lifestyle indeed created controversy. Some of the outlandish claims made about her parallel similar claims about leaders of other dissenting religious communities.

Wilkinson was born on November 29, 1752, the daughter of Jeremiah Wilkinson and Amey Whipple Wilkinson, and the eighth of twelve children. Growing up on a farm in Rhode Island likely contributed to many of the skills Wilkinson became known for as the Publick Universal Friend, including horseback riding and the use of herbs for medical purposes.

Wilkinson also had an outstanding memory. She read the Bible and books of Quaker theology in depth and was reputed to be able to quote at length from both. Her Quaker heritage clearly was a major influence on her later religious messages, particularly the notion that God could make the divine will known directly through the individual.

In the early 1770s, Wilkinson joined a group of New Light Baptists, religious enthusiasts known for emphasizing individual enlightenment through direct connections with God's spirit. Wilkinson's association with this group led to her removal from the Quaker Society in August 1776. Approximately two months after that, the illness that would lead her to become the Publick Universal Friend began. During that pivotal period of illness, which may have been typhus, Wilkinson claimed to see angels proclaiming messages of universal salvation for humanity. She emerged from the illness convinced she was the host of a spirit sent from God to spread that message.

Taking the name Publick Universal Friend, Wilkinson began holding meetings and traveling to nearby towns to spread her message, a remarkable feat for a young woman during the Revolutionary War. Riding sidesaddle, dressed in the black of a clergyman's costume with a white kerchief around her neck, and accompanied by a small but intensely devoted group, Wilkinson preached repentance, advocated celibacy, practiced faith healing, and interpreted dreams and prophecies.

By 1789, her movement, known as the Universal Friends, had grown to a recognized religious group with about 200 members, mostly former Quakers. As her popularity grew, so did the scurrilous charges against her: that she believed she was the second coming of Jesus; that she cheated her followers out of their money; and that she failed to adhere to her own admonitions to be celibate.

In 1788, a small group of Wilkinson's followers established a settlement on Lake Seneca in western New York; Wilkinson herself joined the settlement permanently two years later. In 1794, after a series of land disputes, the group moved 12 miles (19 kilometers) to the west, where the members founded a community known as Jerusalem on Keuka Lake. The Publick Universal Friend and her community thus played an important role in opening western New York to settlement by European Americans. Wilkinson died at her residence in Jerusalem on July 1, 1819.

Jeremy Rapport

See also: Communes; Quakers.

Further Reading

Ahlstrom, Sydney E. *A Religious History of the American People.* New Haven, CT: Yale University Press, 1972.

Hudson, David. *Memoir of Jemima Wilkinson.* 1844. New York: AMS, 1972.

Wiseby, Herbert A., Jr. *Pioneer Prophetess: Jemima Wilkinson, the Publick Universal Friend.* Ithaca, NY: Cornell University Press, 1964.

Williams, Roger (c. 1603–1683)

An early champion of religious freedom and the separation of church and state, Roger Williams was born in London in about 1603 and educated at Cambridge. He sailed with his wife Mary to the Massachusetts Bay Colony, arriving in early 1631.

In Boston, he refused to join the established Puritan congregation on the grounds that it was not fully separated from the Church of England, which he regarded as apostate. Shortly thereafter, he moved to Plymouth, where he ministered to a separatist congregation.

Acquaintance with indigenous leaders in the Plymouth area led Williams to support Native American rights to land more than did other colonial leaders. When the General Court of Massachusetts convicted him of the crime of "teaching dangerous opinions" and banished him from the Massachusetts Bay Colony in 1635, Williams fled to a Native American community. The following year, he settled at the head of Narragansett Bay, buying land from the Narragansett people and establishing a new colony he called Providence. The colony later became known as Rhode Island.

Williams's Rhode Island was founded on a deep suspicion of any alliance between a particular church and the coercive authority of government. He was passionately concerned for the purity of religion. After a brief flirtation with the doctrine of the Baptists, which led him to found the first American Baptist congregation in 1639, Williams seems to have decided that no established congregation could be pure enough. For the rest of his life, he worshipped in his own household rather than as part of any congregation. A millenarian, Williams believed that true churches could be reestablished on earth only by God's agents, as in the days of the apostles.

Williams's generally good relations with Native Americans continued after the founding of Providence. He was the author of one of the first English books on native languages, *A Key to the Language of America* (1643). The work was published in London on the first of two journeys Williams made to get recognition of his new colony from the English government.

During the same trip, Williams also published a rebuttal of "A Letter of Mr. John Cottons" (1643), by the Massachusetts minister John Cotton. In Williams's rebuttal, titled "Mr. Cotton's Letter Lately Printed, Examined and Answered" (1644), he uses biblical language to portray himself as a witness of the truth in his struggles with corrupt Massachusetts ministers. He also published a book attacking persecution, *The Bloudy Tenent of Persecution* (1644).

During Williams's second visit to England, from 1651 to 1653, he became friends with the English Puritan ruler Oliver Cromwell and published another book on persecution, *The Bloudy Tenent yet more Bloody* (1652). On his second return to Rhode Island, Williams served as governor of the colony from 1654 to 1658.

He continued to champion religious freedom as the new sect of Quakers began to enter New England, although he was suspicious of what he regarded as the Quakers' rejection of the Bible in favor of the promptings of the Holy Spirit. Williams published his debates with the Quakers under the title "George Foxe Digg'd out of His Burrows" (1676), punning on the name of the Quaker leader George Fox.

Roger and Mary Williams had six children. She died in 1676, and he died sometime in 1683. Their descendents continued to thrive and help build what would become the state of Rhode Island.

William E. Burns

See also: Native Americans; Puritans; Quakers.

Further Reading

Gaustad, Edwin S. *Liberty of Conscience: Roger Williams in America.* Grand Rapids, MI: W.B. Eerdmans, 1991.

Morgan, Edmund S. *Roger Williams: The Church and the State.* New York: Harcourt, Brace and World, 1967.

Witchcraft and Wicca

The term *witchcraft* is derived from the Old English verb *wiccian,* which referred to the art of bewitching, casting spells, or manipulating the forces of nature in any supernatural way. Until the fifteenth century, witchcraft could hardly be considered countercultural, as it was at first universally, and then widely, practiced in one form or another throughout the West. Thereafter, it was practiced largely in secret and in defiance of the dominant Christian culture, sometimes resulting in bloody persecution.

A more modern form of witchcraft, commonly referred to as Wicca, took root in Europe at the close of the nineteenth century, and flourished in Britain and the United States in the second half of the twentieth century. Estimates by the American Religious Identity Survey in the early twenty-first century set the number of Wiccan adherents in the United States at just over 130,000.

The Great European Witch Hunt

That form of witchcraft with which most in the West are familiar is that wherein beliefs and rituals are associated with Satan, or the devil. This definition, which took 1,500 years to construct, is referred to as the "cumulative concept of witchcraft." It came to dominate Western thought in the fifteenth century and gave rise to the Great European Witch Hunt, which lasted more than two centuries and crossed the Atlantic to the New World.

In the fifteenth century, witches were pictured as women who rose from their beds in the dark of the night to attend the Sabbat, a witches' version of the Christian sabbath. Witches were believed to have renounced their Christian faith and signed a pact with the devil, who presided over them. In exchange for worshipping him, witches were granted supernatural powers, which they used to commit diabolical acts, raise havoc, seduce other Christians into their cult, and otherwise undermine Christianity—and with it the political, social, and cultural structures of Western civilization.

The Great European Witch Hunt, consisting of hundreds of separate incidents, each involving anywhere from one to thousands of suspects, began in the mid-fifteenth century. Many of the incidents were led by professional witch hunters, whose sole job it was to seek out and prosecute witches. The absence of complete records makes it difficult to establish the exact number of prosecutions during the Great European Witch Hunt. Estimates vary greatly for the 250-year period, with the most plausible figures ranging from 110,000 to 180,000 prosecutions and 60,000 to 100,000 executions. As many as 75 percent of witchcraft prosecutions occurred in Central Europe; conviction and execution rates were highest in this area as well. Over time, however, accusations and executions spread to other parts of Europe and the Western Hemisphere.

The largest outbreak of witch trials in British North America occurred in Salem, Massachusetts, in 1692. A total of nineteen people were hanged, one man was pressed to death, and more than 150 others were jailed. Compared to witch hunts in Europe, it was a minor affair, or, as one historian put it, "a small incident in the history of a great superstition." Nevertheless, the Salem witch hunts have never lost their

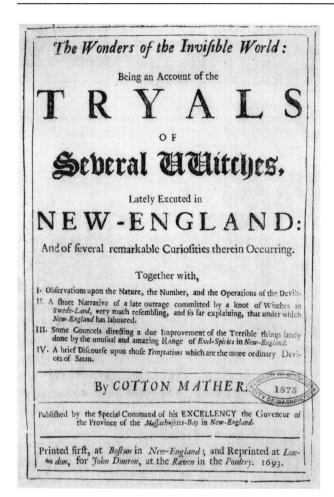

The Wonders of the Invisible World:

Being an Account of the

TRYALS

OF

Several Witches,

Lately Excuted in

NEW-ENGLAND:

And of several remarkable Curiosities therein Occurring.

Together with,

I. Observations upon the Nature, the Number, and the Operations of the Devils.

II. A short Narrative of a late outrage committed by a knot of Witches in Sweds-Land, very much resembling, and so far explaining, that under which New-England has laboured.

III. Some Councels directing a due Improvement of the Terrible things lately done by the unusual and amazing Range of Evil-Spirits in New-England.

IV. A brief Discourse upon those Temptations which are the more ordinary Devices of Satan.

By COTTON MATHER.

Published by the Special Command of his EXCELLENCY the Govenrur of the Province of the Massachusetts-Bay in New-England.

Printed first, at Boston in New-England; and Reprinted at London, for John Dunton, at the Raven in the Poultry. 1693.

Cotton Mather's 1693 pamphlet *The Wonders of the Invisible World* offered an account and defense of the Salem witch trials. The term *witch hunt* still is invoked as a metaphor for the searching out and persecution of persons with unconventional views. *(Library of Congress)*

place in the popular imagination, and the term is still frequently invoked as a metaphor for the extralegal persecution of societal outcasts—such as Communists in cold war America.

Certain elements of the population were disproportionately represented among those accused of witchcraft. Most came from the poorest, weakest, and most vulnerable elements of the population. Seventy-five to 80 percent of the accused were female. Witches commonly identified were women over fifty years of age, and either widowed or never married. They tended to have accumulated a record of what was considered antisocial behavior, including petty crime, and they were seen as sharp-tongued, bad tempered, and prone to quarrels with neighbors and be absent from church.

Some have argued that witchcraft is universally specific to women, but others have shown that such gender identification is more common in the patriarchal societies of the West. Still others point to Christianity's characterization of women as morally weaker than men and therefore more likely to succumb to the diabolical temptations of the devil.

The Salem episode signaled the end of witch hunting, at least as so identified and legally sanctioned in the United States. The people of Massachusetts, like most in the West, continued to believe in witches, but they abandoned any hope of prosecuting them in court. Moreover, as historian John Demos has argued, the very portrayal of witches changed.

Whereas until the seventeenth century witches were portrayed as powerful, formidable, and dangerous adversaries in league with the devil, by the nineteenth century they were identified as "hag-witches," characteristically old, ugly, and decrepit, and living as isolates with little or no human contact. Once a source of fear, they increasingly became a target for contempt, ridicule, and mockery.

Wicca in the Modern World

Beginning in the late nineteenth century, there was a renewed surge of interest, especially among literary and artistic figures, in witchcraft. This interest is sometimes referred to as an occult revival. In the 1920s and 1930s, the Briton Aleister Crowley, who styled himself "the Great Beast," concocted a mix of magic, sorcery, and hedonism often called Satanism, to which, in the 1940s, Margaret Murray added a fertility-cult phenomenon. The two strains were merged and promoted by the English occultist Gerald Gardner beginning in the 1950s.

Gardner gave Wicca its biggest boost with his books *Witchcraft Today* (1954) and *The Meaning of Witchcraft* (1959). He claimed that he had encountered a secret pagan group, into which he had been initiated, that was a remnant of the old witchcraft religion dating to pre-Christian Europe. Thus, Wicca is still commonly referred to as the "Old Religion." Such direct historical roots have been largely discounted, but Gardner's books nevertheless provided the basis upon which modern Wicca has been built.

Modern Wicca became popular in the United States largely due to the efforts of an expatriate Briton, Raymond Buckland, beginning in the early 1960s. The movement evolved eclectically and gained its greatest strength, however, as an outgrowth of the counterculture movements of the 1960s and 1970s. Commonly included in the category of New Age religions, it attracted adherents with its feminine principle and reverence for nature, as opposed to what followers regarded as a patriarchal and environmentally insensitive Christianity. Some found Wicca's rejection of absolute truths appealing.

Modern Wicca is neither a centralized organization nor a single belief system, but rather a wide range of beliefs and practices. In general, Wicca can be divided into two groups. Lineaged Wicca, sometimes called British Traditional Wicca, follows practices outlined by Gardner. Nonlineaged, or Eclectic Wicca, is now the larger of the two groups, especially in the United States. Most Wiccans are organized into largely autonomous covens led by priests and priestesses, many of which have been spun off—or "hived"—from other covens that have grown too large. The ideal size is held to be thirteen members.

In general, Wiccans believe in an ultimate life force called "The One" or "The All," out of which the male and female aspects of life emerged. Most Wiccans worship a goddess and a god, who are seen as complementary in that they represent a balance in nature, sometimes symbolized as the sun and moon. Some Wiccans, especially feminist Wiccans (Dianic Wiccans), reject the male counterpart altogether, preferring to see the goddess as complete in her divinity.

Wiccans believe that the gods are able to manifest themselves in human form through the bodies of the priests or priestesses. In rituals such as drawing down the moon or sun, Wiccans believe that the priestess or priest is able to call down the deity into her or his body in a form of divine possession.

Wiccans practice initiation rites for priests, priestesses, and members, and follow an annual calendar of religious observances or festivals that includes eight Sabbats. Sabbats are Wicca's main religious holidays. Four of them, Samhain, Beltane, Imbolic, and Lammas, are seen as greater than the others; the remaining four are Litha (Summer Solstice), Yule (Winter Solstice), Ostara (Spring Equinox), and Mabon (Autumn Equinox). In addition, Wiccans mark each full moon with a ceremony called Esbats.

Wiccans recognize four elements in nature: earth, air, fire, and water; some add a fifth element, spirit. The five elements are symbolized by the five points on a pentagram, or pentacle, commonly used in Wiccan rituals, with spirit always located at the top. In the casting of the magic circle, the first step in most Wiccan rituals, the four elements are believed to derive their powers from their association with the four cardinal directions of the compass.

Typically, Wiccans fast for a day or ritually bathe before gathering inside the purified circle. Some worship in the nude, or "skyclad"; most wear robes or just street clothing. They pray to the deity or deities, who are welcome guardians of the north, south, east, and west. An altar is erected within the magic circle, on which are placed the tools of the ritual, commonly including a broom, cauldron, chalice, wand, Book of Shadows, altar cloth, athame (a knife use to channel energy), boline (a knife used for cutting), candles, crystals, a pentacle, and incense. The objects have no power in themselves, but each is dedicated to a particular purpose. When the ritual ends, thanks are given to the god and goddess and the circle is closed.

The Wiccan code of ethics is commonly explained as being based on the Wiccan Rede and the Law of Threefold Return, both of which suggest that adherents are free to act as they wish, as long as they take responsibility for their actions and do no harm, lest what they do return to them three times over. More specifically, they adhere to eight virtues—mirth, reverence, honor, humility, strength, beauty, power, and compassion—and 161 laws. Wiccans believe in reincarnation and flatly deny any association between them and practitioners of Black Magic or Satanism. As Wiccans point out repeatedly, they do not believe in the existence of the devil or any similar entity as recognized by Christians. Although misunderstood and viewed with suspicion in some quarters, adherents to this latter-day reincarnation of nature worship coexist relatively peacefully with their Christian neighbors.

Wiccans, despite sometimes inaccurate and negative perceptions and their countercultural status, have attained a certain level of acceptance in American society. In 1986, in the precedent-setting case *Dettmer v. Landon,* the United States Court of Appeals for the Fourth Circuit upheld a lower court decision that ruled that Wicca is a legally recognized religion and therefore to be afforded all the benefits accorded to other recognized religions by law. In 2007, the U.S. Department of Veterans Affairs adopted a policy allowing the pentacle, as an "emblem of belief," to be placed on grave markers in military cemeteries.

Bryan F. Le Beau

See also: New Age.

Further Reading

Adler, Margot. *Drawing Down the Moon: Witches, Druids, Goddess Worshippers and Other Pagans in America Today.* New York: Viking, 1979.

Buckland, Raymond. *The Witch Book: The Encyclopedia of Witchcraft, Wicca, and Neo-Paganism.* Detroit, MI: Visible Ink, 2002.

Demos, John Putnam. *Entertaining Satan: Witchcraft and the Culture of Early New England.* New York: Oxford University Press, 1982.

Gardner, Gerald B. *Witchcraft Today.* 1954. Yucca Valley, CA: Citadel, 2004.

Hall, David D. *Worlds of Wonder, Days of Judgment: Popular Religious Belief in Early New England.* New York: Alfred A. Knopf, 1989.

Hutton, Ronald. *The Triumph of the Moon: A History of Modern Pagan Witchcraft.* Oxford, UK: Oxford University Press, 1999.

Karlsen, Carol. *The Devil in the Shape of a Woman: Witchcraft in Colonial New England.* New York: W.W. Norton, 1987.

Russell, Jeffery. *A History of Witchcraft: Sorcerers, Heretics, and Pagans.* London: Thames and Hudson, 1980.

Wobblies

See Industrial Workers of the World

Woodhull, Victoria (1838–1927)

Between her birth into poverty and her death as the widow of a wealthy British banker, Victoria Claflin Woodhull was a woman who acted in ways that were years ahead of her time. She was a successful newspaper editor, the first American woman stockbroker, and the first woman to be nominated as a candidate for president of the United States. Although her forward-looking activities took their toll on Woodhull's reputation and financial health, she remained steadfast in her resolve to be an example of independence and self-actualization to all women.

Born on September 23, 1838, into a family of nine children in Homer, Ohio, she remained closest to her sister, Tennessee Claflin, throughout her life. Daughters of an alcoholic and abusive braggart, the two girls performed as spiritualists when Victoria was eleven years old in their father's attempt to cash in on that craze. By the age of fifteen, Victoria was married for the first time, to patent-medicine salesman Canning Woodhull, who similarly used the girl to sell his wares.

Eleven years later, she divorced Woodhull, married Colonel James Blood, and moved to New York City along with her sister. The wealthy financier Cornelius Vanderbilt soon provided funding for the sisters to embark on their own careers.

With Vanderbilt's $7,000, the women opened Woodhull, Claflin and Company, a highly successful brokerage firm. Victoria became wealthy and channeled her funds into a candidacy for president under the auspices of the Equal Rights Party in 1872; the abolitionist Frederick Douglass was her running mate. The campaign was doomed because her main supporters—women—did not have the right to vote. Woodhull still spoke out energetically about her beliefs, including the need for woman suffrage, the value of free love, and the evils of racism and economic inequality.

As part of their brokerage venture, the sisters also published a radical newspaper, *Woodhull & Claflin's Weekly,* which advocated on behalf of such countercultural causes as socialism, universal suffrage, free love, birth control, and vegetarianism. In 1872, the newspaper published the first English translation of Karl Marx and Friedrich Engels's *Communist Manifesto.* Most Americans were aghast at the audacity of women engaging such unseemly topics; among those who decried the paper was the popular preacher Henry Ward Beecher.

When Beecher's attacks continued and increased in their ferocity, Woodhull struck back, exposing what would come to be known as the Scandal of the Century: a case of marital infidelity involving Beecher and the wife of his protégé, Theodore Tilton. Anthony Comstock, widely recognized as the nation's self-appointed guardian of morality, took up Beecher's cause. Victoria, Tennessee, and the colonel were repeatedly arrested and charged with libel under the Comstock Act of 1873, a federal law that prohibited sending obscene material through the mail. Although legal fees led to the insolvency of the sisters' brokerage firm and newspaper, they were eventually acquitted of all charges. Interestingly, many who had originally opposed Woodhull came to her defense on the basis of protecting her First Amendment rights.

Despite the defamation and the financial difficulties that came with it, Woodhull never wavered in her belief that women deserved the full recognition and rights accorded to men, including the right to sexual and marital self-fulfillment. By her example and in direct advocacy, Victoria Woodhull was a forerunner of the feminist movements of the late nineteenth and early twentieth centuries. She died on June 9, 1927, in Worcester, England.

Barbara Schwarz Wachal

See also: Communism; Douglass, Frederick; Free Love; Socialism; Suffragists.

Further Reading

Gabriel, Mary. *Notorious Victoria: The Life of Victoria Woodhull, Uncensored.* Chapel Hill, NC: Algonquin, 1998.

Johnston, Johanna. *Satan: The Incredible Saga of Victoria C. Woodhull.* New York: Putnam, 1967.

Woodstock Music and Art Fair

The Woodstock Music and Art Fair, commonly known as the Woodstock festival or simply Woodstock, was held from August 15 to 18, 1969, on a 600-acre (240-hectare) dairy farm in Bethel, New York, owned by Max Yasgur. The concert lineup attracted some of the biggest names in rock music, including Jimi Hendrix, Jefferson Airplane, and the Grateful Dead, along with folk artists such as Joan Baez and Arlo Guthrie. More than 400,000 spectators listened to music in the largest open-air music festival of the 1960s. Much more than a musical concert, however, Woodstock represents the confluence of cultural and social movements concerned with the war in Vietnam, politics, and civil rights.

Four investors organized Woodstock Ventures in March 1969: concert producer Michael Land, recording engineer Artie Kornfeld, and venture capitalists John Roberts and Joel Rosenman. The original idea was to build a recording studio in the small, upstate New York town of Woodstock, where several rock musicians had moved by the late 1960s. The four organizers proposed a concert, and then a two-day festival accommodating 50,000 to 100,000 fans, to fund the studio.

Due to objections from local residents, the town of Woodstock was discarded as a location for the event. A similar fate awaited Woodstock Ventures concerning the town of Wallkill, New York, and its zoning board, whose apprehensions were heightened by rumors of possible marijuana use. Searching for a suitable venue, Woodstock Ventures advertised in local newspapers and finally heard from Yasgur, who responded through a realtor, Morris Abraham. Yasgur's farm featured a natural amphitheater, removed from the urban setting of earlier music festivals, and a deal was struck with the event organizers.

The festival's slogan was "Three Days of Peace and Music . . . An Aquarian Exposition," and the venture group created posters that would draw attention to the event without naming all of the performers. After negotiations with activist Abbie Hoffman and his Youth International Party (whose adherents were called "yippies"), Woodstock Ventures provided a concession for the distribution of leftist literature.

Woodstock took on a character different from previous rock music festivals, which were mostly regional events. With widespread marketing and advertising, Woodstock attracted the attention of the entire nation.

By mid-July 1969, $500,000 worth of tickets had been sold. Due to lack of advance preparation, however, it was not possible to collect tickets—the crowd was estimated at 400,000 people. The audience was predominantly white and middle class, with more males in attendance than females.

When the festival began, highway closures and rainy weather prevented some of the bands from appearing on time. The first performer was folk singer Richie Havens, who performed the antiwar songs "Handsome Johnny" and "Freedom." With several groups continuing to experience difficulty arriving at the venue, Country Joe McDonald sang several solo songs, including the satirical and antiwar "I-Feel-Like-I'm-Fixin'-To-Die Rag." McDonald and John Sebastian performed impromptu sets.

Without ticket booths, Woodstock became a free festival. This sparked rumors that musicians, who had been asked to perform longer sets than originally agreed upon, would not be paid. The Who and the Grateful Dead demanded cash, which was not on hand, although cashier's checks were in a bank. These were retrieved and sent via helicopter to the festival.

The music featured at Woodstock also was influenced by the "back-to-the-land" movement, characterized by a migration from cities to rural locales. This was reflected by Alan Wilson's song "Going Up the Country," performed by Canned Heat. Others who reflected this philosophy were the ensemble Crosby, Stills, Nash and Young, and Joan Baez.

Counterculture values were deeply ingrained in many musicians who performed at Woodstock and wrote, spoke, and sang of social idealism and anticommercialism; among these were Guthrie, Janis Joplin, Jefferson Airplane, and Joe Cocker. Hendrix's solo performance of "The Star-Spangled Banner" carried a powerful antiwar message.

Due to inadequate food and sanitation, the audience adopted a communal approach to life at the festival, with sharing and cooperation. Area resorts helped to alleviate the food shortage with contributions. The eighty farmers of the Hog Farm Collective, an early cooperative commune of the counterculture era, assisted the concertgoers and provided a free kitchen to attendees. Hog Farmer Lisa Law instructed attendees in how to live off the land. Hog Farmer Hugh Romney (later known as activist Wavy Gravy) stood on the stage and announced, "What we have in mind is breakfast in bed for 400,000!" Tom Law taught yoga each morning.

Other Hog Farmers assisted with security. New York Police Department (NYPD) Commissioner How-

Advance ticket sales to attendees of the Woodstock music festival were so great—exceeding 185,000—that organizers were forced to move the venue to a meadow at White Lake in the town of Bethel. More than 200,000 others were let in free. *(Blank Archives/Hulton Archive/Getty Images)*

ard Leary had forbidden NYPD officers' participation as off-duty security. In response, many joined the Woodstock Peace Officers using fictitious names.

Marijuana use was rampant at Woodstock among performers and concertgoers alike. LSD (lysergic acid diethylamide, or acid) also was plentiful. Hog Farmers assisted medical personnel treating those experiencing bad LSD trips in special "freak-out tents." The Hog Farmers had previous experience with negative reactions to LSD.

Rain, mud, and poor sanitation were part of the Woodstock experience. Traffic jams blocked back roads and forced major highways to be closed. Nevertheless, those in attendance regarded the festival as an extension of the communal life that had permeated the early 1960s. Even if many festivalgoers had never taken part in communal living for longer than three days, Woodstock came to epitomize the free-love phi-

losophy and hippie lifestyle. The event, incidentally, lost more than $1 million.

In an effort to re-create some of the original Woodstock experience, organizers launched Woodstock '94, also called Woodstock II, at the 840-acre (340-hectare) Winston farm in Saugerties, New York, about 60 miles (96 kilometers) northeast of the original festival site. While featuring newer bands, a younger audience (about 250,000 attended), and greatly improved sound technology, Woodstock II, by many accounts, re-created much of the drug use experienced at the original event. More commercial in terms of on-site vendors than the first event, this event also was overcrowded for the site and suffered from rain, deep mud, and sanitary issues.

The thirtieth-anniversary festival, Woodstock 1999, was held on the former site of Griffiss Air Force Base in Rome, New York. The three-day July event, carried on pay-per-view television, fell victim to logistical errors, from high ticket prices to inadequate facilities. Incidents of violence and arson finally forced the show to be shut down.

Ralph Hartsock

See also: Baez, Joan; Grateful Dead; Hendrix, Jimi; Hippies; Hoffman, Abbie; Jefferson Airplane; Joplin, Janis; LSD; Marijuana; Rock and Roll; Yippies.

Further Reading

Bennett, Andy, ed. *Remembering Woodstock.* Aldershot, UK: Ashgate, 2004.

Perone, James E. *Music of the Counterculture Era.* Westport, CT: Greenwood, 2004.

———. *Woodstock: An Encyclopedia of the Music and Art Fair.* Westport, CT: Greenwood, 2005.

Woolman, John (1720–1772)

Itinerant Quaker minister John Woolman was one of the first prominent American abolitionists, a leader of the antislavery movement of the eighteenth century, and an advocate of pacifism and radical Christianity both in his writings, including a popular autobiography, and in his life.

He was born in Northampton, New Jersey, on October 19, 1720. In his posthumously published *Journal* (1774), Woolman traced his opposition to slavery to misgivings he had had when an early employer asked him to draw up a bill of sale for a slave woman. He reluctantly acquiesced, but refused any further involvement in slavery and spoke out against it during his travels.

Woolman's concern for the deprived extended to other communities as well. A journey across the Atlantic Ocean led to reflections on the poverty and spiritual deprivation of sailors. In his account of a missionary journey among Native Americans, he viewed native society in a way differently than other white writers of the eighteenth century: not in terms of its differences from Anglo-European society, but emphasizing what the two cultures had in common. In his view, the "warrior spirit," said to have wrought damage to Native Americans, also deformed white society.

Woolman's analyses of the miserable state of slaves, of Native Americans oppressed by white authority, and of the poor all laid blame on the rich for their greed and love of luxury, although he tended to depict his adversaries not as wicked sinners, but as poor creatures in need of truth. His remedy for social evils was individual reformation, which extended to all aspects of life. For instance, he urged nonpayment of taxes if they were to be spent on war.

His hatred of luxury and unnecessary consumption led him to condemn much that others might have seen as harmless diversion, such as colorful clothing. Concerned about the oppression of enslaved workers in the dye trades, Woolman wore only undyed cloth. His disapproval extended even to such "follies" as a magic show at a tavern.

But not all of Woolman's *Journal* was devoted to social analysis. Like other Quaker writers, he recounted his dreams, visions, and spiritual experiences. He wrote very little about his private or family life.

Woolman's first antislavery tract was *Some Considerations on the Keeping of Negroes Recommended to the Professors of Christianity of Every Denomination* (1754), in which he emphasized both the inhumanity of slavery and the insidious way it corrupted the morality of white slave owners. Mastery, he contended, contributed to pride and the love of domination, the vices Woolman most reviled. By being inextricably implicated in the cruelty of slavery, masters hardened their hearts; by living off the labor of slaves, moreover, they and their children became lazy. Slavery could never be justified, Woolman maintained, as black Africans possessed the same natural and god-given right of freedom as white English people.

As implied in his address to "Christians," Woolman made extensive use of the Bible in demonstrating the evil and unlawfulness of slavery. He was a leader in convincing the Quakers' Philadelphia Yearly Meeting to prohibit its members from buying and selling slaves, and, in 1762, he published *Considerations on Keeping Negroes; Recommended to the Professors of Christianity, of Every Denomination, Part Second.*

Woolman died on October 7, 1772, in York, England, while on a missionary journey.

William E. Burns

See also: Abolitionism; Pacifism; Quakers; *Document:* John Woolman's *Journal* (1757).

Further Reading

Rosenblatt, Paul. *John Woolman.* New York: Twayne, 1969.
Shea, Daniel B. *Spiritual Autobiography in Early America.* 2nd ed. Madison: University of Wisconsin Press, 1988.

Wright, Frances (1795–1852)

During the early to mid-1800s, Scottish-born Frances Wright was an active and respected advocate for a range of social reform movements in American, including feminism, the abolition of slavery, universal and equal education, and the rights of children. The freethinking social critic also was an outspoken opponent of organized religion, authoritarianism, and capitalism. Inspired by the utopian socialism of Robert Owen and his son Robert Dale Owen, Wright became an active proponent of cooperative living and social planning. In addition, she is credited with being the first woman to deliver a public lecture before a mixed audience, an Independence Day speech at the Owens's utopian socialist community New Harmony in 1828.

Wright was born in Dundee, Scotland, on September 6, 1795. Orphaned at the age of three, she, along with her younger sister, went to live with their uncle James Mylne, a progressive professor of moral philosophy at the University of Glasgow. In 1818, she visited the United States for the first time. Upon her return to England she published her observations of American cultural life in *Views of Society and Manners in America* (1821), an early and overlooked example of modern sociology. In part a celebration of attempts to define and practice democracy in the United States, the book was taken up by parliamentary reformers in England who sought to transform their own country's politics.

In 1824, Frances Wright and her sister joined the Marquis de Lafayette during his travels to the United States, taking American citizenship the following year. Of great significance was Frances's visit to the community of New Harmony in Indiana. New Harmony was a real-world example of Robert Owen's philosophy of socialism through cooperative labor and communal living.

In 1825, Wright helped found the Nashoba Commune, a 2,000-acre (810-hectare) woodland settlement in western Tennessee that she envisioned as an autonomous, self-sufficient, multiracial community made up of former slaves, free blacks, and whites. Controversially, Wright's undertaking involved the purchase of slaves from their owners, who would be paid from the production of slave labor in the fields of Nashoba. Wright believed that such a venture could be more profitable than slavery, given the greater efficiency of "free" labor over slave labor, and that demonstrating this could help render the slave labor system obsolete.

The experiment was, from the outset, beset by difficulties. Not the least of these was the suspicion with which urban free blacks and slaves viewed the project and its stated goals of recolonization. Slaves were skeptical regarding claims that the people who held their ownership papers, and indeed gained materially from their labor, were devoted to their liberation. Urban free blacks questioned the prospects for practicing sustainable agriculture on unsuitable lands. Slaves and free blacks alike expressed concern about being moved to an unfamiliar part of the country, where the language differed from the dialect they themselves spoke. By 1828, the experiment was largely abandoned; in 1839, Wright chartered a vessel, the *John Quincy Adams,* and accompanied the commune's thirty freed saves to Haiti.

The general failure of Nashoba did not discourage Wright from remaining involved in social activism. She soon embarked on what would be credited as the first public-speaking tour by a woman in the United States. In her lectures, Wright explained her libertarian views on issues such as sexual equality, free love, marriage as domination, and birth control. She also spoke out against the growing tide of religious revivalism, asserting the need for rational debate and empirical observation against the unobservable authorities of faith and tradition.

Following the collapse of Nashoba, Wright moved to New Harmony, which was facing its own imminent demise. There, she joined Robert Dale Owen, who had remained at the commune despite his father's departure, as coeditor of the *New Harmony Gazette.* In 1829, Wright and Owen moved the newspaper to New York City, re-launching it under a new title, the *Free Enquirer.*

During this period, Wright, now in closer contact with the urban poor and working classes, developed her strongest advocacy of socialism and working-class organizations. She viewed cooperative labor and universal education as the dual mechanisms by which the abolition of slavery and the freedom of the working classes might be achieved. Owen and Wright founded the first labor-oriented U.S. political party, the Working Men's Party, in New York. Among the projects Wright developed was a day school for the children of workers and a dispensary for working-class families.

Wright also spoke out against capital punishment in society at large and corporal punishment within the home, linking social punishment with the development of authoritarianism in interpersonal relationships, especially involving the authority of the parent over the child. Wright became an advocate of equal education in free schools in which children would be able to enjoy a holistic education, receiving academic as well as technical training free from any religious doctrine. She envisioned this arrangement as one that freed parents from the economic burdens of raising children, while freeing children from their status as familial possessions. During the 1830s and 1840s, Wright became active in the Popular Health movement, a broad-based social movement that focused on educating individuals about their health and how to prevent disease. The movement aimed its education efforts at women, as the caretakers of their families and communities, and promoted a healthy diet, exercise, dress reform to eliminate corsets, and the use of sexual abstinence in marriage to limit family size.

In 1831, Wright married a French doctor, Guillaume D'Arusmont, with whom she had a daughter; they were divorced in 1850. Following a short time living in Paris, during which time she dropped out of the public sphere, Wright returned to America in 1835 to resume her lecture tours. During the time she had spent abroad, her influence had diminished, however, and the lectures were disappointingly attended.

Wright died in relative obscurity on December 13, 1852. Her epitaph proclaimed her lifelong commitment to social justice: "I have wedded the cause of human improvement, staked on it my fortune, my reputation and my life."

Jeff Shantz

See also: Abolitionism; Feminism, First-Wave; Owen, Robert Dale.

Further Reading

Eckhardt, Celia Morris. *Fanny Wright: Rebel in America.* Cambridge, MA: Harvard University Press, 1984.

Kissel, Susan S. *In Common Cause: The "Conservative" Frances Trollope and the "Radical" Frances Wright.* Bowling Green, OH: Bowling Green State University Popular Press, 1983.

Pease, William H., and Jane H. Pease. "A New View of Nashoba." *Tennessee Historical Quarterly* 19 (1960): 99–109.

Sampson, Sheree. "Reclaiming a Historic Landscape: Frances Wright's Nashoba Plantation in Germantown, Tennessee." *Tennessee Historical Quarterly* 59 (2000): 290–303.

Wright, Richard (1908–1960)

Richard Wright was an acclaimed and controversial African American novelist, short-story writer, essayist, and poet who portrayed and bluntly criticized the racial and social oppression of African Americans in urban societies, espoused Third World liberation, and found solace as an expatriate in France after World War II. Regarded as one of the leading lights of modern African American fiction, Wright is best known for his novel *Native Son* (1940), about the life of a young black man raised in Chicago who falls victim to white-dominated society, and *Black Boy* (1945), an autobiography of his unhappy youth in the Deep South.

Richard Nathaniel Wright was born on September 4, 1908, near Natchez, Mississippi, to Ella Wilson, a teacher, and Nathaniel Wright, a sharecropper. His father abandoned the household when the boy was five, and his mother worked as a maid to support the family. Ella Wilson became ill in 1914, and Wright was shuffled among his maternal relatives until he moved in with his maternal grandmother in Jackson, Mississippi, in 1920. Although his grandmother discouraged his interest in literature, Wright published his first story, "The Voodoo of Hell's Half-Acre" in the *Southern Register,* a local black newspaper, in 1924. After graduating from the ninth grade in 1925, he pursued his literary fascination by reading H.L. Mencken's critiques of racism and the naturalistic fiction then in vogue among American writers.

In 1927, Wright moved to Chicago, where he became involved in radical politics. Drawn to its philosophy of racial and social equality, he joined the Communist party in 1932 and published his proletarian poems in leftist-liberal magazines such as *Left Front* and *Partisan Review.* When, in 1937, a group of Chicago Communists accused him of betraying the party, Wright left for New York.

In New York, he became the editor of Harlem's *Daily Worker* newspaper. Shortly after his arrival, he received an award from the Works Progress Administration (WPA), the New Deal work-relief agency, for *Uncle Tom's Children* (1938), a collection of novellas based on his childhood. He also won a Guggenheim Fellowship in 1939 to finish *Native Son* (1940). In 1941, the National Association for the Advancement of Colored People (NAACP) honored Wright with the Springarn Medal for *Native Son,* a stage version of which he coproduced on Broadway. Wright's literary accomplishments continued with *Twelve Million Voices* (1941), a folk history. About this time, his marriage to Rose Dhima Meadman, a white dancer, ended, and, in 1941, Wright married Ellen Poplar, a daughter of Polish Jewish immigrants and a fellow leftist.

Disappointed with the Communist Party's weakening position against segregation, Wright left the organization in 1944 and wrote "I Tried to Be a Communist" in the *Atlantic Monthly.* He later described his involvement with communism and his encounters with racial prejudice in the acclaimed *Black Boy* (1945).

In 1946, Wright moved to Paris, where he was greeted by existentialist writers Jean-Paul Sartre and

A prominent voice of the modern African American experience, Richard Wright wrote powerful and controversial narratives of racial oppression and social isolation. His work directly influenced younger black novelists and poets. *(Library of Congress)*

Simone de Beauvoir. After returning briefly to the United States, he settled there permanently, becoming a French citizen, in 1947. In France, he supported the Pan-African organization Présence Africaine (African Presence) and backed the anti-Stalin Rassemblement Démocratique Révolutionnaire (Revolutionary Democratic Group). He incorporated his political beliefs into his next two novels, *The Outsider* (1953), which denounces communism and fascism, and *Black Power* (1954), which criticizes British colonialism and espouses African independence. Later texts include *The Color Curtain* (1956), an account of the 1955 conference of nonaligned nations in Bandung, Indonesia; *White Man, Listen!* (1957), a collection of essays on race; and the novel *The Long Dream* (1958).

Despite suffering from amoebic dysentery, which he contracted on a trip to Africa in 1957, Wright organized a final work, the short-story collection *Eight Men,* published posthumously in 1961. He died of a heart attack in Paris on November 28, 1960. He was buried there with a copy of *Black Boy.*

Dorsia Smith

See also: African Americans; Communism.

Further Reading

Kinnamon, Keneth, and Michel Fabre, eds. *Conversations with Richard Wright.* Jackson: University Press of Mississippi, 1993.

Rowley, Hazel. *Richard Wright: The Life and Times.* New York: Henry Holt, 2001.

Wright, Richard. *American Hunger.* New York: Harper & Row, 1977.

X-Files, The

The X-Files was a popular science-fiction television series (1993–2002) created by writer-director-producer Chris Carter that helped solidify the burgeoning Fox Network's market share of evening network television. The 201 shows in the series follow the exploits of Federal Bureau of Investigation (FBI) Special Agents Fox Mulder (played by David Duchovny) and Dana Scully (Gillian Anderson) as they attempt to unravel unsolved cases involving strange, unexplained, or paranormal events.

Set in the contemporary United States, the show featured stories that played to late-twentieth-century fascinations with conspiracy theories, the possibility of extraterrestrial life, and the occult. These phenomena reached a peak in American culture shortly after the premiere of *The X-Files,* which parlayed cold war paranoia into a winning blend of skepticism and conjecture. Building on such real-life events as the assassinations of President John F. Kennedy, civil rights leader Martin Luther King, Jr., and Senator Robert Kennedy in the 1960s, and the Watergate scandal of the 1970s, *The X-Files* painted a picture of a monolithic shadow government dictating domestic and international policy.

By the end of its first season, *The X-Files* had captured a substantial market share and had a loyal fan base. The Internet played a major role in the show's popularity, as hundreds of online fan sites and discussion groups sprang up, and fans lobbied their local Fox Network affiliate stations to carry the new series.

Over subsequent seasons, the appeal and popularity of *The X-Files* broadened even further, and the fan base became even more committed. Eventually acquiring the nickname X-Philes, fans of the show began to hold conventions, publish online newsletters, and speculate about the depth and breadth of the series' conspiratorial storylines. Further fan speculation was encouraged as *The X-Files* featured crossovers and references to other Fox Network shows, such as *Millennium* and *Strange Luck.*

The X-Files reached the zenith of its popularity in 1998 with the release of a feature film that attempted to advance most of the show's important storylines simultaneously. The film, titled *The X-Files,* met with lukewarm reaction from fans and critics alike. Most fans of the TV show, in fact, mark the creative peak in the fifth season (1997–1998), immediately before the film's release. Along with the film came innumerable merchandising efforts, tie-in novels, toys, and games, diluting the program's original niche appeal and alienating many fans. A spin-off series, *The Lone Gunmen,* ran for thirteen episodes in 2001 and featured minor recurring characters from the original show.

The X-Files came to an end after the ninth season, in May 2002. In the final two seasons, according to fans and TV critics, major cast changes and a loss of overall tone and focus contributed to the series' decline. Today, X-Philes continue to hold conventions across the globe, and the Internet fan culture is still active.

Jeffrey Sartain

See also: Science Fiction; UFOs.

Further Reading

Lowry, Brian. *The Truth Is Out There: The Official Guide to* The X-Files. Vol. 1. New York: HarperPrism, 1995.

Yippies

The yippies, members of the Youth International Party (YIP), were a loosely affiliated group of individuals who envisioned themselves as the politically radical answer to hippies—bohemian youth disillusioned with the nature of American life—and aimed to politicize the 1960s counterculture. Known for their use of guerrilla theater, pranks, and outright absurdity to gain the attention of the American public and media, the yippies were among the most imaginative of the 1960s-era activists.

Beginnings

The term *yippie* was coined in 1967 by radical journalist Paul Krassner, to distinguish himself and fellow activists who participated in the youth counterculture from the often apolitical hippies and the radical, student-oriented New Left. *Yippie* was intended as both a play on the word *hippie* and to express the joy members experienced in carrying out their inventive forms of protest.

The de facto leadership of the yippies included Krassner and activists Jerry Rubin, Abbie and Anita Hoffman, and Stewart (Stew) Albert, among others, but there was no formal hierarchy or structure to the group. The yippies also had little unified purpose or philosophy, allowing each individual to determine for himself or herself what being a yippie meant.

Abbie Hoffman and Rubin were the most recognizable figures among the yippies, each spending considerable time writing and speaking, in addition to demonstrating. Though the two are often considered the brains behind the yippies' actions, each had his own opinion about the goals of the Youth International Party.

For Hoffman, the yippies represented a merging of the hippie and New Left philosophies, uniting the counterculture with political action. The intent was to make a statement through what Hoffman termed "revolutionary action-theater" and leave the interpretation of the statement up to the individual. Rubin's view was less structured. He insisted that *yippie* meant "an excuse to rebel" and that there was no specific aim to a yippie's actions. Although their visions of the group did not entirely coincide, both Hoffman and Rubin agreed that *yippie* could mean anything one wanted it to—that the interpretation was in the eye of the beholder.

Tactics

The use of guerrilla theater, which Hoffman learned from the Diggers (a late-1960s San Francisco–based radical community-action group of improvisational actors), was among the most popular of the yippies' tactics to draw attention to what they considered the absurdities of American life and culture in the Vietnam War era. Their actions during 1967 and 1968 ranged from participating in the March on Washington against the Vietnam War in October 1967—during which they promised to "levitate" the Pentagon, using psychic energy in order to exorcise its bad spirits—to nominating a pig ("Pigasus the Immortal") for president of the United States. ("Why vote for half a hog when you can have the whole thing?" they asked.)

Among their most notable actions was an August 1967 demonstration at the New York Stock Exchange in which they sent a shower of dollar bills onto the trading floor from the visitors' gallery. Stock traders stopped their work in shock and scrambled to catch the money falling from above. While it caused only a brief pause in the frantic pace of the stock exchange, the yippies regarded the event as a huge success—they had caused a sort of hiccup in the normal functioning of the American capitalist system. Aside from causing a disruption, however, the demonstration achieved another of their main goals: gaining attention from the news media and the public.

The yippies also relied on dramatic public discourse—exaggerations, provocations, and put-ons—to gain attention and publicity for their demonstrations. During the months leading up to the 1968 Democratic National Convention in Chicago, yippie handbills and speeches invited protesters to a Festival of Life during the convention and suggested that those demonstrating have sex in the streets and release LSD into the water supply, among other propositions. Most incitements were intentionally vague in order to gain more media attention and to allow for broader interpretation—thereby enabling each participant to feel a greater personal connection with the event.

The Festival of Life led to a significant altercation between protesters and police almost immediately. Mayor Richard Daley and the city of Chicago had refused to issue permits for any demonstration, and police began arresting protesters before any trouble began. Believing the yippie provocations, police acted to prevent any public danger, such as drugs in the water supply. The response proved extreme. Early confrontations devolved into what was later termed a "police riot," with law enforcement officers attacking and beating hundreds of protesters, bystanders, and representatives of the news media. The events were captured on film, though not widely broadcast, and word of the police riot spread quickly. The nation was shocked by the brutality of the Chicago police force. Although the violence left many protesters injured, the publicity alone made the demonstration a success for the yippies.

The demonstrations in Chicago also resulted in the arrest and trial of Hoffman and Rubin, along with other demonstration organizers. This group later became known as the Chicago Seven. The demonstrators were charged with conspiracy and inciting a riot. Represented by radical attorney William Kunstler, the defendants became national celebrities for their courtroom antics, including open ridicule of Judge Julius Hoffman and the donning of judges' robes in mockery of the American judicial system.

Legacy

The yippies gradually disbanded, as most members departed to pursue different goals. Following a major drug bust in 1973, Hoffman went underground for almost seven years, initially with the assistance of Weatherman, a radical leftist organization that was composed of former members of the Students for a Democratic Society. He remained politically active

Members of the Youth International Party ("yippies") introduce their presidential candidate for 1968—Pigasus the Immortal—while in Chicago for the Democratic National Convention. *(Julian Wasser/Time & Life Pictures/Getty Images)*

until his suicide in 1989. Rubin, who later became a businessman, died in 1994 after being hit by a car while jaywalking. Others went on to become notable writers, scholars, politicians, and activists.

The yippies pointed to some success in their attempts to politicize the youth of the counterculture. Still, in later years, both Rubin and Hoffman expressed regrets about their yippie pasts. Rubin had altered his political views entirely, while Hoffman lamented how little change they had been able to effect. Regardless, the yippies were among the most noteworthy of the counterculture groups of the 1960s for their ability to convince others to join their fight and to have as much fun as possible in the process.

Kathryn L. Meiman

See also: Chicago Seven; Guerrilla Theater; Hoffman, Abbie; LSD; New Left; Rubin, Jerry; Vietnam War Protests.

Further Reading

Hoffman, Abbie. *Revolution for the Hell of It*. New York: Pocket Books, 1970.

———. *Steal This Book*. New York: Pirate Editions, 1971.

Raskin, Jonah. *For the Hell of It: The Life and Times of Abbie Hoffman*. Berkeley: University of California Press, 1996.

Rubin, Jerry. *Do It! Scenarios of the Revolution*. New York: Simon and Schuster, 1970.

Yoga

Yoga is the practice of physical and mental exercise to promote physical, psychological, and spiritual health. The word *yoga* is a Sanskrit term, and the practice has cultural and historic ties to Hinduism and other Indian belief systems dating back thousands of years. Although there are many varieties of yoga, emphasizing different types of exercise, the form generally practiced outside India in modern times is most closely associated with hatha yoga, emphasizing the practice of physical postures (asanas), slow breathing, relaxation, and meditation. While yoga in contemporary America is a mainstream activity for physical health and relaxation, it has historic roots in countercultural groups seeking to challenge mainstream religious and political beliefs.

The introduction of yoga to the Western world, and the United States in particular, occurred in the late 1800s, corresponding to the introduction of Hinduism. In 1893, Swami Vivekananda spoke in Chicago at the Parliament of World Religions, engaging an audience curious about Eastern practices. In 1894, he established the Vedanta Society of New York, a spiritual organization rooted in Hinduism, for the purpose of sharing spiritual knowledge. The Vedanta Society continues to thrive into the twenty-first century, with study centers located around the world.

Through the 1910s, however, yoga faced a precarious situation in American media and culture, largely due to nativist response to ongoing waves of immigration. Initially regarded as a curiosity, yoga was now demonized, charged with the corruption of youth, enslavement of white women, and other social problems. Interest increased as federal immigration restrictions loosened in the early 1920s, giving limited access to Indian yoga masters, but the practice was largely confined to small circles of adherents from mid-decade through the 1940s.

Yoga underwent a resurgence as a secular form of exercise during the 1950s and 1960s, with books such as *Sport and Yoga* (1953) by Selvarajan Yesudian and *Richard Hittleman's Yoga: 28 Day Exercise Plan* (1969) engaging a wider audience. Classes began to be held at community centers, at Young Men's Christian Associations (YMCAs), and on television. Early celebrity practitioners, including Marilyn Monroe and Gary Cooper, further fueled the public interest. In 1961, the *Los Angeles Times* ran a multipart series, "What's Yoga," which also expanded the audience. Hittleman's *Yoga for Health* began appearing as a daily television program in Los Angeles in 1961, then in New York in 1966. Hittleman's fame was furthered by time spent with countercultural celebrities such as Buddhist philosopher-writer Alan Watts and Beat novelist Jack Kerouac.

During the 1960s, segments of the countercultural movement began to recognize and embrace yoga, seeking not only the physical benefits but also the spiritual uplift it offered. In early 1968, the Beatles became enthralled with meditation and yoga, and they traveled to India to study with the Maharishi Mahesh Yogi—reports of which spread interest in Eastern spiritualism throughout the youth counterculture. The popularity of yoga grew as publicity increased and as more celebrities, such as Mia Farrow, Mick Jagger, Marianne Faithful, and Donovan, helped make it chic. In August 1969, crowds at the Woodstock music festival in upstate New York were introduced to meditation and yoga by Swami Satchidananda, who opened the festival with guided meditation and introduced the sacred Hindu mantra "om" (or "aum") into the counterculture lexicon.

During the 1970s and 1980s, yoga began falling out of favor in American culture, at least in relative terms, re-emerging on the cultural landscape in the early 1990s as the "new" physical fitness fad. Into the twenty-first century, yoga became increasingly commercialized with the establishment of exercise centers and classes throughout the United States, with magazines such as *Yoga, Yoga Journal,* and *Ascent*, with television shows such as *Inhale* and *The Morning Yoga Show,* and a steady stream of instructional home videos. A new round of celebrity practitioners—Madonna, Ricky Martin, and Meg Ryan among them—spoke publicly of their personal experiences with yoga.

From an esoteric practice in the nineteenth century and an expression of the counterculture in the 1950s and 1960s, yoga in America has emerged as a mainstream cultural phenomenon in the 2000s. The number of practitioners has climbed from an estimated 7 million in 1998 to 15 million in 2008, with 75 percent of the nation's health clubs offering yoga classes in the 2000s. Practitioners of yoga come from diverse social and religious backgrounds, taking part for physical development and exercise, stress management, and spiritual growth.

Daniel Farr

See also: Buddhism; Woodstock Music and Art Fair.

Further Reading

Feuerstein, Georg. *The Deeper Dimension of Yoga: Theory and Practice.* Boston: Shambhala, 2003.

Love, Robert. "Fear of Yoga: Super-Love Cults, Commie Swamis, Loose-Limbed Women, and Other Hysteric Headlines." *Utne Reader* (March–April 2007).

Mees, Patricia D. "Yoga Participation Surges." *The Physician and Sportsmedicine* 33:5 (May 2005).

Worthington, Vivian. *A History of Yoga.* Boston: Routledge & Kegan Paul, 1982.

Young, Brigham (1801–1877)

A central figure in the early Mormon movement—the successor to founder Joseph Smith and second president of the Church of Jesus Christ of Latter-day Saints—Brigham Young orchestrated the group's migration to and settlement in Utah in 1847. As head of the church and the first territorial governor of Utah, he played a key role in defending the religion, its people, and its primary prophet against persecution by non-Mormon neighbors and the U.S. government. His leadership stabilized the movement and guided Mormon society in the pursuit of its modern convictions.

Young was born in Whitingham, Vermont, on June 1, 1801. In 1829, he settled in Mendon, New York, near where founder "Prophet" Joseph Smith published *The Book of Mormon* the following year. A carpenter and blacksmith by trade, and a Methodist by faith, Young read *The Book of Mormon* shortly after it appeared and was immediately drawn to its precepts. He took his baptism in April 1832 and set out to Canada as a missionary.

In the succeeding years, Young led a number of successful missionary expeditions in the United States and Canada, extending the church's following and helping dispossessed followers regain lost land. He later succeeded in converting and bringing to America approximately 40,000 English men and women.

Young's organizational skills and devotion to the church and Smith led to his selection as one of the governing body called the Council of Twelve, or Twelve Apostles, in February 1835. When Smith was assassinated in 1844, Young emerged as the Mormons' spiri-

tual leader, directing the great migration of 1846 to 1847. Inspired by Young's idea that building a kingdom of God required more than preaching and converting others to the religion, but also demanded the establishment of a permanent, formal home, the Mormons finally settled in Salt Lake City, Utah.

Young became the director of the Salt Lake City settlement and controlled much of the communal theocracy. The settlement grew at a rapid pace, and Young coordinated the development of codes to govern the actions and behaviors of its members. As president of the Mormon church, he also regularly held hundreds of so-called fireside chats with his followers, reflecting upon clothing, dining, and other cultural concerns.

After the establishment of the Utah Territory and its provisional government, Young also served as governor and superintendent of Indian affairs, extending his influence throughout the region. When fear and resentment of their alternative lifestyle and social philosophies threatened the Mormon community, Young defended Mormons against military and social persecution.

In 1857, Young led a convocation that declared the settlement's independence from the United States. In the Utah War of 1857 to 1858 between the U.S. government and the Mormons—with each side seeking control of Mormon land—Young declared martial law after President James Buchanan appointed a non-Mormon, Alfred Cumming, governor of the Utah Territory. The Mormons, under the displaced Young, fought for their property, periodically attacking the encamped U.S. military.

In April 1858, Buchanan sent representatives to work out a settlement between the parties, and peace was restored. Young's defense of Mormon interests brought praise from within the church and ultimately helped avoid a complete split between the Mormon's Utah territory and the United States.

Mormon society retained a generally self-sustaining lifestyle, producing necessities and providing for each other through communal efforts. Although Young valued the adaptation of current technology for the benefit of Mormon society, the advent of a railroad line connecting the otherwise independent society to outside resources and competition prompted Young to promote local production and encourage education for his community members—efforts to insulate Mormon culture from outside scrutiny. Brigham Young University, founded in 1875 in Provo, remains a prominent and enduring symbol of these efforts.

Although the Mormon church formally ended the practice of plural marriage in 1890, Young had been one of its leading polygamists. He had married a total of twenty-seven women, sixteen of whom bore his fifty-six children. Young divorced some of his wives and some predeceased him. Upon his death on August 29, 1877, he was survived by seventeen wives and forty-seven children.

Sueann M. Wells

See also: Mormonism.

Further Reading

Arrington, Leonard J. *Brigham Young: American Moses.* Urbana: University of Illinois Press, 1986.

Gates, Susa Young. *Brigham Young: Patriot, Pioneer, Prophet and Leader of the Latter Day.* Whitefish, MT: Kessinger, 2004.

Widtsoe, Leah D., and John A. Widtsoe. *Brigham Young the Man of the Hour: Leader of the Latter Day Saints.* Whitefish, MT: Kessinger, 2004.

Zappa, Frank (1940–1993)

One of the most versatile and distinctive figures of rock music, Frank Zappa was known for his talents as a performer and composer, his skills as an audio engineer, and his scathing satire, which targeted both the establishment and the counterculture alike. His compositional style, which he characterized as "conceptual continuity," drew from nearly every genre of music, combining satirical lyrics with pop melodies, jazz improvisation, doo-wop, and rhythm and blues.

Zappa also produced highly original collage, or "pastiche," sequences that mixed sound effects, conversation, and music. And he was known for quoting (later called "sampling") riffs from music that had influenced him, including the perennial favorite "Louie Louie." Zappa sampled works as diverse as television-show themes, advertising jingles, classical masterpieces, and the band Devo's song "Whip It."

As the founder of the "freak band" Mothers of Invention in the 1960s and in his long solo career, Zappa brought a non-mainstream compositional style to popular music and an avant-garde style to performance. He recorded more than fifty albums.

Organized Sound

Frank Vincent Zappa was born in Baltimore, Maryland, on December 21, 1940, to scientist Francis Vincent Zappa and his wife, Rose Marie. Frank was raised in Florida and Maryland before moving to California with his family at age twelve.

His musical career began when he took up the drums in high school. The turning point came in 1954 when he discovered the work of avant-garde classical composer Edgar Varèse, whose music was known for its attempts to sublimate sound through new arrangements of rhythm and timbre. Writing prolifically while he was still in high school, Zappa sought to incorporate new forms of instrumentation and electronic sound into his compositions. He received his first guitar in 1957, and his first band, the Blackouts, played mostly country blues. After high school, Zappa spent a brief period in 1959 studying music theory at Chaffey College in Rancho Cucamonga, California.

His first recordings were scores for low-budget films in the early 1960s, which raised the funds necessary to buy a cheap recording studio in Rancho Cucamonga, called Studio Z. In 1964, he joined a local band called the Soul Giants, which eventually evolved into the Mothers and, after the intervention of nervous record executives, the Mothers of Invention. Their first album, *Freak Out!*, was released in 1966 and parodied the pop music of the day.

Freak Out! was groundbreaking in that it represented the first time Zappa had employed his experimental sound-collage technique in an attempt to capture the freak subculture of Los Angeles. The album was also important because it was one of the first based on a unifying theme, paving the way for such later works as the Who's rock opera *Tommy* (1969) and Pink Floyd's *The Wall* (1979). It also was only the second double LP of rock music ever released. (The first rock double album, and first studio double album, ever released generally is cited as Bob Dylan's *Blonde on Blonde,* also released in 1966.) For all of these reasons, *Freak Out!* established Zappa early on as an inventive new force in rock.

Steady Output

The year 1967 saw the release of three Zappa and Mothers of Invention albums, *Absolutely Free, Lumpy Gravy,* and *Cruisin' with Reuben and the Jets.* The first includes the single "Plastic People," which expresses Zappa's belief that phoniness is an inherent trait in all humans and human establishments. *Absolutely Free* served as a platform for Zappa's sermonizing to the American people; on it he argues that not only is American society inherently hypocritical, but the status quo in America is continually suppressing all alternatives and countercultures. *Lumpy Gravy* was Zappa's first experimentation with orchestral arrangements, while *Cruisin'* was a tribute to and parody of doo-wop music.

These early successes were followed in 1968 by *We're Only in It for the Money.* With a cover parodying that of the Beatles's *Sgt. Pepper's Lonely Hearts Club Band,* the album is regarded as Zappa and the Mothers' seminal work and one of the best rock albums of the 1960s. In addition to showcasing his prowess as an engineer, the album brutally satirizes the hippie movement of the day.

A self-described political and cultural subversive, Zappa was known for standing up against authority in both spheres. In 1985 he testified before a committee of the U.S. Senate that was considering the censorship of music. He was outspoken in his opposition to the Parents' Music Resource Center (PMRC), a group of concerned mothers (led by Tipper Gore, the wife of Democrat Al Gore, then a senator from Tennessee) that had convinced the major record companies to put parental advisory labels on music deemed objectionable. In his testimony before Congress, and throughout his life, Zappa was a prominent advocate of First Amendment protection for all forms of communication. He continued his attack on the PMRC by including audio cuts from the PMRC hearings in the song "Porn Wars" on the 1985 album *Frank Zappa Meets the Mothers of Prevention.*

Throughout his career, Zappa urged his listeners to maintain a healthy skepticism regarding the political and ideological machinations of the status quo. As a social commentator and critic, he constantly pushed against the socially erected barriers of so-called good taste. After his run-in with the PMRC, Zappa's interest in the workings of government increased. In an attempt to correct what he saw as a "fascist bias" in American government, he spent much of 1988 working to get young Americans to register to vote.

In 1990, at the request of Czech Republic President Václav Havel, a lifelong fan, Zappa served as special ambassador of that government on trade, culture, and tourism. Despite pressure from the George H.W. Bush administration, Havel kept Zappa on as cultural attaché until 1991, when he was diagnosed with prostate cancer. Zappa died on December 4, 1993.

Countercultural Legacy

The musicianship and ideology demonstrated on Zappa's steady stream of albums of the 1960s, 1970s, and 1980s, in addition to his onstage theatrics, cemented his reputation as an important underground musician. Zappa and the Mothers of Invention served as the inspiration for a plethora of underground artists who followed, including the Velvet Underground, Nico, and the Tubes. His combination of visual imagery and verbal pastiche established many of the stylistic conventions that would become MTV icons in the 1980s. Perhaps the most interesting aspect of his legacy is the deconstruction-fueled paranoia and caustic satire that has continued to serve as the lyrical base for a multiplicity of contemporary bands that wish to be seen as countercultural.

B. Keith Murphy

See also: Rock and Roll.

Further Reading

Walley, David. *No Commercial Potential: The Saga of Frank Zappa.* New York: Da Capo, 1996.

Zappa, Frank, with Peter Occhiofrosso. *The Real Frank Zappa Book.* New York: Simon and Schuster, 1990.

Zines

In a society notoriously influenced by homogenized mass media and said to be afflicted with impersonal isolation, zines represent a form of written communication that is more scathingly critical of current affairs but significantly less professionally produced or widely read than independent or alternative-media publications such as *The Nation* and *The Atlantic Monthly.* Often the work of one author and either free or nominally priced, zines offer an intensely personal, highly affordable, and often subversive method of independent grassroots communication.

Although many zines are connected to the 1970s hardcore-punk music scene, their roots can be traced to 1920s science fiction fanzines. These independently produced publications distinguished themselves from professionally manufactured magazines by adopting the label "fanzines," a term that has since been shortened simply to "zines." Despite this history, contemporary zine authors, or zinesters, locate themselves not in the sci-fi tradition but in the empowering do-it-yourself ethic of the hardcore-punk music scene.

Although an argument can be made that a zine is any independent publication, there is an obvious difference between Thomas Paine's revolutionary pamphlet *Common Sense* (1776) or the International Socialist Organization's weekly, *Socialist Worker,* and actual zines such as *Punk Planet, Suburban Voice, Slug & Lettuce,* or *Message from the Homeland.* There appears to be no limit to the creativity in format and size of zines. They have been published on everything from intricately folded vellum paper to standard-size newsprint. Despite the availability of affordable offset printing from the Florida-based Small Publisher's Co-Op, which expressly caters to zines, many such publications continue to be illicitly reproduced on photocopy machines, with "donated" copies passed along by a sympathetic shop worker.

Just as zines feature a variety of formats, their content has proven to be nearly unlimited. In general, they feature some blend of personal reflection, social commentary, fringe culture, poetry, incessant babbling, and reviews of or interviews with independent rock bands. Ideologically driven zines such as *Retrogression* and *Impact!* are, or were, published somewhat regularly and combine publicity about the independent music scene with advocacy for gay rights, revolutionizing gender roles, combating racism, and making conscious (anticorporate) consumer choices. Other zines, such as *Thrift Score* and *Mystery Date,* espouse the joys of thrift-store shopping or republish ridiculous sections from 1950s etiquette books. In short, so long as zines are independently published and not profit driven, they can be radical, humorous, or frivolous and still be recognized as a legitimate voice within the zine reading community.

Although there is no centralized clearinghouse for these largely underground publications, *Factsheet Five* (1982–1991) attempted to list and comment on a large sample of zines during its tenure as the zine world's equivalent of the Yellow Pages. Estimates have placed the number of zines in publication as high as 50,000. The accuracy of that figure, however, is made uncertain by the very nature of the publications. Often irregularly published, with press runs ranging from a few dozen to several thousand, many exist under the radar for all but the most dedicated zine aficionados.

David Lucander

See also: Punk Rock; Science Fiction.

Further Reading

Duncombe, Stephen. *Notes from the Underground: Zines and the Politics of Alternative Culture.* New York: Verso, 1997.

Gunderloy, Mike, and Cari Goldberg Janice. *The World of Zines: A Guide to the Independent Magazine Revolution.* New York: Penguin, 1992.

Friedman, R. Seth. *Factsheet Five Reader.* New York: Three Rivers, 1997.

Zoarites

In 1817, a group of 300 religious separatists arrived in Philadelphia from Württemberg in southwest Germany, near Switzerland. Although they were befriended by Quakers, who provided basic necessities and assisted the refugees in locating employment and property, the leader of the new group, Joseph Michael Bäumeler (anglicized to Bimeler), desired a separate community for his followers. Trained as a weaver, Bimeler contracted to buy a 5,500-acre (2,225-hectare) tract of land along the Tuscarawas River in east-central Ohio, agreeing to pay the purchase price over a fifteen-year period. The town was named Zoar, meaning "sanctuary from evil," after the biblical account of Lot, who escaped to Zoar from Sodom. The scarcity of food during the first winter prompted the group to establish a communal society, and on April 19, 1819, the Society of Separatists of Zoar was formed. Members donated all property and material goods to the community, in exchange for food, clothing, and shelter.

The Zoarites were pacifists and refused military service. They did not observe any holidays or traditional religious sacraments, such as baptism or marriage. A couple wishing to marry simply presented themselves before witnesses. One of the most interesting features of the community was the garden, which occupied the entire village square and was designed to represent the New Jerusalem as described in the Book of Revelation. A Norway spruce planted in the center symbolized eternal life; circling the spruce was an arbor representing heaven. Twelve juniper trees, one for each of the apostles, formed a third concentric ring. This area was enclosed by a circular path, with twelve radials signifying the twelve tribes of Israel.

In 1822, concerned that the population might increase too rapidly for its economy, the community adopted the practice of celibacy, which ultimately was abandoned in 1830. For many years, children between the ages of three and fourteen lived in separate nurseries from their families, allowing their mothers to continue to work in the community.

By the mid-1830s, Zoar was almost entirely self-sustaining and sold surplus from its farms to other towns. Its flour mills, two iron foundries, textile factory, and several stores manufactured and sold a variety of goods for general sale. Additional revenue was generated when the Zoarites contracted to build a 7-mile portion of the Ohio and Erie Canal that crossed their property. By 1852, the society's assets were valued at more than $1 million.

Bimeler's death in 1853, combined with the changing social and economic environment, had a major impact on the community. The arrival of the railroad in the 1880s brought greater interaction with the outside world, and the rise of mass production rendered Zoar's small manufacturing businesses obsolete. In 1898, the remaining members decided to dissolve the society. Common property was divided, with each member receiving about 50 acres (20 hectares) and $200.

In 1942, the Ohio Historical Society began acquiring and restoring some of the original town buildings. Today, a number of the Zoarite buildings are open to the public as an historic site.

Denise A. Seachrist

See also: Pacifism; Quakers.

Further Reading

Fernandez, Kathleen M. *A Singular People: Images of Zoar.* Kent, OH: Kent State University Press, 2003.

Zoot-Suiters

Zoot-suiters were an amorphous youth counterculture that emerged in the United States during the late 1930s and early to mid-1940s. They are associated with a style of clothing and grooming popular during that time among African American, Mexican American, and other minority youths.

Zoot-suiters were young men, and some young women, who expressed their individuality, ethnic pride, and resistance to the norms of white society through shared cultural markers. The central component of zoot-suiter style and wardrobe was the flashy, custom-made "zoot suit," designed to express the individuality of the wearer.

The jacket of the basic suit had exaggeratedly broad shoulders and long sleeves that extended over the fingers. It was purposefully baggy and elongated as compared to the business suit fashion of the time, often completely covering the thighs and flaring out from the waist. The pants were loose through the hips and tapered or cuffed at the ankles, to swing and move with the man as he danced or walked in style. A long chain hung from the waist, looping back up to the pocket and generally attached to a watch or knife.

The zoot suit style—a long, broad-shouldered jacket; loose, tapered pants; and a stylish, brimmed hat—exuded a cool, macho air of leisure and maturity. For minorities, it was a means of gaining visibility while defying assimilation. *(Douglas Miller/Hulton Archive/Getty Images)*

The outfit might be topped with a stylish flat-topped hat and dress shoes. African Americans would slick their hair back to make it as smooth as possible; Mexican Americans often chose to comb their hair from the sides to meet in a line at the back of the head called a ducktail. The sum total of the wardrobe was intended to portray a cool, macho air of leisure and maturity.

Much more than a fad, the clothing and lifestyle of the zoot-suiters were linked to serious attempts by African American and Mexican American youths to gain visibility and validation in American society. Social mobility was still very limited for minority youth in America. While many were encouraged by their parents to follow the rules and abide by accepted practices, the zoot-suiters embraced an alternative lifestyle and subculture. Speech was as much a part of this as clothes and grooming, emphasizing street slang and the lingo of jazz and swing.

The popularity of the zoot-suiter counterculture went hand in hand with the rise of dance halls that featured jazz, boogie-woogie, swing, and the like—all music that had yet to receive wide cultural approval. Important performers and bandleaders wore versions of the zoot suit, including Duke Ellington and Count Basie, who rose to fame in the 1930s and 1940s. As African Americans, even such up-and-coming musicians felt the effects of racism, which restricted where they could play music, where they could eat, and where they could find lodging. At the same time, Mexican Americans suffered similarly discriminatory practices in education and the workplace, especially in California. Zoot-suiters looked up to and emulated the bandleaders and pachuco (Latino) gang leaders who had achieved success or cachet in their respective communities.

Mainstream reaction against the zoot-suiters was present from the beginning of the movement, as minority youth in general were painted as delinquents. The public flamboyance of the zoot-suiters, as well as the visibility of their outfits, made them easy targets for local thugs and police alike. This was compounded by the fact that some of the young zoot-suiters in urban areas also had turned to crime.

In 1942, as part of the national rationing of materials during World War II, the War Production Board placed restrictions on fabric used in clothing. All at once, the zoot suit, with its long jacket and flowing slacks, was against federal regulations. This contributed further to the negative view of zoot-suiters, who defiantly continued to wear the extravagant suits. Beginning in Los Angeles, where the City Council successfully petitioned the federal government to make the suit illegal, violent clashes broke out between law enforcement authorities (both the police and military) and zoot-suiters. The fighting spread to urban centers across the country during the next two years.

Over time, the trend spread nationally into "hip" youth culture in the United States. Zoot-suiter culture—or versions of it—also emerged internationally. It was visible in such places as Quebec Province in Canada, Italy, and France during the 1940s, and Great Britain during the 1950s, especially in the Teddy Boys culture.

Indeed, remnants of zoot-suiter style have remained evident in certain entertainers' fashions into the twenty-first century. For most, the original countercultural statement has been subsumed by the mass market. For others, especially African American and Hispanic American entertainers, it remains a way to express personal style and cultural identity.

Jean Anne Lauer

See also: African Americans; Fashion; Jazz.

Further Reading

Alford, Holly. "The Zoot Suit: Its History and Influence." *Fashion Theory* 8:2 (June 2004): 225–36.

Pagán, Eduardo Obregón. *Murder at the Sleepy Lagoon: Zoot Suits, Race, and Riot in Wartime L.A.* Chapel Hill: University of North Carolina Press, 2003.

Tyler, Bruce. "Zoot-Suit Culture and the Black Press." *Journal of American Culture* 17:2 (Summer 1994): 21–33.

Documents

Documents

The Trial of Anne Hutchinson (1637)

Anne Hutchinson, a Puritan layperson, challenged the religious and political orthodoxy of the Massachusetts Bay Colony in the 1630s. In addition to holding informal group discussions that questioned ministerial teachings, Hutchinson openly professed views that were regarded as heretical. Under Governor John Winthrop, Hutchinson was brought to trial in November 1637 at General Court in Newton. She was convicted of sedition and contempt and banished from the colony. The following is an excerpt from her trial transcript.

Mr. {John} Winthrop, Governor: Mrs. Hutchinson, you are called here as one of those that have troubled the peace of the commonwealth and the churches here; you are known to be a woman that hath had a great share in the promoting and divulging of those opinions that are the cause of this trouble, and to be nearly joined not only in affinity and affection with some of those the court had taken notice of and passed censure upon, but you have spoken divers things, as we have been informed, very prejudicial to the honour of the churches and ministers thereof, and you have maintained a meeting and an assembly in your house that hath been condemned by the general assembly as a thing not tolerable nor comely in the sight of God nor fitting for your sex, and notwithstanding that was cried down you have continued the same. Therefore we have thought good to send for you to understand how things are, that if you be in an erroneous way we may reduce you that so you may become a profitable member here among us. Otherwise if you be obstinate in your course that then the court may take such course that you may trouble us no further. Therefore I would intreat you to express whether you do assent and hold in practice to those opinions and factions that have been handled in court already, that is to say, whether you do not justify Mr. Wheelwright's sermon and the petition.

Mrs. Hutchinson: I am called here to answer before you but I hear no things laid to my charge.

Gov.: I have told you some already and more I can tell you.

Mrs. H.: Name one, Sir.

Gov.: Have I not named some already?

Mrs. H.: What have I said or done?

Gov.: Why for your doings, this you did harbor and countenance those that are parties in this faction that you have heard of.

Mrs. H.: That's matter of conscience, Sir.

Gov.: Your conscience you must keep, or it must be kept for you.

Mrs. H.: Must not I then entertain the saints because I must keep my conscience.

Gov.: Say that one brother should commit felony or treason and come to his brother's house, if he knows him guilty and conceals him he is guilty of the same. It is his conscience to entertain him, but if his conscience comes into act in giving countenance and entertainment to him that hath broken the law he is guilty too. So if you do countenance those that are transgressors of the law you are in the same fact.

Mrs. H.: What law do they transgress?

Gov.: The law of God and of the state.

Mrs. H.: In what particular?

Gov.: Why in this among the rest, whereas the Lord doth say honour thy father and thy mother.

Mrs. H.: Ey Sir in the Lord.

Gov.: This honour you have broke in giving countenance to them.

Mrs. H.: In entertaining those did I entertain them against any act (for there is the thing) or what God has appointed?

Gov.: You knew that Mr. Wheelwright did preach this sermon and those that countenance him in this do break a law.

Mrs. H.: What law have I broken?

Gov.: Why the fifth commandment.

Mrs. H.: I deny that for he [Mr. Wheelwright] saith in the Lord.

Gov.: You have joined with them in the faction.

Mrs. H.: In what faction have I joined with them?

Gov.: In presenting the petition.

Mrs. H.: Suppose I had set my hand to the petition. What then?

Gov.: You saw that case tried before.

Mrs. H.: But I had not my hand to [not signed] the petition.

Gov.: You have councelled them.

Mrs. H.: Wherein?

Gov.: Why in entertaining them.

Mrs. H.: What breach of law is that, Sir?

Gov.: Why dishonouring the commonwealth.

Mrs. H.: But put the case, Sir, that I do fear the Lord and my parents. May not I entertain them that fear the Lord because my parents will not give me leave?

Gov.: If they be the fathers of the commonwealth, and they of another religion, if you entertain them then you dishonour your parents and are justly punishable.

Mrs. H.: If I entertain them, as they have dishonoured their parents I do.

Gov.: No but you by countenancing them above others put honor upon them.

Mrs. H.: I may put honor upon them as the children of God and as they do honor the Lord.

Gov.: We do not mean to discourse with those of your sex but only this: you so adhere unto them and do endeavor to set forward this faction and so you do dishonour us.

Mrs. H.: I do acknowledge no such thing. Neither do I think that I ever put any dishonour upon you.

Gov.: Why do you keep such a meeting at your house as you do every week upon a set day?

Mrs. H.: It is lawful for me to do so, as it is all your practices, and can you find a warrant for yourself and condemn me for the same thing? The ground of my taking it up was, when I first came to this land because I did not go to such meetings as those were, it was presently reported that I did not allow of such meetings but held them unlawful and therefore in that regard they said I was proud and did despise all ordinances. Upon that a friend came unto me and told me of it and I to prevent such aspersions took it up, but it was in practice before I came. Therefore I was not the first. . . .

Mrs. H.: If you please to give me leave I shall give you the ground of what I know to be true. Being much troubled to see the falseness of the constitution of the Church of England, I had like to have turned Separatist. Whereupon I kept a day of solemn humiliation and pondering of the thing; this scripture was brought unto me—he that denies Jesus Christ to be come in the flesh is antichrist. This I considered of and in considering found that the papists did not deny him to be come in the flesh, nor we did not deny him—who then was antichrist? Was the Turk antichrist only? The Lord knows that I could not open scripture; he must by his prophetical office open it unto me. So after that being unsatisfied in the thing, the Lord was pleased to bring this scripture out of the Hebrews. He that denies the testament denies the testator, and in this did open unto me and give me to see that those which did not teach the new covenant had the spirit of antichrist, and upon this he did discover the ministry unto me; and ever since, I bless the Lord, he hath let me see which was the clear ministry and which the wrong. Since that time I confess I have been more choice and he hath left me to distinguish between the voice of my beloved and the voice of Moses, the voice of John the Baptist and the voice of antichrist, for all those voices are spoken of in scripture. Now if you do condemn me for speaking what in my conscience I know to be truth I must commit myself unto the Lord.

Mr. Nowel {assistant to the Court}: How do you know that was the spirit?

Mrs. H.: How did Abraham know that it was God that bid him offer his son, being a breach of the sixth commandment?

Dep. Gov. {Thomas Dudley}: By an immediate voice.

Mrs. H.: So to me by an immediate revelation.

Dep. Gov.: How! an immediate revelation.

Mrs. H.: By the voice of his own spirit to my soul. I will give you another scripture, Jer[emiah] 46: 27–28—out of which the Lord showed me what he would do for me and the rest of his servants. But after he was pleased to reveal himself to me I did presently, like Abraham, run to Hagar. And after that he did let me see the atheism of my own heart, for which I begged of the Lord that it might not remain in my heart, and being thus, he did show me this (a twelvemonth after) which I told you of before. . . . Therefore, I desire you to look to it, for you see this scripture fulfilled this day and therefore I desire you as you tender the Lord and the church and commonwealth to consider and look what you do. You have power over my body but the Lord Jesus hath power over my body and soul; and assure yourselves thus much, you do as much as in you lies to put the Lord Jesus Christ from you, and if you go on in this course you begin, you will bring a curse upon you and your posterity, and the mouth of the Lord hath spoken it.

Dep. Gov.: What is the scripture she brings?

Mr. Stoughton {assistant to the Court}: Behold I turn away from you.

Mrs. H.: But now having seen him which is invisible I fear not what man can do unto me. . . .

Gov.: I am persuaded that the revelation she brings forth is delusion.

[The trial text here reads:] All the court but some two or three ministers cry out, we all believe it—we all believe it. [Mrs. Hutchinson was found guilty.]

Gov.: The court hath already declared themselves satisfied concerning the things you hear, and concerning the troublesomeness of her spirit and the danger of her course amongst us, which is not to be suffered. Therefore if it be the mind of the court that Mrs. Hutchinson for these things that appear before us is unfit for our society, and if it be the mind of the court that she shall be banished out of our liberties and imprisoned till she be sent away, let them hold up their hands.

[All but three did so.]

Gov.: Mrs. Hutchinson, the sentence of the court you hear is that you are banished from out of our jurisdiction as being a woman not fit for our society, and are to be imprisoned till the court shall send you away.

Mrs. H.: I desire to know wherefore I am banished?

Gov.: Say no more. The court knows wherefore and is satisfied.

Source: Charles F. Adams, *Antinomianism in the Colony of Massachusetts Bay* (Boston: Prince Society Publications, 1894).

John Woolman's *Journal* (1757)

John Woolman, a Quaker minister from New Jersey, was an early opponent of slavery and an outspoken pacifist. In the 1750s, during a series of missionary expeditions in the Southern, Middle Atlantic, and New England colonies, he witnessed the conditions endured by slaves and began advocating for emancipation with the slaveholders he met. He recounted his travels—as well as other life experiences and personal views—in his classic autobiography, Journal.

Feeling the exercise in relation to a visit to the Southern Provinces to increase upon me, I acquainted our Monthly Meeting therewith, and obtained their certificate. Expecting to go alone, one of my brothers who lived in Philadelphia, having some business in North Carolina, proposed going with me part of the way; but as he had a view of some outward affairs, to accept of him as a companion was some difficulty with me, whereupon I had conversation with him at sundry times. At length feeling easy in my mind, I had conversation with several elderly Friends of Philadelphia on the subject, and he obtaining a certificate suitable to the occasion, we set off in the Fifth Month, 1757. Coming to Nottingham week-day meeting, we lodged at John Churchman's, where I met with our friend, Benjamin Buffington, from New England, who was returning from a visit to the Southern Provinces. Thence we crossed the river Susquehanna, and lodged at William Cox's in Maryland.

Soon after I entered this province, a deep and painful exercise came upon me, which I often had some feeling of since my mind was drawn toward these parts, and with which I had acquainted my brother before we agreed to join as companions. As the people in this and the Southern Provinces live much on the labour of slaves, many of whom are used hardly, my concern was that I might attend with singleness of heart to the voice of the true Shepherd, and be so supported as to remain unmoved at the faces of men.

Ninth of Fifth Month.—A Friend at whose house we breakfasted setting us a little on our way, I had conversation with him, in the fear of the Lord, concerning his slaves, in which my heart was tender; I used much plainness of speech with him, and he appeared to take it kindly. We pursued our journey without appointing meetings, being pressed in my mind to be at the Yearly Meeting in Virginia. In my travelling on the road, I often felt a cry rise from the centre of my mind, thus: "O Lord, I am a stranger on the earth, hide not thy face from me."

On the 11th, we crossed the rivers Patowmack and Rapahannock, and lodged at Port Royal. On the way we had the company of a colonel of the militia, who appeared to be a thoughtful man. I took occasion to remark on the difference in general betwixt a people used to labour moderately for their living, training up their children in frugality and business, and those who live on the labour of slaves; the former, in my view, being the most happy life. He concurred in the remark, and mentioned the trouble arising from the untoward, slothful disposition of the negroes, adding that one of our labourers would do as much in a day as two of their slaves. I replied that free men, whose minds were properly on their business, found a satisfaction in improving, cultivating, and providing for their families; but negroes, labouring to support others who claim them as their property, and expecting nothing but slavery during life, had not the like inducement to be industrious.

After some further conversation I said, that men having power too often misapplied it; that though we made slaves of the negroes, and the Turks made slaves of the Christians, I believed that liberty was the natural right of all men equally. This he did not deny, but said the lives of the negroes were so wretched in their own country that many of them lived better here than there. I replied, "There is great odds in regard to us on what principle we act"; and so the conversation on that subject ended. I may here add that another person, some time afterwards, mentioned the wretchedness of the negroes, occasioned by their intestine wars, as an argument in favour of our fetching them away for slaves. To which I replied, if compassion for the Africans, on account of their domestic troubles, was the real motive of our purchasing them, that spirit of tenderness being attended to, would incite us to use them kindly, that, as strangers brought out of affliction, their lives might be happy among us. And as they are human creatures, whose souls are as precious as ours, and who may receive the same help and comfort from the Holy Scriptures as we do, we could not omit suitable endeavours to instruct them therein; but that while we manifest by our conduct that our views in purchasing them are to advance ourselves, and while our buying captives taken in war animates those parties to push on the war and increase desola-tion amongst them, to say they live unhappily in Africa is far from being an argument in our favour.

I further said, the present circumstances of these provinces to me appear difficult; the slaves look like a burdensome stone to such as burden themselves with them; and that, if the white people retain a resolution to prefer their outward prospects of gain to all other considerations, and do not act conscientiously toward them as fellow-creatures, I believe that burden will grow heavier and heavier, until times change in a way disagreeable to us. The person appeared very serious, and owned that in considering their condition and the manner of their treatment in these provinces he had sometimes thought it might be just in the Almighty so to order it.

Having travelled through Maryland, we came amongst Friends at Cedar Creek in Virginia, on the 12th; and the next day rode, in company with several of them, a day's journey to Camp Creek. As I was riding along in the morning, my mind was deeply affected in a sense I had of the need of divine aid to support me in the various difficulties which attended me, and in uncommon distress of mind I cried in secret to the Most High, "O Lord, be merciful, I beseech Thee, to Thy poor afflicted creature!" After some time I felt inward relief, and soon after a Friend in company began to talk in support of the slave-trade, and said the negroes were understood to be the offspring of Cain, their blackness being the mark which God set upon him after he murdered Abel, his brother; that it was the design of Providence they should be slaves, as a condition proper to the race of so wicked a man as Cain was. Then another spake in support of what had been said.

To all which I replied in substance as follows: that Noah and his family were all who survived the flood, according to Scripture; and as Noah was of Seth's race, the family of Cain was wholly destroyed. One of them said that after the flood Ham went to the land of Nod and took a wife; that Nod was a land far distant, inhabited by Cain's race, and that the flood did not reach it; and as Ham was sentenced to be a servant of servants to his brethren, these two families, being thus joined, were undoubtedly fit only for slaves. I replied, the flood was a judgment upon the world for their abominations, and it was granted that Cain's stock was the most wicked, and therefore unreasonable to suppose that they were spared. As to Ham's going to the land of Nod for a wife, no time being fixed, Nod might be inhabited by some of Noah's family before Ham married a second time; moreover the text saith "That all flesh died that moved upon the earth" (Gen. vii.21). I further reminded them how the prophets repeatedly declare "that the son shall not suffer for the iniquity of the father, but every one be answerable for his own sins."

I was troubled to perceive the darkness of their imaginations, and in some pressure of spirit said, "The love of ease and gain are the motives in general of keeping slaves, and men are wont to take hold of weak arguments to support a cause which is unreasonable. I have no interest on either side, save only the interest which I desire to have in the truth. I believe liberty is their right, and as I see they are not only deprived of it, but treated in other respects with inhumanity in many places, I believe He who is a refuge for the oppressed will, in His own time, plead their cause, and happy will it be for such as walk in uprightness before Him." And thus our conversation ended.

Source: John Woolman, *The Journal and Other Writings of John Woolman* (London: J.M. Dent & Sons, 1910).

Message by Nancy Ward to the Cherokee Council (1817)

Tribal leader Nancy Ward, known for her efforts to establish peace between the Cherokee and white settlers during the 1780s, later attained the status of "Beloved Woman" and held a seat on the Cherokee Council of Chiefs. On May 2, 1817, Ward addressed the council and urged members of the tribe not to give up the land that had sustained them for generations.

Amovey [Tenn.] in Council 2nd May 1817

A True Copy The Cherokee ladys now being present at the meeting of the Chiefs and warriors in council have thought it their duties as mothers to address their beloved Chiefs and warriors now assembled.

Our beloved children and head men of the Cherokee nation we address you warriors in council we have raised all of you on the land which we now have, which God gave us to inhabit and raise provisions we know that our country has once been extensive but by repeated sales has become circumscribed to a small tract and never thought it our duty to interfere in the disposition of it till now, if a father or mother was to sell all their lands which they had to depend on which their children had to raise their living on which would be indeed bad and to be removed to another country we do not wish to go to an unknown country which we have understood some of our children wish to go over the

Mississippi but this act of our children would be like destroying your mothers. You mothers your sisters ask and beg of you not to part with any more of our lands, we say ours you are descendants and take pity on our request, but keep it for our growing children for it was the good will of our creator to place here and you know our father the great president will not allow his white children to take our country away only keep your hands off of paper talks for it is our own country for if it was not they would not ask you to put your hands to paper for it would be impossible to remove us all for as soon as one child is raised we have others in our arms for such is our situation and will consider our circumstance.

Therefore children don't part with any more of our lands but continue on it and enlarge your farms and cultivate and raise corn and cotton and we your mothers and sisters will make clothing for you which our father the president has recommended to us all we don't charge anybody for selling our lands, but we have heard such intentions of our children but your talks become true at last and it was our desire to forewarn you all not to part with our lands.

Nancy Ward to her children Warriors to take pity and listen to the talks of your sisters, although I am very old yet cannot but pity the situation in which you will hear of their minds. I have great many grand children which I wish they to do well on our land.

Nancy Ward

Attested
A McCoy Clk.
Thos. Wilson Secty

Jenny McIntosh	Widow Tarpin
Caty Harlan	Ally Critington
Elizabeth Walker	Cun, o, ah
Susanna Fox	Miss Asty Walker
Widow Gunrod	Mrs. M. Morgan
Widow Woman Holder	Mrs. Nancy Fields

Source: Andrew Jackson Presidential Papers, Library of Congress, Manuscripts Division, Washington, DC.

The Confessions of Nat Turner (1832)

Believing he was the chosen servant of a vengeful god, thirty-year-old Nat Turner led an uprising of Virginia slaves in August 1831 that left hundreds of people dead and caused rampant fear among Southern whites. Tried and convicted that November, Turner recounted

his life story—including his divine revelation—and the details of the rebellion to his lawyer, Thomas R. Gray, while awaiting execution. The published work, The Confessions of Nat Turner, *appeared the following year.*

SIR,—

YOU have asked me to give a history of the motives which induced me to undertake the late insurrection, as you call it—To do so I must go back to the days of my infancy, and even before I was born.

I was thirty-one years of age the 2nd of October last, and born the property of Benj. Turner, of this county. In my childhood a circumstance occurred which made an indelible impression on my mind, and laid the ground work of that enthusiasm, which has terminated so fatally to many, both white and black, and for which I am about to atone at the gallows. It is here necessary to relate this circumstance—trifling as it may seem, it was the commencement of that belief which has grown with time, and even now, sir, in this dungeon, helpless and forsaken as I am, I cannot divest myself of. . . .

And about this time [1825 at age twenty-five] I had a vision—and I saw white spirits and black spirits engaged in battle, and the sun was darkened—the thunder rolled in the Heavens, and blood flowed in streams—and I heard a voice saying, "Such is your luck, such you are called to see, and let it come rough or smooth, you must surely bear it." I now withdrew myself as much as my situation would permit, from the intercourse of my fellow servants, for the avowed purpose of serving the Spirit more fully—and it appeared to me, and reminded me of the things it had already shown me, and that it would then reveal to me the knowledge of the elements, the revolution of the planets, the operation of tides, and changes of the seasons.

After this revelation in the year 1825, and the knowledge of the elements being made known to me, I sought more than ever to obtain true holiness before the great day of judgment should appear, and then I began to receive the true knowledge of faith.

And from the first steps of righteousness until the last, was I made perfect; and the Holy Ghost was with me, and said, "Behold me as I stand in the Heavens"—and I looked and saw the forms of men in different attitudes—and there were lights in the sky to which the children of darkness gave other names than what they really were—for they were the lights of the Savior's hands, stretched forth from east to west, even as they were extended on the cross on Calvary for the redemption of sinners.

And I wondered greatly at these miracles, and prayed to be informed of a certainty of the meaning thereof—and shortly afterwards, while laboring in the field, I discovered drops of blood on the corn as though it were dew from heaven—and I communicated it to many, both white and black, in the neighborhood—and I then found on the leaves in the woods hieroglyphic characters, and numbers, with the forms of men in different attitudes, portrayed in blood, and representing the figures I had seen before in the heavens.

And now the Holy Ghost had revealed itself to me, and made plain the miracles it had shown me—For as the blood of Christ had been shed on this earth, and had ascended to heaven for the salvation of sinners, and was now returning to earth again in the form of dew—and as the leaves on the trees bore the impression of the figures I had seen in the heavens, it was plain to me that the Savior was about to lay down the yoke he had borne for the sins of men, and the great day of judgment was at hand. . . .

And on the 12th of May, 1828, I heard a loud noise in the heavens, and the Spirit was loosened, and Christ had laid down the yoke he had borne for the sins of men, and that I should take it on and fight against the Serpent, for the time was fast approaching when the first should be last and the last should be first.

And by signs in the heavens that it would make known to me when I should commence the great work—and until the first sign appeared, I should conceal it from the knowledge of men—And on the appearance of the sign (the eclipse of the sun last February), I should arise and prepare myself, and slay my enemies with their own weapons.

And immediately on the sign appearing in the heavens, the seal was removed from my lips, and I communicated the great work laid out for me to do, to four in whom I had the greatest confidence, (Henry, Hark, Nelson, and Sam)—

It was intended by us to have begun the work of death on the 4th July last—Many were the plans formed and rejected by us, and it affected my mind to such a degree, that I fell sick, and the time passed without our coming to any determination how to commence— Still forming new schemes and rejecting them, when the sign appeared again, which determined me not to wait longer.

Source: Nat Turner, *The Confessions of Nat Turner* (Richmond, VA: T.R. Gray, 1832).

"Plan of the West Roxbury Community" or Brook Farm (1842), Elizabeth Palmer Peabody

Educator and writer Elizabeth Palmer Peabody operated a bookstore in Boston that became a frequent meeting place and intellectual center for members of the transcendentalist movement. In January 1842, Peabody published an article in The Dial *that articulated the underlying principles of Brook Farm, the transcendentalists' experiment in utopian communal living in West Roxbury, Massachusetts.*

In the last number of *The Dial* were some remarks, under the perhaps ambitious title, of "A Glimpse of Christ's Idea of Society;" in a note to which, it was intimated, that in this number, would be given an account of an attempt to realize in some degree this great Ideal, by a little company in the midst of us, as yet without name or visible existence. The attempt is made on a very small scale. A few individuals, who, unknown to each other, under different disciplines of life, reacting from different social evils, but aiming at the same object,—of being wholly true to their natures as men and women; have been made acquainted with one another, and have determined to become the Faculty of the Embryo University.

In order to live a religious and moral life worthy the name, they feel it is necessary to come out in some degree from the world, and to form themselves into a community of property, so far as to exclude competition and the ordinary rules of trade;—while they reserve sufficient private property, or the means of obtaining it, for all purposes of independence, and isolation at will. They have bought a farm, in order to make agriculture the basis of their life, it being the most direct and simple in relation to nature.

A true life, although it aims beyond the highest star, is redolent of the healthy earth. The perfume of clover lingers about it. The lowing of cattle is the natural bass to the melody of human voices.

On the other hand, what absurdity can be imagined greater than the institution of cities? They originated not in love, but in war. It was war that drove men together in multitudes, and compelled them to stand so close, and build walls around them. This crowded condition produces wants of an unnatural character, which resulted in occupations that regenerated the evil, by creating artificial wants. . . .

The plan of the Community, as an Economy, is in brief this; for all who have property to take stock, and receive a fixed interest thereon; then to keep house or board in commons, as they shall severally desire, at the cost of provisions purchased at wholesale, or raised on the farm; and for all to labor in community, and be paid at a certain rate an hour, choosing their own number of hours, and their own kind of work. With the results of this labor, and their interest, they are to pay their board, and also purchase whatever else they require at cost, as the warehouses of the Community, which are to be filled by the Community as such. To perfect this economy, in the course of time they must have all trades, and all modes of business carried on among themselves, from the lowest mechanical trade, which contributes to the health and comfort of life, to the finest art which adorns it with food or drapery for the mind.

All labor, whether bodily or intellectual, is to be paid at the same rate of wages; on the principle, that as the labor becomes merely bodily, it is a greater sacrifice to the individual laborer, to give his time to it; because time is desirable for the cultivation of the intellect, in exact proportion to ignorance. Besides, intellectual labor involves in itself higher pleasures, and is more its own reward, than bodily labor.

Another reason, for setting the same pecuniary value on every kind of labor, is, to give outward expression to the great truth, that all labor is sacred, when done for a common interest. Saints and philosophers already know this, but the childish world does not; and very decided measures must be taken to equalize labors, in the eyes of the young of the community, who are not beyond the moral influences of the world without them. The community will have nothing done within its precincts, but what is done by its own members, who stand all in social equality;—that the children may not "learn to expect one kind of service from Love and Goodwill, and another from the obligation of others to render it,"—a grievance of the common society stated, by one of the associated mothers, as destructive of the soul's simplicity. Consequently, as the Universal Education will involve all kinds of operation, necessary to the comforts and elegances of life, every associate, even if he be the digger of a ditch as his highest accomplishment, will be an instructor in that to the young members. Nor will this elevation of bodily labor be liable to lower the tone of manners and refinement in the community. The "children of light" are not altogether unwise in their generation. They have an invisible but all-powerful guard of principles. Minds incapable of refinement will not be attracted into this association. It is an Ideal community, and only to the ideally inclined will it be attractive; but these are to be found in every rank of life, under every shadow of circumstance. Even among the diggers in the ditch are to be found some, who through religious cultivation, can look down, in meek superiority, upon the outwardly refined, and the book-learned.

Besides, after becoming members of this community, none will be engaged merely in bodily labor. The hours of labor for the Association will be limited by a general law, and can be curtailed at the will of the individual still more; and means will be given to all for intellectual improvement and for social intercourse, calculated to refine and expand. The hours redeemed from labor by community, will not be reapplied to the acquisition of wealth, but to the production of intellectual goods. This community aims to be rich, not in the metallic representative of wealth, but in the wealth itself, which money should represent; namely, LEISURE TO LIFE IN ALL THE FACULTIES OF THE SOUL. As a community, it will traffic with the world at large, in the products of Agricultural labor; and it will sell education to as many young persons as can be domesticated in the families, and enter into the common life with their own children. In the end, it hopes to be enabled to provide—not only all the necessaries, but all the elegances desirable for bodily and for spiritual health; books, apparatus, collections for science, works of art, means of beautiful amusement. These things are to be common to all; and thus that object, which alone gilds and refines the passion for individual accumulation, will no longer exist for desire, and whenever the Sordid passion appears, it will be seen in its naked selfishness. In its ultimate success, the community will realize all the ends which selfishness seeks, but involved in spiritual blessings, which only greatness of soul can aspire after.

And the requisitions on the individuals, it is believed, will make this the order forever. The spiritual good will always be the condition of the temporal. Every one must labor for the community in a reasonable degree, or not taste its benefits. The principles of the organization therefore, and not its probable results in future time, will determine its members. These principles are cooperation in social matters, instead of competition or balance of interests; and individual self-unfolding, in the faith that the whole soul of humanity is in each man and woman. The former is the application of the love of man; the latter of the love of God, to life. Whoever is satisfied with society, as it is; whose sense of justice is not wounded by its common action, institutions, spirit of commerce, has no business

with this community; neither has any one who is willing to have other men (needing more time for intellectual cultivation than himself) give their best hours and strength to bodily labor, to secure himself immunity therefrom. And whoever does not measure what society owes to its members of cherishing and instruction, by the needs of the individuals that compose it, has no lot in this new society. Whoever is willing to receive from his fellow men that, for which he gives no equivalent, will stay away from its precincts forever.

But whoever shall surrender himself to it[s] principles, shall find that its yoke is easy and its burden light. . . . The principle, with regard to labor, lies at the root of moral and religious life; for it is not more true that "money is the root of all evil," than that *labor is the germ of all good.* . . .

A single farm, in the midst of Massachusetts, does not afford range enough for men to create out of the Earth a living, with no other means; as the wild Indians, or the United States Army in Florida may do. This plan, of letting all persons choose their own departments of action, will immediately place the Genius of Instruction on its throne. Communication is the life of spiritual life. Knowledge pours itself out upon ignorance by a native impulse. All the arts crave response. "Wisdom cries." If every man and woman taught only what they loved, and so many hours as they could naturally communicate, instruction would cease to be a drudgery, and we may add, learning would be no longer a task. The known accomplishments of many of the members of this association have already secured it an interest in the public mind, as a school of literary advantages quite superior. Most of the associates have had long practical experience in the details of teaching, and have groaned under the necessity of taking their method and law from custom and caprice, when they would rather have found it in the nature of the thing taught, and the condition of the pupil to be instructed. Each instructor appoints his hours of study or recitation, and the scholars, or the parents of the children, or the educational committee, choose the studies for the time, and the pupils submit, as long as they pursue their studies with any teacher, to his regulations. . . .

It seems impossible that the little organization can be looked on with any unkindness by the world without it. Those who have not the faith that the principles of Christ's kingdom are applicable to real life in the world will smile at it as a visionary attempt. But even they must acknowledge it can do no harm, in any event. If it realizes the hope of its founders, it will immediately become a manifold blessing. Its moral *aura* must be salutary. As long as it lasts, it will be an example of the beauty of brotherly love.

Source: Elizabeth Palmer Peabody, "Plan of the West Roxbury Community," *The Dial* (1842).

The Declaration of Sentiments, Seneca Falls Convention (1848)

The women's rights movement in America is said to have begun with the Seneca Falls Convention in upstate New York in July 1848. The 100 delegates—sixty-eight women and thirty-two men—signed a document called the Declaration of Sentiments demanding equal rights for women in society. Modeled after the American Declaration of Independence, the text was written by convention organizer Elizabeth Cady Stanton.

When, in the course of human events, it becomes necessary for one portion of the family of man to assume among the people of the earth a position different from that which they have hitherto occupied, but one to which the laws of nature and of nature's God entitle them, a decent respect to the opinions of mankind requires that they should declare the causes that impel them to such a course.

We hold these truths to be self-evident: that all men and women are created equal; that they are endowed by their Creator with certain inalienable rights; that among these are life, liberty, and the pursuit of happiness; that to secure these rights governments are instituted, deriving their just powers from the consent of the governed. Whenever any form of government becomes destructive of these ends, it is the right of those who suffer from it to refuse allegiance to it, and to insist upon the institution of a new government, laying its foundation on such principles, and organizing its powers in such form, as to them shall seem most likely to effect their safety and happiness. Prudence, indeed, will dictate that governments long established should not be changed for light and transient causes; and accordingly all experience hath shown that mankind are more disposed to suffer, while evils are sufferable, than to right themselves by abolishing the forms to which they are accustomed. But when a long train of abuses and usurpations, pursuing invariably the same object, evinces a design to reduce them under absolute despotism, it is their duty to throw off such government, and to provide new guards for their future security. Such has been the patient sufferance

of the women under this government, and such is now the necessity which constrains them to demand the equal station to which they are entitled. The history of mankind is a history of repeated injuries and usurpations on the part of man toward woman, having in direct object the establishment of an absolute tyranny over her. To prove this, let facts be submitted to a candid world.

He has never permitted her to exercise her inalienable right to the elective franchise.

He has compelled her to submit to laws, in the formation of which she had no voice.

He has withheld from her rights which are given to the most ignorant and degraded men—both natives and foreigners.

Having deprived her of this first right of a citizen, the elective franchise, thereby leaving her without representation in the halls of legislation, he has oppressed her on all sides.

He has made her, if married, in the eye of the law, civilly dead.

He has taken from her all right in property, even to the wages she earns.

He has made her, morally, an irresponsible being, as she can commit many crimes with impunity, provided they be done in the presence of her husband. In the covenant of marriage, she is compelled to promise obedience to her husband, he becoming, to all intents and purposes, her master—the law giving him power to deprive her of her liberty, and to administer chastisement.

He has so framed the laws of divorce, as to what shall be the proper causes, and in case of separation, to whom the guardianship of the children shall be given, as to be wholly regardless of the happiness of women—the law, in all cases, going upon a false supposition of the supremacy of man, and giving all power into his hands.

After depriving her of all rights as a married woman, if single, and the owner of property, he has taxed her to support a government which recognizes her only when her property can be made profitable to it.

He has monopolized nearly all the profitable employments, and from those she is permitted to follow, she receives but a scanty remuneration. He closes against her all the avenues to wealth and distinction which he considers most honorable to himself. As a teacher of theology, medicine, or law, she is not known.

He has denied her the facilities for obtaining a thorough education, all colleges being closed against her.

He allows her in church, as well as state, but a subordinate position, claiming apostolic authority for her exclusion from the ministry, and, with some exceptions, from any public participation in the affairs of the church.

He has created a false public sentiment by giving to the world a different code of morals for men and women, by which moral delinquencies which exclude women from society, are not only tolerated, but deemed of little account in man.

He has usurped the prerogative of Jehovah himself, claiming it as his right to assign for her a sphere of action, when that belongs to her conscience and to her God.

He has endeavored, in every way that he could, to destroy her confidence in her own powers, to lessen her self-respect, and to make her willing to lead a dependent and abject life.

Now, in view of this entire disfranchisement of one-half the people of this country, their social and religious degradation—in view of the unjust laws above mentioned, and because women do feel themselves aggrieved, oppressed, and fraudulently deprived of their most sacred rights, we insist that they have immediate admission to all the rights and privileges which belong to them as citizens of the United States.

Source: Elizabeth Cady Stanton, *A History of Woman Suffrage,* vol. 1 (Rochester, NY: Fowler and Wells, 1889).

"Where I Lived, and What I Lived For," *Walden* (1854), Henry David Thoreau

In Henry David Thoreau's classic account of two years living in the woods, Walden, *he offers an idyllic vision of his return to nature and "the essential facts of life." In doing so, Thoreau criticizes the "busyness" of mid-nineteenth-century society and "the lives of quiet desperation" being led by many Americans. In Chapter Two of the book, he describes the setting of his cabin and the values he brought to his life there.*

When first I took up my abode in the woods, that is, began to spend my nights as well as days there, which, by accident, was on Independence Day, or the Fourth of July, 1845, my house was not finished for winter, but was merely a defence against the rain, without plastering or chimney, the walls being of rough, weather-stained boards, with wide chinks, which made it cool at night. The upright white hewn studs and freshly planed door and window casings gave it a clean and airy look, especially in the morning, when its timbers were saturated with dew, so that I fancied that by noon some sweet gum would exude from them. To my imagination it retained throughout the day more or less of this auroral character, reminding me of a certain house on a mountain which I had visited a year before. This was an airy and unplastered cabin, fit to entertain a travelling god, and where a goddess might trail her garments. The winds which passed over my dwelling were such as sweep over the ridges of mountains, bearing the broken strains, or celestial parts only, of terrestrial music. The morning wind forever blows, the poem of creation is uninterrupted; but few are the ears that hear it. Olympus is but the outside of the earth everywhere.

The only house I had been the owner of before, if I except a boat, was a tent, which I used occasionally when making excursions in the summer, and this is still rolled up in my garret; but the boat, after passing from hand to hand, has gone down the stream of time. With this more substantial shelter about me, I had made some progress toward settling in the world. This frame, so slightly clad, was a sort of crystallization around me, and reacted on the builder. It was suggestive somewhat as a picture in outlines. I did not need to go outdoors to take the air, for the atmosphere within had lost none of its freshness. It was not so much within doors as behind a door where I sat, even in the rainiest weather. The Harivansa says, "An abode without birds is like a meat without seasoning." Such was not my abode, for I found myself suddenly neighbor to the birds; not by having imprisoned one, but having caged myself near them. I was not only nearer to some of those which commonly frequent the garden and the orchard, but to those smaller and more thrilling songsters of the forest which never, or rarely, serenade a villager—the wood thrush, the veery, the scarlet tanager, the field sparrow, the whip-poor-will, and many others.

I was seated by the shore of a small pond, about a mile and a half south of the village of Concord and somewhat higher than it, in the midst of an extensive wood between that town and Lincoln, and about two miles south of that our only field known to fame, Concord Battle Ground; but I was so low in the woods that the opposite shore, half a mile off, like the rest, covered with wood, was my most distant horizon. . . .

This small lake was of most value as a neighbor in the intervals of a gentle rain-storm in August, when, both air and water being perfectly still, but the sky overcast, mid-afternoon had all the serenity of evening, and the wood thrush sang around, and was heard from shore to shore. A lake like this is never smoother than at such a time; and the clear portion of the air above it being, shallow and darkened by clouds, the water, full of light and reflections, becomes a lower heaven itself so much the more important. From a hill-top near by, where the wood had been recently cut off, there was a pleasing vista southward across the pond, through a wide indentation in the hills which form the shore there, where their opposite sides sloping toward each other suggested a stream flowing out in that direction through a wooded valley, but stream there was none. That way I looked between and over the near green hills to some distant and higher ones in the horizon, tinged with blue. . . . When I looked across the pond from this peak toward the Sudbury meadows, which in time of flood I distinguished elevated perhaps by a mirage in their seething valley, like a coin in a basin, all the earth beyond the pond appeared like a thin crust insulated and floated even by this small sheet of intervening water, and I was reminded that this on which I dwelt was but *dry land*.

Though the view from my door was still more contracted, I did not feel crowded or confined in the least. There was pasture enough for my imagination. The low shrub oak plateau to which the opposite shore arose stretched away toward the prairies of the West and the steppes of Tartary, affording ample room for all the roving families of men. "There are none happy in the world but beings who enjoy freely a vast horizon," said Damodara, when his herds required new and larger pastures.

Both place and time were changed, and I dwelt nearer to those parts of the universe and to those eras in history which had most attracted me. Where I lived was as far off as many a region viewed nightly by astronomers. We are wont to imagine rare and delectable places in some remote and more celestial corner of the system, behind the constellation of Cassiopeia's Chair, far from noise and disturbance. I discovered that my house actually had its site in such a withdrawn, but forever new and unprofaned, part of the universe. If it were worth the while to settle in those parts near to the Pleiades or the Hyades, to Aldebaran or Altair, then I was really there, or at an equal remoteness from the life which I had left behind, dwindled and twinkling with as fine a ray to my nearest neighbor, and to be seen only in moonless nights by him. . . .

Every morning was a cheerful invitation to make my life of equal simplicity, and I may say innocence, with Nature herself. I have been as sincere a worshipper of Aurora as the Greeks. I got up early and bathed in the pond; that was a religious exercise, and one of the best things which I did. They say that characters were engraven on the bathing tub of King Tching-thang to this effect: "Renew thyself completely each day; do it again, and again, and forever again." I can understand that. Morning brings back the heroic ages. I was as much affected by the faint burn of a mosquito making its invisible and unimaginable tour through my apartment at earliest dawn, when I was sailing with door and windows open, as I could be by any trumpet that ever sang of fame. It was Homer's requiem; itself an Iliad and Odyssey in the air, singing its own wrath and wanderings. There was something cosmical about it; a standing advertisement, till forbidden, of the everlasting vigor and fertility of the world. The morning, which is the most memorable season of the day, is the awakening hour. Then there is least somnolence in us; and for an hour, at least, some part of us awakes which slumbers all the rest of the day and night. Little is to be expected of that day, if it can be called a day, to which we are not awakened by our Genius, but by the mechanical nudgings of some servitor, are not awakened by our own newly acquired force and aspirations from within, accompanied by the undulations of celestial music, instead of factory bells, and a fragrance filling the air—to a higher life than we fell asleep from; and thus the darkness bear its fruit, and prove itself to be good, no less than the light. That man who does not believe that each day contains an earlier, more sacred, and auroral hour than he has yet profaned, has despaired of life, and is pursuing a descending and darkening way. After a partial cessation of his sensuous life, the soul of man, or its organs rather, are reinvigorated each day, and his Genius tries again what noble life it can make. All memorable events, I should say, transpire in morning time and in a morning atmosphere. . . . To him whose elastic and vigorous thought keeps pace with the sun, the day is a perpetual morning. It matters not what the clocks say or the attitudes and labors of men. Morning is when I am awake and there is a dawn in me. Moral reform is the effort to throw off sleep. Why is it that men give so poor an account of their day if they have not been slumbering? They are not such poor calculators. If they had not been overcome with drowsiness, they would have performed something. The millions are awake enough for physical labor; but only one in a million is awake enough for effective intellectual exertion, only one in a hundred millions to a poetic or divine life. To be awake is to be alive. I have never yet met a man who was quite awake. How could I have looked him in the face? . . .

I went to the woods because I wished to live deliberately, to front only the essential facts of life, and see if I could not learn what it had to teach, and not, when I came to die, discover that I had not lived. I did not wish to live what was not life, living is so dear; nor did I wish to practice resignation, unless it was quite necessary. I wanted to live deep and suck out all the marrow of life, to live so sturdily and Spartan-like as to put to rout all that was not life, to cut a broad swath and shave close, to drive life into a corner, and reduce it to its lowest terms, and, if it proved to be mean, why then to get the whole and genuine meanness of it, and publish its meanness to the world; or if it were sublime, to know it by experience, and be able to give a true account of it in my next excursion. For most men, it appears to me, are in a strange uncertainty about it, whether it is of the devil or of God, and have somewhat hastily concluded that it is the chief end of man here to "glorify God and enjoy him forever."

Still we live meanly, like ants; though the fable tells us that we were long ago changed into men; like pygmies we fight with cranes; it is error upon error, and clout upon clout, and our best virtue has for its occasion a superfluous and evitable wretchedness. Our life is frittered away by detail. An honest man has hardly need to count more than his ten fingers, or in extreme cases he may add his ten toes, and lump the rest. Simplicity, simplicity, simplicity! I say, let your affairs be as two or three, and not a hundred or a thousand; instead of a million count half a dozen, and keep your accounts on your thumb-nail. In the midst of this chopping sea of civilized life, such are the clouds and storms and quicksands and thousand-and-one items to be allowed for, that a man has to live, if he would not founder and go to the bottom and not make his port at all, by dead reckoning, and he must be a great calcula-

tor indeed who succeeds. Simplify, simplify. Instead of three meals a day, if it be necessary eat but one; instead of a hundred dishes, five; and reduce other things in proportion. . . . The nation itself, with all its so-called internal improvements, which, by the way are all external and superficial, is just such an unwieldy and overgrown establishment, cluttered with furniture and tripped up by its own traps, ruined by luxury and heedless expense, by want of calculation and a worthy aim, as the million households in the land; and the only cure for it, as for them, is in a rigid economy, a stern and more than Spartan simplicity of life and elevation of purpose. It lives too fast. Men think that it is essential that the Nation have commerce, and export ice, and talk through a telegraph, and ride thirty miles an hour, without a doubt, whether they do or not; but whether we should live like baboons or like men, is a little uncertain. If we do not get out sleepers, and forge rails, and devote days and nights to the work, but go to tinkering upon our lives to improve them, who will build railroads? And if railroads are not built, how shall we get to heaven in season? But if we stay at home and mind our business, who will want railroads? We do not ride on the railroad; it rides upon us. Did you ever think what those sleepers are that underlie the railroad? Each one is a man, an Irishman, or a Yankee man. The rails are laid on them, and they are covered with sand, and the cars run smoothly over them. They are sound sleepers, I assure you. And every few years a new lot is laid down and run over; so that, if some have the pleasure of riding on a rail, others have the misfortune to be ridden upon. And when they run over a man that is walking in his sleep, a supernumerary sleeper in the wrong position, and wake him up, they suddenly stop the cars, and make a hue and cry about it, as if this were an exception. I am glad to know that it takes a gang of men for every five miles to keep the sleepers down and level in their beds as it is, for this is a sign that they may sometime get up again.

Why should we live with such hurry and waste of life? We are determined to be starved before we are hungry. Men say that a stitch in time saves nine, and so they take a thousand stitches today to save nine tomorrow. . . . Hardly a man takes a half-hour's nap after dinner, but when he wakes he holds up his head and asks, "What's the news?" as if the rest of mankind had stood his sentinels. Some give directions to be waked every half-hour, doubtless for no other purpose; and then, to pay for it, they tell what they have dreamed. After a night's sleep the news is as indispensable as the breakfast. . . .

For my part, I could easily do without the post-office. I think that there are very few important communications made through it. To speak critically, I never received more than one or two letters in my life—I wrote this some years ago—that were worth the postage. The penny-post is, commonly, an institution through which you seriously offer a man that penny for his thoughts which is so often safely offered in jest. And I am sure that I never read any memorable news in a newspaper. If we read of one man robbed, or murdered, or killed by accident, or one house burned, or one vessel wrecked, or one steamboat blown up, or one cow run over on the Western Railroad, or one mad dog killed, or one lot of grasshoppers in the winter—we never need read of another. One is enough. If you are acquainted with the principle, what do you care for a myriad instances and applications? . . .

Shams and delusions are esteemed for soundest truths, while reality is fabulous. If men would steadily observe realities only, and not allow themselves to be deluded, life, to compare it with such things as we know, would be like a fairy tale and the Arabian Nights' Entertainments. If we respected only what is inevitable and has a right to be, music and poetry would resound along the streets. When we are unhurried and wise, we perceive that only great and worthy things have any permanent and absolute existence, that petty fears and petty pleasures are but the shadow of the reality. This is always exhilarating and sublime. By closing the eyes and slumbering, and consenting to be deceived by shows, men establish and confirm their daily life of routine and habit everywhere, which still is built on purely illusory foundations. Children, who play life, discern its true law and relations more clearly than men, who fail to live it worthily, but who think that they are wiser by experience, that is, by failure. . . . I perceive that we inhabitants of New England live this mean life that we do because our vision does not penetrate the surface of things. We think that that is which appears to be. . . .

Let us spend one day as deliberately as Nature, and not be thrown off the track by every nutshell and mosquito's wing that falls on the rails. Let us rise early and fast, or break fast, gently and without perturbation; let company come and let company go, let the bells ring and the children cry—determined to make a day of it. Why should we knock under and go with the stream? Let us not be upset and overwhelmed in that terrible rapid and whirlpool called a dinner, situated in the meridian shallows. Weather this danger and you are safe, for the rest of the way is down hill. With unrelaxed nerves, with morning vigor, sail by it, looking another way, tied to the mast like Ulysses. If the engine whistles, let it whistle till it is hoarse for its pains. If the bell rings, why should we run? We will consider what kind of music they are like. Let us settle ourselves, and work and wedge our feet downward through the mud and slush of opinion, and prejudice, and tradition, and delusion, and appearance, that alluvion which covers the globe, through Paris and London, through New York and Boston and Concord, through Church and State, through poetry and philosophy and religion, till we come to a hard bottom and rocks in place, which we can call reality, and say, This is, and no mistake. . . . If you stand right fronting and face-to-face to a fact, you will see the sun glimmer on both its surfaces, as if it were a cimeter, and feel its sweet edge dividing you through the heart and marrow, and so you will happily conclude your mortal career. Be it life or death, we crave only reality. If we are really dying, let us hear the rattle in our throats and feel cold in the extremities; if we are alive, let us go about our business.

Time is but the stream I go a-fishing in. I drink at it; but while I drink I see the sandy bottom and detect how shallow it is. Its thin current slides away, but eternity remains. I would drink deeper; fish in the sky, whose bottom is pebbly with stars. I cannot count one. I know not the first letter of the alphabet. I have always been regretting that I was not as wise as the day I was born. The intellect is a cleaver; it discerns and rifts its way into the secret of things. I do not wish to be any more busy with my hands than is necessary. My head is hands and feet. I feel all my best faculties concentrated in it. My instinct tells me that my head is an organ for burrowing, as some creatures use their snout and fore paws, and with it I would mine and burrow my way through these hills. I think that the richest vein is somewhere hereabouts; so by the divining-rod and thin rising vapors I judge; and here I will begin to mine.

Source: Henry David Thoreau, *Walden, or Life in the Woods* (Boston: Ticknor and Fields, 1854).

Hand-Book of the Oneida Community (1867)

The Oneida Community in central New York State was a Christian utopian settlement established in 1848 by religious and social radical John Humphrey Noyes. Believing in the perfectibility of human life and society, members owned all possessions and property communally, shared the work and governance of the community, and practiced a form of complex (group) marriage. The guiding principles and doctrines were summarized in the Hand-Book of the Oneida Community, *excerpts of which follow.*

Means of Government

The measures relied upon for good government, in these Community families are, first, *daily evening meetings,* which all are expected to attend, and in which religious, social and business matters are freely discussed; and secondly, the system of mutual criticism. This system takes the place of backbiting in ordinary society, and is regarded as one of the greatest means of improvement and fellowship. All of the members are accustomed to voluntarily invite the benefit of criticism from time to time. Sometimes persons are criticized by the entire family; at other times by a committee of six, eight, twelve, or more, selected by themselves from among those best acquainted with them, and best able to do justice to their character. In these criticisms the most perfect sincerity is expected; and in practical experience it is found best for the subject to receive his criticism without replying. There is little danger that the general verdict in respect to his character will be unjust. This ordinance is far from agreeable to those whose egotism and vanity are stronger than their love of truth. It is an ordeal which reveals insincerity and selfishness; but it also often takes the form of commendation, and reveals hidden virtues as well as secret faults. It is always acceptable to those who wish to see themselves as others see them.

These two agencies, viz. daily evening meetings and criticism, are found quite adequate to the maintenance of good order and government in the Communities. Those who join the Communities understanding their principles, and afterward prove refractory and inharmonic, and also those who come into the Communities in childhood, and afterwards develop characters antagonistic to the general spirit, and refuse to yield to the governmental agencies mentioned, either voluntarily withdraw or are expelled. Only one case of expulsion has, however, been recorded. . . .

The Social Organization

of the Oneida Community and its branches, and the intercourse of the sexes, are also easily explained and readily understood. In the first place, the Communities believe, contrary to the theory of the novelists and oth-

ers, that the affections can be controlled and guided, and that they will produce far better results when rightly controlled and rightly guided than if left to take care of themselves without restraint. They entirely reject the idea that love is an inevitable and uncontrollable fatality, which must have its own course. They believe the whole matter of love and its expression should be subject to enlightened self-control, and should be managed for the greatest good. In the Communities it is under the special supervision of the fathers and mothers, or, in other words, of the wisest and best members, and is often under discussion in the evening meetings, and is also subordinate to the institution of criticism. The fathers and mothers are guided in their management by certain general principles which have been worked out, and are well understood in the Communities. One is termed the principle of the ascending fellowship. It is regarded as better for the young of both sexes to associate in love with persons older than themselves, and, if possible, with those who are spiritual and have been some time in the school of self-control, and who are thus able to make love safe and edifying. This is only another form of the popular principle of contrasts. It is well understood by physiologists, that it is undesirable for persons of similar characters and temperaments to mate together. Communists have discovered that it is not desirable for two inexperienced and unspiritual persons to rush into fellowship with each other; that it is far better for both to associate with persons of mature character and sound sense.

Another general principle well understood in the Communities, is, that it is not desirable for two persons, whatever may be their standing, to become exclusively attached to each other—to worship and idolize each other—however popular this experience may be with sentimental people generally. They regard exclusive, idolatrous attachment as unhealthy and pernicious wherever it may exist. The Communities insist that the heart should be kept free to love all the true and worthy, and should never be contracted with exclusiveness or idolatry, or purely selfish love in any form. . . .

The great aim is to teach every one self-control. This leads to the greatest happiness in love, and the greatest good to all. . . .

Free Love

This terrible combination of two very good ideas—freedom and love—was first used by the writers of the Oneida Community about eighteen years ago, and probably originated with them. It was however soon taken up by a very different class of speculators scattered about the country, and has come to be the name of a form of socialism with which we have but little affinity. Still it is sometimes applied to our Communities; and as we are certainly responsible for starting it into circulation, it seems to be our duty to tell what meaning we attach to it, and in what sense we are willing to accept it as a designation of our social system.

The obvious and essential difference between marriage and licentious connections may be stated thus:

Marriage is permanent union. Whoredom is a temporary flirtation.

In marriage, communism of property goes with communism of persons. In whoredom, love is paid for by the job.

Marriage makes a man responsible for the *consequences* of his acts of love to a woman. In whoredom a man imposes on a woman the heavy burdens of maternity, ruining perhaps her reputation and her health, and then goes his way without responsibility.

Marriage provides for the maintenance and education of children. Whoredom ignores children as nuisances, and leaves them to chance.

Now in respect to every one of these points of difference between marriage and whoredom, *we stand with marriage.* Free love with us does *not* mean freedom to love to-day and leave to-morrow; nor freedom to take a woman's person and keep our property to ourselves; nor freedom to freight a woman with our offspring and send her down stream without care or help; nor freedom to beget children and leave them to the street and the poor-house. Our Communities are *families,* as distinctly bounded and separated from promiscuous society as ordinary households. The tie that binds us together is as permanent and sacred, to say the least, as that of marriage, for it is our religion. We receive no members (except by deception or mistake), who do not give heart and hand to the family interest for life and forever. Community of property extends just as far as freedom of love. Every man's care and every dollar of the common property is pledged for the maintenance and protection of the women, and the education of the children of the Community. Bastardy, in any disastrous sense of the word, is simply impossible in such a social state. Whoever will take the trouble to follow our track from the beginning, will find no forsaken women or children by the way. In this respect we claim to be a little ahead of marriage and common civilization.

We are not sure how far the class of socialists called "free lovers" would claim for themselves anything like the above defense from the charge of *reckless* and *cruel* freedom; but our impression is that their position, scattered as they are, without organization or definite separation from surrounding society, makes it impossible for them to follow and care for the consequences of their freedom, and thus exposes them to the just charge of licentiousness. At all events their platform is entirely different from ours, and they must answer for themselves. We are not "free lovers" in any sense that makes love less binding or responsible than it is in marriage.

Source: Hand-Book of the Oneida Community (1867).

Woman's Christian Temperance Union "Do Everything" Policy (1893)

In a speech to the Second Biennial Convention of the World Woman's Christian Temperance Union (WCTU) in October 1893, Frances Willard—president of the American WCTU—declared the necessity of the "Do Everything" policy she had been advocating in the campaign for abstinence and public morals.

Beloved Comrades of the White Ribbon Army:

WHEN we began the delicate, difficult, and dangerous operation of dissecting out the alcohol nerve from the body politic, we did not realize the intricacy of the undertaking nor the distances that must be traversed by the scalpel of investigation and research. In about seventy days from now, twenty years will have elapsed since the call of battle sounded its bugle note among the homes and hearts of Hillsboro, Ohio. We have all been refreshing our knowledge of those days by reading the "Crusade Sketches" of its heroic leader, Mrs. Eliza J. Thompson, "the mother of us all," and we know that but one thought, sentiment and purpose animated those saintly "Praying Bands" whose name will never die out from human history. "Brothers, we beg you not to drink and not to sell!" This was the one wailing note of these moral Paganinis, playing on one string. It caught the universal ear and set the key of that mighty orchestra, organized with so much toil and hardship, in which the tender and exalted strain of the Crusade violin still soars aloft, but upborne now by the clanging cornets of science, the deep trombones of legislation, and the thunderous drums of politics and parties.

The "Do Everything Policy" was not of our choosing, but is an evolution as inevitable as any traced by the naturalist or described by the historian. Woman's genius for details, and her patient steadfastness in following the enemies of those she loves "through every lane of life," have led her to antagonize the alcohol habit and the liquor traffic just where they are, wherever that may be. If she does this, since they are everywhere, her policy will be "Do Everything."

A one-sided movement makes one-sided advocates. Virtues, like hounds, hunt in packs. Total abstinence is not the crucial virtue in life that excuses financial crookedness, defamation of character, or habits of impurity. The fact that one's father was, and one's self is, a bright and shining light in the total abstinence galaxy, does not give one a vantage ground for high-handed behavior toward those who have not been trained to the special virtue that forms the central idea of the Temperance Movement. We have known persons who, because they had "never touched a drop of liquor," set themselves up as if they belonged to a royal line, but whose tongues were as biting as alcohol itself, and whose narrowness had no competitor save a straight line. An all-round movement can only be carried forward by all-round advocates; a scientific age requires the study of every subject in its correlations. It was once supposed that light, heat, and electricity were wholly separate entities; it is now believed and practically proved that they are but different modes of motion. Standing in the valley we look up and think we see an isolated mountain; climbing to its top we see that it is but one member of a range of mountains many of them of well-nigh equal altitude.

Some bright women who have opposed the "Do-Everything Policy" used as their favorite illustration a flowing river, and expatiated on the ruin that would follow if that river (which represents their do-one-thing policy) were diverted into many channels, but it should be remembered that the most useful of all rivers is the Nile, and that the agricultural economy of Egypt consists in the effort to spread its waters upon as many fields as possible. It is not for the river's sake that it flows through the country but for the sake of the fertility it can bring upon adjoining fields, and this is pre-eminently true of the Temperance Reform. . . .

In the conflict with the liquor traffic, the policy of the W.C.T.U. is to attack not only the chief foe, but also its notorious and open allies. This is the course dictated not only by common sense, but by absolute necessity. If the home is to be protected, not only must the dram-shop be made an outlaw, but its allies, the gambling hells, the houses of unreportable infamy, the ignorance of the general population as to alcoholics and other narcotics, the timidity of trade, the venality of portions of the press, and especially the subserviency of political parties to the liquor traffic, must be assailed as confederates of the chief enemy of the home. . . . It is certain that the broad and progressive policy of the W.C.T.U. in the United States makes the whiskey rings and time-serving politicians greatly dread its influence. They honor the Union by frequent and bitter attacks. It is a recognized power in international affairs. If its policy were made narrow and non-partisan, its influence would immensely wane in practical matters of great importance.

The department of Scientific Temperance Instruction, conducted by the W.C.T.U., and led by Mrs. Mary H. Hunt, of Boston, has now made such instruction mandatory in thirty-six States of the Republic. This is a very large and substantial triumph of the broad and progressive policy. Instead of the National W.C.T.U. having lost the confidence of the churches by its broad policy, I believe, after much travel and years of observation, that it never had more of that confidence than at the present hour. At a recent Congressional Hearing, in Washington, I heard a distinguished Presbyterian Professor of Theology, Rev. Dr. Herrick Johnson, of Chicago, call the W.C.T.U. the most powerful, the most beneficent, and the most successful organization ever formed by women. Similar testimony abounds in all the most enlightened circles of the land.

Let us not be disconcerted, but stand bravely by that blessed trinity of movements, Prohibition, Woman's Liberation and Labor's uplift.

Everything is not in the Temperance Reform, but the Temperance Reform should be in everything.

There is no better motto for the "Do-Everything-Policy," than this which we are saying by our deeds: "Make a chain, for the land is full of bloody crimes and the city of violence."

If we can remember this simple rule, it will do much to unravel the mystery of the much controverted "Do-Everything-Policy," viz: that every question of practical philanthropy or reform has its temperance aspect, and with that we are to deal. . . .

Methods that were once the only ones available may become, with the passage of years, less useful because less available. In earlier times the manly art of hunting was most helpful to civilization, because before fields could be cleared and tilled, they had to be free from the danger of wild beasts, and no method of obtaining food was more important than the chase; but when the forests have been cleared away and the pastoral condition of life has supervened, nay, more, when the highest civilization peoples the hills and valleys, it certainly evinces a lack of imagination to present such a spectacle as do the hunters who in England today place a poor stag in a van, convey him on four wheels to a wood, let him out through a door, and set trained dogs upon him, while they follow with guns and halloos, and call it "sport"! The same absurdity has been illustrated by Baron Hirsch, who recently imported 6,000 caged partridges to his country place, let them loose in the groves, and set himself and friends peppering away at them. Surely such conduct is the reverse of manly, and must bring what was once a noble occupation into contempt. But, in a different way, we illustrate the same principle, when we forget that "New occasions teach new duties, Time makes ancient good uncouth." . . .

The Temperance cause started out well nigh alone, but mighty forces have joined us in the long march. We are now in the midst of the Waterloo battle, and in the providence of God the Temperance army will not have to fight that out all by itself. For Science has come up with its glittering contingent, political economy deploys its legions, the woman question brings an Amazonian army upon the field, and the stout ranks of labor stretch away far as the eye can reach. As in the old Waterloo against Napoleon, so now against the Napoleon of the liquor traffic, no force is adequate except the allied forces.

Source: Frances Willard, Address before the Second Biennial Convention of the World Woman's Christian Temperance Union (1893).

Speech at Founding Convention of the Industrial Workers of the World (1905), Eugene V. Debs

Former railroad worker Eugene V. Debs, a leader of the fledgling labor movement and socialist politics in America, was a cofounder of the Industrial Workers of the World (IWW) in 1905. On June 29 of that year, Debs addressed the IWW's founding convention in Chicago, which was attended by some 200 socialists and radical trade unionists.

Fellow Delegates and Comrades:

As the preliminaries in organizing the convention have been disposed of, we will get down to the real work before this body. We are here to perform a task so great that it appeals to our best thought, our united energies, and will enlist our most loyal support; a task in the presence of which weak men might falter and despair, but from which it is impossible to shrink without betraying the working class.

I am much impressed by this proletarian gathering. I realize that I stand in the presence of those who in the past have fought, are fighting, and will continue to fight the battles of the working class economically and politically, until the capitalist class is overthrown and the working class are emancipated from all of the degrading thralldom of the ages. In this great struggle the working class are often defeated, but never vanquished. Even the defeats, if we are wise enough to profit by them, but hasten the day of the final victory.

In taking a survey of the industrial field of today, we are at once impressed with the total inadequacy of working-class organization, with the lack of solidarity, with the widespread demoralization we see, and we are bound to conclude that the old form of pure and simple unionism has long since outgrown its usefulness; that it is now not only in the way of progress, but that it has become positively reactionary, a thing that is but an auxiliary to the capitalist class.

They charge us with being assembled here for the purpose of disrupting the union movement. It is already disrupted, and if it were not disrupted we would not behold the spectacle here in the very city of a white policeman guarding a black scab, and a black policeman guarding a white scab, while the trade unions stand by with their hands in their pockets wondering what is the matter with union labor in America. We are here today for the purpose of uniting the working class, for the purpose of eliminating that form of unionism which is responsible for the conditions as they exist today.

The trades-union movement is today under the control of the capitalist class. It is preaching capitalist economics. It is serving capitalist purposes. Proof of it, positive and overwhelming, appears on every hand. All of the important strikes during the textile workers at Fall River, that proved so disastrous to those who engaged in it; the strike of the subway employees in the city of New York, where under the present form of organization the local leaders repudiated the local leaders and were in alliance with the capitalist class to crush their own followers; the strike of the stockyard's employees here in Chicago; the strike of the teamsters now in progress—all, all of them bear testimony to the fact that the pure and simple form of unionism has fulfilled its mission, whatever that may have been, and that the time has come for it to go.

The American Federation of Labor has numbers, but the capitalist class do not fear the American Federation of Labor; quite the contrary. The capitalist papers here in this very city at this very time are championing the cause of pure and simple unionism. Since this convention met there has been nothing in these papers but a series of misrepresentations. If we had met instead in the interest of the American Federation of Labor these papers, these capitalist papers, would have had their columns filled with articles commending the work that is being done here. There is certainly something wrong with that form of unionism which has its chief support in the press that represents capitalism; something wrong in that form of unionism whose leaders are the lieutenants of capitalism; something wrong with that form of unionism that forms an alliance with such a capitalist combination as the Civic Federation, whose sole purpose it is to chloroform the working class while the capitalist class go through their pockets. There are those who believe that this form of unionism can be changed from within. They are very greatly mistaken. We might as well have remained in the Republican and Democratic parties and have expected to effect certain changes from within, instead of withdrawing from those parties and organizing a party that represented the exploiting working class. There is but one way to effect this great change, and that is for the workingman to sever his relations with the American Federation and join the union that proposes upon the economic field to represent his class, and we are here today for the purpose of organizing that union. I believe that we are capable of profiting by the experiences of the past. I believe it is possible for the delegates here assembled to form a great, sound, economic organization of the working class based upon the class struggle, that shall be broad enough to embrace every honest worker, yet narrow enough to exclude every fakir.

Now, let me say to those delegates who are here representing the Socialist Trade & Labor Alliance that I have not in the past agreed with their tactics. I concede that their theory is right, that their principles are sound; I admit and cheerfully admit the honesty of their membership. But there must certainly be something wrong with their tactics or their methods of propaganda if in these years they have not developed a larger membership than they have to their credit.

Let me say in this connection, I am not of those who scorn you because of your small numbers. I have been taught by experience that numbers do not represent strength. I will concede that the capitalist class does not fear the American Federation of Labor because of their numbers. Let me add that the capitalist class does not fear your Socialist Trade & Labor Alliance. The one are too numerous and the other are not sufficiently numerous. The American Federation of Labor is not sound in its economics. The Socialist Trade & Labor Alliance is sound in its economics, but in my judgment it does not appeal to the American working class in the right spirit. Upon my lips there has never been a sneer for the Socialist Trade & Labor Alliance on account of the smallness of its numbers. I have been quite capable of applauding the pluck, of admiring the courage of the members of the Socialist Trade & Labor Alliance, for though few in numbers, they stay by their colors. . . .

Now, I believe that there is a middle ground that can be occupied without the slightest concession of principle. I believe it is possible for such an organization as the Western Federation of Miners to be brought into harmonious relation with the Socialist Trade & Labor Alliance. I believe it is possible that that element of the organizations represented here have the conviction, born of experience, observation and study, that the time has come to organize a new union, and I believe it is possible for these elements to mingle, to combine here, and to at least begin the work of forming a great economic or revolutionary organization of the working class so sorely needed in the struggle for their emancipation. The supreme need of the hour, as the speaker who preceded me so clearly expressed it in his carefully and clearly thought address—the supreme need of the hour is a sound, revolutionary working-class organization. And while I am not foolish enough to imagine that we can complete this great work in a single convention of a few days' duration, I do believe it is possible for us to initiate this work, to begin it in a way for the greatest promise, with the assurance that its work will be completed in a way that will appeal with increasing force to the working class of the country.

I am satisfied that the great body of the working class in this country are prepared for just such an organization. I know, their leaders know, that if this convention is successful their doom is sealed. They can already see the hand-writing upon the wall, and so they are seeking by all of the power at their command to discredit this convention, and in alliance with the cohorts of capitalism they are doing what they can to defeat this convention. It may fail in its mission, for they may continue to misrepresent, deceive and betray the working class and keep them in the clutches of their capitalist masters and exploiters.

They are hoping that we will fail to get together. They are hoping, as they have already expressed it, that this convention will consist of a prolonged wrangle; that such is our feeling and relations toward each other that it will be impossible for us to agree upon any vital proposition; that we will fight each other upon every point, and that when we have concluded our labors we will leave things in a worse condition than they were before.

If we are true to ourselves we will undeceive those gentlemen. We will give them to understand that we are animated by motives too lofty for them in their baseness and sordidness to comprehend. We will give them to understand that the motive here is not to use unionism as a means of serving the capitalist class, but that the motive of the men and women assembled here is to serve the working class by so organizing that class as to make their organization the promise of the coming triumph upon the economic field and the political field and the ultimate emancipation of the working class. . . .

I have not the slightest feeling against those who in the past have seen fit to call me a fakir. I can afford to wait. I have waited, and I now stand ready to take by the hand every man, every woman that comes here, totally regardless of past affiliations, whose purpose it is to organize the working class upon the economic field, to launch that economic organization that shall be the expression of the economic conditions as they exist today; that organization for which the working class are prepared; that organization which we shall at least begin before we have ended our labors, unless we shall prove false to the object for which we have assembled here.

Now, I am not going to take the time to undertake to outline the form of this organization. Nor should I undertake to try your patience by attempting to elaborate the plan of organization. But let me suggest, in a few words, that to accomplish its purpose this organization must not only be based upon the class struggle, but must express the economic condition of this time. We must have one organization that embraces the workers in every department of industrial activity. It must express the class struggle. It must recognize the class lines. It must of course be class-conscious. It must be totally uncompromising. It must be an organization of the rank and file. It must be so organized and so guided as to appeal to the intelligence of the workers of the country everywhere. And if we succeed, as I believe we will, in forming such an organization, its success is a foregone conclusion.

I have already said the working class are ready for it. There are multiplied thousands in readiness to join it, waiting only to see if the organization is rightly grounded and properly formed; and this done there will be no trouble about its development, and its development will take proper form and expand to its true proportions. If this work is properly begun, it will mean in time, and not a long time at that, a single union upon the economic field. It will mean more than that; it will mean a single party upon the political field; the one the economic expression, the other the political expression of the working class; the two halves that represent the organic whole of the labor movement.

Now, let me say in closing, comrades—and I have tried to condense, not wishing to tax your patience or to take the time of others, for I believe that in such conventions as this it is more important that we shall perform than that we shall make speeches—let me say in closing that you and I and all of us who are here to enlist in the service of the working class need to have faith in each other, not the faith born of ignorance and stupidity, but the enlightened faith of self-interest. We are in precisely the same position; we depend absolutely upon each other. We must get close together and stand shoulder to shoulder. We know that without solidarity nothing is possible, that with it nothing is impossible.

And so we must dispel the petty prejudices that are born of the differences of the past, and I am of those who believe that, if we get together in the true working-class spirit, most of these differences will disappear, and if those of us who have differed in the past are willing to accord to each other that degree of conciliation that we ourselves feel that we are entitled to, that we will forget these differences, we will approach all of the problems that confront us with our intelligence combined, acting together in concert, all animated by the same high resolve to form that great union, so necessary to the working class, without which their condition remains as it is, and with which, when made practical and vitalized and renewed, the working class is permeated with the conquering spirit of the class struggle, and as if by magic the entire movement is vitalized, and side by side and shoulder to shoulder in a class-conscious phalanx we move forward to certain and complete victory.

Source: Industrial Workers of the World Founding Convention Minutes (1905).

The Woman Rebel (1914), Margaret Sanger

In March 1914, reproductive rights crusader Margaret Sanger began publication of an eight-page monthly newspaper called The Woman Rebel. *In its pages, where she coined the term* birth control, *Sanger sought to unite women around the issues of sexual and reproductive freedom, safe contraception, and the feminist movement in general. The following passages appeared in the newspaper's inaugural issue.*

This paper will not be the champion of any "ism."

All rebel women are invited to contribute to its columns.

The majority of papers usually adjust themselves to the ideas of their readers but the WOMAN REBEL will obstinately refuse to be adjusted.

The aim of this paper will be to stimulate working women to think for themselves and to build up a conscious fighting character.

An early feature will be a series of articles written by the editor for girls from fourteen to eighteen years of age. In this present chaos of sex atmosphere it is difficult for the girl of this uncertain age to know just what to do or really what constitutes clean living without prudishness. All this slushy talk about white slavery, the man painted and described as a hideous vulture pouncing down upon the young, pure and innocent girl, drugging her through the medium of grape juice and lemonade and then dragging her off to his foul den for other men equally as vicious to feed and fatten on her enforced slavery—surely this picture is enough to sicken and disgust every thinking woman and man, who has lived even a few years past the adolescent age. Could any more repulsive and foul conception of sex be given to adolescent girls as a preparation for life than this picture that is being perpetuated by the stupidly ignorant in the name of "sex education"!

If it were possible to get the truth from girls who work in prostitution to-day, I believe most of them would tell you that the first sex experience was with a sweetheart or through the desire for a sweetheart or something impelling within themselves, the nature of which they knew not, neither could they control. Society does not forgive this act when it is based upon the natural impulses and feelings of a young girl. It prefers the other story of the grape juice procurer which makes it easy to shift the blame from its own shoulders, to cast the stone and to evade the unpleasant facts that it alone is responsible for. It sheds sympathetic tears over white slavery, holds the often mythical procurer up as a target, while in reality it is supported by the misery it engenders.

If, as reported, there are approximately 35,000 women working as prostitutes in New York City alone, is it not sane to conclude that some force, some living, powerful, social force is at play to compel these women to work at a trade which involves police persecution, social ostracism and the constant danger of exposure to venereal diseases. From my own knowledge of adolescent girls and from sincere expressions of women working as prostitutes inspired by mutual understanding and confidence I claim that the first sexual act of these so-called wayward girls is partly given, partly desired yet reluctantly so because of the fear of the consequences together with the dread of lost respect of the man. These fears interfere with mutuality of expression—the man becomes conscious of the responsibility of the set and often refuses to see her again, sometimes leaving the town and usually denouncing her as having been with "other fellows." His sole aim is to throw off responsibility. The same uncertainty in these emotions is experienced by girls in marriage in as great a proportion as in the unmarried. After the first experience the life of a girl varies. All these girls do not necessarily go into prostitution. They have had an experience which has not "ruined" them, but rather given them a larger vision of life, stronger feelings and a broader understanding of human nature. The adolescent girl does not understand herself. She is full of contradictions, whims, emotions. For her emotional nature longs for caresses, to touch, to kiss. She is often as well satisfied to hold hands or to go arm in arm with a girl as in the companionship of a boy.

It is these and kindred facts upon which the WOMAN REBEL will dwell from time to time and from which it is hoped the young girl will derive some knowledge of her nature, and conduct her life upon such knowledge.

It will also be the aim of the WOMAN REBEL to advocate the prevention of conception and to impart such knowledge in the columns of this paper. . . .

The Prevention of Conception

Is there any reason why women should not receive clean, harmless, scientific knowledge on how to prevent conception? Everybody is aware that the old, stupid fallacy that such knowledge will cause a girl to enter into prostitution has long been shattered. Seldom does a prostitute become pregnant. Seldom does the girl practicing promiscuity become pregnant. The woman of the upper middle class has all available knowledge and implements to prevent conception. The woman of the lower middle class is struggling for this knowledge. She tries various methods of prevention, and after a few years of experience plus medical advice succeeds in discovering some method suitable to her individual self. The woman of the people is the only one left in ignorance of this information. Her neighbors, relatives and friends tell her stories of special devices and the success of them all. They tell her also of the blood-sucking men with M. D. after their names who perform operations for the price of so-and-so. But the working woman's purse is thin. Its far cheaper to have a baby, "though God knows what it will do after it gets here." Then, too, all other classes of women live in places where there is at least a semblance of privacy and sanitation. It is easier for them to care for themselves whereas the large majority of the women of the people have no bathing or sanitary conveniences. This accounts too for the fact that the higher the standard of living, the more care can be taken and fewer children result. No plagues, famine or wars could ever frighten the capitalist class so much as the universal practice of the prevention of conception. On the other hand no better method could be utilized for increasing the wages of the workers.

As is well known, a law exists forbidding the imparting of information on this subject, the penalty being several years' imprisonment. Is it now time to defy this law! And what fitter place could be found than in the pages of the WOMAN REBEL!

Source: Margaret Sanger, *The Woman Rebel* (March 1914).

"I Didn't Raise My Boy to Be a Soldier (1915)"

With the outbreak of World War I in Europe, American pacifists, isolationists, socialists, and other antimilitarists came together in opposition to U.S. involvement. In 1915, "I Didn't Raise My Boy to Be a Soldier" was a popular antiwar song.

Ten million soldiers to the war have gone,
Who may never return again.
Ten million mothers' hearts must break,
For the ones who died in vain.
Head bowed down in sorrow in her lonely
     years,
I heard a mother murmur thro' her tears:

Chorus:
I didn't raise my boy to be a soldier,
I brought him up to be my pride and joy,
Who dares to put a musket on his shoulder,
To shoot some other mother's darling boy?

Let nations arbitrate their future troubles,
It's time to lay the sword and gun away,

There'd be no war today,
If mothers all would say,
I didn't raise my boy to be a soldier.

(Chorus)

What victory can cheer a mother's heart,
When she looks at her blighted home?
What victory can bring her back,
All she cared to call her own?
Let each mother answer in the year to be,
Remember that my boy belongs to me!

(Chorus)

Source: Al Pianadosi and Alfred Bryan, "I Didn't Raise My Boy to Be a Soldier," recording (Edison Collection, Library of Congress).

"Anarchism: What It Really Stands For" (1917), Emma Goldman

With life partner and revolutionary comrade Alexander Berkman, Russian immigrant Emma Goldman was the leading voice and advocate of anarchism in Progressive Era America. Despite her disavowal of violence, Goldman's radical ideas and incendiary rhetoric were a source of fear to the general public and federal government. She expressed her views in countless speeches and published works, including the following exposition in Anarchism and Other Essays.

The history of human growth and development is at the same time the history of the terrible struggle of every new idea heralding the approach of a brighter dawn. In its tenacious hold on tradition, the Old has never hesitated to make use of the foulest and cruelest means to stay the advent of the New, in whatever form or period the latter may have asserted itself. Nor need we retrace our steps into the distant past to realize the enormity of opposition, difficulties, and hardships placed in the path of every progressive idea. The rack, the thumbscrew, and the knout are still with us; so are the convict's garb and the social wrath, all conspiring against the spirit that is serenely marching on.

Anarchism could not hope to escape the fate of all other ideas of innovation. Indeed, as the most revolutionary and uncompromising innovator, Anarchism must needs meet with the combined ignorance and venom of the world it aims to reconstruct.

To deal even remotely with all that is being said and done against Anarchism would necessitate the writing of a whole volume. I shall therefore meet only two of the principal objections. In so doing, I shall attempt to elucidate what Anarchism really stands for.

The strange phenomenon of the opposition to Anarchism is that it brings to light the relation between so-called intelligence and ignorance. And yet this is not so very strange when we consider the relativity of all things. The ignorant mass has in its favor that it makes no pretense of knowledge or tolerance. Acting, as it always does, by mere impulse, its reasons are like those of a child. "Why?" "Because." Yet the opposition of the uneducated to Anarchism deserves the same consideration as that of the intelligent man.

What, then, are the objections? First, Anarchism is impractical, though a beautiful ideal. Second, Anarchism stands for violence and destruction, hence it must be repudiated as vile and dangerous. Both the intelligent man and the ignorant mass judge not from a thorough knowledge of the subject, but either from hearsay or false interpretation.

A practical scheme, says Oscar Wilde, is either one already in existence, or a scheme that could be carried out under the existing conditions; but it is exactly the existing conditions that one objects to, and any scheme that could accept these conditions is wrong and foolish. The true criterion of the practical, therefore, is not whether the latter can keep intact the wrong or foolish; rather is it whether the scheme has vitality enough to leave the stagnant waters of the old, and build, as well as sustain, new life. In the light of this conception, Anarchism is indeed practical. More than any other idea, it is helping to do away with the wrong and foolish; more than any other idea, it is building and sustaining new life.

The emotions of the ignorant man are continuously kept at a pitch by the most blood-curdling stories about Anarchism. Not a thing too outrageous to be employed against this philosophy and its exponents. Therefore Anarchism represents to the unthinking what the proverbial bad man does to the child,—a black monster bent on swallowing everything; in short, destruction and violence.

Destruction and violence! How is the ordinary man to know that the most violent element in society is ignorance; that its power of destruction is the very thing Anarchism is combating? Nor is he aware that Anarchism, whose roots, as it were, are part of nature's forces, destroys, not healthful tissue, but parasitic growths that feed on the life's essence of society. It is merely clearing the soil from weeds and sagebrush, that it may eventually bear healthy fruit.

Someone has said that it requires less mental effort to condemn than to think. The widespread mental indolence, so prevalent in society, proves this to be only too true. Rather than to go to the bottom of any given idea, to examine into its origin and meaning, most people will either condemn it altogether, or rely on some superficial or prejudicial definition of non-essentials.

Anarchism urges man to think, to investigate, to analyze every proposition; but that the brain capacity of the average reader be not taxed too much, I also shall begin with a definition, and then elaborate on the latter.

ANARCHISM:—The philosophy of a new social order based on liberty unrestricted by man-made law; the theory that all forms of government rest on violence, and are therefore wrong and harmful, as well as unnecessary.

The new social order rests, of course, on the materialistic basis of life; but while all Anarchists agree that the main evil today is an economic one, they maintain that the solution of that evil can be brought about only through the consideration of *every phase* of life,—individual, as well as the collective; the internal, as well as the external phases. . . .

Anarchism is the only philosophy which brings to man the consciousness of himself; which maintains that God, the State, and society are non-existent, that their promises are null and void, since they can be fulfilled only through man's subordination. Anarchism is therefore the teacher of the unity of life; not merely in nature, but in man. There is no conflict between the individual and the social instincts, any more than there is between the heart and the lungs: the one the receptacle of a precious life essence, the other the repository of the element that keeps the essence pure and strong. The individual is the heart of society, conserving the essence of social life; society is the lungs which are distributing the element to keep the life essence—that is, the individual—pure and strong.

Source: Emma Goldman, *Anarchism and Other Essays,* 3rd rev. ed. (New York: Mother Earth Publishing, 1917).

Harlem Renaissance Poetry (1922)

A cultural flowering in New York's African American community during the 1920s and 1930s, the Harlem

Renaissance featured works of literature, music, and art that portrayed and celebrated the African American experience in new and vibrant ways. Among the prominent literary voices were those of Langston Hughes, Jean Toomer, and Claude McKay; a sampling of their poems—all published in 1922—appears below.

The Negro Speaks of Rivers
By Langston Hughes

I've known rivers:
I've known rivers ancient as the world and
    older than the flow of human blood in
    human veins.
My soul has grown deep like the rivers.
I bathed in the Euphrates when dawns were
    young.
I built my hut near the Congo and it lulled
    me to sleep.
I looked upon the Nile and raised the
    pyramids above it.
I heard the singing of the Mississippi when
    Abe Lincoln went down to New Orleans,
    and I've seen its muddy bosom turn all
    golden in the sunset.
I've known rivers:
Ancient, dusky rivers.
My soul has grown deep like the rivers.

Reapers
By Jean Toomer

Black reapers with the sound of steel on
    stones
Are sharpening scythes. I see them place the
    hones
In their hip-pockets as a thing that's done,
And start their silent swinging, one by one.
Black horses drive a mower through the
    weeds,
And there, a field rat, startled, squealing
    bleeds,
His belly close to ground. I see the blade,
Blood-stained, continue cutting weeds and
    shade.

America
By Claude McKay

Although she feeds me bread of bitterness,
And sinks into my throat her tiger's tooth,

Stealing my breath of life, I will confess
I love this cultured hell that tests my youth!
Her vigor flows like tides into my blood,
Giving me strength erect against her hate.
Her bigness sweeps my being like a flood.
Yet as a rebel fronts a king in state,
I stand within her walls with not a shred
Of terror, malice, not a word of jeer.
Darkly I gaze into the days ahead,
And see her might and granite wonders there,
Beneath the touch of Time's unerring hand,
Like priceless treasures sinking in the sand.

Source: Poets' Corner, http://www.theotherpages.org/poems/chronidx.html#c1900.

House Committee on Un-American Activities, Testimony of Screenwriter Albert Maltz (1947)

The Hollywood Ten was a group of screenwriters and directors called before the House Committee on Un-American Activities (HUAC) in October 1947 to testify about their own political views and about alleged Communist influence in the motion-picture industry. All ten defied the fervor of the McCarthy era by refusing to state whether or not they were Communists; all ten were held in contempt and served time in jail. What follows is part of the testimony of one of the Hollywood Ten, screenwriter Albert Maltz.

Chairman {Congressman J. Parnell Thomas}: Mr. Maltz, the committee is unanimous in permitting you to read the statement.

Mr. Maltz: Thank you.

I am an American and I believe there is no more proud word in the vocabulary of man. I am a novelist and screen writer and I have produced a certain body of work in the past 15 years. As with any other writer, what I have written has come from the total fabric of my life—my birth in this land, our schools and games, our atmosphere of freedom, our tradition of inquiry, criticism, discussion, tolerance. Whatever I am, America has made me. And I, in turn, possess no loyalty as great as the one I have to this land, to the economic and social welfare of its people, to the perpetuation and development of its democratic way of life.

Now at the age of 39, I am commanded to appear before the House Committee on Un-American Activities. For a full week this committee has encouraged an assortment of well-rehearsed witnesses to testify that I and others are subversive and un-American.

It has refused us the opportunity that any pickpocket receives in a magistrate's court—the right to cross-examine these witnesses, to refute their testimony, to reveal their motives, their history, and who, exactly, they are. Furthermore it grants these witnesses congressional immunity so that we may not sue them for libel for their slanders.

I maintain that this is an evil and vicious procedure; that it is legally unjust and morally indecent—and that it places in danger every other American, since if the right of any one citizen can be invaded, then the constitutional guaranties of every other American have been subverted and no one is any longer protected from official tyranny.

What is it about me that this committee wishes to destroy? My writing? Very well, let us refer to them.

My novel, *The Cross and the Arrow,* was issued in a special edition of 140,000 copies by a wartime Government agency, the armed services edition, for American servicemen abroad.

My short stories have been reprinted in over 30 anthologies, by as many American publishers—all subversive, no doubt.

My film, *The Pride of the Marines,* was premiered in 28 cities at Guadalcanal Day banquets under the auspices of the United States Marine Corps.

Another film, *Destination Tokyo,* was premiered aboard a United States submarine and was adopted by the Navy as an official training film.

My short film, *The House I Live In,* was given a special award by the Academy of Motion Picture Arts and Sciences for its contribution to racial tolerance.

My short story, *The Happiest Man on Earth,* won the 1938 O. Henry Memorial Award for the best American short story.

This, then, is the body of work for which this committee urges I be blacklisted in the film industry—and tomorrow, if it has its way in the publishing and magazine fields also.

By cold censorship, if not legislation, I must not be allowed to write. Will this censorship stop with me? Or with the others now singled out for attack? If it requires acceptance of the ideas of this committee to remain immune from the brand of un-Americanism, then who is ultimately safe from this committee except members of the Ku Klux Klan?

Why else does this committee now seek to destroy me and others? Because of our ideas, unquestionably. In 1801, when he was President of the United States, Thomas Jefferson wrote: "Opinion, and the just maintenance of it, shall never be a crime in my view; nor bring injury to the individual."

But a few years ago, in the course of one of the hearings of this committee, Congressman J. Parnell Thomas said, and I quote from the official transcript: "I just want to say this now, that it seems that the New Deal is working along hand in glove with the Communist Party. The New Deal is either for the Communist Party or it is playing into the hands of the Communist Party."

Very well, then, here is the other reason why I and others have been commanded to appear before this committee—our ideas. In common with many Americans, I supported the New Deal. In common with many Americans I supported, against Mr. Thomas and Mr. Rankin, the anti-lynching bill.

I opposed them in my support of OPA controls and emergency veteran housing and a fair employment practices law. I signed petitions for these measures, joined organizations that advocated them, contributed money, sometimes spoke from public platforms, and I will continue to do so. I will take my philosophy from Thomas Payne, Thomas Jefferson, Abraham Lincoln, and I will not be dictated to or intimidated by men to whom the Ku Klux Klan, as a matter of committee record, is an acceptable American institution.

I state further that on many questions of public interest my opinions as a citizen have not always been in accord with the opinions of the majority. They are not now nor have my opinions ever been fixed and unchanging, nor are they now fixed and unchangeable; but, right or wrong, I claim and I insist upon my right to think freely and to speak freely; to join the Republican Party or the Communist Party, the Democratic or the Prohibition Party; to publish whatever I please; to fix my mind or change my mind, without dictation from anyone; to offer any criticism I think fitting of any public official or policy; to join whatever organizations I please, no matter what certain legislators may think of them. Above all, I challenge the right of this committee to inquire into my political or religious beliefs, in any manner or degree, and I assert that not the conduct of this committee but its very existence are a subversion of the Bill of Rights.

If I were a spokesman for General Franco, I would not be here today. I would rather be here. I would rather die than be a shabby American, groveling before men whose names are Thomas and Rankin, but who now carry out activities in America like those carried out in Germany by Goebbels and Himmler.

The American people are going to have to choose between the Bill of Rights and [this] committee. They cannot have both. One or the other must be abolished in the immediate future.

Chairman {pounding gavel}: Mr. Stripling. Mr. Stripling.

Mr. Stripling: Mr. Maltz, what is your occupation?

Mr. Maltz: I am a writer.

Mr. Stripling: Are you employed in the motion-picture industry?

Mr. Maltz: I work in various fields of writing and I have sometimes accepted employment in the motion-picture industry.

Mr. Stripling: Have you written the scripts for a number of pictures?

Mr. Maltz: It is a matter of public record that I have written scripts for certain motion pictures.

Mr. Stripling: Are you a member of the Screen Writers Guild?

Mr. Maltz: Next you are going to ask me what religious group I belong to.

Chairman: No, no; we are not.

Mr. Maltz: And any such question as that . . . is an obvious attempt to invade my rights under the Constitution.

Mr. Stripling: Do you object to answering whether or not you are a member of the Screen Writers Guild?

Mr. Maltz: I have not objected to answering that question. On the contrary, I point out that next you are going to ask me whether or not I am a member of a certain religious group and suggest that I be blacklisted from an industry because I am a member of a group you don't like.

{The chairman pounds gavel.}

Mr. Stripling: Mr. Maltz, do you decline to answer the question?

Mr. Maltz: I certainly do not decline to answer the question. I have answered the question.

Mr. Stripling: I repeat, Are you a member of the Screen Writers Guild?

Mr. Maltz: And I repeat my answer, sir, that any such question is an obvious attempt to invade my list of organizations as an American citizen and I would be a shabby American if I didn't answer as I have.

Mr. Stripling: Mr. Maltz, are you a member of the Communist Party?

Mr. Maltz: Next you are going to ask what my religious beliefs are.

Mr. {John} Mcdowell: That is not answering the question.

Mr. Maltz: And you are going to insist before various members of the industry that since you do not like my religious beliefs I should not work in such industry. Any such question is quite irrelevant.

Mr. Stripling: I repeat the question. Are you now or have you ever been a member of the Communist Party?

Mr. Maltz: I have answered the question, Mr. Stripling. I am sorry. I want you to know—

Mr. Mcdowell: I object to that statement.

Chairman: Excuse the witness. No more questions. Typical Communist line. . . .

Source: House Committee on Un-American Activities, *Hearings Regarding the Communist Infiltration of the Motion Picture Industry,* 80th Cong., 1st sess., 1947.

Port Huron Statement (1962)

The Port Huron Statement, named for the Michigan convention site where it was written in June 1962, was the founding document of the leftist protest group Students for a Democratic Society (SDS). The manifesto was written chiefly by University of Michigan student Tom Hayden, the first president of the SDS and later one of the Chicago Seven.

We are people of this generation, bred in at least modest comfort, housed now in universities, looking uncomfortably to the world we inherit.

When we were kids the United States was the wealthiest and strongest country in the world: the only one with the atom bomb, the least scarred by modern war, an initiator of the United Nations that we thought would distribute Western influence throughout the world. Freedom and equality for each individual, government of, by, and for the people—these American values we found good, principles by which we could live as men. Many of us began maturing in complacency.

As we grew, however, our comfort was penetrated by events too troubling to dismiss. First, the permeating and victimizing fact of human degradation, symbolized by the Southern struggle against racial bigotry, compelled most of us from silence to activism. Second, the enclosing fact of the Cold War, symbolized by the presence of the Bomb, brought awareness that we ourselves, and our friends, and millions of abstract "others" we knew more directly because of our common peril, might die at any time. We might deliberately ignore, or avoid, or fail to feel all other human problems, but not these two, for these were too immediate and crushing in their impact, too challenging in the demand that we as individuals take the responsibility for encounter and resolution.

While two-thirds of mankind suffers undernourishment, our own upper classes revel amidst superfluous abundance. Although world population is expected to double in forty years, the nations still tolerate anarchy as a major principle of international conduct and uncontrolled exploitation governs the sapping of the earth's physical resources. Although mankind desperately needs revolutionary leadership, America rests in national stalemate, its goals ambiguous and tradition-bound instead of informed and clear, its democratic system apathetic and manipulated rather than "of, by, and for the people."

In a participatory democracy, the political life would be based in several root principles:

- that decision-making of basic social consequence be carried on by public groupings;

- that politics be seen positively, as the art of collectively creating an acceptable pattern of social relations;

- that politics has the function of bringing people out of isolation and into community, thus being a necessary, though not sufficient, means of finding meaning in personal life;

- that the political order should serve to clarify problems in a way instrumental to their solution; it should provide outlets for the expression of personal grievance and aspiration; opposing views should be organized so as to illuminate choices and facilitate the attainment of goals. . . .

The economic sphere would have as its basis the principles:

- that work should involve incentives worthier than money or survival. It should be educative, not stultifying; creative, not mechanical; self-directed, not manipulated, encouraging independence, a respect for others, a sense of dignity and a willingness to accept social responsibility, since it is this experience that has crucial influence on habits, perceptions and individual ethics;

- that the economic experience is so personally decisive that the individual must share in its full determination;

- that the economy itself is of such social importance that its major resources and means of production should be open to democratic participation and subject to democratic social regulation.

Like the political and economic ones, major social institutions—cultural, education, rehabilitative, and others—should be generally organized with the well-being and dignity of man as the essential measure of success.

In social change or interchange, we find violence to be abhorrent because it requires generally the transformation of the target, be it a human being or a community of people, into a depersonalized object of hate. It is imperative that the means of violence be abolished and the institutions—local, national, international—that encourage nonviolence as a condition of conflict be developed.

These are our central values, in skeletal form. It remains vital to understand their denial or attainment in the context of the modern world. . . .

The bridge to political power will be built through genuine cooperation, locally, nationally, and internationally, between a new left of young people, and an awakening community of allies. In each community we must look within the university and act with confidence that we can be powerful, but we must look outwards to the less exotic but more lasting struggles for justice.

To turn these possibilities into realities will involve national efforts at university reform by an alliance of students and faculty. They must wrest control of the educational process from the administrative bureaucracy. They must make fraternal and functional contact with allies in labor, civil rights, and other liberal forces outside the campus. They must import major public issues into the curriculum—research and teaching on problems of war and peace is an outstanding example. They must make debate and controversy, not dull pedantic cant, the common style for educational life. They must consciously build a base for their assault upon the loci of power.

As students, for a democratic society, we are committed to stimulating this kind of social movement, this kind of vision and program in campus and community across the country. If we appear to seek the unattainable, as it has been said, then let it be known that we do so to avoid the unimaginable.

Source: Students for a Democratic Society, 112 East 19th Street, New York, NY.

The Feminine Mystique (1963), Betty Friedan

Betty Friedan's groundbreaking book The Feminine Mystique *was instrumental in reviving American feminism during the 1960s. Calling attention to the boredom and alienation suffered by middle-class American housewives and mothers in the postwar period, the best-selling work prompted women to demand sweeping changes in U.S. society and their own lives. Friedan became recognized as a "founding mother" of the modern women's liberation movement.*

The problem lay buried, unspoken, for many years in the minds of American women. It was a strange stirring, a sense of dissatisfaction, a yearning that women suffered in the middle of the twentieth century in the United States. Each suburban wife struggled with it alone. As she made the beds, shopped for groceries, matched slipcover material, ate peanut butter sandwiches with her children, chauffeured Cub Scouts and Brownies, lay beside her husband at night—she was afraid to ask even of herself the silent question—"Is this all?"

For over fifteen years there was no word of this yearning in the millions of words written about women, for women, in all the columns, books and articles by experts telling women their role was to seek fulfillment as wives and mothers. Over and over women heard in voices of tradition and of Freudian sophistication that they could desire no greater destiny than to glory in their own femininity. Experts told them how to catch a man and keep him, how to breastfeed children and handle their toilet training, how to cope with sibling rivalry and adolescent rebellion; how to buy a dishwasher, bake bread, cook gourmet snails, and build a swimming pool with their own hands; how to dress, look, and act more feminine and make marriage more exciting; how to keep their husbands from dying young and their sons from growing into delinquents. They were taught to pity the neurotic, unfeminine, unhappy women who wanted to be poets or physicists or presidents. They learned that truly feminine women do not want careers, higher education, political rights—the independence and the opportunities that the old-fashioned feminists fought for. Some women, in their forties and fifties, still remembered painfully giving up those dreams, but most of the younger women no longer even thought about them. A thousand expert voices applauded their femininity, their adjustment, their new maturity. All they had to do was devote their lives from earliest girlhood to finding a husband and bearing children. . . .

The suburban housewife—she was the dream image of the young American women and the envy, it was said, of women all over the world. The American housewife—freed by science and labor-saving appliances from the drudgery, the dangers of childbirth and the illnesses of her grandmother. She was healthy, beautiful, educated, concerned only about her husband, her children, her home. She had found true feminine fulfillment. As a housewife and mother, she was respected as a full and equal partner to man in his world. She was free to choose automobiles, clothes, appliances, supermarkets; she had everything that women ever dreamed of.

In the fifteen years after World War II, this mystique of feminine fulfillment became the cherished and self-perpetuating core of contemporary American culture. Millions of women lived their lives in the image of those pretty pictures of the American suburban housewife, kissing their husbands goodbye in front of the picture window, depositing their stationwagonsful of children at school, and smiling as they ran the new electric waxer over the spotless kitchen floor. . . . Their only dream was to be perfect wives and mothers; their highest ambition to have five children and a beautiful house, their only fight to get and keep their husbands. They had no thought for the unfeminine problems of the world outside the home; they wanted the men to make the major decisions. They gloried in their role as women, and wrote proudly on the census blank: "Occupation: housewife." . . .

Gradually I came to realize that the problem that has no name was shared by countless women in America. . . . I heard echoes of the problem in college dormitories and semiprivate maternity wards, at PTA meetings and luncheons of the League of Women

Voters, at suburban cocktail parties, in station wagons waiting for trains, and in snatches of conversation overheard at Schrafft's. The groping words I heard from other women, on quiet afternoons when children were at school or on quiet evenings when husbands worked late, I think I understood first as a woman long before I understood their larger social and psychological implications.

Just what was this problem that has no name? What were the words women used when they tried to express it? Sometimes a woman would say "I feel empty somehow . . . incomplete." Or she would say, "I feel as if I don't exist." Sometimes she blotted out the feeling with a tranquilizer. Sometimes she thought the problem was with her husband or her children, or that what she really needed was to redecorate her house, or move to a better neighborhood, or have an affair, or another baby. Sometimes, she went to a doctor with symptoms she could hardly describe. . . .

Can the problem that has no name be somehow related to the domestic routine of the housewife? When a woman tries to put the problem into words, she often merely describes the daily life she leads. What is there in this recital of comfortable domestic detail that could possibly cause such a feeling of desperation? Is she trapped simply by the enormous demands of her role as modern housewife: wife, mistress, mother, nurse, consumer, cook, chauffeur, expert on interior decoration, child care, appliance repair, furniture refinishing, nutrition, and education? Her day is fragmented as she rushes from dishwasher to washing machine to telephone to dryer to station wagon to supermarket, and delivers Johnny to the Little League field, takes Janey to dancing class, gets the lawnmower fixed and meets the 6:45. She can never spend more than 15 minutes on any one thing; she has no time to read books, only magazines; even if she had time, she has lost the power to concentrate. At the end of the day, she is so terribly tired that sometimes her husband has to take over and put the children to bed. . . .

It is easy to see the concrete details that trap the suburban housewife, the continual demands on her time. But the chains that bind her in her trap are chains in her own mind and spirit. They are chains made up of mistaken ideas and misinterpreted facts, of incomplete truths and unreal choices. They are not easily seen and not easily shaken off. . . .

I think the experts in a great many fields have been holding pieces of that truth under their microscopes for a long time without realizing it. . . . I became aware of a growing body of evidence, much of which has not been reported publicly because it does not fit current modes of thought about women—evidence which throws into question the standards of feminine normality, feminine adjustment, feminine fulfillment and feminine maturity by which most women are still trying to live.

I began to see in a strange new light the American return to early marriage and the large families that are causing the population explosion; the recent movement to natural childbirth and breastfeeding; suburban conformity, and the new neuroses, character pathologies and sexual problems being reported by the doctors. I began to see new dimensions to old problems that have long been taken for granted among women: menstrual difficulties, sexual frigidity, promiscuity, pregnancy fears, childbirth depression, the high incidence of emotional breakdown and suicide among women in their twenties and thirties, the menopause crises, the so-called passivity and immaturity of American men, the discrepancy between women's tested intellectual abilities in childhood and their adult achievement, the changing incidence of adult sexual orgasm in American women, and persistent problems in psychotherapy and in women's education.

If I am right, the problem that has no name stirring in the minds of so many American women today is not a matter of loss of femininity or too much education, or the demands of domesticity. It is far more important than anyone recognizes. It is the key to these other new and old problems which have been torturing women and their husbands and children, and puzzling their doctors and educators for years. It may well be the key to our future as a nation and a culture. We can no longer ignore that voice within women that says: "I want something more than my husband and my children and my home."

Source: From *The Feminine Mystique* by Betty Friedan. Copyright (c) 1983, 1974, 1973, 1963 by Betty Friedan. Used by permission of W.W. Norton & Company, Inc.

"I Have a Dream" (1963), Martin Luther King, Jr.

The Reverend Martin Luther King, Jr., delivered his famous "I Have a Dream" speech on the steps of the Lincoln Memorial during the March on Washington for Jobs and Freedom on August 28, 1963. Galvanizing the crowd of 250,000, the address helped transform the struggle for civil rights into a national movement.

Five score years ago, a great American, in whose symbolic shadow we stand signed the Emancipation Proclamation. This momentous decree came as a great beacon light of hope to millions of Negro slaves who had been seared in the flames of withering injustice. It came as a joyous daybreak to end the long night of captivity. But one hundred years later, we must face the tragic fact that the Negro is still not free.

One hundred years later, the life of the Negro is still sadly crippled by the manacles of segregation and the chains of discrimination. One hundred years later, the Negro lives on a lonely island of poverty in the midst of a vast ocean of material prosperity. One hundred years later, the Negro is still languishing in the corners of American society and finds himself an exile in his own land.

So we have come here today to dramatize an appalling condition. In a sense we have come to our nation's capital to cash a check. When the architects of our republic wrote the magnificent words of the Constitution and the Declaration of Independence, they were signing a promissory note to which every American was to fall heir. . . .

Let us not wallow in the valley of despair. I say to you today, my friends, that in spite of the difficulties and frustrations of the moment, I still have a dream. It is a dream deeply rooted in the American dream.

I have a dream that one day this nation will rise up and live out the true meaning of its creed: "We hold these truths to be self-evident: that all men are created equal." I have a dream that one day on the red hills of Georgia the sons of former slaves and the sons of former slaveowners will be able to sit down together at a table of brotherhood. I have a dream that one day even the state of Mississippi, a desert state, sweltering with the heat of injustice and oppression, will be transformed into an oasis of freedom and justice. I have a dream that my four children will one day live in a nation where they will not be judged by the color of their skin but by the content of their character. I have a dream today.

I have a dream that one day the state of Alabama, whose governor's lips are presently dripping with the words of interposition and nullification, will be transformed into a situation where little black boys and black girls will be able to join hands with little white boys and white girls and walk together as sisters and brothers. I have a dream today. I have a dream that one day every valley shall be exalted, every hill and mountain shall be made low, the rough places will be made plain, and the crooked places will be made straight, and the glory of the Lord shall be revealed, and all flesh

shall see it together. This is our hope. This is the faith with which I return to the South. With this faith we will be able to hew out of the mountain of despair a stone of hope. With this faith we will be able to transform the jangling discords of our nation into a beautiful symphony of brotherhood. With this faith we will be able to work together, to pray together, to struggle together, to go to jail together, to stand up for freedom together, knowing that we will be free one day.

This will be the day when all of God's children will be able to sing with a new meaning, "My country, 'tis of thee, sweet land of liberty, of thee I sing. Land where my fathers died, land of the pilgrim's pride, from every mountainside, let freedom ring." And if America is to be a great nation, this must become true. So let freedom ring from the prodigious hilltops of New Hampshire. Let freedom ring from the mighty mountains of New York. Let freedom ring from the heightening Alleghenies of Pennsylvania! Let freedom ring from the snow-capped Rockies of Colorado! Let freedom ring from the curvaceous peaks of California! But not only that; let freedom ring from Stone Mountain of Georgia! Let freedom ring from Lookout Mountain of Tennessee! Let freedom ring from every hill and every molehill of Mississippi. From every mountainside, let freedom ring.

When we let freedom ring, when we let it ring from every village and every hamlet, from every state and every city, we will be able to speed up that day when all of God's children, black men and white men, Jews and Gentiles, Protestants and Catholics, will be able to join hands and sing in the words of the old Negro spiritual, "Free at last! free at last! thank God Almighty, we are free at last!"

Source: Reprinted by arrangement with The Heirs to the Estate of Martin Luther King, Jr., c/o Writers House as agent for the proprietor, New York, NY. Copyright 1963 Dr. Martin Luther King, Jr.; copyright renewed 1991, Coretta Scott King.

"The Times They Are A-Changin'" (1964), Bob Dylan

Folk and rock musician Bob Dylan (born Robert Zimmerman) was acclaimed as a "spokesman" of his generation and "bard" of the 1960s counterculture—labels he rejected—for such controversial songs as "The Times They Are A-Changin'." Released on his 1964 album of the same name, the composition was said to reflect the spirit of upheaval and generational conflict that characterized the decade. Dylan refused to accept what many came to call the song: an anthem.

Come gather 'round people
Wherever you roam
And admit that the waters
Around you have grown
And accept it that soon
You'll be drenched to the bone.
If your time to you
Is worth savin'
Then you better start swimmin'
Or you'll sink like a stone
For the times they are a-changin'.

Come writers and critics
Who prophesize with your pen
And keep your eyes wide
The chance won't come again
And don't speak too soon
For the wheel's still in spin
And there's no tellin' who
That it's namin'.
For the loser now
Will be later to win
For the times they are a-changin'.

Come senators, congressmen
Please heed the call
Don't stand in the doorway
Don't block up the hall
For he that gets hurt
Will be he who has stalled
There's a battle outside
And it is ragin'.
It'll soon shake your windows
And rattle your walls
For the times they are a-changin'.

Come mothers and fathers
Throughout the land
And don't criticize
What you can't understand
Your sons and your daughters
Are beyond your command
Your old road is
Rapidly agin'.
Please get out of the new one
If you can't lend your hand
For the times they are a-changin'.

The line it is drawn
The curse it is cast
The slow one now
Will later be fast
As the present now
Will later be past
The order is
Rapidly fadin'.
And the first one now
Will later be last
For the times they are a-changin'.

Source: Copyright (c) 1963 by Warner Bros., Inc. Copyright renewed 1991 by Special Rider Music. All rights reserved. International copyright secured. Reprinted by permission.

"An End to History" (1964), Mario Savio

Mario Savio, then a philosophy student at the University of California, Berkeley, was a vocal leader of the Free Speech Movement and a member of its steering committee during the angry student protests that erupted on campus in the fall and winter of 1964. The following article, expressing his views on bureaucracy, democracy, and the fight for free speech, first appeared in a publication called Humanity *in December 1964.*

Last summer I went to Mississippi to join the struggle there for civil rights. This fall I am engaged in another phase of the same struggle, this time in Berkeley. The two battlefields may seem quite different to some observers, but this is not the case. The same rights are at stake in both places—the right to participate as citizens in democratic society and the right to due process of law. Further, it is a struggle against the same enemy. In Mississippi an autocratic and powerful minority rules, through organized violence, to suppress the vast, virtually powerless majority. In California, the privileged minority manipulates the university bureaucracy to suppress the students' political expression. That "respectable" bureaucracy masks the financial plutocrats; that impersonal bureaucracy is the efficient enemy in a "Brave New World."

In our free-speech fight at the University of California, we have come up against what may emerge as the greatest problem of our nation—depersonalized, unresponsive bureaucracy. We have encountered the organized status quo in Mississippi, but it is the same in Berkeley. Here we find it impossible usually to meet with anyone but secretaries. Beyond that, we find functionaries who cannot make policy but can only hide behind the rules. We have discovered total lack of response on the part of the policy makers. To grasp a situation which is truly Kafkaesque, it is necessary to understand the bureaucratic mentality. And we have learned quite a bit about it this fall, more outside the classroom than in.

As bureaucrat, an administrator believes that nothing new happens. He occupies an a-historical point of view. In September, to get the attention of this bureaucracy which had issued arbitrary edicts suppressing student political expression and refused to discuss its action, we held a sit-in on the campus. We sat around a police car and kept it immobilized for over thirty-two hours. At last, the administrative bureaucracy agreed to negotiate. But instead, on the following Monday, we discovered that a committee had been appointed, in accordance with usual regulations, to resolve the dispute. Our attempt to convince any of the administrators that an event had occurred, that something new had happened, failed. They saw this simply as something to be handled by normal university procedures.

The same is true of all bureaucracies. They begin as tools, means to certain legitimate goals, and they end up feeding their own existence. The conception that bureaucrats have is that history has in fact come to an end. No events can occur now that the Second World War is over which can change American society substantially. We proceed by standard procedures as we are.

The most crucial problems facing the United States today are the problem of automation and the problem of racial injustice. Most people who will be put out of jobs by machines will not accept an end to events, this historical plateau, as the point beyond which no change occurs. Negroes will not accept an end to history here. All of us must refuse to accept history's final judgment that in America there is no place in society for people whose skins are dark. On campus students are not about to accept it as fact that the university has ceased evolving and is in its final state of perfection, that students and faculty are respectively raw material and employees, or that the university is to be autocratically run by unresponsive bureaucrats.

Here is the real contradiction: the bureaucrats hold history as ended. As a result significant parts of the population both on campus and off are dispossessed and these dispossessed are not about to accept this a-historical point of view. It is out of this that the conflict has occurred with the university bureaucracy and will continue to occur until that bureaucracy becomes responsive or until it is clear the university cannot function.

The things we are asking for in our civil-rights protests have a deceptively quaint ring. We are asking for the due process of law. We are asking for our actions to be judged by committees of our peers. We are asking that regulations ought to be considered as arrived at legitimately only from the consensus of the governed. These phrases are all pretty old, but they are not being taken seriously in America today, nor are they being taken seriously on the Berkeley campus.

I have just come from a meeting with the Dean of Students. She notified us that she was aware of certain violations of university regulations by certain organizations. University friends of Student Non-violent Coordinating Committee, which I represent, was one of these. We tried to draw from her some statement on these great principles, consent of the governed, jury of one's peers, due process. The best she could do was to evade or to present the administration party line. It is very hard to make any contact with the human being who is behind these organizations.

The university is the place where people begin seriously to question the conditions of their existence and raise the issue of whether they can be committed to the society they have been born into. After a long period of apathy during the fifties, students have begun not only to question but, having arrived at answers, to act on those answers. This is part of a growing understanding among many people in America that history has not ended, that a better society is possible, and that it is worth dying for.

This free-speech fight points up a fascinating aspect of contemporary campus life. Students are permitted to talk all they want so long as their speech has no consequences.

One conception of the university, suggested by a classical Christian formulation, is that it be in the world but not of the world. The conception of Clark Kerr by contrast is that the university is part and parcel of this particular stage in the history of American society; it stands to serve the need of American industry; it is a factory that turns out a certain product needed by industry or government. Because speech does often have consequences which might alter this perversion of higher education, the university must put itself in a position of censorship. It can permit two kinds of speech, speech which encourages continuation of the status quo, and speech which advocates changes in it so radical as to be irrelevant in the foreseeable future. Someone may advocate radical change in all aspects of American society, and this I am sure he can do with impunity. But if someone advocates sit-ins to bring about changes in discriminatory hiring practices, this cannot be permitted because it goes against the status quo of which the university is a part. And that is how the fight began here.

The administration of the Berkeley campus has admitted that external, extra-legal groups have pressured the university not to permit students on campus to organize picket lines, not to permit on campus any speech with consequences. And the bureaucracy went along. Speech with consequences, speech in the area of civil rights, speech which some might regard as illegal, must stop.

Many students here at the university, many people in society, are wandering aimlessly about. Strangers in their own lives there is no place for them. They are people who have not learned to compromise, who for example have come to the university to learn to question, to grow, to learn—all the standard things that sound like cliches because no one takes them seriously. And they find at one point or other that for them to become part of society, to become lawyers, ministers, businessmen, people in government, that very often they must compromise those principles which were most dear to them. They must suppress the most creative impulses that they have; this is a prior condition for being part of the system. The university is well structured, well tooled, to turn out people with all the sharp edges worn off, the well-rounded person. The university is well equipped to produce that sort of person, and this means that the best among the people who enter must for four years wander aimlessly much of the time questioning why they are on campus at all, doubting whether there is any point in what they are doing, and looking toward a very bleak existence afterward in a game in which all of the rules have been made up, which one cannot really amend.

It is a bleak scene, but it is all a lot of us have to look forward to. Society provides no challenge. American society in the standard conception it has of itself is simply no longer exciting. The most exciting things going on in America today are movements to change America. America is becoming ever more the utopia of sterilized, automated contentment. The "futures" and "careers" for which American students now prepare are for the most part intellectual and moral wastelands. This chrome-plated consumers' paradise would have us grow up to be well-behaved children. But an important minority of men and women coming to the front today have shown that they will die rather than be standardized, replaceable and irrelevant.

Source: Humanity, an arena of critique and commitment, no. 2 (December 1964). Reprinted with permission of Lynne Hollander. Copyright 1998 by Lynne Hollander.

Unsafe at Any Speed (1965), Ralph Nader

Consumer and environmental advocate Ralph Nader began his campaign for product safety and consumer rights in the early 1960s. In his book Unsafe at Any Speed, *Nader accused the giant automobile manufacturers of building and selling vehicles with deadly safety defects in the interest of greed. A work of modern muckraking,* Unsafe at Any Speed *was influential in the passage of federal legislation and helped launch the American consumer rights movement.*

For over a half century the automobile has brought death, injury, and the most inestimable sorrow and deprivation to millions of people. With Medea-like intensity, this mass trauma began rising sharply four years ago, reflecting new and unexpected ravages by the motor vehicle. A 1959 Department of Commerce report projected that 51,000 persons would be killed by automobiles in 1975. That figure will probably be reached in 1965, a decade ahead of schedule. . . .

Highway accidents were estimated to have cost this country in 1964, $8.4 billion in property damage, medical expenses, lost wages, and insurance overhead expenses. Add an equivalent sum to comprise roughly the indirect costs and the total amounts to over two percent of the gross national product. But these are not the kind of costs which fall on the builders of motor vehicles (excepting a few successful law suits for negligent construction of the vehicle) and thus do not pinch the proper foot. Instead, the costs fall to users of vehicles, who are in no position to dictate safer automobile designs.

In fact, the gigantic costs of the highway carnage in this country support a service industry. A vast array of services—medical, police, administrative, legal, insurance, automotive repair, and funeral—stand equipped to handle the direct and indirect consequences of accident injuries. Traffic accidents create economic demands for these services running into billions of dollars. It is in the post-accident response that lawyers and physicians and other specialists labor. This is where the remuneration lies and this is where the talent and energies go. Working in the area of prevention of these casualties earns few fees. Consequently our society has an intricate organization to handle direct and indirect aftermaths of collisions. But the true mark of a humane society must be what it does about *prevention* of accident injuries, not the cleaning up of them afterward.

Unfortunately, there is little in the dynamics of the automobile accident industry that works for its reduction. Doctors, lawyers, engineers and other specialists have failed in their primary professional ethic: to dedicate themselves to the prevention of accident injuries. The roots of the unsafe vehicle problem are so entrenched that the situation can be improved only by the forging of new instruments of citizen action. When thirty practicing physicians picketed for safe auto design at the New York International Automobile Show on April 7, 1965, their unprecedented action was the measure of their desperation over the inaction of the men and institutions in government and industry who have failed to provide the public with the vehicle safety to which it is entitled. The picketing surgeons, orthopedists, pediatricians and general practitioners marched in protest because the existing medical, legal and engineering organizations have defaulted.

A great problem of contemporary life is how to control the power of economic interests which ignore the harmful effects of their applied sciences and technology. The automobile tragedy is one of the most serious of these man-made assaults on the human body. The history of that tragedy reveals many obstacles which must be overcome in the taming of any mechanical or biological hazard which is a by-product of industry or commerce. Our society's obligation to protect the "body rights" of its citizens with vigorous resolve and ample resources requires the precise, authoritative articulation and front-rank support which is being devoted to civil rights.

This country has not been entirely laggard in defining values relevant to new contexts of a technology laden with risks. The postwar years have witnessed an historic broadening, at least in the courts, of the procedural and substantive rights of the injured and the duties of manufacturers to produce a safe product. Judicial decisions throughout the fifty states have given living meaning to Walt Whitman's dictum, "If anything is sacred, the human body is sacred." Mr. Justice Jackson in 1953 defined the duty of the manufacturers by saying, "Where experiment or research is necessary to determine the presence or the degree of danger, the product must not be tried out on the public, nor must the public be expected to possess the facilities or the technical knowledge to learn for itself of inherent but latent dangers. The claim that a hazard was not foreseen is not available to one who did not use foresight appropriate to his enterprise."

It is a lag of almost paralytic proportions that these values of safety concerning consumers and economic enterprises, reiterated many times by the judicial branch of government, have not found their way into legislative policy-making for safer automobiles. Decades ago legislation was passed changing the pattern of private business investments to accommodate more fully the safety value on railroads, in factories, and more recently on ships and aircraft. In transport, apart from the motor vehicle, considerable progress has been made in recognizing the physical integrity of the individual. There was the period when railroad workers were killed by the thousands and the editor of *Harper's* could say late in the last century: "So long as brakes cost more than trainmen, we may expect the present sacrificial method of car-coupling to be continued." But injured trainmen did cause the railroads some operating dislocations; highway victims cost the automobile companies next to nothing and the companies are not obligated to make use of developments in science-technology that have demonstrably opened up opportunities for far greater safety than any existing safety features lying unused on the automobile companies' shelves.

A principal reason why the automobile has remained the only transportation vehicle to escape being called to meaningful public account is that the public has never been supplied the information nor offered the quality of competition to enable it to make effective demands through the marketplace and through government for a safe, nonpolluting and efficient automobile that can be produced economically. The consumer's expectations regarding automotive innovations have been deliberately held low and mostly oriented to very gradual annual style changes. The specialists and researchers outside the industry who could have provided the leadership to stimulate this flow of information by and large chose to remain silent, as did government officials.

The persistence of the automobile's immunity over the years has nourished the continuance of that immunity, recalling Francis Bacon's insight. "He that will not apply new remedies must expect new evils, for time is the greatest innovator."

The accumulated power of decades of effort by the automobile industry to strengthen its control over car design is reflected today in the difficulty of even beginning to bring it to justice. The time has not come to discipline the automobile for safety; that time came over four decades ago. But that is not cause to delay any longer what should have been accomplished in the nineteen-twenties.

Source: Ralph Nader, *Unsafe at Any Speed* (New York: Grossman, 1965).

Student Nonviolent Coordinating Committee Position Paper: On Vietnam (1966)

In January 1966, with U.S. escalation of the Vietnam War under way for more than a year, the antiwar movement at home was beginning to mobilize and gain momentum. Among the earliest and most active protest groups was the Student Nonviolent Coordinating Committee (SNCC), a civil rights organization founded in 1960. Under more radical leadership beginning in mid-decade, the SNCC adopted a radical Black Power philosophy and took a strong position against the war. It issued this statement on January 6, 1966.

The Student Nonviolent Coordinating Committee has a right and a responsibility to dissent with United States foreign policy on any issue when it sees fit. The Student Nonviolent Coordinating Committee now states its opposition to the United States' involvement in Vietnam on these grounds:

We believe the United States government has been deceptive in its claims of concern for the freedom of the Vietnamese people, just as the government has been deceptive in claiming concern for the freedom of colored people in other countries as the Dominican Republic, the Congo, South Africa, Rhodesia, and in the United States itself.

We, the Student Nonviolent Coordinating Committee, have been involved in the black peoples' struggle for liberation and self-determination in this country for the past five years. Our work, particularly in the South, has taught us that the United States government has never guaranteed the freedom of oppressed citizens, and is not yet truly determined to end the rule of terror and oppression within its own borders.

We ourselves have often been victims of violence and confinement executed by United States governmental officials. We recall the numerous persons who have been murdered in the South because of their efforts to secure their civil and human rights, and whose murderers have been allowed to escape penalty for their crimes.

The murder of Samuel Young in Tuskegee, Alabama, is no different than the murder of peasants in Vietnam, for both Young and the Vietnamese sought, and are seeking, to secure the rights guaranteed them by law. In each case, the United States government bears a great part of the responsibility for these deaths.

Samuel Young was murdered because United States law is not being enforced. Vietnamese are murdered because the United States is pursuing an aggressive policy in violation of international law. The United States is no respecter of persons or law when such persons or laws run counter to its needs or desires.

We recall the indifference, suspicion and outright hostility with which our reports of violence have been met in the past by government officials.

We know that for the most part, elections in this country, in the North as well as the South, are not free. We have seen that the 1965 Voting Rights Act and the 1966 Civil Rights Act have not yet been implemented with full federal power and sincerity.

We question, then, the ability and even the desire of the United States government to guarantee free elections abroad. We maintain that our country's cry of "preserve freedom in the world" is a hypocritical mask, behind which it squashes liberation movements which are not bound, and refuse to be bound, by the expediencies of United States cold war policies.

We are in sympathy with, and support, the men in this country who are unwilling to respond to a military draft which would compel them to contribute their lives to United States aggression in Vietnam in the name of the "freedom" we find so false in this country.

We recoil with horror at the inconsistency of a supposedly "free" society where responsibility to freedom is equated with the responsibility to lend oneself to military aggression. We take note of the fact that 16 percent of the draftees from this country are Negroes called on to stifle the liberation of Vietnam, to preserve a "democracy" which does not exist for them at home.

We ask, where is the draft for the freedom fight in the United States?

We therefore encourage those Americans who prefer to use their energy in building democratic forms within this country. We believe that work in the civil rights movement and with other human relations organizations is a valid alternative to the draft. We urge all Americans to seek this alternative, knowing full well that it may cost them their lives—as painfully as in Vietnam.

Source: "SNCC: On Vietnam." The Sixties Project. Available at http://www3.iath.virginia.edu/sixties/HTML_docs/Sixties.html.

Black Panther Party Platform and Program (1966)

The transition from the civil rights movement of the 1950s and the early 1960s—an essentially peaceful campaign for integration and equal rights—to the militant Black Power movement of the late 1960s was epitomized by the founding of the Black Panther Party for Self-Defense in October 1966. The Oakland-based organization, which called upon the African American community to take up arms in the struggle against white oppression, issued a statement of founding principles.

What We Want
What We Believe

1. We want freedom. We want power to determine the destiny of our Black Community.

We believe that black people will not be free until we are able to determine our destiny.

2. We want full employment for our people.

We believe that the federal government is responsible and obligated to give every man employment or a guaranteed income. We believe that if the white American businessmen will not give full employment, then the means of production should be taken from the businessmen and placed in the community so that the people of the community can organize and employ all of its people and give a high standard of living.

3. We want an end to the robbery by the white man of our Black Community.

We believe that this racist government has robbed us and now we are demanding the overdue debt of forty acres and two mules. Forty acres and two mules was promised 100 years ago as restitution for slave labor and mass murder of black people. We will accept the payment as currency which will be distributed to our many communities. The Germans are now aiding the Jews in Israel for the genocide of the Jewish people. The Germans murdered six million Jews. The American racist has taken part in the slaughter of over twenty million black people; therefore, we feel that this is a modest demand that we make.

4. We want decent housing, fit for shelter of human beings.

We believe that if the white landlords will not give decent housing to our black community, then the housing and the land should be made into cooperatives so that our community, with government aid, can build and make decent housing for its people.

5. We want education for our people that exposes the true nature of this decadent American society. We want education that teaches us our true history and our role in the present-day society.

We believe in an educational system that will give to our people a knowledge of self. If a man does not have knowledge of himself and his position in society and the world, then he has little chance to relate to anything else.

6. We want all black men to be exempt from military service.

We believe that Black people should not be forced to fight in the military service to defend a racist government that does not protect us. We will not fight and kill other people of color in the world who, like black people, are being victimized by the white racist government of America. We will protect ourselves from the force and violence of the racist police and the racist military, by whatever means necessary.

*7. We want an immediate end to **police brutality** and **murder** of black people.*

We believe we can end police brutality in our black community by organizing black self-defense groups that are dedicated to defending our black community from racist police oppression and brutality. The Second Amendment to the Constitution of the United States gives a right to bear arms. We therefore believe that all black people should arm themselves for self defense.

8. We want freedom for all black men held in federal, state, county and city prisons and jails.

We believe that all black people should be released from the many jails and prisons because they have not received a fair and impartial trial.

9. We want all black people when brought to trial to be tried in court by a jury of their peer group or people from their black communities, as defined by the Constitution of the United States.

We believe that the courts should follow the United States Constitution so that black people will receive fair trials. The 14th Amendment of the U.S. Constitution gives a man a right to be tried by his peer group. A peer is a person from a similar economic, social, religious, geographical, environmental, historical and racial background. To do this the court will be forced to select a jury from the black community from which the black defendant came. We have been, and are being tried by all-white juries that have no understanding of the "average reasoning man" of the black community.

10. We want land, bread, housing, education, clothing, justice and peace. And as our major political objective, a United Nations-supervised plebiscite to be held throughout the black colony in which only black colonial subjects will be allowed to participate for the purpose of determining the will of black people as to their national destiny.

When in the course of human events, it becomes necessary for one people to dissolve the political bands which have connected them with another, and to assume, among the powers of the earth, the separate and equal station to which the laws of nature and nature's God entitle them, a decent respect to the opinions of mankind requires that they should declare the causes which impel them to the separation.

We hold these truths to be self evident, that all men are created equal; that they are endowed by their Creator with certain unalienable rights; that among these are life, liberty, and the pursuit of happiness. That, to secure these rights, governments are instituted among men, deriving their just powers from the consent of the governed; that, whenever any form of government becomes destructive of these ends, it is the right of the people to alter or to abolish it, and to institute a new government, laying its foundation on such principles, and organizing its powers in such form, as to them shall seem most likely to effect their safety and happiness. Prudence, indeed, will dictate that governments long established should not be changed for light and transient causes; and accordingly, all experience hath shown, that mankind are more disposed to suffer, while evils are sufferable, than to right themselves by abolishing the forms to which they are accustomed. But, when a long train of abuses and usurpations, pursuing invariably the same object, evinces a design to reduce them under absolute despotism, it is their right, it is their duty, to throw off such government, and to provide new guards for their future security.

Source: "October 1966 Black Panther Party Platform and Program." The Sixties Project. Available at http://www3.iath.virginia.edu/sixties/HTML_docs/Sixties.html.

National Organization for Women, Statement of Purpose (1966)

A pivotal year in the decade's political and social counterculture, 1966 also saw the establishment of the National Organization for Women (NOW) in Washington, D.C. A formal statement of purpose, written by NOW president Betty Friedan, was adopted at the organization's first national conference on October 29.

We, men and women who hereby constitute ourselves as the National Organization for Women, believe that the time has come for a new movement toward true equality for all women in America, and toward a fully equal partnership of the sexes, as part of the world-wide revolution of human rights. . . .

The purpose of NOW is to take action to bring women into full participation in the mainstream of American society . . . exercising all the privileges and responsibilities thereof in truly equal partnership with men.

We believe the time has come to move beyond the abstract argument, discussion and symposia over the status and special nature of women which has raged in America . . . ; the time has come to confront, with concrete action, the conditions that now prevent women from enjoying the equality of opportunity and freedom of choice which is their right, as individual Americans, and as human beings. . . .

NOW is dedicated to the proposition that women, first and foremost, are human beings, who, like all other people in our society, must have the chance to develop their fullest human potential. We believe that women can achieve such equality only by accepting to the full the challenges and responsibilities they share with all other people in our society, as part of the decision-making mainstream of American political, economic and social life.

We organize to initiate or support action, nationally, or in any part of this nation, by individuals or organizations, to break through the silken curtain of prejudice and discrimination against women in government, industry, the professions, the churches, the political parties, the judiciary, the labor unions, in education, science, medicine, law, religion and every other field of importance in American society. . . .

Despite all the talk about the status of American women in recent years, the actual position of women in the United States has declined . . . to an alarming degree throughout the 1950's and 60's. . . .

Official pronouncements of the advance in the status of women hide not only the reality of this dangerous decline, but the fact that nothing is being done to stop it. . . . Discrimination in employment on the basis of sex is now prohibited by federal law, in Title VII of the Civil Rights Act of 1964. But although nearly one-third of the cases brought before the Equal Employment Opportunity Commission during the first year dealt with sex discrimination and the proportion is increasing dramatically, the Commission has not made clear its intention to enforce the law with the same seriousness on behalf of women as of other victims of discrimination. . . . The National Organization for Women must therefore begin to speak.

WE BELIEVE that the power of American law, and the protection guaranteed by the U.S. Constitution to the civil rights of all individuals, must be effectively applied and enforced to isolate and remove patterns of sex discrimination, to ensure equality of opportunity in employment and education, and equality of civil and political rights and responsibilities on behalf of women, as well as for Negroes and other deprived groups. . . .

WE DO NOT ACCEPT the token appointment of a few women to high-level positions in government and industry as a substitute for serious continuing effort to recruit and advance women according to their individual abilities. To this end, we urge American government and industry to mobilize the same resources of ingenuity and command with which they have solved problems of far greater difficulty than those now impeding the progress of women.

WE BELIEVE that this nation has a capacity . . . to innovate new social institutions which will enable women to enjoy the true equality of opportunity and responsibility in society, without conflict with their responsibilities as mothers and homemakers. . . .

WE BELIEVE that it is as essential for every girl to be educated to her full potential of human ability as it is for every boy—with the knowledge that such education is the key to effective participation in today's

economy and that, for a girl as for a boy, education can only be serious where there is expectation that it will be used in society. . . .

WE REJECT the current assumptions that a man must carry the sole burden of supporting himself, his wife, and family, and that a woman is automatically entitled to lifelong support by a man upon her marriage, or that marriage, home and family are primarily woman's world and responsibility. . . . We believe that proper recognition should be given to the economic and social value of homemaking and child-care. To these ends, we will seek to open a reexamination of laws and mores governing marriage and divorce, for we believe that the current state of "half-equity" between the sexes discriminates against both men and women. . . .

WE BELIEVE that women must now exercise their political rights and responsibilities as American citizens. . . .

IN THE INTERESTS OF THE HUMAN DIGNITY OF WOMEN, we will protest, and endeavor to change, the false image of women now prevalent in the mass media, and in the texts, ceremonies, laws, and practices of our major social institutions. Such images perpetuate contempt for women by society and by women for themselves. . . .

NOW WILL HOLD ITSELF INDEPENDENT OF ANY POLITICAL PARTY in order to mobilize the political power of all women and men intent on our goals. We will strive to ensure that no party, candidate, president, senator, governor, congressman, or any public official who betrays or ignores the principle of full equality between the sexes is elected or appointed to office.

WE BELIEVE THAT women will do most to create a new image of women by acting now, and by speaking out in behalf of their own equality, freedom, and human dignity . . . in an active, self-respecting partnership with men. By so doing, women will develop confidence in their own ability to determine actively, in partnership with men, the conditions of their life, their choices, their future and their society.

Source: National Organization for Women, Washington, DC, 1966. Available at http://www.now.org/history/purpos66.html.

"A Walk on the Wild Side of Stonewall" (1969), Robert Amsel

The gay rights/gay pride movement in America often is said to have begun with the Stonewall riots in New York's Greenwich Village in 1969. In the early morning of June 28, municipal police raided the Stonewall Inn, the city's largest gay bar, and began arresting patrons. The gay clientele, frustrated by ongoing harassment, responded by pelting police with debris. The result was several days of protest and violence. To "set the record straight" on the incident, participant and gay rights activist Robert Amsel wrote a detailed account for the September 15, 1987 edition of The Advocate.

The legend of the Stonewall was born as another legend died. On Sunday, June 22, 1969, Judy Garland was found dead from a pill overdose in her London home. An older generation of homosexuals had idolized Judy, as much for her suffering as her talent. Her unsuccessful marriages, her dependence on pills and liquor, and her resilience—the ability to rise when she was down—gave them hope that whatever their oppression, they too could find the strength to carry on. But now Judy was down and would stay down, and the old gay way of endurance seemed to pass with her.

But while the flags hung at half-mast on Fire Island, new flags were about to be raised on the streets of Greenwich Village. Friday afternoon, June 27, Judy was buried. Saturday morning, June 28, the raid on the Stonewall Inn began. "We will endure" became "We shall overcome."

The Stonewall Inn was located at 53 Christopher Street, off Sheridan Square. It was an after-hours "private club" for members only. Anyone who could scrounge up three bucks could become a member for the evening. The place was reputed to be Mafia-owned (as were most of the gay bars in those days) and liquor was sold on the premises without benefit of a liquor license. This made it a perfect target for the authorities.

There were many gay people at the time who supported the raid on the Stonewall. They wanted gay bars to be gay-owned and operated. They wanted the Mafia out of the business. They failed to appreciate one thing: the reason the Mafia was in the gay bar business to begin with. The Mafia's traditional sphere of influence centered around any illegal activity. Without the Mafia's money, there might not have been any gay bars to legitimize.

This hardly excuses the Stonewall or its condition. The former owners had been burned out and the bar had remained vacant for a year. Its new owners slapped black paint on the already smoke-blackened walls, and with minimum overhauling were ready for business. It was still a firetrap. It was also a dope drop and the suspected source of a minor hepatitis epidemic six months prior to the raid. Its two large rooms—one a dance area, the other a bar—were generally sardine-packed with young men, including drag queens, hippies, street people, and uptown boys slumming. Many customers were under 18, the legal drinking age. Some were runaways, some had nowhere else to go.

For whatever strange reason, the police that summer decided to launch an all-out attack on illegal clubs throughout the city. They did not limit themselves to gay clubs—straight black and Hispanic clubs were also raided. They did, however, seem to specialize in places frequented by members of minorities. Prior to the Stonewall, there had been raids on other gay after-hours clubs, the Sewer and the Snake Pit, both aptly named. The Tele-Star and the Checkerboard had closed down not long before. By the time the cops hit the Stonewall, the customers were angry, frustrated, and, more important, running out of places to go.

Deputy Inspector Seymour Pine led eight plainclothes officers (including two women) into the Stonewall at 3 a.m. It was a hot night and a full moon was shining over Sheridan Square. The employees were arrested for selling liquor without a license. The customers were allowed to leave, one at a time. They waited outside for their friends. Many had been in such raids before, some in the past few weeks.

One straight observer referred to the gathering as "festive," with those exiting the club striking poses, swishing and camping. Then he noted a sudden mood change when the paddywagon arrived and the bartender, doorman, three drag queens and a struggling lesbian were shoved inside. There were catcalls and cries to topple the paddy wagon. Pine hurriedly told the wagon to take off, drop the prisoners off at the Sixth Precinct and rush back. The crowd threw coins at the police and shouted "Pigs!" Coins progressed to bottles. The crowd was closing in. Pine and his detectives moved quickly back into the Stonewall and locked themselves in. . . .

Police reinforcements had arrived en masse. . . . [*Village Voice* reporter] Howard Smith went outside and took notes. He returned inside to discover that the police had vented their anger by smashing all the mirrors, juke boxes, phones, toilets, and cigarette machines. No one but the police had been inside, but the courts would later find them innocent of vandalism.

[Saturday night riot]

Stonewall management found it difficult to keep their customers inside Saturday night, since all the action was outside. Shouts of "Gay Power!" and "Liberate Christopher Street!" echoed along Sixth and Seventh avenues, and Greenwich Avenue (where incarcerated lesbians in the House of Detention shouted support from their barred windows). The battle cry raged the length of Christopher Street.

There was a strong feeling of gay community and a strong fighting spirit, an intoxicating sense of release. It was "us against them, and by God, we're winning." Crowds were growing, as if from the pavement. There was kissing, hugging, fondling. Tanned bodies merged together like some orgy scene in a Cecil B. DeMille epic. Craig Rodwell, owner of a gay bookstore in the Village, reported that some gay men were barricading the streets and not allowing heterosexual drivers to pass. A car of newlyweds was half lifted before the openmouthed bride and groom were allowed to drive on.

New York's Tactical Police Force (TPF) arrived on the scene. They were helmeted and carried clubs. They had rescued Pine and his men the morning before, but were unprepared for the guerrilla warfare that awaited them.

These streets were gay territory. Gay people knew every doorway, alley and side street and where they would lead. They knew how to split up the TPF and run them in circles. Men on roofs or in rooms overlooking Christopher Street hurled bottles at the cops. When the cops looked up, no one could be seen.

Two TPF men chased a gay guy down a side street. Gay bystanders started running with their brother. Before long a large group was running. A man at the head of the group suddenly held out his arms and yelled, "Stop!" The group stopped. "There are two pigs and how many of us?" A moment of meaningful silence. The two cops had also stopped, were looking at one another and then at the crowd. The group leader grinned. "Get the bastards!" About face. The cops were now running at full gallop, a lynch mob on their heels. "Catch'em! Fuck'em!"

The crowd dispersed by 3 a.m.

Sunday night was quiet. Monday and Tuesday nights crowds started to gather again, but outbreaks were few. . . . The next night, Wednesday, July 2, events took a brutal turn. The TPF men used their nightsticks indiscriminately. "At one point," [Dick] Leitsch [of the *Mattachine Newsletter*] wrote, "7th Avenue from Christopher to West 10th looked like a battlefield in Vietnam. Young people, many of them queens, were lying on the sidewalk, bleeding from the head, face, mouth, and even the eyes. Others were nursing bruised and often bleeding arms, legs, backs and necks." . . .

After Wednesday the riots petered out and the politicizing began. [The] Gay Liberation Front (GLF) was a new group of young male and female homosexuals, which formed in late July . . . [The] GLF had a leftist ideology and an anarchic structure. They were sort of a gay SDS, and opted for revolution and whatever means were necessary to achieve it. They aligned themselves with and supported all other radical groups of the period. . . . Many smaller groups sprang up as well. All the groups suffered from infighting, outfighting and egos in conflict. But age-old barriers were breaking down. Gay people in other parts of the country were starting to emerge from their closets. California's heavily gay cities of San Francisco and Los Angeles had their own gay renaissance. New organizations spread throughout the land. A year later, diverse gay groups and independent gays marched in brotherhood and sisterhood. Annual gay pride days would follow. . . .

A decade after Stonewall, in this carefree, extra-fertile soil, a deadly virus was imported. It quietly, swiftly spread before anyone was the wiser.

AIDS produced a backlash stronger and more lethal than anything we knew in our cozy closets. Homophobes always feared that gayness might rub off. Now they fear that death might rub off along with it. . . . And that is why the Stonewall should be remembered today. It doesn't matter that it was a firetrap, that the police may have been doing us a favor. It doesn't matter that the gutsier fighters were drags and street kids. . . . What matters is the communal gay spirit born during that time. . . . Unless we recapture that spirit and do battle, we'll be ripe for a time when "camp" is something that follows "concentration."

Source: Robert Amsel, "A Walk on the Wild Side of Stonewall," *The Advocate* (September 15, 1987).

Bibliography

Books and Articles

Aaron, Daniel. *Men of Good Hope: A Story of American Progressives.* New York: Oxford University Press, 1951.

Abagnale, Frank. *The Art of the Steal: How to Protect Yourself and Your Business From Fraud—America's #1 Crime.* New York: Broadway, 2001.

Abbate, Janet. *Inventing the Internet.* Cambridge, MA: MIT Press, 1999.

Abbot, Keith. *Downstream from* Trout Fishing in America: *A Memoir of Richard Brautigan.* Santa Barbara, CA: Capra, 1989.

Aberle, David F. *The Peyote Religion Among the Navajo.* 2nd ed. Viking Fund Publications in Anthropology, 42. Chicago: University of Chicago Press, 1966.

Abrams, Charles. *Man's Struggle for Shelter in an Urbanizing World.* Cambridge, MA: MIT Press, 1964.

Acker, Kerry. *Everything You Need to Know about the Goth Scene.* New York: Rosen, 2000.

Adam, Barry D. *The Rise of a Gay and Lesbian Movement.* Boston: Twayne, 1997.

Adams, Bluford. *E Pluribus Barnum: The Great Showman and the Making of U.S. Popular Culture.* Minneapolis: University of Minnesota Press, 1997.

Adams, Charles F. *Antinomianism in the Colony of Massachusetts Bay.* Boston: Prince Society Publications, 1894.

Adams, Jad. *Hideous Absinthe: A History of the Devil in a Bottle.* Madison: University of Wisconsin Press, 2004.

Adams, Peter. *The Bowery Boys: Street Corner Radicals and the Politics of Rebellion.* Westport, CT: Greenwood, 2005.

Adams, Rachel. *Sideshow USA: Freak Shows and the American Cultural Imagination.* Chicago: University of Chicago Press, 2001.

Adams, Rebecca, and Robert Sardiello. *Deadhead Social Science: You Ain't Gonna Learn What You Don't Want to Know.* Walnut Creek, CA: AltaMira, 2000.

Adler, Margot. *Drawing Down the Moon: Witches, Druids, Goddess Worshippers and Other Pagans in America Today.* New York: Viking, 1979.

Ahlstrom, Sydney E. *A Religious History of the American People.* New Haven, CT: Yale University Press, 1972.

Alarcón McKesson, Norma. "An Interview with Miguel Piñero." *Revista Chicano-Riqueña* 2:4 (1974): 55–57.

Albert, Peter J., and Ronald Hoffman, eds. *We Shall Overcome: Martin Luther King, Jr., and the Black Freedom Struggle.* New York: Pantheon, 1990.

Alberti, John, ed. *The Simpsons and the Possibility of Oppositional Culture.* Detroit: Wayne State University Press, 2003.

Alcoholics Anonymous World Services. *Alcoholics Anonymous: The Story of How Many Thousands of Men and Women Have Recovered from Alcoholism.* New York: Alcoholics Anonymous World Services, 2001.

Alderman, Pat. *Nancy Ward, Cherokee Chieftainess, Dragging Canoe, Cherokee-Chickamauga War Chief.* Johnson City, TN: Overmountain, 1978.

Aldiss, Brian W. *Billion Year Spree: The True History of Science Fiction.* Garden City, NY: Doubleday, 1973.

Alexander, Paul. *Salinger: A Biography.* Los Angeles: Renaissance, 1999.

Alford, Holly. "The Zoot Suit: Its History and Influence." *Fashion Theory* 8:2 (June 2004): 225–36.

Algarín, Miguel, and Bob Holman, eds. *Aloud: Voices from the Nuyorican Poets Café.* New York: Henry Holt, 1994.

Algarín, Miguel, and Miguel Piñero, eds. *Nuyorican Poetry: An Anthology of Puerto Rican Words and Feelings.* New York: William Morrow, 1975.

Ali, Muhammad. *The Greatest: My Own Story.* New York: Random House, 1975.

Allen, James B., and Glen M. Leonard. *The Story of the Latter-day Saints.* 2nd ed. Salt Lake City: Deseret, 1992.

Alliance for the Arts. *NYC Culture Catalog.* New York: Harry N. Abrams, 1994.

Allsop, Kenneth. *Hard Travellin': The Hobo and His History.* New York: New American Library, 1967.

Allyn, David. *Make Love, Not War: The Sexual Revolution, an Unfettered History.* Boston: Little, Brown, 2000.

Alonso, Karen. *Chicago Seven Political Protest Trial: A Headline Court Case.* Berkeley Heights, NJ: Enslow, 2002.

Alsen, Eberhard. *A Reader's Guide to J.D. Salinger.* Westport, CT: Greenwood, 2002.

Amburn, Ellis. *Pearl: The Obsessions and Passions of Janis Joplin.* New York: Warner, 1992.

American Life Histories: Manuscripts from the Federal Writers' Project, 1936–1940. Washington, DC: Library of Congress, 1998.

Amis, Kingsley. *New Maps of Hell.* New York: Harcourt, Brace, 1960.

Amorth, Gabriele. *An Exorcist Tells His Story.* New York: Ignatius, 1999.

Andelson, Jonathan G. "The Community of True Inspiration from Germany to the Amana Colonies." In *America's Communal Utopias.* Chapel Hill: University of North Carolina Press, 1997.

Andersen, Richard. *Toni Morrison.* New York: Marshall Cavendish Benchmark, 2005.

Anderson, Carlotta R. *All-American Anarchist: Joseph A. Labadie and the Labor Movement.* Detroit: Wayne State University Press, 1998.

Anderson, David D. *Robert Ingersoll.* New York: Twayne, 1972.

Anderson, Edward F. *Peyote: The Divine Cactus.* 1966. Tucson: University of Arizona Press, 1996.

Anderson, Laurie. *Empty Places: A Performance.* New York: Harper Perennial, 1991.

———. *Stories from the Nerve Bible: A Retrospective 1972–1992.* New York: Harper Perennial, 1994.

Anderson, Margaret. *My Thirty Years' War: An Autobiography.* New York: Covici, Friede, 1930.

Anderson, Martin, and Barbara Honegger. *The Military Draft: Selected Readings on Conscription.* Stanford, CA: Hoover Institution Press, 1982.

Anderson, Terry H. *The Movement and the Sixties: Protest in America from Greensboro to Wounded Knee.* New York: Oxford University Press, 1995.

———. *The Sixties.* 2nd ed. New York: Pearson/Longman, 2004.

Anderson, Walter Truett. *The Upstart Spring: Esalen and the Human Potential Movement: The First Twenty Years.* Boston: Addison-Wesley, 1983.

Andrew Jackson Presidential Papers, Library of Congress, Manuscripts Division, Washington, DC.

Andrews, Edward Deming. *The People Called Shakers: A Search for the Perfect Society.* New York: Oxford University Press, 1953.

Andrews, Geoff, et al. *New Left, New Right, and Beyond: Taking the Sixties Seriously.* London: Macmillan, 1999.

Anson, Robert Sam. *Gone Crazy and Back Again: The Rise and Fall of the* Rolling Stone *Generation.* New York: Doubleday, 1981.

Anthony, Gene. *The Summer of Love: Haight-Ashbury at its Highest.* San Francisco: Last Gasp, 1995.

Anzaldúa, Gloria. *Borderlands/La Frontera.* 2nd ed. San Francisco: Aunt Lute, 1999.

Apter, Emily, and William Pietz, eds. *Fetishism as Cultural Discourse.* Ithaca, NY: Cornell University Press, 1993.

Aptheker, Herbert. *Abolitionism: A Revolutionary Movement.* Boston: Twayne, 1989.

Arber, Sara, ed. *The Myth of Generational Conflict: The Family and State in Ageing Societies.* London: Routledge, 2000.

Ariaksinen, Timo. *The Philosophy of H.P. Lovecraft: The Route to Horror.* New York: Peter Lang, 1999.

Armstrong, David. *A Trumpet to Arms: Alternative Media in America.* Los Angeles and Boston: J.P. Tarcher, 1981.

Armstrong, Elizabeth A., and Suzanna M. Crage. "Movements and Memory: The Making of the Stonewall Myth." *American Sociological Review* 71 (October 2006): 724–51.

Arndt, Karl J.R. *George Rapp's Disciples, Pioneers, and Heirs: A Register of the Harmonists in America.* Ed. Donald E. Pitzer and Leigh Ann Chamness. Evansville: University of Southern Indiana Press, 1994.

Arnold, Gina. *Route 666: On the Road to Nirvana.* New York: St. Martin's, 1993.

Arp, Robert, ed. *South Park and Philosophy: You Know, I Learned Something Today.* Malden, MA: Blackwell, 2006.

Arrington, Leonard J. *Brigham Young: American Moses.* Urbana: University of Illinois Press, 1986.

Arrington, Leonard J., and Davis Bitton. *The Mormon Experience: A History of the Latter-Day Saints.* New York: Alfred A. Knopf, 1979.

Ash, Brian, ed. *The Visual Encyclopedia of Science Fiction.* London: Trewin Copplestone, 1977.

Asimov, Isaac. *Asimov on Science Fiction.* New York: Doubleday, 1981.

Atkins, Susan. *Child of Satan, Child of God.* With Bob Slosser. New York: Bantam, 1977.

Atwood, Craig D. *Community of the Cross: Moravian Piety in Colonial Bethlehem.* University Park: Pennsylvania State University Press, 2004.

Austin, Algernon. *Achieving Blackness: Race, Black Nationalism, and Afrocentrism in the Twentieth Century.* New York: New York University Press, 2006.

Austin, Joe. *Taking the Train: How Graffiti Art Became an Urban Crisis in New York City.* New York: Columbia University Press, 2001.

Avrich, Paul. *Anarchist Voices: An Oral History of Anarchism in America.* Oakland, CA: AK, 2005.

———. *The Modern School Movement: Anarchism and Education in the United States.* Princeton, NJ: Princeton University Press, 1980.

Axinn, June, and Mark J. Stern. *Social Welfare: A History of the American Response to Need.* 6th ed. Boston, MA: Pearson/Allyn and Bacon, 2005.

Ayres, Alex, ed. *The Wit and Wisdom of Mark Twain.* New York: HarperPerennial, 2005.

Azerrad, Michael. *Come As You Are: The Story of Nirvana.* New York: Doubleday, 1994.

———. *Our Band Could Be Your Life: Scenes from the American Indie Underground, 1981–1991.* Boston: Little, Brown, 2001.

Bach, Jeffery A. *Voices of the Turtledoves: The Sacred World of Ephrata.* University Park: The Pennsylvania State University Press, 2003.

Bacon-Smith, Camille. *Science Fiction Culture.* Philadelphia: University of Pennsylvania Press, 2000.

Baddeley, Gavin. *Goth Chic: A Connoisseur's Guide to Dark Culture.* Medford, NJ: Plexus, 2002.

Baez, Joan. *And a Voice to Sing With: A Memoir.* New York: Summit, 1987.

Bailey, Beth. *Sex in the Heartland.* Cambridge, MA: Harvard University Press, 1999; 2002.

Bailey, Cathryn. "Making Waves and Drawing Lines: The Politics of Defining the Vicissitudes of Feminism." *Hypatia* 12:3 (1997): 22–28.

Baker, Carlos. *Ernest Hemingway: A Life Story.* New York: Collier, 1988.

———. *Hemingway: The Writer as Artist.* 4th ed. Princeton, NJ: Princeton University Press, 1972.

Baker, Carlos, and James R. Mellow. *Emerson among the Eccentrics: A Group Portrait.* New York: Penguin, 1997.

Baker, Houston. *Modernism and the Harlem Renaissance.* Chicago: University of Chicago Press, 1987.

Baker, Jean-Claude, and Chris Chase. *Josephine: The Hungry Heart.* New York: Random House, 1993.

Balducci, Carolyn Feleppa. *Margaret Fuller: A Life of Passion and Defiance.* New York: Bantam, 1991.

Baldwin, J. *Bucky Works: Buckminster Fuller's Ideas for Today.* New York: John Wiley and Sons, 1996.

Banes, Sally. *Greenwich Village 1963: Avant-Garde Performance and the Effervescent Body.* Durham: Duke University Press, 1993.

Banks, Ann. *First Person America.* New York: Vintage Books, 1981

Barbato, Joseph. "The Rise and Rise of the Small Press." *Publisher's Weekly,* 244, July 1997, 39–48.

Barboza, Steven, ed. *American Jihad: Islam after Malcolm X.* New York: Doubleday, 1994.

Barkun, Michael. *Disaster and the Millennium.* Syracuse, NY: Syracuse University Press, 1986.

Barlow, Philip L. *Mormons and the Bible: The Place of the Latter-Day Saints in American Religion.* New York: Oxford University Press, 1991.

Barnum, P.T. *Humbugs of the World: An Account of Humbugs, Delusions, Impositions, Quackeries, Deceits and Deceivers Generally, in All Ages.* New York: Carleton, 1866.

———. *The Life of P.T. Barnum, Written by Himself.* New York: Redfield, 1855.

Barrera, Mario. *Beyond Aztlán: Ethnic Autonomy in Comparative Perspective.* New York: Praeger, 1988.

Barrett, Leonard E. *The Rastafarians.* 20th anniv. ed. Boston: Beacon, 1997.

Barrow, Steve, and Peter Dalton. *The Rough Guide to Reggae.* 2nd ed. London: Rough Guides, 2001.

Barsky, Robert F. *Noam Chomsky: A Life of Dissent.* Cambridge, MA: MIT Press, 1997.

Barter, James. *Cocaine and Crack.* San Diego, CA: Lucent, 2002.

Barthel, Diane L. *Amana: From Pietist Sect to American Community.* Lincoln: University of Nebraska Press, 1984.

Bartley, William Warren, III. *Werner Erhard: The Transformation of a Man, The Founding of est.* New York: Crown, 1978.

Bascom, William R. "The Focus of Cuban Santería." *Southwestern Journal of Anthropology* 6:1, 1950.

Bast, William. *James Dean: A Biography.* New York: Ballantine, 1956.

Basta, Arno. "Pfaff's on Broadway." *Greenwich Village Gazette* 6:26, 1997. Also found at http://www.gvny.com/content/history/pfaffs.htm.

Battcock, Gregory, ed. *Idea Art: A Critical Anthology.* New York: E.P. Dutton, 1973.

Battcock, Gregory, and Robert Nickas, eds. *The Art of Performance: A Critical Anthology.* New York: E.P. Dutton, 1984.

Battis, Emery John. *Saints and Sectaries: Anne Hutchinson and the Antinomian Controversy in the Massachusetts Bay Colony.* Chapel Hill: Published for the Institute of Early American History and Culture at Williamsburg, Virginia, by the University of North Carolina Press, 1962.

Baumgardner, Jennifer, and Amy Richards. *Manifesta: Young Women, Feminism, and the Future.* New York: Farrar, Straus and Giroux, 2000.

Baxandall, Lee. *World Guide to Nude Beaches and Recreation.* New York: Harmony, 1983.

Baxter, Nancy. *Open the Doors of the Temple: The Survival of Christian Science in the Twentieth Century.* Carmel, IN: Hawthorne, 2004.

Beach, Sylvia. *Shakespeare and Company.* New York: Harcourt, Brace, 1959.

Beale, David O. *In Pursuit of Purity: American Fundamentalism Since 1850.* Greenville, SC: Unusual Publications, 1986.

Beard, Rick, and Leslie Cohen, eds. *Greenwich Village: Culture and Counterculture.* New Brunswick, NJ: Rutgers University Press, 1993.

Beatles, The. *The Beatles Anthology.* New York: Chronicle, 2000.

Beck, Julian. *The Life of the Theatre.* San Francisco: City Lights, 1972.

Bederman, Gail. *Manliness and Civilization: A Cultural History of Gender and Race in the United States, 1880–1917.* Chicago: University of Chicago Press, 1995.

Beemyn, Brett. "The Silence Is Broken: A History of the First Lesbian, Gay, and Bisexual College Student Groups." *Journal of the History of Sexuality* 12:2 (April 2003): 205–23.

Beito, David T. *From Mutual Aid to the Welfare State: Fraternal Societies and Social Services, 1890–1967.* Chapel Hill: University of North Carolina Press, 2000.

Belasco, Warren J. *Appetite for Change.* New York: Pantheon, 1989.

Bell, Daniel. *Marxian Socialism in the United States.* Ithaca, NY: Cornell University Press, 1987; 1996.

Bendroth, Margaret Lamberts. *Fundamentalism and Gender, 1875 to the Present.* New Haven, CT: Yale University Press, 1993.

Bennett, Andy, ed. *Remembering Woodstock.* Aldershot, UK: Ashgate, 2004.

Benston, Kimberly W. *Imamu Amiri Baraka (LeRoi Jones): A Collection of Critical Essays.* Englewood Cliffs, NJ: Prentice Hall, 1978.

Bercovitch, Sacvan. *The Puritan Origins of the American Self.* New Haven, CT: Yale University Press, 1975.

Berger, Dan. *Outlaws of America: The Weather Underground and the Politics of Solidarity.* Oakland, CA: AK, 2006.

Berghaus, Günther. "Happenings in Europe in the '60s: Trends, Events, and Leading Figures." *TDR* 37:4 (Winter 1993): 157–68.

Bergreen, Laurence. *Capone: The Man and the Era.* New York: Touchstone, 1996.

Berkhofer, Robert, Jr. *The White Man's Indian: Images of the American Indian from Columbus to the Present.* New York: Vintage Books, 1979.

Berkman, Alexander. *Now and After: The ABC of Communist Anarchism.* New York: Vanguard, 1929. Reprinted as *What Is Anarchism?* Edinburgh, Scotland: AK, 2003.

———. *Prison Memoirs of an Anarchist.* 1912. Pittsburgh: Frontier, 1970.

Berkove, Lawrence I. *A Prescription for Adversity: The Moral Art of Ambrose Bierce.* Columbus: Ohio State University Press, 2002.

Berlant, Lauren, and Elizabeth Freeman. "Queer Nationality." *boundary 2* 19:1 (Spring 1992): 149–80.

Berlet, Chip, and Matthew N. Lyons. *Right-Wing Populism in America: Too Close for Comfort.* New York: Guilford, 2000.

Berman, Paul. *A Tale of Two Utopias: The Political Journey of the Generation of 1968.* New York: W.W. Norton, 1996.

Bernal, Martin. *Black Athena: The Afroasiatic Roots of Classical Civilization.* New Brunswick, NJ: Rutgers University Press, 1991.

Berne, Emma Carlson, ed. *Cocaine.* Farmington Hills, MI: Greenhaven, 2006.

Bernstein, Matthew. *Controlling Hollywood: Censorship and Regulation in the Studio Era.* Piscataway, NJ: Rutgers University Press, 1999.

Berrigan, Daniel. *The Trial of the Catonsville Nine.* Boston: Beacon, 1970.

Berrigan, Philip. *Widen the Prison Gates: Writing from Jails, April 1970–December 1972.* New York: Simon and Schuster, 1973.

Bershtel, Sara, and Allen Graubard. *Saving Remnants: Feeling Jewish in America.* New York: Free Press, 1992.

Bérubé, Allan, and Jeffrey Escoffier. "Queer/Nation." *Outlook: National Lesbian and Gay Quarterly* 11 (Winter 1991): 12–23.

Bessman, Jim. *Ramones: An American Band.* New York: St Martin's, 1993.

Bibby, John F., and L. Sandy Maisel. *Two Parties—Or More? The American Party System.* Boulder, CO: Westview, 2001.

Bierce, Ambrose. *The Devil's Dictionary.* New York: Bloomsbury, 2003.

Bill, J. Brent. *Holy Silence: The Gift of Quaker Spirituality.* Brewster, MA: Paraclete, 2005.

Birkel, Michael L. *Silence and Witness: The Quaker Tradition.* Maryknoll, NY: Orbis, 2004.

Bisio, Attilio, Adam Weinberg, David Pellow, and Allen Schnaiberg. *Urban Recycling and the Search for Sustainable Community Development.* Princeton, NJ: Princeton University Press, 2000.

Biskind, Peter. *Down and Dirty Pictures: Miramax, Sundance, and the Rise of Independent Film.* New York: Simon and Schuster, 2004.

———. *Easy Riders, Raging Bulls: How the Sex-Drugs-and-Rock 'n' Roll Generation Saved Hollywood.* New York: Simon and Schuster, 1999.

Black, Stephen A. *Eugene O'Neill: Beyond Mourning and Tragedy.* New Haven, CT: Yale University Press, 2002.

Blackett, R.J.M. *Building an Antislavery Wall: Black Americans in the Atlantic Abolitionist Movement, 1830–1860.* Baton Rouge: Louisiana State University Press, 1983.

Blake, David Haven. *Walt Whitman and the Culture of American Identity.* New Haven, CT: Yale University Press, 2006.

Blavatsky, Helena Petrovna. *Isis Unveiled.* 1877. Pasadena, CA: Theosophical University Press, 1972; Wheaton, IL: Theosophical University Press, 1999.

———. *The Key to Theosophy.* 1889. Wheaton, IL: Theosophical University Press, 1998.

———. *The Secret Doctrine: The Synthesis of Science, Religion, and Philosophy.* 1888. Pasadena, CA: Theosophical University Press, 1977; Wheaton, IL: Theosophical University Press, 1999.

Blechman, Max, ed. *Drunken Boat: Art, Rebellion, Anarchy.* Brooklyn, NY, and Seattle, WA: Autonomedia and Left Bank, 1994.

Blee, Kathleen M. *Women of the Klan: Racism and Gender in the 1920s.* Berkeley: University of California Press, 1991.

Bleiler, E.F. "O'Brien, Fitz-James." In *The Guide to Supernatural Fiction.* Kent, OH: Kent State University Press, 1983.

Blight, David W., ed. *Passages to Freedom: The Underground Railroad in History and Memory.* Washington, DC: Smithsonian Institution, 2004.

Blocker, Jack S., Jr., ed. *Alcohol, Reform, and Society: The Liquor Issue in Social Context.* Westport, CT: Greenwood, 1979.

———. *American Temperance Movements: Cycles of Reform.* Boston: Twayne, 1989.

Blodgett, Geoffrey. *Oberlin Architecture, College, and Town: A Social History.* Kent, OH: Kent State University Press, 1985.

Bloodworth, William A. *Upton Sinclair.* Boston: Twayne, 1977.

Bloom, Alexander, ed. *Long Time Gone: Sixties America Then and Now.* New York: Oxford University Press, 2001.

Bloom, Alexander, and Wini Breines, eds. *Takin' It to the Streets.* New York: Oxford University Press, 1995.

Bloom, Harold, ed. *J.D. Salinger.* New York: Chelsea House, 2002.

———. *Nathaniel Hawthorne.* Broomall, PA: Chelsea House, 2000.

Blumhofer, Edith L. *Aimee Semple McPherson: Everybody's Sister.* Library of Religious Biography. Grand Rapids, MI: W.B. Eerdmans, 1993.

Blush, Steven. *American Hardcore: A Tribal History.* Los Angeles: Feral House, 2001.

Bockris, Victor. *Transformer: The Lou Reed Story.* New York: Simon and Schuster, 1994.

———. *Warhol: The Biography.* New York: Da Capo, 2003.

Bockris, Victor, and Gerard Malanga. *Up-Tight: The Story of the Velvet Underground.* London: Omnibus, 1997.

Bode, Carl. *American Lyceum.* New York: Oxford University Press, 1958.

Bodgan, Robert. *Freak Show: Presenting Human Oddities for Amusement and Profit.* Chicago: University of Chicago Press, 1988.

Bodroghkozy, Aniko. *Groove Tube: Sixties Television and the Youth Rebellion.* Durham, NC: Duke University Press, 2001.

Boeri, Miriam Williams, Claire E. Sterk, and Kirk W. Elifson. "Rolling Beyond Raves: Ecstasy Use Outside the Rave Setting." *Journal of Drug Issues* 34:4 (Fall 2004): 831–59.

Bogard, Travis, ed. *O'Neill: Complete Plays.* Vol. 3, *1932–1943.* New York: Library of America, 1988.

Bogdan, Robert. *Freak Show: Presenting Human Oddities for Amusement and Profit.* Chicago: University of Chicago Press, 1990.

Bogues, Anthony. *Caliban's Freedom: The Early Political Thought of C.L.R. James.* London: Pluto, 1997.

Booth, Martin. *Cannabis: A History.* New York: Picador, 2003.

Booth, Stanley. *The True Adventures of the Rolling Stones.* Chicago: Chicago Review, 2000.

Borden, Iain. *Skateboarding, Space and the City: Architecture and the Body.* New York: Berg, 2001.

Bordewich, Fergus M. *Bound for Canaan: The Epic Story of the Underground Railroad, America's First Civil Rights Movement.* New York: Amistad, 2006.

Bordin, Ruth. *Woman and Temperance: The Quest for Power and Liberty, 1873–1900.* Philadelphia: Temple University Press, 1981.

Bordwell, David, et al. *The Classical Hollywood Cinema.* New York: Columbia University Press, 1985.

Bowler, Dave, and Bryan Dray. *R.E.M.: From "Chronic Town" to "Monster."* New York: Carol, 1995.

Bowman, David. *This Must Be the Place: The Adventures of the Talking Heads in the Twentieth Century.* New York: HarperCollins, 2001.

Boyle, Dierdre. *Subject to Change: Guerrilla Television Revisited.* New York: Oxford University Press, 1997.

Bozeman, Theodore Dwight. *The Precisionist Strain: Disciplinary Religion & Antinomian Backlash in Puritanism to 1638.* Chapel Hill: University of North Carolina Press, 2004.

Braden, William. *The Age of Aquarius.* Chicago: Quadrangle. 1970.

Bradford, William. *Of Plymouth Plantation, 1620–1647.* New York: Modern Library, 1967; New York: Alfred A. Knopf, 2001.

Bradley, Richard. *American Political Mythology from Kennedy to Nixon.* New York: Peter Lang, 2000.

Brady, Frank. *Hefner.* London: Weidenfeld and Nicolson, 1975.

Branch, Taylor. *At Canaan's Edge: America in the King Years, 1965–1968.* New York: Simon and Schuster, 2006.

———. *Parting the Waters: America in the King Years, 1954–63.* New York: Simon and Schuster, 1988; New York: Touchstone, 1989.

———. *Pillar of Fire: America in the King Years, 1963–65.* New York: Simon and Schuster, 1998.

Brando, Marlon. *Songs My Mother Taught Me.* New York: Random House, 1994.

Brandon, Ruth. *The Life and Many Deaths of Harry Houdini.* New York: Random House, 2003.

Braude, Ann. *Radical Spirits: Spiritualism and Women's Rights in Nineteenth-Century America.* Boston: Beacon, 1989; Bloomington: Indiana University Press, 2001.

Braunstein, P., and Michael William Doyle, eds. *Imagine Nation: The American Counterculture of the 1960s and '70s.* New York: Routledge, 2002.

Brautigan, Ianthe. *You Can't Catch Death: A Daughter's Memoir.* New York: St. Martin's, 2000.

Breton, André. *Manifestoes of Surrealism.* Trans. Richard Seaver and Helen R. Lane. Ann Arbor: University of Michigan Press, 1972.

Brewer, Gay. *Charles Bukowski.* New York: Twayne, 1997.

Brinkley, Alan. *Voices of Protest: Huey Long, Father Coughlin, and the Great Depression.* New York: Vintage Books, 1983.

Brisbane, Redelia Bates. *Albert Brisbane: A Mental Biography, with a Character Study.* New York: B. Franklin, 1969.

Brock, Erland J., ed. *Swedenborg and His Influence.* Bryn Athyn, PA: Academy of the New Church, 1988.

Brock, Peter. *Pacifism in the United States: From the Colonial Era to the First World War.* Princeton, NJ: Princeton University Press, 1968.

Bromell, Nicholas Knowles. *Tomorrow Never Knows: Rock and Psychedelics in the 1960s.* Chicago: University of Chicago Press, 2000.

Bromley, David G., and Jeffrey K. Hadden. *The Handbook of Cults and Sects in America.* Greenwich, CT: JAI, 1993.

Bromley, David G., and Larry D. Shinn, eds. *Krishna Consciousness in the West.* Cranbury, NJ: Associated University Presses, 1989.

Bromley, David G., and Anson D. Shupe, Jr. *Strange Gods: The Great American Cult Scare.* Boston: Beacon, 1981.

Brook, James, et al. *Reclaiming San Francisco: History, Politics, Culture: A City Lights Anthology.* San Francisco: City Lights, 1998.

Brooke, Michael. *The Concrete Wave: The History of Skateboarding.* Toronto, Ontario, Canada: Warwick, 1999.

Brooks, David. *Bobos in Paradise: The New Upper Class and How They Got There.* New York: Simon and Schuster, 2000.

Brotherton, David C., and Luis Barrios. *The Almighty Latin King and Queen Nation: Street Politics and the Transformation of a New York City Gang.* New York: Columbia University Press, 2004.

Brown, David H. *Santería Enthroned: Art, Ritual, and Innovation in an Afro-Cuban Religion.* Chicago: University of Chicago Press, 2003.

Brown, H. Rap. *Die Nigger Die!* 1969. Chicago: Lawrence Hill, 2002.

Brown, J.D. *Henry Miller.* New York: Ungar, 1986.

Brown, Lloyd W. *Amiri Baraka.* Boston: Twayne, 1980.

Brown, Michael F. *The Channeling Zone: American Spirituality in an Anxious Age.* Cambridge, MA: Harvard University Press, 1999.

Brown, Milton W. *The Story of the Armory Show.* New York: Joseph Hirshhorn Foundation, 1963.

Brown, Slater. *The Heyday of Spiritualism.* New York: Hawthorn, 1970; New York: Pocket Books, 1972.

Broyles-González, Yolanda. *El Teatro Campesino: Theater in the Chicano Movement.* Austin: University of Texas Press, 1994.

Bruccoli, Matthew J. *Some Sort of Epic Grandeur: The Life of F. Scott Fitzgerald.* 1981. Columbia: University of South Carolina Press, 2002.

Bruccoli, Matthew J., and Judith S. Baughman, eds. *Fitzgerald: A Life in Letters.* New York: Simon and Schuster, 1994.

Bruce, Kitty. *The Almost Unpublished Lenny Bruce.* Philadelphia: Running, 1984.

Bruce, Lenny. *How to Talk Dirty and Influence People.* Chicago: Playboy, 1965.

Bruns, Roger A. *Knights of the Road: A Hobo History.* London: Methuen, 1980.

Bryan, Ferald Joseph. *Henry Grady or Tom Watson?: The Rhetorical Struggle for the New South, 1880–1890.* Macon, GA: Mercer University Press, 1994.

Bryan, J., III. *Merry Gentlemen (And One Lady).* New York: Atheneum, 1985.

Buchloh, Benjamin, and Judith F. Rodenbeck. *Experiments in the Everyday: Allan Kaprow and Robert Watts—Events, Objects, Documents.* New York: Miriam and Ira D. Wallach Art Gallery, Columbia University, 1999.

Buckland, Raymond. *The Witch Book: The Encyclopedia of Witchcraft, Wicca, and Neo-Paganism.* Detroit, MI: Visible Ink, 2002.

Buckley, David. *Strange Fascination: David Bowie: The Definitive Story.* London: Virgin Books, 2001.

Buechler, Steven M. *Women's Movements in the United States: Woman Suffrage, Equal Rights, and Beyond.* New Brunswick, NJ: Rutgers University Press, 1990.

Buell, Lawrence. *Emerson.* Cambridge, MA: Belknap Press, 2003.

———. *The Environmental Imagination: Thoreau, Nature Writing, and the Formation of American Culture.* Cambridge, MA: Harvard University Press, 1995.

Bugliosi, Vincent, and Curt Gentry. *Helter Skelter: The True Story of the Manson Murders.* New York: Bantam, 1974.

Buhle, Paul. *C.L.R. James: The Artist as Revolutionary.* New York: Verso, 1988.

———, ed. *History and the New Left: Madison, Wisconsin, 1950–1970.* Philadelphia: Temple University Press, 1990.

———. *Marxism in the United States: Remapping the History of the American Left.* New York: Verso, 1991.

Buhle, Paul, and Nicole Schulman, eds. *Wobblies!: A Graphic History of the Industrial Workers of the World.* London: Verso, 2005.

Buhle, Paul, and E. Sullivan. *Images of American Radicalism.* Hanover, MA: Christopher, 1998.

Bukszpan, Daniel. *The Encyclopedia of Heavy Metal.* New York: Barnes and Noble, 2003.

Bullock, Steven C. *Revolutionary Brotherhood: Freemasonry and the Transformation of the American Social Order, 1730–1840.* Chapel Hill: University of North Carolina Press, 1996.

Bullough, Vern L., ed. *Before Stonewall: Activists for Gay and Lesbian Rights in Historical Context.* New York: Harrington Park, 2002.

Bullough, Vern, and Bonnie Bullough. *Women and Prostitution: A Social History.* New York: Prometheus, 1987.

Bundy, William. *A Tangled Web: The Making of Foreign Policy in the Nixon Presidency.* New York: Hill and Wang, 1998.

Burgess, Stanley M., ed. *Reaching Beyond: Chapters in the History of Perfectionism.* Peabody, MA: Hendrickson, 1986.

Burks, John, Jerry Hopkins, and Paul Nelson. "The Groupies and Other Girls." *Rolling Stone,* February 15, 1969, 11–26.

Burns, Stewart. *Social Movements of the 1960s: Searching for Democracy.* Boston: Twayne, 1990.

———. *To the Mountaintop: Martin Luther King Jr.'s Sacred Mission to Save America, 1955–1968.* San Francisco: HarperCollins, 2004.

Bushman, Claudia Lauper, and Richard Lyman. *Mormons in America.* Religion in American Life. New York: Oxford University Press, 1999.

Bushman, Richard. *Joseph Smith and the Beginnings of Mormonism.* Chicago: University of Illinois Press, 1984.

Butler, Gregory S. *In Search of the American Spirit: The Political Thought of Orestes Brownson.* Carbondale: Southern Illinois University Press, 1992.

Butler, Jon. "Magic, Astrology, and the Early American Religious Heritage, 1600–1760." *American Historical Review* 84 (April 1979): 317–46.

Buzzanco, Robert. *Masters of War: Military Dissent and Politics in the Vietnam Era.* New York: Cambridge University Press, 1996.

———. *Vietnam and the Transformation of American Life.* Malden, MA: Blackwell, 1999.

Caldwell, Mark. *New York Night: The Mystique and Its History.* New York: Scribner's, 2005.

Califia, Pat. *Public Sex: The Culture of Radical Sex.* San Francisco: Cleis, 1994.

Calverton, Victor Francis. *Where Angels Dare to Tread: Socialist and Communist Utopian Colonies in the United States.* Freeport, NY: Books for Libraries, 1941; 1969.

Campbell, Bruce F. *Ancient Wisdom Revived: A History of the Theosophical Movement.* Berkeley: University of California Press, 1980.

Campbell, George R. *An Illustrated Guide to Some Poisonous Plants and Animals of Florida.* Englewood, Florida: Pineapple. 1983.

Campbell, James. *This Is the Beat Generation: New York, San Francisco, Paris.* Berkeley: University of California Press, 1999; London: Vintage Books, 1999.

Campbell, Karlyn Kohrs, ed. *Man Cannot Speak For Her.* New York: Praeger, 1989.

Camus, Albert. *The Stranger.* 1942. New York: Vintage Books, 1989.

Canning, Charlotte. *Feminist Theaters in the U.S.A.: Staging Women's Experience.* New York: Routledge, 1996.

Cantor, Milton. *Max Eastman.* New York: Twayne, 1970.

Capper, Charles, and Conrad Edick Wright, eds. *Transient and Permanent: The Transcendentalist Movement and Its Contexts.* Boston: Massachusetts Historical Society, 1999.

Cardinal, Roger. *Outsider Art.* London: Studio Vista, 1972.

Carless, Jennifer. *Taking Out the Trash: A No-Nonsense Guide to Recycling.* New York: Island, 1992.

Carleton, Jim. *Apple: The Inside Story of Intrigue, Egomania, and Business Blunders.* New York: Times Books, 1997.

Carlin, George. *Brain Droppings.* New York: Hyperion, 1997.

Carlson, Eric, ed. *Companion to Poe Studies.* Westport, CT: Greenwood, 1996.

Carlson, Peter. *Roughneck: The Life and Times of Big Bill Haywood.* New York: W.W. Norton, 1983.

Carlson-Berne, Emma. *Snoop Dogg.* Broomall, PA: Mason Crest, 2006.

Carmichael, Stokely. *Black Power: The Politics of Liberation in America.* New York: Random House, 1967.

Carmichael, Stokely, and Charles V. Hamilton. *Black Power: The Politics of Liberation in America.* New York: Random House, 1967.

Carmichael, Stokely, and Ekwueme Michael Thelwell. *Ready for Revolution: The Life and Struggles of Stokely Carmichael (Kwame Ture).* New York: Scribner, 2003.

Carnes, Bruce. *Ken Kesey.* Boise, ID: Boise State University, 1974.

Caroll, Bret E. *Spiritualism in Antebellum America.* Bloomington: Indiana University Press, 1997.

Carpenter, Humphrey. *A Serious Character: The Life of Ezra Pound.* Boston: Faber and Faber, 1988.

Carpenter, Joel A. *Revive Us Again: The Reawakening of American Fundamentalism.* New York: Oxford University Press, 1997.

Carpenter, Sue. *40 Watts from Nowhere: A Journey into Pirate Radio.* New York: Scribner's, 2004.

Carr, C. *On Edge: Performance at the End of the Twentieth Century.* Hanover, NH: University Press of New England, 1993.

Carr, Ian. *Miles Davis: The Definitive Biography.* London: HarperCollins, 1998.

Carroll, Bret E. *Spiritualism in Antebellum America.* Bloomington: Indiana University Press, 1997.

Carroll, Jim. *The Basketball Diaries.* New York: Penguin, 1987.

Carroll, Joseph Cephas. *Slave Insurrections in the United States, 1800–1865.* Mineola, NY: Dover, 2004.

Carson, Clayborne, ed. *The Autobiography of Martin Luther King, Jr.* New York: Warner, 1998.

———. *In Struggle: SNCC and the Black Awakening of the 1960s.* Cambridge, MA: Harvard University Press, 1981; 1995.

Carson, Gerald. *Cornflake Crusade.* New York: Rinehart, 1957.

Carson, Rachel. *The Sea Around Us.* New York: Oxford University Press, 1951.

———. *Silent Spring.* Boston: Houghton Mifflin, 1962.

———. *Under the Sea Wind: A Naturalist's Picture of Ocean Life.* New York: Oxford University Press, 1962.

Carter, Robert, and Ann Banks. *Survey of Federal Writers' Project Manuscript Holdings in State Depositories.* Washington, DC: American Historical Association, 1985.

Cash, Floris Barnett. "Radicals or Realists: African American Women and the Settlement House Spirit in New York City." *Afro-Americans in New York Life and History* 15:1 (1991): 7–17.

Cash, Johnny. *Cash: The Autobiography.* San Francisco: Harper San Francisco, 1998.

Castaneda, Carlos. *The Teachings of Don Juan: A Yaqui Way of Knowledge.* Berkeley: University of California Press, 1968.

Caws, Mary Ann, ed. *Surrealist Painters and Poets: An Anthology.* Cambridge, MA: MIT Press, 2001.

Chafe, William. *Civilities and Civil Rights: Greensboro, North Carolina, and the Black Struggle for Freedom.* New York: Oxford University Press, 1980.

Chalberg, John. *Emma Goldman: American Individualist.* New York: HarperCollins, 1991.

Chalmers, David M. *Hooded Americanism: The History of the Ku Klux Klan.* New York: New Viewpoints, 1976.

Chan, Sucheng. *Asian Americans: An Interpretive History.* Boston: Twayne, 1991.

Chapman, David. *Sandow the Magnificent: Eugen Sandow and the Beginnings of Bodybuilding.* Urbana: University of Illinois Press, 1994.

Chappell, Ben. *Cruising the Borderlands: Lowrider Style and Gang Scares in Contestation of Urban Space.* Chicago: American Anthropological Association, 1999.

Charpak, Georges, and Henri Broch. *Debunked! ESP, Telekinesis, and Other Pseudoscience.* Baltimore: Johns Hopkins University Press, 2004.

Charters, Ann. *Jack Kerouac: A Biography.* San Francisco: Straight Arrow, 1973.

———. "Marching with The Fugs." *The Review of Contemporary Fiction* 19:1 (1999): 47.

———, ed. *The Penguin Book of the Beats.* London: Penguin, 1992.

Chase, Alston. *Harvard and the Unabomber: The Making of an American Terrorist.* New York: W.W. Norton, 2003.

Chauncey, George. *Gay New York: Gender, Urban Culture, and the Making of the Gay World, 1890–1940.* New York: Basic Books, 1994.

Cheever, Susan. *My Name Is Bill: Bill Wilson—His Life and the Creation of Alcoholics Anonymous.* New York: Simon and Schuster, 2004.

Chenetier, Marc. *Richard Brautigan.* London: Methuen, 1963.

Cherkovski, Neeli. *Ferlinghetti: A Biography.* Garden City, NY: Doubleday, 1979.

———. *Hank: The Life of Charles Bukowski.* New York: Random House, 1991.

Chermayeff, Catherine, Jonathan David, and Nan Richardson. *Drag Diaries.* San Francisco: Chronicle, 1995.

Chidester, David. *Salvation and Suicide: An Interpretation of Jim Jones, the Peoples Temple, and Jonestown.* Bloomington: Indiana University Press, 1988.

Chielens, Edward E., ed. *American Literary Magazines: The Eighteenth and Nineteenth Centuries.* New York: Greenwood, 1986.

Chomsky, Noam. *The Chomsky Reader.* Edited by James Peck. New York: Pantheon, 1987.

Chong, Tommy. *The I Chong: Meditations from the Joint.* New York: Simon Spotlight Entertainment, 2006.

Christian, Diana Leafe. *Creating a Life Together: Practical Tools to Grow Ecovillages and Intentional Communities.* Gabriola Island, Canada: New Society, 2003.

Christo, Karen. *Foreseeing the Future: Evangeline Adams and Astrology in America.* Amherst, MA: One Reed, 2002.

Chryssides, George D. *A Reader in New Religious Movements.* Ed. George D. Chryssides and Margaret Z. Wilkins. New York: Continuum, 2006.

Chuck D. *Fight the Power: Rap, Race, and Reality.* With Yusuf Jah. New York: Delacorte, 1997.

———. *Lyrics of a Rap Revolutionary.* Vol. 1. Ed. Yusuf Jah. Beverly Hills, CA: Offda, 2007.

Churchill, Ward. *Fantasies of the Master Race: Literature, Cinema and the Colonization of American Indians.* San Francisco: City Lights, 1998.

Churchill, Ward, and Jim Vander Wall. *The COINTELPRO Papers: Documents from the FBI's Secret Wars Against Dissent in the United States.* Cambridge, MA: South End, 2002.

Chusid, Irwin. *Songs in the Key of Z: The Curious Universe of Outsider Music.* Chicago: A Cappella, 2000.

Claire, Vivian. *Judy Collins.* New York: Flash, 1977.

Clanton, Gene. *Populism: The Humane Preference in America, 1890–1900.* Boston: Twayne, 1991.

Clapton, Diana. *Lou Reed and the Velvet Underground.* New York: Proteus, 1983.

Clare, Ada. *Only a Woman's Heart.* New York: M. Doolady, 1866.

Clarke, John Henrik, ed. *Marcus Garvey and the Vision of Africa.* New York: Random House, 1974.

Clarke, Peter B. *Black Paradise: The Rastafarian Movement.* San Bernardino, CA: Borgo, 1988.

Cleaver, Kathleen, and George Katsiaficas, eds. *Liberation, Imagination, and the Black Panther Party.* New York: Routledge, 2001.

Clute, John. *Science Fiction: The Illustrated Encyclopedia.* New York: Dorling Kindersley, 1995.

Clute, John, and Peter Nicholls, eds. *The Encyclopedia of Science Fiction.* New York: St. Martin's, 1995.

Clymer, Kenton J., ed. *The Vietnam War: Its History, Literature and Music.* El Paso: Texas Western Press, 1998.

Cody, Pat, and Fred Cody. *Cody's Books: The Life and Times of a Berkeley Bookstore, 1956–1977.* San Francisco: Chronicle, 1992.

Cohen, Ben, and Jerry Greenfield. *Ben & Jerry's Double-Dip: Lead with Your Values and Make Money Too.* New York: Simon and Schuster, 1997.

Cohen, John, ed. *The Essential Lenny Bruce.* New York: Pan Macmillan, 1987.

Cohen, Ronald D. *Rainbow Quest: The Folk Music Revival and American Society.* Amherst: University of Massachusetts Press, 2002.

Cohen, Ronald D., and Reginald E. Zelnik, eds. *The Free Speech Movement: Reflections on Berkeley in the 1960s.* Berkeley: University of California Press, 2002.

Cohen, Stanley. *Folk Devils and Moral Panics: The Creation of the Mods and Rockers.* 3rd ed. New York: Routledge, 2002.

Cohn, Lawrence, ed. *Nothing But the Blues: The Music and the Musicians.* New York: Abbeville, 1999.

Coiner, Constance. *Better Red: The Writing and Resistance of Tillie Olson and Meridel Le Sueur.* New York: Oxford University Press, 1995.

Coleman, Joe. *Cosmic Retribution: The Infernal Art of Joe Coleman.* Seattle, WA: Fantagraphics, 1992.

Coleman, Ray. *Lennon: The Definitive Biography.* New York: HarperCollins, 1992.

Coleman, Simon, and Leslie Carlin, eds. *The Cultures of Creationism: Anti-Evolution in English Speaking Countries.* Burlington, VT: Ashgate, 2004.

Collins, John James. *Native American Religions: A Geographical Survey.* Lewiston, NY: Edwin Mellen, 1991.

Collins, Judy. *Sanity and Grace: A Journey of Suicide, Survival, and Strength.* New York: J.P. Tarcher/Penguin, 2003.

———. *Singing Lessons.* New York: Pocket Books, 1998.

———. *Trust Your Heart.* Boston: Houghton Mifflin, 1987.

Collins, Patricia Hill. *Black Feminist Thought.* 2nd ed. New York: Routledge, 2000.

Collins, Randall, and Michael Makowsky. *The Discovery of Society.* New York: Random House, 1972.

Conason, Joe. *It Can Happen Here.* New York: St. Martin's, 2007.

Conford, Philip. *The Origins of the Organic Movement.* Edinburgh, Scotland: Floris, 2001.

Conkin, Paul. *American Originals: Homemade Varieties of Christianity.* Chapel Hill: University of North Carolina Press, 1997.

Conlin, Joseph R., ed. *The American Radical Press, 1880–1960.* Westport, CT: Greenwood, 1974.

———. *Big Bill Haywood and the Radical Union Movement.* Syracuse, NY: Syracuse University Press, 1969.

Conrad, Barnaby. *Absinthe: History in a Bottle.* San Francisco: Chronicle, 1988.

Conrad, Winston. *Hemingway's France: Images of the Lost Generation.* Emeryville, CA: Woodford, 2000.

Conyers, James L. *Civil Rights, Black Arts, and the Black Power Movement in America: A Reflexive Analysis of Social Movements in the United States.* New York: Ashgate, 2002.

Cook, Blanche Wiesen. *Crystal Eastman on Women and Revolution.* New York: Oxford University Press, 1978.

Cook, Bruce. *The Beat Generation.* New York: Scribner, 1971.

Cook, David A. *A History of Narrative Film.* New York: W.W. Norton, 2004.

Cook, James W. *The Arts of Deception: Playing with Fraud in the Age of Barnum.* Cambridge, MA: Harvard University Press, 2001.

Co-op Handbook Collective, The. *The Food Co-op Handbook: How to Bypass Supermarkets to Control the Quality and Price of Your Food.* Boston: Houghton Mifflin, 1975.

Cooper, Marc. "Interview: George Carlin." *The Progressive,* July 2001.

Corliss, Richard. "The World According to Michael: Taking Aim at George W., a Populist Agitator Makes Noise, News, and a New Kind of Political Entertainment." *Time,* July 12, 2004, 62–70.

Corydon, Bent, and L. Ron Hubbard, Jr. *L. Ron Hubbard: Messiah or Madman?* Secaucus, NJ: Lyle Stuart, 1987.

Cotkin, George. *Existential America.* Baltimore: Johns Hopkins University Press, 2002.

Cott, Nancy F. *The Grounding of Modern Feminism.* New Haven, CT: Yale University Press, 1987.

Cottrell, Robert. *Roger Nash Baldwin and the American Civil Liberties Union.* New York: Columbia University Press, 2000.

Coulson, William R. *Groups, Gimmicks, and Instant Gurus: An Examination of Encounter Groups and Their Distortions.* New York: Harper & Row, 1972.

Coupland, Douglas. *Generation X: Tales for an Accelerated Culture.* New York: St. Martin's, 1991.

Cowan, Douglas E. *Cults and New Religions: A Brief History.* Malden, MA: Blackwell, 2008.

Cowley, Malcolm. *Exile's Return: A Literary Odyssey of the 1920s.* New York: Viking, 1951; New York: Penguin, 1994.

———. *A Second Flowering.* New York: Viking, 1973.

Cox, Harvey. *Fire from Heaven: The Rise of Pentecostal Spirituality and the Reshaping of Religion in the Twenty-First Century.* Reading, MA: Addison-Wesley, 1995.

Cox, Robert S. *Body and Soul: A Sympathetic History of American Spiritualism.* Charlottesville: University of Virginia Press, 2003.

Coyote, Peter. *Sleeping Where I Fall.* New York and Washington, DC: Counterpoint, 1998.

Cramer, C.H. *Royal Bob: The Life of Robert G. Ingersoll.* Indianapolis, IN: Bobbs-Merrill, 1952.

Craven, Wayne. *American Art: History and Culture.* New York: McGraw-Hill, 2003.

Cray, Ed. *Ramblin' Man: The Life and Times of Woody Guthrie.* New York: W.W. Norton, 2004.

Crocker, Kathleen, and Jane Currie. *Chautauqua Institution.* Charleston, SC: Arcadia, 2001.

Cronon, Edmund David. *Black Moses: The Story of Marcus Garvey and the Universal Negro Improvement Association.* Madison: University of Wisconsin Press, 1968.

Cross, Charles R. *Heavier Than Heaven: A Biography of Kurt Cobain.* New York: Hyperion, 2001.

Crow, Thomas. *Modern Art in the Common Culture.* New Haven, CT: Yale University Press, 1996.

Crowe, Charles. *George Ripley: Transcendentalist and Utopian Socialist.* Athens: University of Georgia Press, 1967.

Crumb, Robert. *The Complete Crumb Comics.* 17 vols. Seattle: Fantagraphics, 1987–2005.

Cuneo, Michael W. *American Exorcism: Expelling Demons in the Land of Plenty.* New York: Broadway, 2002.

Cunningham, C., S. Brown, and J.C. Kaski. "Effects of Transcendental Meditation on Symptoms and Electrocardiographic Changes in Patients with Cardiac Syndrome X." *American Journal of Cardiology* 85:5 (March 2000): 653–55.

Curran, Douglas. *In Advance of the Landing: Folk Concepts of Outer Space.* Rev. ed. New York: Abbeville, 2001.

Curtis, Edward E., IV. *Islam in Black America: Identity, Liberation, and Difference in African-American Islamic Thought.* Albany: State University of New York Press, 2002.

Curtis, Susan. *A Consuming Faith: The Social Gospel and Modern American Culture.* Columbia: University of Missouri Press, 2001.

D'Emilio, John. *Sexual Politics, Sexual Communities.* Chicago: University of Chicago Press, 1998.

D'Emilio, John, and Estelle B. Freedman. *Intimate Matters: A History of Sexuality in America.* New York: Harper & Row, 1988.

Dallek, Robert. *Flawed Giant: Lyndon Johnson and His Times, 1961–1973.* New York: Oxford University Press, 1998.

———. *An Unfinished Life: John F. Kennedy, 1917–1963.* Boston: Little, Brown, 2003.

Dalton, David. *Piece of My Heart: A Portrait of Janis Joplin.* New York: Da Capo, 1991.

Daly, Markate, ed. *Communitarianism: A New Public Ethics.* Belmont, CA: Wadsworth, 1994.

Danto, Arthur. *Playing with the Edge: The Photographic Achievement of Robert Mapplethorpe.* Berkeley: University of California Press, 1996.

Darder, Antonia, and Rodolfo D. Torres, eds. *The Latino Studies Reader: Culture, Economy, and Society.* Malden, MA: Blackwell, 1998.

Darnton, Robert. *Mesmerism and the End of the Enlightenment in France.* Cambridge, MA: Harvard University Press, 1968.

Davidson, Sue. *A Heart in Politics: Jeannette Rankin and Patsy T. Mink: Women Who Dared.* Seattle, WA: Seal, 1994.

Davies, Hunter. *The Beatles.* New York: McGraw-Hill, 1985.

Davis, Allen F. *Spearhead for Reform: The Social Settlements and the Progressive Movement 1890–1914.* New York: Oxford University Press, 1967.

Davis, Angela Y. *Angela Davis: An Autobiography.* New York: Random House, 1974.

———. *Blues Legacies and Black Feminism: Gertrude "Ma" Rainey, Bessie Smith, and Billie Holiday.* New York: Vintage Books, 1998.

Davis, Fred. *Fashion, Culture, and Identity.* Chicago: University of Chicago Press, 1992.

Davis, James. *Skateboarding Is Not a Crime: Fifty Years of Street Culture.* Richmond Hill, Canada: Firefly, 2004.

Davis, James Kirkpatrick. *Assault on the Left: The FBI and the Sixties Antiwar Movement.* Westport, CT: Praeger, 1997.

Davis, Janet M. *The Circus Age: Culture and Society Under the American Big Top.* Chapel Hill: University of North Carolina Press, 2002.

Davis, John T. *Austin City Limits: Twenty-Five Years of American Music.* New York: Billboard, 2000.

Davis, Mike. *City of Quartz.* New York: Vintage Books, 1990.

Davis, Miles, with Quincy Troupe. *Miles: The Autobiography.* New York: Simon and Schuster, 1989.

Davis, Stephen. *Old Gods Almost Dead: The 40-Year Odyssey of the Rolling Stones.* New York: Broadway, 2001.

Dawson, Lorne L. *Comprehending Cults: The Sociology of New Religious Movements.* New York: Oxford University Press, 2006.

Day, Bell. "R(apid)evolution Begins at Home: (Where You'd Least Expect It)." *Inner City Light* 1:2 (July–Sept 1979): 9.

Day, Dorothy. *The Long Loneliness: An Autobiography.* New York: Harper and Row, 1952.

Dayton, Donald W. *The Higher Christian Life: Sources for the Study of the Holiness, Pentecostal, and Keswick Movements.* New York: Garland, 1985.

De Mille, Richard. *Castaneda's Journey: The Power and the Allegory.* Brooklyn, NY: Capra, 1976.

Deaver, William O. "Miguel Piñero (1946–1988)." In *Latino and Latina Writers,* ed. Alan West-Durán. New York: Scribner's, 2004.

DeBenedetti, Charles. *An American Ordeal: The Anti-War Movement of the Vietnam War.* New York: Syracuse University Press, 1990.

Debord, Guy. *Society of the Spectacle.* 1967. Detroit, MI: Black and Red Books, 1983.

Debs, Theodore. *Sidelights: Incidents in the Life of Eugene V. Debs.* Terre Haute, IN: Eugene V. Debs Foundation, 1973.

Decurtis, Anthony, et. al. *The Rolling Stone Illustrated History of Rock & Roll.* New York: Random House, 1992.

Deetz, James, and Patricia Scott Deetz. *The Times of Their Lives: Life, Love, and Death in Plymouth Colony.* New York: W.H. Freeman, 2000.

DeKoven, Marianne. *Utopia Limited: The Sixties and the Emergence of the Postmodern.* Durham, NC: Duke University Press, 2004.

Delano, Sterling F. *Brook Farm: The Dark Side of Utopia.* Cambridge, MA: Belknap Press, 2004.

Delany, Martin R. *The Condition, Elevation, Emigration, and Destiny of the Colored People of the United States.* 1852. Amherst, NY: Humanity, 2004.

Dellums, Ronald V. *Lying Down with the Lions: A Public Life from the Streets of Oakland to the Halls of Power.* Boston: Beacon, 1999.

Deloria, Philip. *Playing Indian.* New Haven, CT: Yale University Press, 1998.

Deloria, Vine, Jr. *Custer Died for Your Sins: An Indian Manifesto.* Norman: University of Oklahoma Press, 1988.

Delp, Robert W. "Andrew Jackson Davis: Prophet of American Spiritualism." *Journal of American History* 54 (June 1967): 43–56.

D'Emilio, John. *Sexual Politics, Sexual Communities: The Making of a Homosexual Minority in the United States, 1940–1970.* Chicago: University of Chicago Press, 1998.

Demos, John Putnam. *Entertaining Satan: Witchcraft and the Culture of Early New England.* New York: Oxford University Press, 1982.

Dempsey, Jack. *Thomas Morton of "Merrymount": The Life and Renaissance of an Early American Poet.* Scituate, MA: Digital Scanning, 2000.

Dennis, Matthew. *Cultivating a Landscape of Peace: Iroquois-European Encounters in Seventeenth-Century America.* Ithaca, NY: Cornell University Press, 1993.

Denson, Charles. *Coney Island: Lost and Found.* Berkeley, CA: Ten Speed, 2002.

DeRogatis, Jim. *Turn on Your Mind: Four Decades of Great Psychedelic Rock.* Milwaukee, WI: Hal Leonard, 2003.

DeVeaux, Scott. *The Birth of Bebop: A Social and Musical History.* Berkeley: University of California Press, 1997.

Devor, Holly. *FTM: Female-to-Male Transsexuals in Society.* Bloomington: Indiana University Press, 1999.

Dewey, John. *Democracy and Education: An Introduction to the Philosophy of Education.* New York: Macmillan, 1919.

Dick, Philip K. *The Collected Stories of Philip K. Dick.* Los Angeles: Underwood/Miller, 1987.

Dickson, Paul. *Slang: The Popular Dictionary of Americanisms.* New York: Walker, 2006.

Dietz, Roger. "Peter, Paul and Mary: Harmony from an Era of Protest." *Sing Out* 44:2 (Winter 2000): 34–40, 43.

Diggins, John Patrick. *The Rise and Fall of the American Left.* New York: W.W. Norton, 1992.

DiGirolamo, Vincent. "Such Were the B'hoys." *Radical History Review* 90 (2004): 123–41.

Dikkers, Scott, ed. The Onion *Presents Our Dumb Century: 100 Years of Headlines from America's Finest News Source.* New York: Three Rivers, 1999.

DiSanto, Ronald L., and Thomas J. Steele. *Guidebook to* Zen and the Art of Motorcycle Maintenance. New York: William Morrow, 1990.

Disch, Thomas M. *The Dreams Our Stuff Is Made Of: How Science Fiction Conquered the World.* New York: Touchstone, 1998.

Dixon, Winston Wheeler, and Gwendolyn Audrey Foster, eds. *Experimental Cinema: The Film Reader.* New York: Routledge, 2002.

Doggett, Peter. *Lou Reed: Growing Up in Public.* New York: Omnibus, 1992.

Doherty, Thomas Patrick. *Cold War, Cool Medium: Television, McCarthyism, and American Culture.* New York: Columbia University Press, 2003.

Dohrn, Bernardine, Bill Ayers, and Jeff Jones, eds. *Sing a Battle Song: The Revolutionary Poetry, Statements, and Communiqués of the Weather Underground, 1970–1974.* New York: Seven Stories, 2006.

Dollar, George W. *A History of Fundamentalism in America.* Greenville, SC: Bob Jones University Press, 1973.

Dominick, Joseph R. *Broadcasting, Cable, the Internet, and Beyond: An Introduction to Modern Electronic Media.* Boston: McGraw-Hill, 2008.

Donaldson, Gary. *Liberalism's Last Hurrah: The Presidential Campaign of 1964.* Armonk, NY: M.E. Sharpe, 2003.

Dorrien, Gary. *Soul in Society: The Making and Renewal of Social Christianity.* Minneapolis, MN: Fortress, 1995.

Dos Passos, John. *Adventures of a Young Man.* New York: Houghton Mifflin, 1939.

Doss, Erika. *Elvis Culture: Fans, Faith, and Image.* Rev. ed. Lawrence: University Press of Kansas, 1999.

———. *Twentieth-Century American Art.* New York: Oxford University Press, 2002.

Douglas, Susan J. *Listening In: Radio and the American Imagination: From Amos 'n' Andy and Edward R. Murrow to Wolfman Jack and Howard Stern.* New York: Times Books, 1999.

Dowd, Gregory Evans. *A Spirited Resistance: The North American Indian Struggle for Unity, 1745–1814.* Baltimore: Johns Hopkins University Press, 1992.

Dowhower, Richard L. "Clergy and Cults: A Survey." *Cult Observer* 11:3, 1994.

Downing, John D.H., Tamara Villarreal Ford, Genève Gil, and Laura Stein. *Radical Media: Rebellious Communication and Social Movements.* Thousand Oaks, CA: Sage, 2002.

Doyle, Michael William. "Staging the Revolution: Guerrilla Theater as a Countercultural Practice, 1965–1968." In *Imagine Nation: The American Counterculture of the 1960s and '70s,* edited by Peter Braunstein and Michael William Doyle. New York: Routledge, 2002.

Drake, Jennifer. "Feminist Generation and Listen Up: Voices from the Next Feminist Generation." *Feminist Studies* 23:2 (1997): 97.

Draper, Robert. Rolling Stone *Magazine: The Uncensored History.* New York: Doubleday, 1990.

Draper, Theodore. *The Origins of American Communism.* New York: Elephant, 1989.

Draves, Bill. *The Free University.* Chicago: Association Press/Follett, 1980.

Dray, Philip. *At the Hands of Persons Unknown: The Lynching of Black America.* New York: Modern Library, 2003.

Dreifus, Claudia. *Woman's Fate: Raps from a Feminist Consciousness-Raising Group.* New York: Bantam, 1973.

Drinnon, Richard. *Rebel in Paradise: A Biography of Emma Goldman.* Chicago: University of Chicago Press, 1961.

Duberman, Martin. *Black Mountain College: An Exploration in Community.* New York: E.P. Dutton, 1972.

———. *Paul Robeson: A Biography.* New York: W.W. Norton, 2005.

———. *Stonewall.* New York: Plume, 1994.

Duberman, Martin M., Martha Vicinus, and George Chauncey, Jr., eds. *Hidden from History: Reclaiming the Gay and Lesbian Past.* New York: NAL, 1989.

Dubin, Steven C. *Arresting Images: Impolitic Art and Uncivil Actions.* London and New York: Routledge, 1992.

Dudar, Helen, and Enrico Ferorelli. "It's Home Sweet Home for Geniuses, Real or Would-be: New York's Chelsea Hotel." *Smithsonian* 14 (December 1983): 94–105.

Dudley, Wade G. *Splintering the Wooden Wall: The British Blockade of the United States, 1812–1815.* Annapolis, MD: Naval Institute Press, 2003.

Dudley, William, ed. *The 1960s.* San Diego, CA: Greenhaven, 2000.

Duke, David C. *John Reed.* Boston: Twayne, 1987.

Dulchinos, Donald P. *Pioneer of Inner Space: The Life of Fitz Hugh Ludlow, Hasheesh Eater.* New York: Autonomedia, 1998.

Dumenil, Lynn. *Freemasonry and American Culture, 1880–1930.* Princeton, NJ: Princeton University Press, 1984.

Dun, Elizabeth E. "Backus, Isaac." In *American National Biography,* ed. John A. Garraty and Mark C. Carnes. New York: Oxford University Press, 1999.

Dunaway, David King. *How Can I Keep from Singing: Pete Seeger.* New York: McGraw-Hill, 1981.

Duncombe, Stephen. *Notes From the Underground: Zines and the Politics of Alternative Culture.* London and New York: Verso, 1997.

Dunn, Roy Sylvan. "The KGC in Texas, 1860–1861." *Southwestern Historical Quarterly* 70 (1967): 543–73.

Duyck, John. *Larry Rivers: Paintings and Drawings, 1951–2001.* New York: Marlborough Gallery, 2006.

Dyck, Cornelius J. *An Introduction to Mennonite History.* 3rd ed. Scottdale, PA: Herald, 1993.

Dylan, Bob. *Chronicles.* New York: Simon and Schuster, 2004.

Dyson, Michael Eric. *Between God and Gangsta Rap: Bearing Witness to Black Culture.* New York: Oxford University Press, 1996.

———. *Holler If You Hear Me: Searching for Tupac Shakur.* New York: Basic Civitas, 2001.

Early, Gerald, ed. *The Muhammad Ali Reader.* Hopewell, NJ: Ecco, 1998.

Eastman, Max. *Reflections on the Failure of Socialism.* 1955. Westport, CT: Greenwood, 1982.

———. *Since Lenin Died.* 1925. Westport, CT: Hyperion, 1973.

Ebin, Victoria. *The Body Decorated.* London: Blacker Calmann Cooper, 1979.

Echols, Alice. *Daring to Be Bad: Radical Feminism in America, 1967–1975.* Minneapolis: University of Minnesota Press, 1989.

———. *Scars of Sweet Paradise: The Life and Times of Janis Joplin.* New York: Metropolitan, 1999.

———. *Shaky Ground: The '60s and Its Aftershocks.* New York: Columbia University Press, 2002.

Eckhardt, Celia Morris. *Fanny Wright: Rebel in America.* Cambridge, MA: Harvard University Press, 1984.

Edmonds, Anthony O. *Muhammad Ali.* Westport, CT: Greenwood, 2005.

Edmonds, Ben. *What's Going On? Marvin Gaye and The Last Days of The Motown Sound.* Edinburgh: MOJO, 2001.

Edmonds, Ennis Barrington. *Rastafari: From Outcasts to Culture Bearers.* New York: Oxford University Press, 2003.

Egan, Leona Rust. *Provincetown as a Stage: Provincetown, the Provincetown Players, and the Discovery of Eugene O'Neill.* New York: Parnassus Imprints, 1994.

Ehrmann, Eric. "Toking Down with MC5." *Rolling Stone,* January 4, 1969. Reprint. *Rolling Stone,* June 11, 1992, 35.

Eisele, Albert. *Almost to the Presidency: A Biography of Two American Politicians.* Blue Earth, MN: Piper, 1972.

Elbaum, Max. *Revolution in the Air: Sixties Radicals Turn to Lenin, Mao, and Che.* London: Verso, 2002.

Eldridge, John. *C. Wright Mills.* New York: Tavistock, 1983.

Eliot, Marc. *Death of a Rebel.* Garden City, NY: Anchor, 1979.

Ellis, Jacqueline. *Silent Witnesses: Representations of Working-Class Women in the United States.* Bowling Green, OH: Bowling Green State University Popular Press, 1998.

Ellison, Harlan, ed. *Again, Dangerous Visions.* New York: Doubleday, 1972.

———. *Dangerous Visions.* New York: Doubleday, 1967.

Ellsberg, Daniel. *Secrets: A Memoir of Vietnam and the Pentagon Papers.* New York: Viking, 2001.

Ellwood, Robert S. *The Sixties Spiritual Awakening: American Religion Moving from Modern to Postmodern.* New Brunswick, NJ: Rutgers University Press, 1994.

Emerson, Ralph Waldo. *Selected Writings of Emerson.* Ed. Donald McQuade. New York: Random House, 1981.

Entwistle, Joan. *The Fashioned Body: Fashion, Dress and Modern Social Theory.* Malden, MA: Blackwell, 2000.

Epstein, Daniel Mark. *Sister Aimee: The Life of Aimee Semple McPherson.* New York: Harcourt Brace Jovanovich, 1993.

———. *What Lips My Lips Have Kissed: The Loves and Love Poems of Edna St. Vincent Millay.* New York: Henry Holt, 2001.

Erickson, Hal. *From Beautiful Downtown Burbank: A Critical History of* Rowan and Martin's Laugh-In, *1968–1973.* Jefferson, NC: McFarland, 2000.

Ernst, Robert. *Weakness Is a Crime: The Life of Bernarr Macfadden.* Syracuse, NY: Syracuse University Press, 1991.

Esslin, Martin. *The Theatre of the Absurd.* New York: Vintage Books, 2004.

Esterberg, Kristin G. "From Accommodation to Liberation: A Social Movement Analysis of Lesbians in the Homophile Movement." *Gender and Society* 8:3 (September 1994): 424–43.

Estren, Mark James. *A History of Underground Comics.* 1974. Berkeley, CA: Ronin, 1993.

Evanier, Mark. *Mad Art: A Visual Celebration of the Art of MAD Magazine and the Idiots Who Create It.* New York: Watson-Guptill, 2002.

Evans, David, and Scott Michaels. *Rocky Horror: From Concept to Cult.* London: Sanctuary, 2002.

Evans, Sara. *Personal Politics: the Roots of Women's Liberation in the Movement and the New Left.* New York: Random House, 1979.

Evanzz, Karl. *The Judas Factor: The Plot to Kill Malcolm X.* New York: Thunder's Mouth, 1992.

Eyerman, Ron, and Scott Barretta. "From the 30s to the 60s: The Folk Music Revival in the United States." *Theory and Society* 25:4 (August 1996): 501–43.

Faderman, Lillian. *Odd Girls and Twilight Lovers: A History of Lesbian Life in Twentieth-Century America.* New York: Columbia University Press, 1991.

———. *Surpassing the Love of Men: Romantic Friendship and Love Between Women from the Renaissance to the Present.* New York: William Morrow, 1981.

Fantina, Robert. *Desertion and the American Soldier: 1776–2006.* New York: Algora, 2006.

Farber, David. *Chicago '68.* Chicago: University of Chicago Press, 1988.

Farrell, Amy Erdman. *Yours in Sisterhood: Ms. Magazine and the Promise of Popular Feminism.* Chapel Hill: University of North Carolina Press, 1998.

Farrell, James J. *The Spirit of the Sixties: The Making of Postwar Radicalism.* New York: Routledge, 1997.

Fatout, Paul. *Ambrose Bierce: The Devil's Lexicographer.* Norman: University of Oklahoma Press, 1951.

Fausto-Sterling, Anne. *Sexing the Body: Gender Politics and the Construction of Sexuality.* New York: Basic Books, 2000.

Fax, Elton C. *Garvey: The Story of a Pioneer Black Nationalist.* New York: Dodd, Mead, 1972.

Felton, David, Robin Green, and Dalton David, eds. *Mindfuckers: A Source Book on the Rise of Acid Fascism in America, Including Material on Charles Manson, Mel Lyman, Victor Baranco, and Their Followers.* San Francisco: Straight Arrow, 1972.

Felton, Harold W. *Nancy Ward: Cherokee.* New York: Dodd Mead, 1975.

Fenster, Mark. *Conspiracy Theories.* Minneapolis: University of Minnesota Press, 1999.

Ferguson, Robert. *Henry Miller: A Life.* New York: W.W. Norton, 1991.

Ferlinghetti, Lawrence. *These Are My Rivers: New and Selected Poems, 1955–1993.* New York: New Directions, 1993.

Ferlinghetti, Lawrence, and Nancy J. Peters. *Literary San Francisco: A Pictorial History from Its Beginnings to the Present Day.* San Francisco: City Lights and Harper & Row, 1980.

Fernandez, Kathleen M. *A Singular People: Images of Zoar.* Kent, OH: Kent State University Press, 2003.

Ferree, Mayra Marx, and Beth B. Hess. *Controversy and Coalition: The New Feminist Movement.* Boston: Twayne, 1985.

Fett, Sharla M. *Working Cures: Healing, Health, and Power on Southern Slave Plantations.* Chapel Hill: University of North Carolina Press, 2002.

Feuerlicht, Roberta Strauss. *Justice Crucified: The Story of Sacco and Vanzetti.* New York: McGraw-Hill, 1997.

Feuerstein, Georg. *The Deeper Dimension of Yoga: Theory and Practice.* Boston: Shambhala, 2003.

Field, Andrew. *Djuna: The Formidable Miss Barnes.* Austin: University of Texas Press, 1985.

Fields, Rick. *How the Swans Came to the Lake: A Narrative History of Buddhism in America.* Boulder, CO: Shambhala, 1981; London: Shambhala, 1992.

Fike, Rupert. *Voices from the Farm: Adventures in Community Living.* Summertown, TN: Book Publishing, 1998.

Fikes, Jay Courtney. *Carlos Castaneda, Academic Optimism and the Psychedelic Sixties.* Victoria, Canada: Millennia, 1996.

Filene, Benjamin. *Romancing the Folk: Public Memory and American Roots Music.* Chapel Hill: University of North Carolina Press, 2000.

Fine, Gary Alan. *Shared Fantasy: Role Playing Games as Social Worlds.* Chicago: University of Chicago Press, 1983.

Finestone, Aaron. "Free University." Collegiate Press Service 44–1. Washington, DC: U.S. Student Press Association, January 25, 1966.

Finney, Ben, and James D. Houston. *Surfing: A History of the Ancient Hawaiian Sport.* Rohnert Park, CA: Pomegranate Artbooks, 1996

Fishbein, Leslie. *Rebels in Bohemia: The Radicals of* The Masses, *1911–1917.* Chapel Hill: University of North Carolina Press, 1982.

Fisher, James Terence. *The Catholic Counterculture in America, 1933–1962.* Chapel Hill: University of North Carolina Press, 1989.

Fitch, Noel Riley. *Sylvia Beach and the Lost Generation: A History of Literary Paris in the Twenties and Thirties.* New York: W.W. Norton, 1985.

Fitzgerald, F. Scott. *The Crack-up.* New York: New Directions, 1993.

———. *Tender Is the Night.* New York: Scribner, 1996.

Fitzgerald, Zelda. *The Collected Writings of Zelda Fitzgerald.* Ed. Matthew J. Bruccoli. Tuscaloosa: University of Alabama Press, 1991.

Flamming, Douglas. *Bound for Freedom: Black Los Angeles in Jim Crow America.* Berkeley: University of California Press, 2005.

Fleisher, Julian. *The Drag Queens of New York: An Illustrated Field Guide.* New York: Riverhead, 1996.

Flexner, Eleanor. *Century of Struggle: The Woman's Rights Movement in the United States.* 1959. Cambridge, MA: Harvard University Press, 1975; enlarged ed. with Ellen Fitzgerald, Cambridge, MA: Belknap Press, 1996.

Flink, James J. *The Car Culture.* Cambridge, MA: MIT Press, 1975.

Florence, Namulundah. *Bell Hooks' Engaged Pedagogy.* Westport, CT: Bergin & Garvey, 1998.

Flores, William V., and Rina Benmayor, eds. *Latino Cultural Citizenship: Claiming Identity, Space, and Rights.* Boston: Beacon, 1997.

Flynn, George Q. *Conscription and the Military: The Draft in France, Great Britain, and the United States.* Westport, CT: Greenwood, 2002.

Fogleman, Aaron S. "Jesus Is Female: The Moravian Challenge in the German Communities of British North America." *William and Mary Quarterly* 60 (2003): 295–332.

Foner, Phillip S., ed. *The Black Panthers Speak.* New York: Da Capo, 2002.

———. *History of the Labor Movement in the United States.* Vol. 4, *The Industrial Workers of the World, 1905–1917.* New York: International, 1965.

———, ed. *The Life and Writings of Frederick Douglass.* 4 vols. New York: International, 1950–1955.

———, ed. *W.E.B. Du Bois Speaks.* 2 vols. New York: Pathfinder, 1970.

Ford, Linda G. *Iron-Jawed Angels.* Lanham, MD: University Press of America, 1991.

Fortea, Jose Antonio. *Interview with an Exorcist.* New York: Ascension, 2006.

Foster, Lawrence. *Religion and Sexuality: The Shakers, the Mormons, and the Oneida Community.* Urbana: University of Illinois Press, 1981.

Foster, Stephen. *The Long Argument: English Puritanism and the Shaping of New England Culture, 1570–1700.* Chapel Hill: University of North Carolina Press, 1991.

Fowler, Robert B. *The World of Jack T. Chick (The History of the World According to Jack T. Chick).* San Francisco: Last Gasp, 2001.

Francis, Richard. *Transcendental Utopias: Individual and Community at Brook Farm, Fruitlands, and Walden.* Ithaca, NY: Cornell University Press, 1997.

Frank, Thomas. *The Conquest of Cool: Business Culture, Counterculture, and the Rise of Hip Consumerism.* Chicago: University of Chicago Press, 1997.

Frankfort, Ellen. *The Voice: Life at* The Village Voice. New York: William Morrow, 1976.

Franklin, H. Bruce. *The Vietnam War: In American Stories, Songs, and Poems.* Boston: St. Martin's/Bedford, 1996.

Franklin, John Hope, and Loren Schweninger. *Runaway Slaves: Rebels on the Plantation.* New York: Oxford University Press, 1999.

Franzese, Robert J., Herbert C. Covey, and Scott Menard. *Youth Gangs.* 3rd ed. Springfield, IL: Charles C. Thomas, 2006.

Frascina, Francis, ed. *Pollock and After: The Critical Debate.* 2nd ed. New York: Routledge, 2000.

Frazer, Winifred L. *Mabel Dodge Luhan.* Boston: Twayne, 1984.

Freedman, Estelle B. "Boston Marriage, Free Love, and Fictive Kin: Historical Alternatives to Mainstream Marriage." *OAH Newsletter* 32:3 (August 2004): 1, 16.

Freedman, Jane. *Feminism.* Philadelphia: Open University Press, 2001.

Friedan, Betty. *The Feminine Mystique.* New York: W.W. Norton, 1963.

———. *It Changed My Life: Writings on the Women's Movement.* New York: Random House, 1976.

———. *The Second Stage.* New York: Summit, 1981.

Friedman, Ken, ed. *The Fluxus Reader.* New York: Academy Editions, 1998.

Friedman, Myra. *Buried Alive: The Biography of Janis Joplin.* New York: William Morrow, 1973.

Friedman, R. Seth. *Factsheet Five Reader.* New York: Three Rivers, 1997.

Friesen, John W., and Virginia Lyon Friesen. *The Palgrave Companion to North American Utopias.* New York: Palgrave Macmillan, 2004.

Fromartz, Samuel. *Organic, Inc.: Natural Foods and How They Grew.* Orlando, FL: Harcourt, 2006

Frost, Jennifer. *"An Interracial Movement of the Poor": Community Organizing and the New Left in the 1960s.* New York: Bedford/St. Martin's, 2004.

Fuchs, Rudi, and Jan Hein Sassen. *Dennis Hopper (a Keen Eye): Artist, Photographer, Filmmaker.* Rotterdam, The Netherlands: RAI, 2001.

Fuller, Robert C. *Mesmerism and the American Cure of Souls.* Philadelphia: University of Pennsylvania Press, 1982.

———. *Spiritual But Not Religious: Understanding Unchurched America.* New York: Oxford University Press, 2001.

Furlong, Monica. *Zen Effects: The Life of Alan Watts.* Woodstock, VT: Skylight Paths, 2001.

Furlong, William. *Laurie Anderson: An Overview.* Audio Arts, 1981. Audiocassette.

Furlough, Ellen, and Carl Strikwerda. "From Cooperative Commonwealth to Cooperative Democracy: The American Cooperative Ideal, 1880–1940." In *Consumers Against Capitalism? Consumer Cooperation in Europe, North America, and Japan, 1840–1990,* ed. Ellen Furlough and Carl Strikwerda. Lanham, MD: Rowman & Littlefield, 1999.

Gaar, Gillian G. *She's a Rebel: The History of Women in Rock & Roll.* Seattle: Seal, 1992.

Gabriel, Mary. *Notorious Victoria: The Life of Victoria Woodhull, Uncensored.* Chapel Hill, NC: Algonquin, 1998.

Gahr, David. *The Faces of Folk Music.* New York: Citadel, 1968.

Gaines, James R. *Wit's End: Days and Nights of the Algonquin Round Table.* New York: Harcourt Brace Jovanovich, 1977.

Gallo, Marcia M. *Different Daughters: A History of the Daughters of Bilitis and the Rise of the Lesbian Rights Movement.* Emeryville, CA: Seal, 2006; New York: Carroll & Graf, 2006.

Garber, Marjorie. *Vested Interests: Cross-dressing and Cultural Anxiety.* New York: Routledge, 1992.

Garcia, Ignacio M. *Chicanismo: The Forging of a Militant Ethos Among Mexican Americans.* Tucson: University of Arizona Press, 1997.

Garcia, John A. *Latino Politics in America: Community, Culture, and Interests.* Lanham, MD: Rowman & Littlefield, 2003.

Garcia, Richard A., ed. *The Chicanos in America 1540–1974: A Chronology and Fact Book.* Dobbs Ferry, NY: Oceana, 1977.

Gardner, Gerald B. *Witchcraft Today.* 1954. Yucca Valley, CA: Citadel, 2004.

Gardner, Martin. *The Healing Revelations of Mary Baker Eddy: The Rise and Fall of Christian Science.* New York: Prometheus, 1993.

Garner, Gerald C. *The Streaking Book.* New York: Bantam, 1974.

Garofalo, Reebee, ed. *Rockin' the Boat: Mass Music and Mass Movements.* Boston: South End, 1992.

Garrison, Dee. *Mary Heaton Vorse: The Life of an American Insurgent.* Philadelphia: Temple University Press, 1989.

Garrison, William Lloyd. *William Lloyd Garrison and the Fight Against Slavery: Selections from* The Liberator. Bedford Series in History and Culture. New York: St. Martin's, 1994.

Garrow, David J. *Bearing the Cross: Martin Luther King, Jr., and the Southern Christian Leadership Conference.* New York: William Morrow, 1986.

Gaspar de Alba, Alicia. *Chicano Art: Inside/Outside the Master's House.* Austin: University of Texas Press, 1998.

Gately, Iain. *Tobacco: A Cultural History of How an Exotic Plant Seduced Civilization.* New York: Grove, 2003.

Gates, Henry Louis, Jr. "Afterword." In *Their Eyes Were Watching God,* by Zora Neale Hurston. New York: HarperPerennial, 1990.

Gates, Henry Louis, Jr., and Cornell West, eds. *The African-American Century: How Black Americans Have Shaped Our Country.* New York: Free Press, 2002.

Gates, Katherine. *Deviant Desires: Incredibly Strange Sex.* New York: Juno, 2000.

Gates, Susa Young. *Brigham Young: Patriot, Pioneer, Prophet and Leader of the Latter Day.* Whitefish, MT: Kessinger, 2004.

Gaustad, Edwin S. *Liberty of Conscience: Roger Williams in America.* Grand Rapids, MI: Eerdmans, 1991.

Gavin, James. *Deep in a Dream: The Long Night of Chet Baker.* New York: Alfred A. Knopf, 2002.

Geerdes, Clay. "The Dating of *Zap Comix #1.*" *Comics Journal* 218 (December 1999): 117–20.

Genat, Robert. *Lowriders.* Minneapolis, MN: MBI, 2001.

Genovese, Eugene D. *Roll, Jordan, Roll: The World the Slaves Made.* New York: Pantheon, 1974.

George, Nelson. *Hip Hop America.* New York: Penguin, 1999; 2005.

Getz, Leonard. *From Broadway to the Bowery: A History and Filmography of the Dead End Kids, Little Tough Guys, East Side Kids and the Bowery Boys Films.* Jefferson, NC: McFarland, 2006.

Gibbon, Sean. *Run Like an Antelope: On the Road with Phish.* New York: St. Martin's/Griffin, 2001.

Gibson, Morgan. *Revolutionary Rexroth: Poet of East-West Wisdom.* North Haven, CT: Shoe String, 1986.

Gifford, Barry, and Lawrence Lee. *Jack's Book: An Oral Biography of Jack Kerouac.* New York: St. Martin's, 1978.

Giles, Kevin. *Flight of the Dove: The Story of Jeannette Rankin.* Beaverton, OR: Touchstone, 1980.

Gilfoyle, Timothy J. *City of Eros: New York City, Prostitution, and the Commercialization of Sex.* New York: W.W. Norton, 1992.

Gilhooley, Leonard. *Contradiction and Dilemma: Orestes Brownson and the American Idea.* New York: Fordham University Press, 1972.

Gill, Crispin. *Mayflower Remembered: A History of the Plymouth Pilgrims.* New York: Taplinger, 1970.

Gill, Gillian. *Mary Baker Eddy.* Radcliffe Biography Series. New York: Perseus, 1999.

Gillies, James, and R. Cailliau. *How the Web Was Born: The Story of the World Wide Web.* Oxford, UK: Oxford University Press, 2000.

Gilmore, Lee, and Mark Van Proyen, eds. *AfterBurn: Reflections on Burning Man.* Albuquerque: University of New Mexico Press, 2005.

Ginsberg, Allen. *Howl and Other Poems.* San Francisco: City Lights, 1956.

Ginzburg, Lori D. *Women and the Work of Benevolence: Morality, Politics, and Class in the Nineteenth-Century United States.* New Haven, CT: Yale University Press, 1992.

Gioia, Ted. *The History of Jazz.* New York: Oxford University Press, 1997.

Gitlin, Todd. *The Sixties: Years of Hope, Days of Rage.* Toronto, Canada: Bantam, 1987; New York: Bantam, 1989.

———. *The Whole World Is Watching: Mass Media in the Making and Unmaking of the New Left.* Berkeley: University of California Press, 1980.

Giuliano, Geoffrey, and Brenda Giuliano. *The Lost Lennon Interviews.* Holbrook, MA: Adams Media, 1996.

Gladstein, Mimi Reisel, and Chris Matthew Sciabarra. *Feminist Interpretations of Ayn Rand.* University Park: Pennsylvania State University Press, 1999.

Glass, L.L., M.A. Kirsch, and F.N. Parris. "Psychiatric Disturbances Associated with Erhard Seminars Training." *American Journal of Psychiatry* 134:3, 1977.

Glassie, John. "The Pugilist Novelist." *New York Times Magazine,* September 29, 2002, 21.

Glazier, Loss Pequeño. *Small Press: An Annotated Guide.* Westport, CT: Greenwood, 1992.

Gleason, Ralph J. *The Jefferson Airplane and the San Francisco Sound.* New York: Ballantine, 1969.

Glessing, Robert. *The Underground Press in America.* Bloomington: Indiana University Press, 1970.

Goffman, Ken, and Dan Joy. *Counterculture through the Ages: From Abraham to Acid House.* New York: Villard, 2004.

Goines, David Lance. *The Free Speech Movement: Coming of Age in the 1960s.* Berkeley, CA: Ten Speed, 1993.

Goldberg, RoseLee. *Performance: Live Art 1909 to the Present.* New York: Harry N. Abrams, 1979.

———. *Performance: Live Art Since 1960.* New York: Harry N. Abrams, 1998.

Goldblatt, Gloria. "The Queen of Bohemia Grew Up in Charleston." *Carologue* (Autumn 1988): 10–11, 28.

Goldman, Albert. *Elvis.* New York: McGraw-Hill, 1981.

———. *Ladies and Gentlemen, Lenny Bruce!!* New York: Random House, 1974.

Goldman, Emma. *Anarchism and Other Essays.* 3rd rev. ed. New York: Mother Earth, 1917.

———. *Living My Life.* Garden City, NY: Garden City, 1936.

———. *Red Emma Speaks: Selected Writings and Speeches.* Ed. Alix Kates Shulman. New York: Random House, 1972.

Goldsmith, Barbara. *Other Powers: The Age of Suffrage, Spiritualism, and the Scandalous Victoria Woodhull.* New York: Alfred A. Knopf, 1998.

Golemba, Henry L. *George Ripley.* Boston: Twayne, 1977.

Gonzales, Rodolfo. *Message to Aztlán: Selected Writings of Rodolfo "Corky" Gonzales.* Houston: Arte Público, 2001.

Gonzalez-Wippler, Migene. *Santería: The Religion, Faith, Rites, Magic.* St. Paul, MN: Llewellyn, 1994.

Gooch, Brad. *City Poet: The Life and Times of Frank O'Hara.* New York: Alfred A. Knopf, 1993.

Goodman, Paul. *Towards a Christian Republic: Antimasonry and the Great Transition in New England, 1826–1836.* New York: Oxford University Press, 1988.

Goodwyn, Lawrence. *Democratic Promise: The Populist Movement in America.* New York: Oxford University Press, 1976.

———. *The Populist Moment: A Short History of the Agrarian Revolt in America.* New York: Oxford University Press, 1978.

Gordon, Linda. *The Moral Property of Women: A History of Birth Control Politics in America.* Urbana: University of Illinois Press, 2002.

Gordon, Terrence W. *Marshall McLuhan: Escape into Understanding.* Toronto: Stoddart, 1997.

Gordon, William A. *The Mind and Art of Henry Miller.* Baton Rouge: Louisiana State University Press, 1967.

Gossage, Howard Luck. *Is There Any Hope for Advertising?* Ed. Kim Rotzoll, Jarlath Graham, and Barrows Mussey. Urbana: University of Illinois Press, 1986.

Gottfried, Ted. *Drugs: The Facts about Marijuana.* New York: Benchmark, 2005.

Gottlieb, Joanne, and Gayle Wald. "Smells Like Teen Spirit: Riot Grrrls, Revolution, and Women in Independent Rock." In *Microphone Fiends: Youth Music and Youth Culture,* edited by Andrew Ross and Tricia Rose. New York: Routledge, 1994.

Gottschalk, Stephen. *The Emergence of Christian Science in American Religious Life.* Berkeley: University of California Press, 1974.

———. *Rolling Away the Stone: Mary Baker Eddy's Challenge to Materialism.* Bloomington: Indiana University Press, 2005.

Goulart, Ron. *Cheap Thrills: An Informal History of the Pulp Magazines.* New Rochelle, NY: Arlington House, 1972.

Gould, Joseph E. *The Chautauqua Movement: An Episode in the Continuing American Revolution.* Albany: State University of New York, 1961.

Gracia, Jorge J.E., and Pablo de Greiff, eds. *Hispanics/Latinos in the United States: Ethnicity, Race, and Rights.* New York: Routledge, 2000.

Graham, Herman, III. *The Brothers' Vietnam War: Black Power, Manhood, and the Military Experience.* Gainesville: University Press of Florida, 2003.

Graham, Jenny. *Revolutionary in Exile: The Emigration of Joseph Priestley to America, 1794 to 1804.* Philadelphia: American Philosophical Society, 1995.

Graña, César, and Marigay Graña, eds. *On Bohemia: The Code of the Self-Exiled.* New Brunswick, NJ: Transaction, 1990.

Granger, David A. *John Dewey, Robert Pirsig, and the Art of Living: Revisioning Aesthetic Education.* New York: Palgrave Macmillan, 2006.

Grathwohl, Larry. *Bringing Down America: An FBI Informant with the Weathermen.* New Rochelle, NY: Arlington House, 1976.

Gray, Jonathan. *Watching with the Simpsons: Television, Parody, and Intertextuality.* New York: Routledge, 2006.

Greeley, Robert E. "Robert Ingersoll." In *The Encyclopedia of Unbelief,* ed. Gordon Stein, 349–50. Buffalo, NY: Prometheus, 1985.

Green, Harvey. *Fit for America: Health, Fitness, Sport, and American Society.* New York: Pantheon, 1986.

Green, Jared F., ed. *DJ, Dance, and Rave Culture.* Detroit, MI: Greenhaven, 2005.

Green, Jonathon. *Cannabis.* New York: Thunder's Mouth, 2002.

Greenberg, Kenneth S., ed. *Nat Turner: A Slave Rebellion in History and Memory.* New York: Oxford University Press, 2003.

Greenfeld, Howard. *Gertrude Stein: A Biography.* New York: Crown, 1973.

Greenfield, Robert. *Timothy Leary: A Biography.* New York: Harcourt, 2006.

Greenwald, Andy. *Nothing Feels Good: Punk Rock, Teenagers and Emo.* New York: St. Martin's, 2003.

Gregory, Dick, and Robert Lipsyte. *Nigger: An Autobiography.* New York: E.P. Dutton, 1964.

Gregory, Dick, and Shelia P. Moses. *Callus On My Soul: A Memoir.* Atlanta: Longstreet, 2000.

Gridley, Mark C. *Jazz Styles: History and Analysis.* Upper Saddle River, NJ: Prentice Hall, 2003.

Griffin, Farah Jasmine. *If You Can't Be Free, Be a Mystery: In Search of Billie Holiday.* New York: Ballantine, 2002.

Griffith, Robert, and Athan Theoharis, eds. *The Specter: Original Essays on the Cold War and the Origins of McCarthyism.* New York: Franklin Watts, 1974.

Groce, Nancy. *New York: Songs of the City.* New York: Billboard/Watson-Guptill, 1999.

Grof, Stanislav. *LSD Psychotherapy.* Sarasota, FL: Multidisciplinary Association for Psychedelic Studies, 2001.

Grogan, Emmett. *Ringolevio (A Life Played for Keeps).* Boston: Little, Brown, 1972.

Gross, Michael. *My Generation: Fifty Years of Sex, Drugs, Rock, Revolution, Glamour, Greed, Valor, Faith, and Silicon Chips.* New York: Cliff Street, 2000.

Grover, Kathryn, ed. *Fitness in American Culture: Images of Health, Sport, and the Body, 1830–1940.* Amherst: University of Massachusetts Press, and Rochester, New York: Margaret Woodbury Strong Museum, 1989.

Grunenberg, Christoph, and Jonathan Harris, eds. *Summer of Love: Psychedelic Art, Social Crisis and Counterculture in the 1960s.* Liverpool, UK: Liverpool University Press, 2005.

Guarneri, Carl J. *The Utopian Alternative: Fourierism in Nineteenth-Century America.* Ithaca, NY: Cornell University Press, 1991.

Guerrilla Girls. *Confessions of the Guerrilla Girls.* With an essay by Whitney Chadwick. New York: HarperPerennial, 1995.

———. *The Guerrilla Girls' Bedside Companion to the History of Western Art.* New York: Penguin, 1998.

Guillermo, Kathy Snow. *Monkey Business: The Disturbing Case that Launched the Animal Rights Movement.* Washington, DC: National Press, 1993.

Gunderloy, Mike, and Cari Goldberg Janice. *The World of Zines: A Guide to the Independent Magazine Revolution.* New York: Penguin, 1992.

Gunn, James. *Alternate Worlds: The Illustrated History of Science Fiction.* Englewood Cliffs, NJ: Prentice Hall, 1975.

———, ed. *Inside Science Fiction: Essays on Fantastic Literature.* I.O. Evans Studies in the Philosophy and Criticism of Literature, No. 11. San Bernardino, CA: Borgo, 1992.

———. *The New Encyclopedia of Science Fiction.* New York: Viking Penguin, 1988.

Guthrie, Woody. *Bound for Glory.* Garden City, NY: Doubleday, 1943.

Gutiérrez, David G. *Walls and Mirrors: Mexican Americans, Mexican Immigrants, and the Politics of Ethnicity.* Berkeley: University of California Press, 1995.

Guy-Sheftall, Beverly, ed. *Words of Fire: An Anthology of African-American Feminist Thought.* New York: New Press, 1995.

Habell-Pallán, Michelle. *Loca Motion: The Travels of Chicana and Latina Popular Culture.* New York: New York University Press, 2005.

Habell-Pallán, Michelle, and Mary Romero, eds. *Latino/a Popular Culture.* New York: New York University Press, 2002.

Hackett, Pat, ed. *The Andy Warhol Diaries.* New York: Random House, 1991.

Haden-Guest, Anthony. *The Last Party: Studio 54, Disco, and the Culture of the Night.* New York: William Morrow, 1997.

Haenfler, Ross. *Straight Edge: Clean-Living Youth, Hardcore Punk, and Social Change.* New Brunswick, NJ: Rutgers University Press, 2006.

Hagedorn, John M. *Gangs in the Global City: Alternatives to Traditional Criminology.* Urbana: University of Illinois Press, 2007.

Hahn, Emily. *Mabel: A Biography of Mabel Dodge Luhan.* Boston: Houghton Mifflin, 1997.

Hahne, Ron. *Black Mask and Up Against the Wall Motherfucker: The Incomplete Works of Ron Hahne, Ben Morea, and the Black Mask Group.* London: Unpopular Books and Sabotage Editions, 1993.

Haining, Peter. *The Classic Era of American Pulp Magazines.* London: Prion, 2000.

Hajdu, David. *Positively 4th Street: The Lives and Times of Joan Baez, Bob Dylan, Mimi Baez Farina, and Richard Farina.* New York: Farrar, Straus and Giroux, 2001.

Haley, Alex, and Malcolm X. *The Autobiography of Malcolm X.* New York: Ballantine, 1992.

Hall, David D. *The Antinomian Controversy, 1636–1638: A Documentary History.* 2nd ed. Durham, NC: Duke University Press, 1990.

———. *Worlds of Wonder, Days of Judgment: Popular Religious Belief in Early New England.* New York: Alfred A. Knopf, 1989.

Hall, Gwendolyn Midlo. *Africans in Colonial Louisiana: The Development of Afro-Creole Culture in the Eighteenth Century.* Baton Rouge: Louisiana State University Press, 1995.

Hall, James C. *Mercy, Mercy Me: African-American Culture and the American Sixties.* New York: Oxford University Press, 2001.

Hall, John R. *Gone from the Promised Land: Jonestown in American Cultural History.* New Brunswick, NJ: Transaction, 1987.

Halleck, DeeDee. *Hand-Held Visions: The Impossible Possibilities of Community Media.* New York: Fordham University Press, 2002.

Halper, Jon. *Gary Snyder: Dimensions of a Life.* New York: Random House, 1991.

Hamalian, Linda. *A Life of Kenneth Rexroth.* New York: W.W. Norton, 1991.

Hamilton, Blair. *Free Universities, Experimental Colleges and Free Schools.* Yellow Springs, OH: Antioch College Department of Educational Research/Union for Research and Experimentation in Higher Education, 1968.

Hamm, Mark S. *American Skinheads: The Criminology and Control of Hate Crime.* Westport, CT: Praeger, 1993.

Hamm, Thomas D. *The Quakers in America.* New York: Columbia University Press, 2003.

Hammond, William M. *Public Affairs: The Military and the Media, 1968–1973.* Washington, DC: Center of Military History, 1996.

Han, Arar, and John Hsu, eds. *Asian American X: An Intersection of Twenty-First-Century Asian American Voices.* Ann Arbor: University of Michigan Press, 2004.

Hand-Book of the Oneida Community. 1867. Oneida, NY: Office of Oneida Circular, 1875.

Hanegraaff, Wouter J. *New Age Religion and Western Culture: Esotericism in the Mirror of Secular Thought.* Albany: State University of New York Press, 1998.

Haney, Ian F. *Racism on Trial: The Chicano Fight for Justice.* Cambridge, MA: Belknap Press, 2003.

Haney-López, Ian F. *Racism on Trial: The Chicano Fight for Justice.* Cambridge, MA: Belknap Press, 2003.

Hanson, Dian. *Naked as a Jaybird.* New York: Taschen, 2003.

Harmond, Richard. "Progress and Flight: An Interpretation of the American Cycle Craze of the 1890s." *Journal of Social History* 5:2 (1971–1972): 235–57.

Harold, Christine. *OurSpace: Resisting the Corporate Control of Culture.* Minneapolis: University of Minnesota Press, 2007.

Harris, Leon. *Upton Sinclair: American Rebel.* New York: Crowell, 1975.

Harris, Neil. *Humbug: The Art of P.T. Barnum.* Boston: Little, Brown, 1973.

Harris, Oliver, ed. *The Letters of William S. Burroughs: 1945–1959.* New York: Viking, 1993.

Harris-Fain, Darren. *Understanding Contemporary American Science Fiction: The Age of Maturity, 1970–2000.* Columbia: University of South Carolina Press, 2005.

Harrison, Cynthia. *On Account of Sex: The Politics of Women's Issues, 1945–1968.* Berkeley: University of California Press, 1988.

Harrison, Harry P. *Culture Under Canvas: The Story of Tent Chautauqua.* As told to Karl Detzer. New York: Hastings House, 1958.

Harrold, Stanley. *American Abolitionists.* Harlow, UK: Pearson Education, 2001.

Hattunen, Karen. *Confidence Men and the Painted Women: A Study of Middle Class Culture in America 1830–1870.* New Haven, CT: Yale University Press, 1982.

Hawes, Elizabeth. *Why Is a Dress? Who? What? When? Where?* New York: Viking, 1942.

Hay, Harry. *Radically Gay: Gay Liberation in the Words of Its Founder.* Ed. Will Roscoe. Boston: Beacon, 1996.

Hayden, Tom. *Reunion: A Memoir.* New York: Random House, 1988.

Hayes, David, and Brent Walker. *The Films of the Bowery Boys: A Pictorial History of the Dead End Kids.* New York: Citadel, 1987.

Heale, M.J. *The Sixties in America: History, Politics and Protest.* Chicago: Fitzroy Dearborn, 2001.

Heath, Joseph. *Nation of Rebels: Why Counterculture Became Consumer Culture.* New York: HarperBusiness, 2004.

Hebdige, Dick. *Cut 'n' Mix: Culture, Identity, and Caribbean Music.* London: Methuen, 1987.

———. *Subculture: The Meaning of Style.* London: Methuen, 1979; New York: Routledge, 1987.

Heckman, Don. "Folk Singer Carolyn Hester Is Back—Still Feisty, Still Full of Concerns." *Los Angeles Times,* February 11, 1989, part V.

Heidenry, John. *What Wild Ecstasy: The Rise and Fall of the Sexual Revolution.* New York: Simon and Schuster, 1997.

Heirich, Max. *The Beginning: Berkeley, 1964.* New York: Columbia University Press, 1971.

Hellmann, John. *Fables of Fact: The New Journalism as New Fiction.* Urbana: University of Illinois Press, 1981.

Hemingway, Ernest. *A Moveable Feast.* New York: Charles Scribner's Sons, 1964.

Hendra, Tony. *Going Too Far.* New York: Doubleday, 1987.

Hennessee, Judith. *Betty Friedan: Her Life.* New York: Random House, 1999.

Henry, Astrid. *Not My Mother's Sister: Generational Conflict and Third-Wave Feminism.* Bloomington: Indiana University Press, 2004.

Henry, Tricia. *Break All Rules!: Punk Rock and the Making of a Style.* Studies in the Fine Arts. Ann Arbor, MI: UMI Research Press, 1989.

Herlihy, David V. *Bicycle: The History.* New Haven, CT: Yale University Press, 2004.

Herndon, Venable. *James Dean: A Short Life.* Garden City, NY: Doubleday, 1974.

Hersch, Charles. *Democratic Artworks: Politics and the Arts from Trilling to Dylan.* Albany: State University of New York Press, 1998.

Hess, David J. *Science in the New Age: The Paranormal, Its Defenders and Debunkers, and American Culture.* Madison: University of Wisconsin Press, 1993.

Hewitt, Kim. *Mutilating the Body: Identity in Blood and Ink.* Madison: University of Wisconsin Press, 1997.

Heylin, Clinton. *All Yesterdays' Parties: The Velvet Underground in Print: 1966–1971.* Cambridge, MA: Da Capo, 2005.

Heymann, C. David. *Ezra Pound, The Last Rower: A Political Profile.* New York: Viking, 1976.

Heywood, Leslie, and Jennifer Drake, eds. *Third Wave Agenda: Being Feminist, Doing Feminism.* Minneapolis: University of Minnesota Press, 1997.

Hickey, Isabel M. *Astrology: A Cosmic Science.* Sebastopol, CA: CRCS, 1992.

Hickman, Timothy A. "Heroin Chic: The Visual Culture of Narcotic Addiction." *Third Text* 16:2 (2002): 119–36.

Hicks, Jimmie, ed. "Some Letters Concerning the Knights of the Golden Circle in Texas, 1860–1861." *Southwestern Historical Quarterly* 65 (1961): 80–86.

Higgins, Dick. "The Origin of Happening." *American Speech* 51:3/4 (Autumn–Winter 1976): 268–71.

Higgs, John. *I Have America Surrounded: The Life of Timothy Leary.* Fort Lee, NJ: Barricade, 2006.

Hill, Marvin S. *Quest for Refuge: The Mormon Flight from American Pluralism.* Salt Lake City: Signature, 1989.

Hill, Robert A., ed. *The Marcus Garvey and Universal Negro Improvement Association Papers.* Berkeley: University of California Press, 1987.

Hilliard, David, and Donald Weise, eds. *The Huey P. Newton Reader.* New York: Seven Stories, 2002.

Hilt, Michael L., and Jeremy H. Lipschultz. *Mass Media, An Aging Population and the Baby Boomers.* New York: Lawrence Erlbaum, 2005.

Himmelstein, Hal. *Television Myth and the American Mind.* New York: Praeger, 1984.

Hinckley, Jim, and Jon G. Robinson. *Big Book of Car Culture: The Armchair Guide to Automotive Americana.* St. Paul, MN: Motorbooks, 2005.

Hinds, William Alfred. *American Communities and Co-operative Colonies.* 2nd ed. Philadelphia: Porcupine, 1959.

Hine, Robert V. *California's Utopian Colonies.* Berkeley: University of California Press, 1983.

Hirsch, Jerrold. *Portrait of America: A Cultural History of the Federal Writers' Project.* Chapel Hill: University of North Carolina Press, 2003.

Hitchens, Christopher. "On the Imagination of Conspiracy." In *For the Sake of Argument: Essays and Minority Reports.* London: Verso, 1993.

Hixson, Richard. *Pornography and the Justices: The Supreme Court and the Intractable Obscenity Problem.* Carbondale: Southern Illinois University Press, 1996.

Hixson, Walter L, ed. *The Vietnam Antiwar Movement.* New York: Garland, 2000.

Hoberman, J., and Jonathon Rosenbaum. *Midnight Movies.* New York: Harper & Row, 1983.

Hobhouse, Janet. *Everybody Who Was Anybody: A Biography of Gertrude Stein.* New York: Putnam, 1975.

Hoffman, Abbie. *The Autobiography of Abbie Hoffman.* 2nd ed. New York: Four Walls Eight Windows, 2000.

———. *Revolution for the Hell of It.* New York: Dial, 1968; New York: Pocket Books, 1970.

———. *Soon to Be a Major Motion Picture.* New York: Putnam, 1980.

———. *Steal This Book.* New York: Pirate Editions, 1971.

Hoffman, Abbie, and Daniel Simon. *The Best of Abbie Hoffman.* New York: Four Walls Eight Windows, 1989.

Hoffman, Frederick, J. Charles Allen, and Carolyn F. Ulrich. *The Little Magazine: A History and a Bibliography.* Princeton, NJ: Princeton University Press, 1947.

Hofmann, Albert. *LSD: My Problem Child.* Los Angeles: Jeremy P. Tarcher, 1983.

Hofstadter, Richard. "The Paranoid Style in American Politics." *Harper's,* November 1964.

Hogeland, Lisa Marie. *Feminism and Its Fictions: The Consciousness-Raising Novel and the Women's Liberation Movement.* Philadelphia: University of Pennsylvania Press, 1998.

Hogrefe, Jeffrey. *O'Keeffe: The Life of an American Legend.* New York: Bantam, 1992.

Holiday, Billie, with William Dufty. *Lady Sings the Blues.* 1956. New York: Penguin, 1984.

Holland, Julie, ed. *Ecstasy: The Complete Guide. A Comprehensive Look at the Risks and Benefits of MDMA.* Rochester, NY: Park Street, 2001.

Hollenweger, Walter. *Pentecostalism: Origins and Developments Worldwide.* Peabody, MA: Hendrickson, 1997.

Holloway, Joseph E., ed. *Africanisms in American Culture.* Bloomington and Indianapolis: Indiana University Press, 1990.

Holm, D.K., ed. *R. Crumb: Conversations.* Jackson: University Press of Mississippi, 2004.

———. *Robert Crumb.* Rev. ed. London: Pocket Essentials, 2005.

Holsworth, Robert D. *Public Interest Liberalism and the Crisis of Affluence: Reflections on Nader, Environmentalism, and the Politics of a Sustainable Society.* Boston: G.K. Hall, 1980.

Holt, John. *Instead of Education: Ways to Help People Do Things Better.* New York: Dutton, 1976.

Holtz, Geoffrey T. *Welcome to the Jungle: The Why Behind "Generation X."* New York: St. Martin's, 1995.

Homberger, Eric. *American Writers and Radical Politics, 1900–39: Equivocal Commitments.* London: Macmillan, 1986.

———. *John Reed.* Manchester, UK: Manchester University Press, 1990.

———, ed. *John Reed and the Russian Revolution: Uncollected Articles, Letters, and Speeches on Russia.* New York: St. Martin's, 1992.

———. *New York City: A Cultural and Literary Companion.* New York: Interlink, 2003.

Honoré, Carl. *In Praise of Slow: How a Worldwide Movement Is Challenging the Cult of Speed.* New York: HarperSanFrancisco, 2004.

Hopfer, Christian, Bruce Mendleson, James M. Van Leeuwen, Susan Kelly, and Sabrina Hooks. "Club Drug Use Among Youths in Treatment for Substance Abuse." *The American Journal of Drug Addictions* 15:1 (2006): 94–99.

Hopkins, Jerry. *Elvis: A Biography.* New York: Simon and Schuster, 1971.

Hopkins, Jerry, and Danny Sugerman. *No One Here Gets Out Alive.* New York: Warner, 1995.

Horn, Barbara Lee. *The Age of Hair: Evolution and Impact of Broadway's First Rock Musical.* New York: Greenwood, 1991.

Horne, Gerald. *Black and Red: W.E.B. Du Bois and the Afro-American Response to the Cold War, 1944–1963.* Albany: State University of New York Press, 1986.

Horowitz, Irving Louis, ed. *Science, Sin, and Scholarship: The Politics of Reverend Moon and the Unification Church.* Cambridge, MA: MIT Press.

Hoskyns, Barney. *Glam: Bowie, Bolan and the Glitter Rock Revolution.* New York: Pocket Books, 1998.

Hostetler, John A., ed. *Amish Roots: A Treasury of History, Wisdom, and Lore.* Baltimore: Johns Hopkins University Press, 1989.

———. *Amish Society.* 4th ed. Baltimore: Johns Hopkins University Press, 1993.

Houdini, Harry. *Houdini: A Magician among the Spirits.* New York: Fredonia, 2002.

———. *Houdini on Magic.* New York: Dover, 1953.

Houellebecq, Michel. *H.P Lovecraft: Against the World, Against Life.* Trans. Dorna Khazeni. San Francisco, CA: Believer, 2005.

House Committee on Un-American Activities. *Hearings Regarding the Communist Infiltration of the Motion Picture Industry.* 80th Cong., 1st sess., 1947.

Howard, Albert. *The War in the Soil.* Emmaus, PA: Rodale, 1946.

Howe, Daniel Walker. *The Unitarian Conscience: Harvard Moral Philosophy, 1805–1861.* Cambridge, MA: Harvard University Press, 1970.

Howe, Irving, and Kenneth Libo. *World of Our Fathers: The Journey of the East European Jews to America and the Life They Found and Made.* New York: Simon and Schuster, 1976.

Howe, Neil, and William Strauss. *Millennials Rising: The Next Great Generation.* New York: Random House, 2000.

———. "The New Generation Gap." *The Atlantic Monthly,* December 1992, 67–87.

Howell, John. *Laurie Anderson.* New York: Thunder's Mouth, 1992.

Howlett, John. *James Dean: A Biography.* New York: Simon and Schuster, 1975.

Howorth, Lisa N. "Graffiti." In *Handbook of American Popular Culture,* ed. Thomas M. Inge. 2nd. ed. New York: Greenwood, 1989.

Hoye, Jacob, ed. *MTV Uncensored.* New York: Pocket Books, 2001.

Hoyser, Catherine E., and Lorena Laura Stookey. *Tom Robbins: A Critical Companion.* Westport, CT: Greenwood, 1997.

Hrebeniak, Michael. *Action Writing: Jack Kerouac's Wild Form.* Carbondale: Southern Illinois University Press, 2006.

Hubbard, L. Ron. *Scientology: The Fundamentals of Thought.* Los Angeles: Bridge, 1997.

Hubbard, Richard. *The Jesus Freaks.* New York: Pyramid, 1972.

Hudson, David. *Memoir of Jemima Wilkinson.* 1844. New York: AMS, 1972.

Huerta, Jorge A. *Chicano Theater: Themes and Forms.* Tempe, AZ: Bilingual Press/Editorial Bilingue, 1982.

Huggins, Nathan. *Harlem Renaissance.* New York: Oxford University Press, 1971.

Hughes, Langston. *The Collected Works of Langston Hughes.* Ed. Arnold Rampersad. Columbia: University of Missouri Press, 2001–2004.

Humes, D. Joy. *Oswald Garrison Villard, Liberal of the 1920s.* Syracuse, NY: Syracuse University Press, 1960.

Hunt, Dana. "Rise of Hallucinogen Use." In *National Institute of Justice: Research in Brief.* Washington, DC: United States Department of Justice, 1997.

Hurston, Zora Neale. *Tell My Horse.* New York: HarperPerennial, 1990.

Hutchinson, George. *The Harlem Renaissance in Black and White.* Cambridge, MA: Belknap Press, 1995.

Hutton, Ronald. *The Triumph of the Moon: A History of Modern Pagan Witchcraft.* Oxford, UK: Oxford University Press, 1999.

Huxley, Aldous. *Selected Letters.* Chicago: Ivan R. Dee, 2007.

Iacobbo, Karen, and Michael Iacobbo. *Vegetarian America: A History.* Westport, CT: Praeger, 2004.

Industrial Workers of the World. *Proceedings of the First Convention of the Industrial Workers of the World.* New York: Merit, 1969.

Inglis, Brian. *Natural and Supernatural: A History of the Paranormal.* Garden City Park, NY: Avery, 1992.

International Forum on Globalization. *Alternatives to Economic Globalization: A Better World Is Possible.* San Francisco: Berrett-Koehler, 2002.

Israel, Betsy. *Bachelor Girl: The Secret History of Single Women in the Twentieth Century.* New York: HarperCollins, 2002.

Isserman, Maurice. *If I Had a Hammer: The Death of the Old Left and the Birth of the New Left.* Urbana: University of Illinois Press, 1993.

Iversen, Leslie. *Speed, Ecstasy, Ritalin: The Science of Amphetamines.* New York: Oxford University Press, 2006.

Jackman, Ian, ed. *Con Men.* New York: Simon and Schuster, 2003.

Jacobs, Louis. *Their Heads in Heaven: Unfamiliar Aspects of Hasidism.* Portland, OR: Vallentine-Mitchell, 2005.

Jacobs, Ron. *The Way the Wind Blew: A History of the Weather Underground.* New York: Verso, 1997.

Jacoby, Susan. *Freethinkers: A History of American Secularism.* New York: Metropolitan Books, 2004.

Jagger, Mick, Keith Richards, Charlie Watts, and Ronnie Wood. *According to the Rolling Stones.* San Francisco: Chronicle, 2003.

James, C.L.R. *Marxism for Our Times: C.L.R. James On Revolutionary Organization.* Ed. Martin Glaberman. Jackson: University Press of Mississippi, 1999.

Jay, Karla. *Out of the Closets: Voices of Gay Liberation.* New York: New York University Press, 1992.

———. *Tales of the Lavender Menace: A Memoir of Liberation.* New York: Basic Books, 2000.

Jeansonne, Glen. *Transformation and Reaction: America, 1921–1945.* New York: HarperCollins, 1993.

Jeffreys-Jones, Rhodri. *Peace Now! American Society and the Ending of the Vietnam War.* New Haven, CT: Yale University Press, 1999.

Jeffries, Judson L. *Huey P. Newton: The Radical Theorist.* Jackson: University Press of Mississippi, 2002.

Jehovah's Witnesses: Proclaimers of God's Kingdom. Brooklyn: Watchtower Bible and Tract Society of New York, 1993.

Jenkins, Philip. *Decade of Nightmares: The End of the Sixties and the Making of Eighties America.* New York: Oxford University Press, 2006.

Jezer, Marty. *Abbie Hoffman: American Rebel.* New Brunswick, NJ: Rutgers University Press, 1993.

Joachimides, Christos, and Norman Rosenthal, eds. *American Art in the 20th Century: Painting and Sculpture 1913–1993.* New York: Neues, 1993.

Johnson, Ford. *Confessions of a God Seeker: A Journey to Higher Consciousness.* Silver Spring, MD: ONE, 2003.

Johnson, Tracy, ed. *Encounters with Bob Dylan.* Daly City, CA: Humble Press, 2000.

Johnson-Woods, Toni. *Blame Canada!: South Park and Contemporary Culture.* New York: Routledge, 2006.

Johnston, Johanna. *Mrs. Satan.* New York: G.P. Putnam's Sons, 1967.

———. *Satan: The Incredible Saga of Victoria C. Woodhull.* New York: Putnam, 1967.

Johnston, Robert D., ed. *The Politics of Healing: Histories of Alternative Medicine in Twentieth-Century North America.* New York: Routledge, 2004.

Jones, Charles E., ed. *The Black Panther Party Reconsidered.* Baltimore: Black Classic, 1998.

Jones, Landon Y. *Great Expectations: America and the Baby Boom Generation.* New York: Coward-McCann, 1980; New York: Ballantine, 1986.

Jones, LeRoi. *The Baptism and The Toilet.* New York: Grove, 1966.

Joost, Nicolas, and Alvin Sullivan. *D.H. Lawrence and* The Dial. Carbondale: Southern Illinois University Press, 1970.

Joseph, Jamal. *Tupac Shakur Legacy.* New York: Simon and Schuster, 2006.

Joseph, Miriam, and Julian Durlacher. *Speed: Its History and Lore.* London: Carlton, 2002.

Joseph, Peniel, E. *Waiting 'Till the Midnight Hour' A Narrative History of Black Power in America.* New York: Henry Holt & Company, 2006.

Joshi, S.T. *A Dreamer and a Visionary: H.P. Lovecraft and His Time.* Liverpool: Liverpool University Press, 2001.

Judah, J. Stillson. *Hare Krishna and the Counterculture.* New York: John Wiley and Sons, 1974.

Judis, John B., and Ruy Teixeira. *The Emerging Democratic Majority.* New York: Scribner's, 2002.

Jules-Rosette, Bennetta. *Josephine Baker in Art and Life.* Urbana: University of Illinois Press, 2007.

Juno, Andrea, ed. *Dangerous Drawings: Interviews with Comix and Graphix Artists.* New York: Juno, 1997.

Kaiser, Charles. *1968 in America: Music, Politics, Chaos, Counterculture, and the Shaping of a Generation.* New York: Weidenfeld and Nicolson, 1988.

Kaiser, David. *American Tragedy: Kennedy, Johnson, and the Origins of the Vietnam War.* Cambridge, MA: Harvard University Press, 2000.

Kalush, William, and Larry Sloman. *The Secret Life of Houdini: The Making of America's First Superhero.* New York: Holiday House, 2000.

Kaminski, Marek M. *Games Prisoners Play.* Princeton, NJ: Princeton University Press, 2004.

Kanellos, Nicolás, ed. *The Hispanic Literary Companion.* Detroit, MI: Visible Ink, 1997.

Kanter, Rosabeth Moss. *Commitment and Community: Communes and Utopias in Sociological Perspective.* Cambridge, MA: Harvard University Press, 1972.

———. *Communes: Creating and Managing the Collective Life.* New York: Harper & Row, 1973.

Kaplan, Judy, and Linn Shapiro. *Red Diapers: Growing Up in the Communist Left.* Carbondale: University of Illinois Press, 1998.

Kaprow, Allan. *Essays on the Blurring of Art and Life.* Ed. Jeff Kelley. Berkeley: University of California Press, 2003.

———. *Some Recent Happenings.* New York: Something Else Press, 1966.

Karch, Steven B. *A Brief History of Cocaine.* 2nd ed. Boca Raton, FL: CRC, 2006.

Kardou, Janet. *Robert Mapplethorpe: The Perfect Moment.* Philadelphia: Institute of Contemporary Art, 1990.

Karlsen, Carol. *The Devil in the Shape of a Woman: Witchcraft in Colonial New England.* New York: W.W. Norton, 1987.

Karp, Josh. *A Futile and Stupid Gesture: How Doug Kenney and National Lampoon Changed Comedy Forever.* Chicago: Chicago Review, 2006.

Kars, Marjoleine. *Breaking Loose Together: The Regulator Rebellion in Pre-Revolutionary North Carolina.* Chapel Hill: University of North Carolina Press, 2002.

Katz, Eric, Andrew Light, and David Rothenberg, eds. *Beneath the Surface: Critical Essays in the Philosophy of Deep Ecology.* Cambridge, MA: MIT Press, 2000.

Katz, Vincent, ed. *Black Mountain College: Experiment in Art.* Essays by Martin Brody. Cambridge, MA: MIT Press, 2002.

Kazin, Michael. *The Populist Persuasion: An American History.* New York: Basic Books, 1995.

Kehoe, Alice Beck. *The Ghost Dance: Ethnohistory and Revitalization.* San Francisco: Holt, Rinehart and Winston, 1989.

Kelley, Trevor, and Leslie Simon. *Everybody Hurts: An Essential Guide to Emo Culture.* New York: HarperEntertainment, 2007.

Kellner, Douglas. *Herbert Marcuse and the Crisis of Marxism.* Berkeley: University of California Press, 1984.

Kelly, Robert J. *Encyclopedia of Organized Crime in the United States: From Capone's Chicago to the New Urban Underworld.* Westport, CT: Greenwood, 2000.

Keltz, Iris. *Scrapbook of a Taos Hippie: Tribal Tales from the Heart of a Cultural Revolution.* El Paso, TX: Cinco Puntos, 2000.

Kendrick, Walter. *The Secret Museum: Pornography in Modern Culture.* Berkeley: University of California Press, 1987.

Kennedy, David M. *Birth Control in America: The Career of Margaret Sanger.* New Haven, CT: Yale University Press, 1970; 2001.

Kennedy, Elizabeth Lapovsky, and Madeline D. Davis. *Boots of Leather, Slippers of Gold: The History of a Lesbian Community.* New York: Routledge, 1993.

Kennedy, George, Jr., ed. *A Historical Guide to Edgar Allan Poe.* New York: Oxford University Press, 2001.

Kennedy, Richard S., ed. *Selected Poems: E.E. Cummings.* New York: Liveright, 1994.

Kerouac, Jack. *The Dharma Bums.* New York: Penguin Modern Classics, 2000.

———. *On the Road.* New York: Viking, 1957.

———. "The Roaming Beatniks." In *Kerouac and Friends: A Beat Generation Album,* ed. Fred W. McDarrah and Timothy S. McDarrah. New York: Thunder's Mouth, 2002.

Kerr, Howard. *Mediums and Spirit-Rappers and Roaring Radicals: Spiritualism in American Literature, 1850–1900.* Urbana: University of Illinois Press, 1973.

Kershaw, Alex. *Jack London: A Life.* London: HarperCollins, 1997.

Kersnowski, Frank L., and Alice Hughes, eds. *Conversations with Henry Miller.* Jackson: University Press of Mississippi, 1994.

Kersten, Andrew E. *A. Philip Randolph: A Life in the Vanguard.* Lanham, MD: Rowman & Littlefield, 2006.

Kesey, Ken. *One Flew Over the Cuckoo's Nest.* New York: Signet, 1962.

Keyes, Cheryl L. *Rap Music and Street Consciousness.* Music in American Life. Urbana: University of Illinois Press, 2004.

Kim, Sojin. *Chicano Graffiti and Murals: The Neighborhood Art of Peter Quezada.* Jackson: University of Mississippi Press, 1995.

Kimball, Roger. *The Long March: How the Cultural Revolution of the 1960s Changed America.* San Francisco: Encounter, 2000.

Kimeldorf, Howard. *Battling for American Labor: Wobblies, Craft Workers, and the Making of the Union Movement.* Berkeley: University of California Press, 1999.

Kimmel, Michael, and Michael Kaufman. "Weekend Warriors: The New Men's Movement." In *The Politics of Manhood: Profeminist Men Respond to the Mythopoetic Men's Movement (and the Mythopoetic Leaders Answer),* ed. Michael Kimmel. Philadelphia: Temple University Press, 1995.

Kinnamon, Keneth, and Michel Fabre, eds. *Conversations with Richard Wright.* Jackson: University Press of Mississippi, 1993.

Kirby, Michael. *Happenings: An Illustrated Anthology.* New York: E.P. Dutton, 1965.

Kirk, Andrew. *Counterculture Green: The Whole Earth Catalog and American Environmentalism.* Lawrence: University Press of Kansas, 2007.

Kisch, John, and Edward Mapp. *A Separate Cinema: Fifty Years of Black-Cast Posters.* New York: Noonday, 1992.

Kissel, Susan S. *In Common Cause: The "Conservative" Frances Trollope and the "Radical" Frances Wright.* Bowling Green, OH: Bowling Green State University Popular Press, 1983.

Kitwana, Bakari. *The Rap on Gangsta Rap: Who Run It? Gangsta Rap and Visions of Black Violence.* Chicago: Third World, 1994.

Klatch, Rebecca E. *A Generation Divided: The New Left, the New Right, and the 1960s.* Berkeley: University of California Press, 1999.

Klaw, Spencer. *Without Sin: The Life and Death of the Oneida Community.* New York: Allen Lane, 1993.

Klein, Joe. *Woody Guthrie: A Life.* New York: Random House, 1980.

Klein, Malcolm W., and Cheryl L. Maxson. *Street Gang Patterns and Policies.* New York: Oxford University Press, 2006.

Kline, Benjamin. *First Along the River: A Brief History of the U.S. Environmental Movement.* Lanham, MD: Rowman & Littlefield, 2007.

Kline, David, Daniel Burstein, Arne J. De Keijzer, and Paul Berger. *Blog!: How the Newest Media Revolution Is Changing Politics, Business, and Culture.* New York: CDS, 2005.

Klinkowitz, Jerome. *The Vonnegut Effect.* Columbia: University of South Carolina Press, 2004.

Kluger, Richard. *Ashes to Ashes: America's Hundred-Year Cigarette War, the Public Health, and the Unabashed Triumph of Philip Morris.* New York: Alfred A. Knopf, 1996.

Knight, Peter. *Conspiracy Culture: From the Kennedy Assassination to The X-Files.* New York: Routledge, 2000.

Koekkoek, Brad, and Mike Helm. *The First Eugene, Oregon Coloring Book.* Eugene, OR: Rainy Day, 1979.

Kolata, Gina. *Ultimate Fitness: The Quest for Truth About Exercise and Health.* New York: Picador, 2004

Kopay, David, and Perry Dean Young. *The David Kopay Story: The Coming-out Story that Made Football History.* Los Angeles: Advocate, 2001.

Kopp, James J. "Looking Backward at Edward Bellamy's Influence in Oregon, 1888–1936." *Oregon Historical Quarterly* 104:1 (Spring 2003).

Kornfeld, Eve. *Margaret Fuller: A Brief Biography with Documents.* Boston: Bedford, 1997.

Kozak, Robert. *This Ain't No Disco: The Story of CBGB.* Boston: Faber and Faber, 1988.

Kristal, Hilly. *CBGB & OMFUG: Thirty Years from the Home of Underground Punk.* New York: Harry N. Abrams, 2005.

Kramer, Peter. "Post-Classical Hollywood." In *The Oxford Guide to Film Studies,* ed. John Hill and Pamela Church Gibson. New York: Oxford University Press, 1998.

Krassner, Paul. *How a Satirical Editor Became a Yippie Conspirator in Ten Easy Years.* New York: Putnam, 1971.

———. *Murder at the Conspiracy Convention and Other American Absurdities.* Fort Lee, NJ: Barricade, 2000.

———. *One Hand Jerking: Reports From an Investigative Satirist.* New York: Seven Stories, 2005.

———. *Paul Krassner's Impolite Interviews.* New York: Seven Stories, 1999.

Kraybill, Donald B. *The Riddle of Amish Culture.* Rev. ed. Baltimore: Johns Hopkins University Press, 2001.

Kraybill, Donald B., and Carl D. Bowman. *On the Backroad to Heaven: Old Order Hutterites, Mennonites, Amish, and Brethren.* Baltimore: Johns Hopkins University Press, 2002.

Kraybill, Donald B., and Steven M. Nolt. *Amish Enterprise: From Plows to Profits.* 2nd ed. Baltimore: Johns Hopkins University Press, 2004.

Kriedberg, Marvin A., and Merton G. Henry. *History of Military Mobilization in the United States Army, 1775–1945.* Stockton, CA: University Press of the Pacific, 2005.

Kripal, Jeffrey John, and Glenn W. Schuck, eds. *On the Edge of the Future: Esalen and the Evolution of American Culture.* Bloomington: Indiana University Press, 2005.

Krohn, Claus-Dieter. *Intellectuals in Exile: Refugee Scholars and the New School for Social Research.* Trans. Rita and Robert Kimber. Amherst: University of Massachusetts Press, 1993.

Kruchkow, Diane, and Curt Johnson, eds. *Green Isle in the Sea: An Informal History of the Alternative Press, 1960–85.* Highland Park, IL: December, 1986.

Kubica, Chris, and Will Hochman, eds. *Letters to J.D. Salinger.* Madison: University of Wisconsin Press, 2002.

Kuehn, Robert, ed. *Aldous Huxley: A Collection of Critical Essays.* Englewood Cliffs, NJ: Prentice Hall, 1974.

Kuersteiner, Kurt. *The Unofficial Guide to the Art of Jack T. Chick: Chick Tracts, Crusader Comics, and Battle Cry Newspapers.* Atglen, PA: Schiffer, 2004.

Kuhn, Cynthia, Scott Swartzwelder, and Wilkie Wilson. *Buzzed: The Straight Facts about the Most Used and Abused Drugs from Alcohol to Ecstasy.* New York: W.W. Norton, 1988.

Kuhn, Maggie. *No Stone Unturned: The Life and Times of Maggie Kuhn.* New York: Ballantine, 1991.

Kuhn, Maggie, and Margaret Kuhn. *Get Out There and Do Something about Injustice.* New York: Friendship, 1972.

Kunen, James Simon. *The Strawberry Statement: Notes of a College Revolutionary, 1968/69.* St. James, NY: Brandywine, 1995.

Kunstler, William Moses, and Sheila Isenberg. *My Life as a Radical Lawyer.* Secaucus, NJ: Carol, 1994.

Kurtz, Paul. *A Skeptic's Handbook of Parapsychology.* Buffalo, NY: Prometheus, 1985.

Kutolowski, Kathleen Smith. "Antimasonry Reexamined: Social Bases of the Grass-Roots Party." *Journal of American History* 71 (1984): 269–93.

La Barre, Weston. *The Peyote Cult.* 5th ed. Norman: University of Oklahoma Press, 1989.

Ladd, Jim. *Radio Waves: Life and Revolution on the FM Dial.* New York: St. Martin's, 1991.

Laffan, Barry. *Communal Organization and Social Transition: A Case Study from the Counterculture of the Sixties and Seventies.* New York: Peter Lang, 1997.

Lager, Fred "Chico." *The Inside Scoop: How Two Real Guys Built a Business with a Social Conscience and a Sense of Humor.* New York: Crown, 1994.

Lalich, Janja. *Bounded Choice: True Believers and Charismatic Cults.* Berkeley: University of California Press, 2004.

Lalicki, Tom. *Spellbinder: The Life of Harry Houdini.* New York: Atria, 2006.

Lamb, Christopher. "Changing With the Times: The World According to 'Doonesbury.'" *Journal of Popular Culture* 23 (1990): 113–29.

Lamy, Philip. *Millennium Rage: Survivalists, White Supremacists, and the Doomsday Prophecy.* New York: Plenum, 1996.

Land, Jeff. *Active Radio: Pacifica's Brash Experiment.* Minneapolis: University of Minnesota Press, 1999.

Landay, Lori. "The Flapper Film: Comedy, Dance, and Jazz Age Kinaesthetics." In *A Feminist Reader in Early Cinema,* ed. Jennifer M. Bean and Diane Negra. Durham, NC: Duke University Press, 2002.

Landis, Arthur H. *The Abraham Lincoln Brigade.* New York: Citadel, 1967.

———. *Death in the Olive Groves: American Volunteers in the Spanish Civil War, 1936–1939.* New York: Paragon House, 1989.

Lane, David Christopher. *The Making of a Spiritual Movement: The Untold Story of Paul Twitchell and Eckankar.* New York: Garland, 1993.

Lang, Amy Schrager. *Prophetic Woman: Anne Hutchinson and the Problem of Dissent in the Literature of New England.* Berkeley: University of California Press, 1987.

LaPlante, Eve. *American Jezebel: The Uncommon Life of Anne Hutchinson, the Woman Who Defied the Puritans.* New York: HarperCollins, 2004.

Larson, Christine A. *Alternative Medicine.* Westport, CT: Greenwood, 2007.

Lasar, Matthew. *Pacifica Radio: The Rise of an Alternative Network.* Philadelphia: Temple University Press, 2000.

Lasn, Kalle. *Culture Jam: How to Reverse America's Suicidal Consumer Binge—and Why We Must.* New York: Quill/HarperCollins, 2000.

"Laugh Trackers." Readings. *Harper's Magazine* (March 2006).

Lauter, Paul, and Florence Howe. *Conspiracy of the Young.* Cleveland, OH: World, 1970.

Lawrence, Tim. *Love Saves the Day: A History of American Dance Music Culture, 1970–1979.* Durham, NC: Duke University Press, 2003.

Lawson, Don. *The Abraham Lincoln Brigade: Americans Fighting Fascism in the Spanish Civil War.* New York: T.Y. Crowell, 1989.

Le Beau, Bryan F. *The Atheist: Madalyn Murray O'Hair.* New York: New York University Press, 2003.

Le Blanc, Paul. *A Short History of the U.S. Working Class: From Colonial Times to the Twenty-First Century.* Amherst, NY: Humanity, 1999.

Leach, Joseph. *Bright Particular Star: The Life and Times of Charlotte Cushman.* New Haven, CT: Yale University Press, 1970.

Lear, Linda. *Rachel Carson: Witness for Nature.* New York: Henry Holt, 1997.

Learner, Laurence. *The Paper Revolutionaries: The Rise of the Underground Press.* New York: Simon and Schuster, 1972.

Lears, Jackson. *Fables of Abundance: A Cultural History of Advertising in America.* New York: Basic Books, 1994.

Leary, Timothy. *High Priest.* New York: World, 1968.

LeBaron, Sarah, and Jessica Pecsevne, eds. *Oberlin College: Off the Record.* Pittsburgh: College Prowler, 2005.

Lee, Martha M. *Earth First!: Environmental Apocalypse.* Syracuse, NY: Syracuse University Press, 1995.

Lee, Martin A., and Bruce Shalin. *Acid Dreams: The Complete Social History of LSD: The CIA, the Sixties and Beyond.* New York: Grove, 1985.

Leeds, Barry H. *Ken Kesey.* New York: Frederick Ungar, 1981.

Lefever, Harry G. "When the Saints Go Riding In: Santería in Cuba and the United States." *Journal for the Scientific Study of Religion* 35:3, 1998.

Leftkowitz, Mary R., and Guy Maclean. *Black Athena Revisited.* Chapel Hill: North Carolina University Press, 1996.

Lehnert, Tomek. *Rogues in Robes.* Nevada City, CA: Blue Dolphin, 1997.

Leikin, Steven. "The Citizen Producer: The Rise and Fall of Working-Class Cooperatives in the United States." In *Consumers Against Capitalism? Consumer Cooperation in Europe, North America, and Japan, 1840–1990,* ed. Ellen Furlough and Carl Strikwerda. Lanham, MD: Rowman & Littlefield, 1999.

Lembcke, Jerry. *The Spitting Image: Myth, Memory, and the Legacy of Vietnam.* New York: New York University Press, 1998.

Lemmon, Sarah McCulloh. *Frustrated Patriots: North Carolina and the War of 1812.* Chapel Hill: University of North Carolina Press, 1973.

Leopold, Richard. *Richard Dale Owen: A Biography.* Cambridge, MA: Harvard University Press, 1967.

Lesh, Phil. *Searching for the Sound: My Life with the Grateful Dead.* New York: Little, Brown, 2005.

Lester, Julius. *Look Out Whitey! Black Power's Gon Get Your Mam.* London: Alison & Busby, 1970.

Lesueur, Stephen C. *The 1838 Mormon War in Missouri.* Columbia: University of Missouri Press, 1987.

Leuchtenberg, William E. *Franklin D. Roosevelt and the New Deal.* New York: Harper & Row, 1963.

Lev, Peter. *American Films of the 70s: Conflicting Visions.* Austin: University of Texas Press, 2000.

Levine, David. *Defending the Earth: Debate Between Murray Bookchin and Dave Foreman.* Montreal, Canada: Black Rose, 1991.

Levine, Lawrence W. *Black Culture and Black Consciousness: Afro-American Folk Thought from Slavery to Freedom.* New York: Oxford University Press, 1977.

Levine, Robert S. *Martin R. Delany: A Documentary Reader.* Chapel Hill: University of North Carolina Press, 2003.

Levinson, Paul. *Digital McLuhan: A Guide to the Information Millennium.* London: Routledge, 1999.

Levitas, Daniel. *The Terrorist Next Door: The Militia Movement and the Radical Right.* New York: Thomas Dunne, 2002.

Lévy, Maurice. *Lovecraft: A Study in the Fantastic.* Trans. S.T. Joshi. Detroit: Wayne State University Press, 1988.

Lewis, David Levering. *W.E.B. Du Bois: Biography of a Race, 1868–1919.* New York: Henry Holt, 1993.

———. *When Harlem Was in Vogue.* New York: Random House, 1981.

Lewis, James R. *Legitimating New Religions.* New Brunswick, NJ: Rutgers University Press, 2003.

———. *Odd Gods: New Religions and the Cult Controversy.* New York: Prometheus, 2001.

Lewis, James R., and J. Gordon Melton, eds. *Perspectives on the New Age.* Albany: State University of New York Press, 1992.

Lewis, Rupert, and Patrick Bryan, eds. *Garvey: His Work and Impact.* Trenton, NJ: Africa World Press, 1991.

Lewisohn, Mark. *EMI's The Complete Beatles Recording Sessions: The Official Story of the Abbey Road Years.* London: Hamlyn, 1990.

Lhamon, W.T., Jr. *Jump Jim Crow: Lost Plays, Lyrics, and Street Prose of the First Atlantic Popular Culture.* Cambridge, MA: Harvard University Press, 2003.

Lichtenberg, Jacqueline, Sondra Marshak, and Joan Winston. *Star Trek Lives! Personal Notes and Anecdotes.* New York: Bantam, 1975.

Lichtman, Jane. *Bring Your Own Bag: A Report on Free Universities.* Washington, DC: American Association for Higher Education, 1973.

Lieberman, Robbie. *My Song Is My Weapon: People's Songs, American Communism, and the Politics of Culture, 1930–1950.* Urbana: University of Illinois Press, 1989.

Liebman, Arthur. *Jews and the Left.* New York: John Wiley and Sons, 1979.

Light, Alan. *The Vibe History of Hip Hop.* New York: Three Rivers, 1999.

Lighter, Jonathan E., ed. *Historical Dictionary of American Slang.* 2 vols. New York: Random House, 1994, 1997.

Lincoln, E. Eric. *The Black Muslims in America.* 3rd ed. Grand Rapids, MI: William B. Eerdmans, 1994.

Lindenmeyer, Kriste. *The Greatest Generation Grows Up: American Childhood in the 1930s.* New York: Ivan Dee, 2005.

Lindsay, Vachel. *Adventures while Preaching the Gospel of Beauty.* New York: Kennerley, 1914.

Linzmayer, Owen W. *Apple Confidential: The Real Story of Apple Computer, Inc.* Berkeley, CA: No Starch, 1999.

Lippard, Lucy R. *Pop Art.* New York: Thames and Hudson, 1985.

Lipton, Peggy. *Breathing Out.* New York: St. Martin's, 2005.

Livingstone, Marco. *Pop Art: A Continuing History.* New York: Harry N. Abrams, 1990.

Loewenstein, Dora, and Philip Dodd. *According to the Rolling Stones.* London: Weidenfeld & Nicolson, 2003.

Lomax, Alan. *The Land Where the Blues Began.* New York: New Press, 2002.

Long, Carolyn Morrow. *Spiritual Merchants: Religion, Magic, and Commerce.* Knoxville: University of Tennessee Press, 2001.

Lopach, James J., and Jean A. Luckowski. *Jeannette Rankin: A Political Woman.* Boulder: University Press of Colorado, 2005.

Lott, Eric. *Love and Theft: Blackface Minstrelsy and the American Working Class.* New York: Oxford University Press, 1993.

Loughery, John. *John Sloan: Painter and Rebel.* New York: Henry Holt, 1995.

Love, Robert. "Fear of Yoga: Super-Love Cults, Commie Swamis, Loose-Limbed Women, and Other Hysteric Headlines." *Utne Reader* (March–April 2007).

Lovelock, James. *Gaia: A New Look at Life on Earth.* 3rd ed. New York: Oxford University Press, 2000.

Loving, Jerome. *Walt Whitman: The Song of Himself.* Berkeley: University of California Press, 1999.

Lowry, Brian. *The Truth Is Out There: The Official Guide to* The X-Files. Vol. 1. New York: HarperPrism, 1995.

Luhan, Mabel Dodge. *Edge of Taos Desert: An Escape to Reality.* Albuquerque: University of New Mexico Press, 1987.

Lumsden, Linda J. *Rampant Women.* Knoxville: University of Tennessee Press, 1997.

Lundquist, James. *Jack London: Adventures, Ideas, and Fiction.* New York: Ungar, 1987.

Lundwall, Sam J. *Science Fiction: What It's All About.* New York: Ace, 1971.

Lynd, Staughton, and Alice Lynd, eds. *Nonviolence in America: A Documentary History.* Rev. ed. Maryknoll, NY: Orbis, 1995.

Lynn, Kenneth S. *Hemingway.* Cambridge, MA: Harvard University Press, 1987.

Lytle, Mark H. *The Gentle Subversive: Rachel Carson, Silent Spring, and the Rise of the Environmental Movement.* New York: Oxford University Press, 2007.

Maaga, Mary McCormick. *Hearing the Voices of Jonestown.* Syracuse, NY: Syracuse University Press, 1998.

Maas, Peter. *The Valachi Papers.* New York: G.P. Putnam's Sons, 1968.

MacAuliffe, Kevin M. *The Great American Newspaper: The Rise and Fall of* The Village Voice. New York: Scribner's, 1978.

MacFarquhar, Larissa. "The Populist: Michael Moore Can Make You Cry." *The New Yorker,* February 16 and 23, 2004.

Machado, Manuel, Jr. *Listen Chicano! An Informal History of the Mexican-American.* Chicago: Nelson-Hall, 1978.

Maciel, David R., and Isidro D. Ortiz, eds. *Chicanas/Chicanos at the Crossroads: Social, Economic, and Political Change.* Tucson: University of Arizona Press, 1996.

MacIntyre, Alasdair C. *After Virtue: A Study in Moral Theory.* 3rd ed. Notre Dame, IN: University of Notre Dame Press, 2007.

Mackay, Daniel. *The Fantasy Role-Playing Game: A New Performing Art.* Jefferson, NC: McFarland, 2001.

MacLean, Nancy. *Behind the Mask of Chivalry: The Making of the Second Ku Klux Klan.* New York: Oxford University Press, 1994.

Madden, David. *Proletarian Writers of the Thirties.* Carbondale: Southern Illinois University Press, 1968.

Mahesh Yogi, Maharishi. *Science of Being and Art of Living: Transcendental Meditation.* New York: Plume, 2001.

Maier, Thomas. *Dr. Spock: An American Life.* New York: Basic Books, 2003.

Mailer, Norman. *The Fight.* Boston: Little, Brown, 1975.

Malcolm X, with Alex Haley. *The Autobiography of Malcolm X.* New York: Grove, 1965.

Malone, Michael. *Infinite Loop.* New York: Doubleday, 1999.

Mandel, Jerry, and Harvey W. Feldman. "The Social History of Teenage Drug Use." In *Teen Drug Use,* ed. George Beschner and Alfred S. Friedman. Lexington, MA: Lexington, 1986.

Mankowitz, Wolf. *Mazeppa, the Lives, Loves, and Legends of Adah Isaacs Menken: A Biographical Quest.* New York: Stein and Day, 1982.

Manso, Peter. *Brando: The Biography.* New York: Hyperion, 1994.

Mantooth, Wes. *You Factory Folks Who Sing This Rhyme Will Surely Understand: Culture, Ideology, and Action in the Gastonia Novels of Myra Page, Grace Lumpkin, and Olive Dargan.* New York: Routledge, 2006.

Manzarek, Ray. *Light My Fire: My Life with the Doors.* New York: G.P. Putnam's Sons, 1998.

Marchand, Phillip. *Marshall McLuhan: The Medium and the Messenger.* Cambridge, MA: MIT Press, 1998.

Marcus, Griel. *Like a Rolling Stone: Bob Dylan at the Crossroads.* New York: PublicAffairs, 2005.

———. *The Old, Weird America: The World of Bob Dylan's Basement Tapes.* New York: Picador, 2001.

Marcuse, Herbert. *One-Dimensional Man: Studies in the Ideology of Advanced Industrial Society.* Boston: Beacon, 1964.

Marek, Jayne E. *Women Editing Modernism: Little Magazines and Literary History.* Lexington: University Press of Kentucky, 1995.

Margolick, David. *Strange Fruit: The Biography of a Song.* New York: Ecco/HarperCollins, 2001.

Marks, Barry A. *E.E. Cummings.* New York: Twayne, 1964.

Marotta, Toby. *The Politics of Homosexuality.* Boston: Houghton Mifflin, 1981.

Marqusee, Mike. *Muhammad Ali and the Spirit of the Sixties.* New York: Verso, 1999.

Marsden, George M. *Fundamentalism and American Culture: The Shaping of Twentieth-Century Evangelicalism, 1870–1925.* 2nd ed. New York: Oxford University Press, 2006.

Marshall, Peter. *Demanding the Impossible: A History of Anarchism.* London: Fontana, 1993.

Marshall, Richard. *Robert Mapplethorpe.* New York: Whitney Museum of American Art, 1988.

Martin, Carolyn A. *Managing Generation Y: Global Citizens Born in the Late Seventies and Early Eighties.* Amherst, MA: HRD, 2001.

Martin, James J. *Men Against the State: The Expositors of Individualist Anarchism in America, 1827–1908.* Colorado Springs, CO.: Ralph Myles, 1970.

Martin, Jay. *The Dialectical Imagination: A History of the Frankfurt School and the Institute of Social Research, 1923–1950.* Berkeley: University of California Press, 1996.

Martin, Malachi. *Hostage to the Devil: The Possession and Exorcism of Five Americans.* New York: Harper, 1992.

Martin, Susan. *Decade of Protest: Political Posters from the United States, Viet Nam, Cuba, 1965–1975.* Santa Monica, CA: Smart Art Press, 1996.

Martin, Tony. *Race First: The Ideological and Organizational Struggles of Marcus Garvey and the Universal Negro Improvement Association.* Westport, CT: Greenwood, 1976.

Martin, Walter R. *The Kingdom of the Cults.* Minneapolis, MN: Bethany House, 1965.

Marvin, Thomas F. *Kurt Vonnegut: A Critical Companion.* Westport, CT: Greenwood, 2002.

Mascia-Lees, Frances E., and Patricia Sharpe, eds. *Tattoo, Torture, Mutilation, and Adornment: The Denaturalization of the Body in Culture and Text.* Albany: State University of New York Press, 1992.

Masters, Robert E.L., and Jean Houston. *The Varieties of Psychedelic Experience.* New York: Dell, 1966.

Maurer, David W. *The American Confidence Man.* Springfield, IL: Charles C. Thomas, 1974.

Mauskopf, Seymour H., and Michael R. McVaugh. *The Elusive Science: Origins of Experimental Psychical Research.* Baltimore: Johns Hopkins University Press, 1980.

Max, Peter. *Peter Max Superposter Book.* New York: Crown, 1971.

May, Elaine Tyler. *Homeward Bound: American Families in the Cold War Era.* New York: Basic Books, 1988.

May, Robert E. *Manifest Destiny's Underworld: Filibustering in Antebellum America.* Chapel Hill: University of North Carolina Press, 2002.

Mayer, Henry. *All on Fire: William Lloyd Garrison and the Abolition of Slavery.* New York: St. Martin's, 1998.

Maynard, John Arthur. *Venice West: The Beat Generation in Southern California.* New Brunswick, NJ: Rutgers University Press, 1993.

McAlmon, Robert. *Being Geniuses Together.* London: Secker and Warburg, 1938.

McCall, Tara. *This Is Not a Rave: In the Shadow of a Subculture.* New York: Thunder's Mouth, 2001.

McCarraher, Eugene. *Christian Critics: Religion and the Impasse in Modern American Social Thought.* Ithaca, NY: Cornell University Press, 2000.

McCarthy, David. *Pop Art.* London: Tate Gallery, 2000.

McCarthy, Eugene J. *The Year of the People.* Garden City, NY: Doubleday, 1969.

McCarthy, Timothy Patrick, and John McMillian, eds. *The Radical Reader: A Documentary History of the American Radical Tradition.* New York: New Press, 2003.

McCartney, John T. *Black Power Ideologies.* Philadelphia: Temple UP, 1992.

McClay, Wilfred M. "Edward Bellamy and the Politics of Meaning." *American Scholar* 64:2 (Spring 1995): 264–72.

McDarrah, Fred W., and Gloria S. McDarrah. "Cedar Street Tavern." In *Beat Generation: Glory Days in Greenwich Village.* New York: Schirmer, 1997.

McFeely, William S. *Frederick Douglass.* New York: W.W. Norton, 1991.

McGloin, John Bernard. *San Francisco: The Story of a City.* San Rafael, CA: Presidio, 1978.

McGrath, Alister. *The Twilight of Atheism: The Rise and Fall of Disbelief in the Modern World.* New York: Doubleday, 2004.

Mcgrath, Tom. *MTV: The Making of a Revolution.* Philadelphia: Running Press, 1996.

McGuire, John Thomas. "From the Courts to the State Legislatures: Social Justice Feminism, Labor Legislation, and the 1920s." *Labor History* 45:2 (Spring 2004): 225–46.

McKeen, William. *Hunter S. Thompson.* Boston: Twayne, 1991.

McKenna, Terence K. *The Archaic Revival: Speculations on Psychedelic Mushrooms, the Amazon, Virtual Reality, UFOs, Evolution, Shamanism, the Rebirth of the Goddess, and the End of History.* San Francisco: HarperSanFrancisco, 1991.

McKennon, Joe. *Pictorial History of the American Carnival.* Sarasota, FL: Carnival, 1971.

McLeod, Kate. *Beetlemania: The Story of the Car that Captured the Hearts of Millions.* New York: Smithmark, 1999.

McLoughlin, William G., ed. *The Diary of Isaac Backus.* 3 vols. Providence, RI: Brown University Press, 1979.

———. *Isaac Backus and the American Pietistic Tradition.* Boston: Little, Brown, 1967.

———. *Isaac Backus on Church, State, and Calvinsim: Pamphlets, 1754–1789.* Cambridge, MA: Harvard University Press, 1968.

McMath, Robert C. *Populist Vanguard: A History of the Southern Farmers' Alliance.* Chapel Hill: University of North Carolina Press, 1975.

McMillian, John. "Electrical Bananas: An Epistemological Inquiry into the Great Banana Hoax of 1967." *The Believer* 25 (June/July 2005): 18–26.

McMillian, John, and Paul Buhle, eds. *The New Left Revisited.* Philadelphia: Temple University Press, 2003.

McNamara, Brooks, and Jill Dolan, eds. *The Drama Review: Thirty Years of Commentary on the Avant-Garde.* Ann Arbor, MI: UMI Research Press, 1986.

McNeil, Legs, and Gillian McCain, eds. *Please Kill Me: The Uncensored Oral History of Punk.* New York: Penguin, 1997.

McQuillar, Tayannah Lee. *When Rap Music Had a Conscience: The Artists, Organizations and Historic Events That Inspired and Influenced the "Golden Age" of Hip-Hop from 1987 to 1996.* New York: Thunder's Mouth, 2007.

McWilliams, John C. *The 1960s Cultural Revolution.* Westport, CT: Greenwood, 2000.

Meeker, Martin. "Behind the Mask of Respectability: Reconsidering the Mattachine Society and Male Homophile Practice, 1950s and 1960s." *Journal of the History of Sexuality* 10:1 (January 2001): 78–116.

Mees, Patricia D. "Yoga Participation Surges." *The Physician and Sportsmedicine* 33:5 (May 2005).

Meier, August, John Bracey, Jr., and Elliot Rudwick. *Black Protest in the Sixties.* New York: M. Wiener, 1991.

Meier, Matt S., and Feliciano Ribera. *Mexican Americans/American Mexicans: From Conquistadors to Chicanos.* New York: Hill and Wang, 1993.

Mele, Christopher. *Selling the Lower East Side: Culture, Real Estate, and Resistance in New York City.* Minneapolis: University of Minnesota Press, 2000.

Melton, J. Gordon. *The Church of Scientology.* Studies in Contemporary Religions. Salt Lake City: Signature Books in cooperation with CESNUR, 2000.

Melville, Keith. *Communes in the Counter Culture; Origins, Theories, Styles of Life.* New York: Morrow, 1972.

Mercer, Mick. *Hex Files: The Goth Bible.* Woodstock, NY: Overlook, 1997.

Merrett, Christopher D., and Norman Walzer. *Cooperative and Local Development: Theory and Applications for the 21st Century.* Armonk, NY: M.E. Sharpe, 2004.

Merrill, Lisa. *When Romeo Was a Woman: Charlotte Cushman and Her Circle of Female Spectators.* Ann Arbor: University of Michigan Press, 1999.

Merrill, Walter M. *Against Wind and Tide: A Biography of William Lloyd Garrison.* Cambridge, MA: Harvard University Press, 1963.

Messner, Michael. *Politics of Masculinities: Men in Movements.* Thousand Oaks, CA: Sage, 1997.

Meyer, Ursula, ed. *Conceptual Art.* New York: E.P. Dutton, 1972.

Meyerowitz, Joanne. *How Sex Changed: A History of Transsexuality in the United States.* Cambridge, MA: Harvard University Press, 2002.

Meyers, Jeffrey. *Hemingway: A Biography.* New York: Da Capo, 1999.

———. *Scott Fitzgerald: A Biography.* New York: HarperCollins, 1994.

Mickler, Michael L. *A History of the Unification Church in America 1959–1974.* New York: Garland, 1993.

Middlekauff, Robert. *The Mathers: Three Generations of Puritan Intellectuals, 1596–1728.* Berkeley: University of California Press, 1999.

Miles, Barry. *Ginsberg: A Biography.* London: Viking, 1989; London: Virgin Books, 2001.

———. *William Burroughs: El Hombre Invisible.* London: Virgin Books, 2002.

Miles, Dione. *Something in Common: An IWW Bibliography.* Detroit, MI: Wayne State University Press, 1986.

Milford, Nancy. *Savage Beauty: The Life of Edna St. Vincent Millay.* New York: Random House, 2001.

———. *Zelda: A Biography.* New York: Harper & Row, 1970.

Miller, Bobby. *Fabulous!: A Photographic Diary of Studio 54.* New York: St. Martin's, 1998.

Miller, Jim. *Democracy Is in the Streets: From Port Huron to the Siege of Chicago.* Cambridge, MA: Harvard University Press, 1994.

Miller, Perry. *The New England Mind: The Seventeenth Century.* Cambridge, MA: Harvard University Press, 1954.

———. *Orthodoxy in Massachusetts, 1630–1650: A Genetic Study.* Cambridge, MA: Harvard University Press, 1933.

———. *Visible Saints: The History of a Puritan Idea.* New York: New York University Press, 1963.

Miller, Russell. *Bunny: The Real Story of* Playboy. New York: New American Library, 1984.

Miller, Stephen. *Johnny Cash: The Life of an American Icon.* London: Omnibus, 2003.

Miller, Terry. *Greenwich Village and How It Got That Way.* New York: Crown, 1990.

Mills, Kathryn, and Pamela Mills, eds. *C. Wright Mills: Letters and Autobiographical Writings.* Berkeley: University of California Press, 2000.

Mintz, Jerome. *Hasidic People: A Place in the New World.* Cambridge, MA: Harvard University Press, 1992.

Mitchell, Juliet, and Ann Oakley, eds. *What Is Feminism?* Oxford, UK: Basil Blackwell, 1986.

Mitchell, Richard G., Jr. *Dancing at Armageddon: Survivalism and Chaos in Modern Times.* Chicago: University of Chicago Press, 2004.

Mitnick, Kevin D. *The Art of Intrusion: The Real Stories Behind the Exploits of Hackers, Intruders and Deceivers.* Indianapolis, IN: Wiley, 2005.

Mockingbird Foundation. *The Phish Companion: A Guide to the Band and Their Music.* San Francisco: Backbeat, 2004.

Molesworth, Charles. *Marianne Moore: A Literary Life.* New York: Atheneum, 1990.

Monaghan, Jay. *The Great Rascal: The Life and Adventures of Ned Buntline.* New York: Bonanza, 1952.

Montessori, Maria. *The Montessori Method*. Cambridge, MA: R. Bentley, 1965.

Montgomery, David. *The Fall of the House of Labor: The Workplace, the State, and American Labor Activism, 1865–1925*. New York: Cambridge University Press, 1987.

Mooney, James. *The Ghost Dance Religion and the Sioux Outbreak of 1890*. Lincoln: University of Nebraska Press, 1991.

Moore, Joan, and John M. Hagedorn. *Female Gangs: A Focus on Research*. Washington, DC: U.S. Department of Justice, Office of Justice Programs, Office of Juvenile Justice and Delinquency Prevention, 2001.

Moore, Lucia W. *The Story of Eugene*. New York: Stratford House, 1949.

Moore, Mike. *A World Without Walls: Freedom, Development, Free Trade and Global Governance*. New York: Cambridge University Press, 2003.

Moore, R. Laurence. *In Search of White Crows: Spiritualism, Parapsychology, and American Culture*. New York: Oxford University Press, 1977.

Moore, Rebecca. *A Sympathetic History of Jonestown: The Moore Family Involvement in Peoples Temple*. Lewiston, NY: Edwin Mellen, 1985.

Moore, Robin C. "Adam Purple's Garden: Art and Science in Action Research." Proceedings of the 6th annual conference of the Environmental Design Research Association at the City University of New York's Graduate Center, New York, NY, June 10–13, 1985.

Moore, Thomas. *The Style of Connectedness: Gravity's Rainbow and Thomas Pynchon*. Columbia: University of Missouri Press, 1987.

Moraga, Cherríe, and Gloria Anzaldúa, eds. *This Bridge Called My Back: Writings by Radical Women of Color*. 2nd ed. New York: Kitchen Table: Women of Color, 1984.

Morgan, Bill. *The Beat Generation in San Francisco: A Literary Tour*. San Francisco: City Lights, 2003.

———. *I Celebrate Myself: The Somewhat Private Life of Allen Ginsberg*. New York: Penguin, 2006.

Morgan, Edmund S. *The Puritan Family: Essays on Religion and Domestic Relations in Seventeenth-Century New England*. Boston: Boston Public Library, 1944.

———. *Roger Williams: The Church and the State*. New York: Harcourt, Brace and World, 1967.

Morgan, H. Wayne. *Drugs in America: A Social History, 1800–1980*. Syracuse, NY: Syracuse University Press, 1981.

Morgan, Richard G., ed. *Kenneth Patchen: A Collection of Essays*. New York: AMS, 1977.

Morgan, Ted. *Literary Outlaw: The Life and Times of William S. Burroughs*. New York: Henry Holt, 1988.

———. *Reds: McCarthyism in Twentieth-Century America*. New York: Random House, 2003.

Moro, Pamela, James Myers, and Arthur Lehmann. *Magic, Witchcraft, and Religion: An Anthropological Study of the Supernatural*. New York: McGraw-Hill, 2006.

Morris, Roy, Jr. *Ambrose Bierce: Alone in Bad Company*. New York: Crown, 1995.

Morrison, Toni. *Beloved*. New York: Random House, 1987.

———. *The Bluest Eye*. New York: Holt, Rinehart and Winston, 1970.

Morrow, Lance, Nancy Gibbs, Richard Lacayo, and Jill Smolowe. *Mad Genius: The Odyssey, Pursuit and Capture of the Unabomber Suspect*. New York: Warner, 1996.

Morse, Donald E. *The Novels of Kurt Vonnegut: Imagining Being an American*. Westport, CT: Praeger, 2003.

Morton, Margaret. *The Tunnel: The Underground Homeless of New York City*. New Haven, CT: Yale University Press, 1995.

Morton, Marian J. *Emma Goldman and the American Left: "Nowhere at Home."* New York: Twayne, 1992.

Morton, Thomas. *New English Canaan*. 1637. New York: Da Capo, 1969.

Moskowitz, Sam. "The Fabulous Fantasist—Fitz-James O'Brien." In *Explorers of the Infinite*. Cleveland, OH: World, 1963.

Moss, John, and Linda M. Morra. *At the Speed of Light There Is Only Illumination: A Reappraisal of Marshall McLuhan*. Toronto: University of Ottawa Press, 2004.

Mott, Wesley T. *Encyclopedia of Transcendentalism*. Westport, CT: Greenwood, 1996.

Muesse, Mark W. "Religious Studies and 'Heaven's Gate': Making the Strange Familiar and the Familiar Strange." In *The Insider/Outsider Problem in the Study of Religion: A Reader*, ed. Russell T. McCutcheon. New York: Cassell, 1999.

Mullen, Bill, and Sherry Lee Linkon, eds. *Radical Revisions: Rereading 1930s Culture*. Urbana: University of Illinois Press, 1996.

Mullen, Brendan. *Lexicon Devil: The Fast Times and Short Life of Darby Crash and the Germs*. With Don Bolles and Adam Parfrey. Los Angeles: Feral House, 2002.

Muñoz, Carlos, Jr. *Youth, Identity, Power: The Chicano Movement*. New York: Verso, 1989.

Munt, Sally. "The Personal, Experience, and the Self." In *Out in Culture: Gay, Lesbian, and Queer Essays on Popular Culture*, ed. Corey K. Creekmur and Alexander Doty. Durham, NC: Duke University Press, 1995.

Murphy, Alexandra K., and Sudhir Alladi Venkatesh. "Vice Careers: The Changing Contours of Sex Work in New York City." *Qualitative Sociology* 29 (2006): 129–54.

Murphy, Bren Ortega, and Jeffery Scott Harder. "1960s Counterculture and the Legacy of American Myth: A Study of Three Films." *Canadian Review of American Studies* 23:2 (Winter 1993): 57–79.

Murphy, Joseph M. *Santería: African Spirits in America*. Boston: Beacon, 1993.

Myerson, Joel, ed. *The Brook Farm Book: A Collection of First-Hand Accounts of the Community*. New York: Garland, 1987.

———. *The New England Transcendentalists and* The Dial. Rutherford, NJ: Fairleigh Dickinson University Press, 1980.

———, ed. *Selected Letters of Nathaniel Hawthorne*. Columbus: Ohio State University Press, 2002.

———, ed. *Transcendentalism: A Reader*. New York: Oxford University Press, 2000.

Nachman, Gerald. *Seriously Funny: The Rebel Comedians of the 1950s and 1960s*. New York: Pantheon, 2003.

Nadeau, Maurice. *The History of Surrealism*. Trans. Richard Howard. New York: Macmillan, 1965.

Nader, Ralph. *Crashing the Party: Taking on the Corporate Government in an Age of Surrender*. New York: St. Martin's, 2002.

———. *Unsafe at Any Speed: The Designed-In Dangers of the American Automobile*. New York: Grossman, 1965; 1972.

Nader, Ralph, and Barbara Ehrenreich. *The Ralph Nader Reader*. New York: Seven Stories, 2000.

Næss, Arne. *Ecology, Community and Lifestyle*. Cambridge, UK: Cambridge University Press, 1989.

Nagel, Joane. *American Indian Ethnic Renewal: Red Power and the Resurgence of Identity and Culture.* New York: Oxford University Press, 1996.

Namias, June. *White Captives: Gender and Ethnicity on the American Frontier.* Chapel Hill: University of North Carolina Press, 1993.

Nash, Gary B. *The Unknown American Revolution: The Unruly Birth of Democracy and the Struggle to Create America.* New York: Viking, 2005.

Nash, Robert Jay. *Hustlers and Con Men: An Anecdotal History of the Confidence Man and His Games.* New York: M. Evans, 1976.

National Collection of Fine Arts. *Images of an Era: The American Poster 1945–1975.* Washington, DC: National Collection of Fine Arts, 1975.

Navasky, Victor S. "The Merger That Wasn't." *The Nation,* January 1, 1990.

Neale, Steve, and Murray Smith, eds. *Contemporary Hollywood Cinema.* London: Routledge, 1998.

Neider, Charles, ed. *The Complete Short Stories of Mark Twain.* New York: Bantam, 1984.

Neill, A.S. *Summerhill: A Radical Approach to Child Rearing.* New York: Hart, 1960.

Neilli, Humbert S. *The Business of Crime: Italians and Syndicate Crime in the United States.* New York: Oxford University Press, 1976.

Nelson, Eugene. *Break Their Haughty Power: Joe Murphy in the Heyday of the Wobblies.* San Francisco: ISM, 1993.

Nelson, Rob. *Revolution X: A Survival Guide for Our Generation.* New York: Penguin, 1994.

Nestle, Marion. *Food Politics.* Berkeley: University of California Press, 2002.

Newport, Kenneth G.C. *The Branch Davidians of Waco: The History and Beliefs of an Apocalyptic Sect.* New York: Oxford University Press, 2006.

Newton, Huey P. *To Die for the People: The Writings of Huey P. Newton.* Ed. Toni Morrison. New York: Writers and Readers, 1995.

Nicholson, Stuart. *Billie Holiday.* Boston: Northeastern University Press, 1995.

Nies, Judith. *Native American History: A Chronology of a Culture's Vast Achievements and Their Links to World Events.* New York: Ballantine, 1996.

Nilsen, Per, and Dorothy Sherman. *The Wild One: The True Story of Iggy Pop.* London: Omnibus, 1988.

Nissenbaum, Stephen. *Sex, Diet, and Debility in Jacksonian America: Sylvester Graham and Health Reform.* Chicago: Dorsey, 1988.

Noakes, Bob. *Last of the Pirates: A Saga of Everyday Life on Board Radio Caroline.* Edinburgh, Scotland: P. Harris, 1984.

Nordhoff, Charles. *The Communistic Societies of the United States.* New York: Hillary House, 1960.

Nordin, Dennis S. *Rich Harvest: A History of the Grange, 1867–1900.* Jackson: University Press of Mississippi, 1974.

Noriega, Chon A. *Shot in America: Television, the State, and the Rise of Chicano Cinema.* Minneapolis: University of Minnesota Press, 2000.

Norman, Philip. *Shout! The Beatles in Their Generation.* New York: Fireside, 2005.

Norton, David Fate. "Francis Hutcheson in America." *Studies in Voltaire and the Eighteenth Century* 154 (1976): 1547–68.

Notes from Nowhere, eds. *We Are Everywhere: The Irresistible Rise of Global Anti-capitalism.* London: Verso, 2003.

Noyes, George, and Lawrence Foster. *Free Love in Utopia: John Humphrey Noyes and the Origin of the Oneida Community.* Urbana: University of Illinois Press, 2001.

Numbers, Ronald L. *The Creationists: From Scientific Creationism to Intelligent Design.* Exp. ed. Cambridge, MA: Harvard University Press, 2006.

Numbers, Ronald L., and Jonathan M. Butler, eds. *The Disappointed: Millerism and Millenarianism in the Nineteenth Century.* Bloomington: Indiana University Press, 1987.

Nybakken, Elizabeth. "Alison, Francis." In *American National Biography,* ed. John A. Garraty and Mark C. Carnes. New York: Oxford University Press, 1999.

O'Brien, David J. *Isaac Hecker: An American Catholic.* Mahwah, NJ: Paulist Press, 1991.

O'Brien, Geoffrey. "Is It All Just a Dream?: *Fahrenheit 9/11,* a Film by Michael Moore." *The New York Review of Books,* August 12, 2004, 17–19.

O'Connor, Francis V., ed. *Art for the Millions: Essays from the 1930s by Artists and Administrators of the WPA Federal Art Project.* Greenwich, CT: New York Graphic Society, 1973.

O'Hara, Craig. *The Philosophy of Punk: More Than Noise.* 2nd ed. San Francisco: AK, 1999.

Ogbar, O.G. *Black Power: Radical Politics and African American Identity.* Baltimore: Johns Hopkins University Press, 2004.

Olds, Mason. "Unitarian-Universalism: An Interpretation Through Its History." In *America's Alternative Religions,* ed. Timothy Miller. Albany: State University of New York Press, 1995.

Omer, Stewart. *Peyote Religion: A History.* Norman: University of Oklahoma Press, 1987.

Oppenheim, James. "The Story of the *Seven Arts.*" *American Mercury* 20 (1930): 156–64.

Orr, Catherine. "Charting the Currents of the Third Wave." *Hypatia* 12:3 (1996): 29–45.

Osborn, Reuben. *Marxism and Psychoanalysis.* New York: Delta, 1965.

Osgerby, Bill. " 'Chewing Out a Rhythm on My Bubble-Gum': The Teenage Aesthetic and Genealogies of American Punk." In *Punk Rock: So What?* ed. Roger Sabin. New York: Routledge, 1999.

Ostling, Richard N., and Joan K. Ostling. *Mormon America: The Power and the Promise.* New York: HarperCollins, 1999.

Owen, Robert Dale. *Robert Dale Owen at New Lanark: Two Booklets and One Pamphlet, 1824–1838.* New York: Arno, 1972.

———. *Threading My Way: An Autobiography.* 1874. New York: A.M. Kelley, 1967.

Owen, Ted, and Denise Dickson. *High Art: A History of the Psychedelic Poster.* London: Sanctuary, 1999.

Owens, Thomas. *Bebop: The Music and Its Players.* New York: Oxford University Press, 1995.

Ozieblo, Barbara, ed. *The Provincetown Players: A Choice of the Shorter Works.* Sheffield, MA: Sheffield Academic Press, 1996.

Packard, Vance. *The Hidden Persuaders.* New York: D. McKay, 1957.

Pagán, Eduardo Obregón. *Murder at the Sleepy Lagoon: Zoot Suits, Race, and Riot in Wartime L.A.* Chapel Hill: University of North Carolina Press, 2003.

Palahniuk, Chuck. Interview. By Andrew Phillips. *Newsweek,* September 1, 2003, 10.

Palast, Greg. *Armed Madhouse.* New York: Penguin, 2006.

———. *The Best Democracy Money Can Buy: The Truth About Corporate Cons, Globalization and High-Finance Fraudsters.* New York: Penguin, 2002.

Palmer, Bruce. "Man Over Money": The Southern Populist Critique of American Capitalism. Chapel Hill: University of North Carolina Press, 1980.

Panchyk, Richard. American Folk Art for Kids. Chicago: Chicago Review Press, 2004.

Parfrey, Adam, ed. Apocalypse Culture. Portland, OR: Feral House, 1990.

Park, Robert L. Voodoo Science: The Road from Foolishness to Fraud. New York: Oxford University Press, 2000.

Parker, Derek, and Julia Parker. The New Compleat Astrologer. New York: Cresent, 1971.

Parmet, Herbert S. The Democrats: The Years After FDR. New York: Macmillan, 1976.

Parrish, Michael E. Anxious Decades: America in Prosperity and Depression, 1920–1941. New York: W.W. Norton, 1992.

Parry, Albert. Garrets and Pretenders: A History of Bohemianism in America. New York: Dover, 1960.

Partridge, Eric. A Dictionary of Slang and Unconventional English. 8th ed. Ed. Paul Beale. New York: Macmillan, 1984.

Passet, Joanne E. Sex Radicals and the Quest for Women's Equality. Urbana: University of Illinois Press, 2003.

Patai, Daphne, ed. Looking Backward, 1988–1888: Essays on Edward Bellamy. Amherst: University of Massachusetts Press, 1988.

Patchen, Kenneth. The Collected Poems of Kenneth Patchen. New York: New Directions, 1967

Patterson, Clayton, ed. Resistance: A Radical Social and Political History of the Lower East Side. New York: Seven Stories, 2007.

Paul, Ellen Frankel, Fred D. Miller, and Jeffrey Paul. The Communitarian Challenge to Liberalism. New York: Cambridge University Press, 1996.

Paul, Sherman. Emerson's Angle of Vision: Man and Nature in American Experience. Cambridge, MA: Harvard University Press, 1952.

Peabody, Elizabeth Palmer. "Plan of the West Roxbury Community." The Dial. 1842.

Pearce, Richard, ed. Critical Essays on Thomas Pynchon. Boston: G.K. Hall, 1982.

Pearce, Roy Harvey. Savagism and Civilization: A Study of the Indian and the American Mind. Berkeley: University of California Press, 1988.

Pearson, Hugh. The Shadow of the Panther: Huey Newton and the Price of Black Power in America. Redding, MA: Addison-Wesley, 1994.

Peary, Danny. Cult Movies. New York: Delta, 1981.

Pease, William H., and Jane H. Pease. "A New View of Nashoba." Tennessee Historical Quarterly 19 (1960): 99–109.

Peck, Abe. Uncovering the Sixties: Life and Times of the Underground Press. New York: Pantheon, 1985.

Peck, M. Scott. Glimpses of the Devil: A Psychiatrist's Personal Accounts of Possession, Exorcism, and Redemption. New York: Free Press, 2005.

Peckham, Howard H. Pontiac and the Indian Uprising. Chicago: University of Chicago Press, 1961.

Pela, Robert. Filthy: The Weird World of John Waters. Los Angeles: Alyson, 2002.

Penland, Paige R. Lowrider: History, Pride, Culture. St. Paul, MN: Motorbooks, 2003.

Perkin, Eric William. Droppin' Science: Critical Essays on Rap Music and Hip Hop Culture. Philadelphia: Temple University Press, 1996.

Perkins, John. The Secret History of the American Empire: Economic Hit Men, Jackals, and the Truth About Global Corruption. New York: Dutton, 2007.

Perlman, Bennard B. Painters of the Ashcan School: The Immortal Eight. New York: Dover, 1979; Mineola, NY: Dover, 1988.

Perone, James E. Music of the Counterculture Era. Westport, CT: Greenwood, 2004.

———. Songs of the Vietnam Conflict. Westport, CT: Greenwood, 2001.

———. Woodstock: An Encyclopedia of the Music and Art Fair. Westport, CT: Greenwood, 2005.

Perrin, Dennis. Mr. Mike: The Life and Work of Michael O'Donoghue—The Man Who Made Comedy Dangerous. New York: Avon, 1998.

Perry, Charles. The Haight-Ashbury: A History. New York: Random House, 1984; 2005.

Perry, George. San Francisco in the Sixties. London: Pavilion, 2002.

Perry, Imani. Prophets of the Hood: Politics and Poetics in Hip Hop. Durham, NC: Duke University Press, 2004.

Perry, Lewis. Radical Abolitionism: Anarchy and the Government of God in Antislavery Thought. Ithaca, NY: Cornell University Press, 1973; Knoxville: University of Tennessee Press, 1995.

Perry, Paul. On the Bus: The Complete Guide to the Legendary Trip of Ken Kesey and the Merry Pranksters and the Birth of the Counterculture. New York: Thunder's Mouth, 1996.

Peters, Casey. "Peace and Freedom Party from 1967 to 1997." Synthesis/Regeneration 12 (Winter 1997).

Peters, Nancy J. "The Beat Generation and San Francisco's Culture of Dissent." In Reclaiming San Francisco History, Politics, Culture, ed. James Brook, Chris Carlsson, and Nancy J. Peters. San Francisco: City Lights, 1998.

Peters, Shawn Francis. Judging Jehovah's Witnesses. Lawrence: University Press of Kansas, 2000.

Petrini, Carlo. Slow Food Revolution: A New Culture for Eating and Living. With Gigi Padovani. Trans. Francesca Santovetti. New York: Rizzoli, 2006.

Petros, George, ed. The Exit Collection. Chicago: Tacit, 1998.

Pfeffer, Paula F. A. Philip Randolph: A Pioneer of the Civil Rights Movement. Baton Rouge: Louisiana State University Press, 1990.

Philbrick, Nathaniel. Mayflower: A Story of Courage, Community, and War. New York: Penguin, 2007.

Picknett, Lynn. The Mammoth Book of UFOs. New York: Carroll & Graf, 2001.

Piehl, Mel. Breaking Bread: The Catholic Workers and the Origins of Catholic Radicalism in America. Philadelphia: Temple University Press, 1982.

Pierson, John. Spike, Mike, Slackers, and Dykes: A Guided Tour Across a Decade of American Independent Cinema. New York: Hyperion, 1996.

Pike, Sarah. New Age and Neopagan Religions in America. New York: Columbia University Press, 2004.

Pipes, Daniel. Conspiracy: How the Paranoid Style Flourishes and Where It Comes From. New York: Free Press, 1997.

Piro, Sal, Merylene Schneider, and Richard O'Brien. Creatures of the Night: The Rocky Horror Experience. Livonia, MI: Stabur, 1990.

Pitts, Victoria L. In the Flesh: The Cultural Politics of Body Modification. New York: Palgrave Macmillan, 2003.

Pitzer, Donald E., ed. America's Communal Utopias. Chapel Hill and London: University of North Carolina Press, 1997.

Plagens, Peter. Sunshine Muse: Art on the West Coast, 1945–1970. Berkeley: University of California Press, 1999.

Plasencias, Luis F.B. "Lowriding in the Southwest: Cultural Symbols in the Mexican American Community." In History, Culture and Society: Chicano Studies in the 1980s, ed. National Association for

Chicano Studies. Ypsilanti, MI: Bilingual Press/Editorial Bilingue, 1983.

Platt, Charles. *Anarchy Online.* New York: HarperPrism, 1997.

Platt, Susan Noyes. "*The Little Review:* Early Years and Avant-Garde Ideas." In *The Old Guard and the Avant Garde: Modernism in Chicago, 1910–1940,* ed. Sue Ann Prince. Chicago: University of Chicago Press, 1990.

Pleasant, George. *The Joy of Streaking: A Guide to America's Favorite Pastime.* New York: Ballantine, 1974.

Pletscher, A., and D. Ladewig, eds. *Fifty Years of LSD: Current Status and Perspectives of Hallucinogens.* New York: Parthenon, 1994.

Plimpton, Ruth Talbot. *Mary Dyer: Biography of a Rebel Quaker.* Boston: Branden, 1994.

Poblete, Juan, ed. *Critical Latin American and Latino Studies.* Minneapolis: University of Minnesota Press, 2003.

Polhemus, Ted. "Psychobillies." In *Streetstyle: From Sidewalk to Catwalk.* New York: Thames and Hudson, 1994.

Pollitzer, Anna. *A Woman on Paper: Georgia O'Keeffe.* New York: Simon and Schuster, 1988.

Polner, Murray, and Jim O'Grady. *Disarmed and Dangerous: The Radical Lives and Times of Daniel and Philip Berrigan.* New York: Basic Books, 1997.

Pond, Frederick Eugene. *The Life and Adventures of Ned Buntline.* London: Cadmus Book Shop, 1919.

Pop, Iggy, with Anne Wehrer. *I Need More.* New York: Karz-Cohl, 1982.

Porter, Horace A. *Stealing the Fire: The Art and Protest of James Baldwin.* Middletown, CT: Wesleyan University Press, 1989.

Porter, Jack Nusan, and Peter Dreier, eds. *Jewish Radicalism: A Selected Anthology.* New York: Grove, 1973.

Portier, William. *Isaac Hecker and the First Vatican Council.* Ceredigion, UK: Edwin Mellen, 1985.

Potash, Chris, ed. *Reggae, Rasta, Revolution: Jamaican Music from Ska to Dub.* New York: Schirmer, 1997.

Powell, William. *The Anarchist Cookbook.* Fort Lee, NJ: Barricade, 1989.

Powers, Ann. "The Love You Make: Fans and Groupies." In *Trouble Girls: The* Rolling Stone *Book of Women in Rock,* ed. Barbara O'Diar. New York: Random House, 1997.

Powers, Ron. *Mark Twain: A Life.* New York: Free Press, 2005.

Powers, Thomas. *The War at Home: Vietnam and the American People, 1964–1968.* New York: Grossman, 1973.

Powers-Beck, Jeffrey. *The American Indian Integration of Baseball.* Lincoln: University of Nebraska Press, 2004.

Pressman, Steven. *Outrageous Betrayal: The Dark Journey of Werner Erhard from est to Exile.* New York: St. Martin's, 1993.

Pribram, E. Deidre. *Cinema and Culture: Independent Film in the United States, 1980–2001.* New York: Peter Lang, 2002.

Price, E. Hoffmann. *Book of the Dead: Friends of Yesteryear: Fictioneers and Others (Memories of the Pulp Fiction Era).* Sauk City, WI: Arkham House, 2001.

Pringle, David. *The Ultimate Guide to Science Fiction.* New York: Pharos, 1990.

Pryor, Richard, and Todd Gold. *Pryor Convictions and Other Life Sentences.* New York: Pantheon, 1995.

Pryse, Marjorie. "Archives of Female Friendship and the 'Way' Jewett Wrote." *New England Quarterly* 66:1 (March 1993): 47–66.

Pulido, Laura. *Black, Brown, Yellow and Left: Radical Activism in Los Angeles.* Berkeley: University of California Press, 2006.

Pye, Michael. *Maximum City: The Biography of New York.* London: Sinclair-Stevenson, 1991.

Quarles, Benjamin. *Frederick Douglass.* Washington, DC: Associated, 1948.

Quinn, Arthur Hobson. *Edgar Allan Poe: A Critical Biography.* New York: D. Appleton-Century, 1941.

Quinn, Eithne. *Nuthin' But a "G" Thang: The Culture and Commerce of Gangsta Rap.* New York: Columbia University Press, 2004.

Quinn, James F. "Angels, Bandidos, Outlaws, and Pagans: The Evolution of Organized Crime among the Big Four 1 percent Motorcycle Clubs." *Deviant Behavior* 22:4 (July 2001): 379–99.

Quinn, James F., and Shane D. Koch. "The Nature of Criminality within One-Percent Motorcycle Clubs." *Deviant Behavior* 24:3 (May 2003): 281–306.

Raab, Selwyn. *Five Families: The Rise, Decline, and Resurgence of America's Most Powerful Mafia Empires.* New York: Thomas Dunne, 2005.

Rabin, Robert L., and Stephen D. Sugarman. *Regulating Tobacco.* New York: Oxford University Press, 2005.

———. *Smoking Law Policy: Law, Politics, and Culture.* New York: Oxford University Press, 1993.

Rabinowicz, Harry M. *Hasidism: The Movement and Its Master.* New York: Jason Aronson, 1988.

Raeburn, Daniel K. *The Imp 2: The Holy Book of Chick with the Apocrypha and Dictionary-Concordance.* Chicago: Imp, 1998.

Rafferty, Patricia. "Discourse on Differences: Street Art/ Graffiti of Youth." *Visual Anthropology Review* 7:2 (1991): 77–83.

Rafferty, Sean, and Rob Mann, eds. *Smoking and Culture: The Archeology of Tobacco Pipes in Eastern North America.* Knoxville: University of Tennessee Press, 2004.

Ramone, Dee Dee. *Poison Heart: Surviving the Ramones.* Wembly, UK: Firefly, 1997.

Rampersad, Arnold. *The Art and Imagination of W.E.B. Du Bois.* New York: Schocken, 1990.

———. *The Life of Langston Hughes.* 2 vols. New York: Oxford University Press, 1986–1988.

Raskin, Jonah. *American Scream: Allen Ginsberg's* Howl *and the Making of the Beat Generation.* Berkeley: University of California Press, 2004.

———. *For the Hell of It: The Life and Times of Abbie Hoffman.* Berkeley: University of California Press, 1996.

Ratcliffe, Donald J. "Antimasonry and Partisanship in Greater New England, 1826–1836." *Journal of the Early Republic* 15 (1995): 199–239.

Rawlings, Terry. *Mod: A Very British Phenomenon.* London: Omnibus, 2001.

Ray, Angela G. *The Lyceum and Public Culture in the Nineteenth-Century United States.* East Lansing: Michigan State University Press, 2005.

Ray, Man. *Self Portrait.* London: André Deutsch, 1963.

Reed, Adolph. *W.E.B. Du Bois and American Political Thought: Fabianism and the Color Line.* New York: Oxford University Press, 1997.

Reed, Bill. *Early Plastic.* Los Angeles: Cellar Door, 2000.

Reed, Jeremy. *Waiting for the Man: A Biography of Lou Reed.* London: Picador, 1994.

Reich, Charles A. *The Greening of America.* 1970. New York: Three Rivers, 1995.

Reid, Jan. *The Improbable Rise of Redneck Rock.* Austin: University of Texas Press, 2004.

Reidelbach, Maria. *Completely Mad: A History of the Comic Book and Magazine.* Boston: Little, Brown, 1991.

Reiser, Andrew. *The Chautauqua Movement: Protestants, Progressives and the Culture of Modern Liberalism.* New York: Columbia University Press, 2003.

Remnick, David. *King of the World: The Rise of an American Hero.* New York: Random House, 1998.

Renshaw, Patrick. *The Wobblies: The Story of Syndicalism in the United States.* Chicago: Ivan R. Dee, 1999.

Reppetto, Thomas A. *American Mafia: A History of Its Rise to Power.* New York: Henry Holt, 2004.

Rexroth, Kenneth. *World Outside the Window: The Selected Essays of Kenneth Rexroth.* Ed. Bradford Morrow. New York: New Directions, 1987.

Reynolds, Simon. *Generation Ecstasy: Into the World of Techno and Rave Culture.* New York: Routledge, 1999.

Rheingold, Howard, ed. *The Millennium Whole Earth Catalog: Access to Tools and Ideas for the Twenty-first Century.* San Francisco: Harper San Francisco, 1994.

Rhine, J.B. *Extra-Sensory Perception.* Boston: Bruce Humphries, 1934.

Rhodes, Colin. *Outsider Art: Spontaneous Alternatives.* London: Thames and Hudson, 2000.

Rhodes, Lisa. *Electric Ladyland: Women and Rock Culture.* Philadelphia: University of Pennsylvania Press, 2005.

Riccio, Barry D. *Walter Lippmann: Odyssey of a Liberal.* Somerset, NJ: Transaction, 1994.

Rich, Adrienne. "Compulsory Heterosexuality and Lesbian Existence." In *Blood, Bread, and Poetry: Selected Prose 1979–1985.* New York: W.W. Norton, 1986.

Richardson, Robert D., Jr. *Emerson: The Mind on Fire.* Berkeley: University of California Press, 1995.

———. *Henry Thoreau: A Life of the Mind.* Berkeley: University of California Press, 1986.

Richter, Daniel K. *The Ordeal of the Longhouse: The Peoples of the Iroquois League in the Era of Colonization.* Chapel Hill: University of North Carolina Press, 1992.

Ridgeway, James. *Blood in the Face: The Ku Klux Klan, Aryan Nations, Nazi Skinheads, and the Rise of a New White Culture.* New York: Thunder's Mouth, 1990.

Ridley, Jasper. *The Freemasons: A History of the World's Most Powerful Secret Society.* New York: Arcade, 2001.

Riggenbach, Jeff. *In Praise of Decadence.* Amherst, NY: Prometheus, 1998.

Riley, Charles A., II. *The Art of Peter Max.* New York: Harry N. Abrams, 2002.

Riley, Tim. *Hard Rain: A Dylan Commentary.* New York: Da Capo, 1999.

Rinaldo, Peter M. *Atheists, Agnostics, and Deists in America: A Brief History.* Briarcliff Manor, NY: DorPete, 2000.

———. *Trying to Change the World.* Briarcliff Manor, NY: DorPete, 1992.

Riordan, James, and Jerry Prochnicky. *Break on Through: The Life and Death of Jim Morrison.* New York: HarperCollins, 1992.

Rips, Geoffrey. *Unamerican Activities: The Campaign Against the Underground Press.* San Francisco: City Lights, 1981.

Ritz, David. *Divided Soul: The Life of Marvin Gaye.* New York: Da Capo, 1991.

Rivers, Larry, and Arnold Weinstein. *What Did I Do: The Unauthorized Biography of Larry Rivers.* New York: Thunder's Mouth, 2001.

Robbins, Fred, and David Ragan. *Richard Pryor: This Cat's Got Nine Lives.* New York: Delilah, 1982.

Robbins, Mary Susannah, ed. *Against the Vietnam War: Writings by Activists.* Syracuse NY: Syracuse University Press, 1999.

Roberts, Nora Ruth. *Three Radical Women Writers: Class and Gender in Meridel Le Sueur, Tillie Olsen, and Josephine Herbst.* New York: Garland, 1996.

Robinson, Jack. *Captain Otway Burns and His Ship* Snap Dragon. Wilmington, NC: Lulu, 2006.

Robinson, Jackie, and Alfred Duckett. *I Never Had It Made: An Autobiography of Jackie Robinson.* New York: HarperPerennial, 2003.

Robinson, JoAnn Gibson. *The Montgomery Bus Boycott and the Women Who Started It.* Knoxville: University of Tennessee Press, 1990.

Robinson, Paul A. *The Freudian Left: Wilhelm Reich, Geza Roheim, Herbert Marcuse.* New York: Harper & Row, 1969.

Robinson, Roxana. *Georgia O'Keeffe: A Life.* New York: Harper & Row, 1989.

Rochester, Stuart I. *American Liberal Disillusionment: In the Wake of World War.* University Park: Pennsylvania State University Press, 1977.

Rock, Mick. *Glam! An Eyewitness Account.* London: Vision on Publishing, 2006.

Rock, Mick, and David Bowie. *Blood and Glitter.* London: Vision On, 2002.

Rockwell, John. "Art-Rock, Black vs. White and Vanguard Cross-Pollination." In *All American Music: Composition in the Twentieth Century,* edited by John Rockwell. New York: Alfred A. Knopf, 1983.

Rodale, J.I. *Paydirt: Farming and Gardening with Composts.* New York: Devin-Adair, 1945.

Rodriguez, Ellen. *Dennis Hopper: A Madness to His Method.* New York: St. Martin's, 1988.

Rodzvilla, John, ed. *We've Got Blog: How Weblogs Are Changing Our Culture.* Cambridge, MA: Perseus, 2002.

Rogers, Carl R. *Carl Rogers on Encounter Groups.* New York: Harper-Collins, 1970.

Rogin, Michael. *Blackface, White Noise: Jewish Immigrants in the Hollywood Melting Pot.* Berkeley: University of California Press, 1998.

Rolfe, Edwin. *The Lincoln Battalion.* New York: Veterans of the Abraham Lincoln Brigade, 1974.

Roman Catholic Church. *The Rites of the Catholic Church.* New York: Liturgical Press, 1999.

Rome, Adam. "Conservation, Preservation, and Environmental Activism: A Survey of the Historical Literature." *National Parks Service* (September 26, 2006).

———. "Give Earth a Chance: The Environmental Movement and the Sixties." *Journal of American History* 90:2 (September 2003): 525–54.

Rorabaugh, W.J. *Berkeley at War: The 1960s.* New York: Oxford University Press, 1989.

———. *Kennedy and the Promise of the Sixties.* New York: Cambridge University Press, 2002.

Rose, Phyllis. *Jazz Cleopatra: Josephine Baker in Her Time.* New York: Doubleday, 1997.

Rose, Tricia. *Black Noise: Rap Music and Black Culture in Contemporary America.* Middletown, CT: Wesleyan University Press, 1994.

Rosen, Moishe, and Bill Proctor. *Jews for Jesus.* Old Tappan, NJ: Fleming H. Revell, 1974.

Rosen, Ruth. *The World Split Open: How the Modern Women's Movement Changed America.* New York: Penguin, 2000.

Rosenberg, Jessica, and Gitana Garo. "Riot Grrrl: Revolutions from Within." *Signs: Journal of Women in Culture and Society* 23:3 (1998): 809–41.

Rosenblatt, Paul. *John Woolman.* New York: Twayne, 1969.

Rosenkranz, Patrick. *Rebel Visions: The Underground Comix Revolution 1963–1975.* Seattle, WA: Fantagraphics, 2002.

Rosenstone, Robert. *Crusade of the Left: The Lincoln Battalion in the Spanish Civil War.* New York: Pegasus, 1969.

Rosset, Barney, ed. *Evergreen Review Reader, 1957–1966.* New York: Arcade, 1994.

———. *Evergreen Review Reader, 1967–1973.* New York: Four Walls Eight Windows, 1998.

Rossinow, Doug. *The Politics of Authenticity: Liberalism, Christianity, and the New Left in America.* New York: Columbia University Press, 1998.

Rossman, Michael. *On Learning and Social Change.* New York: Random House, 1972.

Rostker, Bernard. *I Want You!: The Evolution of the All-Volunteer Force.* Santa Monica, CA: RAND Corporation, 2006.

Roszak, Theodore. *The Making of a Counter Culture: Reflections on the Technocratic Society and Its Youthful Opposition.* Berkeley: University of California Press, 1995.

Rothman, Stanley, and S. Robert Lichter. *Roots of Radicalism: Jews, Christians, and the New Left.* New York: Oxford University Press, 1982.

Rowe, David L. *Thunder and Trumpets: Millerites and Dissenting Religion in Upstate New York, 1800–1850.* Chico, CA: Scholars, 1985.

Rowley, Hazel. *Richard Wright: The Life and Times.* New York: Henry Holt, 2001.

Rozwenc, Edwin Charles. *Cooperatives Come to America: The American Utopian Adventure.* Philadelphia: Porcupine, 1975.

Rubenstein, Richard E. *Left Turn: Origins of the Next American Revolution.* Boston: Little, Brown, 1973.

Rubin, Arnold. *Marks of Civilization: Artistic Transformation of the Human Body.* Los Angeles: Museum of Cultural History, University of California, 1988.

Rubin, Jerry. *Do It! Scenarios of the Revolution.* New York: Simon and Schuster, 1970.

———. *Growing (Up) at Thirty-Seven.* Toronto: M. Evans, 1976.

Rubin, Richard L. *Party Dynamics: The Democratic Coalition and the Politics of Change.* New York: Oxford University Press, 1976.

Rudnick, Lois Palken. *Mabel Dodge Luhan: New Woman, New Worlds.* Albuquerque: University of New Mexico Press, 1984.

———. *Utopian Vistas: The Mabel Dodge Luhan House and the American Counterculture.* Albuquerque: University of New Mexico Press, 1996.

Ruiz, Vicki L., and Virginia Sánchez Korrol, eds. *Latina Legacies: Identity, Biography, and Community.* New York: Oxford University Press, 2005.

Rusk, Ralph. *The Life of Ralph Waldo Emerson.* Charles Scribner's Sons, 1949.

Russell, Francis. *Tragedy in Dedham: The Story of the Sacco-Vanzetti Case.* New York: McGraw-Hill, 1971.

Russell, Jeffery. *A History of Witchcraft: Sorcerers, Heretics, and Pagans.* London: Thames and Hudson, 1980.

Russell, Mark, ed. *Out of Character: Rants, Raves, and Monologues from Today's Top Performance Artists.* New York: Bantam, 1997.

Ruth, David E. *Inventing the Public Enemy: The Gangster in American Culture, 1918–1934.* Chicago: University of Chicago Press, 1996.

Rutkoff, Peter M., and William B. Scott. *New School: A History of the New School for Social Research.* New York: Free Press, 1986.

Rycroft, Charles. *Wilhelm Reich.* New York: Viking, 1971.

Sabin, Roger. *Punk Rock, So What?: The Cultural Legacy of Punk.* New York: Routledge, 1999.

Sagan, Carl, and Thornton Page, eds. *UFOs: A Scientific Debate.* Ithaca, NY: Cornell University Press, 1972.

Sakolsky, Ron, ed. *Surrealist Subversions: Rants, Writings and Images by the Surrealist Movement in the United States.* Brooklyn, NY: Autonomedia, 2003.

Sale, Kirkpatrick. *SDS.* New York: Vintage Books, 1974.

Sale, Kirkpatrick, and Eric Foner. *The Green Revolution: The American Environmental Movement, 1962–1992.* New York: Hill & Wang, 1993.

Sales, William. *From Civil Rights to Black Liberation: Malcolm X and the Organization of Afro-American Unity.* Boston: South End, 1994.

Salvatore, Nick. *Eugene V. Debs: Citizen and Socialist.* Urbana: University of Illinois Press, 1982; 2007.

Sampson, Sheree. "Reclaiming a Historic Landscape: Frances Wright's Nashoba Plantation in Germantown, Tennessee." *Tennessee Historical Quarterly* 59 (2000): 290–303.

Sandbrook, Dominic. *Eugene McCarthy and the Rise and Fall of Postwar American Liberalism.* New York: Anchor, 2005.

Sandeen, Ernest R. *The Roots of Fundamentalism: British and American Millenarianism, 1800–1930.* Chicago: University of Chicago Press, 1970.

Sandel, Michael J. *Liberalism and the Limits of Justice.* 2nd ed. New York: Cambridge University Press, 1998.

Sanders, Clinton. *Customizing the Body: The Art and Culture of Tattooing.* Philadelphia: Temple University Press, 1989.

Sanders, Ed. *The Family.* New York: Thunder's Mouth, 2002.

Sanger, Margaret. *The Selected Papers of Margaret Sanger.* Ed. Esther Katz. Urbana: University of Illinois Press, 2003.

———. *The Woman Rebel.* March 1914. The Selected Papers of Margaret Sanger.

Sante, Luc. *Low Life: Lures and Snares of Old New York.* New York: Farrar, Straus and Giroux, 2003.

Santelli, Robert, and Emily Davidson. *Hard Travelin': The Life and Legacy of Woody Guthrie.* Hanover, NH: University Press of New England, 1999.

Sartre, Jean-Paul. *Being and Nothingness.* New York: Routledge Classics, 2003.

Saul, Scott. *Freedom Is, Freedom Ain't: Jazz and the Making of the Sixties.* Cambridge, MA: Harvard University Press, 2003.

Savage, Barbara Dianne. *Broadcasting Freedom: Radio, War, and the Politics of Race, 1938–1948.* Chapel Hill: University of North Carolina Press, 1999.

Sawyer, Dana. *Aldous Huxley: A Biography.* New York: Crossroad, 2002.

Sawyer-Laucanno, Christopher. *E.E. Cummings: A Biography.* Naperville, IL: Sourcebooks, 2004.

Saxton, Alexander. *Bright Web in the Darkness.* New York: St. Martin's, 1958.

———. *The Great Midland.* 1948. Reprint, Urbana: University of Illinois Press, 1997.

Scarce, Rik. *Eco-Warriors: Understanding the Radical Environmental Movement.* Walnut Creek, CA: Left Coast, 2006.

Schaffer, Ingrid. *The Essential Man Ray.* New York: Harry N. Abrams, 2003.

Schickel, Richard. *Marlon Brando: A Life in Our Times.* New York: Atheneum, 1991.

Schlesinger, Arthur. *Orestes A. Brownson: A Pilgrim's Progress.* Boston: Little, Brown, 1939.

Schnapp, Jeffrey T. *Revolutionary Tides: The Art of the Political Poster 1914–1989.* New York: Rizzoli, 2005.

Schneider, Herbert W., and George Lawton. *A Prophet and a Pilgrim: Being the Incredible History of Thomas Lake Harris and Laurence Oliphant; Their Sexual Mysticisms and Utopian Communities, Amply Documented to Confound the Skeptic.* New York: Columbia University Press, 1942.

Schneider, Mark R. *"We Return Fighting": The Civil Rights Movement in the Jazz Age.* Boston: Northeastern University Press, 2002.

Schneider, Richard J. *Henry David Thoreau.* Boston: Twayne, 1987.

Schoenwald, Jonathan M. *A Time for Choosing: The Rise of Modern American Conservatism.* New York: Oxford University Press, 2001.

Schofield, R.E. *The Enlightened Joseph Priestley: A Study of His Life and Work from 1773 to 1804.* University Park: Pennsylvania State University Press, 2004.

Schrecker, Ellen. *Many Are the Crimes: McCarthyism in America.* Boston: Little, Brown, 1998.

Schreiner, Samuel A., Jr. *The Concord Quartet: Alcott, Emerson, Hawthorne, Thoreau, and the Friendship That Freed the American Mind.* New York: John Wiley and Sons, 2006.

Schultes, Richard Evans, and Albert Hoffman. *Plants of the Gods: Their Sacred, Healing and Hallucinogenic Powers.* Rochester, VT: Healing Arts, 1992.

Schultz, John. *The Chicago Conspiracy Trial.* New York: Da Capo, 1993.

Schulze, Suzanne. *Horace Greeley: A Bio-Bibliography.* New York: Greenwood, 1992.

Schumacher, Michael. *Dharma Lion: A Biography of Allen Ginsberg.* New York: St. Martin's, 1994.

———. *There But for Fortune: The Life of Phil Ochs.* New York: Hyperion, 1996.

Schwarz, Christa A.B. *Gay Voices of the Harlem Renaissance.* Bloomington: Indiana University Press, 2003.

Sciabarra, Chris Matthew. *Ayn Rand, Homosexuality, and Human Liberation.* Cape Town, South Africa: Leap, 2003.

———. *Ayn Rand: The Russian Radical.* University Park: Pennsylvania State University Press, 1995.

Scott, John W., Mike Dolgushkin, and Stu Nixon. *Deadbase XI: The Complete Guide to Grateful Dead Songlists.* Cornish, NH: Deadbase, 1999.

Scott, Marian. *Chautauqua Caravan.* New York: D. Appleton-Century, 1939.

Seale, Bobby. *Seize the Time: The Story of the Black Panther Party and Huey P. Newton.* New York: Random House, 1970; Baltimore: Black Classics, 1991.

Seale, Ervin. *Mingling Minds: Phineas Parkhurst Quimby's Science of Health and Happiness.* Camarillo, CA: DeVorss, 1997.

Sears, Clara Endicott, ed. *Bronson Alcott's Fruitlands, with Louisa May Alcott's Transcendental Wild Oats.* 1915. Whitefish, MT: Kessinger, 2003.

Seaver, James E. *A Narrative of the Life of Mrs. Mary Jemison.* New York: Random House, 1929.

Seeger, Pete. *Where Have All the Flowers Gone: A Musical Autobiography.* Ed. Peter Blood. Bethlehem, PA: Sing Out, 1997.

Segaller, Stephen. *Nerds 2.0.1: A Brief History of the Internet.* New York: TV Books, 1998.

Selzer, Jack. *Kenneth Burke in Greenwich Village: Conversing with the Moderns, 1915–1931.* Madison: University of Wisconsin Press, 1996.

Senelick, Laurence. *The Changing Room: Sex, Drag, and Theatre.* New York: Routledge, 2000.

Sentilles, Renée M. *Performing Menken: Adah Isaacs Menken and the Birth of American Celebrity.* New York: Cambridge University Press, 2003.

Seretan, Glenn L. *Daniel De Leon: The Odyssey of an American Marxist.* Cambridge, MA: Harvard University Press, 1979.

Service, Robert. *Comrades: A History of World Communism.* Cambridge, MA: Harvard University Press, 2007.

Sessions, George, ed. *Deep Ecology for the 21st Century: Readings on the Philosophy and Practice of the New Environmentalism.* Boston: Shambhala, 1995.

Sessions, George, and Bill Devall. *Deep Ecology: Living as if Nature Mattered.* Layton, UT: Gibbs Smith, 2001.

Seume, Keith. *VW New Beetle Performance Handbook.* St. Paul, MN: MBI, 2001.

Shadwick, Keith, and Douglas J. Nobel. *Jimi Hendrix: Musician.* San Francisco: Backbeat, 2003.

Shambaugh, Bertha M.H. *Amana: The Community of True Inspiration.* 1908. Iowa City, IA: Penfield, 1988.

Shank, Theodore. *Beyond the Boundaries: American Alternative Theater.* Ann Arbor: University of Michigan Press, 2002.

Shapiro, Harry. *Waiting for the Man: The Story of Drugs and Popular Music.* London: Helter Skelter, 1999.

Shapiro, Harry, and Caesar Glebbek. *Electric Gypsy: Jimi Hendrix.* New York: St. Martin's, 1995.

Shapiro, Peter. *Turn the Beat Around: The Secret History of Disco.* New York: Faber & Faber, 2005.

Sharaf, Myron. *Fury on Earth: A Biography of Wilhelm Reich.* New York: Da Capo, 1994.

Sharon, Adam, and Greg Sharon. *The Cheech and Chong Bible.* Harrison, NY: Brown Stane, 2002.

Shea, Daniel B. *Spiritual Autobiography in Early America.* 2nd ed. Madison: University of Wisconsin Press, 1988.

Shea, John G. *The American Shakers and Their Furniture.* New York: Van Nostrand Reinhold, 1971.

Shelton, Robert. *No Direction Home: The Life and Music of Bob Dylan.* New York: Ballantine, 1987.

Shepard, Odell. *Pedlar's Progress: The Life of Bronson Alcott.* Boston: Little, Brown, 1938.

Shermer, Michael. *Why People Believe Weird Things: Pseudoscience, Superstition, and Other Confusions of Our Time.* New York: W.H. Freeman, 1997.

Shi, David E. *The Simple Life: Plain Living and High Thinking in American Culture.* New York: Oxford University Press, 1985.

Shipps, Jan. *Mormonism: The Story of a New Religious Tradition.* Urbana: University of Illinois Press, 1985.

Shreve, Anita. *Women Together, Women Alone: The Legacy of the Consciousness-Raising Movement.* New York: Viking, 1989.

Siegel, Deborah L. "The Legacy of the Personal: Generating Theory in Feminism's Third Wave." *Hypatia* 12:3 (1997): 46–75.

Siegel, Robert, ed. *Dispatches from the Tenth Circle: The Best of* The Onion. New York: Three Rivers, 2001.

Silesky, Barry. *Ferlinghetti: The Artist in His Time.* New York: Warner, 1990.

Silver, Richard. 'The Spiritual Kingdom in America: The Influence of Swedenborg on American Society and Culture, 1815–1860." Ph.D. diss., Stanford University, 1983.

Silverman, David. *Reading Castaneda: A Prologue to the Social Sciences.* London: Routledge, 1975.

Silverman, Kenneth. *Houdini!!!: The Career of Ehrich Weiss.* New York: HarperCollins, 1997.

Simon, Geoffrey, and Trout, Grafton. "Hippies in College 1967 from Teeny Boppers to Drug Freaks." *Transaction* December 1967, 27–32.

Simon, Linda. *Gertrude Stein Remembered.* Lincoln: University of Nebraska Press, 1994.

Simpson, George E. "Political Cultism in West Kingston." *Social and Economic Studies* 4 (June 1955): 133–49.

Simpson, Jeffrey. *Chautauqua: An American Utopia.* New York: Harry N. Abrams, 1999.

Sinclair, Andrew. *Jack: A Biography of Jack London.* New York: Harper & Row, 1977.

Singer, Peter. *Animal Liberation.* New York: Ecco, 2002.

Sitkoff, Harvard. *The Struggle for Black Equality: 1954–1992.* Rev. ed. New York: Hill and Wang, 1993.

Skelton, Tracy, and Gill Valentine, eds. *Cool Places: Geographies of Youth Cultures.* London and New York: Routledge, 1998.

Sklar, Kathryn Kish, Anja Schuler, and Susan Strasser, eds. *Social Justice Feminists: A Dialogue in Documents, 1885–1933.* Ithaca, NY: Cornell University Press, 1999.

Slick, Darby. *Don't You Want Somebody to Love: Reflections on the San Francisco Sound.* Berkley, CA: SLG, 1991.

Slick, Grace. *Somebody to Love? A Rock and Roll Memoir.* New York: Warner, 1998.

Sloan, Douglas. *The Scottish Enlightenment and the American College Ideal.* New York: Teachers College Press, 1971.

Sloan, John. *The Gist of Art: Principles and Practise Expounded in the Classroom and Studio.* Mineola, NY: Dover, 1977.

Small, Melvyn. *Antiwarriors: The Vietnam War and the Battle for America's Hearts and Minds.* Wilmington, DE: Scholarly Resources, 2002.

Smedley, Audrey. *Race in North America: Origin and Evolution of a Worldview.* 3rd ed. Boulder, CO: Westview, 2007.

Smethurst, James Edward. *The Black Arts Movement: Literary Nationalism in the 1960s and 1970s.* Chapel Hill: University of North Carolina Press, 2005.

Smith, Frank. *Robert Ingersoll: A Life.* Buffalo, NY. Prometheus, 1985.

Smith, Greg. "'And All the Sinners, Saints': Patti Smith, Pioneer Musician and Poet." *Midwest Quarterly: A Journal of Contemporary Thought* 41:2 (Winter 2000): 173–90.

Smith, Larry R. *Kenneth Patchen.* Boston: Twayne, 1978.

———. *Lawrence Ferlinghetti: Poet-at-Large.* Carbondale and Edwardsville: Southern Illinois University Press, 1983.

Smith, Paul Chaat, and Robert Allen Warrior. *Like a Hurricane: The Indian Movement from Alcatraz to Wounded Knee.* New York: New Press, 1996.

Smoak, Gregory. *Ghost Dances and Identity: Prophetic Religion and American Indian Ethnogenesis in the Nineteenth Century.* Berkeley: University of California Press, 2006.

Snodgrass, Mary Ellen. *The Underground Railroad: An Encyclopedia of People, Places, and Operations.* Armonk, NY: M.E. Sharpe, 2007.

Snoop Dogg. *Tha Doggfather: The Times, Trials, and Hardcore Truths of Snoop Dogg.* With Davin Seay. New York: William Morrow, 1999.

Snyder, Gary. *The Gary Snyder Reader: Prose, Poetry, and Translations, 1952–1998.* Washington, DC: Counterpoint, 1999.

———. Interview. By Peter Barry Chowka. *East–West Journal* (Summer 1977).

Sobieszek, Robert A. *Ports of Entry: William S. Burroughs and the Arts.* Los Angeles: Los Angeles County Museum of Art, 1996.

Sochen, Julie. *Herstory: A Woman's View of American History.* New York: Alfred, 1974.

Sokolow, Jayme A. *Eros and Modernization: Sylvester Graham, Health Reform, and the Origins of Victorian Sexuality in America.* Rutherford, NJ: Fairleigh Dickinson University Press, 1983.

Sollors, Werner. *Amiri Baraka/LeRoi Jones: The Quest for a Populist Modernism.* New York: Columbia University Press, 1978.

Sonn, Richard D. *Anarchism.* New York: Twayne, 1992.

Spann, Edward K. *Democracy's Children: The Young Rebels of the 1960s and the Power of Ideals.* Wilmington, DE: Scholarly Resources, 2003.

Sparkman, David. "Laurie Anderson Interviewed by David Sparkman." *Washington Review* (October–November 1981): 25–26.

Spears, Richard A. *American Slang Dictionary.* 4th ed. New York: McGraw-Hill, 2006.

Spence, Clark C. "Knights of the Tie and Rail—Tramps and Hoboes in the West." *Western Historical Quarterly* 2:1 (January 1971): 4–19.

Spencer, Colin. *Vegetarianism: A History.* New York: Four Walls Eight Windows, 2002.

Spigel, Lynn, and Michael Curtin, eds. *The Revolution Wasn't Televised: Sixties Television and Social Conflict.* New York: Routledge, 1997.

Spitz, Bob. *The Beatles: The Biography.* New York: Little, Brown, 2005.

Spock, Benjamin. *The Common Sense Book of Baby and Child Care.* New York: Pocket Books, 1957.

Spock, Benjamin, and Mary Morgan. *Spock on Spock: A Memoir of Growing Up with the Century.* New York: Pantheon, 1989.

Sprigg, June. *Shaker Design.* New York: Whitney Museum of American Art, 1986.

Staloff, Darren. *The Making of an American Thinking Class: Intellectuals and Intelligentsia in Puritan Massachusetts.* New York: Oxford University Press, 1998.

Stambler, Leah G. "The Lyceum Movement in American Education, 1826–1845." *Paedagogica Historica* 21:1 (1981): 157–85.

Standley, Fred L., and Nancy V. Burt, eds. *Critical Essays on James Baldwin.* Boston: G.K. Hall, 1988.

Stansell, Christine. *American Moderns: Bohemian New York and the Creation of a New Century.* New York: Henry Holt, 2000.

Stanton, Elizabeth Cady. *A History of Woman Suffrage.* Vol. 1. Rochester, NY: Fowler and Wells, 1889.

Stark, Rodney, and William Sims Bainbridge. *The Future of Religion: Secularization, Revival, and Cult Formation.* Berkeley: University of California Press, 1985.

Starr, Kevin. *The Dream Endures: California Enters the 1940s.* New York: Oxford University Press, 2002.

Staub, Michael E. *Torn at the Roots: The Crisis of Jewish Liberalism in Postwar America.* New York: Columbia University Press, 2002.

Stavans, Ilan. *The Hispanic Condition: Reflections on Culture and Identity in America.* New York: HarperPerennial, 1996.

Stavis, Benedict. *We Were the Campaign: New Hampshire to Chicago for McCarthy.* Boston: Beacon, 1969.

Stebbins, Emma, ed. *Charlotte Cushman: Her Letters and Memories of Her Life.* 1878. New York: Blom, 1972.

Stecyk, C.R., III, and Glen E. Friedman. *DogTown: The Legend of the Z-Boys.* New York: Burning Flags, 2002.

Steele, Ronald. *Walter Lippmann and the American Century*. Boston: Little, Brown, 1980.

Steele, Valerie. *Fetish: Fashion, Sex, and Power*. New York: Oxford University Press, 1996.

Stefoff, Rebecca. *The American Environmental Movement*. 10th ed. New York: Facts on File, 1995.

Steger, Manfred B. *Judging Nonviolence: The Dispute Between Realists and Idealists*. New York: Routledge, 2003.

Steiker, Lowell D. *The Jesus Trip: Advent of the Jesus Freaks*. Nashville, TN: Abingdon, 1971.

Stein, Arlene, ed. *Sisters, Sexperts, Queers: Beyond the Lesbian Nation*. New York: Plume, 1993.

Stein, Judith. *The World of Marcus Garvey: Race and Class in Modern Society*. Baton Rouge: Louisiana State University Press, 1986.

Stein, Kathi. *Beyond Recycling: A Re-User's Guide*. Santa Fe, NM: Clear Light, 1997.

Stein, Rebecca L., and Philip L. Stein. *Anthropology of Religion, Magic, and Witchcraft*. New York: Allyn and Bacon, 2004.

Stein, Stephen J. *The Shaker Experience in America: A History of the United Society of Believers*. New Haven, CT: Yale University Press, 1992.

Steinbeck, John. *The Grapes of Wrath*. New York: Viking, 1939.

Steinem, Gloria. *Outrageous Acts and Everyday Rebellions*. 2nd ed. New York: Owl, 1995.

Steinhorn, Leonard. *The Great Generation: In Defense of the Baby Boom Legacy*. New York: Thomas Dunne, 2006.

Sterling, Bruce, ed. *Mirrorshades: The Cyberpunk Anthology*. Westminster, MD: Arbor House, 1986.

Stern, Madeleine B. *The Pantarch: A Biography of Stephen Pearl Andrews*. Austin: University of Texas Press, 1968.

Stevens, Jay. *Storming Heaven: LSD and the American Dream*. New York: Harper & Row, 1988.

Stewart, Omar Call. *Peyote Religion: A History*. Norman: University of Oklahoma Press, 1987.

Stich, Sidra. *Made in U.S.A.: An Americanization in Modern Art, The '50s and '60s*. Berkeley: University of California Press, 1987.

Still, William. *The Underground Railroad: Authentic Narratives and First-Hand Accounts*. 1872. Ed. Ian Frederick Finseth. Mineola, NY: Dover, 2007.

Stoehr, Taylor. *Nay Saying in Concord: Emerson, Alcott, and Thoreau*. Hamden, CT: Shoe String (Archon), 1979.

Streissguth, Thomas. *Hoaxers and Hustlers*. Minneapolis, MN: Oliver, 1994.

Strong, Douglas M. *Perfectionist Politics: Abolitionism and the Religious Tensions of American Democracy*. Syracuse, NY: Syracuse University Press, 1999.

Stroup, Herbert Hewitt. *The Jehovah's Witnesses*. New York: Russell & Russell, 1945.

Stryker, Susan, and Stephen Whittle, eds. *The Transgender Studies Reader*. New York: Routledge, 2006.

Stuart, Tristram. *The Bloodless Revolution: A Cultural History of Vegetarianism from 1600 to Modern Times*. New York: W.W. Norton, 2007.

Suarez, Juan. *Bike Boys, Drag Queens, and Superstars: Avant-Garde, Mass Culture, and Gay Identities in the 1960s Underground Cinema*. Bloomington: Indiana University Press, 1996.

Suleiman, Susan R. *Subversive Intent: Gender, Politics, and the Avant-Garde*. Cambridge, MA: Harvard University Press, 1990.

Sullivan, Denise. *R.E.M.: Talk About the Passion: An Oral History*. New York: Da Capo, 1998.

Sullivan, James. *Jeans: A Cultural History of an American Icon*. New York: Gotham, 2006.

Suthrell, Charlotte. *Unzipping Gender: Sex, Cross-Dressing and Culture*. Oxford, UK: Berg, 2004.

Sutin, Lawrence. *Divine Invasions: A Life of Philip K. Dick*. New York: Harmony, 1989.

Sutton, Robert P. *Communal Utopias and the American Experience: Religious Communities, 1732–2000*. Westport, CT: Praeger, 2003.

———. *Communal Utopias and the American Experience: Secular Communities, 1824–2000*. Westport, CT: Praeger, 2004.

Sutton, Walter, ed. *Pound, Thayer, Watson, and* The Dial: *A Story in Letters*. Gainesville: University Press of Florida, 1994.

Swan, Daniel C. *Peyote Religious Art: Symbols of Faith and Belief*. Jackson: University Press of Mississippi, 1999.

Swarts, Katherine. *Club Drugs*. The History of Drugs. Farmington Hills, MI: Greenhaven, 2006.

Sylvan, Robin. *Trance Formation: The Spiritual and Religious Dimensions of Global Rave Culture*. New York: Routledge, 2005.

Sylvander, Carolyn W. *James Baldwin*. New York: Ungar, 1980.

Synan, Vinson. *The Holiness-Pentecostal Tradition: Charismatic Movements in the Twentieth Century*. 2nd ed. Grand Rapids, MI: Eerdmans, 1997.

Szatmary, David P. *Rockin' in Time: A Social History of Rock-and-Roll*. 4th ed. Englewood Cliffs, NJ: Prentice Hall, 2000.

Szwed, John F. *So What: The Life of Miles Davis*. New York: Simon and Schuster, 2002.

Szymanski, Ann-Marie. *Pathways to Prohibition: Radicals, Moderates, and Social Movement Outcomes*. Durham, NC: Duke University Press, 2003.

Tabor, James D., and Eugene V. Gallagher. *Why Waco? Cults and the Battle for Religious Freedom in America*. Berkeley: University of California Press, 1995.

Taggett, Sherry Clayton, and Ted Schwarz. *Paintbrushes and Pistols: How the Taos Artists Sold the West*. Santa Fe, NM: John Muir, 1990.

Tapscott, Don. *Growing Up Digital: The Rise of the Net Generation*. New York: McGraw-Hill, 1999.

Tarzian, Charles. "Performance Space P.S. 122." *The Drama Review: TDR* 29:1 (Spring 1985): 84–91.

Taylor, Cynthia. *A. Philip Randolph: The Religious Journey of an African-American Labor Leader*. New York: New York University Press, 2006.

Taylor, Derek. *It Was Twenty Years Ago Today*. New York: Simon and Schuster, 1987.

Taylor, Eugene. *Shadow Culture: Psychology and Spirituality in America*. Washington, DC: Counterpoint, 1999.

Tester, Jim. *A History of Western Astrology*. New York: Ballantine, 1987.

Theall, Donald F. *The Virtual Marshall McLuhan*. Montreal: McGill-Queen's University Press, 2001.

Third World Gay Revolution. "The Oppressed Shall Not Become the Oppressor." 1970. Reprinted in *We Are Everywhere: A Historical Sourcebook of Gay and Lesbian Politics*, ed. Mark Blasius and Shane Phelan. New York: Routledge, 1997.

Thom, Mary. *Inside* Ms.: *Twenty-five Years of the Magazine and the Feminist Movement*. New York: Henry Holt, 1997.

Thomas, Douglas. *Hacker Culture*. Minneapolis: University of Minnesota Press, 2002.

Thomas, Dwight, and David Jackson, eds. *The Poe Log*. Boston: G.K. Hall, 1987.

Thomas, Janet. *The Battle in Seattle: The Story Behind and Beyond the WTO Demonstrations.* Golden, CO: Fulcrum, 2003.

Thomas, Robert Davis. *The Man Who Would Be Perfect: John Humphrey Noyes and the Utopian Impulse.* Philadelphia: University of Pennsylvania Press, 1977.

Thompson, Bob. "The Ballad of Carolyn Hester: Four Decades After Stardom Passed Her By, She's Singing Her Heart Out." *The Washington Post,* January 12, 2005, sec. C.

Thompson, Hunter S. *Fear and Loathing in Las Vegas: A Savage Journey to the Heart of the American Dream.* New York: Random House, 1971.

———. *Fear and Loathing: On the Campaign Trail '72.* San Francisco: Straight Arrow, 1973.

———. *Hell's Angels: A Strange and Terrible Saga.* New York: Random House, 1967.

———. *Kingdom of Fear: Loathsome Secrets of a Star-Crossed Child in the Final Days of the American Century.* New York: Simon and Schuster, 2003.

Thompson, Keith. *Angels and Aliens: UFOs and the Mythic Imagination.* Reading, MA: Addison-Wesley, 1991.

Thomson, David. *Marlon Brando.* New York: DK, 2003.

Thoreau, Henry David. *The Portable Thoreau.* Ed. Carl Bode. New York: Penguin, 1977.

———. *Walden, or Life in the Woods.* Boston: Ticknor and Fields, 1854.

Thorp, Daniel B. *The Moravian Community in Colonial North Carolina: Pluralism on the Southern Frontier.* Knoxville: University of Tennessee Press, 1989.

Thrasher, Frederic M. *The Gang: A Study of 1,313 Gangs in Chicago.* Chicago: University of Illinois Press, 1927.

Timmons, Stuart. *The Trouble with Harry Hay: Founder of the Modern Gay Movement.* Boston: Alyson, 1990.

Todd, Jan. "Bernarr Macfadden: Reformer of Feminine Form." *Journal of Sport History* 14:1 (Spring 1987): 61–75.

Toksvig, Signe. *Emanuel Swedenborg, Scientist and Mystic.* New York: Swedenborg Foundation, 1983.

Tollefson, James W. *The Strength Not to Fight: An Oral History of Conscientious Objectors of the Vietnam War.* Boston: Little, Brown, 1993.

Tomkins, Calvin. "Comment." *The New Yorker,* 27 April 1987, 27–28.

Toon, Elizabeth, and Janet Golden. " 'Live Clean, Think Clean, and Don't Go to Burlesque Shows': Charles Atlas as Health Advisor." *Journal of the History of Medicine and Allied Sciences* 57:1 (2002): 39–60.

Torgoff, Martin. *Can't Find My Way Home: America in the Great Stoned Age, 1945–2000.* New York: Simon and Schuster, 2004.

Toth, Jennifer. *The Mole People: Life in the Tunnels Beneath New York City.* Chicago: Chicago Review Press, 1993.

Tracy, Steven, ed. *A Historical Guide to Langston Hughes.* New York: Oxford University Press, 2004.

Trelease, Allen W. *White Terror: The Ku Klux Klan Conspiracy and Southern Reconstruction.* New York: Harper & Row, 1971.

Tremlett, George. *David Bowie: Living on the Brink.* New York: Carroll and Graf, 1997.

Treviño, Jesús Salvador. *Eyewitness: A Filmmaker's Memoir of the Chicano Movement.* Houston, TX: Arte Público, 2001.

"Tripping on Banana Peels." *Time* (April 7, 1967): 52.

Trobridge, George. *Swedenborg: Life and Teaching.* New York: Swedenborg Foundation, 1968.

Trogdon, Robert W., ed. *Ernest Hemingway: A Literary Reference.* New York: Carroll and Graff, 2002.

Tucker, Ruth A. *Not Ashamed: The Story of Jews for Jesus.* Sisters, OR: Multnomah, 2000.

Tulloch, John. *Science Fiction Audiences: Watching* Doctor Who *and* Star Trek. New York: Routledge, 1995.

Turan, Kenneth, and Stephen F. Zito. *Sinema: American Pornographic Films and the People Who Make Them.* New York: Praeger, 1974.

Turner, Chris. *Planet Simpson: How a Cartoon Masterpiece Defined a Generation.* Cambridge, MA: Da Capo, 2005.

Turner, Florence. *At the Chelsea Hotel.* San Diego, CA: Harcourt Brace Jovanovich, 1987.

Turner, Fred. *From Counterculture to Cyberculture: Stewart Brand, the Whole Earth Network, and the Rise of Digital Utopianism.* Chicago: University of Chicago Press, 2006.

Turner, James. *Without God, Without Creed: The Origins of Unbelief in America.* Baltimore: Johns Hopkins University Press, 1985.

Turner, Nat. *The Confessions of Nat Turner.* Richmond, VA: T.R. Gray, 1832.

Turner, Ron, ed. *Kustom Kulture: Von Dutch, Ed "Big Daddy" Roth, Robert Williams and Others.* San Francisco: Last Gasp, 1993.

Turner, Steve. *Trouble Man: The Life and Death of Marvin Gaye.* New York: Ecco, 2000.

Tussey, Jean Y., ed. *Eugene V. Debs Speaks.* New York: Pathfinder, 1972.

Twenge, Jean M. *Generation Me: Why Today's Young Americans Are More Confident, Assertive, Entitled—and More Miserable Than Ever Before.* New York: Free Press, 2006.

Twitchell, Paul. *Eckankar: The Key to Secret Worlds.* San Diego, CA: Illuminated Way, 1969.

Tworkov, Helen. *Zen in America.* San Francisco: North Point, 1989.

Tyler, Bruce. "Zoot-Suit Culture and the Black Press." *Journal of American Culture* 17:2 (Summer 1994): 21–33.

Tyler, Robert L. *Rebels of the Woods: The IWW in the Pacific Northwest.* Eugene: University of Oregon Press, 1967.

Tyrell, Ian R. *Sobering Up: From Temperance to Prohibition in Antebellum America, 1800–1860.* Westport, CT: Greenwood, 1979.

Tytell, John. *Ezra Pound: The Solitary Volcano.* New York: Anchor, 1987.

———. *The Living Theatre: Art, Exile and Outrage.* New York: Grove, 1995.

U.S. Department of Agriculture Rural Business-Cooperative Service. *Co-ops 101: An Introduction to Cooperatives.* Cooperative Information Report 55. June 1997.

Ullman, Sharon. *Sex Seen: The Emergence of Modern Sexuality in America.* Berkeley: University of California Press, 1997.

Ullman, Victor. *Martin R. Delany: The Beginnings of Black Nationalism.* Boston: Beacon, 1971.

Ulrich, John M., and Andrea L. Harris, eds. *GenXegesis: Essays on Alternative Youth (Sub) Culture.* Madison: University of Wisconsin Press, 2003.

Unterberger, Richie. "The Great Folk-Rock Clash: The 1965 Newport Folk Festival." In *Turn! Turn! Turn!: The '60s Folk-Rock Revolution.* San Francisco: Backbeat, 2002.

Vale, V., and Andrea Juno, eds. *RE/Search #6/7: Industrial Culture Handbook.* San Francisco: RE/Search, 1983.

Valk, Jereon de. *Chet Baker: His Life and Music.* Berkeley, CA: Berkeley Hills, 2000.

Van Deburg, William. *New Day in Babylon: The Black Power Movement and American Culture, 1965–1975.* Chicago: University of Chicago Press, 1992.

Varon, Jeremy. *Bringing the War Home: The Weather Underground, the Red Army Faction, and Revolutionary Violence in the Sixties and Seventies.* Berkeley: University of California Press, 2004.

Vaughn, Stephen. *Freedom and Entertainment: Rating the Movies in an Age of New Media.* New York: Cambridge University Press, 2005.

Vaughn, William Preston. *The Antimasonic Party in the United States, 1826–1843.* Lexington: University Press of Kentucky, 1983.

Venables, Robert W. *American Indian History: Five Centuries of Conflict and Coexistence.* Santa Fe, NM: Clear Light, 2004.

Veysey, Laurence R. *The Communal Experience: Anarchist and Mystical Communities in Twentieth-Century America.* Chicago: University of Chicago Press, 1978.

Vicinus, Martha. *Intimate Friends: Women Who Loved Women, 1778–1928.* Chicago: University of Chicago Press, 2004.

Viehmeyer, L. Allen. *An Index to Hymns and Hymn Tunes of the Ephrata Cloister 1730–1766.* Ephrata, PA: Ephrata Cloister Associates, 1995.

Vincent, Peter. *Hot Rod: An American Original.* St. Paul, MN: Motorbooks, 2002.

Von Eschen, Penny M. *Race Against Empire: Black Americans and Anticolonialism, 1937–1957.* Ithaca, NY: Cornell University Press, 1997.

von Schmidt, Eric, and Jim Rooney. *Baby, Let Me Follow You Down: The Illustrated Story of the Cambridge Folk Years.* 2nd ed. Amherst: University of Massachusetts Press, 1994.

von Schmidt, Eric, and Jim Rooney. *Baby, Let Me Follow You Down: A History of the Cambridge Folk Years.* 2nd ed. Amherst: University of Massachusetts Press, 1994.

Vorse, Mary Heaton. *A Footnote to Folly: Reminiscences of Mary Heaton Vorse.* 1935. Rev. ed., with Mary H. Borse. New York: Arno, 1980.

Wacker, Grant. *Heaven Below: Early Pentecostals and American Culture.* Cambridge, MA: Harvard University, 2003.

Wagner, Herbert. *Harley-Davidson 1930–1941: Revolutionary Motorcycles and Those Who Rode Them.* Atglen, PA: Schiffer, 1996.

Walker, Jesse. *Rebels on the Air: An Alternative History of Radio in America.* New York: New York University Press, 2001.

Walker, Michael. *Laurel Canyon.* New York: Faber & Faber, 2006.

Walker, Rebecca, ed. *To Be Real: Telling the Truth and Changing the Face of Feminism.* New York: Anchor, 1995.

Walker, Samuel. *In Defense of American Liberties: A History of the American Civil Liberties Union.* Carbondale: Southern Illinois University Press, 1990.

Walker, Stanley. *The Night Club Era.* New York: Frederick A. Stokes, 1933.

Wall, Robert Emmet. *Massachusetts Bay: The Crucial Decade 1640–1650.* New Haven, CT: Yale University Press, 1972.

Walley, David. *No Commercial Potential: The Saga of Frank Zappa.* New York: Da Capo, 1996.

Walljasper, Jay. "Radical, Mama!: *Mother Jones* Gets a Makeover." *Utne Reader* 90 (November–December 1998): 101–6.

Ward, Geoffrey C. *Jazz: A History of America's Music.* New York: Alfred A. Knopf, 2000.

———. *Unforgivable Blackness: The Rise and Fall of Jack Johnson.* New York: Vintage Books, 2006.

Ward, Martha. *Voodoo Queen: The Spirited Lives of Marie Laveau.* Jackson: University Press of Mississippi, 2004.

Ware, Kate. *Man Ray: 1890–1976.* Cologne, Germany: Taschen, 2000.

Wark, McKenzie. *A Hacker Manifesto.* Cambridge, MA: Harvard University Press, 2004.

Warlaumont, Hazel G. *Advertising in the 60s: Turncoats, Traditionalists, and Waste Makers in America's Turbulent Decade.* Westport, CT: Praeger, 2001.

Warner, Michael, ed. *Fear of a Queer Planet: Queer Politics and Social Theory.* Minneapolis: University of Minnesota Press, 1993.

Warren, Heather A. *Theologians of a New World Order: Reinhold Niebuhr and the Christian Realists, 1920–1948.* New York: Oxford University Press, 1997.

Warshaw, Matt. *Surfriders: In Search of the Perfect Wave.* Del Mar, CA: Tehabi, 1997.

Washington, James M., ed. *I Have a Dream: Writings and Speeches that Changed the World.* San Francisco: HarperCollins, 1992.

Washington, Mary Helen. "Introduction: Zora Neale Hurston: A Woman in Half Shadow." In *I Love Myself When I Am Laughing . . . And Then Again When I Am Looking Mean and Impressive: A Zora Neale Hurston Reader,* ed. Alice Walker. New York: Feminist Press, 1979.

Washington, Peter. *Madame Blavatsky's Baboon: A History of the Mystics, Mediums, and Misfits Who Brought Spiritualism to America.* New York: Schocken, 1996.

Waterman, Dick. *Between Midnight and Day: The Last Unpublished Blues Archive.* New York: Thunder's Mouth, 2003.

Waters, John. *Shock Value: A Tasteful Book About Bad Taste.* New York: Thunder's Mouth, 1995.

Watkins, Elizabeth Siegel. *On the Pill: A Social History of Oral Contraceptives, 1950–1970.* Baltimore: Johns Hopkins University Press, 1998.

Watkins, S. Craig. *Hip Hop Matters: Politics, Pop Culture and the Struggle for the Soul of a Movement.* Boston: Beacon, 2006.

Watkins, T.H. *The Hungry Years: A Narrative History of the Great Depression in America.* New York: Owl, 2000.

Watson, Mary Ann. *Defining Visions: Television and the American Experience Since 1945.* Fort Worth, TX: Harcourt Brace College, 1998.

Watson, Steven. *The Birth of the Beat Generation: Visionaries, Rebels and Hipsters, 1944–1960.* New York: Pantheon, 1995.

———. *Factory Made: Warhol and the Sixties.* New York: Pantheon, 2003.

Watts, Alan. *In My Own Way: An Autobiography, 1915–1965.* New York: Pantheon, 1972.

———. *The Way of Zen.* 1957. New York: Vintage Spiritual Classics, 1999.

Watts, Jill. *God, Harlem U.S.A.: The Father Divine Story.* Berkeley: University of California Press, 1992.

Wavy Gravy. *The Hog Farm and Friends.* By Wavy Gravy as told to Hugh Romney and vice versa. New York: Links, 1974.

———. *Something Good for a Change: Random Notes on Peace Thru Living.* New York. St Martin's, 1992.

Webber, Everett. *Escape to Utopia: The Communal Movement in America.* New York: Hastings House, 1959.

Weber, Max. *The Protestant Ethic and the "Spirit" of Capitalism and Other Writings.* Trans. and ed. Peter Baehr and Gordon C. Wells. New York: Penguin, 2002.

Wei, William. *The Asian American Movement.* Philadelphia: Temple University Press, 1993.

Weil, Ellen, and Gary K. Wolfe. *Harlan Ellison: The Edge of Forever.* Columbus: Ohio State University Press, 2002.

Weingarten, Gene. "Doonesbury's War." *Washington Post Magazine,* October 22, 2006.

Weinreich, Regina. "Ed Sanders: The Un-fuzzy Fug." *The Review of Contemporary Fiction* 19:1 (1999): 57.

Weinstein, Deena. *Heavy Metal: The Music and Its Culture.* New York: Da Capo, 2000.

Weisbrot, Robert. *Father Divine and the Struggle for Racial Equality.* Urbana: University of Illinois Press, 1983.

Weisenburger, Steven C. *A Gravity's Rainbow Companion: Sources and Contexts for Pynchon's Novel.* Athens: University of Georgia Press, 1988.

Weitzer, Ronald. *Sex for Sale: Prostitution, Pornography, and the Sex Industry.* New York: Routledge, 1999.

Wertkin, Gerard C. *The Four Seasons of Shaker Life.* New York: Simon and Schuster, 1986.

Wessinger, Catherine. *How the Millennium Comes Violently: From Jonestown to Heaven's Gate.* New York: Seven Bridges, 2000.

West, Mike. *The Lives and Crimes of Iggy Pop.* Manchester, UK: Babylon, 1982.

Wetzsteon, Ross. *Republic of Dreams: Greenwich Village, the American Bohemia, 1910–1960.* New York: Simon and Schuster, 2007.

Wexler, Alice. *Emma Goldman in America.* Boston: Beacon, 1984.

Wheatley, Richard. *The Life and Letters of Mrs. Phoebe Palmer.* New York: Garland, 1984.

Whissen, Thomas R. *Classic Cult Fiction: A Companion to Popular Cult Literature.* New York: Greenwood, 1992.

Whitburn, Joel. *The Billboard Book of Top 40 Hits.* 8th ed. New York: Billboard, 2004.

White, Charles Edward. *The Beauty of Holiness: Phoebe Palmer as Theologian, Revivalist, Feminist, and Humanitarian.* Grand Rapids, MI: Francis Asbury, 1986.

White, Deborah Gray. *Ar'n't I a Woman?: Female Slaves in the Plantation South.* New York: W.W. Norton, 1999.

White, James. *Sketches of the Christian Life and Public Labors of William Miller.* Battle Creek, MI: Steam, 1875.

White, Ralph. *Nobody Wanted War: Misconceptions in Vietnam and Other Wars.* New York: Doubleday, 1970.

White, Vibert L., Jr. *Inside the Nation of Islam: A Historical and Personal Testimony by a Black Muslim.* Gainesville: University Press of Florida, 2001.

Whitely, Sheila, ed. *Sexing the Groove: Gender and Popular Music.* New York: Routledge, 1997.

Whitfield, Stephen, and Gene Roddenberry. *The Making of* Star Trek. New York: Ballantine, 1968.

Whitmer, Peter O. *Aquarius Revisited: Seven Who Created the Sixties Counterculture That Changed America—William Burroughs, Allen Ginsberg, Ken Kesey, Timothy Leary, Norman Mailer, Tom Robbins, Hunter S. Thompson.* With Bruce VanWyngarden. New York: Macmillan, 1987.

———. *When the Going Gets Weird: The Twisted Life and Times of Hunter S. Thompson: A Very Unauthorized Biography.* New York: Hyperion, 1993.

Whorton, James C. *Nature Cures: The History of Alternative Medicine in America.* New York: Oxford University Press, 2002.

Widtsoe, Leah D., and John A. Widtsoe. *Brigham Young the Man of the Hour: Leader of the Latter Day Saints.* Whitefish, MT: Kessinger, 2004.

Wiener, Jon. *Come Together: John Lennon in His Time.* New York: Random House, 1984.

Wiggershaus, Rolf. *The Frankfurt School: Its History, Theories, and Political Significance.* Cambridge, MA: MIT Press, 1994.

Willard, Frances. "Address before the Second Biennial Convention of the World Woman's Christian Temperance Union." 1893. Available at http://gos.sbc.edu/w/willard.html.

William, Donald Lee. *Border Crossings: A Psychological Perspective on Carlos Castaneda's Path of Knowledge.* Toronto, Canada: City, 1981.

Williams, Clifford. *One More Train to Ride: The Underground World of Modern American Hoboes.* Bloomington: Indiana University Press, 2003.

Williams, John A., and Dennis A. Williams. *If I Stop, I'll Die: The Comedy and Tragedy of Richard Pryor.* New York: Thunder's Mouth, 1991.

Williams, Juan. *Eyes on the Prize: America's Civil Rights Years, 1954–1965.* New York: Viking Penguin, 1987.

Williams, Juan, and Julian Bond. *Eyes on the Prize: America's Civil Rights Years, 1954–1965.* New York: Penguin, 1988.

Williams, Linda. *Hard Core: Power, Pleasure, and the "Frenzy of the Visible."* Berkeley: University of California Press, 1989.

Williams, Robert C. *Horace Greeley: Champion of American Freedom.* New York: New York University Press, 2006.

Wilson, Edwin. *Living Theatre: A History.* Boston: McGraw-Hill, 2000.

Wilson, Elizabeth. *Bohemians: The Glamorous Outcasts.* New Brunswick, NJ: Rutgers University Press, 2000.

Wilson, Lloyd Lee. *Wrestling with Our Faith Tradition: Collected Public Witness, 1995–2004.* Philadelphia: Quaker Press of Friends General Conference, 2005.

Wilson, Morrow, and Suzanne Wilson. *Drugs in American Life.* New York: H.W. Wilson, 1975.

Wilson, Susan. *The Literary Trail of Greater Boston: A Tour of Sites in Boston, Cambridge, and Concord.* Rev. ed. Boston: Commonwealth Editions, 2005.

Wilson, William Julius. *The Truly Disadvantaged: The Inner City, the Underclass, and Public Policy.* Chicago: University of Chicago Press, 1987.

Wineapple, Brenda. *Hawthorne: A Life.* New York: Alfred A. Knopf, 2003.

Winship, Michael P. *Making Heretics: Militant Protestantism and Free Grace in Massachusetts, 1636–1641.* Princeton, NJ: Princeton University Press, 2002.

———. *The Times and Trials of Anne Hutchinson: Puritans Divided.* Lawrence: University Press of Kansas, 2005.

Wiseby, Herbert A., Jr. *Pioneer Prophetess: Jemima Wilkinson, the Publick Universal Friend.* Ithaca, NY: Cornell University Press, 1964.

Witoszek, Nina, and Andrew Brennan, eds. *Philosophical Dialogues: Arne Næss and the Progress of Ecosophy.* Lanham, MD: Rowman & Littlefield, 1999.

Wixson, Douglas C. *Worker-Writer in America: Jack Conroy and the Tradition of Midwestern Literary Radicalism, 1898–1990.* Urbana: University of Illinois Press, 1994.

Wojcik, Daniel. *The End of the World as We Know It: Faith, Fatalism, and Apocalypse in America.* New York: New York University Press, 1997.

———. *Punk and Neo-Tribal Body Art.* Jackson: University Press of Mississippi, 1995.

Wolfe, Tom. *The Electric Kool-Aid Acid Test.* New York: Farrar, Straus and Giroux, 1968; New York: Bantam, 1989.

Wolfenstein, Eugene Victor. *Psychoanalytic-Marxism: Groundwork.* New York: Guilford, 1993.

Wolle, Francis. *Fitz-James O'Brien: A Literary Bohemian of the Eighteen-Fifties.* Boulder: University of Colorado Press, 1944.

Wollman, Elizabeth L. *The Theater Will Rock: A History of the Rock Musical from* Hair *to* Hedwig. Ann Arbor: University of Michigan Press, 2006.

Wood, John. "Hells Angels and the Illusion of the Counterculture." *Journal of Popular Culture* 37:2 (Fall 2003): 336–52.

Wood, Peter H. *Black Majority: Negroes in Colonial South Carolina from 1670 through the Stono Rebellion.* New York: Alfred A. Knopf, 1974.

Wood, Robert. *Straightedge Youth: Complexity and Contradictions of a Subculture.* Syracuse, NY: Syracuse University Press, 2006.

Woodhull, Victoria C. *Free Lover: Sex, Marriage and Eugenics in the Early Speeches of Victoria Woodhull.* Seattle, WA: Inkling, 2005.

Woods, Thomas. *Knights of the Plow: Oliver H. Kelley and the Origins of the Grange in Republican Ideology.* Ames: Iowa State University Press, 1991.

Woodward, C. Vann. *Tom Watson: Agrarian Rebel.* Savannah, GA: Beehive, 1973.

Woolman, John, *The Journal and Other Writings of John Woolman.* London: J.M. Dent & Sons, 1910.

Worcester, Kent. *C.L.R. James: A Political Biography.* Albany: State University of New York Press, 1996.

World Publishing. Rowan and Martin's Laugh-In: *The Burbank Edition.* New York: World, 1969.

Worrall, Arthur J. *Quakers in the Colonial Northeast.* Hanover, NH: University Press of New England, 1980.

Worthington, Vivian. *A History of Yoga.* Boston: Routledge & Kegan Paul, 1982.

Wright, Kai, ed. *The African-American Archive: The History of the Black Experience through Documents.* New York: Black Dog & Leventhal, 2001.

Wright, Richard. *American Hunger.* New York: Harper & Row, 1977.

Wright, Stuart A. *Armageddon in Waco: Critical Perspectives on the Branch Davidian Conflict.* Chicago: University of Chicago Press, 1995.

Wrobel, Arthur. *Pseudo-Science and Society in Nineteenth-Century America.* Lexington: University Press of Kentucky, 1987.

Wunderlich, Roger. *Low Living and High Thinking at Modern Times, New York.* Syracuse, NY: Syracuse University Press, 1992.

Wynn, Charles M., Arthur W. Wiggins, and Sidney Harris. *Quantum Leaps in the Wrong Direction: Where Real Science Ends—and Pseudoscience Begins.* Washington, DC: Joseph Henry, 2001.

X, Malcolm. *The Autobiography of Malcolm X.* With Alex Haley. New York: Grove, 1965.

X, Malcolm, and George Breitman, eds. *Malcolm X Speaks: Selected Speeches.* New York: Grove Weidenfeld, 1990.

Yalom, Irvin D., and Molyn Leszcz. *The Theory and Practice of Group Therapy.* New York: Basic Books, 2005.

Yankelovich, Daniel. *The New Morality: A Profile of American Youth in the '70s.* New York: McGraw-Hill, 1974.

Yarbro-Bejarano, Yvonne. "The Female Subject in Chicano Theatre: Sexuality, 'Race,' and Class." *Theatre Journal* 38 (1986): 389–407.

Yates, Brock. *Outlaw Machine: Harley-Davidson and the Search for the American Soul.* Boston: Little, Brown, 1999.

Yinger, J. Milton. *Countercultures: The Promise and the Peril of a World Turned Upside Down.* New York: Free Press, 1982.

Yoder, Andrew. *Pirate Radio Stations: Tuning In to Underground Broadcasts in the Air and Online.* 3rd ed. New York: McGraw-Hill, 2002.

Yoder, Jon A. *Upton Sinclair.* New York: Ungar, 1975.

Yordon, Judy E. *Experimental Theatre: Creating and Staging Texts.* Long Grove, IL: Waveland, 1997.

Young, Gray, ed. *The Internet.* Bronx, NY: H.W. Wilson, 1998.

Zablocki, Benjamin David. *Alienation and Charisma: A Study of Contemporary American Communes.* New York: Free Press, 1980.

Zappa, Frank, with Peter Occhiofrosso. *The Real Frank Zappa Book.* New York: Simon and Schuster, 1990.

Zephaniah, Benjamin. *Gangsta Rap.* New York: Bloomsbury, 2004.

Zinn, Howard. *SNCC: The New Abolitionists.* 1964. Cambridge, MA: South End, 2002.

Zirin, Dave. *What's My Name, Fool? Sports and Resistance in the United States.* New York: Haymarket, 2005.

Zung, Thomas T.K., ed. *Buckminster Fuller: Anthology for a New Millennium.* New York: St. Martin's, 2001.

Zurier, Rebecca. *Art for the Masses: A Radical Magazine and Its Graphics, 1911–1917.* Philadelphia: Temple University Press, 1988.

———. *Picturing the City: Urban Vision and the Ashcan School.* Berkeley: University of California Press, 2006.

Web Sites

ACT UP (AIDS Coalition to Unleash Power). http://www.actupny.org.

The Advocate. http://www.advocate.com.

Alcoholics Anonymous. http://www.alcoholics-anonymous.org.

Amana Society. http://www.amanasociety.com.

American Civil Liberties Union. http://www.aclu.org.

American Holistic Medical Association. http://holisticmedicine.org.

American Indian Movement. http://www.aimovement.org.

American Museum of Beat Art. http://www.beatmuseum.org.

Andy Warhol Foundation for the Visual Arts. http://www.warholfoundation.org.

Archive of Folk Culture, American Folklife Center at the Library of Congress. http://www.loc.gov/folklife.

The Beatles. http://www.beatles.com.

Birmingham Civil Rights Institute Archives. http://www.bcri.org/archives/index/index.htm.

Black Mountain College. http://www.blackmountaincollege.org.

The Black Panther Party. http://www.blackpanther.org.

Blue Man Group. http://www.blueman.com.

Bob Dylan. http://www.bobdylan.com.

Burning Man Project. http://www.burningman.com.

Catholic Worker Movement. http://www.catholicworker.org.

Center for the Study of Responsive Law. http://www.csrl.org.

Chick Publications. http://www.chick.com.

Church of Christ, Scientist. http://www.tfccs.com.

Church of Jesus Christ of Latter-day Saints. http://www.lds.org.

Church of Scientology. http://www.scientology.org.

City College of New York. http://www.ccny.cuny.edu.

City Lights Books. http://www.citylights.com.

Civil Rights in Mississippi Digital Archive. http://www.lib.usm.edu/~spcol/crda.

Columbia University. http://www.columbia.edu.

Coney Island Polar Bear Club. http://www.polarbearclub.org.

The Diggers Archives. http://www.diggers.org.

Doonesbury Town Hall @ Slate. http://www.doonesbury.com.

Earth First! http://earthfirst.org.

Earth Liberation Front. http://earthliberationfront.com.

Eckankar. http://www.eckankar.org.

Esalen Institute. http://www.esalen.org.

Evergreen Review. http://www.evergreenreview.com.

Extext Archives/Zines. http://www.etext.org/Zines.

The Farm. http://www.thefarm.org.

Fellowship for Intentional Community. http://fic.ic.org.

Folk Music Archives. http://folkmusicarchives.org.

Foursquare Church. http://www.foursquare.org.

Free Speech Movement Digital Archive. http://bancroft.berkeley.edu/FSM.

Freemasonry.org. http://www.freemasonry.org.

Fruitlands Museum. http://www.fruitlands.org.

The Fugs. http://www.thefugs.com.

Gender Public Advocacy Coalition. http://www.gpac.org.

Grand Comicbook Database Project. http://www.comics.org.

Grateful Dead. http://www.gratefuldead.com.

Gray Panthers. http://www.graypanthers.org.

Greenpeace. http://www.greenpeace.org.

Guerrilla Girls. http://www.guerrillagirls.com.

Haight-Ashbury Home Page. http://www.lovehaight.org.

Hells Angels Motorcycle Club. http://www.hells-angels.com.

Industrial Workers of the World. http://www.iww.org.

International Peace Mission. http://www.libertynet.org/fdipmm.

International Society for Krishna Consciousness. http://www.iskcon.com.

Jehovah's Witnesses. http://www.watchtower.org.

Jews for Jesus. http://jewsforjesus.org.

John Birch Society. http://www.jbs.org.

The Kitchen. http://www.thekitchen.org.

The Knights Party, USA (Ku Klux Klan). http://www.kkk.com.

League of American Bicyclists. http://www.bikeleague.org.

Living Theatre, The. http://www.livingtheatre.org.

MAD Magazine. http://www.dccomics.com/mad.

Martin Luther King, Jr. Research and Education Institute at Stanford University. http://www.stanford.edu/group/King/index.htm.

The MC5. http://www.MC5.org.

Michigan State University Libraries Comic Art Collection Home Page. http://www.lib.msu.edu/comics/index.htm.

Mother Jones. http://www.motherjones.com.

Ms. Foundation for Women. http://www.ms.foundation.org.

Ms. Magazine. http://www.msmagazine.com.

MTV. http://www.mtv.com.

Naropa University. http://www.naropa.edu.

The Nation. http://www.thenation.com.

Nation of Islam. http://www.noi.org.

National Association for the Advancement of Colored People. http://www.naacp.org.

National Organization for Women. http://www.now.org.

The New School. http://www.newschool.edu.

1969 Woodstock Festival & Concert. http://www.woodstock69.com.

Nuyorican Poets Café. http://www.nuyorican.org.

Oberlin College. http://www.oberlin.edu.

ONE National Gay & Lesbian Archives. http://www.onearchives.org.

The Onion: America's Finest News Source. http://www.theonion.com.

Pacifica and Affiliates Network. http://pacificanetwork.org.

Pacifica Radio Foundation. http://www.kpfk.org.

Peace and Freedom Party. http://www.peaceandfreedom.org.

People for the Ethical Treatment of Animals. http://www.peta.org.

Performance Space 122. http://www.ps122.org.

Peter Max Online. http://www.petermax.com.

Planned Parenthood Federation of America. http://www.plannedparenthood.org.

Poets' Corner. http://www.theotherpages.org/poems.

Promise Keepers. http://www.promisekeepers.com.

Public Citizen. http://www.citizen.org.

Public Enemy. http://www.publicenemy.com.

Public Interest Research Groups. http://www.uspirg.org.

The Realist Archive Project. http://www.ep.tc/realist.

The Register-Guard on the Web. http://www.registerguard.com.

Rolling Stone. http://rollingstone.com.

The Rolling Stones. http://www.rollingstones.com.

Sierra Club. http://www.sierraclub.org.

The Simpsons. http://www.thesimpsons.com/index.html.

The Sixties Project. http://www2.iath.virginia.edu/sixties/HTML_docs/Sixties.html.

Society for Creative Anachronism. http://www.sca.org.

South Park. http://www.southparkstudios.com.

Southern California Library for Social Studies and Research. http://www.socallib.org.

Theosophical Society in America. http://www.theosophical.org.

Transcendental Meditation Program. http://www.tm.org.

Unitarian Universalist Association of Congregations. http://www.uua.org.

United Farm Workers of America. http://ufw.org.

The Universal Negro Improvement Association and African Communities League. http://www.unia-acl.org.

University of California, Berkeley. http://berkeley.edu.

The Village Voice. http://www.villagevoice.com.

Wavy Gravy. http://www.wavygravy.net.

Whole Earth Catalog. http://www.wholeearth.com.

Wilderness Society. http://wilderness.org.

Wolfgang's Vault (Home to the Bill Graham Archives). http://www.wolfgangsvault.com.

Yoga Journal. http://www.jogajournal.com.

Filmography

The feature films, documentaries, and experimental works contained in this filmography correspond to the broadest possible definition of what this encyclopedia identifies as countercultural. In addition to providing information on each of the films included in the encyclopedia's main text, the list includes movies relevant to entries that do not explicitly mention motion pictures. Selections include mainstream feature films, television documentaries, experimental short films, art films, international coproductions (most of which treat American themes or were made in part with American funding), agitprop documentaries, historically censored works, and a number of cult classics. Many of the works depict or comment on movements, people, ideas, or historical references relevant to multiple entries in *American Countercultures*.

Adventures of Priscilla, Queen of the Desert, The. Directed by Stephan Elliot. 1994. Available on DVD from MGM Home Entertainment, 2000. A dramatized road movie about two drag queens and a transsexual encountering an unprepared world.

Alice's Restaurant. Directed by Arthur Penn. 1969. Available on DVD from MGM Home Entertainment, 2001. A cinematic adaptation of Arlo Guthrie's satiric, antiwar song-story of 1967.

All the President's Men. Directed by Alan J. Paluka. 1976. Available on DVD from Warner Home Video, 2006. The dramatization of Carl Bernstein and Bob Woodward's investigative work that led to the breaking of the Watergate scandal and the impeachment and resignation of President Richard M. Nixon.

Almost Famous. Directed by Cameron Crowe. 2000. Available on DVD from Universal Home Entertainment, 2001. This semi-autobiographical feature film explores the experiences of a young rock and roll journalist in the early 1970s.

Altered States. Directed by Ken Russell. 1980. Available on DVD from Warner Home Video, 1998. A cult film about a scientist's experiments with primal consciousness.

American Roots Music. Directed by Jim Brown. 2001. Available on DVD from Palm Pictures, 2001. A documentary about emerging musical styles in the twentieth century.

American Splendor. Directed by Shari Springer Berman and Robert Pulcini. 2003. Available on DVD from Warner Home Video, 2004. This stylized biopic of comic book personality Harvey Pekar combines documentary footage and fictional dramatization.

Amistad. Directed by Steven Spielberg. 1997. Available on DVD from Dreamworks/Universal Home Entertainment, 1999. A historical feature film about an 1839 uprising aboard a Spanish slave ship and the aftermath.

An Inconvenient Truth. Directed by Davis Guggenheim. 2006. Available on DVD from Paramount Home Video, 2006. A documentary about global warming that urges environmental activism.

Apocalypse Now. Directed by Francis Ford Coppola. 1979. Available on DVD from Paramount Home Video, 2006. This lyrical film about the Vietnam War doubles as a re-imagination of Joseph Conrad's 1902 novel *Heart of Darkness*.

Assault on Gay America: The Life and Death of Billy Jack. Directed by Claudia Pryor Malis. 2000. Available on DVD from PBS Home Video, 2006. A television documentary about the roots of homophobia in the United States.

Atomic Café, The. Directed by Kevin Rafferty. 1982. Available on DVD from Docurama, 2002. An experimental antinuclear documentary comprising footage from 1940s and 1950s U.S. government–issued propaganda films.

Autobiography of Miss Jane Pittman, The. Directed by John Korty. 1974. Available on DVD from Classic Media, 2005. This celebrated television drama explores an African American woman's memories, often of struggle, from the Civil War through the civil rights era.

Basket Case. Directed by Frank Henenlotter. 1982. Available on DVD from Something Weird Video, 2001. A cult horror film about a vengeful set of former conjoined twins.

Beat Generation, The: An American Dream. Directed by Janet Forman. 1987. Available on VHS from Fox Lorber Home Video, 1998. A documentary about the lives and views of major players in the Beat movement, including Allen Ginsberg, Neal Cassady, and Jack Kerouac.

Beat Street. Directed by Stan Lathan. 1984. Available on DVD from MGM Home Entertainment, 2003. A dramatic youth film about the street-level cultural scene—including hip-hop, break dancing, and graffiti—in 1980s New York City.

Before Stonewall: The Making of a Gay and Lesbian Community. Directed by John Scagliotti, et al. 1984. Available on DVD from First Run Features, 2004. A documentary concerned with the practice and reception of homosexuality in America up to 1969.

Beloved. Directed by Jonathan Demme. 1998. Available on DVD from Touchstone Home Video, 1998. This feature film adaptation of the Pulitzer Prize–winning Toni Morrison novel of the same title examines the costs of slavery through the story of an escaped slave and the persistent reexamination of her past.

Berkeley in the Sixties. Directed by Mark Kitchell. 1990. Available on DVD from First Run Features, 2002. A political documentary that examines the campus and community activist movements of the University of California, Berkeley, in the 1960s.

Big Lebowski, The. Directed by Ethan Coen and Joel Coen. 1998. Available on DVD from Universal Home Entertainment, 2005. An offbeat comedy about a mystical loser know as "The Dude."

Billy Jack. Directed by Tom Laughlin. 1971. Available on DVD from Warner Home Video, 2004. A feature film about a half-Indian Vietnam veteran and loner who protects an endangered school.

Birth of a Nation, The. Directed by D.W. Griffith. 1915. Available on DVD from Kino Video, 2002. This groundbreaking narrative feature film contrasts the effects of the American Civil War on two families and is notorious for its portrayal of the Ku Klux Klan.

Black Gold. Directed by Marc Francis and Nick Francis. 2006. Available on DVD from California Newsreel, 2006. A documentary about the cultural history and economic legacy of coffee.

Black Mountain Revisited. Directed by Joe Cardarelli. 1990. Available on VHS from Maisonneuve Press and Viridian Video Productions, 1996. A retrospective documentary chronicling the glory years of North Carolina's famous Black Mountain College.

Black Press, The: Soldiers Without Swords. Directed by Stanley Nelson. 1999. Available on DVD from Half Nelson Productions/California Newsreel, 1999. A documentary history of black newspapers.

Blackboard Jungle. Directed by Richard Brooks. 1955. Available on DVD from Warner Home Video, 2005. A dramatic literary adaptation about a dedicated teacher working at a troubled urban school.

Blowup. Directed by Michelangelo Antonioni. 1966. Available on DVD from Warner Home Video, 2004. Set amid the verve of swinging London, this trendsetting art film is about a hip photographer's unraveling of what seems to be a murder mystery.

Blue Collar and Buddha: A Documentary. Directed by Taggart Siegel. 1987. Available on VHS from NAATA Distribution, 1996. A documentary concerning Laotian immigrants and the cultural clashes that occur with their resettlement in the American Midwest.

Bluegrass Journey. Directed by Ruth Oxenberg. 2003. Available on DVD from Blue Stores Films, 2004. A documentary about the contemporary bluegrass scene told through interviews and performances.

Bob & Carol & Ted & Alice. Directed by Paul Mazursky. 1969. Available on DVD from Columbia Tristar Home Video, 2004. An offbeat 1960s feature film about repression and liberation through sexual coupling.

Bonnie and Clyde. Directed by Arthur Penn. 1967. Available on DVD from Warner Home Video, 1999. Youth, exuberance, and graphic violence color this romanticized retelling of the story of outlaws Bonnie Parker and Clyde Barrow in this celebrated revival of the gangster genre.

Bound for Glory. Directed by Hal Ashby. 1976. Available on DVD from MGM Home Entertainment, 2000. This film about the life of folksinger Woody Guthrie was adapted from his autobiography.

Boys Don't Cry. Directed by Kimberly Peirce. 1999. Available on DVD from 20th Century Fox Home Entertainment, 2000. A dramatized feature film about a transgendered youth's life and struggles with sexual identity.

Bukowski: Born into This. Directed by John Dullaghen. 2003. Available on DVD from Magnolia Home Entertainment, 2006. A documentary biography of controversial Los Angeles street poet Charles Bukowski.

Burning Man Festival. Directed by Joe Winston. 1997. Available on DVD from Ow Myeye Productions, 2001. A documentary about Nevada's Burning Man Festival, a celebration of collective consciousness, artistic and musical expression, and unfettered creativity.

Cabinet of Dr. Caligari, The. Directed by Robert Weine. 1920. Special Collector's Edition available on DVD from Image Entertainment, 1997. A classic silent film in the horror genre.

Carter Family, The: Will the Circle Be Unbroken?. Directed by Kathy Conkwright. 2005. Available on DVD from PBS Home Video, 2005. A television documentary about the life and times of country music's Carter family.

Cat's Cradle. In *By Brakhage: An Anthology.* Directed by Stan Brakhage. 1959. Available on DVD from Criterion Collection, 2003. An avant-garde experimental short featuring a couple, a cat, and the inside of a house.

Cecil B. DeMented. Directed by John Waters. 2000. Available on DVD from Artisan Entertainment, 2001. A cult film about an insane independent motion picture director and his renegade group of teenage filmmakers who kidnap an A-list Hollywood actress and force her to star in their underground film.

Celebration at Big Sur. Directed by Johanna Demetrakas. 1971. This documentary about the 1969 Big Sur Folk Festival in California features such performing artists as Joan Baez, Joni Mitchell, and Graham Nash.

Chappaqua. Directed by Conrad Rooks. 1966. Available on DVD from Fox Lorber Home Video, 1997. A psychedelic 1960s feature film about expanded consciousness through the use of alcohol and drugs and metaphysical experimentation.

Cheech & Chong's Still Smokin. Directed by Tommy Chong. 1983. Available on DVD from Paramount Home Video, 2000. Following the success of *Up in Smoke,* this film includes more marijuana-fueled pratfalls from the comedy duo Cheech & Chong.

Cheech & Chong's Up in Smoke. Directed by Lou Adler and Tommy Chong. 1978. Available on DVD from Paramount Home Video, 2000. The comedy duo Cheech Marin and Tommy Chong embark on a series of drug-induced hijinks in this feature film.

Chelsea Girls. Directed by Paul Morrissey and Andy Warhol. 1966. Available on DVD from Raro Video, 2003. A banal, experimental epic (over four hours in length) that serves as a time capsule for participants in Warhol's studio, The Factory, and examines their lives at the famous Hotel Chelsea.

Chicago 10. Directed by Brett Morgen. 2007. Available on DVD from Participant Productions, 2007. A hybrid film that uses animation, dramatized voice acting, archival footage, and music to explore the antiwar protests at the 1968 Democratic National Convention, the arrest and trial of several leaders of the protests, including Abbie Hoffman, Jerry Rubin, David Dellinger, and Tom Hayden, and the legacy of those events.

Chicano! History of the Mexican-American Civil Rights Movement. Various directors. 1996. Available on VHS from NLCC Educational Media, 1996. This polyvocal documentary about the struggle for Mexican American rights during the 1960s and 1970s focuses on the legacy of César Chávez and the need for labor solidarity.

City Kids Meet Ashcan Art. Directed by Robert W. Snyder. 1998. Available on VHS from Carousel Film & Video, 1998. A documentary about students from the Bronx in New York City viewing and reacting to artwork created by the Ashcan school of American painters.

Clerks. Directed by Kevin Smith. 1994. Available on DVD from Miramax Home Entertainment, 2004. A quirky independent comedy about a day in the life of retail workers in suburban New Jersey.

Confessions of a Nazi Spy. Directed by Anatole Litvak. 1939. A somewhat propagandistic dramatic feature about the discovery of a Nazi spy ring in the United States.

Conspiracy Theory. Directed by Richard Donner. 1997. Available on DVD from Warner Home Video, 1998. A thriller about an offbeat New York City taxi driver/conspiracy theorist who finds himself caught up in a real-life conspiracy.

Convention City. Directed by Archie Mayo. 1933. Released before the Hays Code on moral standards was in effect, this feature was noted for its salacious subject matter.

Cradle Will Rock. Directed by Tim Robbins. 1999. Available on DVD from Touchstone Home Video, 2000. A broad dramatization of changing mores, cultural production, and the pervasiveness of New Deal programs in 1930s New York City.

Cruising. Directed by William Friedkin. 1980. Available on DVD from Warner Home Video, 2007. A controversial police drama about a murder investigation in the sadomasochist haunts of New York's 1980s gay subculture.

Crumb. Directed by Terry Zwigoff. 1994. Available on DVD from Sony Home Entertainment, 2006. A documentary portrayal of the life, loves, and obsessions of iconoclastic cartoonist R. Crumb.

Cry-Baby. Directed by John Waters. 1990. Available on DVD from Universal Home Entertainment, 2005. This cult classic about a group of juvenile delinquents parodies teen musicals and 1950s Elvis Presley movies.

Desistfilm. In *By Brakhage: An Anthology.* Directed by Stan Brakhage. 1954. Available on DVD from Criterion Collection, 2003. A short, surrealistic film in the horror genre, focusing on a group of young adults isolated in a house in the woods.

Dirty Pictures. Directed by Frank Pierson. 2000. Available on DVD from MGM Home Entertainment, 2000. A dramatization of the 1990 trial of controversial photographer Robert Mapplethorpe.

Dirty Shame, A. In *Very Crudely Yours: John Waters Collection.* Directed by John Waters. 2004. Available on DVD from New Line Home Entertainment, 2005. A repressed middle-aged Baltimore woman turns into a sex addict and becomes part of the city's underground subculture.

Do the Right Thing. Directed by Spike Lee. 1989. Available on DVD from Criterion Collection, 2001. An explosive drama about a day of mounting racial tension in Brooklyn, New York.

Don't Look Back. Directed by D.A. Pennebaker. 1967. Available on DVD from New Video Group, 2007. A groundbreaking rock documentary about Bob Dylan's 1965 tour of England.

Dr. Strangelove or: How I Learned to Stop Worrying and Love the Bomb. Directed by Stanley Kubrick. 1964. Available on DVD from Sony Home Entertainment, 2001. A suspense comedy in which an insane general initiates a process leading to nuclear holocaust that a room full of politicians and generals frantically try to stop.

Drugstore Cowboy. Directed by Gus Van Sant. 1989. Available on DVD from Lions Gate Home Entertainment, 1999. A gritty road movie about a group of drug addicts and their descent into crime.

Easy Rider. Directed by Dennis Hopper. 1969. Available on DVD from Columbia Tristar Home Video, 2004. A road movie of the 1960s about two free spirits on a cross-country quest for an "authentic" American experience, famously doused in sex, drugs, and rock and roll.

Eat a Bowl of Tea. Directed by Wayne Wong. 1989. Available on DVD from Columbia Tristar Home Video, 2003. A dramatic saga of Chinese American assimilation in the 1940s.

Edward Scissorhands. Directed by Tim Burton. 1990. Available on DVD from 20th Century Fox Home Entertainment, 2000. A modern fairy tale that tells the story of Edward, a man created by an inventor who dies before finishing Edward and leaves him with scissors in place of hands.

El Mariachi. Directed by Robert Rodriguez. 1992. Available on DVD from Sony Home Entertainment, 2003. A seminal low-budget action film that is part of the celebrated independent film movement of the 1990s.

El Topo. In *The Films of Alejandro Jodorowsky.* Directed by Alejandro Jodorowsky. 1970. Available on DVD from ABKCO Films/Anchor Bay Entertainment, 2007. A quintessential cult film—part European art film and part revisionist Western—about a transcendental hero who undertakes a mythopoetic vision quest.

Elephant Man, The. Directed by David Lynch. 1980. Available on DVD from Paramount Home Entertainment, 2001. An American auteur's take on the story of a physically deformed man rescued from a life as a freak show attraction.

Eraserhead. Directed by David Lynch. 1977. Available on DVD from Absurda/Subversive Cinema, 2005. A stylistically obscure midnight movie about an odd man's domestic hell.

Eternal Sunshine of the Spotless Mind. Directed by Michel Gondry. 2004. Available on DVD from Universal Home Entertainment, 2004. A wacky drama about a couple that undergoes a procedure to erase each other from their memories when their relationship turns sour.

Even Cowgirls Get the Blues. Directed by Gus Van Sant. 1993. Available on DVD from New Line Home Entertainment, 2004. The film adaptation of a Tom Robbins novel about a hitchhiker with a comically enlarged thumb who ends up participating in a feminist rebellion.

Ever Since the World Ended. Directed by Calum Grant and Joshua Atesh Lee. 2001. Available on DVD from BFS Entertainment and Multimedia, 2007. A pseudo-documentary about establishing a commune in postapocalyptic San Francisco.

Exorcist, The. Directed by William Friedkin. 1973. Available on DVD from Warner Home Video, 2000. This feature horror film, based on William Peter Blatty's 1971 novel of the same name, fictionalizes the allegedly true story of a young girl who is possessed by the devil.

Eyes on the Prize. Directed by Henry Hampton. 1986, 1990. Available on DVD from PBS Home Video, 2006. A multipart documentary that chronicles the civil rights movement.

Faces. In *John Cassavetes: Five Films.* Directed by John Cassavetes. 1968. Available on DVD from Criterion Collection, 2004. This seminal independent feature film explores the passion of a marriage gone awry.

Fahrenheit 9/11. Directed by Michael Moore. 2004. Available on DVD from Columbia Tristar Home Video, 2004. This polemical documentary about President George W. Bush's conflicted allegiances and problematic foreign ties is set in the immediate post-9/11 period.

Far From Heaven. Directed by Todd Haynes. 2002. Available on DVD from Universal Home Entertainment, 2003. A dramatic feature film about a racially mixed relationship in the 1950s.

Fear and Loathing in Las Vegas. Directed by Terry Gilliam. 1998. Available on DVD from Universal Home Video, 1998. Based on the counterculture classic by Hunter S. Thompson, an oddball journalist and his psychopathic lawyer travel to Las Vegas for a series of psychedelic escapades.

Female Trouble. In *Very Crudely Yours: John Waters Collection.* Directed by John Waters. 1974. Available on DVD from New Line Home Entertainment, 2005. A cult classic about a spoiled schoolgirl who runs away from home, gets pregnant, and ends up as a fashion model for a pair of beauticians who like to photograph women committing crimes.

Festival Express. Directed by Bob Smeaton. 1970, 2004. Available on DVD from New Line Home Entertainment, 2004. This documentary about a concert tour of Canada by San Francisco–scene bands traveling by train features Janis Joplin, the Grateful Dead, The Band, and others.

54. Directed by Mark Christopher. 1998. Available on DVD from Miramax Home Entertainment, 1999. A fictional account of New York's famous Studio 54 discotheque.

Fight Club. Directed by David Fincher. 1999. Available on DVD from 20th Century Fox Home Entertainment, 2000. A cult literary adaptation about a man's dissatisfaction with his mainstream lifestyle and foray into a semisecret underground movement.

Fight in the Fields, The: Cesar Chavez and the Farmworkers' Struggle. Directed by Rick Tejada-Flores and Ray Telles. 1996. Available on DVD from Cinema Guild, 2003. A documentary chronicling the legacy of César Chávez and the fight for Chicano self-determination.

Film About a Woman Who . . . Directed by Yvonne Rainer. 1974. Available on VHS from Zeitgeist Films, 1990. An experimental film concerned with attempts to construct a feminist form of subjectivity.

Fireworks. In *The Films of Kenneth Anger, Volume 1.* Directed by Kenneth Anger. 1947. Available on DVD from Fantoma Films, 2007. A classic experimental film infamous for its exploration of the intersections between homosexuality and sadomasochism.

Flaming Creatures. Directed by Jack Smith. 1964. Available on VHS from Facets Video, 1997. This mid-length experimental film is known for its lyrical and polymorphous screen sexuality.

Forrest Gump. Directed by Robert Zemeckis. 1994. Available on DVD from Paramount Home Video, 2001. A well-meaning man, limited in IQ, finds himself unwittingly part of counterculture events and meets key figures from the 1950s through the 1970s.

Freaks. Directed by Tod Browning. 1932. Available on DVD from Warner Home Video, 2004. A shocking cult movie about real circus sideshow performers who take revenge on a "normal" couple after suffering sustained degradation.

Friendly Persuasion. Directed by William Wyler. 1956. Available on DVD from Warner Home Video, 2000. Based on a 1945 novel of the same title by Jessamyn West, this acclaimed film stars Gary Cooper as the patriarch of a family of pacifist Quakers living in Indiana during the American Civil War.

Fritz the Cat. Directed by Ralph Bakshi. 1972. Available on DVD from MGM Home Entertainment, 2001. An animated feature film about an amorously bold and anthropomorphized cat in early 1970s New York.

Gang War: Bangin' in Little Rock. Directed by Marc Levin. 1971. Available on DVD from HBO Home Video, 2006. A documentary about the encroachment of gang activity in Little Rock, Arkansas.

Getting Straight. Directed by Richard Rush. 1970. Drama of a frustrated, liberal teacher in the era of campus violence.

Gimme Shelter. Directed by Albert Maysles and David Maysles. 1970. Available on DVD from Criterion Collection, 2003. A rock music documentary about the 1969 Rolling Stones tour, including the tragic events that took place at the Altamont Speedway concert in Northern California.

Glorifying the American Girl. Directed by John Harkrider and Millard Webb. 1929. Available on VHS from Alpha Video Distributors, 1997. A narrative feature film about a department store salesgirl's rise to fame.

Glory. Directed by Edward Zwick. 1989. Available on DVD from Sony Home Entertainment, 2006. A dramatized account of the 54th Massachusetts Infantry, the first all-black regiment in the American Civil War.

Godfather, The. Directed by Francis Ford Coppola. 1972. Available on DVD from Paramount Home Video, 2001. The Academy Award–winning drama of the Corleones, a fictional New York Mafia family, based on Mario Puzo's novel of the same name.

Graduate, The. Directed by Mike Nichols. 1967. Available on DVD from MGM Home Entertainment, 2007. This feature film stars Dustin Hoffman in the critically acclaimed role of Benjamin Braddock, a confused college graduate who has an affair with a much older woman.

Grapes of Wrath, The. Directed by John Ford. 1940. Available on DVD from 20th Century Fox Home Entertainment, 2004. An acclaimed film adaptation of John Steinbeck's novel of the same name about Dust Bowl migrants during the Great Depression of the 1930s.

Grateful Dead Movie, The. Directed by Jerry Garcia and Leon Gast. 1977. Available on DVD from Monterey Video, 2004. The laboriously edited concert documentary of the Grateful Dead's first round of farewell concerts in October 1974.

Great Day in Harlem, A. Directed by Jean Bach. 1994. Available on DVD from Image Home Entertainment, 2005. A documentary that examines the personalities and social circumstances responsible for the most famous jazz photograph in history: a group photograph of the top jazz musicians in New York City in 1958, which was taken for a piece in *Esquire* magazine.

Grindhouse. Directed by Robert Rodriguez and Quentin Tarantino. 2007. Available on DVD from Weinstein Company, 2007. A two-part exploitation feature film, consisting of *Planet Terror* (Rodriguez) and *Death Proof* (Tarantino).

Groove. Directed by Greg Harrison. 2000. Available on DVD from Columbia Tristar Home Video, 2000. A dramatic feature about one crazy night in the throes of San Francisco's burgeoning rave scene.

Hackers. Directed by Iain Softley. 1995. Available on DVD from MGM Home Entertainment, 1998. A technologically overloaded action film about computer hackers who find themselves embroiled in a sinister plot involving big business and the Federal Bureau of Investigation.

Hag in a Black Leather Jacket. Directed by John Waters. 1964. A dark farce about an African American man who courts a Caucasian woman by carrying her around in a trash can and later marries her in a ceremony conducted by a Ku Klux Klansman.

Hairspray. In *Very Crudely Yours: John Waters Collection.* Directed by John Waters. 1989. Available on DVD from New Line Home

Entertainment, 2005. A campy film that addresses racial segregation with the director's signature humor.

Happiness. Directed by Todd Solondz. 1998. Available on DVD from Lions Gate Home Entertainment, 2003. An edgy independent feature film about the dissatisfactions and sexual transgressions of three middle-class New Jersey sisters.

Harder They Come, The. Directed by Perry Henzell. 1972. Available on DVD from Xenon, 2006. This midnight movie following the precipitous rise of an upstart con man in Jamaica features music by Jimmy Cliff.

Harlan County, U.S.A. Directed by Barbara Kopple. 1976. Available on DVD from Criterion Collection, 2006. A documentary about a group of miners who are pitted against an exploitive corporation.

Hearts and Minds. Directed by Peter Davis. 1974. Available on DVD from Criterion Collection, 2002. A controversial documentary about the failures and immediate legacy of the war in Vietnam.

Heavy Traffic. Directed by Ralph Bakshi. 1973. Available on DVD from MGM Home Entertainment, 2000. An experimental animated feature chronicling a randy teenager's hopes of leaving home and living on his own terms.

Henry & June. Directed by Philip Kaufman. 1990. Available on DVD from Universal Home Video, 1999. A dramatized re-creation of the relationship between writers Henry Miller and Anaïs Nin.

Hester Street. Directed by Joan Micklin Silver. 1975. Available on DVD from Home Vision Entertainment, 2004. The tale of a young Jewish woman coming to terms with 1890s American culture.

High Noon. Directed by Fred Zinnemann. 1952. Available on DVD from Republic Pictures, 1998. An iconic Western starring Gary Cooper as a frontier lawman and the newlywed husband of a pacifist Quaker (Grace Kelly) who finds himself standing alone against a revenge-seeking enemy.

Hitchhiker's Guide to the Galaxy. Directed by Garth Jennings. 2005. Available on DVD from Buena Vista Home Entertainment, 2005. A feature film based on the sci-fi comedy book series by Douglas Adams, which follows the adventures of hapless Englishman Arthur Dent, who escapes the demolition of Earth by a bureaucratic alien race called the Vogons.

Hollywood Aliens and Monsters. Directed by Kevin Burns. 1997. Available on VHS from A&E Home Video, 1997. A history of science fiction moviemaking, with an emphasis on the relationship between political and social paranoia and the subject matter of the films.

Holy Mountain, The. In *The Films of Alejandro Jodorowsky.* Directed by Alejandro Jodorowsky. 1973. Available on DVD from ABKCO Films/Anchor Bay Entertainment, 2007. A cult film about the trials and destiny of a messianic figure (portrayed by the director).

Homeless in Paradise. Directed by Chuck Braverman and Marilyn Braverman. 2006. Available on DVD from New Day Films, 2006. A documentary portrayal of four homeless people in the Santa Monica, California, area.

Hooked: Illegal Drugs and How They Got That Way. Directed by Thom Yaroschuk. 2000. Available on DVD from A&E/New Video, 2002. This multipart television documentary examines the rise of drug use in America.

Hunger, The. Directed by Tony Scott. 1983. Available on DVD from Warner Home Video, 2004. A horror movie, largely praised by the goth subculture, about a female vampire.

Hunting of the President, The. Directed by Nickolas Perry and Harry Thomason. 2004. Available on DVD from 20th Century Fox Home Entertainment, 2004. An investigative documentary about the widespread effort to attack, discredit, and impeach President Bill Clinton.

I Am Chicano. Directed by Jesús Salvador Treviño. 1972. An early documentary about the Chicano Movement of the 1960s and early 1970s.

I Am Joaquin. Directed by Luis Valdez. 1969. Available on VHS from CFI Video, 1995. The adaptation of a seminal Chicano poem about the exploitation of Mexican labor in the United States.

I Shot Andy Warhol. Directed by Mary Harron. 1995. Available on DVD from MGM Home Entertainment, 2001. Biopic about Valerie Solanas, a militant feminist who shot and wounded Andy Warhol.

In the Grip of Evil. Directed by Charles Vanderpool. 1997. Available on DVD from WinStar Home Entertainment, 1998. An investigative documentary about exorcism and the historical motivation for William Peter Blatty's 1971 horror novel *The Exorcist* and 1973 film of the same name.

In the Heat of the Night. Directed by Norman Jewison. 1967. Available on DVD from MGM Home Entertainment, 2001. A police drama about a murder investigation in the Deep South that prompts an uneasy racial alliance.

Incident at Oglala: The Leonard Peltier Story. Directed by Michael Apted. 1992. Available on DVD from Artisan Home Entertainment, 2004. A documentary that re-creates the controversy surrounding the 1975 police invasion of Pine Ridge Indian Reservation in South Dakota.

Inside Islam. Directed by Mark Hufnail. 2002. Available on DVD from New Video Group, 2002. A documentary about the history, rise, and reception of Islam.

Inside Life Outside. Directed by Sachiko Hamada and Scott Sinkler. 1988. Available on VHS from New Day Films, 1988. A documentary about the daily struggles of a group of homeless people in New York.

Introspection. In *Viva la Dance: The Beginnings of Ciné-Dance.* Directed by Sara Kathryn Arledge. 1941 and 1946. Available on DVD from Image Entertainment, 2005. A poetic dance film that is considered a benchmark in the genre.

Invasion of the Body Snatchers. Directed by Don Siegel. 1956. Available on DVD from Republic Entertainment, 2002. This science fiction film about the surreptitious invasion of a small American town by aliens is noted for its typification of cold war paranoia and the apocalyptic beliefs of the Red Scare.

Iron Jawed Angels. Directed by Katja von Garnier. 2004. Available on DVD from HBO Home Video, 2004. A dramatization of historical events and key figures in the struggle for woman suffrage.

Jailhouse Rock. Directed by Richard Thorpe. 1957. Available on DVD from Warner Home Video, 2007. An iconic early rock and roll film starring Elvis Presley as a musician with a rags-to-riches story.

Jaws. Directed by Steven Spielberg. 1975. Available on DVD from Universal Home Entertainment, 2005. The super thriller and box office hit adapted from Peter Benchley's best-selling 1974 novel of the same title.

Jesus Camp. Directed by Heidi Ewing and Rachel Grady. 2006. Available on DVD from Magnolia Home Entertainment, 2006. A documentary that chronicles the attitudes found at evangelical

Christian summer camps through the lives of the children as they study and play.

Kids. Directed by Larry Clark. 1995. Available on DVD from Trimark Home Entertainment/Lions Gate Home Entertainment, 2000. A seminal, candid 1990s independent film about the lives of nihilistic adolescents.

Kill Bill: Vol. 1 and *Kill Bill: Vol. 2.* Directed by Quentin Tarantino. 2003, 2004. Available on DVD from Miramax Home Entertainment/Buena Vista Home Entertainment, 2004. This two-part feature film is positioned as a send-up of kung fu revenge narratives.

Land of Look Behind. Directed by Alan Greenberg. 1982. Available on DVD from Subversive Cinema, 2006. A documentary film about the life and times of reggae artist Bob Marley.

Laramie Project, The. Directed by Moisés Kaufman. 2002. Available on DVD from HBO Home Video, 2002. The dramatization of a small town's direct confrontation with its own intolerance in the wake of the homophobic murder of Matthew Shepard.

Last Waltz, The. Directed by Martin Scorsese. 1978. Available on DVD from MGM Home Entertainment, 2004. A rock concert documentary detailing the star-studded, final hurrah of The Band.

Life and Times of Allen Ginsberg, The. Directed by Jerry Aronson. 1994. Available on DVD from New Yorker Video, 2006. This documentary investigates the life, work, and legacy of Beat poet Allen Ginsberg.

Lone Star. Directed by John Sayles. 1996. Available on DVD from Warner Home Video, 1999. A dramatic feature film about a murder investigation in a Texas border town.

Malcolm X. Directed by Spike Lee. 1992. Available on DVD from Warner Home Video, 2000. This epic biopic dramatizes the life of Malcolm X, a leader in the Nation of Islam whose ideas helped inspire the Black Power movement.

Manhatta. In *Avant-Garde: Experimental Cinema of the 1920s and '30s.* Directed by Charles Sheeler and Paul Strand. 1921. Available on DVD from Kino Video, 2005. An early avant-garde short film that explores the aesthetic potential for representing the New York cityscape.

Manufacturing Consent: Noam Chomsky and the Media. Directed by Mark Achbar and Peter Wintonick. 1992. Available on DVD from Zeitgeist Video, 2002. A biographical documentary about Noam Chomsky's work in assessing the hidden ideological manipulations employed by Western democracies.

*M*A*S*H.* Directed by Robert Altman. 1970. Available on DVD from 20th Century Fox Home Entertainment, 2004. A dark comedy about staff members of a Korean War field hospital who use humor and hijinks to keep their sanity amid the horror of war.

Matewan. Directed by John Sayles. 1987. Available on DVD from Artisan Home Entertainment, 2001. This historical feature film dramatizes the hostilities toward organized labor in West Virginia's coal-mining country in 1920.

Matrix, The. Directed by Andy Wachowski and Larry Wachowski. 1999. Available on DVD from Warner Home Video, 2001. A cyberpunk science fiction film about the enslavement of humanity by its own computer creations that is, by turns, technophobic and technophilic.

Mazes and Monsters. Directed by Steven Hilliard Stern. 1982. Available on DVD from Trinity/905 Entertainment, 2005. This dramatic youth film about the pleasures and pains of role-playing games was made during the height of concern over the game *Dungeons & Dragons*.

Medium Cool. Directed by Haskell Wexler. 1969. Available on DVD from Paramount Home Video, 2001. A highly political dramatic feature film about a cameraman's engagement with the events of the 1968 Democratic National Convention.

Men with Guns. Directed by John Sayles. 1997. Available on DVD from Columbia Tristar Home Entertainment, 2003. This dramatic feature film underscores the difficulties of effecting change in poor, agricultural communities.

Meshes of the Afternoon. In *Maya Deren: Experimental Films.* Directed by Maya Deren. 1943. Available on DVD from Mystic Fire Video, 2002. A revelatory avant-garde short film by one of America's leading female filmmakers.

Midnight Cowboy. Directed by John Schlesinger. 1969. Available on DVD from Sony Home Entertainment, 2006. A dramatic feature film about a would-be male prostitute thrust into an unlikely friendship with a streetwise hustler.

Mighty Wind, A. Directed by Christopher Guest. 2003. Available on DVD from Warner Home Video, 2003. A largely improvised pseudo-documentary about the staging of a folk music tribute concert.

Miles of Smiles, Years of Struggle. Directed by Paul Wagner and Jack Santino. 1983. Available on VHS from California Newsreel, 1983. A documentary about the unionization of African American porters and their impact on the civil rights movement.

Mod Squad, The. Directed by Scott Silver. 1999. Available on DVD from MGM Home Entertainment, 1999. This feature-film remake of the popular 1960s television show follows three young undercover agents infiltrating the Los Angeles underworld.

Mondo Trasho. Directed by John Waters. 1969. A day in the lives of a hit-and-run driver and her victim, featuring an array of bizarre events.

Monterey Pop. Directed by D.A. Pennebaker. 1967. Available on DVD from Criterion Collection, 2002. A documentary film about hijinks—onstage and off—at the famous 1968 rock, pop, blues, and jazz festival.

Mormons, The. Directed by Helen Whitney. 2007. Available on DVD from PBS Home Video, 2007. A television documentary about the history and contemporary practice of Mormonism.

Mothlight. In *By Brakhage: An Anthology.* Directed by Stan Brakhage. 1963. Available on DVD from Criterion Collection, 2003. An experimental short film featuring so-called found bits of insects, leaves, and other detritus sandwiched between two strips of perforated tape.

Motorcycle Diaries, The. Directed by Walter Salles. 2004. Available on DVD from Universal Home Entertainment, 2005. The dramatization of a motorcycle road trip that Cuban revolutionary Che Guevara took with a friend in his youth, which revealed his life's calling.

MTV Uncensored. Directed by David P. Levin. 1999. This documentary features stories about MTV, as told by the people who were a part of the cable television network, including producers, video jockeys, and stars such as Cindy Crawford, Janeane Garafalo, and Jon Stewart.

National Lampoon's Animal House. Directed by John Landis. 1978. Available on DVD from Universal Home Entertainment, 2003. A feature-film comedy known for its riffs on the tropes of American fraternity and sorority life.

Night of the Living Dead. Directed by George A. Romero. 1968. Available on DVD from Elite Entertainment, 2002. This cult horror feature about the mysterious animation of dead bodies has been praised for its allegorization of racism, the Vietnam War, and the political climate of late-1960s America.

Not a Love Story: A Motion Picture About Pornography. Directed by Bonnie Sherr Klein. 1981. Available on VHS from National Film Board of Canada Video, 1991. A strongly feminist documentary about the harmful effects of pornography on American cultural discourse.

On the Waterfront. Directed by Elia Kazan. 1954. Available on DVD from Columbia Tristar Home Video, 2001. A feature-film drama about labor and organized crime in postwar urban America.

One Flew Over the Cuckoo's Nest. Directed by Milos Forman. 1975. Available on DVD from Warner Home Video, 2002. The acclaimed film adaptation of Ken Kesey's cult novel, grounded in a man's challenges to the oppressive governance of a mental institution.

Oneida Family of John Humphrey Noyes, The. Directed by Milton H. Jannone. 1975. Available on VHS from M.H. Jannone Video, 1991. A documentary about the history of the Oneida utopian community in upstate New York and its founder.

Outlaw, The. Directed by Howard Hughes and Howard Hawks. 1943. Available on VHS from Front Row Entertainment, 1993. A scandalous Western noted for its circumvention of Hays Code moral strictures.

Panic in Needle Park, The. Directed by Jerry Schatzberg. 1971. Available on DVD from on 20th Century Fox Home Entertainment, 2007. An unglamorized portrayal of life among a group of heroin addicts who frequent New York City's "Needle Park."

Parallax View, The. Directed by Alan J. Pakula. 1974. Available on DVD from Paramount Home Entertainment, 1999. A dramatic thriller centered around the witnessing of the assassination of a political candidate.

Parting Glances. Directed by Bill Sherwood. 1986. Available on DVD from First Run Features, 1999. This dramatic feature film tells a gay love story set amid the ravages of the AIDS virus.

Party Monster. Directed by Fenton Baily and Randy Barbato. 2003. Available on DVD from 20th Century Fox Home Entertainment, 2004. A dramatic feature film about the New York club scene of the 1980s and 1990s.

Pecker. In *Very Crudely Yours: John Waters Collection.* Directed by John Waters. 1998. Available on DVD from New Line Home Entertainment, 2005. A comedy about a Baltimore sandwich shop employee who becomes an overnight sensation when his family photographs become the latest rage in the art world.

Philadelphia. Directed by John Demme. 1993. Available on DVD from Columbia Tristar Home Video, 1997. A man with AIDS, fired by a conservative law firm, hires a homophobic small-time lawyer for a wrongful dismissal suit.

Pink Flamingos. Directed by John Waters. 1972. Available on DVD from New Line Home Entertainment, 2004. A transvestite vies for the title of "filthiest person alive" in this cult classic glorified for its transcendence of so-called good taste.

Planet of the Apes. Directed by Franklin J. Schaffner. 1968. Available on DVD from 20th Century Fox Home Entertainment, 2006. Astronauts crash land on a planet in the distant future, where intelligent talking apes are the dominant species and humans are the oppressed and enslaved.

Plow that Broke the Plains, The. Directed by Pare Lorentz. 1936. Available on DVD from Naxos, 2007. A New Deal–era documentary about the plight of America's agricultural West due to abuse of the land.

Poison. Directed by Todd Haynes. 1991. Available on DVD from Fox Lorber Home Video, 1999. This obscure, poetic feature film tells three intercut stories of murder, transgressive sexuality, and alienation.

Polyester. In *Very Crudely Yours: John Waters Collection.* Directed by John Waters. 1981. Available on DVD from New Line Home Entertainment, 2005. A cult classic about a suburban housewife's breakdown when her husband admits he's been unfaithful.

President's Analyst, The. Directed by Theodore J. Flicker. 1967. Available on DVD from Paramount Home Entertainment, 2004. A cold war comedy about attempts to wrestle national secrets out of the U.S. president's former psychotherapist.

Psych-Out. Directed by Richard Rush. 1968. Available on DVD from MGM Home Entertainment, 2003. A hippie exploitation feature chronicling a runaway girl's introduction to the communal philosophies of the free love generation as she searches for her long-lost brother.

Pull My Daisy. Directed by Robert Frank. 1959. Available on VHS from Kultur Video, 1998. A short film created by and starring members of the Beat movement, including Allen Ginsberg, Larry Rivers, and Jack Kerouac.

Pulp Fiction. Directed by Quentin Tarantino. 1994. Available on DVD from Miramax Home Entertainment, 2002. A seminal film of the 1990s independent movement showcasing several interwoven tales of life, death, drugs, and sex.

Pump Up the Volume. Directed by Allan Moyle. 1990. Available on DVD from New Line Home Video, 1999. A dramatic feature about a teenager's liberation through his persona on pirate radio.

Pumping Iron. Directed by George Butler and Robert Fiore. 1977. Available on DVD from Warner Home Video, 2003. A documentary about bodybuilding, which is famous for helping to launch Arnold Schwarzenegger's celebrity career.

Punishment Park. Directed by Peter Watkins. 1971. Available on DVD from New Yorker Video, 2005. An incendiary pseudo-documentary about the U.S. government's interrogation and abuse of those it identifies as politically undesirable.

Putney Swope. Directed by Robert Downey, Sr. 1969. Available on DVD from Image Entertainment, 2006. A satirical feature film in which a group of black militants takes over a Madison Avenue advertising firm and stages an ideological assault on white America.

Quadrophenia. Directed by Franc Roddam. 1979. Available on DVD from Rhino/WEA, 2001. The story of a working-class London mod, set against the soundtrack of the Who's 1973 concept album *Quadrophenia.*

Queen of Sheba Meets the Atom Man, The. Directed by Ron Rice. 1963. Available on VHS from Arthouse, 1996. This experimental feature film criticizes mainstream representational modes and subjects.

Rainbow Bridge. Directed by Chuck Wein. 1972. Available on DVD from Rhino Home Video, 2000. This fictional feature film—built around documentary concert footage—tells a story about a center for alternative consciousness that extends its message by hosting a Jimi Hendrix concert near a volcano.

Rebel Without a Cause. Directed by Nicolas Ray. 1955. Available on DVD from Warner Home Video, 2005. This dramatic James Dean vehicle details a rebellious teenager's desire to fit in with his peers, to the dismay of his family.

Rebels With a Cause. Directed by Helen Garvy. 2000. Available on DVD from Zeitgeist Films, 2003. A documentary history of Students for a Democratic Society.

Reds. Directed by Warren Beatty. 1981. Available on DVD from Paramount Home Video, 2006. A dramatic love story that portrays the relationship between radical American journalist John Reed and activist-feminist Louise Bryant, set in the epic milieu of the 1917 Bolshevik Revolution.

Reefer Madness. Directed by Louis J. Gasnier. 1936. Available on DVD from 20th Century Fox Home Entertainment, 2004. Ostensibly about the dangers of marijuana use, this midnight movie is beloved by audiences for its camp, kitsch, and ineptly didactic style.

Repo Man. Directed by Alex Cox. 1984. Available on DVD from Universal Home Entertainment, 2006. A thoroughly punk science fiction feature about a man who repossesses cars and his brushes with a conspiracy by an extraterrestrial government.

River, The. Directed by Pare Lorentz. 1938. Available on DVD from Naxos, 2007. A New Deal–era documentary about the role of the Mississippi River in American life.

Rock 'n' Roll High School. Directed by Allan Arkush. 1979. Available on DVD from Buena Vista Home Entertainment, 2005. A comedic tale of youthful rebelliousness, starring the iconoclastic rock group the Ramones.

Rocky Horror Picture Show, The. Directed by Jim Sharman. 1975. Available on DVD from 20th Century Fox Home Entertainment, 2002. The quintessential cult musical, noted for the persistence of its theatrical screenings and for its audience-participation element.

'Round Midnight. Directed by Bertrand Tavernier. 1986. Available on DVD from Warner Home Video, 2001. A feature film about a fictional American jazz musician's life and music in 1950s Paris.

Sacco and Vanzetti. Directed by Peter Miller. 2005. Available on DVD from First Run Features/Icarus Films, 2006. A documentary film about two of America's most well-known anarchists, Nicola Sacco and Bartolomeo Vanzetti.

Saturday Night Fever. Directed by John Badham. 1977. Available on DVD from Paramount Home Entertainment, 2002. This dramatic feature film is largely responsible for bringing disco music and culture into the mainstream.

Scorpio Rising. In *Kenneth Anger, Volume II.* Directed by Kenneth Anger. 1964. Available on VHS from BFI Video, 2000. A keystone work of the American avante-garde, largely responsible for the profusion of the combination of "high" (formal playfulness, stylistic excess) and "low" (popular music, comic books, the icon of James Dean) culture in film.

Scratch. Directed by Doug Pray. 2000. Available on DVD from Palm Pictures, 2002. This concert documentary, featuring world-renowned disk jockeys in competition, doubles as a history of the turntablist in popular music.

Serial Mom. Directed by John Waters. 1994. Available on DVD from HBO Home Video, 1999. A dark comedy about a suburban housewife who murders her neighbors and creates a media sensation as the town's serial killer mom.

Seven Days in May. Directed by John Frankenheimer. 1964. Available on DVD from Warner Home Video, 2000. A dramatic feature film in which a bold general contemplates a coup d'état during a crucial moment in the cold war.

sex, lies, and videotape. Directed by Steven Soderbergh. 1989. Available on DVD from Columbia Tristar Home Video, 1998. This dramatic feature, widely recognized as the catalyst and prototype for the American independent film movement of the 1990s, tells a frank story of sexual intimacy and dissolving relationships.

Shadows. In *John Cassavetes: Five Films.* Directed by John Cassavetes. 1959. Available on DVD from Criterion Collection, 2004. An artistic feature film about an interracial relationship at the height of the Beat era.

Shaft. Directed by Gordon Parks. 1971. Available on DVD from Warner Home Video, 2000. This iconic blaxploitation film follows the adventures of Detective John Shaft.

Shakers, The: Hands to Work, Hearts to God. Directed by Amy Stechler Burns and Ken Burns. 1984. Available on DVD from PBS Home Video, 2004. An historical documentary about the religious beliefs, cultural practices, and national legacy of the Shakers.

Shaolin Ulysses: Kungfu Monks in America. Directed by Martha Burr and Mei-Juin Chen. 2002. Available on DVD from Docurama/New Video Group, 2004. A documentary about a group of Buddhist monks who are engaged in spreading their religion and the practice of kung fu across America.

She's Gotta Have It. Directed by Spike Lee. 1986. Available on VHS from Polygram Pictures, 1995. A dramatic feature film about an African American woman's confused relationships.

Shock of the New, The. Directed by David Richardson. 1980. Available on DVD from Ambrose Video, 2001. A documentary television series on the history of modernism in the arts.

Single Beds and Double Standards. Directed by Kevin Brownlow and David Gill. 1980. Available on VHS from HBO Home Video, 1980. A documentary about Hollywood's move to self-censorship through the institution of the Motion Picture Production Code (also known as the Hays Code) of 1930.

Sir! No Sir! Directed by David Zeiger. 2005. Available on DVD from Docurama/New Video Group, 2006. A documentary about attempts by GIs to oppose the Vietnam War through subversion, peaceful demonstration, and other methods.

Sit Down and Fight: Walter Reuther and the Rise of the Auto Workers Union. Directed by Charlotte Zwerin. 1992. Available on VHS from PBS Home Video, 1992. A documentary recollecting Reuther's struggle for workers' rights amidst resistant management in the automobile industry.

Slacker. Directed by Richard Linklater. 1991. Available on DVD from Criterion Collection, 2004. An experimental, independent feature that seamlessly follows the lives of a cornucopia of peripheral characters in Austin, Texas.

SLC Punk! Directed by James Merendino. 1999. Available on DVD from Columbia Tristar Home Video, 1999. A gritty film that details the daily routine and social tribulations of two Salt Lake City punk rockers.

Smoke Signals. Directed by Chris Eyre. 1998. Available on DVD from Miramax Home Entertainment/Buena Vista Home Entertainment, 1999. A feature comedy about a trip by two Native Americans to collect the remains of one's recently deceased father.

Smothered: The Censorship Struggles of the Smothers Brothers Comedy Hour. Directed by Maureen Muldaur. 2002. Available on DVD from New Video Group, 2003. A documentary profiling the censorship issues surrounding the CBS comedy/variety program.

Star Wars. In *Star Wars Trilogy.* Directed by George Lucas. 1977. Available on DVD from 20th Century Fox Home Entertainment, 2004. The original film in the blockbuster saga set in outer space.

Stop Making Sense. Directed by Jonathan Demme. 1984. Available on DVD from Palm Pictures, 1999. A concert documentary of the rock group Talking Heads.

Story of Jazz, The. Directed by Matthew Seig. 1991. Available on VHS from BMG Video, 1993. This documentary details the historical and cultural origins of jazz music in America.

Storytelling. Directed by Todd Solondz. 2001. Available on DVD from New Line Home Video/Warner Home Video, 2002. An independent film consisting of two unrelated stories of youths working through sexual, social, and familial alienation.

Stranger Than Paradise. Directed by Jim Jarmusch. 1984. Available on DVD from MGM Home Entertainment, 2000. An early independent film about a hip New Yorker's relationship with his visiting Hungarian cousin.

Strawberry Statement, The. Directed by Stuart Hagmann. 1970. Available on VHS from MGM Home Entertainment, 1993. A feature film about a young man's road to involvement in radical politics during the Columbia University protests of the late 1960s.

Struggles in Steel: A Story of African-American Steelworkers. Directed by Tony Buba. 1996. Available on VHS from California Newsreel Video, 1996. A labor documentary that examines personal remembrances of the struggle for racial equality in the steel industry.

Style Wars. Directed by Tony Silver and Henry Chalfant. 1983. Available on DVD from Plexifilm/Passion River, 2005. A documentary on the graffiti subculture emerging in New York City in the 1980s.

Suburbia. Directed by Penelope Spheeris. 1984. Available on DVD from New Horizons Home Video, 2000. A family of homeless teens unite in a throwaway society.

Superfly. Directed by Gordon Parks, Jr. 1972. Available on DVD from Warner Home Video, 2004. A blaxploitation feature about a drug dealer desperate to make one last major sale before abandoning the lifestyle.

Sweet Sweetback's Baadasssss Song. Directed by Melvin Van Peebles. 1971. Available on DVD from Xenon Pictures, 2002. A highly political action film that is widely considered to have instigated the blaxploitation cycle in movies.

Terminator, The. Directed by James Cameron. 1984. Available on DVD from MGM Home Entertainment, 2001. A science fiction thriller in which a computer takes over the future world and its cyborg terminators threaten the existence of humanity.

Thelonious Monk: Straight No Chaser. Directed by Charlotte Zwerin. 1988. Available on DVD from Warner Home Video, 2001. This documentary about jazz musician Thelonious Monk mixes contextual footage, personal testimony, and concert segments.

Thin Blue Line, The. Directed by Errol Morris. 1988. Available on DVD from MGM Home Entertainment, 2005. This investigative documentary is concerned with obtaining justice for a man wrongfully convicted in a 1976 murder.

This Divided State. Directed by Steven Greenstreet. 2005. Available on DVD from Disinformation, 2005. A documentary about the controversy surrounding a speaking engagement in Utah for filmmaker Michael Moore.

This Film Is Not Yet Rated. Directed by Kirby Dick. 2006. Available on DVD from Genius Entertainment, 2007. A documentary that traces the practices and follies of the Motion Picture Association of America's process of rating movies.

This Is Spinal Tap. Directed by Rob Reiner. 1984. Available on DVD from MGM Home Entertainment, 2000. A mock documentary about the waning prowess of a fictional hard rock band.

Thousand Pieces of Gold. Directed by Nancy Kelly. 1990. Available on VHS from Hemdale Video, 1992. This dramatized feature film is based on the true story of a young Chinese woman's encounter with oppressive sexual politics in late-nineteenth-century America.

To Kill a Mockingbird. Directed by Robert Mulligan. 1962. Available on DVD from Universal Home Entertainment, 2005. The Hollywood adaptation of Harper Lee's novel of the same name, in which a black man is put on trial for the rape of a white woman in the Deep South.

Trekkies. Directed by Roger Nygard. 1997. Available on DVD from Paramount Home Entertainment, 1999. A comedic documentary about the internal debates and outward images of Star Trek fan culture.

Trip, The. Directed by Roger Corman. 1967. Available on DVD from MGM Home Entertainment, 2003. A far-out exploitation feature about a stressed-out television director's first encounters with LSD.

Tupac: Resurrection. Directed by Lauren Lazin. 2003. Available on DVD from Paramount Home Entertainment, 2004. A documentary about the life of rapper Tupac Shakur.

Velvet Goldmine. Directed by Todd Haynes. 1998. Available on DVD from Miramax Home Entertainment, 1998. This dramatic feature is about an investigative journalist's search for signs of life from a faded glam rocker.

Walk the Line. Directed by James Mangold. 2005. Available on DVD from 20th Century Fox Home Entertainment, 2006. A fictionalized biopic of iconic musician Johnny Cash.

Walker. Directed by Alex Cox. 1987. Available on VHS from MCA/Universal Home Video, 1988. A highly subversive fictionalized account of a coup d'etat in Nicaragua staged by nineteenth-century American William Walker in the name of U.S. corporate interests. The film deliberately uses anachronisms to link the atrocities of the past to the contemporary moment.

War at Home, The. Directed by Glenn Silber and Barry Alexander Brown. 1979. Available on DVD from First Run Features, 2003. This documentary features interviews with people involved with and leading resistance to the Vietnam War in the Madison, Wisconsin area.

Wattstax. Directed by Mel Stuart. 1973. Available on DVD from Warner Home Video, 2004. This documentary, chronicling the famous 1972 Wattstax festival and concert, also tells the story of cultural attitudes in Los Angeles's Watts neighborhood in the wake of the 1965 riots.

Weather Underground, The. Directed by Sam Green. 2003. Available on DVD from New Video Group, 2004. A documentary of members of the radical Weatherman group that examines their rise, fall, and legacy.

Wedlock House: An Intercourse. In *By Brakhage: An Anthology.* Directed by Stan Brakhage. 1959. Available on DVD from Criterion Collection, 2003. An experimental short film showcasing an abstract look at the personal and sexual life of a young couple (played by Brakhage and his wife).

Where the Day Takes You. Directed by Mark Rocco. 1992. Available on DVD from Columbia Tristar Home Video, 2003. A dramatization of abject poverty and its ill effects on a group of wayward youth.

Who Killed the Electric Car? Directed by Chris Paine. 2006. Available on DVD from Sony Home Entertainment, 2006. A political documentary exploring the unrealized potential of the electric car through examination of the governmental and corporate interests opposed to its very existence.

Who's Afraid of Virginia Woolf? Directed by Mike Nichols. 1966. Available on DVD from Warner Home Video, 2006. Known for its psychological realism and sometimes vulgar language, this feature film adaptation of Edward Albee's play exposes the problems of a troubled bourgeois couple.

Wild in the Streets. Directed by Barry Shear. 1968. Available on DVD from MGM Home Entertainment, 2004. A topical youth exploitation film about the institution of a rock star as president of the United States and his subsequent punishment of citizens over the age of thirty.

Wild One, The. Directed by Laszlo Benedek. 1953. Available on DVD from Columbia Tristar Home Video, 1998. A dramatic feature film about a rebellious biker gang that comes into conflict with a rival gang and the residents of a small California town.

Wild Style. Directed by Charlie Ahearn. 1983. Available on DVD from Rhino Home Video, 2002. A feature-length drama that showcases the emerging street culture of graffiti, break dancing, and rap music.

Window Water Baby Moving. In *By Brakhage: An Anthology.* Directed by Stan Brakhage. 1962. Available on DVD from Criterion Collection, 2003. An experimental documentary in which Brakhage films the birth of his child.

Winter Soldier. Directed by Winterfilm Collective. 1972. Available on DVD from Milliarium Zero, 2006. This collectively authored film presents the testimony of angry Vietnam veterans and reveals blunders of the U.S. government and transgressions committed against innocent Vietnamese citizens.

With Babies and Banners: Story of the Women's Emergency Brigade. Directed by Lorriane Gray. 1978. Available on VHS from New Day Films, 1990. This documentary about the role women played in the General Motors sit-down strike of 1936 and 1937 mixes archival footage and personal testimony.

Wobblies, The. Directed by Stewart Bird and Deborah Shaffer. 1979. Available on DVD from Docudrama/New Video Group, 2006. A documentary on the history of the Industrial Workers of the World (IWW) and the concessions they helped win for workers in the United States.

Woman Under the Influence, A. In *John Cassavetes: Five Films.* Directed by John Cassavetes. 1974. Available on DVD from Criterion Collection, 2004. This independent drama explores a woman's mental illness and the challenges it brings to her family's life.

Woodstock. Directed by Michael Wadleigh. 1970. Available on DVD from Warner Home Video, 1997. A concert documentary presenting a kaleidoscopic view of the Woodstock music festival held in Bethel, New York, in August 1969.

X-Files. Directed by Rob Bowman. 1998. Available on DVD from 20th Century Fox Home Entertainment, 2002. In this feature film based on the science-fiction television series of the same name, FBI Special Agents Fox Mulder and Dana Scully oppose the U.S. government in a conspiracy and discover the truth about an alien colonization of Earth.

Year of the Communes. Directed by Chris Munger. 1970. A documentary study of urban and rural communes in Northern California and Southern Oregon, the film deals with religious, social, and economic forces in these experimental societies.

Yellow Submarine. Directed by George Dunning. 1968. Available on DVD from MGM Home Entertainment, 1999. The Beatles star in and provide the soundtrack for this animated feature, in which the rock group is spirited away in a yellow submarine to save Pepperland from the dreaded Blue Meanies and bring music back to the land.

Zoolander. Directed by Ben Stiller. 2001. Available on DVD from Paramount Home Entertainment, 2002. A comedic feature film about the cutthroat worlds of fashion and male modeling in America.

Zoot Suit. Directed by Luis Valdez. 1981. Available on DVD from Universal Home Entertainment, 2003. The adaptation of a play (also by Valdez) about the zoot suit riots in Los Angeles in the 1940s.

Kevin M. Flanagan and Gina Misiroglu

Index

A